All Cloudless Glory

All Cloudless Glory

THE LIFE OF
GEORGE WASHINGTON

FROM YOUTH TO YORKTOWN

Harrison Clark

REGNERY PUBLISHING, INC.
Washington, D.C.

Clark, E. Harrison
    All cloudless glory : the life of George Washington / E. Harrison Clark
        p.   cm.
    Includes bibliographical references (p.   ) and index.
    Contents: v. 1. From youth to Yorktown
    ISBN 0-89526-466-8 (v. 1)
    1. Washington, George, 1732–1799. 2. Presidents—United States—Biography.
    3. Generals—United States—Biography. 4. United States. Continental Army—Biography.
    I. Title.
    E312.C56   1995
    973.4'1'092—dc2   95-37393
    [B]   CIP

Published in the United States by Regnery Publishing, Inc.
An Eagle Publishing Company
422 First Street, SE, Suite 300
Washington, DC 20003

Distributed to the trade by National Book Network
4720-A Boston Way
Lanham, MD 20706

Printed on acid-free paper.
Manufactured in the United States of America

10 9 8 7 6 5 4 3 2 1

Books are available in quantity for promotional or premium use. Write to Director of Special Sales, Regnery Publishing, Inc., 422 First Street, SE, Suite 300, Washington, DC 20003, for information on discounts and terms or call (202) 546-5005.

Designed by Dori Miller
Maps by Chris Capell Computer Graphics

Endpapers: Paintings of Mount Vernon attributed to Edward Savage, 1792. Front: the west front with the circular driveway in the foreground. Back: the east front overlooking the Potomac. (Courtesy of the Mount Vernon Ladies' Association of the Union)

George Washington had thanks and naught beside,
Except the all-cloudless glory (which few men's is)
To free his country.

Byron *Don Juan*, Canto the Ninth.

For
Agnes Mason Clark

CONTENTS

PART THREE: FARMER 1759–1775

PART FOUR: GENERAL AND FARMER 1775–1781

LIST OF MAPS

ACKNOWLEDGEMENTS

T HE AUTHOR IS indebted to many for advice and help, not least to those who critically reviewed the manuscript at Mount Vernon and elsewhere. His thanks go to Dr. William B. Allen, the late John A. Castellani, Professor North Callahan, Mrs. Ellen McCallister Clark, Mr. Frank Hammond, the late Edgar M. Hinchcliffe, Professor Codman Hislop, the late Colonel Francis Pickens Miller, Mrs. Helen Hill Miller, Mr. Robert Nash, Mr. John P. Riley, Dr. Heinz H. E. Scheidemandel, Mrs. Clara J. Schleh, Mrs. Robert Channing Seamans, Jr., Mr. Paul G. Sifton, the late Charles C. Wall, and the late Mathilde Williams. His particular thanks go to Mr. John Augustine Washington, the late Frank E. Morse, Mr. Franz M. Oppenheimer, and Miss Barbara McMillan.

The following institutions kindly provided copies of their original documents: the Boston Public Library, the Houghton Library of Harvard University, the Historical Society of Minnesota, the Historical Society of Pennsylvania, the Manuscript Division of the Library of Congress, the Mount Vernon Ladies Association of the Union, the Virginia State Library, the Alderman Library of the University of Virginia, and the George Washington Birthplace National Monument.

All Cloudless Glory

PART ONE

FAMILY AND BOYHOOD
1657–1748

ONE

THE ANGLO-AMERICAN WASHINGTONS

1657–1732

THE ENGLISH WASHINGTONS, an ancient gentry family and dutiful subjects of their Tudor and Stuart monarchs, gained rewards suitable to their stations. In 1539 Lawrence Washington, a former mayor of Northampton, purchased from the Crown for a modest sum a priory at Sulgrave, where he built a house. Two generations later, another Lawrence Washington of Sulgrave produced seven sons to serve their sovereigns. One died in Spain while page to the Prince of Wales. Two were knighted, one becoming the father of Colonel Sir Henry Washington, hero of the armies of Charles I. Sir William, Henry's father, married an aunt of the duchess of Richmond. From this it appears that it was another kinsman, George Washington, who was recorded under Charles I as "waiting on the Duke of Richmond to be sworn of the Privy Chamber to the King."

The Reverend Lawrence Washington, the only cleric among these seven sons, was to suffer in mind, body, and estate for his loyalty to church and Crown. An Oxford graduate, he became in 1633 the "modest, sober" rector of All Saints Church in Purleigh, Essex. When civil war broke out in 1642, he supported the sovereign and denounced the "Traytors" of the parliamentary army. Shortly after the second Lord Fairfax broke the cavaliers' siege of Hull, Parliament ejected the "Malignant Royalist," as it called Lawrence, from his parish. Parliament added the common Puritan charge that he was guilty of a "beastly vice, dayly tippling" in alehouses, in which he encouraged others to participate.

Lawrence found haven with friendly royalists in nearby Maldon. Sometime thereafter Thomas Roberts, lord of Little Braxted Manor, five miles away, permitted him to preach in his small parish church. So impoverished was the family that Lawrence's wife and children were forced to move in with her stepfather at Tring. Lawrence died in 1653, four years after the king's execution; he was buried in All Saints Church in Maldon. His widow survived him only until 1655. Her oldest son, John, after obtaining authority in 1656 to administer her estate, set out to make an adventurous living.

The following year John Washington signed as second officer aboard the *Sea Horse of London*, a ketch carrying cargo to Danzig, Lübeck, and Copenhagen. Part of the cargo was tobacco; from his subsequent deposition filed in Virginia, it is known that he traveled overland to sell the weed in Elsinore. The ship thereafter sailed directly for Virginia to pick up more tobacco. It arrived there late in 1656 or early in 1657. On February 28, 1657, the ship ran aground on an inland shoal of the Potomac River, later sinking in a violent storm with the loss of all cargo. John helped to raise and repair the ship but this ended his career in the merchant navy. He stayed in Virginia and founded a family.

After a dispute over his share of the wages and profits, John filed an attachment against the ship's master, Edward Prescott. In May the case was heard before the justices of the peace of Westmoreland County. Its final disposition is not known but one of the justices was Nathaniel Pope, a Virginia burgess, who had previously served in the Maryland Assembly, and had a daughter named Anne. Sometime the following year John married her. Pope gave his son-in-law seven hundred acres at Bridges Creek, on the Potomac River, and lent him enough money to start farming. Bridges Creek was to be, for several generations, the seat of the Washingtons in Virginia. John's brother Lawrence, after making several trips between England and Virginia between 1659 and 1665, also settled permanently in the area.

John, twenty-five when he married, set out vigorously to improve his position. He became a vestryman, burgess, justice of the peace, and, as a militia colonel, helped to suppress Bacon's Rebellion. Washington Parish, with its upper and lower churches, was named for him, a rare instance of an individual being so honored. In his twenty years in the colony, he added more than 8,000 acres to the land deeded by his father-in-law, including among his purchases what he and his immediate descendants described in their wills as 2,500 acres at Hunting Creek, much farther up the Potomac, in near wilderness. Three generations later, its meticulous heir, George

Washington, surveyed his Mount Vernon farm and found that it contained 2,126 acres.

John's will assigned his property to his wife, his daughter Martha, and two sons, Lawrence and John. Lawrence, the elder, inherited the original Pope land at Bridges Creek as well as the Hunting Creek tract.

Lawrence Washington, in the course of his rather short life, added only modestly to his inherited acreage. Like his father, he served in the House of Burgesses, and like his father made a good marriage, to Mildred, daughter of Augustine Warner, once speaker of the House of Burgesses. He died in 1698 at about thirty-seven.

Although the documentation is uncertain, around 1690 Lawrence may have erected a small house at Hunting Creek, which may have been enlarged over the next century into the Mount Vernon mansion house. Lawrence's 1698 will mentioned that two women were then living at the farm, though it is not known whether they were in this house or elsewhere on the property.

Within a year or so of her husband's death, Lawrence's widow—and George Washington's grandmother—Mildred Washington married George Gale of an English tobacco-importing family, with whom she soon moved to Whitehaven, England, along with her children by Lawrence: John, Augustine (Gus), and Mildred. In 1701 George Gale enrolled the two boys, John, age ten, and Augustine, seven, at the Appleby Grammar School in Westmorland, but in 1704, in response to a Virginia court order, he returned the three Washington children to the colony. In accordance with their father's will, his cousin John assumed the guardianship of the two boys and their sister.

AUGUSTINE WASHINGTON

The younger boy, Gus, whose English education was brief, grew into a tall young man, of whose characteristics only tradition remains. His fourth son, George, had a vague memory of him as a blond and husky man who was very fond of his children. He was a county judge at twenty-two, the age at which George was to be Virginia's commander in chief. Subsequently he became a vestryman, church warden, militia captain, and sheriff. He farmed, bought and traded land, and promoted iron ore mining and smelting through the Principio Company. Among his land purchases was the Hunting Creek property, which he acquired from his sister in 1726.

In 1715, probably the year he came of age, Gus married his first wife, Jane Butler, by whom he had four children: Butler and Jane, who died in infancy and youth, and Lawrence and Augustine (Austin). Perhaps feeling that his own English schooling at Appleby had too quickly ended, Gus gave Lawrence and Austin the advantages of a full English public school education.*

Richard Appleby stressed the classics. Although the school was small, headmaster Richard Yates took pride in its library, which he continued to expand during his fifty-eighty-year tenure. It was well-equipped in such diverse fields as history, mathematics, geography, and theology. Among the books were Addison's *Cato* and two copies of a Latin translation of Baldassare Castiglone's *Il Libro del Cortegiano*, first published in Venice in 1528, containing rules for courtly manners. The students read *The Spectator* of Addison and Steele and also used it as a basis for translations into Latin. By the time the brothers returned to Virginia, they were well-equipped to supervise the education of their stepbrother, Mary Ball Washington's oldest son.

MARY BALL WASHINGTON

When Augustine Washington returned to Virginia in 1730 from a trip to England, he learned that his first wife, Jane, had died the previous November. On March 6, 1730, the widower, about thirty-seven, married Mary Ball, who was around twenty-one.

Joseph Ball, George's maternal grandfather, was a relatively prosperous farmer who served as burgess, vestryman, and justice of the peace. A widower

---

* Thanks to an intensive search of its archives by Edgar Hinchcliffe, late master and librarian of the school, it is possible to give an approximation of the curriculum of the era as well as the dates the brothers were enrolled in and taught at the school.

Richard Yates, Appleby's headmaster for fifty-eight years (1723-1781) was, according to Hinchcliffe, "a remarkable man, a scholar of no mean ability, who made the School the most notable Grammar School in the North at the time." Surviving correspondence indicates that Gus Washington and his two sons were on the friendliest of terms with Yates for many years. It appears to have been in 1729 that Gus took Lawrence with him on a trip to England, in connection with his colonial iron works, and enrolled him at Appleby School where, for the next three years, he was on the honor rolls. Lawrence is also recorded as having donated a half-guinea to Yates' library fund on December 4, 1732. The manuscript is too defaced to determine whether, at this time, he returned for a visit to Virginia.

In 1732, the year of George Washington's birth and probably after the event, Austin joined Lawrence at Appleby, where he was recorded as being on the honor rolls in the ensuing years. No further documentation was found for Lawrence, although it appears probable that Gus saw his two sons at Appleby in 1737. Since the brothers were there well beyond the usual school-leaving age, Hinchcliffe concluded that, as honor students, they had become "ushers" (assistant masters) for what was a customary three-year term. His statement was supported by two facts: (1) Austin, about twenty-one or twenty-two, gave the library fund a half-guinea, December 3, 1741, "on his leaving the school," and (2) Yates wrote to Lawrence at Mount Vernon in the humorous terms used to a colleague rather than as a headmaster to a former pupil.

approaching sixty, he married a widow, Mary Johnson, sometime before 1709, fathered Mary Ball, and died while his daughter was still in infancy. Her mother survived only until she was entering her teens. The orphaned child became the ward of George Eskridge, the lawyer who had unsuccessfully defended George Gale in the action brought to return his Washington stepchildren to their Virginia relations. One of the boys sent back from Westmorland, England, to Westmoreland, Virginia, became her husband. When Mary Ball came of age, she had substantial inheritances in land, livestock, and slaves from her father, mother, and brother. No portraits of Mary Ball are extant and perhaps none was ever made, but there is little reason to doubt the statement given to Mason Weems by John Fitzhugh, a longtime friend of Mary's, that she had been a famous beauty in her youth.

During the Victorian period, Mary Ball Washington tended to be canonized by American and even English writers. In reaction, perhaps, a few twentieth-century historians and writers have tried to paint her as something of a monster, unloved by George and her other children. Her slim surviving correspondence, however, indicates the warmth of her feeling for all her family. To her oldest son she wrote: "I am, my dear George, your loving and affectionate mother." He, in turn, publicly referred to her as "my revered Mother; by whose Maternal hand (early deprived of a Father) I was led from childhood." A cousin of his recalled how "very kind" she was yet sufficiently forceful to keep the young "mute as mice" when she was nearby. Her grandson, Lawrence Lewis, when in his sixties, gratefully remembered his walks with her to see the beauties of the Rappahannock, while she urged him to express his love to the God who had given them to the world. On behalf of her neighbors, the mayor of Fredericksburg, addressing her oldest son, called her "amiable," a word often applied to George Washington.

Mary Ball Washington had a difficult life, early orphaned and, at thirty-five, widowed with five children, the oldest age eleven. In 1781, sick and well past her threescore and ten, she traveled over the Blue Ridge Mountains, apparently on the news that her son, Samuel, was dying. She stayed on through a hard winter to help care for his seven children and stepchildren, all under age fourteen. In so doing, she missed seeing another son, George, on his way north from Yorktown. She wrote him how much this distressed her, for she might never again have the pleasure of seeing him.

The earlier tradition that she was a Spartan mother was based on fact. She lived a longer life than her parents, children, or grandchildren. Her forty-six-year widowhood almost equalled her husband's life span of forty-nine years. Her firstborn, George, the last of her children to die, clearly inherited his robust constitution from her, outliving his half brothers and four preceding Washington forebears by nearly two to three and one-half decades. Mary Ball Washington added a needed vigor to the previously short-lived Washington stock.

TWO

THE EARLY YEARS

1732–1748

I N 1798, MARTHA WASHINGTON, sitting by her tea service at Mount Vernon, recalled to a Polish visitor the primitive Virginia of her childhood. She remembered, nearly but not quite accurately, that there had been only one carriage in the entire colony, and that she and her friends always traveled by horseback. There was little trade except in and for tobacco. A package of tea was considered "a very great present."

The Virginia of 1732, the year George Washington was born, contained about 125,000 people, three-quarters of them white. The residents were confined, for the most part, to the tidewater regions. Specie was scarce, and tobacco was the principal medium of exchange. And yet Virginia had been self-governing for 113 years. Its legislature, the second-oldest parliament, functioned almost uninterruptedly during the years when its London mother was frequently suspended. Virginia also appears to have been the most fecund of the colonies. British travelers before the revolution commented on the numbers of children to be seen everywhere. From 1732 to 1775 Virginia's population quadrupled to nearly 500,000, though immigration was not large and slaves were imported at a rate averaging a thousand or so a year. Long before the idea of revolution entered the head of any American, Virginia was producing a surplus of vigorous young, accustomed to self-government, who began moving westward in increasing numbers. George Washington was born while the movement inland was gaining momentum. By the time he was twenty-three, Governor Dinwiddie was reporting to London that the colony wanted all the land to the west, including California.[*]

THE FAMILY

Gus Washington's ten children were not unusually numerous by Virginia standards. George, fifth of the ten to appear in approximately twenty-three years, was born near Pope's Creek, Washington Parish, Westmoreland County. Though a bill exists for a house built by Gus Washington some ten years before, there is no certainty that this was the house of George's birth. He himself wrote of his "numerous" relatives who had reproduced for several generations in the area.

A family Bible at Mount Vernon records the births of Mary Washington's six children and the deaths of a daughter and stepdaughter. Written by some unknown person, the information is of such a character as to appear that it came from Mary Washington. George was baptized on April 5. The unsubstantiated story that George was named for his mother's guardian, George Eskridge, has been frequently repeated, but the possibility lingers that George II was the inspiration. The Bible thereafter records the births of Betty in 1732, Samuel in 1735, John Augustine in 1736, Charles in 1738, and Mildred in 1739. In 1735 Jane, Gus' child by his first wife, died; in 1740 his last-born, Mildred, was buried.

Gus traveled to England, probably in 1736, to discuss his iron ore mining and smelting operations. He returned to Virginia and fathered Charles, who was born on May 1, 1738. In October he purchased from the widow of Anthony Strother a 260-acre farm on the Rappahannock. Mason Weems noted, in the early 1800s, that it was "a plantation... opposite to Fredericksburg. It lifts its low and modest front of faded red, over the turbid waters of Rappahannock." He added that it was an object of pilgrimage, many thinking it was George Washington's birthplace.

In 1739 Great Britain declared war on Spain and, subsequently, France. George II's later refusal to commission Americans was to annoy George Washington, but, at this period, the king encouraged colonials to serve the Crown by granting them regular British commissions. In calling for three

---

[*] In 1849, Benjamin Franklin Washington, great-grandson of Samuel, born in 1734 at Bridges Creek, settled in California. The tenth Lord Fairfax may have migrated there about the same time since he is recorded in *Burke's Peerage* as speaker of California's lower house in 1853.

thousand American reinforcements of British troops in the Caribbean, the king, in April 1740, forwarded to Sir William Gooch, acting governor of Virginia, and to the proposed commander, Major General Alexander Spotswood, company grade commissions for officers selected. Lawrence Washington, George's elder half-brother, was quick to abandon farming for military service, carrying to Gooch all the recommendations he could accumulate. He was the first officer chosen, thereby becoming senior captain in the Virginia contingent. When Spotswood died, Gooch assumed command of the American Regiment.

Lawrence received his commission August 6, 1740. William Byrd's diary indicates that the Virginia Assembly called on Gooch near the end of the month to say farewell, presumably not long before he sailed. The American Regiment joined the land forces of Major General Thomas Wentworth, operating with the British fleet under Vice Admiral Edward Vernon. The expedition, to capture Spanish-held Cartagena, was to be the first of the two major military disasters in which the Washington brothers participated on the British side, the other being Braddock's defeat.

Lawrence spent much of his time on Admiral Vernon's flagship. He was the hero of an early British attack on Panama's Puerto Bello, which he had dashingly captured in two days' fighting. When the fleet arrived off Cartagena on March 3, Wentworth, to Vernon's dismay, temporized for three weeks before he undertook a land assault. The Spanish were given ample time to prepare, and the result was a bloody rout for the British, who were forced to retire to Jamaica. In a letter home dated May 30, Lawrence Washington estimated that six hundred men had been killed in battle but tropical diseases had decimated the fleet and army in even greater number. A further attempt to capture Santiago, Cuba, was soon abandoned. The American Regiment was ordered broken up.

In October 1741, the headmaster of Appleby wrote to Gus to commiserate with him on his "late calamity suffered by fire," which no one has satisfactorily identified. At the same time, he congratulated Gus on Lawrence's escape at Cartagena, where so many had died. Yates added that Austin, who was finishing his teaching term, had set his heart on studying law, but he was a boy of such "goodness" that he would reconcile himself to another career if his father thought best. Joseph Deane, of Whitehaven, a friend of the Washington boys at Appleby, informed Lawrence in the Caribbean that his brother had become "a pretty [fine] young fellow." Austin returned to Virginia in 1742, while his family was still concerned about Captain Lawrence Washington.

Lawrence may have reached Virginia about the end of the year or perhaps in early 1743. Although he had not been in the shore fighting, his long volunteer service made him a hero to the colony, while his British commission was to give him half-pay for life. He subsequently became adjutant general of Virginia's militia with the rank of major.

AUGUSTINE WASHINGTON'S DEATH

Gus Washington had sent his two oldest sons to England for schooling when they reached the age of about eleven or twelve. In later life George Washington claimed that plans for sending him also to England changed with the sudden death of his father. According to the family's recollections to Weems, George was visiting cousins in Choptank, in the next county, when he was called back to his dying father's bedside.

On April 11, 1743, the day before he died, Gus drafted—hastily and rather loosely—an extensive will providing for the distribution of property to his wife and seven living children. This was complicated because he owned many square miles of land scattered through Maryland and four counties of Virginia.

As the oldest son, Lawrence received title to all Gus' ironworks, together with the land at Little Hunting Creek. Along with this went the house, live-stock, and watermill on the property. This indicates that what was to be Mount Vernon was a farm in full operation. Austin, next in seniority, inherited the lands between Bridges and Pope's Creeks, subject to the clause that Gus' widow be given "the Liberty of working my Land at Bridges Creek Quarter for the term of five years next after my Decease during which time she may fix a Quarter on Deep Run." John, the fifth living son, received most of Gus' remaining peninsular land between Bridges and Mattox Creeks, amounting to seven hundred acres.

George inherited the Strother farm on the Rappahannock, described by his father as "the Land I now live on." In addition he and his brother Samuel were given half of Gus' lands on Deep Run, which George later estimated to amount to five thousand acres, and George received three lots in Fredericksburg, two with houses. Other farms, totaling some twenty-four hundred acres, went to Samuel, Austin, Charles, and John.

Shortly after Gus' death, Lawrence renamed his newly inherited house "Mount Vernon," in respect of the marks of favor he had received from his former commanding admiral. The first documented use of the term is in Lawrence's July 19 letter to Richard Yates at Appleby. In it he announced that he was married that day to Anne Fairfax, daughter of William Fairfax, who owned Belvoir, the next large plantation down the Potomac River. His former headmaster replied to Lawrence in November with a Latin pun on Mount Vernon and his marriage.

Although the onset of Lawrence's tuberculosis, from which he suffered an early death, cannot be determined with precision, the probability is that he had the disease when he was married and that he had contracted it in the ship's close quarters in the Caribbean.

GEORGE WASHINGTON'S EDUCATION

Following Gus' death, Mary Washington and her five surviving children, ages three to eleven, returned to her husband's Bridges Creek plantations, where so many of the children's relatives lived. It had one of the few schools beyond the elementary, available to planters' sons. In addition Austin had returned to the area after his three years' teaching at Appleby Grammar School.

Mason Weems, who interviewed many members of the Washington family as well as George's old schoolmates, reported that Mary sent her oldest son to live with Austin, now married to Anne Aylett. This provided him with the nearest approach to the English public school education that his father had planned for him prior to his death. He also attended Henry Williams' school, located by the National Park Service as on or near the Mattox Creek lands inherited by John. It seems that he took practical courses under Williams, while being tutored in the finer arts by Austin.

Old schoolmates told Weems that Williams taught "reading, spelling, English grammar, arithmetic, surveying, book-keeping and geography." Their statements are confirmed by George's notebooks, which show that he studied arithmetic, geography, geometry, trigonometry, and surveying. He learned bookkeeping in the form he would use all his life for his personal and official accounts. Numerous exercises in penmanship resulted in his graceful handwriting, so easy to read two centuries later. As an exercise he copied out the Italian rules of civility, a Latin version of which had been in the Appleby library. Probably Austin lent an English translation to Williams. George's schoolmates remembered how the powerful youth beat them all in running, wrestling, pole vaulting, weight throwing, and broad jumping.

George made notes on his studies in history and literature, presumably in Austin's library and under his direction. These show he read English history, most of the *Spectator*, as well as Addison's *Cato*, a play which greatly influenced American eighteenth-century writing, including George's. His later letters and general library indicate that he was a fast reader who absorbed writers as diverse as Goldsmith, Voltaire, Sterne, Adam Smith, and

Arthur Young. In his middle teens he studied military history, strategy, and tactics with his brother Lawrence.

George thus had the advantage of two substitute fathers as friendly guides in his development to manhood. He probably spent the greater part of his adolescent years at the house of one or the other. He easily absorbed the social graces. His superb horsemanship and dancing skill, his charm and humor, made him welcome everywhere.

Further developments in George's education were undoubtedly connected to his brother's marriage to Anne Fairfax and to the claims of her father's cousin to the Northern Neck of Virginia. Charles II had granted the vaguely defined neck to seven men who had defended his father, Charles I, against Cromwell and the Fairfaxes. In the course of time, the proprietary claims passed to Lord Culpeper, whose daughter married Thomas, fifth Lord Fairfax. These, in turn, were inherited by his son, Thomas. The sixth lord vigorously pressed his claim to a territory far more extensive than the Virginia government considered justified by the original grant. Lord Fairfax's 1736-1737 survey was made in order to present his claim to the privy council in London. Virginia fought Fairfax thereafter for years, but he was well provided with friends at court.

After long study, the council handed down its decision in April 1745, confirming most of his claim. The sixth Lord Fairfax became the assured proprietor of eighty-one hundred square miles of Virginia and what is now West Virginia. The territory extended from below the point where George was born to the headwaters of the Potomac and Rappahannock Rivers in the Allegheny Mountains. Larger than Wales, the domain was subject only to his recognition of earlier grants made by Virginia. Lord Fairfax's agent in Virginia was his cousin, William Fairfax, father-in-law of Lawrence Washington.

How soon George or Lawrence heard of the council's decision is not known but the news reached the governor at Williamsburg in June 1745. Shortly thereafter, in August, George undertook an intensive course in surveying, a skill that would be much needed in the Fairfax grants. His course lasted at least until the following March. He wrote his notebooks in duplicate. The first were neat working papers. The second were models of esthetic and professional accuracy and are the first evidence of George's precocity and early maturity. Among his extant surveys is one of the ancestral lands at Bridges Creek.

Not long after he completed this course and before he did advanced surveying, there was a curious episode in which Lawrence suggested that George go to sea. England was still at war. Lawrence had admired the Royal Navy and he or his Fairfax connections obtained a midshipman's berth for George. William Fairfax was engaged by Lawrence to tell his brother about the plan.

Fairfax's September 9, 1746, letter to Lawrence produced George's first quoted statement that "he will be steady and thankfully follow your advice as his best friend." Lawrence also engaged Robert Jackson to intercede with Mary Washington but he reported nine days later: "I am afraid Mrs. Washington will not keep to her first resolution. She seems to intimate a dislike to George's going to sea and says several persons told her that it is a very bad Scheme. She offers several trifling objections such as fond and unthinking mothers suggest, and I find that one word against his going has more weight than ten for it. Colo. Fairfax seems desirous he should go and desired me to acquaint you with Mrs. Washington's sentiments." Colonel Fairfax's own midshipman son, Thomas, had been killed in action the preceding June, which was not a heartening inducement for a mother to send her son to war.

In December Mary Washington wrote her half-brother, Joseph Ball, then in England, about two problems: the coming end of her tenure at Bridges Creek and George's proposed maritime career. His May 19 reply scorned the idea of her oldest son going to sea. If George entered the merchant marines, he would be subject to impressment in the Royal Navy, which would "cut him and staple him and use him like a Negro, or rather, like a dog. And as for any considerable preferment in the Navy, it is not to be expected, there are always too many grasping for it here, who have interest and he has none." He added that any planter, if he were industrious, lived much better than a master of a Virginia ship. He included some sound advice, which George did not follow for a long time: "Neither must he send his Tobacco to England to be sold here, and goods sent him; if he does, he will soon get in the merchant's debt, and never get out again. He must not be hasty to be right; but must go on gently and with patience as things will naturally go. This method, without aiming at being a fine gentleman before his time, will carry a man more comfortably and surely through the world than going to sea, unless it be a great chance indeed. I Pray God help you and yours... Your Loving Brother J. B."

The year 1747, when George may have completed his formal schooling, was noteworthy for the arrival of the lord proprietor at Belvoir. At about this time young Washington's professional skill was checked by James Genn, one of Lord Fairfax's principal surveyors. George earned his first fees thereafter from private landowners in the neck. Cryptic notes among his papers indicate he may have traveled that year as far afield as Frederick Town (now Winchester).

Possibly this same year Mary Washington moved to her own land, where she built a house big enough to accommodate her five children, ranging in age from nine to fifteen. The only surviving document referring to this is the May 19, 1747, letter to her from Joseph Ball. This disclosed that, in addition to discussing the proposal to send George to sea, she had written about her future plans. He wrote: "I think you are in the Right to leave the house where you are, and to go upon your own Land; but as for Timber I have scarce enough for my own plantations; so can spare you none of that; but as for stone, you may take what you please to build you a House." The letter was addressed to her "nigh the falls, Rappahannock River," indicating that she was building a house north of Falmouth.

Her eldest son, mature beyond his years, was soon off to make his living. Later George was to give endless praise to the joys of farming, but its drudgery clearly repelled him in his youth when he set out for western adventures. From 1747 on, he passed part of each year with Lawrence and Anne Washington at Mount Vernon. To the list of clothing he made for a trip he added at the top, as an afterthought, "Razor," to emphasize his growing manhood. Being with his brother was ideal for an ambitious youth. His surveying services were soon employed by Lord Fairfax, William and George William Fairfax, and Lawrence Washington, the most important people of the Northern Neck and of great influence in the colony itself. William Fairfax was a member of the governor's council and later its president. His son George, Lawrence's brother-in-law, was burgess for Frederick County, where he had large land holdings. Lawrence, Virginia's adjutant general, represented Fairfax County in the Virginia Assembly and was also a justice of the peace. In addition, he and his friends, who included the lieutenant governor, Robert Dinwiddie, had organized a company to promote land purchases and settlement in the Ohio Valley, beyond the Fairfax grants.

That autumn and winter Lord Fairfax and James Genn planned new surveys in the western portion of his territory. It was undoubtedly Genn, highly experienced in wilderness survey work, who recommended the inclusion of young Washington in the team he was to head. Since George does not appear to have been paid for this, it may have been a field internship, qualifying him to be a registered surveyor. Both Lawrence Washington and George Fairfax gave him special assignments in addition to his work for Genn. Lawrence did not live to see it but his half-brother, barely sixteen when he first went over the mountains, was to become commander of Virginia's military forces six years later.

PART TWO

FRONTIERSMAN
1748–1758

THREE

YOUTH

1748–1753

T HE IMPORTANT ROLE of the Fairfaxes in opening up settlement of the West has never received adequate attention. George joined them in an active capacity when their work was already well advanced.

In mapping his claimed domain in 1736 and 1737, Lord Fairfax ordered the territory surveyed to the headwaters of the Rappahannock and the Potomac. The headspring of the latter was traced to the Allegheny Mountains. In 1742, while Fairfax's appeal to the privy council was still pending, a party of Virginians penetrated what is now West Virginia and Kentucky. At the Mississippi, they were captured by the French and imprisoned at New Orleans.

In 1744 the governments of Virginia, Maryland, and Pennsylvania entered into a treaty at Lancaster, Pennsylvania, with the Six Nations, the loose confederacy of Indian tribes who were often called "Iroquois." Through a long process of extermination or conquest of weaker tribes, the Six Nations had extended their claims well into the Ohio Valley regions. There, tributary Shawnees and Delawares settled after 1720. During the negotiations, the Iroquois claimed that they had conquered all the tribes along the Susquehannah and the Potomac, as well as those who had settled on the lands far beyond these rivers. They did admit that the English had beaten one tribe and had a justifiable claim to a portion of the area. In the end, the Indians sold the lands that Virginia wanted, with the understanding that further territories could be purchased as needed.

In 1746, Colonel William Fairfax led a new surveying party to map the western boundary of the Fairfax territory, from the Rappahannock to the headwaters of the Potomac. It was while he was en route that he stopped to tell George Washington of the plan to send him to sea. Colonel Fairfax had with him numerous attendants, his own son George, and James Genn. The Fairfax party, which placed a still extant headstone at the originating spring of the Potomac, found that a nearby stream apparently flowed into a tributary of the Ohio River which, in turn, joined the Mississippi. This close link between the two fired Lawrence Washington's imagination.

In 1747 the Ohio Company was organized to promote trade and settlement beyond the Fairfax domain. Lawrence Washington was one of its original organizers. Over the next years additional shareholders included Thomas Lee, who, as head of the governor's council, was called the president of Virginia, Austin Washington, various other Lees, and George Mason, who in 1758 moved to Gunston Hall near Mount Vernon.

In 1748 France and England signed a peace treaty. These powers, by long habit, passed peaceful years aggressively pushing territorial claims in a way as to ensure further war. The Ohio Valley was one such place where they were moving to collision. France had been far ahead of England in the area between the Alleghenies and the Rockies. La Salle had claimed the Mississippi and all its tributaries for France as early as 1682, effectively adding the whole area to Canada. By 1748 French priests and soldiers had astonishingly accurate maps of the Great Lakes, the Mississippi, and the river which they called "l'Oyo" or "la Belle Rivière." They were well aware of the important strategic point where the Allegheny and the Monongahela joined to become the Ohio, which they named "Trois Rivières." There, on French-claimed territory, Lawrence Washington hoped to establish a British fort and trading post.

TO THE MOUNTAINS

George Washington began both his first extended trip westward and a lifelong diary on March 11 (O.S.), 1748, with two passages scarcely designed to ring down through the ages:

> Began my Journey in Company with George Fairfax, Esqr.; we travell'd this day 40 Miles to Mr. George Neavels in Prince William County.

This Morning Mr. James Genn the surveyor came to us. We travell'd over the Blue Ridge to Capt. Ashby's on Shannondoa River. Nothing remarkable happen'd.

From this date, the previously unknown George Washington emerges with vigor. The wit and humor, which bubble through his writings, appear for the first time. In echoing his mother's love for natural beauty, he began to develop a theme which was to recur in his presidential diaries more than forty years later.

Genn's surveying party stopped first at Lord Fairfax's quarter, marked on its original survey as the Manor of Leeds, in honor of an English family holding. Fairfax's house, built the following year, was given the name Greenway Court. In riding up the Shenandoah Valley, George wrote that "we went through the most beautiful Groves of Sugar Trees & spent the best part of the Day in admiring the Trees & richness of the Land." Next day, on their way to Frederick Town, Washington again commented on the land as "exceeding Rich & Fertile all the way produces abundance of Grain Hemp Tobacco." That day the surveyors laid off lots. George continued the following day:

15th We set out early with Intent to Run around the said Land but being taken in a Rain & it Increasing very fast obliged us to return, it clearing about one oclock & our time being too Precious to Lose, we a second time ventur'd out & Worked hard till Night & then return'd to Penningtons. We got our Suppers & was lighted into a Room & I not being so good a Woodsman as the rest of my Company stripped myself very orderly & went into the Bed as they called it when to my Surprize I found it to be nothing but a Little Straw-Matted together without Sheets or any thing else but only one thread Bear blanket with double its Weight of Vermin such as Lice Fleas ec. I was glad to get up (as soon as the Light was carried from us) & put on my Cloths & Lay as my Companions. Had we not been very tired I am sure we should not have slep'd much that night I made a Promise not to Sleep so from that time forward chusing rather to sleep in the open Air before a fire as will appear hereafter.

16th We set out early & finish'd about one oClock & then Travell'd up to Frederick Town where our Baggage came to us we cleaned ourselves (to get Rid of the Game we had catched the Night before) & took a Review of the Town and thence return'd to our Lodgings where we had a good Dinner prepar'd for us Wine and Rum Punch in Plenty & a good Feather Bed with clean Sheets which was a very agreeable regale.

18th We Travell'd about 35 Miles to Thomas Berwicks on Potomack where we found the River so excessively high by Reason of the Great Rains that had fallen up about the Allegany Mountains, so they told us, which was then bringing down the melted Snow & that it would not be fordable for several Days it was then above Six foot Higher than usual and was rising. We agreed to stay till Monday.

23d Rain'd till about two oClock & Clear'd when we were agreeably surpris'd at the sight of thirty odd Indians coming from War with only one Scalp. We had some Liquor with us of which we gave them Part it elevating there Spirits put them in the Humour of Dauncing of whom we had a War Daunce. There manner of Dauncing is as follows Viz They clear a Large Circle make a Great Fire in the Middle then seats themselves around it the Speaker makes a grand speech telling them in what Manner they are to Daunce after he has finished the best Dauncer Jumps up as one awaked out of a Sleep and Jumps about the Ring in a most comical Manner he is followed by the Rest then begins there Musicians to Play. The Musick is a Pot half of Water with a Deerskin Stretched over it as tight as it can go & a goard with some Shott in it to Rattle & a Piece of an horses Tail tied to it, to make it look fine, the one keeps Rattling and the other Drumming all the while the others is Dauncing.

The surveyors rode through the cold spring rains up the South Branch of the Potomac. By March 29 they were surveying acreage and laying off lots to be sold by Fairfax's agents. On April 3 a gusty storm blew their tent away and they had to lie the rest of the night in the open. The next day they were watched by German-speaking curiosity seekers. Many Germans had poured into the Fairfax grant with Virginia titles or as squatters. This group may have been among those whose settlement was arranged by Joist Hite, who refused to recognize Lord Fairfax's ownership. He raised so much commotion that in 1749 Lord Fairfax temporarily closed his Frederick County land office.

In continued spring rain the Genn surveying party moved on, occasionally stopping to shoot wild turkeys weighing as much as twenty pounds. On April 8 George wrote:

We rode down below the Trough in order to Lay off Lots... The Trough is [a] couple of Ledges of Mountain Impassable running side and side together for above 7 or 8 Miles & the River down between them you must Ride Around the back of the Mountain for to get below them. We Camped this Night in the Woods near a Wild Meadow where was a Large Stack of Hay. After we had Pitch'd our Tent and made a very Large Fire we pull'd out our Knapsack in order to Recruit ourselves. Every[one] was his own Cook, our Spits was Forked Sticks, our Plates was a Large Chip, as for Dishes we had none.

On April 9 the party began the return trip, reaching Frederick Town two days later. Washington wrote briefly of the last stage to Mount Vernon: "12th We set off... in order to go over Wms. Gap about 20 Miles and after Riding about 20 miles, we had 20 to go for we had lost ourselves... This day [we] see a Rattle Snake the first we had seen in all our Journey. Wednesday the 13th of April 1748 Mr. Fairfax got safe home and I myself safe to my Brothers which concludes my Journal."

APPOINTMENT TO OFFICE

While George, aided by his own ability as well as by powerful friends, was rising into trusted and active work, his half brother Lawrence, full of dreams of the future, was increasingly ill from chronic tuberculosis. His four children apparently caught it also, for each died in infancy. Thus five tragedies were to make George Washington the eventual owner of Mount Vernon. In December 1749, nine months after the survey party returned, Lawrence asked for sick leave from the House of Burgesses. George spent at least part of that winter with his ill brother at Mount Vernon. On May 5, 1749, George wrote to Lawrence in Williamsburg, where he had resumed his seat, to express the hope that his cough was mending and that he would not have to go to England. He had hoped to meet him in the capital to register some deeds, but his horse, through lack of fodder, was too weak to make the journey.

That same month William Fairfax engaged George as assistant surveyor to lay out what was to be the most important town in the Northern Neck, Alexandria, north of Mount Vernon and Belvoir. Either before or during this period Lawrence sailed for England on Ohio Company business. William Fairfax wrote his son-in-law from Mount Vernon on July 17 that he was there with Lawrence's wife, his brothers Austin and George, and his sister Betty. They had been joined by Mr. Carlyle and Sarah (Fairfax's daughter) as well as George Fairfax and his wife and a "Miss Molly" [McCarthy]. This large house party toasted the success of Lawrence in England. Colonel Fairfax mentioned that George was writing him to enclose his plat of Alexandria and his ideas as to the proposed sale of lots.

With the completion of his apprenticeship, George rode to William and Mary College at Williamsburg. There, on July 30, 1749, he received his formal commission, at seventeen, as surveyor for Culpeper County. He went to his new post almost immediately to take his oaths and conduct his first licensed survey. Thereafter his notebooks show rough notes for each survey, which he converted into the elegant designs he had learned to draw. From the date of receipt of his commission, he signed himself "G. Washington SCC." Generally he had with him a crew of two chainmen and a marker.

For the next months, until winter cut his work short, George did surveying over a vast area. He spent time with Lord Fairfax, receiving instructions about work Lord Fairfax wanted performed. An undated note, found among his papers, is a request to "Mr. Washenton" to look for a lost horse with a white face and bell, on the South Branch of the Potomac. This and other evidence indicate that he was far afield, north of what was to be the frontier post of Cumberland and up the Shenandoah to Augusta County. Some idea of the roughness of his life is contained in an undated letter (probably November) which he wrote to "Robin," possibly a Washington cousin:

> *The receipt of your kind favour of the 2d of this Instant afforded me unspeakable pleasure... I receiv'd it amongst a parcel of Barbarian's and an uncooth set of People... Since you receiv'd my Letter in October Last I have not sleep'd above three Nights or four in a bed after walking a good deal all the Day. I lay down before the fire upon a Little Hay Straw Fodder or bairskin whichever is to be had with Man Wife Children like a Parcel of Dogs or Catts... Happy's he that gets the Birth nearest the fire... Nothing would make it pass off tolerably but a good Reward. A Dubloon is my constant gain every Day that the Weather will permit my going out and sometimes Six Pistoles. The coldness of the weather will not allow my making a long stay as the Lodging is rather too cold... I have never had my cloths off but lay and sleep in them like a Negro except the few nights I have lay'n in Frederick Town.*

George's fees were high, since six pistoles equalled around twenty-two Spanish dollars; land in the Shenandoah Valley could be bought for less than a dollar an acre. George waited carefully to find good farms. When he was eighteen, he began buying in quantity, picking up nearly fifteen hundred acres in 1750 and 1751.

George's first signs of illness appeared during this frontier surveying. In writing that autumn to his sister-in-law, Anne Washington, he said how glad he was to hear that his brother had arrived safely "*in health*" in England. The fever and ague which he himself had "to Extremety" prevented him from calling on her at Mount Vernon. Though his description might cover malaria, his close association with Lawrence makes it more likely that this was the initial onset of George Washington's own long battle with tuberculosis.

THE OHIO COMPANY

Late in 1749 Lawrence returned from a successful trip to London. George received from him a full report of the proposed operations of his company, which had been granted five-hundred thousand acres in the Ohio Valley. Lawrence prepared a rough map of the area, indicating how he thought the Potomac and Ohio Rivers might nearly interlock. Years later, George, inspecting the area, confirmed that their headwaters were only a few miles apart. Along with his map, Lawrence sent to England a letter describing the area beyond this point as "vastly rich."

English traders, he added, had not been able to penetrate because of a lack of goods. Once the Ohio Company established its post at the junction of the Allegheny and Monongahela Rivers, they could travel hundreds of miles into the interior. The Virginians had a great advantage over the French, since they could supply goods by way of the Potomac, while the Saint Lawrence was at a much greater distance and frozen for a large part of the year. He added: "The further we extend our Frontier, the safer we render the interior Dominions, and the French, having possession of the Ohio, might easily invade Virginia, for our mountains are not so formidable as to be much security... The Indians are our Friends... Nothing can more contribute to keeping them our Friends than contriving them the necessaries of Life at the easiest rates... The Indians... esteem those honestest who sell the cheapest."

Lawrence also pleaded that the new area be entirely free in religion in order to attract settlers: "Restrictions on conscience are cruel in regard to those on whom they are imposed and injurious to the country imposing them... This Colony was greatly settled in the latter part of Charles the First's time and during the usurpation, by the zealous churchmen; and that spirit which was then brought in, has ever since continued... What has been the consequence? We have increased by slow degrees while our neighboring communities, whose natural advantages are greatly inferior to ours, have become populous."

While Lawrence greatly underestimated the growth of Virginia's population, which his friends and relatives were stimulating, his views were remarkable for their vision and tolerance. Lawrence's dreams influenced his brother, who became the first Washington to reach the Monongahela, go down the Ohio River, and own land in that valley.

In 1750 Thomas Lee, president of the Ohio Company, died, and Lawrence became his successor. That same year Dr. Thomas Walker and a party of Virginians explored as far west as Kentucky. Shortly afterwards, the company dispatched Christopher Gist, long experienced in work with the Indians, on an extended trip through present-day Ohio, Indiana, and Kentucky. He found the Indians averse to any settlement north of the Ohio. In consequence Gist was dispatched in 1751 and 1752 on another extensive investigation along the southern areas of the valley, as far as the present Wheeling, West Virginia. He wrote long reports for the Ohio Company, which were available to George at Mount Vernon.

The Ohio Company built its first storehouse in 1750 at Will's Creek (Cumberland). The following year the company started construction of a road to the forks of the Ohio River. In 1752 the governor of Virginia empowered Christopher Gist to hold treaty talks with the Indians at Logstown, about thirteen miles from the junction of the three rivers. Gist successfully negotiated title to lands south of the Ohio. In the meantime, the French were also active. They had charted the Ohio River in 1746, burying plates at various points, claiming the territory for France. By 1752 the French had plans for a series of forts south of Lake Erie. The most important of these was to be at the forks of the Ohio, the proposed terminus of the Ohio Company's road. The stage was being set for conflict and for Washington's early rise to international fame.

TO BARBADOS

Meanwhile, Lawrence Washington's active tenure as president of the Ohio Company was cut short as his health grew steadily worse. In July 1750, George took Lawrence to the warm waters at Bath, Virginia (now Berkeley Springs, West Virginia), but they did him no good. In 1751 Lawrence decided, as a last desperate remedy, to proceed to Barbados which, though hot and sticky, had a favorable reputation for pulmonary disorders. His wife, Anne, at home with her one surviving child, a sickly girl of about eleven months, could not travel. George became Lawrence's companion.

The trip to Barbados would be George's only venture outside of continental America. The brothers sailed from Fredericksburg for Bridgetown towards the end of September 1751. George was gone for four months, nearly half the time at sea. His diary survives only in mutilated form but enough remains to provide an indication of their activities.

George had spent most of his early years on or near rivers. Now he spent much of his first five weeks on a larger ship, learning as much more as he could of seamanship. His extant papers include a ship's log in his neat handwriting, wherein he recorded every two hours the course, latitude and longitude, the distance run, and the wind and weather. His curiosity as powerful as his intellect, George was soon writing learnedly of reefing and double-reefing the sails and of hauling the foresail.

The voyage in hurricane season was unmercifully rough. Between October 16 and 22 the ship passed close to what the ship's officers assumed was "a violent hurricane." George wrote first of a "Strong wind" and then over several days of a "Hard gale and a disturb'd and large Sea which imminently endangered our Masts... Hard Squalls of Wind and Rain... The Compass not remaining two hours in any point. The Seamen seemed disheartend confessing they had never seen such weather... A Constant succession of hard Winds, Squalls of Rain... a large Tumbling Sea."

On the twenty-second the wind lightened enough for the sailors to repair the damaged rigging. The next day the sun came out, and George remarked that it showed that the bread "was almost Eaten up by Weavels & Maggots." By October 30 there was "a certain & steady trade Wind which after near five Weeks buffiting and being toss'd by a fickle & Merciless Ocean was gladening news." They landed at Bridgetown on November 3 or 4.

Upon arrival they were greeted by Major Gedney Clarke, a member of the Barbados governor's council and a relation of the first husband of Mrs. William Fairfax. He recommended a physician who, after examining Lawrence, was quite optimistic as to a cure. Thus encouraged, George gave his attention to the scenery as they rode in search of a house to rent. Barbados, in its wet season, was lush, and George records himself as "perfectly ravished by the beautiful prospects which on every side [were] presented to our View. The fields of Cain, Corn, Fruit Trees, &c., in a delightful Green."

Major Clarke invited the Washingtons to breakfast and dinner with him. George recorded going without much enthusiasm, since there was a case of smallpox in the house. By the eighth, the brothers had rented a house for the "extravagantly dear" price of fifteen pounds per month. Lawrence found the hot and humid climate very trying, and was forced to keep mainly to the house except early in the morning or in the cool of the evening.

George, however, now nineteen, blossomed in his new life. His natural charm, about which so many persons were to comment in later life, made him a sought-after guest. With his brother he was invited to the Beefsteak and Tripe Club, which met each Saturday night at the house of a member. Thereafter George was asked everywhere. He dined with the military, judges, and the surveyor general. He attended church as well as the theatre. On November 17 the gay life abruptly stopped. His December 12 diary made a brief note of what happened:

Was strongly attacked with the small Pox: sent for Dr. Lanahan whose attendance was very constant till my recovery, and going out which was not 'till thursday the 12th of December.

Not another word did he write of the miseries of two sick brothers far from home. George was soon dining out again, with a commodore, a general, members of the governor's council, and the governor of Tortola. He took everyone in stride, and poked into everything in Barbados. He inspected the island fortifications. He read a natural history of the island. He noted all the local produce, particularly the fruits, which he sampled: granadella, sapodilla, pomegranate, orange, lemon, forbidden fruit, apple, guava, pineapple, avocado, yam, plantain, potato, rice, and Guinea corn. He enjoyed most the taste of fresh pineapple. He commented on the richness and blackness of much of the soil and expressed wonder that so many people could be in debt when the farms were more productive than those of Virginia. He made notes on manuring practices. The women, he wrote, were very agreeable but behaved rather too much like negroes. The men had florid complexions. The climate was healthy for those who stayed temperate. He attended a trial for rape. He remarked on the behavior of the governor, who stayed too aloof from the people. Barbadians, too, complained of the rapacity of British officials, whose fees were regarded as far out of line with the work they performed.

Lawrence Washington subsequently informed William Fairfax that the climate was too hot for him and he proposed to proceed to Bermuda. George sailed on the *Industry* for Virginia on December 22, very probably with instructions to give Anne Washington news of her husband and to bring her and her daughter, if it seemed desirable, to Bermuda. This sea trip home was even rougher than his outward voyage. Though Christmas Day was "fine and clear and pleasant with moderate Sea," and the occasion for a feast of goose and roast beef, on the last day of the year the *Industry* ran into "violent winds... with excessive rain [and] mountainous running [seas which prevented] carrying Sail." On the third and fourth of January there were more storms and heavy seas. On the eighth the ship was marooned; next day there were such huge winds and seas that the ship had to proceed with masts almost bare. Soon snow and hail were added to the rain. On January 16 the *Industry* encountered HMS *Glasgow*, which had been trying for two weeks to make the Virginia coast in the storms. They also met a merchant vessel, which had been five weeks on its way from Saint Kitts to Philadelphia.

On January 23 George wrote that the mate, with the weather moderating, was "inticed... from his Cabbin (as a snail enlivened by the genial heat of the Sun) who since the third or fourth day after leaving Barbados has been coop'd up with a fashionable disorder contracted there." On January 26 the waters grew shallower, and birds and marsh weed appeared; late that night the ship reached the mouth of the York River. Upon landing, George proceeded to Williamsburg to deliver his brother's letters to Governor Dinwiddie.

This was the first encounter between the sixty-year-old governor (technically lieutenant governor) and the nineteen-year-old youth, whom he was soon to make Virginia's military commander. George wrote that Dinwiddie received him "Graceously. He enquired kindly after the health of my Brother and invited me to stay and dine." It is a reasonable surmise that George raised the question whether, since Lawrence's health made it desirable that he resign as adjutant general, he could have the job. If the governor expressed surprise, history has no record of it.

Shortly after his return, George rode west to Frederick County to resume surveying. While there, he increased his landholdings at Bullskin Creek, not far from the present-day Charles Town, which was to be named for his youngest brother. He returned to the tidewater in the spring, as increasingly worried letters from Lawrence reached Mount Vernon. If Lawrence had any hope of recovery, he would stay in Bermuda and ask George to bring his wife and baby there. If not, he would return to Mount Vernon "to my grave."

George had heard that the Virginia adjutancy, held by his brother, was considered too large a task for one man. In consequence, at least three district adjutants were to be appointed. Colonel William Fitzhugh, who was living in Maryland, was under consideration for the Northern Neck. George stopped in Maryland to call on Fitzhugh to see whether he wanted the job. The colonel gave him a letter to forward to the governor, stating conditions to be met if he were to accept. On June 10 George sent Fitzhugh's letter to Dinwiddie, requesting at the same time that, if the colonel were not appointed, he might have the Northern Neck adjutancy. If Fitzhugh got it, he would be happy to have one of the other districts. George added that he would "take the greatest pleasure in punctually obeying, from time to time, your Honour's commands; and by a strict observance of my Duty, render myself worthy of the trust reposed in me: I am sensible my best endeavors will not be wanting, and doubt not, but by a constant application to fit myself for the Office, could I presume Your Honour had not in view a more deserving person."

Very shortly afterwards, Lawrence, a dying man, reached Virginia. Mary Washington and her children went to Mount Vernon to see him. Lawrence rewrote his will, as quickly and loosely as his father had done. He left Mount Vernon to his daughter, or to George in the event of her death (a possibility he mentioned three times in his will), subject to his wife's life tenancy. Lawrence died on July 26, 1752. His daughter lived for only a short time thereafter and George became the heir about 1754.

On November 6 the governor of Virginia, by and with the advice and consent of his council, appointed George Washington major of militia and adjutant for the southern district. Major Washington was sworn in just before his twenty-first birthday. Although Dinwiddie could not foresee this, the young officer was to be his principal interest and irritant for the next five years.

FOUR

LIEUTENANT COLONEL WASHINGTON

1753–1754

MAJOR WASHINGTON AT twenty-one had presumably reached his full height of six feet, two-and-one-half inches. He was a giant in an age when Americans were much shorter on the average. A tabulation of the heights of 1,134 men in Virginia's colonial regiment showed that two-fifths were between four feet eleven inches and five feet five inches. Only one man exceeded Washington in height; probably none did in strength. He had an unusually powerful build, with hands that Lafayette and Timothy Pickering described as the largest they had ever seen on a man. He was very light in coloring with eyes described by Weems as cerulean blue. Dr. James Craik recalled in later years that when he and Washington attended church in the frontier days, the eyes of the ladies were more likely to be on Washington than on the preacher.

The governor-in-council had defined the adjutant's duties as "instructing the officers and soldiers in the use and exercise of their arms... bringing the militia to a more regular discipline, besides improving the meaner people." The young major, in addition to his military reading at Mount Vernon, had attended his brother in some of his duties as adjutant. Washington's training in mathematics, topography, and surveying would also be helpful.

The construction in 1752 of two French forts in what is now western Pennsylvania abruptly brought Washington into high responsibility. Dinwiddie, increasingly alarmed, reported France's action to London in June. The British government reacted with uncharacteristic speed. In August, George II approved the construction of forts by Virginia and announced that British ordnance supplies were on their way. The king ordered Dinwiddie diplomatically to request all intruders to depart peaceably. Should they be answered with force, Dinwiddie was to drive the French out of the territory. He was assured that the British government would give him the fullest backing.

In October of 1753, shortly after the governor received his instructions, Major Washington was in Williamsburg, volunteering to proceed to the French forts. With the council's approval, Dinwiddie drafted Washington's orders and handed him a passport as well as a letter to the commander of the French forces in the territory. Without experience in war or diplomacy, Washington faced a difficult and dangerous mission that included intelligence work, since the governor instructed him to find out all he could of French fortifications and numerical strength.

Washington started north on October 31. In Fredericksburg he picked up the Dutch-born Jacob van Braam, who had some knowledge of French. In Alexandria and Winchester the pair purchased supplies and horses. At Will's Creek, Christopher Gist, the experienced agent of the Ohio Company, joined them, along with four Indian traders and servants. From November 15, the party picked its way through the forbidding passes of the Alleghenies. On November 22, sixteen months after his brother's death, George reached the forks of the Ohio, where Lawrence had planned to establish his trading post. He wrote:

> *I spent some time in viewing the Rivers and the Land in the Fork which I think extremely well situated for a Fort, as it has the absolute Command of both Rivers. The Land at the Point is 20 or 25 Feet above the common Surface of the Water; and a considerable Bottom of flat, well-timbered land all around it, very convenient for Building: The Rivers are each a Quarter of a Mile, or more, and run here very near at right Angles; Aligany bearing N. E. and Monongahela S. E. The former of these two is a very rapid and swift running Water; the other deep and still, without any perceptible Fall.*

Washington spent the days of November in discussions with Indians friendly to the English, including an Oneida and Mingo chief, Monakatoocha, and a Seneca chief, the Half-King, so-called because of allegiances he owed the Six Nations. The Half-King informed Washington that he had complained to the French of their movements in the region and they had treated him with contempt. He, the Shanoahs, and Delawares promised therefore to support the English. He offered Washington an escort on his visit to the French commander, which was gladly accepted, and the expedition resumed its progress:

[Venango, December 4.] This is an old Indian Town, situated at the Mouth of French Creek on Ohio... We found the French Colours hoisted at a House which they drove Mr. John Frazier, an English Subject, from; I immediately repaired to it, to know where the Commander resided: There were three Officers, one of whom, Capt. Joncaire, informed me that he had the Command of the Ohio, but that there was a General Officer at the near Fort, where he advised me to apply for an Answer. He invited us to sup with them, and treated us with the greatest Complaisance. The Wine, as they dosed themselves pretty plentifully with it, soon banished the Restraint which at first appeared in their Conversation, and gave a License to their Tongues to reveal their Sentiments more freely. They told me, That it was their absolute Design to take Possession of the Ohio, and by G— they would do it; For that altho' they were sensible the English could raise two Men for their one; yet they knew their Motions were too slow and dilatory to prevent any Undertaking of theirs. They pretend to have an undoubted Right to the River, from a Discovery made by one LaSalle 60 Years ago; and the Rise of this Expedition is to prevent our settling on the River or Waters of it, as they had heard of some Families moving-out in Order thereto.

7th Monsieur La Force, Commissary of the French Stores, and three other Soldiers came over to accompany us up [to Fort Le Boeuf near Waterford, Pennsylvania]... At 11 oClock we set out for the Fort, and were prevented from arriving there till the 11th by excessive Rains, Snows and bad Travelling, through many Mires and Swamps... We passed over much good Land... and through several extensive and very rich Meadows...

12th I prepared early to wait upon the Commander... I acquainted him with my Business, and offered my Commission and Letter: Both of which he desired me to keep till the arrival of Monsieur Riparti [de Repentigny]... At 2 oClock... [he] arriv'd, when I offered the Letter, &c. again; which they receiv'd, and adjourn'd into a private Apartment for the Captain to translate, who understood a little English; after he had done it, [Legardeur de Saint Pierre,] the Commander, desir'd I would walk in, and bring my Interpreter to peruse and correct it, which I did.

13th The chief Officers retired, to hold a Council of War; which gave me an Opportunity of taking the Dimensions of the Fort, and making what Observations I could.

Washington estimated that the fort held about a hundred men. He instructed his guides and Indians to count all canoes. They numbered 220, with others building. By December 14 snow was falling heavily and the horses grew so weak Washington had them sent on ahead. The next day the commandant gave him a reply to Dinwiddie, along with ample supplies and liquor for his trip. He also attempted to bribe his Indians to desert. Washington commented: "I can't say that ever in my life I suffer'd so much Anxiety as I did in this Affair." Washington then made what he described as "a very fatiguing passage" upriver by canoe. He wrote that a number of times they were

nearly staved against Rocks, and many Times were obliged all Hands to get out and remain in the Water Half an Hour or more, getting over the Shoals. At one Place the Ice had lodged and made it impassable by Water; therefore we were obliged to carry our Canoe across a Neck of Land, a quarter of a Mile over. We did not reach Venango, till the 22nd, where we met with our Horses.

The horses however "were now so weak and feeble," and the progress of the main party so slow over snow and ice-bound roads that Washington became "uneasy to get back to make Report of my Proceedings to his Honour the Governor," and "determined to prosecute my Journey the nearest Way through the Woods, on foot." Setting out with Gist alone, the two men were the very next day waylaid by "a Party of French Indians," one of whom "fired at Mr. Gist or me, not 15 steps off, but fortunately missed." The next day the two men reached the Allegheny River, which they had hoped vainly to find frozen so they could walk across it. Instead they built a raft with but "one poor Hatchet" for a tool. "Just after Sun-setting, after a whole Day's Work; we got it launched, and on board of it, and set off; but before we were Half Way over, jammed in the Ice, in such a Manner that we expected every Moment our Raft to sink, and ourselves to perish; I put out my setting pole to try to stop the Raft, that the Ice might pass by, when the Rapidity of the Stream threw it with so much Violence against the Pole, that it jerked me out into ten Feet Water." Washington fortunately saved himself by catching hold of one of the raft logs. But the travellers could not get the raft to either shore and were forced to swim for an island.

Gist had all his fingers and some of his toes frozen. By morning the river was solid and they made for John Frazier's house. There they met "20 Warriors who were going to the southward to War, but coming to a Place upon the head of the Great Cunnaway [Kanawha], where they found seven People killed and scalped, all but one Woman with very light hair, they turned about and ran back, for Fear the Inhabitants should rise and take them as the

Authors of the Murder... By the Marks that were left, they say they were French Indians of the Ottaway Nation."

Obtaining horses, they made a visit to "Queen Aliquippa, who had expressed great Concern that we passed her in going to the Fort. I made her a Present of a Matchcoat and a Bottle of Rum, which latter was thought much the best Present of the Two." In the face of continued extreme weather the two men made Belvoir by January 11 and Williamsburg January 16, where Washington "waited upon his Honour the Governor with the Letter I had brought from the French Commandant."

The December 15 letter from Legardeur de St. Pierre, which Washington delivered to the governor, was politely blunt:

> *I have the honor, Sir, to be commander-in-chief here. Monsieur Washington transmitted to me the letter which you wrote to the commandant of French troops.*
>
> *As for your summons to me to retire, I do not feel any obligation to do so, whatever may be your instructions. I am here by orders of my general and I beg you, Sir, not to doubt for an instant that I have the fixed resolution to conform to them with the exactness and firmness expected of the best officer.*
>
> *I made it my particular duty to receive Monsieur Washington with a distinction, equal to your position and to his own quality and great merit."*

The letter achieved the distinction, which was to be rare among the French, of spelling Washington's name correctly.

Although the House of Burgesses had adjourned without voting defense funds, the council was in session when George returned. The governor asked him to prepare a report of his trip, giving him only twenty-four hours to do so. Dinwiddie was sufficiently impressed to subsequently order it printed for the Virginia Assembly. He gave Major Washington barely enough time to write a preface, in which Washington apologized for the "numberless imperfections" that were consequent on the haste with which he had written it. He was given no time for redrafting nor had he even known it was to be printed until the Assembly, called for February 14, was already in session. He added: "There is nothing can recommend it to the Public, but this. Those Things which came under the Notice of my own Observation, I have been explicit and just in a Recital of. Those which I have gathered from Report, I have been particularly cautious not to augment, but collected the Opinions of the several Intelligencers, and selected from the whole, the most probable and confident Account."

The printed version omitted Washington's careful drawing of the whole region from the Alleghenies to Lake Erie, which he had made from his compass reckonings. Later surveys showed the map to be remarkably accurate, considering the primitive conditions under which his notes were made. The drawing contained designs of the existing French forts, with an outline of their further plans: "The French are coming from their Forts on and near the Lake Erie to Venango [at the junction of French Creek and the Allegheny River] to erect another Fort. From thence they design to the Forks of the Monongahela and to the Logs Town and so to continue down the River building at the most convenient places in order to prevent our Settlements, &ca. NB. A little below the Shanapin Town [Pittsburgh] in the Forks is the place where we are going immediately to Build a Fort as it Commands the Ohio and Monongahela."

Dinwiddie sent copies of the printed document to members of the council and House and to other colonial governors. He also transmitted a copy to London where it was immediately reprinted. Thus the twenty-one-year-old major became known for the first time internationally. The report indicated that he was a tough, resourceful officer and an acute observer who could gather and accurately evaluate intelligence under unusually adverse conditions.

While waiting for the House to convene, Dinwiddie dispatched Washington to the Shenandoah Valley to recruit militia for service at the forks of the Ohio. Washington, on his return, reported that the militia system was a paper organization and little recruiting had taken place, although Lord Fairfax himself was the county lieutenant. When the Assembly reconvened, the governor urged immediate action to provide funds for defense of the frontier, using the Washington report as his most powerful argument. The Assembly itself promptly voted praise and fifty pounds to the young major for his mission.

In spite of the clear emergency, the governor had no easy time getting funds for a regular military force. There were outcries in the House of Burgesses that the ten thousand pounds he requested was for the protection of a private enterprise, the Ohio Company. Questions were raised as to whether the forks of the Ohio were in Virginia or Pennsylvania. This was important since Virginia law forbade the militia (needed to reinforce the regular troops) to serve outside the colony. Others wondered whether the territory was even British. Since Dinwiddie had direct orders from London to protect the frontiers, the debates made him very uneasy. In the end, the burgesses voted the money but appointed a committee to control its expenditure jointly with the governor. Dinwiddie signed the act but complained bitterly to London that it was unconstitutional. The governor, as the Crown's representative, had the clear prerogative of allocating supplies.

Washington had asked Dinwiddie to appoint him adjutant of the Northern

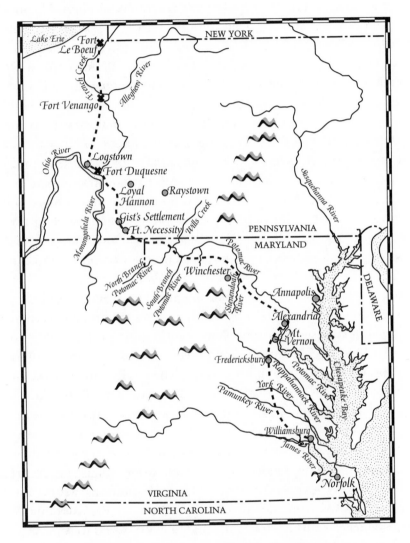

Washington's Journey to Fort Le Boeuf, 1753

Neck if he did not find a man more suitable for the position. During Washington's absence in the Ohio regions, the governor transferred him there. Once the military bill authorizing the recruiting of three hundred men passed, young Washington made known to Richard Corbin, of the governor's council, his desire to join the regular military service. As John Marshall put it, Corbin's reply was laconic: "Dear George—I enclose you your commission. God prosper you with it."

Dinwiddie, who was to complain of the shortage of experienced officers in the colony, selected Joshua Fry as colonel and commander of what was to become the Virginia Regiment. Fry, a surveyor and mapmaker, had been a county lieutenant in charge of militia, with additional experience in Indian negotiations. Shortly thereafter Washington, who described Fry many years later as "old and corpulent," was appointed lieutenant colonel and second in command, a commission he held in addition to his majority in the militia. Other appointments included George Muse as major and Christopher Gist and Adam Stephen as captains. James Craik joined as physician. In order to reward the officers, and to stimulate the recruitment of enlisted men, the governor authorized a future grant to them of two hundred thousand acres of land in the Ohio Valley. The officers were ordered to various points to recruit: Fry to the tidewater region, Washington to Alexandria, and Stephen to Winchester.

Before Washington reached Alexandria, a company under Captain William Trent, largely composed of frontiersmen, had begun to erect the first fort at the Ohio forks. On March 20 Washington received urgent orders from the governor to proceed immediately there with such men as he had enlisted. Dinwiddie had a dispatch from Trent to the effect that he anticipated a French attack. Washington reported to the governor that he and others had assembled around seventy-five soldiers, many of the "loose, idle" type who often had no shoes or shirts. The commissary, Major Carlyle, was prepared to clothe them, if the colony could guarantee credit and the men would gladly repay from their wages. As soon as wagons could be assembled, Washington set off for his first military venture. On April 2, with around 150 officers and men, he began the march to Winchester, which he completed in about seven days.

At Winchester a few men under Captain Adam Stephen joined Washington. From this frontier post the young lieutenant colonel had to get his men and supplies to Will's Creek and thence over the Allegheny Mountains to the Ohio River. He stretched his impressment powers, as he wrote the governor, to the limit, to get wagons. He thought his authority would not "be questioned, unless some busybody interferes." In spite of all efforts he could gather only ten of seventy-four requisitioned wagons. At Will's Creek, while Washington held council with the Indians, Ensign Edward Ward, who had been left in charge of the Ohio fort, arrived with the news that he and thirty-three soldiers had surrendered to French forces, which he estimated to be at least one thousand. Neither Captain Trent nor his lieutenant had been present at the time of the surrender, though Ward had informed them that Indian scouts had seen the French moving down the river in overwhelming force. Washington, with a handful of untrained troops, was now the entire force of the British empire opposing French control of the Ohio Valley.

FIVE

COLONEL WASHINGTON
PUSHES WAR

1754

A T THIS CRITICAL PERIOD, there were no British troops in Virginia and relatively few elsewhere in the colonies. Although George II had commanded Dinwiddie to use force to eject the French from the Ohio if they did not depart peaceably, and had promised the fullest military support, for an extended time this remained a paper assurance. London moved slowly in crises. Nearly five years would elapse before Washington led a British army into Fort Duquesne. His military service during the period was to be as long as that from Long Island to Yorktown and proved a rehearsal for the main event, when once again he would struggle with inadequate supplies and funds, undisciplined militia, provincial jealousies, and long marches with infrequent battles. His experience now with guerrilla tactics and British commanders and troops was to be of the greatest future value to him.

Ensign Ward reported to Washington that their Indian ally, the Half-King, had been among those captured at the forks. He brought with him the Half-King's letter, renewing his loyalty and expressing his readiness to "fall upon" the French. He added: "If you do not come to our assistance now, we are entirely undone... I speak with a heart full of grief." Washington replied with some exaggeration that his troops were clearing the roads for "a great number of our warriors, who are ready to follow us, with our great guns, our ammunition and provisions." He signed himself "George Washington

Conotocarious," an Indian name meaning 'towntaker,' which had been conferred on him by the Half-King.

Washington dispatched Ward to Williamsburg with a letter for Dinwiddie. He informed the governor that he would do his best for the "good of my country; whose rights, while they are asserted in so just a cause, I will defend to the last remains of my life." He had determined to push ahead to Redstone Creek, a tributary of the Monongahela, some thirty-seven miles from the fort the French had taken. He continued:

> *I doubt not that we can maintain a possession there, till we are reinforced, unless the rising of the waters shall admit the enemy's cannon to be conveyed up in canoes, and then I flatter myself we shall not be so destitute of intelligence, as not to get timely notice of it, and make a good retreat.*

> *I hope you will see the absolute necessity for our having, as soon as our forces are collected, a number of cannon, some of heavy metal, with mortars and grenades to attack the French, and put us on an equal footing with them.*

Washington suggested that Dinwiddie make every effort to induce the Cherokees, Catawbas, and Chickasaws to come to his assistance, as well as to conclude a treaty with the English allies, the Six Nations. He also informed him that he was writing for help directly to the governors of Pennsylvania and Maryland because of the time it would take to get mail to their capitals by way of Williamsburg.

Washington's letters to Governor Horatio Sharpe of Maryland and to Governor James Hamilton of Pennsylvania recapitulated much of the information given to Dinwiddie, stressing the strong French forces already in the area as well as the intelligence that additional French troops were on the way and would be joined by six hundred Indians. To Sharpe he added:

> *I ought first to have begged pardon of your excellency for this liberty of writing... It was the glowing zeal I owe my country that influenced me to impart these advices and my inclination prompted me to do it to you as I know you are solicitous for the public weal and warm in this interesting cause; that should rouse from the lethargy we have fallen into, the heroick spirit of every free-born English man to attest the rights and privileges of our king (if we don't consult the benefits of our selves) and resque [rescue] from the invasion of a usurping enemy, our Majesty's property, his dignity, and land.*

*I hope, sir, you will excuse the freeness of my expressions, they are the pure
sentiments of the heart.*

On May 9, twelve days after Washington had written to the neighboring governors, he reported again to Dinwiddie. He complained that the horses
Captain Trent had promised for his arrival at Will's Creek were not there and
that they had had to send forty miles for wagons. His men were building and
widening the road north. So difficult was the task they were able to move only
two to four miles each day. Intelligence from traders fleeing the French indicated their increasing reinforcements, with a heavy concentration fortifying
Duquesne. A few days later he wrote Fry that he had canoed thirty miles down
the Youghiogheny River, to see if it were navigable, but he had encountered
two miles of rapids and then a forty-foot fall. He asked for trading goods to
give to the Indians whose "friendship is not so warm as to prompt them to
services gratis."

FIGHT WITH THE FRENCH

On May 27 Washington learned that Dinwiddie had gone to Winchester, hoping to see the Half-King and other chiefs. Washington transmitted to the governor, verbatim, the following message, which he had received from the
Half-King:

To the forist [first of], his Majesties Commander Offiverses to hom this meay concern:

*On acc't of a freench armey to meat Miger Georg Wassiontton therfor my Brotheres I
deesir you to be awar of them for deisin'd to strik ye forist English they see ten days
since they marchd I cannot tell what nomber the half King and the rest of the Chiefs
will be with you in five dayes to consel, no more at present but give my serves to my
Brothers the English*

> *The Half-King*
> *John Davison (interpreter)*

Washington noted that he was writing from Great Meadows, eighteen miles
beyond his previous camp, and that French scouts had been seen: "We have,
with Nature's assistance, made a good Intrenchment, and, by clearing the
Bushes out of these Meadows, prepar'd a charming field for an encounter."
He added that his previous intelligence on the size of the French forces had

probably been exaggerated. The next day Washington encountered the French. He wrote immediately to Colonel Fry, saying:

> *I send to inform you, that Yesterday I engag'd a party of French, whereof 11 were killed and 20 taken, with the loss of only 1 of mine killed and 2 or 3 wounded... By some of their Papers we can discover, that large detach'ts. are expected every day, which we can reasonably suppose are to attack us, especially since we have began.*

He asked for immediate reinforcements. Colonel Fry died after being thrown from his horse two days after this was written. At twenty-two Washington became acting and then commissioned colonel and commander in chief of His Majesty's Virginia Regiment. The same day George wrote a full account of the battle to Dinwiddie:

> *I had detach'd a party of 75 Men to meet with 50 of the French, who, we had Intelligence, were upon their March towards us to Reconnoitre, &ca. Ab't 9 O'clock the same night, I receiv'd an express from the Half King, who was Incamp'd with several of his People ab't 6 Miles off, that he had seen the Track of two French Men X'ing the road, and believ'd the whole body were lying not far off, as we had an acc't of that number passing Mr. Gist's.*

> *I set out with 40 Men before 10, and was from that time till near Sun rise before we reach'd the Indian's Camp, hav'g March'd in [a] small path, a heavy Rain, and a Night as Dark as it is possible to conceive.*

> *When we came to the Half King, I council'd with him, and got his assent to go hand in hand and strike the French... When we came to the place where the Tracks were, the Half King sent two Indians to follow their tracks, and discover their lodgement, which they did ab't half a mile from the Road, in a very obscure place surrounded with Rocks. I thereupon... form'd a disposition to attack them on all sides, which we accordingly did, and, after an Engagement of ab't 15 minutes, we killed 10, wounded one, and took 21 Prisoners. Amongst those that were killed was Monsieur Jumonville, the Commander, princip'l Officers taken is Monsieur Druillong and Mons'r La force, who your Honour has often heard me speak of as a bold Enterprising Man, and a person of great sublity and cunning.*

> *These Officers pretend they were coming on an Embassy; but the absurdity of this pretext is too glaring, as your Honour will see by the Instructions and Summons inclos'd. These Instructions were to reconnoitre the Country... to get intelligence which they were to send Back by some brisk dispatches.*

The Half King... has declared to send these Frenchmen's Scalps with a Hatchet to all the Nations of Indians in union with them.

I shall expect every hour to be attack'd, and by unequal numbers, which I must withstand if there are 5 to 1 or else I fear the Consequence will be we shall lose the Indians if we suffer ourselves to be drove Back... I doubt not if you hear I am beaten, but you will at the same [time] hear that we have done our duty in fighting.

This small skirmish, which followed the French seizure of a British fort, was often wrongly credited as the cause of the ensuing war between France and Britain, which spread to Europe and as far east as India. Horace Walpole called it a "trifling incident, but one which gave date to the war," while Voltaire expressed surprise that "a cannon-shot fired in America could give the signal that set Europe in a blaze." Washington was sufficiently pleased with his success to describe it further in a letter of June 3 to Dinwiddie:

If the whole Detch't of the French behave with no more Resolution than this chosen Party did, I flatter myself we shall have no g't trouble in driving them to Montreal. Tho' I took 40 Men under my com'd when I marched out, yet the darkness of the night was so great, that by wandering a little from the main body 7 were lost, and but 33 ingag'd. There was also but 7 Indians with arms, two of which were Boys, one Dinwiddie, your Honour's God Son, who behav'd well in action. There were 5 or 6 Indians who served to knock the poor, unhappy wounded in the head, and bereiv'd them of their scalps.

We have just finish'd a small pallisado'd Fort, in which, with my small numbers, I shall not fear the attack of 500 men.

Following Dinwiddie's appeal for aid, London ordered the governors of South Carolina and New York to send regular troops to Virginia. North Carolina added a regiment of provincials. The New York companies were much delayed in reaching Virginia. When they finally arrived, Dinwiddie found them not only undermanned but many too old to march. In addition, they had thirty women and children along but were lacking in provisions, tents, and blankets. The North Carolinians arrived with insufficient arms and money. When their payroll stopped, the units disbanded before getting near the front. Only the South Carolina regulars under Captain James Mackay saw action; they would join Washington just in time to be beaten.

Dinwiddie had appointed Washington a full colonel and commander of the Virginia Regiment in early June of 1754. To coordinate the troops from the four colonies Dinwiddie chose as commander in chief a fellow Scot, Colonel James Innes, with whom Lawrence Washington had served at Cartagena. Washington was to rank second, while Dinwiddie gave brevet commissions as lieutenant colonels to the regular captains from New York and South Carolina. This was ingenious but unworkable. The holders of a king's commission, however low, maintained they outranked even a colonel appointed by a provincial governor. About June 10 Washington wrote Dinwiddie a long letter balanced between appreciation and complaints:

> I... return your Honour my hearty thanks for your kind congratulations on our late success, which I hope to improve without risquing the imputation of rashness... I rejoice that I am likely to be under the command of an experienced Officer and Man of Sense, it is what I have most ardently wished for. I shall here beg leave to return my grateful thanks for your favour in promoting me to the Command of the Regiment.

> I hope Captain McKay will have more sense than to insist upon any unreasonable distinction, tho' he and His have Commissions from his Majesty... yet we have the same Spirit to serve our Gracious King as they have; and are as ready and willing to sacrifice our lives for our Country's good.

> Since writing the foregoing, Captain McKay with the Independent Company has arrived... Having Commissions from the King, they look upon themselves as a distinct Body.

> It now behooves, Honourable Sir, that you lay your absolute commands on one or another to obey. This is indispensably necessary.

Then Washington went to a major point which was to rankle him in all his associations with the British army until he retired from this war. As he pointed out to Dinwiddie, British officers would automatically order "a Regular attack which would expose us to almost immediate death without hope of damaging them, as the French all fight in the Indian method which, by this, we have got some experience in." The Americans under Washington had begun to learn from the French and Indians and hence knew better than the British how to deal with them. The youthful Washington could never persuade his British superiors on this point; more than two decades later he would drive the point home somewhat more effectively.

LETTERS FROM TIDEWATER

Some cheerful letters from friends reached Washington on the frontier, conveying the respect he had won throughout Virginia. Colonel Charles Carter, father-in-law of Light Horse Harry Lee, said that he was "charmed" by the bravery of Washington in his first engagement with the French. Daniel Campbell wrote that his victory "gave me and your other friends such satisfaction as is only felt by those who have hearts full of mutual affection and friendship." Major Carlyle explained what he was doing to get supplies to the troops. He added: "We have great Rejoicings on Yr Good Success." William Fairfax enclosed two *Gazettes*, "wherein you'l observe, your mem'ble Acts are not forgot." Some of the letters were still on their way to him when Colonel Washington suffered his first military defeat.

SIX

"SOUNDLY BEATEN"

1754

THE YOUNG VIRGINIA COLONEL, with too few troops, guns, and even supplies to maintain an adequate defense, decided to undertake the kind of high-risk offensive against superior forces that would later earn a reprimand from General Washington.

The Virginia garrison, in its "small palisado'd Fort" at Great Meadows, had fewer than three hundred men. When Captain Mackay refused to cooperate, the Virginians established two forward posts, one at Redstone Creek, which flowed into the Monongahela, the other thirteen miles from Great Meadows at the house of Captain Christopher Gist. Washington hauled guns and supplies to Gist's house and began negotiations with the Shawnees, Delawares, and Six Nations. He was assisted by the Half-King and Andrew Montour, friendly Indians, and George Croghan, a frontier trader. Washington had only meager presents and not much apparent strength. The Indians were shrewd at guessing the size of opposing forces and one by one they disappeared. Even the Half-King slipped back to Fort Necessity. A friendly Indian warned George that twelve hundred French and allied Indians were on their way to attack him.

Washington asked for the help of Mackay, who moved to Gist's house with his detachment. Their council of June 28 concluded that they should "decamp directly" to Fort Necessity. Once they arrived they worked rapidly at the small, hastily constructed fort, building defensive trenches, but the enemy allowed them little time. The French and Indians, nine hundred or so in number, swiftly moved south on June 26 from Fort Duquesne. Their commander, Coulon de Villiers, a brother of Jumonville, wanted particularly to punish Washington. By July 2 they were at Gist's settlement and next morning at Fort Necessity, which Coulon described as advantageously situated. Washington's 1786 summation from memory was brief and reasonably accurate:

> *About 9 Oclock on the 3d. of July the Enemy advanced with Scouts, and dismal Indian yells to our Intrenchment, but was opposed by so warm, spirited and constant a fire, that to force the works in that way was abandoned by them. [T]hey then, from every little rising tree, stump, Stone, and bush kept up a constant galling fire upon us; which was returned in the best manner we could till late in the Afternoon. [Then] fell the most tremendous rain that can be conceived, filled our trenches with Water, Wet not only the Ammunition in the Cartouche boxes and firelocks, but that which was in a small temporary Stockade in the middle of the Intrenchment called Fort Necessity... and left us nothing but a few (for all were not provided with them) Bayonets for defence. In this situation and <u>no</u> prospect of bettering it, terms of capitulation were offered to us by the enemy which, with some alterations that were insisted upon were the more readily acceded to, as we had no Salt provisions, and but indifferently supplied with fish; which from the heat of the weather, would not keep; and because a full third of our numbers, Officers as well as privates were, by this time, killed or wounded. The next Morning we marched out with the Honours of War, but were soon plundered contrary to the Articles of capitulation of a great part of a our Baggage by the Savages.*

The main fighting took place between 11 A.M. and 8 P.M. when the French called to talk. Washington had with him only two French-speaking officers, the chevalier de Peyroney who had been wounded and Jacob van Braam, the Dutch-born officer whose French was limited. The French offered their terms which van Braam then had to translate into English. The fact that neither French nor English were van Braam's first language would later be a source of some confusion. After discussions and changes in the wet night, Mackay and Washington signed for the English and Coulon for the French.

The fight, the capitulation, and the surrender brought Washington into international controversy, and earned him severe criticism from some sources. The governor of Virginia said Washington was undoubtedly brave, but he should not have pushed towards the Redstone Creek without waiting for the additional troops and supplies that had been ordered. The governor of Maryland, Horatio Sharpe, made some tart comments. Sir William Johnson, a well-known Indian agent in New York, said Washington appeared to be too anxious for glory. Horace Walpole said he was a fanfaron. The loudest complaints came from France.

The articles of capitulation included a statement, twice repeated, that the killing of Jumonville, bearer of a diplomatic letter, was a murder. The French had outmaneuvered the translator who, according to Washington, rendered this as "loss" or "death." The French court published the capitulation, with an edited version of Washington's papers and diaries, and circulated them throughout Europe. They called their future ally "the cruel Washington," while a minor poet, Antoine Thomas, added an epic denunciation of the killing of Jumonville at "l'Oyo."

The British ambassador to Versailles, Lord Albemarle, was also titular governor of Virginia. (Titular governorships were an old British custom to give court favorites extra income. The real governor, in this case Dinwiddie, did all the work but bore the title of lieutenant governor and shared his salary with the ambassador.) Albemarle, after receiving the French protests, complained about Washington to Dinwiddie. The lieutenant governor defended him, saying that the translator had been incompetent and a poltroon, and had misled Washington.

The ambassador also wrote to the colonial secretary: "Washington and many such may have courage and resolution but they have no knowledge or experience in our profession; consequently there can be no dependence on them. Officers and good ones, must be sent to discipline the militia and to lead them... We may then (and not before) drive the French back to their settlements and encroach on them as they do at present upon us." Albemarle penned this in September. He died in December, a few months before the Braddock disaster.

Another controversy developed around Article VII in the capitulation, which provided that the prisoners taken in the "murder" of Jumonville would be returned. Van Braam and Robert Stobo were left with the French as hostages until this could be arranged.

When the treaty reached Dinwiddie, he declared that Washington had no authority to surrender French prisoners and refused their release. In consequence van Braam and Stobo spent several years in a Canadian prison. Stobo's exploits were legendary. While still a prisoner at Fort Duquesne, he drew a map of the fort with an estimate of its garrison and smuggled it to Virginia. These papers were found in Braddock's baggage and Stobo was sentenced to death in Quebec. He escaped instead with valuable information that he gave to Wolfe. He returned to Virginia in 1759 to a hero's welcome. Van Braam was released when the English took Quebec in 1760.

FRICTION WITH DINWIDDIE

Though criticism was widespread outside Virginia, his fellow countrymen regarded Washington as their greatest military hero. He had stood off nine hundred French and Indians with a third that number throughout a day's fighting until his ammunition had been lost in heavy rains. Virginians believed, incorrectly, that each side had lost a third in killed and wounded and that the numerical advantage in enemies struck was greatly on the side of the local regiment.

Virginians made their feelings about Colonel Washington abundantly clear in the ensuing months. The chevalier de Peyroney wrote from Williamsburg that there was praise for Washington "from every mouth," and all the burgesses united to vote additional funds for his regiment. Nevertheless a breach had developed between Dinwiddie and Washington that widened over the years. Washington never realized that Dinwiddie had secret dreams of military glory. The governor had asked London for a royal commission for himself but, to this time, none for the local colonel.

Washington reached Williamsburg about two weeks after the battle. Captain Mackay, who went with him, mentioned that he was not a very gay companion on the return journey. The remnants of Washington's troops gradually drifted into Alexandria. The governor and council gave a reward of one pistole to each man who had fought the French.

On July 20 Dinwiddie ordered Colonel James Innes to build a fort at Will's Creek large enough to hold six months' provisions, advising him that he ought to have sufficient troops, food, and ammunition before attempting to remount an offensive against the French. Some days later Dinwiddie abruptly changed his mind. He wrote Washington on August 1 that his "Forces should immediately start over the Allegheny mountains either to dispossess the French at Fort Duquesne or to build a new fort in the area." He ordered him to raise his regiment to its authorized strength of 300, to march immediately such troops as he had to Will's Creek, and to proceed from there "with despatch" to destroy the French corn supplies at Logstown, northwest of Duquesne. This strange order may be attributed to what Dinwiddie described as the "monstrous fatigues" he had undergone. Washington mulled over the letter for a week or more and then complained to his friend, William Fairfax. After quoting the governor in full, he said:

> *Thus, Sir, you will see I am ordered, with the utmost dispatch, to repair to Will's Creek with the regiment; to do which, under the present circumstances, is as impracticable, as it is... to dispossess the French of their fort.*

Consider, I pray you, Sir, under what unhappy circumstances the men at present are; and their numbers, compared with those of the enemy, are so inconsiderable, that we should be harassed and drove from place to place at their pleasure... Before our force can be collected, with proper stores of provisions, ammunition, working-tools, &c., it would bring on a season in which horses cannot travel over the mountains on account of snows, want of forage... high waters... Neither can men, unused to that life, live there, without some other defence from the weather than tents. This I know of my own knowledge, as I was out last winter... The cold was so intense that it was scarcely supportable.

I have orders to compleat my regiment, and not a 6d. is sent for that purpose. Can it be imagined, that subjects fit for this purpose, who have been so much... alarmed at our want of provisions, which was a main objection to enlisting before, will more readily engage now without money, than they did before with it?... [There are] great deficiencies of Men, Arms, Tents, Kettles, Screws (which was a fatal want before), Bayonets, Cartouche-Boxes, &c., &c.,... Scarcely a man has either shoes, stockings, or hat. These things the merchants will not credit them for; the country has made no provision; they have not money themselves... There is not a man that has a Blanket.

If we depend on Indian assistance, we must have a large quantity of proper Indian goods to reward their services... It is by this means alone, that the French command such an interest among them, and that we had so few. This, with the scarcity of Provisions, was proverbial; would induce them to ask, when they were to join us, if we meant to starve them as well as ourselves.

Washington also informed Captain Mackay of his orders, to which the captain whimsically, if bitterly, replied:

I was favourd with yours of the 15 Inst. by Mr. Cowper which was the first I heard of the Sudden Resolves. [Y]our being So Well provided to enable you to Comply wt. your Instructions gives grate hope of the Success of the Interpraise what ever it is. Not doubting but that every other thing upon which an expedition of Such Importance depends Will be equely taken care of; Some days ago we had 12 head of Cattle but they went away and I Suppose after the example of the No. Carolina Regt. have gon home but this is not all our dependance for we have about 40 lb of Bacon and 3 Milk Cows one of which we have caught this day. So if we go Soon on this new Sceam there is no doubt of our being well supplyed there being Such large provision made for it.

So far as is known Washington did not express his displeasure directly to the governor. He did take up the affair with Innes, who said he was unable to countermand the orders to proceed to Will's Creek. Innes could settle the vexing problem of Washington's rank, since he held a king's commission as captain, which was senior to the other regular officers. He was thus in a position to keep the Virginia command independent of the others.

Dinwiddie's scheme collapsed following a dispute with the House of Burgesses. In older days the governor had been entitled to a fee for signing each land patent but this had gone into abeyance. After Dinwiddie reinstituted its collection, the house protested and sent an agent to England to argue the matter. When the governor asked for twenty thousand pounds for the colony's defense, the burgesses tacked onto the supply bill a clause paying the agent's expenses. The governor refused to sign and dissolved the house. He suggested to London that the British Parliament pass an act "to compel the subjects here to obedience to His Majesty's commands."

Thereafter Dinwiddie wrote Washington: "No doubt You have heard that our Assembly is progrogu'd without granting any Supplies; Under this unexpected disappointment, I fear we are not Numbers sufficient to attack the Fort taken from Us by the French." Instead he directed Washington to send Captain Lewis and forty or fifty men to protect the frontier from Indian raiding parties. With the rest of the regiment, Washington was ordered "to march to Will's Creek, to join the other forces in executing such Orders as I may see proper to direct... The late Disappointment from the Assembly has entirely defeated the Operations I had proposed."

COLONEL WASHINGTON RESIGNS

Shortly after Dinwiddie cancelled his orders, the House of Burgesses passed a resolution commending Washington, his officers, and men "for their late gallant and brave Behaviour in the Defence of their Country." Washington replied:

We, the Officers of the Virginia Regiment, are highly sensible of the particular Mark of Distinction, with which you have honoured Us... and can not help testifying our grateful Acknowledgements for your high <u>sense</u> of what We shall always esteem a Duty to our Country and the best of Kings.

Favoured with your Regard, We shall zealously endeavor to deserve your Applause, and, by our future Actions, strive to convince the Worshipful House of Burgesses, *how much We Esteem their Approbation; and, as it ought to be, Regard <u>it</u>, as the Voice of our Country.*

Whether the underlining of "it" can be considered a slap at the royal governor cannot now be determined. It is of some significance in view of the dispute that had developed between Dinwiddie and both burgesses and troops. All the officers of the regiment except Muse and van Braam were individually mentioned in the resolution. Muse had retreated from the French fire and was considered a coward. Van Braam came under a cloud because of his interpretation from the French, which many thought treacherous. The assembly made amends years later when van Braam returned to the colony.

It is not entirely clear who was responsible for Washington's resignation from the Virginia Regiment. In October Governor Sharpe of Maryland received a king's commission and was given authority over the armed forces of the continent. This was understood to be temporary until a general officer could come out from England. Dinwiddie broke the regiment into companies and informed Washington that he was to have captain's rank until the question of royal commissions for Americans could be settled. Washington blamed Dinwiddie and the machinations of the regular officers stationed at Will's Creek for this demotion. In this he may have been wrong, for not long afterwards an order arrived, signed by George II, decreeing that all officers appointed by colonial governors were to rank below those having the king's commission. Even general officers, when joined to regular troops, if holding provincial commissions, were to have no recognized rank above that of captain. Colonel Washington resigned; he would not submit to officers whom he had previously commanded.

Governor Sharpe attempted to persuade Washington to continue. Although Washington wrote to Colonel William Fitzhugh, the governor's assistant, that his inclinations were "strongly bent to arms," he declined, adding:

You made mention in your letter of my continuing in the Service, and retaining my Colo's Commission. This idea has filled me with surprise; for if you think me capable of holding a commission that has neither rank nor emolument annexed to it, you must entertain a very contemptible opinion of my weakness... I must be reduced to a very low command, and subjected to that of many who have acted as my inferior Officers. In short, every Captain, bearing the King's Commission, every half-pay Officer, or other, appearing with such a commission, would rank before me... I shall have the consolation of knowing, that I have opened the way when the smallness of our numbers exposed us to the attack of a Superior Enemy; that I have hitherto stood the heat and brunt of the Day, and escaped untouched in time of extreme danger; and that I have the Thanks of my Country, for the Services I have rendered it.

Within a few months Washington's actions at Braddock's defeat would bring him Virginia's unanimous recall to service.

SEVEN

THE BRADDOCK DEFEAT

1755

O N FEBRUARY 20, 1755, Edward Braddock, a Scot newly elevated from colonel to major general in the foot guards, arrived in Virginia as commander in chief of His Majesty's forces in America. Dinwiddie wrote to the Scots-Irish governor of North Carolina to say that he was "mighty glad" that Braddock had come.

Braddock had with him two regiments under Colonels Sir Peter Halkett and Thomas Dunbar. His aides, Captains Roger Morris and Robert Orme, and his military secretary, Captain William Shirley, son of the governor of Massachusetts, were to become Washington's good friends when he joined Braddock's staff. Two other officers, Horatio Gates and Thomas Gage, would later play important roles during the revolution. A teamster grandson of a baronet, Daniel Morgan, was to be an outstanding American guerrilla leader.

Braddock seems to have been selected for his reputation as a strict discipli-narian, an asset with British troops but less so with the more undisciplined Americans. He was also a brusque no-nonsense man who could get things done. But things did not get done so easily in America, and this evoked his belligerence. He possessed a good deal of European military knowledge, an innate kindness in dealing with his staff and an unshakable bravery and self-confidence. He came to admire only two Americans, Washington and Franklin, which indicates good judgment of men. Franklin's verdict that he would have made "a good Officer in some European war" is perhaps the most just that has been made.

WASHINGTON RETURNS TO DUTY

After resigning his commission Washington returned to farming. His sister-in-law, the widow of Lawrence Washington, had a life tenancy of Mount Vernon but she had remarried and was living elsewhere. George rented the property from her in December 1754. It remained his permanent residence until his death.

Although retired, the twenty-two-year-old former soldier followed the news of British moves with intense interest. As soon as he heard of Braddock's arrival Washington sent him a note of congratulation. Three weeks after his twenty-third birthday, he received a polite reply from Captain Orme, Braddock's aide: "The General having been inform'd that you exprest some desire to make the Campaigne, but that you declin'd it upon the disagreableness that you thought might arise from the Regulation of Command, has order'd me to acquaint you that he will be very glad of your Company in his Family [on his staff] by which all Inconveniences of that kind will be obviated. I shall think myself very happy to form an acquaintance with a person so universally esteem'd." Farmer Washington replied enthusiastically:

Mount Vernon, March 15, 1755

Sir: I was not favoured with your agreeable letter, (of the 2d) till yesterday, acquainting me with the notice his Excellency is pleased to honour me with, by kindly desiring my Company in his Family. It's true, Sir, I have ever since I declined a command in this Service express'd an Inclination to serve the Ensuing Campaigne as a Volunteer; and this believe me Sir, is not a little encreased, since its likely to be conducted by a Gentleman of the General's great good Character...

I shall do myself the pleasure of waiting upon his Excellency, as soon as I hear of his arrival at Alexandria.

It appears that Washington first met Braddock at Alexandria late in March 1755, explaining that he was eager to serve but had to arrange for the management of his property. Braddock agreed that there was no pressing need for Washington to join him before he moved his troops to Will's Creek.

THE GOVERNORS' CONFERENCE

Under the leadership of Braddock, a conference was held at Alexandria in April consisting of Captain Augustus Keppel, his naval commander, and the governors of Virginia, Maryland, Pennsylvania, New York, and Massachusetts. This was an all-British conference to discuss strategic plans devised in London. The ablest man present was William Shirley of Massachusetts. English-born, he had lived for nearly a quarter of a century in America and got along well with the colonists and his legislature. Shirley's planning had earlier been responsible for a major British victory at Louisburg, using New England troops. Franklin said of him: "Tho Shirley was not a bred soldier, he was sensible and sagacious in himself, attentive to good Advice from others, capable of forming judicious Plans, quick and active in carrying them into Execution." Shirley had been designated a major general and second in command to Braddock.

The conference approved a four-pronged attack against the French. Braddock was to take Fort Duquesne and then proceed north to Niagara. Shirley and William Pepperell, the New England hero of Louisburg who had received a baronetcy and a royal commission as major general, were to proceed west to Niagara to meet Braddock. A third force was designated to proceed to Crown Point on Lake Champlain, while a fourth was assigned to retake Louisburg, which to the annoyance of New England had been returned by the British to the French. On April 23 Washington wrote from Mount Vernon to William Fairfax to tell him of the conference:

> *I have had the honour to be introduced to the Governors; and of being well receiv'd by them all, especially Mr. Shirley, whose character and appearance has perfectly charmed me, as I think every word and every action discovers the Gent'n. and great Politician. I heartily wish something of such unanimity amongst us, as appear'd to Reign between him and his Assembly.*

Washington's brother John agreed to take charge of his affairs while he was on Braddock's staff. The brothers visited his Bullskin plantation across the Blue Ridge, and George then proceeded to Frederick, Maryland, where he found Braddock in a frenzy. Braddock had dispatched one regiment through Maryland and the other through Virginia hoping to speed the troops on separate routes, but the Maryland road on which Braddock had come with the regiment sent through that state ended at Frederick. The troops had to backtrack across the Potomac to get to Winchester. Contractors failed to deliver supplies. Wagons, horses, and forage were scarce. The roads were dreadful, and the heat had turned un-English. Braddock began to curse the Americans, especially the assemblies of Pennsylvania, Maryland, and Virginia, which he felt were not cooperating with him on roads or supplies.

BENJAMIN FRANKLIN

Washington appears to have reached Frederick after Benjamin Franklin had left. Franklin was then an important member of the Pennsylvania Assembly as well as deputy postmaster general of the colonies. During the initial stages of trouble in the Ohio River region, Pennsylvania had contributed little in the way of money or provisions. This was partly a reflection of Quaker pacifism but more the result of friction between the Quaker-dominated Assembly and the proprietaries who, Franklin noted, refused with "incredible Meanness" to let "their vast Estates" be taxed. The Assembly in turn refused to pass defense bills unless the proprietaries were taxed, and a permanent deadlock ensued. Hearing of Braddock's low opinion of Pennsylvania, the Assembly sent Franklin, ostensibly in his capacity as deputy postmaster, to confer with him. In his autobiography, Franklin described this trip, on which his son accompanied him:

> We found the General at Frederick Town, waiting impatiently for the Return of those he had sent thro' the back Parts of Maryland and Virginia to collect Waggons. I staid with him several Days, Dined with him daily, and had full Opportunity of removing his prejudices, by the Information of what the Assembly had before his Arrival actually done and were still willing to do to facilitate his Operations. When I was about to depart, the Returns of Waggons to be obtained were brought in, by which it appeared that they amounted only to twenty-five, and not all of these were in serviceable Condition. The General and the Officers were surprised, declared the Expedition was then at an End, being impossible, and exclaimed against the Ministers for ignorantly sending them in a Country destitute of the Means of conveying their Stores, Baggage, &c., not less than 150 Waggons being necessary.

> I happened to say, I thought it was a pity they had not been landed in Pennsylvania, as in that Country almost every Farmer had his Waggon. The General eagerly laid hold of my Words, and said, "Then you, Sir, who are a Man of Interest there, can probably procure them for us; and I beg you will undertake it."

Franklin and Braddock settled on terms for horses and Conestoga wagons. Braddock provided eight hundred pounds as an advance. Franklin and his son went to York, Lancaster, and Cumberland and placed advertisements in the local gazettes, offering to hire on a per diem basis men, horses, and wagons. In offering the king's gold and silver Franklin added that Sir John St. Clair, "the Hussar," a word chosen to strike terror into the German farmers, was prepared to enter Pennsylvania to seize what he needed. Within two weeks Franklin had 150 wagons and 259 horses ready for Braddock. He had given his personal bond to the farmers guaranteeing them against losses. This action caused him much subsequent trouble. He also made cash advances from his own pocket, only part of which he ever recovered.

Braddock was overjoyed with Franklin's effectiveness and wrote to London to say that he had done his job "with great punctuality and Integrity, and [it] is almost the only Instance of Ability and Honesty I have known in these provinces." There were those who later complained that Franklin was too efficient and that Braddock's army should not have been burdened with so heavy a supply train. Franklin did not stop with wagons. The army also received 6,000 bushels of oats and corn for fodder. In addition, after hearing that the British officers lacked amenities, he got the Pennsylvania Assembly to provide food parcels for them consisting of tea, coffee, sugar, biscuits, condiments, chocolate, rice, raisins, cheeses, plus 40 hams, 400 pounds of butter, 40 gallons of rum, and nearly 500 bottles of old Madeira.

Franklin's autobiography, written years after the event, noted another conversation with Braddock:

He [gave] me some Account of his intended Progress. "After taking Fort Duquesne," says he, "I am to proceed to Niagara; and, having taken that, to Frontenac, if the Season will allow time, and I suppose it will; for Duquesne can hardly detain me above three or four Days; and then I see nothing that can obstruct my March to Niagara."... I had conceived some Doubts and Fears of the Campaign. But I ventured only to say, "To be sure, Sir, if you arrive well before Duquesne, with these fine troops so well provided with Artillery, that Place, not yet compleatly fortified, and as we hear with no very strong garrison, can probably make but a short Resistance. The only Danger I apprehend of Obstruction to your March, is from Ambuscades of Indians, who, by constant practice, are dextrous in laying and executing them. And the slender Line, near four Miles long, which your Army must make, may expose it to be attacked by Surprize on its Flanks, and to be cut like a Thread into several Pieces, which, from their Distance, cannot come up to support each other."

He smiled at my Ignorance, and replied, "These Savages may indeed be a formidable Enemy to your raw American Militia, but upon the King's regular and disciplined Troops, Sir, it is impossible they should make any Impression." I was *conscious of an Impropriety in my Disputing with a military Man in Matters of his Profession, and said no more.*

In 1786, in a brief memoir, Washington indicated that he had said almost the same thing: "He... used every proper occasion... to impress the Genl. and the principal officers" with the need to take defensive measures suitable to the tactics the Canadian French, and their Indians would use against a column of British regulars on the "March through the Mountains and covered Country." But "so prepossessed were they in favr. of *regularity* and *discipline* and in such absolute contempt were *these people held*, that the admonition was suggested in vain."

THE NEW ADC

On May 10 Washington was "appointed Aid-de-Camp to His Excellency General Braddock." Washington, without a command, enjoyed himself. The serious, lengthy, and complaining letters he had written as colonel were replaced by lighthearted notes. He wrote his mother from camp: "I am very happy in the General's Family, and I am treated with a complaisant Freedom which is quite agreeable." His letter to Major Carlyle said that he had "infinite satisfaction" that Braddock had had to turn his troops back to Virginia from Maryland. Washington had apparently warned him that this would happen. He also informed Mrs. George Fairfax that he had found out why General Braddock regarded Mrs. Wardrop much more favorably than Mrs. Fairfax, for Mrs. Wardrop had sent him a present of cake and "potted woodcocks." He wrote his brother John that it was "quite the mode" to wear boots in the army. His wore out, and he asked for another pair. After telling about his trip, he said: "I shou'd be glad to hear you live in Harmony and good fellowship with the family at Belvoir, as it is in their power to be very serviceable upon many occasions to us, as young beginners. I would advise your visiting often... To that Family I am under many obligations, particularly to the old Gentleman [Colonel William Fairfax]." He then asked his brother to fish around "with indifference and unconcern" to see what George's prospects might be and how much support he would get from the leading citizens if he decided to run for the House of Burgesses from Fairfax. He had heard in Williamsburg that the county was to be divided and two new seats would soon be available.

THE ARMY MOVES FORWARD

Washington may have been the only cheerful person around the camp. William Shirley, Braddock's secretary, wrote gloomily to his friend, the governor of Pennsylvania:

We have a general most judiciously chosen for being disqualified for the service he is employed in, in almost every respect. He may be brave for aught I know, and he is honest in pecuniary matters. But as the King said of a neighboring governor of yours [Sharpe of Maryland] when proposed for the command of the American forces about a month ago & recommended as a very honest man though not remarkably able... "A little more ability & a little less honesty upon the present occasion might serve our turn better." It is a joke to suppose that secondary officers can make amends for the defects of the first... As to these I don't think we have much to boast. Some are insolent, others capable, but rather aiming at showing their abilities than making a proper use of them. I have a great love for my friend Orme. I think it uncommonly fortunate for our leader that he is under the influence of so honest and capable a man. But I wish for the sake of the Public that he had some more experience in business, particularly in America... You will think me out of humour. I own I am so. I am greatly disgusted at seeing our expedition (as it is called) so ill concerted originally in England & so ill appointed; so improperly conducted since in America.

Washington, in a letter to Colonel Fairfax, described Braddock's state of mind: "The General, by frequent breaches of contracts, has lost all degree of patience... [I]nstead of blameing the individual as he ought... he... looks upon the Country... as void of both Honour and Honesty; we have frequent disputes on this head which are maintained with warmth on both sides, especially on his, who is incapable of Arguing with't; or giving up any point he asserts."

Washington thought the expedition had too many wagons and too few packhorses. He noted an increase in dysentery among the twenty-six hundred men of the army. As the expedition proceeded, June heat, chiggers, and flies added to the discomfort. Friendly Indians appeared but, covered as they were with greasepaint and smelling to heaven, they failed to cheer the English. They became drunk on the general's rum and did what the British described as horrible dances with barbarous yells. Nor were the English regulars' dispositions improved by the not-so-tall American tales of Indian atrocities; stray English soldiers were found scalped.

WASHINGTON'S ILLNESS

George missed most of the army's march. On June 14 he came down with an acute attack of what may have been tuberculosis. Two weeks later, still very weak, he wrote his brother John, explaining that he had been left behind to wait for the rear group under Colonel Dunbar.

The rear detachment had been formed in part because of Washington's own advice to Braddock. Alarmed that the column's three- to four-mile wagon train was an invitation to ambush, he urged Braddock to move ahead quickly with a strong force of men and the artillery but only the most necessary supplies. The train, adequately guarded, could then come on at its own pace. The plan was adopted, at least in theory, Braddock moving on with roughly half the men and fewer than "30 Carriages... and all of those strongly Horsed; which was a prospect that convey'd the most infinite delight to me tho' I was excessively ill at the time." Very soon, however, Washington became disenchanted with the British notion of a quick march. "[A]ll my sanguine hopes [were] brought very low when I found, that instead of pushing on with vigour, without regarding a little rough Road, they were halting to level every Mole Hill, and to erect Bridges over every Brook; by which means we were 4 Days gett'g 12 miles." In any event Washington was now too sick to travel at all and "was left by the Doct'r's Advice and the Genl's absolute orders" to follow later with the rear guard. Meanwhile the main column continued nervously having "had frequent Alarms, and several Men scalp'd."

In spite of his problems, the irascible general looked after his young aide like an old mother hen; on June 19 Roger Morris wrote to Washington to say that it was "the general's positive Commands to you are not to stir but by the advice of the person under whose care you are."

On June 30 Washington informed Orme that he was still with the rear of Colonel Dunbar's detachment, adding: "My Fevers are very moderate, and I hope are near a Crisis; when I shall have nothing to encounter but excessive weakness, and the difficulty in getting to you; which I wou'd not fail in doing ere you reach Duquesne, for £500."

THE BATTLE

On July 8, a wagon with Washington lying in it arrived at Braddock's camp. He was hardly strong enough to get up and ride but he did so the next day in time for the fight. He bore up thereafter for thirty or more sleepless hours of activity.

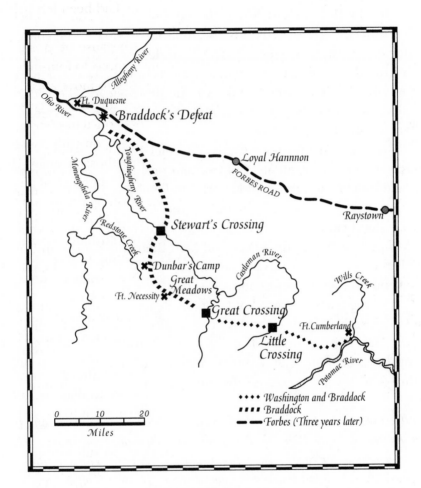

Braddock's Defeat, 1755

Approximately 1,400 British troops were assigned to the attack on Fort Duquesne. The total number at the fort is not exactly known but it may not have exceeded 400 French and Canadians, of whom perhaps 100 were untrained boys. In addition about 800 Indians (termed "savages" or "Americans" by the French) had gathered from many tribes to help their French brothers. Despite such odds, the audacity of a few French officers who knew the terrain was to win the day. The Sieur de Contrecoeur, who had taken the fort from the English, received daily reports of the advance. He knew that they were in sufficient force to take Duquesne by siege. The Indians were alarmed at their numbers, and for a while there was a serious question as to whether they would fight or run.

At the suggestion of young Captain Daniel Beaujeu, who had reached Duquesne with reinforcements, Contrecoeur decided to send out most of his troops and Indians to ambush and attack Braddock at one of the two crossings of the Monongahela. The Indians took a great deal of persuasion to join and it appears that Beaujeu told them he would have to fight without them. They agreed to go, but by the time they had held their war dances and prepared themselves emotionally, it was too late to cut off the British at the river itself. Beaujeu and his men therefore improvised.

The attacking party consisted of Captains Beaujeu, Dumas, and Ligneris, a few subalterns, slightly over 200 French and Canadians, and fewer than 650 Indians. The British plan of march called for two crossings of the Monongahela through shallow fords. Washington recalled in detail, more than thirty-three years later, the subsequent events as he saw them:

> *About 10 Oclock... after the Van had crossed the Monongahela the <u>second time</u>... and the rear yet in the River, the front was attacked, and by the unusual Hallooing and whooping of the enemy, whom they could not see, were so disconcerted and confused, as soon to fall into irretrievable disorder. [A British officer later wrote: "The yell of the Indians is fresh on my ear, and the terrific sound will haunt me till the hour of my dissolution."] The rear was forced forward to support them but, seeing no enemy, and themselves falling every moment from the fire, a general panic took place among the [English] troops, from which no exertions of the Officers could recover them.*

Gage's forward troops succeeded in killing the French commander, Beaujeu, and turning cannon on the French and Indians. Many Canadians fled and the Indians wavered, but Dumas, who took over the command, directed them to spread out on both flanks of the British. Numerous Indians took command of a hill above the main British forces where they could see but not be seen.

When some Virginians, under Captain Thomas Waggener, moved up the hill in Indian fashion, the British troops fired on them, bringing down many. Washington continued:

Before it was <u>too late</u>, and the confusion became general, an offer was made by George Washington to head the provincials, and engage the enemy in their own way, but the propriety of it was not seen, until it was too late for execution. After this, many attempts were made to dislodge the enemy from an eminence on the Right, but they all proved ineffectual, and fatal to the Officers who, by great exertions and good examples, endeavoured to accomplish it. In one of these the General received the Wound of which he died but, previous to it, had several horses killed and disabled under him. Captains Orme and Morris, his two Aids de Camp, having received wounds which rendered them unable to attend, George Washington remained the sole Aid throughout the Day. He also had one horse killed and two wounded under him. A ball [went] through his hat and several through his clothes, but [he] escaped unhurt. [Here Washington named various officers killed or wounded.] No person knowing, in the disordered State things were, nor who the surviving Senior Officer was, and the Troops by degrees going off in confusion, without a ray of hope of further opposition from those that remained, George Washington placed the General in a small covered cart, which carried some of his most essential equipage, and in the best order he could, with the best Troops... brought him over the <u>first</u> ford of the Monongahela. There they were formed in the best order circumstances would admit, on a piece of rising ground, after which, by the General's orders, he rode forward to halt those who had been earlier in the retreat. Accordingly, after crossing the Monongahela the <u>second time</u> and ascending the heights, he found Lieutenant Colonel Gage engaged in this business, to whom he delivered the General's order, and then returned to report the situation he found them in. When he was again requested by the General, whom he met coming on in his litter, with the first halted troops, to proceed (it then being after sundown) to the second division under the command of Colonel Dunbar, to make arrangements for covering the retreat, and forwarding on provisions and refreshments to the retreating and wounded Soldiery.

To accomplish this, for the second division was 40 odd miles in the rear, took up the whole night, and part of the next Morning, which from the weak state in which he was, and the fatigues and anxiety of the [previous] 24 hours, rendered him in a manner wholly unfit for the execution of the duty he was sent upon, when he arrived at Dunbar's camp. To the best of his power, however, he discharged it, and remained with the second division, till the other joined it. The shocking Scenes

which presented themselves in this Nights March are not to be described. The dead,
the dying, the groans, lamentation, and crys along the Road of the wounded for
help... were enough to pierce a heart of admanant, the gloom and horror of which
was not a little encreased by the impervious darkness occasioned by the close shade
of thick woods which in places rendered it impossible for the two guides which
attended to know when they were in, or out of the track but by groping on the
ground with their hands.

The British killed and wounded 977 out of 1,469 troops present. French and
Indian casualties were probably no more than 50. Fortunately, as Washington
noted, the Indians did not follow or the remaining survivors would have been
massacred. They had stopped to scalp the wounded and the dead (including
eight women) and to gather all the loot they could before retiring in triumph
to Duquesne. That night the French fort was a joyful place. The Indians
burned twelve of their English prisoners at the stake, their dying screams min-
gling with the delighted yells of the Indians. The next day they abandoned the
French, fearing the British would attack again.

Bad news traveled fast even in a wilderness. News of the defeat had reached
Dunbar's camp before Washington's arrival. Colonel Innes at Will's Creek had
a garbled version the following day, whereupon he sent out dispatches "To
whom this may concern," a phrase that later provoked Washington's sarcasm.
Dunbar's version reached Dinwiddie in Williamsburg on July 14. Shirley, the
new British commander in chief, whose son was killed in the battle, learned
of it in Albany on July 22.

Washington found Dunbar's camp in a state of panic. Though the rear
camp was far from the enemy, many of the men fled when "To Arms" was
beaten. Washington was too fatigued to do more than deliver Braddock's
request for help. Braddock arrived in camp the next night after a terrible
ordeal. Colonel Dunbar immediately ordered the destruction of all guns,
most supplies, and the Pennsylvania farmers' wagons, to speed the retreat.
The still-large army, seventeen hundred strong, marched off rapidly for
Cumberland. Braddock died on July 13, his last words were: "We shall better
know how to deal with them another time." Washington saw to his proper burial and had wagons driven over the grave, to obliterate it. Dunbar did not tarry
long, even at Will's Creek, 100 miles from Duquesne. Not until he reached
Philadelphia, some 350 miles by the route he took, did he set up a permanent
encampment. There, as Franklin put it, he felt safe, knowing that the inhabitants would protect him.

The news of Braddock's defeat spread horror in Pennsylvania, Maryland,
and Virginia. Not for some time did these colonies hear that Dunbar had

abandoned the frontier upon which, as Parkman wrote, there will burst "a storm of blood and fire." The British army had provided a most convenient road across the mountains for the French and Indians.

EIGHT

MR. WASHINGTON IS REAPPOINTED COLONEL

1755

WITHIN A WEEK the bulk of the surviving Virginia troops were in Cumberland. After two days' rest, Washington sent Dinwiddie an account of the proceedings at the Monongahela. Because the French and Indians had kept so well hidden, Washington and the other participants greatly underestimated the size of the opposing force:

We were attacked (very unexpectedly I must own) by abt. 300 French and Ind'ns; Our numbers consisted of abt. 1300 well arm'd Men, chiefly Regulars, who were immediately struck with such a deadly Panick, that nothing but confusion and disobedience of order's prevail'd amongst them: The Officers in gen'l behaved with incomparable bravery, for which they greatly suffered, there being near 60 kill'd and wound'd. A large proportion out of the number we had! The Virginian Companies behav'd like Men and died like Soldiers; for I believe out of the 3 Companys that were there that day, scarce 30 were left alive; Captn. Peyrouny and all his Officers, down to a Corporal, were kill'd; Captn. Polson shar'd almost as hard a Fate, for only one of his Escap'd: In short, the dastardly behaviour of the English Soldier's expos'd all those who were inclin'd to do their duty to almost certain Death; and at length, in despight of every effort to the contrary, broke and run as Sheep before the Hounds, leav'g the Artillery, Ammunition, Provisions, and every individual thing we had with us a prey to the Enemy; and when we endeavour'd to rally them in hopes of regaining our invaluable loss, it was with as much success as if we had attempted to have stop'd the wild Bears of the Mountains... I luckily escap'd with't a wound tho' I had four Bullets through my Coat and two Horses shot under me. It is supposed we left 300 or more dead in the Field; about that number we brought off wounded; and it is imagin'd... that two thirds of both... received their shott from our own cowardly English Soldiers who gather'd themselves into a body contrary to orders 10 or 12 deep, wou'd then level, Fire and shoot down the men before them.

I tremble at the consequence this defeat may have upon our back settlers, who I suppose will all leave their habitations unless there are proper measures taken for their security.

Colo. Dunbar, who commands at present, intends so soon as his Men are recruited at this place, to continue his March to Phila. into Winter Quarters: so that there will be no Men left here unless it is the poor remains of the Virginia Troops.

Washington wrote a similar letter to his mother, adding that after the other aides were wounded, "I was the only person left to distribute the Genl's. Orders which I was scarcely able to do, as I was not half recovered from a violent illness... I am still in a weak and Feeble cond'n."

Captain Orme, severely wounded in the thigh, also sent letters to Governors Dinwiddie, Morris, and Shirley, which because of his weakness he dictated. In his letter to Morris of Pennsylvania, which was similar to the one to Dinwiddie, he said:

The Officers were absolutely sacrificed by their unparalleled good behaviour, advancing some times in bodies and sometimes separately hoping by such examples to engage the soldiers to follow them, but to no purpose. The General had five horses killed under him, and at last received a wound through his right arm into his lungs of which he died the 13th instant. Poor Shirley [William Jr., the governor's son] was shot through the head. Mr. Washington had two horses shot under him, and his clothes shot through in several places behaving the whole time with the greatest courage and resolution. Sir Peter Halkett was killed upon the Spot. Colonel Burton and Sir John St. Clair wounded.

In writing Governor Shirley, Orme said it had been his understanding that the continental command devolved on him, whereas Dunbar maintained that he had a status independent of Shirley. He noted that all the general's papers had been lost on the battlefield. These were to give the French the British plan of campaign against them.

DUNBAR MOVES DECISIVELY

Dinwiddie received Washington's and Orme's letters on July 24. They were his first official reports and necessarily a shock. He told Orme he had read his letter with tears in his eyes, and he offered him a room at the governor's house for his convalescence. In replying to Washington, Dinwiddie first congratulated him on his gallant behavior and then chided him for his remarks about Dunbar. "Surely you must mistake. Colonel Dunbar will not march to winter-quarters in the middle of summer... No, he is a better officer, and I have a different opinion of him." Nonetheless, the governor was sufficiently perturbed to write to Dunbar, referring to British honor and to his "character as a brave officer." Dunbar replied that he was leaving the next day for Philadelphia. Dinwiddie called this "monstrous," a cry quickly echoed in Pennsylvania and Maryland. Dinwiddie complained that Dunbar was removing not only his own troops but the independent companies that had arrived long before Braddock.

At this point the difficulties of long-distance command became apparent. William Shirley was moving from Albany to Lake Ontario, to conduct the offensive that had been planned at Alexandria. Since he was in New York, that province pressed him for additional troops and he ordered Dunbar to proceed north. When urgent appeals rolled in from the colonies to the south, however, Shirley ordered Dunbar to return to the attack on Duquesne. But he left a loophole through which Dunbar would crawl. Shirley noted that if it were "absolutely impracticable" to do so, then Dunbar was to bring his troops to Albany. Since he had already decided this at Fort Cumberland, Dunbar ignored the order to return to Duquesne and stayed in Philadelphia for a month.

While there he and his officers gave a ball at the State House to celebrate the victory of American troops at Crown Point. He then moved north, but so slowly that Shirley complained that he arrived too late to do any good there either. He was eventually relieved of his command and sent to Gibraltar. He died a lieutenant general. John Shirley, William's son, whose brother William Jr. had been killed with Braddock and who was himself to die three months later in the campaign against Oswego, wrote to the governor of Pennsylvania: "Col. Dunbar's retreat is tho't by many here to be a greater Misfortune than the late Genl. Braddock's unhappy defeat. What Dishonour is thereby reflected on the British army."

THE INQUEST

William Shirley had earlier received instructions from London to make "Enquiry into the Causes and Circumstances of the late bad Behaviour of the King's Troops upon the Monongahela." When Dunbar reached Albany in October, Shirley ordered him and Gage to prepare a report. Their document was without value. In an understatement, Shirley said that it "doth not seem so distinct and clear as it might be." He himself, as a trained lawyer and a man with some military experience, interviewed the surviving officers. He also instructed an engineer, Patrick Mackellar, who had been at the battle, to draw maps of the terrain and the positions of the troops. These have been regarded as the most reliable documents of the engagement. Two major points were brought out by Shirley in his report dated November 5. The first concerned the destruction of the supplies that had been hastily ordered by Dunbar:

> *As to the Consequences of the General's Defeat, after his Troops who were concerned in that Action, had join'd the Division, I find that <u>now</u> the immediate Destruction of great Quantities of the Artillery Stores and Provisions is Condemned by some of the Field Officers. The Copy of an Order from the late General, signed by Capt. Dobson his fourth Aid de Camp hath been produced to me by Col. Dunbar in his own Justification, yet it seems difficult to say how that Order, which was given out from the General at a time, when the Colonel looked upon him, as he says, as a dying man, and consequently incapable of Command, came to be so readily complied with.*

Shirley further commented on Braddock's defeat: "The Baron de Dieskau [a German-born French general captured at Lake George by American troops] in speaking of General Braddock's defeat, said that none of their Officers were in the least Surprized at it, as it was a Maxim with them never to Expose Regulars in the Woods, without a sufficient number of Indians and Irregulars for any Attack that might be Expected. The inclosed Extract of a Paper dated at Montreal July 25th will further shew, Sir, what use the French make of Irregulars, when join'd with Regulars in Marching through the Woods; Vizt. for Scouts, Ranging Parties and Outguards upon their Flanks to prevent Ambuscade or Surprize, which Services, the French call 'la petite Guerre.'" Less than ten percent of the forces at the Braddock defeat were French regulars.

WASHINGTON GOES TO MOUNT VERNON

On the day he wrote Dinwiddie, Washington informed his brother John: "As I have heard since my arriv'l at this place, a circumstantial acct. of my death and dying speech, I take this early opportunity of contradicting both... We have been scandalously beaten by a trifling body of men." From Mount Vernon on June 28 he dropped a note to Orme: "It is impossible to relate the difft. accts. that was given of our late unhappy Engagem't; but all tend'd greatly to the disadvantage of the poor deceas'd Gen'l., who is censured on all hands." To this Orme replied a month later from Philadelphia:

My dear George:

Your letter gave me infinite Pleasure as every Mark of your Friendship & Remembrance ever will do... The Part of your Letter mentioning the Reflections upon the General gives me much uneasiness tho' I feel a Contempt for the Detractors. I know the ignorant and rascally C D (Dunbar) is one promoter through Resentment and Malevolence, and the thick head Baronet [St. Clair] another intending to build his Character upon the Ruins of one much more amiable than his can be. For my Part I judge it a Duty to vindicate the Memory of a Man whom I greatly and deservedly esteemed... I am convinced the Affection he bore you as well as your Integrity and good Nature will make you assiduous in removing these abominable Prejudices... I am...

> *My dear George*
> *Yr. most affectionate friend*
> *Robert Orme.*

The salutation and conclusion are unusually warm for letters between military men and indicate the esteem Washington had won. Orme soon thereafter returned to England and resigned his commission.

CONGRATULATIONS

Despite the defeat, Washington received various letters of congratulation for his own behavior and that of the colonial troops. Joseph Ball, his uncle, who had lived in England for many years, commended Washington on his "Martial Spirit," and added: "We have heard of General Braddock's Defeat. Every body Blames his Rash Conduct. Every body Commends the Courage of the Virginia and Carolina Men: which is very Agreeable to me." Charles Lewis wrote of the "good Opinion the Governour Assembly &c. entertain of Yr. Conduct, I assure you Sir scarce anything else is talked of here," while Philip Ludwell said that he had told the governor that he ought to give a new command to Colonel Washington who "deserved everything his Country could do for him."

As magazines and newspapers arrived from England, to his embarrassment Washington found that they were sometimes too enthusiastic about the colonists. One account said that after the regulars fled, three hundred Virginians held off sixteen hundred French and Indians for three hours and then successfully brought Braddock off the field.

Still quite ill during his sojourn at Mount Vernon, Washington expressed bitterness about his military life and his treatment by Innes and Dinwiddie, blaming the latter for his demotion from colonel to captain. His August 2 letter to his brother Austin, a member of the House of Burgesses, summed up his feelings in a way that appears to have been intended for the legislature:

> I am always ready and always willing, to do my Country any Service that I am capable of; but never upon the Terms I have done, having suffer'd much in my private fortune, besides impairing one of the best of Constitutions.

> I was employed to go a journey in the Winter (when I believe few or none wou'd have undertaken it) and what did I get by it? my expenses borne! I then was appointed with trifling Pay to conduct an handful of Men to the Ohio. What did I get by this? Why, after putting myself to a considerable expence in equipping and providing necessarys for the Campaigne I went out, was soundly beaten, lost them all—came in, and had my Commission taken from me or, in other words my Com'd reduced, under pretence of an Order from home. I then went out a volunteer with Genl. Braddock and lost all my Horses and many other things, but this being a voluntary act, I shou'd not have mentioned it, was it not to shew that I have been upon the losing order ever since I enter'd the Service, which is now near two year's; so that I think I can't be blam'd, shou'd I, if I leave my Family again, and end'vr. to do it upon such terms as to prevent my sufferg., (to gain by it, is the least of my expectation).

> You ask whether I think the forces can March this Fall. I must answer, I think it impossible, for them to do the French any damage (unless it be by starv'g) for want of a proper train of Artillery.

On August 14 Washington wrote to Warner Lewis to say that if he were to accept any command he would have to have the final say on the selection of his officers. Appointments made without his advice and consent had brought him unnecessary trouble.

COMMANDER IN CHIEF AGAIN

Washington's mother quickly got word, four weeks after his worrisome letter from Cumberland, that he might be off again to fight the French and Indians. She wrote, asking him not to go, but he replied on August 14: "If the Command is press'd upon me by the genl. voice of the Country, and offer'd upon such terms as can't be objected against, it would reflect eternal dishonour upon me to refuse it and that, I am sure must, or ought, to give you greater cause of uneasiness." That same day Dinwiddie finished drafting his "Instructions for Colonel George Washington, Commander-in-Chief of the Virginia Regiment."

Washington arrived in Williamsburg on August 27 to discuss the matter with the governor and the Assembly. He knew exactly what he wanted and was tough enough, at twenty-three, to express his demands. He got almost everything he asked. The Assembly had voted forty thousand pounds for a regiment of one thousand men to be divided into sixteen companies. Dinwiddie had already appointed many of the company captains by the time Washington got to Williamsburg. He insisted that he nominate all field officers and that he be provided with an adjutant, an aide-de-camp, and proper batmen. He also demanded a good salary and allowances. The governor and the Assembly yielded all along the line. His pay was set at thirty shillings a day against his earlier 12/6, and he was given a table allowance of one hundred pounds a year. He also seems, then or possibly somewhat later, to have been given a commission of 2 percent on all the funds he handled for the regiment. Having won his points, Washington agreed to take the command and the governor gave him his commission about September 1. Washington quickly appointed Adam Stephen as lieutenant colonel and Andrew Lewis as major. Captain George Mercer became his aide.

Colonel Washington was again in command of His Majesty's principal force in defense of the Virginia frontiers. His was a slim enough command, with probably no more than two hundred men on active duty. He was now supposed to recruit eight hundred more troops, equip and train them, and erect defenses along an enormous border country open to Indian attacks at any point.

NINE

COMMAND TROUBLES

1755–1756

S HORTLY AFTERWARDS THE governor wrote to London in an attempt
to get Washington a royal commission. In his letter to Sir Thomas
Robinson, he said:

*I have granted commissions to raise sixteen companies, to augment our forces to one
thousand men, and have incorporated them into a regiment. The command thereof
is given to Colonel George Washington, who was one of General Braddock's aides-
de-camp, and I think a man of great merit and resolution. Our officers are greatly
disturbed for want of his Majesty's commissions, that, when they join the regulars
they may have some rank; and I am persuaded it would be of infinite service, if his
Majesty would graciously please to honour them with his commissions, the same as
General Shirley's and Sir William Pepperell's regiments; and I am convinced, if
General Braddock had survived, he would have recommended Mr. Washington to
the royal favour, which I beg your interest in recommending.*

Washington remained hopeful for some time that he would get his royal commission, particularly as the undeclared hostilities between Britain and France
were giving way to full-scale war. With his governor's commission only, he
quickly ran into trouble with a captain holding a British commission who
turned out to be more annoying than Captain Mackay.

DIFFICULTIES

Washington took over the new command with his usual seriousness, but the tasks facing him were more wearisome than those of 1754. Recruiting turned out to be the most troublesome problem of all. Every prospective soldier had heard in fullest detail of the Braddock defeat and of Indian atrocities; even the jobless preferred starvation to service on the frontier. A few unemployed were rounded up in Fredericksburg, but they caused so much commotion that they were jailed. Their friends broke in to release them. At the first Alexandria recruiting not a single man volunteered. Officers had to be sent into Maryland and Pennsylvania to look for recruits.

George's commissary, Charles Dick, decided he did not want to continue in a thankless post, complaining that he had not received his pay and had not even been reimbursed for supplies purchased from his own pocket. He informed Washington that he was being sued for having trusted the government. He added: "As this is the Case besides 50 things more too tedious to mention, I leave you to Judge what Man can bare such usage."

Officers were given strict and detailed orders by Washington, but, as he wrote to Dinwiddie, some of them paid not the least attention to them. He was soon writing to the governor to complain of a lack of "Tents, Kettles, Arms, Ammunition, Cartridge, Paper, &c."

On August 14 Washington had reported that he was still in a "weak and feeble condition." Once reappointed to command, however, he came to full and vigorous life. In September and early October he galloped some twelve hundred miles throughout Virginia and its frontiers, inspecting, advising, commanding, and exhorting. His route took him from Williamsburg to Fredericksburg, Alexandria, Winchester, Cumberland, back to Winchester, up the Shenandoah Valley to Augusta Court House (now Staunton), then across the Alleghenies to Fort Dinwiddie (five miles west of Warm Springs), and thence to the Greenbrier River in what is now West Virginia. He then retraced his route via Winchester and Alexandria to Williamsburg.

From Augusta westward, Washington got his first glimpse of what the Indian raids meant to settlers in the far areas of Virginia. The farms lay deserted and the corn was unharvested. A few weeks before his arrival the Indians had attacked a group of settlers at a fort on the Greenbrier River, killed a dozen of them, and captured two girls. They also burned a dozen farmhouses. Before he got back to Williamsburg he received an urgent dispatch from Adam Stephen, in command at Fort Cumberland. Stephen had been reporting increased Indian patrols and scouting expeditions around the fort. The situation had suddenly worsened. He wrote worriedly to Washington on October 4:

> *Matters are in the most deplorable Situation at Fort Cumberland—Our Communication with the Inhabitants is Cut off—By the best Judges of Indian affairs, it's thought there are at least 150 Indians about us—They divided into Small parties, have Cut off the Settlement of Paterson Creek, Potomack. Above Cresops, and the People on Town Ck about four miles below his house—They go about and Commit their Outrages at all hours of the Day and nothing is to be seen or heard of, but Desolation and murder heightened with all Barbarous Circumstances, and unheard of Instances of Cruelty. They Spare the lives of the Young Women, and Carry them away to gratify the Brutal passions of Lawless Savages. The Smoke of the Burning Plantations darken the day, and hide the neighboring mountains from our sight—*
>
> *Unless Relief is Sent to the Back inhabitants immediately None will Stay on this side Monocasy or Winchester—*
>
> *The Magazine is Secured, and a Watch Set about on the Fort—So many Alarms prevented the Work Going on with dispatch. I have reason to believe Capt Dagworthy will look upon himself as Commanding Officer after You have joined the troops... The Province he Serves has 30 effective men in the Service. I was attacked by the Indians on my way down, and lost a man. I saved my Bacon by retreating to the Fort.*
>
> *I was apprisd of the Indians design to Attack, and Sent to My Lord Fairfax for 200 militia—alarming the South Branch and all the Neighborhood... I heard my Lord was very Urgent, and assiduous in the Affair, but there is only a few sent up under Capt. Vorne—Had my directions been observed by Harry Vanmeter, or the Militia Come from Frederick, The Lives and Liberty of 100 people would have been saved.*

The Indians, according to Washington's reports, killed or captured some seventy settlers and burned a number of houses. Washington took prompt action with his tiny command and such additional militia as he could raise. He dispatched sixty officers and men from Fredericksburg to Cumberland, but as this was a two weeks' march, he decided to go himself to the latter post with the few recruits available in Alexandria and, on the way, pick up Shenandoah militia. He reported to speaker of the house John Robinson that he intended to "Repair to Winchester with all imaginable Dispatch, and full hopes of having it in my power to Repel those Barbarous and insolent Invaders, of our Country." From Winchester, on October 11, he sent Dinwiddie a graphic account of the panic produced by Indian raids and the compounding influence of rumors:

> *I rid post to this place, passing by Lord Fairfax's who was not at home, but here, where I arrived Yesterday about noon, and found everything in the greatest hurry and confusion, by the back Inhabitants flocking in, and those of the Town removing out, which I have prevented as far as it was in my power. I was desirous of proceeding immediately, at the head of some Militia, to put a stop to the Ravages of the Enemy; believing their Numbers to be few; but was told by Colo. Martin, who had attempted to raise the Militia for the same purpose, that it was impossible to get above 20 or 25 Men; they having absolutely refused to stir; choosing as they say to die, with their Wives and Familys... In all things I meet with the greatest opposition. No Orders are obey'd, but what a Party of Soldiers, or my own drawn Sword, Enforces; without this, a single Horse, for the most urgent occasion cannot be had: to such a pitch has the Insolence of these People arrived, by having every point hitherto submitted to them; however, I have given up none where his Majesty's Service requires the Contrary, and where my proceedings are justified by my Instructions; nor will I, unless they execute what they threaten, i.e., "to blow out my Brains."*

Washington complained to the governor about the lack of a proper military law, which made it impossible to take action against "the Indolence" of the officers and "the growing Insolence" of the enlisted men. He had again thought of resigning, since he could "never answer one expectation of the Assembly." He noted that legislation was also needed to provide fines and corporal punishment for civilians who harbored deserters. He reported one comic interlude:

> *Last night at 8 o'clock, arriv'd an express, just spent with fatigue and fear, reporting that a party of Indians were seen about the plantation of one Isaac Julian ab't 12 Miles off and that the Inhabitants were flying in the most promiscuous manner from their dwellings... This morning, before we could parade the Men, to March upon the last Alarm, arrived a Second Express, ten times more terrified than the former, with information that the Indians had got within four Miles of the Town, and were killing and destroying all before them; for that he had heard constant Firing, and the Shrieks of the unhappy Murder'd! Upon this, I immediately collected what Force I could which consisted*

of 22 Men, recruited from the Rangers, and 19 of the Militia and Marched therewith directly to the place where those horrid Murders were said to be committed. When we came there, whom shou'd we find occasioning all this disturbance but 3 drunken Soldiers of the Light-Horse, carousing, firing their Pistols, and uttering the most unheard-of Imprecations; Those we took and Marched Prisoners to Town, where we met the Men I sent out last Night, and learned that the party of Indians, discovered by Isaac Julian, proved to be a Mulatto and Negro, seen hunting of Cattle by his Son, who alarmed the Father, and the Father the Neighbourhood.

Washington reported that he was taking all available militia and rangers to Fort Cumberland, although he had received information that the Indians, who had been killing and harassing settlers in the area, had probably departed. He also informed the governor that Captain Waggener, who had brought recruits from Alexandria, could hardly pass over the Blue Ridge Mountains "for the Crowds of People, who were flying as if every moment were death... they firmly believing that Winchester was in Flames." In consequence he ordered public notices posted informing the people that no Indians had been seen for about ten days. He urged everyone to return home, especially as this was harvest time.

On the march to Cumberland the colonel saw unpleasant evidence of the Indian raids. One farmhouse had been burned and the owner killed. Neighbors had buried the body but wolves had dug it up and eaten it. Not far away they found the body of a woman who had been scalped, and nearby a dead boy and young man. On arriving at Cumberland, Washington took immediate steps to assist the settlers. Where farms were deserted, he ordered his troops to gather the crops for public use. He assigned armed guards to farmers who were afraid to work their fields. Burial and scouting parties were organized. He ordered Captain Christopher Gist to Harris's Ferry (Harrisburg) to raise Indian allies against the enemy and to recruit "Woods-men." Gist had been in Philadelphia and reported to Washington on October 15 the impression he had made. "Yr. Name Is More talked of in Pennsylvania than any Other person of the Army and everybody Seems willing to Venture under Your command and if you could Send Some descreet person doubt not but They will Inlist a good Nomber... The Assembly of Pennsylvania is now Sitting and for a fortnight. Mr. Franklin and Indeed Mr. Peters both Told me if you was to write a pressing letter to them informing them of the Damage and Murder and Desire their Assistance you would now get it Sooner than any one in America."

Captain Hog, stationed at the lonely outpost of Camp Dinwiddie, southwest of what is now Staunton, wrote that he had no salt, iron for axes, or nails, and winter had reached the valley. With the humor of the frontiersman, he described his experience with the local militia on October 13:

> *The Louisa Company under Capt. Fox marched out from Dickison's fort abt 10 days ago, with 4 of the Inhabitants of Green Briar and the first night after they got there one of the Country Men was killed and scalped, Supposed by the Indians. They continued 2 or 3 days there & returned complaining of Hunger and Hardships after devouring 2 beeffs & a sufficient quantity of potatoes this is all the good they have done... notwithstanding they were fired with Military Courage & greatly desirous of doing something Glorious for their King and Country, when Mr. John Todd preached to them a Military Sermon.*

Washington continued, burdened with details. He issued strict orders to control looting by his troops. He had to arrange for wagons, barrels, flour, pork, and beef and to meet the ever-present need for salt to preserve meat. He was concerned with cartridges, powder, and scarce paper for making cartridges. He stressed the need to be careful and sparing of supplies. He was watchful of such minor details as windows insufficiently secured on powder magazines.

The problem of cooking kettles involved even the governor. Captain Hog wrote to Washington: "I did not gett any kettles at Fredericksburg and the Men suffer prodigiously for want of them." Colonel Stephen appended a simple footnote to one of his reports: "Memoranda, We want Kettles much." Eventually the governor wrote Washington: "I hope by this You have more Camp Kettles &c. from N York which were forwarded from Hampton ten days ago."

The governor agreed fully with Washington as to the need for a military law and called a special Assembly for this purpose. He asked Washington to come to Williamsburg to present his views. Washington made it in seven days' hard riding. His proposals had been conveyed verbally to Colonel William Fairfax and by letter to the governor and speaker. The law, as passed, was inadequate from Washington's viewpoint but it did provide the death penalty for desertion, mutiny, and other military offenses. The governor had to approve all executions before they could be carried out. At Washington's request, Dinwiddie gave him signed blank warrants for his use.

WASHINGTON IN POLITICS

When Washington, as Braddock's aide, went to Williamsburg he picked up a rumor that Fairfax County was to be divided; this would mean two additional seats in the House of Burgesses. He immediately wrote to his brother to see what support he could get were he to run. When a seat unexpectedly became vacant in Frederick County on the frontier, Washington's friends entered his name at the last minute for the December election. He drew only forty votes in this first try for elective office. He was never defeated thereafter.

THE CASE OF CAPTAIN DAGWORTHY

In his October 4 letter to Washington, Adam Stephen hinted that Captain John Dagworthy would attempt to take command at Fort Cumberland. His prediction was correct and Dagworthy caused George much misery.

Dagworthy was an American-born officer who, for a brief period, had held the king's commission as captain. He was then put on half-pay, which he settled for a lump-sum payment. When Braddock came to America, Governor Sharpe of Maryland appointed Dagworthy head of a company that joined Braddock's forces. Dagworthy showed Braddock his old royal commission, which for some reason he had not been required to surrender. Braddock said that he would have to recognize him as a senior captain. This laid the groundwork for later trouble. When James Innes took leave as governor of Fort Cumberland, he handed the command to Lieutenant Colonel Adam Stephen of the Virginia Regiment. Around the beginning of October Dagworthy turned up at Cumberland with around thirty men of his Maryland company. He claimed the overall command as holder of the king's commission, though his orders came from Maryland's governor. Dagworthy was able to make his claim stick for a surprising length of time, in spite of the outrage expressed by Washington, Stephen, Dinwiddie, and the Virginia Assembly. Dagworthy went so far as to commandeer the provisions supplied the fort by Virginia and to say that none could be used without his express order. Washington, totally fearless in battle, quivered at the royal commission and refused thereafter to go near Fort Cumberland, leaving the burden of the dispute to Stephen.

The officers at Cumberland took sides; at least one Virginia officer refused to obey Stephen, asserting only Dagworthy could issue orders. Washington made urgent appeals to Dinwiddie, who wrote to Shirley, the British commander in chief. Shirley in turn asked Sharpe to settle the matter. Sharpe instructed Dagworthy that he was in command of the fort but not of the Virginia troops. But Dagworthy gave out only that part of Sharpe's letter that referred to the fort.

ORDERS AND COMPLAINTS

From the beginning of November until early February Washington sent a series of letters, orders, and memoranda to his officers and to the governor. These cover sixty pages of print. They were dated from Williamsburg, Fredericksburg, Mount Vernon, Alexandria, and Winchester but never from Cumberland. They included issues great and small. He wrote his paymaster to deduct sixpence each month from the pay of the drummers for their instruction and the repair of their drums. He informed him that the pay of any man who died was to continue for twenty-eight days in order to pay for his coffin. He begged the governor for copies of the military act. The governor replied that the printer had been so busy making paper money for the troops that he had not had time to print the bill but the governor would send copies when this was done.

Washington frequently chided delinquent officers. He informed Captain Hog: "The Governor complains of your laying in provisions for twenty months, instead of the twelve which I ordered; and takes notice of an extraordinary charge of ten pounds, for a Trough, which amazes me: the like sure was never heard of." To Captain John Ashby he wrote on December 28: "I am very much surprized to hear the great irregularities which were allowed of in your Camp... There are continual complaints to me of the misbehaviour of your Wife; who I am told sows sedition among the men, and is chief of every mutiny. If she is not immediately sent from the Camp, or I hear any more complaints of such irregular Behaviour upon my arrival there; I shall take care to drive her out myself, and suspend you."

Washington wrote to Stephen that the various officers he sent out for recruiting had returned after more than a month's absence. "Yesterday being the time appointed to Rendezvous here, came in ten Officers, with twenty recruits; which make up the number at this place, twenty-five. Great!" He ordered Stephen to see that officers chose proper men for new sergeants in their companies. "I think there are many more of the new ones that will grace the Officers better than the old dirty ones." He ordered his commanders to read the mutiny bill to the men and to inform them that if they deserted they would be hanged, even if they returned voluntarily.

Throughout the dispute with Dagworthy his desire for a king's commission preyed much on his mind. To Stephen he wrote:

> I shall wait [at Alexandria] a few days, in hopes of receiving the express from
> General Shirley, who the Governor sent to for commissions for the Field Officers... We
> have advices [these turned out to be mistaken] the King return'd to London from

Hanover on the 25th. of September, that War was Proclaim'd the 29th., and that we have already taken 5 of their Men of War and 120 Sail of Merchant Men; a bold stroke by jove; a glorious beginning... The Man of War mention'd in my last is not yet arriv'd, tho' hourly expected; it is said... that she has commissions for us... I have sanguine expectation's we shall soon receive them... The express that was sent to Genl. Shirley returned without seeing him... The Governor is very strongly of opinion that Captn. Dagworthy has no right to contend the Command... He is not there by order of his Majesty... He can have no better pretention's than a visiting half pay Officer who transiently passes thro' the Camp, to assume the Com'd. I wish you would sound him out on this h'd, and hear how he will answer these things.

TO BOSTON

Washington thus passed the problem to his subordinate, who got nowhere with Dagworthy. Washington then appealed to Dinwiddie for permission to present his case (along with a letter from the governor and a memorial from his officers) to Shirley in Boston. Dinwiddie, as annoyed as Washington, approved the request and wrote a kindly letter on his behalf to Shirley. To this point, except for his voyage to Barbados, numerous visits to Williamsburg, and trips to Frederick and Annapolis, Washington had seen little but rough frontier country. Now, with Dinwiddie's leave, he was able to visit the north and its three major towns.

Washington began the long ride in early February, accompanied by his aide, Captain George Mercer; another favorite officer, Captain Robert Stewart; as well as two batmen, John Alton and William Bishop. Mercer's appointment had caused some Virginia talk about the twenty-three-year-old colonel. Dinwiddie said he had never before heard of a man below general's rank having an aide, while William Fairfax remarked that the Burgesses found it extraordinary that he had not only an aide but a secretary.

Washington kept no diary of his trip but his expense accounts give clues to his activities. In Philadelphia, America's largest town, he spent twenty-four pounds at the tailors and hatters. He remained there for four or five days before moving on to New York, carrying introductory letters to two prominent men, Oliver De Lancey and Beverley Robinson, who were to uphold the British cause in the revolution. He seems to have passed part of his time at the house of Robinson, a son of Virginia's speaker. He noted in his accounts that he took "ladies," presumably Mrs. Robinson and her sister, Mary Philipse, to see "that elaborate and celebrated piece of mechanism, called the Microcosm, or the World in Miniature," as the press called it. This had moving ships, birds, coaches, and other objects. He also lost at cards, bought three horses, and properly tipped the servants.

Washington and his officers reached Boston about February 27. How often he saw Shirley is not known but the governor informed Sharpe that he had taken some days to make up his mind on the Dagworthy affair. While waiting, Washington played cards at the governor's house and again lost money. He bought a hat, gloves, and quantities of silver lace for the uniforms of himself and his Virginia officers, and paid a tailor's bill. On March 5 Shirley gave Washington the paper for which he had come so far:

> Governor Dinwiddie at the Instance of Colonel Washington having referred to me concerning the right of Command, between him and Capt. Dagworthy, and desiring that I would determine it, I do thereupon give it as my Opinion that Capt. Dagworthy who now acts under a Commission from the Governor of the Province of Maryland, and where there are no regular Troops join'd, can only take Rank as Provincial Captain and of Course is under the Command of all Provincial Field Officers, and in case it shall happen, that Col. Washington and Capt. Dagworthy should join at Fort Cumberland. It is my Orders that Colonel Washington should take the Command.

Instead of directly confronting Dagworthy as Dinwiddie had advised, Washington, with great expenditure of time and money, had won a minor victory but had gained no major objective. While in Boston he heard that Shirley had appointed Governor Sharpe of Maryland, whom George did not very much like, as commander of all the southern forces. Shirley wrote to Sharpe on February 23 outlining his campaign plans against the French. He proposed that the provinces of Pennsylvania, Maryland, Virginia, and South Carolina raise 7,300 men, keeping 4,000 for their own defenses and shipping 3,300 men north. He expressed the view that smashing the enemy at Niagara and Lake Ontario would stop supplies to the French and Indians in the Ohio Valley. Shirley concluded:

> As it is necessary that an Officer of Rank in his Majesty's Army should be appointed to take upon him the Command of all the Forces rais'd in the Colonies of Pennsylvania, Maryland, and Virginia and South Carolina to be emply'd in the Expedition against Fort Duquesne, I have appointed you, Sir, to that Command, and now inclose your Commission.

When Dagworthy heard of Sharpe's appointment, Stephen wrote Washington, "He is by with Hopes and Expectations, Exults for Joy at the Change, Struts like a Bull Frog." What Sharpe, Dagworthy, Dinwiddie, and Washington did not know was that Shirley's days of power were ending. He had many enemies in New York, including the De Lancey family and the Indian commissioner, Sir William Johnson. A month after Washington saw him, Shirley learned that he was to be relieved both as commander in chief and as governor of Massachusetts. In his place Lord Loudoun was appointed commanding general; he was also made titular governor of Virginia. Loudoun was to be one of the most blundering generals ever sent to America, and this meant more trouble for the British forces as well as for Colonel Washington.

Washington headed south for Williamsburg, returning somewhat more rapidly than he had ridden north. He reached the Virginia capital on March 30. He had hardly arrived before expresses came from the frontier to say that, with spring, strong Indian attacks had begun and he was urgently needed in the West. Three days later he was on his way back to his command.

TEN

FORT BUILDING

1756

WASHINGTON HAD BEEN annoyed by the appointment of Governor Sharpe as head of the southern military forces. He planned to resign his commission as soon as he got to Williamsburg. The news of renewed Indian attacks on the frontier made this impossible. Instead, he wrote to Sharpe and Shirley asking to be made second in command. Washington's letter, dispatched on April 4 to Sharpe, was forwarded by him to Shirley on April 14 with a generous endorsement: "As Mr. Washington is much esteemed in Virginia and really seems a gentleman of merit, I should be exceedingly glad to learn that Your Excellency is not averse to favoring his application and request."

By the time Sharpe's letter reached Shirley, the latter had learned that he was to be relieved as commanding general. He was informed that a Colonel Daniel Webb, just raised to major general, would be coming to assume temporary command until General James Abercromby or Lord Loudoun could arrive. If Abercromby came before Loudoun he was to take command from Webb until Loudoun's arrival. This was a confusing situation for Shirley, who was given no inkling of their proposed plans. In the meantime, Pennsylvania, Maryland, and Virginia had rejected his proposal that they assign troops to the northern campaign. They could barely raise enough men for their own defense, they said. Shirley wrote Sharpe that under the circumstances it

seemed useless to consider an attack against Fort Duquesne. He added kind
words about Washington:

> *In the mean time I beg you would be pleas'd to acquaint Col Washington, that the*
> *Appointment of him to the second Command in the propos'd Expedition upon the*
> *Ohio, will give me great satisfaction and pleasure; that I know no Provincial*
> *Officer upon this Continent, to whom I would so readily give it as to himself; that I*
> *shall do it, if there is nothing in the King's Orders, which I am in continual*
> *expectation of, that interferes with it; and that I will have the pleasure of*
> *answering his Letter immediately after my receiving them.*

The situation with respect to Dagworthy settled itself quite independently of
Washington's trip to Boston. Colonel James Innes returned in April from
North Carolina. He was reconfirmed by Sharpe as commander of the fort,
which he then took from Dagworthy. Stephen reported to Washington that
Innes did not thereafter interfere with the Virginia troops.

PANIC AT WINCHESTER

Washington returned to Winchester to find endless troubles. On April 7 he
wrote separate letters to Dinwiddie and to Robinson:

> *I arrived here yesterday, and though not a little fatigued, and incessantly hurried*
> *by the afflicting news from the back inhabitants, who are hourly importuning me*
> *for assistance, which is not in my power to give... The people in general are greatly*
> *intimidated, and so apprehensive of danger, that I really believe the Blue Ridge*
> *Mountains will in time become the Frontiers of Virginia. If the <u>fears</u> of the people do*
> *not magnify <u>numbers</u>, those of the Enemy are not inconsiderable. They have made*
> *many ineffectual attempts upon several of our Forts; destroyed Cattle, burned*
> *Plantations; and this in defiance of our smaller parties, while they dextrously avoid*
> *the larger.*

> *Our Detachments, by what I can learn, have sought them diligently; but the*
> *cunning and vigilance of Indians in the woods are no more to be conceived, than*
> *they are to be equalled by our people. Indians are the only match for Indians; and*
> *without these, we shall ever fight upon unequal terms.*

> *I find it impossible to continue on to Fort Cumberland, until a body of men can be*
> *raised, in order to do which I have advised with Lord Fairfax, and other officers of*

the militia... in hopes that this expedient may meet with wished-for success. If it should, I shall, with such men as are ordered from Fort Cumberland to Join these, scour the woods and suspected places, in all the mountains, valleys, &c. on this part of our frontiers.

It seemed to be the sentiment of the House of Burgesses when I was down, that a chain of forts should be erected on our frontiers, for the defense of the people. This expedient, in my opinion, without an inconceivable number of men, will not answer their expectations.

Your Honour may in some measure penetrate into the daring designs of the French by their instructions, where orders are given to <u>burn</u>, if possible, our magazine at Conococheague, a place that is in the midst of a thickly settled country.

The people of this town are under dreadful apprehension of an attack, and all the roads between this and Fort Cumberland are much infested.

Washington's acute intellect enabled him in a day to take in all aspects of a bad situation throughout western Virginia. On April 16 he wrote again to Dinwiddie to say that all his hopes of raising men to scour the mountains had vanished. Only fifteen had shown up in response to orders. As the officers put it, their exhortations to the militia had failed. He therefore had to wait for reinforcements from Cumberland. Having heard that the Assembly had voted funds to raise two thousand men, he proposed that the size of companies be raised from fifty to eighty-seven enlisted men. This followed the British pattern and would be less expensive than the Virginia system. He pointed to the need for drafting men who would be under military laws, but Landon Carter, his friend and supporter, wrote back: "Should we talk of obliging men to serve the Country, you are sure to have a fellow mumble over the words Liberty & Property a thousand times."

HIS OFFICERS ACCUSED

The expresses ran almost continuously between Williamsburg and the valley that spring and summer. On the day that Washington sent his first gloomy reports back, the speaker and governor were preparing letters that were to cause Washington great anguish. The speaker referred to "complaints... of the Behaviour of some of the Officers of the Fort," while Dinwiddie said: "I hope the Affairs of the Regimt. are not in so bad a Condition as represented here. The

Assembly were greatly inflamed being told that the greatest Immoralities & Drunkenness have been much countenanced and proper Discipline neglected." Even his loyal old friend, William Fairfax, worried him: "It's talked of among the Burgesses that an Enquiry is intended relating to the Misbehaviour of some of your Officers." Speaker Robinson, after receiving Washington's letter on the desperate situation in the Winchester area, replied that he thought that it was partly caused by the bad conduct of the officers at Fort Cumberland.

While his friends and supporters were cutting at his morale, Washington received word that Indians had attacked Edward's Fort, only twenty miles from Winchester where Washington had but a small garrison. Three families were murdered by hostile Indians at Patterson Creek. When George assigned a force under Captain John Mercer to search Warm Springs Mountain for Indians, they halted at Edward's Fort, which suffered a further attack. Mercer, his ensign, and fifteen men were killed and scalped.

In the midst of all the alarums and excursions, at a time when Washington did not know whether Winchester would be the next objective, he sat down on April 18 and wrote the governor and speaker agonized letters concerning the charges from Williamsburg against the officers at Fort Cumberland. To Robinson he said:

> It gave me infinite concern to hear by several letters, that the Assembly are incensed against the Virginia Regiment; and think they have cause to accuse the officers of all inordinate vices; but more especially of drunkenness and profanity! How far any _one_ individual may have subjected himself to such reflections, I will not pretend to determine, but this I am certain of; and can with the highest safety call my conscience, my God! and (what I suppose will still be a more demonstrable proof, at least in the eye of the World) the Orders and Instructions which I have given, to evince the purity of my own intentions and to shew on the one hand, that my incessant endeavours have been directed to discountenance Gaming, drinking, swearing, and other vices, with which all camps too much abound... I have been more explicit, Sir, on this head than I otherwise shou'd, because I find that my own character must of necessity be involved in the general censure, for which reason I can not help observing, that if the country think they have cause to condemn my conduct, and have a person in view that will act; that _he_ may do. But who will endeavour to act more for her Interests than I have done? It will give me the greatest pleasure to resign a command which I solemnly declare I accepted against my will.
>
> For which reasons I shou'd ever be content in retirement, and reflect with no little pleasure, that no sordid views have influenced my conduct, nor have the hopes of

unlawful gains swerved me in any measure from the strictest dictates of Honour! I have diligently sought the public welfare; and have endeavoured to inculcate the same principles on all that are under me. These reflections will be a cordial to my mind so long as I am able to distinguish between Good and Evil.

Washington sent a copy of the governor's letter to Adam Stephen, who made a dignified reply and defense. The whole affair was a temporary tempest in a winecup but it had been mishandled in Williamsburg at a critical moment in the colony's history. The threat of resignation brought immediate and encouraging letters. Landon Carter said: "I find by your letter to Colo. Carter that you have suffered yourself to be affected with some reflections that at most were only hinted at, some few of the Officers who perhaps may have behaved like disorderly young men. When you can't but know that it can only be the want of more power in your Country to have added every honr. & reward that even Perfect Merit could have entitled itself to, how we are grievd. to hear Colo. George Washington hinting to his country he is willing to retire Sir Merit begets Envy... No Sir rather let Braddocks bed be your aim than anything that might discolour those Laurels that I promise my self are kept in store for you... A whole crowd of Females have ordered me to tender their best wishes for yr. success & I don't doubt but this night will in a great measure be dedicated to heaven for yr. protection."

Charles Carter wrote: "The House of Burgesses have the greatest expectations from your personal appearance on our Frontiers and are so far from imputing any mistakes or irregularities of the Officers to you that I am satisfied they would have resented it to your satisfaction if any person had... From my constant attendance in the House I can with great truth say I never heard your conduct questioned. Whenever you are mentioned tis with the greatest respect. I hope you will therefore arm your Self with patience." And William Fairfax, who had sent a note that disturbed George, wrote: "Your good Health and Fortune is the Toast at every Table, Among the Romans Such a general Acclamation and public Regard shown to any of their Chieftains were always esteemd a high Honour and gratefully accepted."

Dinwiddie did not apologize for his letter but replied: "I observe Colo. Stephen's Letters vindicating his Character, & I hope the Reports were without Foundation & [of] course malitious." There the matter rested and Washington continued attempting to defend the frontiers. Later in the year a gazette in Williamsburg published an attack on the Virginia Regiment using similar material, and this brought about the threatened resignation of the entire officers' corps.

MORE PANIC

In letters of April 22 and 24 Washington further described to Dinwiddie the conditions in and around Winchester:

> *This encloses several letters... Your Honour may see to what unhappy straits the distressed inhabitants, as well as I, am reduced. I am too little acquainted, Sir, with pathetic language, to attempt a description Of the people's distresses, though I have a generous soul, sensible of wrongs and swelling for redress, But what can I do? If bleeding, dying! would glut their insatiate revenge, I would be a willing offering to savage fury, and die by inches to save a people! I see their situation, know their danger, and participate in their sufferings, without having it in my power to give them further relief than uncertain promises, In short, I see inevitable destruction in so clear a light that, unless vigorous measures are taken by the Assembly, and speedy assistance sent from below, the poor inhabitants that are now in forts, must unavoidably fall, while the remainder of the country are flying before the barbarous foe.*

> *(Two days later) Not an hour, nay scarcely a minute, passes, that does not produce fresh alarms and melancholy accounts... The inhabitants are removing daily, and in a short time will leave this country as desolate as Hampshire, where scarcely a family lives. Three families were murdered the night before last, at the distance of less than twelve miles from this place; and every day we have accounts of such cruelties and barbarities, as are shocking to human nature... No road is safe to travel.*

> *I have just been informed that numbers about the neighborhood hold councils and cabals to very dishonourable purposes... They talk of capitulating and coming upon terms with the French and Indians, rather than lose their lives and fortunes through obstinacy.*

Dinwiddie's letters show that he was as shocked by events as Washington was. Never during his term of office did he work harder to get help to the man on the front. On April 29 he sent an express to Washington to say: "Your letter of the 24th was delivered to me by Capt. Peachy, which Letter with his Information gives me great Pain and Uneasiness for the back Settlements, & your present distress'd Situation, I have and continue to do every Thing in my Power for Your relief. The Militia of ten Counties are ordered to march directly for Winchester, Small Arms, Powder, Shott &c. have been sent from this to Fredericksburg two Days ago... Commissary Walker is sent up to forward the Ammunition to You, to provide Provisions & any other necessary

Services... The Cherokees left this on Monday for Augusta Court House, & I send an Express to Major Lewis to hasten them to Winchester."

Further letters from Dinwiddie informed Washington that he was pushing a new military bill through the Assembly; he was sure that if Washington used army provisions for the relief of distressed civilians, he would receive full government approval; and he had obtained Assembly consent to build a fort at Winchester. He was sending more powder and small arms. "I have ordered everything in my Power that I cou'd conceive necessary for Your relief." He added that no less a person than the attorney general of the province planned to accompany "one hundred Gentlemen" who would gallop to his aid. Such action "will give great Spirits to our Common People." Washington's letters, however, make no reference to their having arrived.

Washington's appeals for militia help through the county lieutenants who attended his meetings were almost too effective. Dinwiddie too sent urgent orders and their efforts brought unexpected results when the militia poured in. On April 29, 86 men arrived and Washington was informed 100 more were nearing town. On May 2 he had 173, and more came each day. On May 8 he ordered a detachment of 200 men to halt outside the town, as Winchester was full and the militia had begun quarreling. On May 10 more than 200 officers and men arrived to which were added 262 the following day.

On May 17 expresses arrived reporting that the Indians were attacking three nearby forts. Though this was a false alarm the militia fled as fast as they had come. By morning Washington found that he had only a handful left. Sixty-four of 70 men from the Louisa company departed, 50 of the 58 in the Stafford company, and so it went down the line. Not only farmers panicked; Washington had the distressing task of telling the governor of the militia's retreat.

Fortunately about this time the Indians left as quickly as the militia. Washington informed the governor that they had returned to Duquesne: "The roads over the Allegany Mountains are as much beaten, as they were last year by General Braddock's army. From these and other circumstances we may judge their numbers were considerable. Whether they are gone for the season, or only to bring in a larger party, I am at a loss to determine."

Remembering the comments from Williamsburg on his troops, Washington issued orders that any soldier fighting or quarreling was to be given five hundred lashes. The penalty for being drunk was set at one hundred. Shortly afterward he decreed that the use of profane language should cost the offender twenty-five strokes. In addition he ordered a court-martial for a sergeant who had retreated at Edward's Fort. He was sentenced to death. Two deserters received the same sentence.

A new military law had passed authorizing a regiment of fifteen hundred men but it had defects. Men were to be drafted but could obtain exemption on payment of ten pounds. Many paid and, in consequence, Washington got the colony's dregs. Draftees were not to be sent out of the colony, which meant they could not serve at Cumberland, on the Maryland side of the Potomac. Finally, they were to be released on December 1 after relatively short service.

The law authorized the commander to build a series of small forts from Will's Creek southward to the North Carolina border. With few men and tools, Washington complained he was given inadequate instructions. He heard from Williamsburg that (since he had designed the fort at Winchester) they had left the decisions to him. With the valley grown temporarily more peaceful, he rode down to the capital for further discussions.

Washington had been kept somewhat posted on the expected arrival in America of three additional British generals, with reinforcing troops, and, it was hoped, the long-sought royal commissions for Americans. Colonel Gage, who had been in Braddock's command, wrote on May 10 that Shirley was in Albany, waiting for them. He added a description of his American soldiers: "The greatest Boasters and werst Soldiers on the Continent... I never Saw any in My Life So infamously bad as those that come from New England." This was a bit unkind, since Gage's English troops had panicked at Braddock's defeat, while New England troops at Beauséjour had won one of the only two British victories of 1755. Twenty years later, when Washington took command of the New England troops who held Gage in a tight net in Boston, his first impression of them, which soon vanished, was not much higher.

Dinwiddie had written to General Abercromby to try to obtain Washington's royal commission, even before the inevitable plea to do so came from the colonel: "Good Sir, give me leave to pray your interest with his Lordship in favour of Colonel George Washington, who, I will venture to say, is a very deserving gentleman, and has from the beginning commanded the forces of this dominion. General Braddock had so high an esteem for his merit, that he made him one of his aides-de-camp, and, if he had survived, I believe he would have provided handsomely for him in the regulars. He is a person much beloved here, and he has gone through many hardships in the service, and believe he can raise more men here, than any one present I know."

By the time Washington's later letter reached his desk, the governor could reply: "You need not have wrote me to recommend You to the Earl of Loudoun." The Virginia Assembly also petitioned the king for his royal favor to the officers of the Virginia Regiment. When Washington subsequently saw Dinwiddie in Williamsburg, he found him at the beginning of an illness that forced his retirement the following year. He had suffered paralytic disorders which, with the fatigue of his work, made him less and less capable of directing affairs.

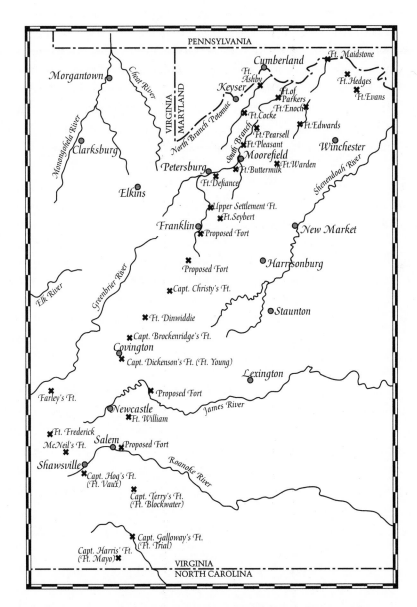

The Virginia Frontier, including Washington's Proposed Forts,
1756–1758

On his return to Winchester, Washington reappraised the situation for the governor's benefit. In May the Virginia Regiment had only 321 regulars. The draft law had added 246 men but some of these had deserted and others were unfit for service. With the scarcity of tools and the few men available, fort building was a slow process. Since each had not only to be built but garrisoned, he could erect only one at a time. It is probable that all the forts were personally designed by Washington. On July 21 he wrote to Captain Waggener: "I now enclose you the plans promised in my last; which if you observe, you can not possibly err. The one shows the Ground-Work of foundation of the Fort. The *other*, the Houses and conveniences therein; with such plain and easy directions for constructing these Buildings, that you can not mistake the design." By August 4 the colonel could report progress to the governor:

Giving the necessary orders and directions, about the chain of forts to be built on the frontiers, has kept me so closely employed, that I could not write fully to your Honour until this. But I have got that trouble now pretty well off my hands.

By the enclosed council held at Fort Cumberland, you will see our determination... where it is necessary to erect the forts. Although we have not kept strictly to the act of Assembly, I hope it will be overlooked, as I am sensible this will be the best chain that can possibly be erected for the defense of the people, and that the Assembly aimed at that, but, being unacquainted with the situation of the country, had fallen into an error.

I could wish we were clear of Fort Cumberland. It takes a great part of our small force to garrison it, and I see no service it is to our colony; for since the Indians have drove the inhabitants so low down, they do not hesitate to follow them as far as Conogochiege and this place. There have been several families murdered within two miles of the mouth of the Conogochiege, on the Maryland side, this week; and Fort Cumberland is now so much out of the way that they seldom hear of these things within a month after they are done.

DECLARATION OF WAR

On May 17, 1756, London announced the long-expected war with France, pretending as the cause the French seizure two years previous of the forks of the Ohio. Washington asked the governor how to announce it to his troops. Dinwiddie replied: "The method, you are to declare war, is at the head of your companies, with three vollies of small arms for his Majesty's health and a successful war." In addressing his troops on August 15, after paraphrasing the pompous statements of the royal proclamation, Washington added: "Let us show our willing obedience to the best of kings, and, by a strict attachment to his royal commands, demonstrate the love and loyalty we bear to his sacred person." Twenty years later he wrote to Joseph Reed from Cambridge: "Do not neglect... to bring us the shirts, medicines, &c. from New York; they are much wanting here, and cannot be had, I should think, upon better terms than on a loan from the best of Kings, so anxiously disposed to promote the welfare of his American subjects."

ELEVEN

AFFAIRS AT FORT CUMBERLAND

1756

T O BUILD CIRCULATION the *Virginia Gazette*, Williamsburg's only newspaper, engaged in a series of attacks on the government. They were written under the head of "The Virginia-Centinel." The tenth article, taking the Virginia Regiment apart, was published on September 3, 1756. It appeared just after Washington's August 29 appeal to Lord Fairfax for immediate help in saving "the most valuable and flourishing part of this country from immediate destruction." The *Gazette* said in part: "When raw Novices and Rakes, Spendthrifts and Bankrupts... are honoured with Commissions in the Army... and... give their Men an Example of all Manner of Debauchery, Vice and Idleness; when they lie sculking in Forts... instead of searching out the enemy... when nothing brave is so much as attempted... when Men whose Profession it is to endure hardships, and encounter Dangers, cautiously shun them, and suffer their Country to be ravaged... Censure cannot be silent nor can the Public receive much Advantage from a Regiment of such dastardly Debauchees. Their country calls; and see! the Heroes run / To save her—if the Game or Dance is done."

The entire officers' corps exploded and presented an ultimatum to Colonel Stephen, demanding "Publick Satisfaction" for such "groundless and barb'rous Aspersions." They said that otherwise they would hand in a mass resignation. They added that "The Printer wou'd never have dar'd to insert such a Paper" without the governor's approval.

The officers also drew up a petition to the Assembly, noting their long service and many battles and their endeavors to build new forts under difficult conditions. They pointed out that, unlike regular British troops, they never went into winter quarters. They also referred sarcastically to their "luxurious and dainty living," adding that the authors of the article were "malicious, wilfull and (as they fear to discover themselves) cowardly Lyars." They demanded that the Assembly give them a vote of thanks in order to wipe out the stain. Although his letters have been lost, it appears that Washington wrote to his brother Austin, as well as others, to see whether he ought to resign. His brother replied:

> It is [the Speaker's] opinion, mine & all your friends you ought not to give up your commission, as your country never stood more in need of your assistance & we are all apprehensive if you give up Innes will succeed & then only consider how disagreeable it will be to the whole Colony (a few Scotchmen excepted) & I must believe as much so to you as any in particular... I hope Sir for the above reasons you will calmly consider of it & not at this time of imminent danger give up your commission in doing of which it will in some measure be giving up your Country... You will give a handel to that Scandalous Centinel. I am sensible you will be blamed more for that than every other action of yr. life.

Having been persuaded to forget the matter by numerous letters from Williamsburg, Washington succeeded in calming the ruffled feelings of his officers.

VALLEY TOUR

The colonel repeatedly complained to the capital about the ineffectiveness of the fortifications he had been ordered to garrison. He disliked Cumberland because it was an ill-defended storage point that took 150 men from more active scenes of war. He decided that it was a waste to have small troop units in a long chain of posts in the Shenandoah Valley. He advocated combining them into three or four large forts, each with a garrison strong enough for ranging, scouting, and defensive and offensive action.

On hearing of new Indian action near Augusta, Washington set off on September 28 to examine his chain of posts. On this trip southward, he came within a few miles of the North Carolina border. He was almost ambushed near what is now Christiansburg by Indians who shortly afterward killed and scalped two men at the spot. His reports were full of gloom. He wrote Stephen on October 23: "Last night I returned from a very long and troublesome jaunt on the Frontiers, as far as Mayo; affairs seem to be in a dangerous situation: and to add to our misfortunes, I find our neighbourhood here on the wing; you and your Garrison in great distress and danger; the Enemy ravaging the country about Conogochieg, Stony-Run, and South Branch; loud and general complaints for protection; few or no men to send abroad for any Service. In short, so melancholy a scene, without the power of changing it to our satisfaction and interest, fills me with the greatest anxiety and uneasiness." Washington wrote to Speaker Robinson on November 9 pointing out weaknesses of the militia system:

1st. The bad order of the Militia and the insufficiency of defending the Inhabitants by them... The difficulty of collecting them in time of danger is so prejudicial, that the Enemy have every opportunity to plunder, kill, scalp and escape before they appear.

2nd. The Garrison I found weak for want of men; but more so thro' indolence and want of order. None I saw were in a posture of defence; and few that might not be surprized with the greatest ease. An instance whereof happened at Dickerson's fort; when the Indians ran down, caught several children playing under the Walls, and had got to the Fort gate before they were discovered. Thus Vass's fort was surprized and lost with the Garrison... Their diligence and resolution in pursuit are exemplified in Capt. Hunt... who was persuaded by Capt. McNeil, on seeing a poor man inhumanly massacred... to go in search of the Savages. They followed the tracks, and came to a run, thro' which they had just passed... Here the Captain stopped, and finding he came up fast with them, thought proper to desist.

From these and other circumstances too tedious to mention, it must appear a very natural conclusion, that the situation of the Frontiers is much to be pitied... The ruinous state of the frontiers, and the vast extent of land we have lost since this time twelvemonth, must appear incredible to those who are not eye-witnesses of the desolation. Upwards of fifty miles of a rich and (once) thick-settled country is now deserted and abandoned, from the Maryland to the Carolina lines.

THE EARL AND THE TROUBLED WATERS

To add to Washington's problems, the question of Fort Cumberland now arose to plague him further. His proposal to abandon the outpost, for which he advanced cogent reasons, was overruled by Lord Loudoun. This was only a tiny fraction of Loudoun's continent-wide bumbling, but it caused much misery to Virginia and to Washington. Washington had written on August 5 to John Robinson, the speaker, who was on the house committee for military affairs, to explain why he considered Cumberland a liability:

> *I could heartily wish the governor and Committee would resolve me, whether Fort Cumberland is to be garrisoned with any of the Virginia forces or not. It lies in a most defenceless posture, and I do not care to be at expence in erecting <u>new</u>, or repairing the old works, until I am satisfied on this point.*

> *This place [Cumberland] at present contains all our provisions and valuable stores, and is not capable of an hour's defence, if the enemy were to bring only one single half-pounder against it; which they might do with great ease on horseback. Besides, it lies so remote <u>now</u> from this, as well as the neighbouring inhabitants, and at the same time is not a whit more convenient than Cocke's Fort, on Patterson's Creek, to the enemy, which is twenty five miles nigher this way, that it requires as much force to keep the communication open to it, as a fort at the Meadows would do, and employs 150 men, who are a <u>dead</u> charge to the country, as they can be of no other use than just to protect and guard the stores, which might as well be lodged at Cox's; indeed better, for these reasons—it would then be more contiguous to this, to the inhabitants, and to the enemy, if we should ever carry an expedition over the mountains, by opening a road the way the Indians have <u>blazed</u>. A strong garrison there would not only protect the stores, but also the few remaining inhabitants on the Branch, and at the same time waylay, and annoy the enemy as they pass and repass the mountains. Whereas, those at Fort Cumberland, lying out in a corner, quite remote from the inhabitants, to where the Indians always repair to do their murders, can have no intelligence of any thing that is doing, but remain in total ignorance of all transactions. When I was down, I applied to the Governor for his particular and positive directions in this affair. The following is an exact copy of his answer. "Fort Cumberland is a King's fort, and built chiefly at the charge of the colony, therefore properly under our direction, until a governor is appointed." Now whether I am to understand this ay or no, to the plain simple question asked, vizt. "Is the fort to be continued or removed?" I know not. But in all important matters I am directed in this ambiguous and uncertain way.*

Robinson took up Washington's letter with his committee, which supported his case, but Dinwiddie overruled it. Washington said that Dinwiddie was unclear but the governor's letter was to the point. He had written: "As to Fort Cumberland, its a King's Fort & a Magazine for Stores, its not in my Power to order it to be deserted, & if we did it wou'd encourage the Enemy to be more audacious; when Lord Loudon comes here... he has full Powers to do what he thinks proper & a Representation to him will be regular, at present it must be properly supported with Men."

On Washington's repeated insistence, Dinwiddie reconsidered, writing on September 30 to say that he thought it would be "disagreeable... to me to give up any Place of strength, as it would raise the Spirits of the Enemy... but as You are on the Spot & You think it very prejudicial to the Service to keep that Fortress, I desire You may call a Council of Officers & consult whether the most adviseable to keep it or demolish it." He added that if the decision were made to abandon the fort the officers should be most explicit in their reasoning since Dinwiddie would report it to Loudoun. But before the council had time to meet, the governor received a letter from Loudoun: "[I] do hope & trust the Government of Virginia will not suffer the Post of Fort Cumberland to be wrested from them."

Washington did not participate in the war council of his Cumberland officers. After two days' deliberation their report questioned the use of the fort in its current state but proposed additional works and an increased garrison if it were to be maintained. The officers suggested that the three neighboring provinces contribute to its support. This was quite different from what Washington had in mind but he forwarded the decision to the governor with his own comments and recommendations on November 2. The governor placed them before his council. In doing so Dinwiddie noted that additional troops would be needed to fortify Cumberland properly and persuaded the council that this was what was really required. He then sent a peremptory command to Washington: "I hereby order You immediately to march one hundred Men to Fort Cumberland, from the forces you have at Winchester, & make the Place as strong as You can in Case of an Attack... These orders I expect you will give due obedience to."

Dinwiddie had been increasingly ill; this partly explains an approach to Washington quite different from his past treatment. For some reason, not clear now, he suspected Washington of ingratitude and snapped at phrases in his letters that he felt reflected upon his judgment.

The letter reached Washington in Alexandria about November 24. In response to his orders he hurried immediately to Winchester. There he found that, with all draftees scheduled to be released December 1, he had only eighty-one men to meet the governor's order and to protect both Winchester and Cumberland. The governor had mistaken the size of the garrison because he had included draftees in his count. Washington reported to Dinwiddie that the "late and unexpected order has caused the utmost terror and consternation in the people. The stores of every kind have all been brought from Fort Cumberland, save those indispensably necessary there, at a very great expense, and lie in the court-house and other public buildings... I am convinced, if your Honour were truly informed of the situation of this place, of its importance and danger, you would not think it prudent to leave such a quantity of valuable stores... In the next place... the works, which have been begun and continued with labor and hardship... [will be] in a manner totally abandoned." The governor, prodded by Lord Loudoun, now further intervened to make the situation more wretchedly complicated. He wrote Washington on December 10:

> *The Returns of Your Strength at Fort Loudoun surpriz'd me... I tho't You might have march'd 100 Men from thence for reinforcing Fort Cumberland, & left a sufficient Garrison at Fort Loudoun, but as Capt. Mercer's Information was wrong, I on receipt of Yr. Letter call'd the Council, not caring to act in an Affair of that Consequence without their Advice, Copy of the Minutes, of Council You have enclos'd; by which You may observe, that it's tho't absolutely necessary to reinforce Fort Cumberland; at same Time to leave a proper Garrison at Winchester; in order thereto it's further thought proper to call in the Forces from the Stockade Forts, to qualify You to march a proper Number of Men to Fort Cumberland, & to leave a proper Garrison at Fort Loudoun with Officers suitable, also to appoint a Person to command, who may continue the Finishing of the Fort.*

> *I rec'd a letter from Ld. Loudoun, a Paragraph thereof in regard to Fort Cumberland is as follows. "As to the Affair of Fort Cumberland; I own it gives me great Uneasiness, & I am of the same opinion with You, that it was very material to have supported that Fort this Winter, & after that, we cou'd easily have made it a better Post than ever it has been, from what I hear of it; I cannot agree with Col. Washington in not drawing unto him, the Posts from the Stockade Forts, in order to defend that advanced one; & I shou'd imagine, much more of the Frontier will be expos'd, by retiring Your advanc'd Posts near Winchester, where I understand he is retired, for from Your Letter, I take it for granted, that he has before this executed his Plan, without waiting for any Advice; If he leaves any of the great Quantity of Stores behind, it will be very unfortunate; & he ought to consider, that it must lie at his own door—This Proceeding, I am afraid will have a bad Effect as to the Dominion; & will not have a good Appearance at Home [England]."*

Washington quickly forwarded to Dinwiddie his comments on Loudoun's obtuse appraisal: "I have read over that paragraph in Lord Loudoun's letter... over and over again, but am unable to comprehend the meaning of it. What scheme it is, I was carrying into execution without awaiting advice, I am at a loss to know, unless it was building the chain of forts along our frontiers, which I not only took conformably to an act of Assembly, and by your own orders... If, under these circumstances, my 'conduct is responsible for the fate of Fort Cumberland,' it must be confessed, that I stand upon a tottering foundation indeed. I cannot charge my memory with either proposing, or intending, to draw the forts nearer to Winchester... Nothing gives me greater uneasiness and concern, than that his Lordship should have imbibed prejudices so unfavourable to my character."

The governor, doubly afraid of Loudoun, who was titular governor of Virginia and British commander in chief, had overreacted to Loudoun's thoughtless remarks. Sick and distracted, he tended to hide behind Loudoun and his council. He had forced the issue of Cumberland against the advice of his field commander. He then ordered a new garrison to Cumberland larger than the number of men at Winchester. To correct his initial mistakes he compounded them by requesting Washington to strip the forts in the Shenandoah Valley. As Dinwiddie became more foolish, Washington turned icily polite and more willing than ever to obey orders if he could decipher them:

I am at a little loss to understand the meaning of your Honour's orders, and the opinion of the Council, when I am directed to evacuate all the stockade forts, and at the same time to march only one hundred men to Fort Cumberland, and to continue the like number here to garrison Fort Loudoun. If the stockade forts are all abandoned, there will be more men than are required for these two purposes, and the communications between them, of near eighty miles, will be left without a soldier, unguarded and exposed. But I mean nothing more by asking the question, than to know your Honour's intentions, which I would willingly pay strict obedience to.

Dinwiddie now ordered that any surplus men be retained for the frontier posts. This backing and filling by royally appointed officials, their disregard of Washington's advice, and the callous treatment of the Shenandoah Valley's inhabitants created much resentment in Williamsburg. Speaker John Robinson wrote Washington on December 31, 1756:

I am truly concerned at the uneasiness you are under in your present Situation, and the more so, as I am sensible You have too much reason for it. The Resolution of defending Fort Cumberland, and evacuating the other Forts was taken before I knew... any thing of the Matter... I took the Liberty to expostulate with many of the Council upon it, who gave me for Answer that Lord Loudoun had insisted that

Fort Cumberland be preserved at all Events; and as we had so few troops, it could not be done without breaking up the small Forts... It was no Purpose to tell them that our Frontiers would thereby be intirely exposed to our Cruel and Savage Enemy, and that they could receive no protection from Fort Cumberland... in another province, and so remote from any of our inhabitants... They persisted in their Resolution without any other reason for it than it was in pursuance of Lord Loudoun's desire, it can't be any difficult matter to guess who was the Author and Promoter of this Advice and Resolution, or by whom my Lord Loudoun has been persuaded the Place is of such importance.

The affair of Fort Cumberland was not finally corrected until a meeting of royal governors in Philadelphia determined that Maryland should garrison the fort. It was nearly summer before that province provided the needed troops. Although Dinwiddie had given far more attention to the views of the British commander in chief than to those of Virginia, this did not prevent Loudoun from subsequently trying to have Dinwiddie removed from office.

TWELVE

FORT LOUDOUN

1757

WILLIAM PITT CAME to power in late 1757 but not until the following year was he able to recall Lord Loudoun from the American command. Loudoun had lost a major battle at Oswego in August 1756, shortly after taking over from Shirley. He subsequently endeavored to place the blame for the disaster on his predecessor. He scrapped Shirley's strategic plans, which were very similar to those that would be adopted by Pitt and his generals. Loudoun concentrated, instead, on taking Louisburg, far from the northern French fortresses at Niagara, Oswego, and Ticonderoga, and farthest of all from Duquesne. Washington, patiently hoping for a visit from the commander in chief, waited in vain. Nonetheless, he kept to a simple faith that Loudoun had the power to save Virginia. In January 1757, Washington drafted a letter to him which is ten pages long in print. He reviewed the history of relations with the French from the days of his expedition to Fort Le Boeuf down to the time of writing. It was Washington's finest state paper to date, dispassionate and without rancor, although at times he was emotional about the sufferings of the Virginia Regiment. The letter bears evidence of careful polishing and redrafting, but he slipped in some soldier's slang in referring to his men thinking they were "bubbled" (swindled) when they failed to receive their pay. Washington described his troops thus:

However, under these disadvantageous restraints, I must beg leave to say, that the Regiment has not been inactive; on the contrary, it has performed a vast deal of work, and has been very alert in defending the people, which will appear by observing, that, notwithstanding we are more contiguous to the French and their Indian allies, and more exposed to their frequent incursions, than any of the neighbouring colonies, we have not lost half the inhabitants, which others have done, but considerable more soldiers in their defence. For in the course of this campaign, since March, I mean, (as we have had but one constant campaign, and continued scene of action, since we first entered the service), our troops have been engaged in upwards of twenty skirmishes, and we have had near an hundred men killed and wounded, from a small regiment dispersed over the country.

Washington said that the regiment had experienced "a dawn of hope" when it heard of Loudoun's appointment and of his high character. He enclosed a memorial from his officers, which, in calling Loudoun their noble patron, expressed "the deep sense We have of His Majesty's great WISDOM and paternal care for His Colonies, in sending your Lordship to their protection at this critical juncture."

Washington received a polite acknowledgement from Loudoun's aide, who said that the general "seems very much pleased with the Accounts you have given him." Since they were uniformly gloomy, this indicated that Loudoun had not bothered to read the letter. Nine months later, Washington wrote to the speaker of the House of Burgesses, suggesting means by which "we may be able to draw a little of Lord Loudoun's attention to the preservation of these colonies."

Washington, having heard that various colonial governors would meet with Loudoun in Philadelphia to discuss southern military affairs, asked Dinwiddie for permission to attend. The governor replied: "I cannot conceive what service you can be of in going there, as the plan concerted will in course be communicated to you and the other officers. However, as you seem so earnest to go, I now give you leave."

THE CONFERENCE

Washington arrived in Philadelphia around February 21, the day before his twenty-fifth birthday. He was accompanied by Captain Robert Stewart and by his servant, Thomas Bishop. Franklin's autobiography said that indecision and procrastination were Loudoun's most characteristic features. He quoted a messenger as telling him that the general was "like St. George on the Signs always on horseback, and never rides on." The governors of Maryland, Virginia, and North Carolina, to say nothing of Colonel Washington, consequently had a tedious wait until his excellency appeared on March 14.

Washington met Franklin briefly in Philadelphia and appears to have heard him speak in the Assembly. His expense account notes bottles of wine he shared with Governor Sharpe of Maryland. Washington also learned while there that his old notes and diaries (which had been captured by the French at Fort Necessity who then translated and published them in French) had been retranslated into English and were in process of publication. He subscribed to a copy.

Loudoun was quite secretive with the governors about his northern plans. He was in Philadelphia primarily to get as many troops as he could and he had little interest in southern problems. The governors were told that he had no plan for an attack on Duquesne in 1757, and they were urged to raise additional troops for defensive purposes. Because an assault by the French on South Carolina was feared, Loudoun persuaded Dinwiddie to send four hundred men from the small Virginia regiment to Charleston. In return he got Sharpe of Maryland to agree to take over Fort Cumberland.

Washington presented carefully drafted facts about Virginia to the conference but his work was largely wasted. He won a concession at Cumberland but lost a part of the Virginia troops needed for frontier defense. And he obtained no recognition from Loudoun for himself or for the officers of the Virginia Regiment.

During this period the Pennsylvania Assembly appointed Benjamin Franklin its agent in London. Shortly afterwards Loudoun ordered all shipping along the coast and outward to cease in order to maintain secrecy for his northern expedition. Franklin had to wait almost three months in New York and nearly ran out of money. His encounters with Loudoun, his endeavors to be reimbursed for his expenses in raising horses and wagons for Braddock, and his comments on the Louisburg expedition are recorded in his autobiography:

While I was... detained at New York, I received all the Accounts of the Provisions, &c., that I had furnished to Braddock... I presented them to Lord Loudoun, desiring to be paid the balance. He caused them to be examined by the proper Officer who, after comparing every Article with its Voucher, certified them to be right, and the Balance due, for which his Lordship promised to give me an Order on the Paymaster. This, however, was put off from time to time; and, tho' I called often for it by Appointment, I did not get it. At length, just before my Departure, he told me he had on better consideration concluded not to mix his Accounts with those of his

Predecessors. "And you," said he, "when in England, have only to exhibit your Accounts at the Treasury, and you will be paid immediately."

I mentioned, but without Effect, a great and unexpected Expense I had been put to by being delayed so long at N. York, as a Reason for my desiring to be presently paid; and on observing, that it was not right I should be put to any further Trouble or Delay in obtaining the Money I had advanced, as I charged no Commission for my Service. "O, Sir," says he, "you must not think of persuading us that you are no Gainer. We understand better those Affairs, and know that every one concerned in supplying the Army finds means in the doing it to fill his own Pockets." I assured him that this was not my Case, and that I had not pocketed a Farthing; but he appeared clearly not to believe me... As to my balance I am not paid it to this Day.

At length the Fleet sailed, the General and all his Army on board, bound to Louisburg, with Intent to besiege and take that Fortress; all the Packet Boats in Company, ordered to attend the General's Ship ready to receive his Despatches when those should be ready. We were out 5 Days before we got a Letter with Leave to part... The other two Packets he still detained, carried them with him to Halifax, where he staid some time to exercise the Men in sham Attacks upon sham Forts, then altered his Mind as to besieging Louisburg, and returned to New York, with all his Troops, together with the two Packets above mentioned, and all their Passengers. During his Absence the French and savages had taken Fort George on the Frontier of that Province, and the Savages had massacred many of the Garrison after Capitulation... On the whole I wondered much how such a Man came to be Entrusted with so important a Business as the Conduct of a great Army... General Shirley, on whom the Command of the Army devolved upon the Death of Braddock, would in my opinion if continued in Place, have made a much better Campaign than that of Loudoun in 1757, which was frivolous, expensive, and disgraceful beyond Conception.

DINWIDDIE REBUKED

Virginia was the only province that deliberately ignored Lord Loudoun's embargo. The Virginia Assembly begged Dinwiddie for permission to export current crops of wheat and tobacco, some of which were already on ship-board, saying that the province's entire livelihood was at stake. The Assembly strongly hinted that they could not afford to pay taxes for defense unless this was done. With the advice and consent of his council, Dinwiddie ordered the embargo lifted. Lord Loudoun was so furious at this breach of orders that he endeavored to have Dinwiddie recalled by London. Eventually this storm blew over but it did not improve Dinwiddie's disposition.

BACK TO THE FRONTIER

In early April Washington was again on his weary frontier beat. He described it to his English tobacco agent, Richard Washington, in a letter dated April 15: "I have been posted then for twenty Months Past upon our cold and Barren Frontiers, to perform I think I may say impossibilitys that is, to protect from the cruel Incursions of a Crafty Savage Enemy a line of Inhabitants of more than 350 Miles in extent with a force inadequate to the task, by this means I am become in a manner an exile and Seldom inform'd of those oppertunitys which I might otherwise embrace, of corrisponding with my friends."

Virginia's commander now ran into more trouble with Fort Cumberland. Maryland's independent-minded Assembly declared that the British commander in chief had no right to give orders to the province's own troops. Lord Loudoun's cry of outrage was instantly seconded by Dinwiddie. Washington was caught in a bind when Virginia's governor ordered him on April 5 and 7 to detach two hundred men, under Colonel Stephen, and send them from Cumberland via Fredericksburg for further shipment to Charleston, South Carolina. The governor, more querulous than ever, was now always determined that all his commands be obeyed instantly. Maryland delayed sending in its forces, leaving Washington in a position of risking the fort or the governor's displeasure. Not long after the redoubtable Captain John Dagworthy took the Cumberland command, he alarmed the whole frontier with false reports that the French were coming in great force to attack his fort. Washington, back at Fort Loudoun in Winchester, was forced to send urgent letters to Dinwiddie, his forward posts, and the militia. He was disgusted once more at Dagworthy, when it turned out that Dagworthy had misunderstood what his Indians had reported.

Dinwiddie now issued orders whose effect was further to reduce the morale of the Virginia Regiment. It seems to have been his answer to a lengthy petition sent by the officers on April 16. They complained that they had been the longest in wartime service of any troops in the colonies, yet they had no regular status nor the perquisites of British officers. To emphasize this, they continued: "We can not conceive that because we are Americans, we shou'd therefor be deprived of the Benefits common to British subjects, nor that it shou'd lessen our claim to preferment. And we are certain, that no Body of regular Troops ever before served three bloody Campaigns, without royal notice." Complaining of "the great expence" of the officers to the colony, Dinwiddie ordered all but seven captains to be reduced to lieutenant's rank. He also cut Washington's allowances and the number of his servants. He directed Washington to have nothing further to do with Indian affairs, indicating he had appointed Edmund Atkin for this purpose.

On June 16 Washington reported to the governor that his regiment, exclusive of those who had gone to Charleston, consisted of 384 men stationed at nine forts distributed over 200 miles of territory. Since he estimated that the whole frontier was 350 miles in length, this meant slightly over one man to the mile. To add to his burdens, he had trouble with friendly as well as hostile Indians. Atkin was slow in arriving, and the allied Indians complained they were not getting their goods. The colonel informed the governor on May 24: "A party of Cherokees under Warhatchie is come in with 4 Scalps and 2 Prisoners: They are much dissatisfied that the presents are not here. Look upon Capt. Mercers going off [to South Carolina] as a trick to evade performance of the promise that has been made to them; will not believe that Mr. Atkin is coming; and in short, they are the most insolent, most avaricious, and most dissatisfied wretches that I have ever had to deal with. If any thing shou'd detain Mr. Atkins arrival, it will not be in my power to convince them that it is not a mere *hum* [humbug]."

After Atkin's arrival Washington said that the Indians seemed to be both more pleased and more displeased than ever. Washington had sent out scouting parties to search for the French and their Indian allies. One group killed two French officers and brought back another officer and an Indian as captives. This produced a quarrel between Atkin, who claimed the sole right to question Indians, and the officers of the Virginia Regiment. Both sides complained to Washington. Atkin said that the officers had dared to question the authority of "his Majesty's Agent & Superintendent of Indian Affairs," while they in turn said that they "imagin'd he had been better acquainted with the Rules of good Manners than to send such a Message to Gentlemen who from their Station in Life their Births & Education ought to be treated with Respect."

Washington intervened to soothe everyone and then questioned the prisoners in the company of the agent. Atkin, later suspecting some of the Cherokees, had them arrested and confined in prison. Their brethren immediately sent out messengers ordering a general Cherokee uprising, to free them. Washington again had to straighten out this situation.

Since Stanwix's Pennsylvania command extended to the southern British forces, Washington was technically under his orders. He asked Dinwiddie how he should act with respect to Stanwix. The governor replied that Washington was to obey Stanwix without regard to orders that might have originated with him. However, the governor continued to send instructions as though Stanwix did not exist. In one instance Washington asked both for urgent leave for some private affairs. Stanwix sent a polite reply saying that it was unnecessary to ask him as he knew that Washington would never take time off unless there were an emergency. Dinwiddie denied the request.

NEWS FROM CHARLESTON

During the summer Captain George Mercer, who had been Washington's aide, wrote from Charleston to tell him how the Virginia detachment fared. He praised the Swiss-born British commanding officer, Colonel Henry Bouquet, as "a good natured, sensible Man, very obliging to all under his Command." The following year Bouquet was transferred to Pennsylvania; Washington was to serve under him in the final campaign against Duquesne.

Mercer reported that the Virginians got along well with the regular British officers. They had expected to see a parcel of disorderly people "like the rest of the Provincials," but they found that the Virginians "made a good and soldierlike Appearance and performed in every particular as well as could be expected from any Troops." The English, having found Washington's officers to be gentlemen, became very friendly. They stopped calling them "provincials," referring to them instead as "the Detachment of the Virginia Regiment." Captain Mercer summed up Charleston:

> *I never... was so much disappointed. The Town Is little larger than Williamsburg no buildings in it to compare with our public ones. The town is on a point of land... There are some very good houses [there.] The rest of the Town is indifferently improved, many very bad low clapboard House upon their Principal Streets which are in general narrow & confined... I have not yet mentioned the fair Ones I wish I could call Them so, I assure you they are very far inferior to the Beauties of our own Country, & as much on the Reserve as in any Place I ever was, occasioned by the Multiplicity of Scandal which prevails here; for the chief of your Entertainment even in the best Houses & as the first Introduction is upon that agreeable Subject. Then you hear the Termagant & the Inconstant, the Prude & the Coquette the fine Gent & the fine Lady laid off in their most beautiful Colours.*

Mercer added that he was sure that Washington would hardly believe that Colonel Stephen, who had been so long at the frontier post of Cumberland, "never appears here but in full dressed laced Suits—so great a change has

Carolina produced." The Virginia detachment, having encountered no enemy, returned to Washington's command in time for the campaign of 1758 against Duquesne.

DINWIDDIE AND WASHINGTON QUARREL

The governor and his commander had worked together since late 1753, when Dinwiddie had appointed the young man as major. Now the governor was sick and testy, and Washington himself, during the latter part of the year, became desperately ill. Their final relationship ended on an unhappy note. Early in June the colonel wrote to the speaker of the house: "I am convinced it would give pleasure to the Governor to hear I am involved in trouble, however undeservedly, such are his dispositions towards me."

In July Dinwiddie complained of the slowness in building Fort Loudoun and of Washington's failure to transmit information he had received from Stanwix. On August 13, a sharp letter reached the colonel from Williamsburg. The governor said Washington was very loose in sending his accounts. He added that Washington had not mentioned the number of men sent to Augusta, nor did he acknowledge receipt of small arms, and he had failed to report trouble with the friendly Indians. "You must allow this is a loose way of Writing & it's Your Duty to be more particular to me." Washington replied on August 27:

I must beg leave, however, before I conclude, to observe, in justification of my own conduct, that it is with pleasure I receive reproof, when reproof is due, because no person can be readier to accuse me, than I am to acknowledge an error, when I am guilty of one; nor more desirous of atoning for a crime, when I am sensible of having committed it. But, on the other hand, it is with concern I remark that my best endeavours lose their reward, and that my conduct, although I have universally studied to make it as unexceptionable as I could, does not appear to you in a favourable light. Otherwise your Honour would not have accused me of loose behaviour and remissness of duty, in matters where, I believe, I have rather exceeded than fallen short of it. This, I think, is evidently the case in speaking of Indian affairs at all after being instructed not to have any concern with or "management of Indian affairs"... I really thought it unnecessary to say more than that "the detachment for Augusta was marched," because your Honour gave me a copy of the council held at Philadelphia, which directed one hundred and fifty men to be posted at Dickinson's, and one hundred at Vauses, which direction I observed, and thought it would be sufficiently understood when I wrote as above... I should have acknowledged the receipt of the arms had they come, but they were not arrived when my last was wrote... However, if I have err'd in these points, I am sorry for it, and shall endeavour for the future to be as particular and satisfactory, in my accounts of these things, as possible.

The Indian agent, provided by Dinwiddie, had proved so ineffective that he turned many friendly Indians against the English. On September 17 twenty settlers were killed twelve miles from Fort Loudoun. Fifteen more were massacred a few days later. On September 24 Washington informed Dinwiddie that the inhabitants of the valley were "terrified beyond expression. Some have abandoned their plantations, and many are packing... Another irruption into the heart of this settlement will be fatal. The only method of effectually defending such a vast extent of mountains covered with thick woods, as our frontiers, against such an enemy, is by carrying the war into their country." On being denied leave to come to Williamsburg, the colonel wrote the governor on October 24 that he wanted to go to the capital to beg for help in his dire straits; the Virginia Assembly, Lord Loudoun, or Colonel Stanwix had to do something. If no farmers were left in the valley, there would be no food for the garrison.

On November 2 the governor wrote Washington: "I am much indisposed." It probably reached headquarters after the colonel's collapse with a dangerous illness. It was a recurrence of tuberculosis on top of severe dysentery with which he had suffered off and on, since August 1. The long relations between the two ended, with both men very sick.

THE RETURN TO MOUNT VERNON

On November 9 Captain Robert Stewart wrote to Dinwiddie from Fort Loudoun: "For upwards of three Months past Colo. Washington has labour'd under a Bloody Flux, about a week ago his Disorder greatly increas'd attended with bad Fevers the day before yesterday he was seiz'd with Stitches & violent Pleurtick Pains upon which the Doctor Bled him and yesterday he twice repeated the same operation... The Doctor has strongly recommended his immediately changing his air and going some place where he can be kept quiet (a thing impossible here) being the best chance that now remains for his Recovery, the Colo. objected to following this Advice before he could procure Yr. Hons. Liberty but the Doctor [Craik] gave him such reasons as convinc'd him it might be too late and he has at length with reluctance agreed to it; therefore has Directed me to acquaint Yr. Honr. (as he is not in condition to write himself) of his resolution of leaving this immediately."

Dinwiddie promptly replied to Stewart: "The violent Complaint Colo. Washington labors under gives me great Concern, it was unknown to me or he shou'd have had Leave of Absence sooner, & I am very glad he did not delay following the Doctor's advice, to try a Change of Air, I sincerely wish him a speedy Recovery."

Harboring a chronic disease, and worn down by fatigue, criticisms, and frustrations, Washington collapsed. For five months he was unable to resume his command.

THIRTEEN

BRIGADIER WASHINGTON REACHES DUQUESNE

1758

GEORGE WASHINGTON HAD moved into his brother's tubercular household when he was about sixteen. His first severe illness occurred the following year. His next bout with the disease appears to have taken place not long after his twentieth birthday. He was again ill for several months when he was twenty-three. Midsummer of 1757 was the beginning of the longest serious illness of Washington's life. Even near the end of his bitter fight, he missed death by the narrowest margin. When he realized that he was finally free of the disease, perhaps in late 1762, he was a changed man whose goal was no longer glory but the happiness of living.

When Washington returned to Mount Vernon he received as good medical advice as could be given even in a much later age. James Craik, though he had followed the barbarous practice of bleeding a very sick man, wrote to him at Mount Vernon to say that God was the best of all physicians. Nothing would be more conducive to his recovery than complete rest and quiet and turning his mind from all public business. At home he was under the care of a remarkable man, Charles Green, a physician who had taken Holy Orders and was also his rector. Green confined Washington to strict rest, told him to avoid meats, and assigned a bland diet of jellies, tea, and wine mixed with gum arabic.

Washington's brother John and his wife, who were taking care of Mount Vernon, were away when he returned. He therefore appealed to Mrs. George

Fairfax, his neighbor, for help. William Fairfax, who so long supported Washington, had died two months previously. George Fairfax was in England to settle his father's estate and perhaps to look into other matters, for he was now in line for the family title, after Lord Fairfax's aging brother.

Shortly after Christmas Washington had sufficiently recovered to write a few letters to his London merchants. He soon indicated that he wanted to return to his post. He may have been influenced by a report he received of a Christmas night brawl that his regiment had started at Winchester. The details are obscure, but from a January 30 letter to Washington by John Baylis, a militia major, it appears that Washington's soldiers beat up a man they thought was Baylis, and Lord Fairfax was threatened with mayhem, with the result that numerous soldiers were jailed. At least one duel was subsequently offered. The news that he was struggling to return to his post reached his neighbor George Mason, who chided him on January 4: "I hope You will comply with the Opinion & Advice of all Your Friends, & not risque a Journey to Winchester till a more favourable Season of the Year, or a better State of Health, will permit You to do it with Safety; & give Me Leave Sir to mention another Consideration, which I am sure will have Weight with You—in attempting to attend the Duty of Your Post at a Season of the Year when there is no Room to expect an Alarm, or anything extraordinary to require Your Presence, You will, in all probability, bring on a Relapse, & render Yourself incapable of Serving the Public at a time when there may be the utmost Occasion; & there is nothing more certain than that a Gentlemen in Your Station owes the Care of his Health & Life not only to Himself & his Friends, but to his Country."

Around February 11 Washington made an attempt to travel to Williamsburg to talk to John Blair, acting governor after Dinwiddie's departure, but he had such severe pains and fevers that he returned to Mount Vernon and to bed. It was almost three weeks before he could go south again. In March he was at the capital, combining business with a fast and successful courtship.

MRS. CUSTIS

Washington was 27 in February. He knew that his condition was so critical that if he resumed service at all, it could be for only a short period. It was better for him, therefore, to have a wife who could help restore his health. With her he could go back to farming, adding public service on the side.

He unerringly picked the right woman, though reliable details as to how he did it are lacking. She was a widow, a few months older than he, with two small children. From all the later descriptions of Martha Dandridge Custis it is possible to surmise why she accepted the colonel. She spoke of herself as "a fine, healthy girl... cheerful as a cricket and busy as a bee." Others said of Martha that "her soul overflows with kindness." She was never happier than when she could nurse sick people, children, servants, and soldiers to health. Sometime that March, five-foot-high Martha agreed to take the towering colonel as her husband. A year later he wrote of the happiness he had with the "agreeable Partner" who was finally to restore him to health.

BACK TO BATTLE

On March 4 Washington resumed correspondence about the war with France. Lord Loudoun had forwarded to Colonel Stanwix the proposal of a Major John Smith to take Detroit. Stanwix sent the letter to Washington for comment. He replied:

> *You condescend to ask my opinion of Major Smith. Pray, does not his plan sufficiently indicate the man? Can there be a better index to his abilities, than his scheme for reducing the enemy on the Ohio? and his expeditious march of a thousand men to Detroit? Surely, he intended to provide them with wings to facilitate their passage over so mountainous and extensive a country, or what way else could he accompany it in?*

> *I have not had the pleasure of seeing Major Smith, though I have been favoured with a letter from him, in which he politely professes some concern at hearing of my indisposition, as it prevented him from seeing me at Winchester; but desires, at the same time that I will <u>attend him at his house</u> in Augusta, about two hundred miles hence! or in Williamsburg by the 20th instant, when, I suppose he intends to honour me with his <u>orders</u>.*

> *I have never been able to return to my command, since I wrote to you last, my disorder at times returning obstinately upon me, in spite of the efforts of all the sons of Aesculapius. At certain periods I have been reduced to great extremity.*

> *I am now under a strict regimen, and shall set out tomorrow for Williamsburg to receive the advice of the best physicians there. My constitution is certainly greatly impaired, and as nothing can retrieve it, but the greatest care and the most circumspect conduct, as I now have no prospect left of preferment in the military*

way, and as I despair of rendering that immediate service, which my country may require from the person commanding their troops, I have some thoughts of quitting my command, and retiring from all public business, leaving my post to be filled by some other person more capable of the task, and who may, perhaps, have his endeavours crowned with more success than mine have been. Wherever I go, or whatever becomes of me, I shall always possess the sincerest and most affectionate regard for you.

Colonel Stanwix, throughout their association, always treated Washington with great consideration and politeness, which Washington warmly recipro-cated. While in Williamsburg the colonel learned of new developments in the French war. Pitt had recalled Loudoun and assigned Jeffrey Amherst to take Louisburg. The brilliant Lord Howe was ordered to smash Ticonderoga while an unknown Scot, John Forbes, was selected to capture Fort Duquesne. Pitt promised the Americans that the British would provide arms, ammunition, and equipment, and the colonies need only raise and pay their soldiers. He removed a great American grievance in which colonial field officers, when with regular British troops, were reduced to captain's rank. They were now permitted to retain their rank through colonel. Pitt appealed with generosity to Americans who responded with enthusiasm.

Virginia, like England, sprang into fresh life. On April 7 the colony voted to increase its forces to two thousand men, to add three ranger companies and a second regiment, and to call up additional militia for local defense. The colony agreed to send the regiments wherever they were needed. Colonel William Byrd III was appointed to command the second regiment. On April 5, two days before the act passed the Assembly, Colonel Washington was back at Fort Loudoun.

John Forbes, just created brigadier general, took over his command in Philadelphia in March. It consisted of Scots Highlanders on their way from Britain, the Royal Americans, and provincial regiments from Pennsylvania, Maryland, Virginia, and North Carolina. To these were added the detachment of the Virginia Regiment that had been in South Carolina.

Washington at once began his usual maneuvers to assure his becoming an important figure in the campaign. He wrote to Stanwix, just promoted to brigadier, on April 10:

Permit me, at the same time I congratulate you... upon the promotion you have met with and justly merited, to express my concern at the prospect of parting with you. I can truly say, it is a matter of no small regret to me! and that I should have thought myself happy in serving this campaign under your immediate command...

I... Beg that you will add one more kindness, and that is, to mention me in
favorable terms to General Forbes... not as a person who would depend upon him
for further recommendation to military preferment, for I have long conquered all
such expectancies... but as a person who would be gladly distinguished in some
measure from the <u>common run</u> of provincial officers, as I understand there will be
a motley herd of us.

Washington also requested Colonel Thomas Gage, with whom he had served
in the Braddock campaign, to put in a good word for him with the southern
commander in chief. All this showed the kind of modesty on which people
were to comment for years after he had won international fame. Forbes, in
fact, had heard all about him and, not long after assuming command, wrote
of him in complimentary terms to the acting governor of Virginia. When Blair
forwarded the letter to the colonel, Washington dropped a line to Forbes:
"Permit me to return you my sincere thanks for the honour you were pleased
to do me, in a letter to Mr. President Blair, and to assure you that, to merit a
continuance of the good opinion you have therein expressed for me, shall be
one of my principal studies. I have no higher ambition than to act my part well
during the campaign, and if I should *thereby* merit your approbation, it would
be the most pleasing reward for the toils I shall undergo." He added that his
men were scattered over some two hundred miles of territory and he would
have considerable trouble assembling them after his orders arrived.

Washington stressed repeatedly to Forbes, St. Clair, and Bouquet the importance of their Indian allies, the need to encourage them with gifts, and the
desirability of frequently counselling with their chiefs. Forbes was new to
America but St. Clair had long experience in the country. This time the
British worked with patience to secure Indian support, thereby delaying the
campaign so long that Washington chafed with impatience.

To replace the men of the Virginia Regiment, who were scheduled to go
north, the law authorized the governor or the commander in chief of the regiment to call out the militia. The acting governor suggested that Washington
do this but he felt it politically too delicate and believed that such orders
should come from Williamsburg; hence Blair took on the responsibility.

On April 27 Washington wrote to St. Clair that Blair had ordered the
Virginia Regiments placed under Forbes' command and that he expected his
companies from South Carolina shortly. He thanked St. Clair for his good
opinion saying that "the Esteem of my Friends" would be his only reward
other than the consciousness of doing his duty. St. Clair dropped a line on
May 7 to say he would proceed to Winchester to help Washington in any way
he could. In the meantime, he was "busy about Roads, Hay, Oats, Indian Corn,

& Waggons." He asked Washington to arrange for a room in Winchester. Washington replied: "I have engaged Lodgings for you at Mr. P. Buchby's, much the best House in this Town."

Increasingly Washington urged training and discipline for his officers and men. He asked Major Lewis to read as widely as he had done to qualify for his majority. He enjoined his officers to put the men through exercises, to see that their arms were well repaired, they had adequate target practice, and their uniforms were carefully mended. He took time to procure leggings for his men, as well as a hair-trunk, a traveling writing case, cups and saucers, and English saddles for himself.

When St. Clair came to Winchester he gave Washington orders for his regiments to march. He also sent him to Williamsburg for supplies and pay for the troops. Washington left Winchester about May 24, returning on June 13 by way of Martha Custis' house. The new governor, Francis Fauquier, reached the capital just after Washington's departure. Washington dropped him a note of welcome and congratulations from Winchester.

The first Virginia Regiment set off on June 24 from Fort Loudoun for Fort Cumberland, with the second marching the following day. Washington reached Cumberland on July 2. There he had to sit and wait in agony while the entire summer slipped away. He wrote to Bouquet that his officers and men were short of regimental uniforms. He therefore proposed putting them into the hunting shirt and leggings of the woodsmen. Bouquet, more flexible than most British officers—having seen men of Major Lewis' Virginia detachment in this dress—gave his approval. In thanking Bouquet, Washington said this would save many pack horses for the expedition to Duquesne.

THE NEW BURGESS

Since 1755 Washington had wanted to be in the House of Burgesses. Now that his military career was ending he was more anxious than ever to win a seat. Though it was difficult for him to campaign in Frederick County while he was in Cumberland, he entered his name for the July 24 election.

Bouquet gave Washington permission to campaign, but Washington decided to leave the election in the hands of his friends. His managers, however, urged him to return since his absence gave a handle to talk that he could not be fighting and representing the district at the same time. They added that the promises of the common herd to vote for him could not be trusted and that he should personally see them. Others reported that his friends were pushing everything with the greatest ardor, "even... Will the Hatter and his

Oyly Spouse Show the greatest Spirit in the Cause." Old friends such as John Carlyle and his brother-in-law, George Fairfax, came up from Alexandria to assist. Lord Fairfax also helped and was recorded as voting for Washington. Letters soon reached Fort Cumberland headed "Dear Burgess," informing him that he had won by a wide margin. Lieutenant Charles Smith of his command said: "I have the Happiness to Inform You your Friends have been Very Sincere So that you were carried by a Number of Votes more than any Candidate... Colo. James Wood Sat on the Bench, and Represented Your Honour, and was Carried round the Town with a General applause, Huzawing Colo. Washington." The Virginia Assembly had not yet forbidden the candidates to give out liquor during the campaigns. Washington asked his managers to spare no expense on this. His bills showed they distributed seventy-two gallons of rum, thirty-four of wine, and forty-six of beer.

The balloting was open and by voice. Washington later copied out the names and choices of all voters. A few selected only one of the four men running. It would appear that, without a single speech or public appearance, the young colonel received 309 votes, or 78 percent of the total. The other successful candidate, Thomas Bryan Martin, nephew of Lord Fairfax, had 239 votes. Captain Robert Stewart wrote Washington that it was a remarkable display of confidence in one who had "so long Commanded the whole of that Country in the worst of times."

Washington's frontier constituents and military officers were a tough and skeptical lot but they expressed an equally high faith in him. From letters of his officers, it appears that he had the knack of making each one feel that he was his particular friend. Strangers who visited the camp at Fort Cumberland were treated with such courtesy that Colonel Washington's hospitality became legendary throughout the frontier posts of Maryland and Pennsylvania.

Following his election, the colonel dropped numerous letters of thanks to his campaign managers and friends. To James Wood he wrote that his heart was full of "joy and gratitude... I don't like to touch upon our Public Affairs... I will therefore say little... Backwardness appears in all things but the approach of Winter—that jogs on apace."

COLONEL WASHINGTON VERSUS THE BRITISH ARMY

When Washington was born, Americans thought themselves English and the British armies invincible. When George was nine, Captain Lawrence Washington, R. A., watched the Cartagena disaster, the result of fumbling by the British army command. Four years later, New Englanders, led by the

American general William Pepperell, successfully brought off the siege and capture of Louisburg. At twenty-two, Washington became the only American aide to General Braddock, British commander in chief in America. When disaster struck down Braddock, and his English troops panicked, the little glory of the day was reserved for Washington and his Virginians. Braddock's defeat and Dunbar's flight opened Virginia's frontiers to bloody Indian attacks, which Colonel Washington had to fight off with pitifully small means. He then had to bear bumbling interference in his operations by the succeeding British commander in chief. Lord Loudoun subsequently failed in the mismanaged siege of Louisburg.

The new commander in chief, Major General James Abercromby, to whom Brigadier John Forbes reported, had been planning an attack on Ticonderoga in 1758, while Bouquet was moving on Duquesne. When the American Lieutenant Colonel John Bradstreet offered to lead a simultaneous expedition against Fort Frontenac (Kingston, Ontario), Forbes overruled him but was persuaded by his war council to permit Bradstreet to have a small force. Abercromby moved north with about fifteen hundred troops, the majority American. After his second in command, the popular Lord Howe, was killed, the British were humiliatingly beaten by Montcalm's French army, which was a quarter its size. Abercromby fled southward in a manner that was to be as long remembered in New England and New York as Dunbar's flight was in the middle colonies. Colonel Washington had this news at approximately the time he received the election returns from Winchester. He was now to encounter an even lower level of competence in the commander in chief of the southern forces of North America, General Forbes, who had been Lord Loudoun's adjutant general. On June 25 Francis Halkett, Forbes' brigade major, informed Washington that the general did not "debar any body from telling their way of thinking, when at the same time he only makes use of that part of their way of thinking, which corrisponds with his own."

It is not clear why Forbes landed at Philadelphia, which was much farther from Fort Duquesne than Alexandria, Virginia, but it can be presumed to have been a blunder by the war office in London. Nearly everyone assumed that, in spite of this initial mistake, he would march his fourteen hundred regulars to Fort Cumberland to join the more than five thousand troops from Pennsylvania, Maryland, Virginia, and the Carolinas. There a road existed almost to Duquesne itself. Forbes was dilatory, taking nearly three months to reach Carlisle, Pennsylvania, one hundred miles to the west. There he fell seriously ill, far too much so to lead an expedition, where speed, strength, and stamina were required. Nonetheless he persisted in maintaining his command, moving slowly by litter with frequent stops for rest.

About the time Washington reached Cumberland at the beginning of July, rumors floated through Maryland and Virginia that General Forbes planned to go straight across Pennsylvania to Duquesne. Even Pennsylvanians found this difficult to believe. Their own western trade went through Cumberland, since little more than Indian trails existed from a point ten miles west of Shippensburg across the rest of the colony. The planned direct western course required that more than 162 miles of road be hacked through wilderness and over numerous mountain ridges. Reports to Washington by his own officers indicate that it sometimes took a day to clear a half mile of wagon roads.

Colonel Washington, having been ordered to move his two regiments to Cumberland and to detach approximately five hundred men under Lieutenant Colonel Adam Stephen to Ray's Town (Bedford) in Pennsylvania, was himself asked to proceed to Ray's Town, but this order was subsequently cancelled. In the meantime the Virginia troops were ordered to work on the roads leading east from Ray's Town and northeast from Cumberland to that place. Soon loud howls were heard from Virginia's volunteer troops that they were being made day laborers for Maryland and Pennsylvania. They were also engaged, as they knew, in building roads away from the enemy. At one point, Bouquet did instruct Washington to repair the Braddock road, but the Virginia colonel replied that all the troops he could spare were working elsewhere.

Although mountain frosts were only three months off, Bouquet sent men out in July to reconnoitre the paths westward. On the fourteenth he informed Washington that he was unacquainted with the country and asked whether Washington thought an expedition could be sent against the Indians in the Ohio Valley. Washington replied that such an undertaking with a large body of troops and provisions was not feasible. The Indians would quickly discover them and the enterprise would fail. Washington had early discerned the plans of Forbes (along with most other unbelieving Virginians), but he was among the last to be officially informed. Bouquet's letter of July 24 giving Washington a hint is missing, but the colonel's reply suggests its contents:

> *I shall most chearfully proceed on any Road; pursue any Route; or enter upon any service; that the General or yourself can think me usefully employ'd in; and shall never have a Will of my own, when a duty is required of me; but since you desire me to speak; permit me to observe this that after having convers'd with all the Guides, and been convinced by them and every other who has knowledge of the Country, that a Road comparable to General Braddock's (or indeed fit for any Service at all even for carrying Horses) cannot be made... I shou'd be extremely glad of one hours conference with you and that when the General arrives.*

About July 30 Washington saw Bouquet in Ray's Town. It was a frustrating meeting for him, since Bouquet not only showed no understanding of the issues raised by the colonel, who had fought and traveled over the area for six years, but also reported sourly on his plans to Forbes. Upon his return to camp at Cumberland, Washington composed one of his most able papers, with only a day or two of work. His brilliant mind enabled him to summarize the situation with respect to the roads as well as to prepare a plan to move nearly seven thousand troops and three months' reserve supplies of food, to build fortified deposits along the way, and to capture Duquesne within fifty-two days.

Washington's letter, dispatched on August 2, pointed out that the Cumberland-Duquesne road had been selected by Pennsylvanians and Virginians after long discussions with experienced Indians who knew every inch of the land. All having agreed that it was the best route to the Ohio, its construction had begun five years earlier. His own and Braddock's troops had put it into good shape to a point near Duquesne. Washington emphasized that it was not practical or possible to construct so good a road west from Ray's Town over "such monstrous Mountains, covered with woods and Rocks." Time pressed because the troops of the middle colonies would be out of service in the autumn. How, he asked, could the argument be advanced that it was easier to build the one hundred miles of road, still needed, than to use a road already existing. He pointed out, further, that Cumberland was a central point for supplies from Virginia and Maryland, which could come by water as well as road. Washington then came to the heart of his proposal, to achieve success in a little over seven weeks:

1. The troops should never be divided, and proposals to use both roads would not work. However, the existing trails over the mountains of Pennsylvania could be used for the quick return of unloaded packhorses, which could then bring supplies down the regular road. Scarce forage would thereby be saved.

2. Since time was short, the building of fortified places of deposit along the way had to be limited. Washington proposed the first fort at the Great Crossing. He suggested that fifteen hundred men could march there immediately, with wagons loaded to carry about thirty days of supplies for six thousand men. The remaining army would follow with ample provisions. He inserted detailed calculations of the number of wagons required for food supplies. For the march and the erection of a fort, he estimated that twenty-six days would be required.

3. At Salt Lick, his next proposed fort, thirty-five miles and four days' march beyond, he suggested sending 2,500 men to build a strong work. From this point, 3,000–4,000 men could be sent on to investigate Duquesne. In the meantime, packhorses would be returning over the mountains to bring more supplies.

Washington's final calculation was that the whole army could move in thirty-four days to the two forts and on to Duquesne, with nearly three months' supplies on hand. This would be an overwhelming reserve for a siege, which should not require more than eighteen days to complete.* At the outside, even allowing for errors, everything would be finished by October 15. With his papers is a file copy of a note that Washington may or may not have sent to Forbes' brigade major, Halkett, to say that if the other route were taken, they would be stopped at "Laurel Hill this Winter; not to gather Laurels, by the by."

It is safe to say that Forbes had never before, during his British army career, encountered brilliance. Moreover, it was displayed by a colonial colonel who not only thought carefully of logistics, strategy, and tactics, but who was also quite prepared to lead the whole enterprise while the general rested at a point far from the scene. Before his letter was forwarded to Forbes, Bouquet simply told Washington the general had ordered the Pennsylvania road built. Forbes was subsequently furious at Washington and eventually took his umbrage out on all American officers and men. Washington, he wrote, was "taking the lead in this ridiculous way" and "his behavior about the roads was no ways like a soldier." More than three months later, Forbes voted to abandon the expedition at Laurel Hill, but it was Colonel Washington who saved him from this final humiliation.

To Bouquet, Washington wrote further on August 6: "The General's orders... will, when once given, be a Law to me. I shall never hesitate in obeying them; but, till this Order came out, I thought it incumbent upon me to say what I cou'd... If I am deceived in my opinion, I shall acknowledge my Error as a Gentleman, led astray from judgment, and not by prejudice, in opposing a measure so conducive to the Publick Weal as you seem to have conceiv'd this to be. If I unfortunately am right, my conduct must acquite me of having discharg'd my Duty on this Important occasion; on the good Success of which, Our All, in a manner, Depends."

From this point on, Washington, still doomed to inactivity at Cumberland, received conflicting intelligence. Bouquet, euphoric, wrote him on August 10: "The Road will be cut tomorrow night to the foot of the mountain." He

---

* For those interested in parallels, the siege and conquest of Yorktown were to take nineteen days.

followed on August 26: "The first division of the artillery is over the Allegheny and had no Stop or difficulty to go over the Gap; The Road will be cut tonight to the foot of L. Hill and in three days Sir John promises to be over to Loyal Hannon. The second division will follow immediately and I expect with impatience the arrival of the General to move on myself. We must shortly enter upon action, and I know that we have time enough to carry our Point, if we meet with no new difficulties."

At the same time, William Ramsay, a Virginian in Bouquet's camp, said that even Pennsylvanians thought the road from Shippensburg to Ray's Town was far worse than anything on the Cumberland-Duquesne route, and that the British were encountering great difficulties in constructing the advance portion. "The road up the Allegheny Mountains is Steep, Stony & of very difficult access, even Alpine difficulties attend the lightest carriages." He added that he did not see how artillery could ever be taken over this or the next large ridge. In the meantime, General Forbes was resting at Shippensburg, with what he called "a most violent and tormenting distemper."

On August 19 Ensign Coleby Chew of the Virginia forces reported that he had reconnoitered Fort Duquesne and found that its French and Indian garrison was much weaker than the British thought. Washington had subsequent confirmatory reports from his Indian scouts. He concluded that the total enemy force was around eight hundred, towards which an army of nearly seven thousand was inching forward.

Nine days later Washington received abrupt orders from General Forbes to move forward on the Braddock road and to take a position at Salt Lick, a procedure that Washington had previously termed fatal. At the same time Forbes asked to see him in Ray's Town, towards which Forbes was proceeding so slowly that he did not reach there until September 15. On September 2 Washington gave the governor of Virginia, Francis Fauquier, an objective appraisal of the situation, including his own arguments for the Cumberland road and the progress that had been made to that point on the Pennsylvania road. He noted that Forbes had made it appear to everyone that the Virginians "were the partial people." He said he heard that the contractor was ordered to lay in supplies for four thousand men that winter at Loyal Hannon, at the foot of Laurel Hill. He added: "I think *now* nothing but a miracle can procure Success." Sometime thereafter he received a letter from Joseph Chew, dated New York, September 11, informing him that the American Colonel Bradstreet had taken Fort Frontenac and thereby cut all French communications with their western forts and settlements. He hoped this would make the conquest of Duquesne easy. This was to be, in fact, one of the two miracles supplied by Americans that saved the expedition.

On September 16, two American gentlemen, Colonels George Washington and William Byrd, appeared before Forbes in Ray's Town. The commanding general was in an ugly mood. During the preceding two weeks, he had denounced Americans to Bouquet as "scoundrels." He wrote to Pitt, the British prime minister, that the Virginia and Pennsylvania Regiments were a disappointment. American officers were, with a few exceptions, "a collection of broken inn-keepers, horse jockeys and Indian traders," while the enlisted men were "scum." Now he coarsely chided Washington for being a provincial partisan whose sole objective in wanting the Cumberland road was Virginia's good. He said he did not care "twopence" for colonial jealousies and suspicions. He cancelled his previous order to proceed up the Braddock road. Washington was commanded, instead, to march to Ray's Town, now a backwater post. As Forbes' additional punishment, Washington had to wait there for more weeks of inaction combined with further schooling in British army methods.

NOT TO REASON WHY

On September 13, very shortly after his arrival at Ray's Town, Washington received news of a major disaster devised by Bouquet and Major James Grant of the Highlanders in which sixty-seven Virginia officers and men were killed and many wounded. As he was soon to find out, Forbes had no idea the battle was even to take place, so Washington was not in a position to complain that no one had consulted him. On September 25 he informed George Fairfax:

I greatly bewail the misfortune that gives rise to the following relation. Major Grant... with a chosen detachment of 800 Marchd from Our advancd Post at Loyal Hannon the 12th Instt. for Fort Duquesne what to do there I cannot certainly say, but it is reported and I suppose justly, to Annoy the Enemy and to gain Intelligence. In the Night of the 13th, he took Post with his Troops in several Columns on a Hill just above the Fort, from whence he sent out to Reconnoitre the Works, this they did, and burnt a Log House just by the Walls. Not content with this Success Majr. Grant must needs send an Engineer in full view of the Fort next morning with a covering Party to take a Plan of the place... and while this was doing causd the Reveille to beat in different places; which caused the Enemy to Salle upon them in great numbers.

Washington did not then know the extent to which the Highlanders had panicked. The Virginians, under Major Lewis, who had been left as baggage guards, pushed forward on hearing the firing. They were caught in the retreating tide but succeeded in partly saving the situation. Washington noted that General Forbes had "complimented me publickly on their good behaviour, and that every Mouth resounds their Praises." Forbes himself reported to Amherst that the Virginians alone had saved the day. Majors Lewis and Grant were captured and sent to Montreal. The disaster did not prevent Grant's subsequent rise to full general in the British army. In reporting the battle to the governor on September 25, Washington mentioned that Major Lewis had been very much opposed to the whole idea but "there was no dissuading Colonel Bouquet." He thought that this affair added "a greater gloom than ever" to the campaign.

Not long afterwards, the Virginia Assembly, fed up with British army bungling, nearly voted to abolish the Virginia Regiments. At the last minute they were saved but ordered back to the colony by December 1.

DUQUESNE FALLS

In the meantime Washington continued at Ray's Town, ten days' march from the forward post at Loyal Hannon. His only known activity was a brisk memorandum to General Forbes, instructing him on how to march troops through wooded country while protecting themselves against Indian or French attacks by promptly heading for the trees. There is no indication that Forbes paid him much attention, for he was too busy with the increasing difficulties of the road beyond Loyal Hannon, fifty miles from Duquesne. By October 15 Forbes was writing Bouquet that his descriptions of the road pierced him to the soul. On October 20 he reported to Pitt that heavy rains and snow had made the road a morass. "If the weather does not favour, I shall be absolutely locked up in the mountains." On October 13 Washington began the march for Loyal Hannon, arriving there on October 23. On November 11 Forbes and his war council agreed that the expedition had to be given up as hopeless. The next day Washington barely escaped being killed. In 1788, still remembering it vividly after thirty years, he described what happened:

> During the time the Army lay at Loyal haning a circumstance occurred which involved the life of G W in as much jeopardy as it had ever been before or since. The enemy sent out a large detachment to reconnoitre our Camp, and to ascertain our strength; in consequence of Intelligence that they were within 2 miles of the Camp a party commanded by Lt. Colo. Mercer of the Virginia line (a gallant and good officer) was sent to dislodge them between whom a severe conflict and hot firing ensued which lasting some time and appearing to approach the Camp it was

*conceived that our party was yielding the ground upon which G W. with
permission of the Genl. called (for dispatch) for Volunteers and immediately
marched at their head to sustain, as was conjectured the retiring troops. Led on by
the firing till he came within less than half a mile, and it ceasing, he detached
Scouts to investigate the cause and to communicate his approach to his friend Colo.
Mercer, advancing slowly in the meantime. But it being near dusk and the
intelligence not having been fully disseminated among Colo. Mercer's Corps, and
they taking us, for the enemy who had retreated approaching in another direction
commenced a heavy fire upon the relieving party which drew fire in return, in spite
of all the exertions of the Officers, one of whom and several privates were killed and
many wounded, before a stop could be put to it. To accomplish which G W never
was in more imminent danger by being between two fires, knocking up with his
sword the presented pieces.*

In addition to this miraculous escape, Washington had the good luck to capture three of the enemy. These, according to his November 26 letter to the
governor, indicated how weak the enemy fortress was, and that provisions
were running low. A new note of cheer appeared in camp, and the decision
was made to go forward. Here at last Washington came into his own. Forbes
assigned him the advance brigade, honoring him with the short-lived title
"Brigadier Washington." In the meantime, Virginia's governor, unaware of
the decision to halt and fearing criticism if Washington's troops were recalled,
summoned the Assembly to meet. On November 13 the speaker sent an
express to Washington to tell him that the Assembly had proceeded with a dispatch never before known and in three days "passed an Act to empower the
Govr. to continue the Forces in the Pay of this Colony" until January 1. This
was done "not from any Expectation many of us had that an Attempt would
be made, after so many repeated delays, to rescue the Fort at this Season, but
as I said before that the blame might not lie at our door... I heartily pity our
poor men who must be now very illy provided to stand the severity of the
Season."

As he advanced over the last of the mountains, Washington wrote dispatch
after dispatch to Forbes and Bouquet. From Chestnut Ridge he reported that,
though it was nearly midnight on his arrival on the fifteenth, he had ordered
out working parties for the road. He urgently asked for more axes. Two days
later he reported that constant labor from daybreak till nightfall had opened
seven or eight miles of road. The next day he wrote of more progress, informing the general that he would set out, with a thousand men, at three the next
morning. He asked for additional meat for his hard-working soldiers and
assured the general that he was sending out scouting parties to prevent

surprises. He reported that they were still about thirty miles from Duquesne.

On November 24 returning Indian scouts reported that they had seen great columns of smoke arising from the fort. The French, in accordance with orders previously received, had abandoned Duquesne rather than risk a siege. They destroyed such provisions and arms as they could not carry away. On November 28 Washington wrote to Governor Fauquier to say: "I have the pleasure to inform you, that Fort Duquesne, or the ground rather on which it stood, was possessed by his Majesty's troops on the 25th instant... The possession of this fort has been a matter of great surprise to the whole army." General Forbes promptly renamed it Fort Pitt in honor of the man who had made the victory possible, he said, thereby placing "this noble, fine country, to all perpetuity, under the dominion of Great Britain."

With characteristic generosity, Washington reported to the governor of Virginia: "General Forbes has great merit (which I hope will be rewarded) for the happy issue which he has brought our affairs to, infirm and worn down as he is." Bouquet, on the other hand, wrote to William Allen, chief justice of Pennsylvania: "After God, the success of this expedition is due entirely to the General... Yielding to the urging instances for taking Braddock's Road... would have been our destruction."

Washington had carried himself through the five months of strain on adrenaline alone. Almost the moment he reached Duquesne and planted the British colors, he fell back into illness. To maintain the fort through the winter, Forbes asked that a detachment of Virginians be stationed there. Since they were ragged and ill equipped, as usual, he requested Washington to proceed immediately to Williamsburg to arrange for supplies. Washington began the long exhausting ride from Fort Pitt to Virginia's capital about December 1, stopping en route at Mount Vernon. He arrived in Williamsburg before the year's end. After taking care of Forbes' affairs he tendered his resignation as commander in chief of the Virginia Regiments.

THE REGIMENT'S ADDRESS

On December 31 twenty-seven officers of the first Virginia Regiment drafted a memorandum on his retirement and sent it to Washington by officer messenger. It said, in part:

To GEORGE WASHINGTON, Esqr. Collo. of the Virginia Regiment &
Commander of all the Virginia Forces—

We your most obedient and affectionate Officers, beg leave to express our great Concern, at the disagreeable News we have received of your Determination to resign the Command of that Corps, in which we have under you long served.

The happiness we have enjoy'd, and the Honour we have acquir'd, together with the mutual Regard that has always subsisted between you and your Officers, have implanted so sensible an Affection in the Minds of us all, that we cannot be silent on this critical occasion...

Judge then, how sensibly we must be Affected with the loss of such an excellent Commander, such a sincere Friend, and so affable a Companion. How rare it is to find these Amiable Qualifications blended together in one Man? How great the loss of such a Man?... We with the greatest Deference, presume to entreat you to suspend those Thoughts (of Retirement) for another Year, and to lead us on to assist in compleating the Glorious Work of extirpating our Enemies, towards which so considerable Advances have already been made. In you we place the most implicit Confidence. Your Presence only will cause a steady Firmness and Vigour to actuate in every Breast, despising the greatest Dangers, and thinking light of Toils and Hardship, while led on by the man we know and Love.

Captain Robert Stewart, formerly Washington's aide, said it more simply in his letter of January 16: "The regret, dejection and grief your Resignation has occasion'd in the whole Corps is too melancholy a Subject to enter on." Washington replied to his officers and men with an emotional appreciation of their letter and services. In 1788, after he had received endless praise, he remembered their salute well: "The solicitation of the Troops which he commanded to Continue, their Affectionate farewell address to him, when they found the Situation of his health and other circumstances would not allow it, affected him exceedingly and in grateful sensibility he expressed the warmth of his attachment to them on that, and his inclination to serve them on every other future occasion."

PART THREE

FARMER
1759–1775

FOURTEEN

MARRIAGE AND PEACE

1759–1765

EIGHTEENTH-CENTURY AMERICANS of the governing class, in contrast to their British cousins, led generally pure private and public lives. Such exceptions as Daniel Parke and his son-in-law, William Byrd, were the more memorable on that account. Parke, the American aide to Marlborough, who brought the news of Blenheim to Queen Anne, received numerous rewards from her, including the governorship of the Leeward Islands. He was murdered in Antigua in 1710, as a consequence of one of his liaisons. His complex will provoked decades of litigation among his legitimate and unsanctified descendants in the courts of Antigua, England, and Virginia. Parke's two legitimate daughters married William Byrd and John Custis of Virginia. Byrd's diary contained enough scandalous passages about his stay in London for his descendants to hide it many years. The eccentric Custis, before his death, ordered a famed epitaph, still on Virginia's Eastern Shore: "John Custis... aged 71 years, and yet lived but seven years, which was the space of time he kept a bachelor's home... This inscription put on his tomb was by his own positive orders." Shortly before John's death in 1749 his son, Daniel Parke Custis, a bachelor of thirty-eight, married the eighteen-year-old Martha Dandridge. Daniel died in 1757, leaving his widow and two surviving children, John Parke (Jacky) and Martha (Patsy or Pat), who were then around two-and-a-half and a few months old, respectively.

Martha Dandridge Custis had been a widow for about eighteen months when she remarried. Her union with George Washington, which was to last nearly forty-one years, took place on January 6, 1759, at the White House, her country farm some thirty miles from Williamsburg. The absence of any extant correspondence on the part of Washington until May makes it appear probable that his wife made him rest as much as possible until they settled at Mount Vernon.

The myth that Martha was rich, and that this was an attraction for her new husband, has persisted down the years. Since Daniel Custis died intestate, she received by law only one-third of his estate. A portion of her share of $40,000 or so was for life only. The inheritance was subject to severe shrinkage if continuing litigation against it were successful. Suit for around $43,000 had been filed, including interest, but plus costs. In addition Martha had paid extensive legal fees for the defense of her children's and her interests. By an April court order Washington became administrator of the estates of Jacky and Patsy. He managed these without charge over the years, doubling their values in about fifteen years. No adverse judgment materialized against the Custis properties.

Washington was sworn in as Burgess for the frontier county of Frederick on his twenty-seventh birthday. Four days later the House voted its thanks to him "for his brave and steady behaviour, from the first Encrouchments and hostilities of the French and their Indians, to his resignation, after the happy Reduction of Fort Duquesne." He was assigned to the committee on propositions and grievances but his main work was on military matters. The new British commander in chief, Jeffrey Amherst, had called on Virginia for troops to assist him in taking French Canada. A bill for this passed the House in April. Washington, still ill, then asked for leave to return to Mount Vernon.

The colonel, who had ridden so long on the frontier with his hard-bitten officers, was now leader of a different flock: Martha, and two little children who had begun to call him "Poppa." On his way home, Washington sent a note ahead to his overseer, John Alton, asking him to get the key to the house from George Fairfax; make fires and air the place; set up beds; polish the tables, chairs, and stairs; and buy eggs and chickens.

The Washingtons reached their house on April 6, as the early spring blossoms were at their height. Mount Vernon had been raised a story the preceding year, but it lacked the wings and waterfront piazza that the master subsequently added. Its furnishings were presumably of the spare kind suitable for a bachelor officer. It was soon made a hospitable place, as indicated by Washington's August 9 note to Colonel Henry Churchill: "I was in hopes we should have had the pleasure of seeing you at Mount Vernon. Mrs. Washington impeaches you of a breach of promise in failure of this, and I don't know a better method of atonement, than coming soon and doubling the intended times of staying."

PLANTER

At this point Washington had to take on an essentially new career. He had left farming for other work in early youth. Mount Vernon, still rented from Lawrence Washington's widow, had little chance to attain efficiency, even by rather low Virginia standards. Gus Washington lived there only briefly, turning it over to Lawrence who soon went off to the wars. When George first leased it, he too departed for five years' military service. His brother John looked after the farm until his marriage, when he moved to his own quarters. The outbuildings, fencing, stock, and lands showed signs of long neglect.

Farming became for Washington the most absorbing of all his lifelong interests. With the zest which led him to read all he could on military management, he set out to be what was rare in the colonies, a man who studied the latest advances in British agricultural sciences. For the next forty years Washington lavished—insofar as his long absences permitted—hard work, intense study, and much capital on his property.

In the years before the revolution, Washington corresponded extensively with his London agents who sold his crops and sent him the goods he needed. He wrote his principal agent, Robert Cary, on May 1, enclosing copies of his appointment as administrator of the Custis estates. Mrs. Washington was clearly not satisfied with the sparseness of the furnishings. In addition to lists of wanted clothing, grass seed, and treatises on agriculture, gardening, and horses, Washington ordered a tester bedstead, curtains, carpets, and a firescreen. On May 7 he wrote to Richard Washington: "I have quit a Military Life; and Shortly shall be fix'd at this place with an agreeable Partner, and then shall be able to conduct my own business with more punctuality than heretofore as it will pass under my own inspection; a thing impracticable in the Publick service."

A great deal of Washington's London correspondence thereafter was given over to complaints of low tobacco prices and of shoddy goods shipped in return. Some of the clothing sent from London, he wrote his merchants, might have been worn by his forefathers. As early as June 12, in his first spring at Mount Vernon, he complained to Capel and Osgood Hanbury of London that they had got poor prices for him, though tobacco was scarce, while they had sent no accounts since the death of Colonel Custis. He informed them that these were particularly necessary now that he had to make twice yearly trustee reports to the General Court of Virginia.

On September 20 he wrote to Cary, asking him to set up three accounts, one for himself and one for each of his stepchildren. "The whole will remain under my management whose particular care it shall be to distinguish always either by Letter or Invoice from whom Tobacco are ship'd, and for whose use Goods are Imported in Order to prevent any mistakes arising." He continued:

> I am possess'd of several Plantations, on this River (Potomack) and the fine Lands of Shenandoah, and shou'd be glad if you wou'd ingenuously tell me what prices I might expect you to render for Tobacco's made thereon of the same seed of that of the estate's and managed in every respect in the same manner as the best Tobacco's on James or York River's are. I ask this question for my own private Information, and my Shipping of these Crops will be govern'd in a great measure by the answer you may give; therefore you will excuse me I hope, if I again desire the favour of you to take some pains to inform yourselves exactly, because shou'd the prices differ from those of the Estate I might possibly think myself deceiv'd and be disgusted of Course.
>
> Please to send the Goods contain'd in the Inclos'd Invoices and charge them as there directed. I flatter myself that particular care will be taken in choosing them, the want of which gives some Tradesmen an oppertunity of Imposing upon us most Vilely.

There followed a shopping list running to more than six printed pages. A sampling of this huge market basket indicates the difficulties early Americans had where the supplier was at such distances:

- *Food*—Cheese, tea, anchovies, capers, olive oil, raisins, almonds, sugar, oats for oatmeal, candy, mustard, pepper, and biscuits.

- *Household and Farm*—Starch, bluing, candles, pins, soap, medicines, blankets, saws, axes, scythes, hinges, chisels, compasses, gimlets, files, thread, playing cards, brushes, bridles, scissors, and writing paper.

- *Clothing*—Suits, hats, handkerchiefs, aprons, hose, and shoes for the Washington household, including the servants. Toys and dolls for the children were added.

Washington also ordered busts of various military heroes, including Alexander, Caesar, Charles XII, Marlborough, and the King of Prussia

(Frederick the Great). The art dealer to whom this order was referred regretted that he had none of these, but offered in their place Virgil, Homer, Shakespeare, Milton, Locke, and Newton.

On November 25 Washington wrote to Cary in London that he was shipping between fifty and sixty hogsheads of tobacco (usually averaging a thousand pounds each). On November 30 a further letter commented that his long shopping lists had gone by ships that had probably foundered and he was forwarding duplicates. He added that he needed a neat grate (for coal or wood) for his fireplace, saying that he understood grates were now made of steel. He thanked them for their "polite Congratulations on my Marriage, as I likewise am for your Dispatch of my Goods." On the same day he wrote to another London merchant to suggest the shoes they sent were of "Dog leather," for the two pairs he received had worn out in four days.

THE DIARY

Washington had started a diary when he first went over the mountains at sixteen. At twenty-seven he began a new one which ran, with gaps, until the day before his death. Many of his notes are of trivial events and weather changes, but others reflect Washington's humor and inquiring mind. Some of the best travel records of eighteenth-century America are contained in them. Washington's neighbor Daniel French received this opening comment on January 1, 1760: "Visited my Plantations and receiv'd an Instance of Mr. French's great Love of Money in disappointing me of some Pork, because the price had risen to 22/6 after he had engaged to let me have it at 20/." Washington was forced to accept, since he needed the meat for his overseers and other personnel. The hogs arrived on January 8, Washington noted, "one being lost on the way—as the others might as well have been for their goodness." The animals, when killed, weighed 751 pounds as dressed meat. In spite of his complaints, he bought seventeen more hogs from French on the twenty-second.

Washington noted homely items. They were out of butter; an oysterman, tied up at his dock, plagued him with "disorderly behavior," and Washington had to order him away "in the most pre-emptory manner." Mrs. Washington had measles and several of the household caught the disease. The Reverend Charles Green, who had ministered to him when he was laid up with dysentery and tuberculosis, treated Mrs. Washington. Mrs. Fairfax came over from neighboring Belvoir to look after her. She stayed till evening and Washington sent her home in a carriage. He complained that she did not return it the next day, Sunday, until it was too late to go to church. The opening pages included much humor:

> *We spent a very lonesome Evening at Colo. Champe's, not any Body favouring us with their Company but himself... Found Richd. Stephen's hard at Work with an ax—very extraordinary this... Went to a ball at Alexandria, where Musick & Dancing was the chief Entertainment. However in a convenient Room detach'd for the purpose abounded great plenty of Bread and Butter, some Biscuits with Tea, & Coffee which the Drinkers oft coud not Distinguish from Hot water sweeten'd. Be it remembered that pocket handkerchiefs serv'd the purposes of Table Cloths & Napkins... I shall... distinguish this Ball by the Stile of the Bread & Butter Ball... Doctr Laurie came here. I may add Drunk.*

Much of his time was spent looking after sick slaves. "Cupid," ill of pleurisy at the Dogue Run plantation, was brought to Mount Vernon for better care. Washington sent for Dr. Laurie to take care of "Beechy." Two other slaves were ordered blooded or "physicked." A smallpox epidemic reached his Bullskin farm. He rode there, ordered the sick slaves placed in his own rooms, and employed a nurse to look after them.

Washington wrote of moving out his tobacco crops and of purchasing corn, hay, tallow, and shingles. He mentioned that he had made more than a thousand bottles of cider. He set a horse's broken leg in accordance with directions in a handbook he had. After placing the leg in a sling that did not hold, he had to destroy the horse.

Washington noted that he made an agreement with his neighbor William Clifton to buy 806 acres of his land for 1,150 pounds sterling, subject to Mrs. Clifton's approval. Later Clifton came by to say that his wife had refused but "his shuffling behaviour on the occasion convinced me of his being the trifling body represented." A few days later Washington learned that Clifton had sold the land to Thomson Mason for 1,200 pounds. In his diary he called Clifton "a thorough paced Rascall, disregardful of any Engagements of Words or Oaths." Eventually after "much discourse," Washington offered him 50 pounds above Mason's price, saying the land had been promised him. The case was settled on this basis.

Washington resurveyed his lands, finding many inaccuracies in the deeds. With his blacksmith he tried, unsuccessfully, to design a new type of plow. However, he continued working at it; some of his later inventive experiments succeeded. Shortly after this, he began grafting cherry and plum trees, and then "a pretty little pearky June Pear." Subsequently he grafted apples.

In April Washington was out plowing and seeding lucerne, rye grass, oats, and barley. He experimented with compost on marked fields, mixing in various combinations earth, sand, mud, marl, and black loam with horse, cow, and sheep dung to "a tolerable degree of fineness & jumbling them well together in a cloth." From these experiments he went on to animal breeding and sheepshearing.

Washington's diaries include long tables of tobacco, corn, and wheat yields from various fields, the rent paid him from his many properties; and records of his tobacco shipments. On April 3, 1761, he wrote Robert Cary to complain that he had been paid only 11d. for his tobacco while other planters got 12d. He added: "Certain I am no Person in Virginia takes more pains to make their Tobo. fine than I do and tis hard then I should not be as well rewarded for it."

THE WAR

The Seven Years' War, which George Washington had a role in starting, continued for more than four years after his retirement to Mount Vernon. While he was haggling over tobacco prices, the British were achieving great victories on the American continent. His former officers Robert Stewart and George Mercer sent him welcome reports of their frontier service.

Mercer, commanding at Fort Pitt, informed Washington in September that the French, after burning the posts at Venango and Le Boeuf, which he had visited as Dinwiddie's emissary, had retired to Detroit. The British were building a brick fortress at Pittsburgh large enough to hold a garrison of four thousand.

Stewart, also stationed at Fort Pitt, said that the Shawnee and Delaware tribes were still so angry at Washington, whom they considered to be the cause of all their misfortunes, that they always spoke of him as "The Great Knife." Stewart was enraptured by Pittsburgh: "A view of three glorious Rivers, and the many Beauties Nature has been so lavish in adorning this place... A most delightful prospect, terminated by many high, romantic Mountains... The more I see of this charming Country, the more I'm enamoured with it." He asked what had happened to the bounty lands along the Ohio River that had been promised those who had volunteered to serve Virginia in 1754.

In July Ticonderoga and Crown Point fell to Amherst. In September Wolfe captured Quebec, ending French rule in Canada. Billy Fairfax, Washington's neighbor and prospective heir to the Fairfax title and lands, died with Wolfe. On September 20, before he had news of this victory, Washington wrote his London correspondent, Richard Washington: "The Scale of Fortune is turn'd greatly in our favour, and Success is become the boon companion of our Fortunate Generals." He added that his brother Austin, who had gone to

England for his health, had not benefited from his trip. He himself longed to see the great metropolis of London, "but I am now tied by the Leg and must set Inclination aside."

TWO DEATHS

At the end of 1760, word reached Virginia of the death of George II. The new monarch, George III, young and well-meaning, though not very bright or well-educated, was warmly greeted in England. He inserted into his first speech to Parliament the phrase "Born and educated in this country, I glory in the name of *Britain.*" Some of the older courtiers regarded the sentences as slightly unkind to his German-born predecessors, while others thought the word "Britain" was too deferential to the Scots. His subjects generally viewed it for what it was, a simple declaration of pride in country. A few years later an American newspaper predicted that not many generations would elapse before the royal family would move to the center of the growing empire and the monarch would declare: "Born and educated among you, I glory in the name of AMERICA."

On February 11, 1761, Governor Francis Fauquier proclaimed the new king in the capital of Virginia, "amidst the joyful acclamations of the people, at the capitol, the market place, and the college." On March 5 he appeared before the Burgesses to say that there was "the greatest reason to form the most sanguine expectations of enjoying the blessing of freedom, in the same full latitude we experienced under his grandfather, in the person of his successor, his present Majesty." No sooner was the king crowned and sanctified, however, than he moved to displace Pitt from power, thus beginning twenty years of personal reign.

Washington was not present at this session of the Burgesses. He may have been detained because of the critical illness of Lawrence Washington's widow, Anne Fairfax, wife of George Lee. She died on March 14, very probably from the disease that had killed her first husband and four children. By her death Washington became the sole owner of Mount Vernon, which he had previously leased.

ELECTION

The succession of a new king led to the automatic dissolution of the House of Burgesses and a new election. This meant additional trouble and expense for

Washington, who represented a frontier constituency. Thomas Bryan Martin, Lord Fairfax's nephew, decided not to run again in Frederick. Two men, Adam Stephen, Washington's former lieutenant colonel, and George Mercer, his one-time aide, announced their candidacy. Stephen was the more aggressive and energetic of the two and quickly got to work. This provided an additional complication for Washington since he mistrusted Stephen and liked Mercer. It also meant a more active campaign than he would have had to make with only two candidates.

Captain Robert Stewart soon warned Washington that Stephen was making headway. He "is incessantly employ'd in traversing this County and... practices every method of making Interest with it's Inhabitants for Electing him their Representative in Assembly, his claims to disinterestedness, Public Spirit and genuine Patriotism are Trumpeted in the most turgid manner." Stephen proposed to introduce "various Commercial Schemes, which are to diffuse Gold & opulency thro' Frederick, and prove... as Sovereign a Remedy against Poverty and Want as Glen's red root was in removing hunger and imbecility from our Horses in Campaign 58... He has attracted the attention of the Plebeians, whose unstable Minds are agitated by every Breath of Novelty." Stewart urged Washington to come to Frederick as soon as possible.

Washington followed this advice in May 1761. He attended a cockfight and a wedding, and made long, rough rides through his enormous constituency. For reasons that are now obscure, Washington was furious at Stephen. He wrote to Captain Van Swearingen, the sheriff, to say:

> *Col. Stephens proceedings is a matter of the greatest amazement to me. I have come across sundry of his letters directed to the Freeholders wherein he informs them that he acquitted himself of what was charged to him in the Streets of Winchester while you were present, and goes on to draw Comparisons to prove his Innocence... However His conduct throughout the whole is very obvious to all who will be convinced, but I find there are some that do not choose to have their Eyes opened.*

> *I hope my Interest in your Neighbourhood still stands good, and as I have the greatest reason to believe you can be no Friend to a Person of Colo. Stephens Principles; I hope, and indeed make no doubt you will contribute your aid towards shutting him out of the Public trust he is seeking.*

The election, held on May 18, 1761, resulted in 505 votes for Washington (88 percent), 399 for Mercer, and 299 for Stephen. The first two were declared the Frederick Burgesses.

ILLNESS

The strenuous campaign brought Washington what seemed at first to be a feverish cold. He soon became acutely ill from what was the most severe of his many tubercular attacks. He consulted Drs. Craik and Laurie and the Reverend Charles Green. He sent an account of his illness and symptoms to Captain Stewart in Philadelphia, who there saw a Dr. Macleane, whom Stewart called the ablest physician in America. Macleane advised Washington to proceed to Philadelphia. At Dr. Green's advice, he went instead to Warm Springs (Berkeley) where he had once taken his very ill brother, Lawrence. On August 26 he wrote to Green of the waters and of his disagreeable trip:

We found of both sexes about 200 people at this place, full of all manner of diseases and complaints... The Springs... are situated very badly on the East side of a steep Mountain, and inclosed by hills on all sides, so that the afternoon's Sun is hid by 4 o'clock and the fogs hang over us till 9 or 10 which occasion great damps, and the mornings and evening to be cool.

I was much overcome with the fatigue of the ride and weather together. However, I think my fevers are a good deal abated, although my pains grow rather worse, and my sleep equally disturbed. What effect the waters may have upon me I can't say at present, but I expect nothing from the air—this certainly must be unwholesome.

Washington stayed there about three weeks and then returned to Mount Vernon. The exact course of the disease is not now known, but he referred to the fact that he had been critically ill in a letter of October 20 to Richard Washington: "Since my last of the 14th. July I have in appearance been very near my last gasp; the Indisposition then spoken of Increased upon me and I fell into a very low and dangerous State. I once thought the grim King would certainly master my utmost efforts and that I must sink in spite of a noble struggle but thank God I have now got the better of the disorder and shall soon be restor'd I hope to perfect health again."

In early November Washington thought he had recovered sufficiently to attend the House of Burgesses. On November 9 he informed Peter Stover that he had introduced the bill to establish Stover's Town (now Strasburg) in the valley, but he had been so ill he had to withdraw from the House. He asked another Burgess to manage it for him.

There is little documentation on the next months of his illness. It is known that he paid rather large bills to two Williamsburg physicians. Thereafter it can be assumed that he returned to Mount Vernon for a long period of Mrs.

Washington's nursing care. His full recovery took many months. This is indicated by the fact that not until May 28 did he answer long accumulated correspondence from Robert Cary and Company in London. He noted that he was responding to their letters of the previous June, August, September, and October. In the spring he attended the funeral of his half brother Austin. About all that can be said from the evidence available is that Washington's longest critical illness lasted from May of 1761 to about May of the following year.

Washington brushed close to death during this period but his strong heart pulled him through and enabled him forever to break the hold of tuberculosis. In passing through the valley of the shadow of death he changed greatly. The Colonel Washington of thirty was a man mature beyond his years, mellow, humane, and happy to be alive.

On August 28, 1762, long recovered, he wrote to Burwell Bassett, who had married Martha Washington's sister, the kind of sprightly letter he usually confined to close friends:

> *I was favoured with your Epistle wrote on a certain 25th of July when you ought to have been at Church, praying as becomes every good Christian Man who has as much to answer for as you have; strange it is that you will be so blind to truth that the enlightening sounds of the Gospel cannot reach your Ear, nor no examples awaken you to a sense of Goodness; could you but behold with what religious Zeal I hye me to Church on every Lords day, it would do your heart good, and fill it I hope with equal fervency; I am told you have lately introduced into your Family, a certain production which you are lost in admiration of... It is thought you will have little time to animadvert upon the prospect of your crops; pray how will this be reconciled to that... vigilance which is so essentially necessary at a time when our growing Property, meaning the Tobacco, is assailed by every villainous worm that has had an existence since the days of Noah... Perhaps you may be as well off as we are; that is, have no Tobacco for them to eat and there I think we nicked the Dogs, as I think to do you if you expect any more... I shall see you I expect about the first of November.*

THE GREAT DISMAL SWAMP AND THE MISSISSIPPI

After his recovery, Washington's great energy could not be entirely channelled into being a farmer, head of household, churchman, and legislator. He engaged in two ventures as far apart as the eastern Virginia swamps and the Mississippi River.

In June 1763 he became one of the fifty sponsors and organizers of the Mississippi Company. Its charter authorized the dispatch of an agent to

London to obtain a Crown grant of 2.5 million acres along the Mississippi River. The royal proclamation line prohibiting settlement beyond the Alleghenies, established later in the year, killed this scheme, but Washington's interest in obtaining land as far west as the Mississippi continued for years.

The second Washington venture was a proposal to drain and irrigate land in the Great Dismal Swamp. Washington made his first examination in May 1763. He found some very rich land and farmers already established on higher ground. He made a further trip in October. The Dismal Swamp Company was chartered by the Virginia Assembly and given canal access rights across privately owned lands. The company itself acquired some forty thousand acres, and Washington bought additional acreage for himself. Nothing productive ever came of this venture though a start was made on canal digging.

DIVERSIFICATION

Washington was one of the first American farmers, and perhaps the first on a large scale, to experiment with crop diversification and to plan his crops in accordance with future market demands. As early as 1763 his livestock included sheep, pigs, cattle, and horses. He caught substantial supplies of herring and shad. His fruit trees consisted of apples, peaches, plums, pears, and cherries. He grew turnips, peas, and, a little later, potatoes. His grain crops included wheat, barley, and spelt, a form of wheat. According to his diary, he also planted around 180,000 stands of corn. He produced cider and brandy. All of this was in addition to tobacco.

What eventually made Washington a modestly prosperous farmer was his decision to abandon tobacco growing. Tobacco was Virginia's largest cash crop, which provided the sterling exchange needed for necessities and luxuries. Washington's continued complaints to his London merchants on the prices they obtained indicate his dissatisfaction with its handling. His tobacco was not as good quality as he thought and his 1762 crop was skimpy. In 1763, Washington signed a seven-year contract with Carlyle and Adams, merchants of Alexandria, for sales of wheat to them at a fixed price. From 1765 on, after initial experiments with small crops, he rapidly expanded his wheat acreage. Later he entered the milling business for his own and for others' grain and found that his diversification program provided greater stability of income than a single cash crop.

The advantages of American economic subordination to Great Britain were not entirely one-sided. Britain offered bounties on American flax and hemp.

Washington experimented with these crops, and, although conditions for them at Mount Vernon were not ideal, he did collect some small hemp bounties.

By 1763, Washington had worked four years to build up his family's farms and fortunes. An April 27, 1763, letter to Captain Robert Stewart indicates how far he still had to go. Stewart had served long and honorably with the Virginia Regiment, which had been disbanded. He asked Washington to lend him four hundred pounds so that he could purchase a captain's commission in the British army. Washington replied:

> *I wish my dear Stewart that the circumstances of my Affairs wou'd have permitted me to have given you an order... for £400 with as much ease and propriety as you seem to require it, or even for twice that Sum if it would make you easy; but alas! to shew my inability in this respect, I inclose you a copy of Mr. Cary's last Acct. currt. against me, which upon my honour and the faith of a Christian is a true one, and transmitted to me with the additional aggravation of a hint at the largeness of it.*

> *...I doubt not but you will be surprized at the badness of their condition unless you will consider under what terrible management and disadvantages I found my Estate when I retired from the Publick Service of this Colony; and that besides some purchases of Lands and Negroes I was necessitated to make adjoining me (in order to support the Expenses of a large Family), I had Provision's of all kinds to buy for the first two or three years; and my Plantation to stock in short with every thing; Buildings to make, and other matters, which swallowed up before I well knew where I was, all the money I got by Marriage nay more, brought me in Debt, and I believe I may appeal to your own knowledge of my Circumstances before.*

> *I do not urge these things my dear Sir in order to lay open the distresses of my own Affairs, on the contrary they should forever have remained profoundly secret to your knowledge did it not appear necessary at this time to acquit myself in your esteem, and to evince my inability of exceeding £300 a sum I am now labouring to procure by getting money to purchase Bills of that amt. to remit to yourself, that Mr. Cary may have no knowledge of the transaction, and for which my regard for you will disappoint him. A Regard of that high nature that I coud never see you uneasy without feeling a pain and wishing to remove the cause; and therefore when you complained of the Mortification of remaining a Subaltern in a Corp you had frequently commanded the Subs of, I wanted you out, and hope it might be effected; but I shall have done on the Subject giving me leave to add only that in case you shoud not have a call for the money (and your Letter speaks of this) you will then be so good as to pay it to Mr. Cary to whom I believe it will be no disagreeable tender and advise me thereof.*

Stewart subsequently had a rather checkered career, but in 1768 he was appointed collector of customs at Kingston, Jamaica. From there he wrote to Washington saying that he could now draw on London "for the amount of the money you was generously pleas'd in the handsomest and most Friendly manner to advance to me... for which and your invariable and polite attention to my welfare my heart will never cease to glow with the most lively ardour of the strongest Friendship and genuine gratitude."

Washington, though he himself had to pay interest on his London debits, drew only the principal amount, but he ran into difficulties in collecting it. He complained about this to Robert Cary, his London merchant, noting that he had loaned the money many years before without security. This matter was finally settled, and Stewart wrote to Washington: "I observe with the utmost Gratitude that you have Drawn only for the Principal... I really want words to convey the Ideas of what I feel on this *Noble Act* and fresh mark of your uncommon Friendship... Accept my dear Friend of my most Gratefull Thanks."

PEACE AND HIGHER TAXES

An England at the height of glory signed the 1763 peace treaty by which all French Canada became British. George III's government proceeded that year, and in the two following, to irritate his American subjects into near-rebellion. Virginia, praised in 1762 by Fauquier as composed of "loyal, faithful and dutiful subjects... dear to your royal Sovereign" and in 1763 by Amherst, the British commander in chief, as a "public-spirited colony, full of Honour," was the first to suffer. This brought from Burgess Washington his first known outcry against London's directives.

Although peace had come to Europe, the French-oriented Indians in North America rose up in fury against their new British rulers. Included among the rebellious tribes were the Shawnees and Delawares, who had singled out Colonel Washington as the source of their woes. An Indian war, led in the West by Pontiac, broke out almost simultaneously with the peace. The Indians seized many of the British posts in Pennsylvania, Indiana, Ohio, and Michigan, and nearly captured Detroit and Fort Pitt. Washington reported to Robert Stewart on August 13, 1763, that "another tempest has arose upon our Frontiers, and the alarm spread wider than ever... No families stand above the Conogocheage road... In Augusta many people have been killed, and numbers fled, and confusion and despair prevails in every Quarter."

Virginia had been financing its defense by forced loans in the form of emissions of treasury bills that were to be redeemed from future taxes. Virginia's currency was far below sterling, and British merchants were afraid they would be paid in depreciated pounds rather than in sterling. Accordingly, they persuaded the British government to order Virginia to desist. Washington had reported this to Stewart on May 2: "Our Assembly is suddenly called, in consequence of a Memorial of the British Merchts. to the Board of Trade representing the Evil consequences of our Paper emissions, and their Lordships report and orders thereupon which I suppose will set the whole Country in Flames; this stir of the Merchts. seems to be ill timed and cannot be attended with any good effects."

In August, after reporting the Indian troubles to Stewart, Washington said that he had expected the Assembly would be called to provide for the province's defense. Since it was to be "an Assembly without money," the governor had not summoned it and had relied instead on militia "under the Command of Colo. Stephen whose Military Courage and Capacity (says the Governor) is well established."

Virginia felt aggrieved again when George III issued a proclamation on October 2, 1763, establishing the Allegheny Mountains as a limit beyond which no American settlement could take place and forbidding private or provincial purchases of Indian lands without the king's permission. Trading with the Indians was to be by license. All the area from Florida to the Great Lakes and from the Atlantic watershed to the Mississippi was declared out of bounds to settlers. Virginia claimed all of the territory involved, from Tennessee north to the Great Lakes. The proclamation was regarded as an intolerable interference in Virginia's domestic affairs and by none more than those who hoped for riches from land speculation. It was also well-known that the British government was so corrupt that those close to the king could still get land. Americans paid only modest heed to the proclamation. Within seven years of its issue, some seventeen thousand settlers were in Kentucky and Tennessee.

As early as 1762 the British government had decided to keep an army of ten thousand men in America, though standing armies had been unpopular in England and almost unknown in the colonies. Captain Stewart, in a chatty note of early 1764, gave Washington a forecast of what was next in store: "It is said I'm afraid from too good authority that the Colonies will be saddled with a Tax of not less than three hundred thousand Pounds Sterling per annum in order to support the Troops Judg'd necessary for their Defence." The revenue act of 1764 increased duties paid in America on such luxury imports as silk and Madeira and raised the tax on non-British sugar, much needed by New England for its rum manufactures. This feature aroused particular opposition in Massachusetts. Samuel Adams, a radical, and Thomas Hutchinson, a Tory, thought the act impolitic and unconstitutional.

On March 22, 1765, the House of Commons passed a stamp act introduced by George Grenville, the king's first minister, which placed excises in English, not depreciated colonial, pounds on all American legal documents, licenses, and publications, as well as on cards and dice. The tax hit at everyone but hardest at the two most strident groups of society, lawyers and newspaper publishers. The reactions to the 1764 tax had been mild in Virginia but not so to that of 1765. Virginia had been self-governing and self-taxing for almost a century and a half. This blow, following the proclamation line and the prohibition against paper money, brought the first Virginia moves towards rebellion.

Two months after the Stamp Act passed, a new member, Patrick Henry, took his seat in the House of Burgesses. Henry, youthful and rustic, had already won a famous case, the Parson's Cause, in which he objected to the Crown overruling acts of the Virginia Assembly. Some of his remarks to the jury at that time had brought cries of "treason" from the spectators. The older Burgesses, until now, had held the House under tight control. The speaker, John Robinson, also treasurer of the colony, was one of Virginia's most influential persons. It was not then known, or not to most people, that he had used the provincial treasury as a loan office for his friends. When he died the next year, his accounts were found to be a hundred thousand pounds short. Three days or so after Henry became a Burgess, a bill was introduced to establish a Virginia land loan office, to be financed by borrowing in London. Very probably this proposal was connected with Robinson's peculations. Henry rose to oppose it. Jefferson, who heard him speak, reported his saying that it had been indicated that "men of property had contracted debts which, if exacted suddenly, must ruin them and their families, but with a little indulgence of time, might be paid with ease. What, Sir, is it proposed, then, to reclaim the spendthrift from his dissipation and extravagance by filling his pockets with money?" While the House passed the bill, the council, the upper body, refused assent.

Hardly had Patrick Henry engaged the enmity of the controlling group than he proceeded again to the attack. A copy of the proposed stamp act had reached the Burgesses. With many members absent, including, in all probability, Washington, the House formed itself into a committee of the whole to consider what measures to take. On his twenty-ninth birthday, Henry rose to introduce the Virginia Resolves: that Virginians had all the basic privileges of Englishmen, that they had uninterruptedly governed themselves since ancient times, and that the Virginia Assembly had the sole right to tax Virginians. Debate in the House, as Jefferson later reported, was "most bloody." The older members cried out against the resolves; Henry received a great deal of personal abuse. On the second day, in an impassioned harangue against the Stamp Act, Henry made his legendary statement: "Caesar had his Brutus;

Charles the First, his Cromwell, and George the Third..." At this point Speaker Robinson shouted "Treason" and the cry was echoed by the speaker's supporters. Jefferson, who had been enthralled by Henry's "sublime eloquence," heard him conclude, "and George the Third may profit by their example. If this be treason, make the most of it." He then apologized to the House for his language. Five of his resolves passed by a small margin, and Henry left for western Virginia. The older members, as soon as he was gone, struck out the fifth resolve, but the essential deed was done.

The royal governor of Massachusetts, Francis Bernard, wrote to London: "Two or three months ago, I thought this people would have submitted to the Stamp Act... But the publishing the Virginia Resolves, proved an alarmed bell to the Disaffected." The British commander in chief, now General Gage, called them a signal for a general outcry throughout the continent. "The Lawyers," he added, "are the Source from whence the Clamours have flowed in every Province."

The governor of Virginia, Francis Fauquier, dissolved the House and ordered new elections. This proved a blessing for Washington. A seat became vacant in Fairfax County where he lived, and he ran there instead of Frederick. He was elected without difficulty; he thus severed his political connections with the frontier, which he had represented for seventeen years.

WASHINGTON COMMENTS ON THE STAMP ACT

Washington, who had missed the debate, remained calm about the act. One of his few known references to it was in a September 20 letter to the portrait painter Francis Dandridge, his wife's uncle who lived in England.

The Stamp Act Imposed on the Colonies by the Parliament of Great Britain engrosses the conversation of the Speculative [i.e. philosophical] part of the Colonists, who look upon this unconstitutional method of Taxation as a direful attack upon their Liberties, and loudly exclaim against their Violation; what may be the result of this and some other (I think I may add) ill judged Measures, I will not undertake to determine; but this I may venture to affirm, that the advantage accrueing to the Mother Country will fall greatly short of the expectations of the Ministry for certain it is, our whole Substance does already in a manner flow to Great Britain and that whatsoever contributes to lessen our Importations must be hurtful to their Manufacturers. And the Eyes of our People, already beginning to open, will perceive, that many Luxuries which we lavish our substance to Great Britain for, can well be dispensed with whilst the necessaries of Life are (mostly) to be had within ourselves. This consequently will introduce frugality, and be a necessary stimulation to Industry.

COLONEL MERCER RETURNS TO AMERICA

George Mercer, Washington's old aide and friend, had left Virginia in 1763 to seek political preferment in England. There is no reason to suppose he particularly sought the post of stamp distributor for Virginia, but having been offered it, he accepted. Captain Stewart wrote to Washington from London, on August 18, 1765, to report: "As for News I beg leave to refer you to the Bearer Colo. Mercer who returns to Collect a Tax upon his native Land, the Mode of Imposing which, we are told, the people of America in general, and the Virginians in particular, look on as in infringement of their Priviledges, which has occasioned such a ferment that a Majority of their Representatives in a Legislative Capacity, made some Very warm and bold Resolves, Printed Copies of which are handed about in this place but it is asserted that the last and most violent of them is spurious."

The resolve to which Stewart refers was most probably the one which was stricken out as soon as Patrick Henry left town. By the time Mercer got to Virginia, nine of the colonies had met in Congress in New York to pass resolutions more restrained than those of Virginia, requesting Parliament to repeal the act.

Colonel Mercer arrived in Virginia two days before November 1, the date the act was to take effect. As soon as his presence was known, an immense crowd assembled. The governor, who was popular with Virginians and noted for his tact, handled the situation with such skill that there was no violence. He reported to London that there had been a "concourse of people, I should call a mob, did I not know that it was chiefly if not altogether composed of gentlemen of property." After discussions and negotiations lasting two days, Mercer resigned and soon thereafter returned to England. When no litigants appeared at the general court, the governor adjourned it.

In New York and Massachusetts mob violence got out of hand. The first stages of revolution had begun. Soon, Virginia as well as the other colonies had their "Sons of Liberty," a term first employed in Parliament by Colonel Isaac Barré in a speech opposing the stamp tax. Eleven years later, Patrick Henry, who had precipitated the disturbance, became the first republican governor of Virginia.

FIFTEEN

RELATIVE TRANQUILITY

1766–1769

T HE STAMP ACT, described by the British minister, George Grenville, "as an experiment towards further aid," that is, American financial aid to Britain, casually passed an indifferent Parliament in March 1765. The king was then in a state of illness, diagnosed by Paul Wold, professor of pathology, University of California, San Diego, as "the congenital metabolic disease, acute intermittent porphyria. This condition causes agonizing abdominal pain, manic overactivity, skin rash, red urine, paralysis, delirium and psychosis." The king was unfit to make important decisions.

The king snapped out of it in time to encounter Parliament's consternation at the ferocity of American opposition. By then Lord Rockingham's Whig cabinet, more sympathetic to Americans, was in power but holding on precariously. In December 1765, George III wrote to General Henry Seymor Conway, the cabinet's manager in the House of Commons: "I am more and more grieved at the accounts from America. Where this spirit will end is not to be said. It is undoubtedly the most serious matter that ever came before Parliament. It requires more deliberation, candour, and temper, than I fear it will meet with." The king saw the situation correctly, but this did not prevent his own bumbling interference.

The reactions in Parliament ranged from those who wanted to dispatch the British army and navy instantly to America to enforce the laws, to those who asked for immediate repeal and a declaration that Britain would never again impose such a tax. The Whigs devised a bad compromise that carried both houses. Parliament first resolved that the king "by and with the advice and consent of the Lords Spiritual and Temporal and Commons of Great Britain in Parliament Assembled, had, hath, and of Right ought to have full power and authority to make Laws and Statutes of sufficient force and validity to bind the Colonys and People of America, subjects of the Crown of Great Britain, in all cases whatsoever."

Ensuing resolutions contained much talk of "the power and dignity" of Great Britain, the violation by Americans of the laws and authority of that country, and of the passage by American legislatures of resolutions derogatory to "the legal and constitutional dependency of the colonys." One resolution, instructing the British governors in America to bring the offenders to "condign punishment," was stricken out. Practically the only opposing voices in either house were those of Pitt and Lord Camden. The House of Commons did not even divide on the resolves. Only four lords, one of whom was Earl Cornwallis, voted with Camden. The House of Commons, with practical unanimity, also refused to receive the petition of the Stamp Act Congress.

Rockingham and Conway supposed that the assertion of Parliament's absolute authority over America would clear the way to an easy repeal of the stamp tax, but the bill ran into trouble. Grenville was all for using force in America but he was voted down. The king wavered and wobbled. Rockingham had the king's assurance that he favored repeal, but when Lord Strange, a friend of Grenville, asked him whether he was for repeal, enforcement, or modification, the king said modification. Rockingham was in great distress, but George III, after a brief nervous collapse, said he was for modification as opposed to repeal or enforcement; however, if he had to choose between the latter two, he was for repeal. Conway finally carried it through Commons, but Rockingham had a rough time before the House of Lords passed it over vigorous opposition, on its third reading, March 17, 1766.

The king and Pitt became great heroes to America. New York erected a statue of George III, which stayed on the Bowery, until July 9, 1776, when it was wrecked and large portions melted into bullets for use against the king's troops. On July 21, 1766, Washington, in one of his letters of complaint to Robert Cary and Company, London (they had, he said, sent too many shoes, their scythes and chisels were often crooked, while the hoes they forwarded were as bad as those he had returned the year before), added:

the Repeal of the Stamp Act, to whatsoever causes owing, ought much to be rejoiced at, for had the Parliament of Great Britain resolv'd upon enforcing it the

*consequences I conceive wou'd have been more direful than is generally
apprehended both to the Mother Country and to her Colonies. All therefore who
were instrumental in procuring the Repeal are entitled to the Thanks of every
British Subject and have mine cordially.*

Washington's letter reduced the constitutional issue to its element. Was
Parliament supreme in the empire, as the Declaratory Act implied, or was it, as
Washington called it, "the Parliament of Great Britain"? Already that year,
Richard Bland, his colleague in the House of Burgesses, had written a pamphlet
which called the king sovereign in America but not the king and Parliament.

For the next three years, except for a 1767 reference to the stamp tax as an
"Act of Oppression," Washington's scanty surviving correspondence takes
little note of political affairs. Then, in writing to George Mason, he said that
Americans might yet, as a last resort, have to take up arms in defense of their
rights.

DEPENDENCE ON BRITAIN

Mature politically, America was still highly economically dependent on
England. Washington's London shopping lists included the most elemental
manufactures, as well as luxury items that could be sacrificed without essential
harm. The increased attention to spinning and weaving on Washington's
farms after 1765 was an effort to reduce British imports. His decision to grow
no tobacco at Mount Vernon in 1766, while part of a long-range plan of
diversification, was influenced by British measures to tax the colonists. It
reflected a general American desire to lessen the economic ties that, more
than the political, kept the country tied to mother's apron strings.

Later agreements not to import British goods, in which Washington took
the lead in Virginia, were almost universally supported. For Virginians they
had the added advantage that many planters had lived beyond their means.
This had been fashionable, but it became equally so to dress and live simply.
In 1770 there was a feminine declaration of independence when the ladies at
the governor's ball in Williamsburg all dressed in homespun rather than in
London silks. In many ways it was a fortunate movement. Nearly ten years
before the war, America began increasingly to make its own cloths, hats, shirts,
and, finally, muskets and gunpowder. The Washington plantations were
among the first to participate, spinning, weaving, milling, distilling, and, when
required, giving up goods taxed by Britain.

The growth of American population, instead of being a source of pride to

England, alarmed many Englishmen who could see America deigning to "wrestle with us for Preeminence." As early as 1766, the increase of population led them to think independence was on its way unless "we wisely take the power out of their hands." Keeping settlers behind the Alleghenies and controlling American trade were two weapons. Americans, including Washington, were already thinking in terms of destiny. A favorite game was to estimate future population. Americans believed they were doubling roughly every twenty-five years and would eventually catch up with England. It was only a matter of time before hordes of Americans would go smashing over the mountains whatever London might order.

MRS. WASHINGTON'S CHILDREN

Washington tried to provide his stepson, Jacky Custis, with a good classical and general education; in this program he had rather limited cooperation from Jacky. Mrs. Washington's daughter ("my little Patt") was more worrying because her epileptic fits occurred more frequently as she grew older. The Washingtons consulted physicians in Williamsburg, Fredericksburg, and Alexandria. They also took her to the waters at Warm Springs and even tried a man who attached an iron ring to her to bring out the devil.

Late in 1761, Washington engaged a tutor, Walter Magowan, who stayed with the family until 1768 when he left to take Holy Orders in England. Washington, after his marriage, ordered books from London for a child just learning to read and then, in 1761, a more impressive array, which included works by Horace and Terence, and Latin grammars and dictionaries. Washington wrote to his subsequent tutor that Jacky had read Virgil by the time he was twelve. Young Martha Custis was not fit for intense study. She received some tutoring from Magowan, but when he left, instruction, except in music and dancing, appears to have been abandoned.

When Jacky was fourteen, Washington persuaded his wife that Jacky ought to go to a school where disciplined study could be enforced. He selected the school of the Reverend Jonathan Boucher in Caroline County, Virginia. On May 30, 1768, he wrote to Boucher:

> *Mr. Magowan who lived several years in my Family, Tutor to Master Custis (my Son-in-Law and Ward) having taken his departure for England leaves the young Gentleman without any master at this time. I should be glad therefore to know if it would be convenient for you to add him to the number of your Pupils. He is a boy of good genius, about 14 yrs. of age, untainted in his morals, and of innocent manners...*

*Now Sir, if you incline to take Master Custis I should be glad to know what
conveniences it may be necessary for him to bring, and how soon he may come. For
as to Board and Schooling (provender for his Horses he may lay in himself) I do
not think it necessary to enquire into and will cheerfully, pay Ten or Twelve
pounds a year extraordinary to engage your peculiar care of and a watchful eye to
him as he is a promising boy; the last of his Family and will possess a very large
Fortune; add to this my anxiety to make him fit for more useful purposes, than a
horse Racer.*

Washington was too honest not to imply that Jacky Custis was a bit of a problem child. Boucher, then about thirty and having a struggle to survive, was
delighted to add such a pupil.

The Church of England, through the bishop of London who had charge of
American branches, tended to ship out clergymen who were not suitable for
appointment to an English parish. Boucher had not received a rectorship to
his liking in Virginia and turned to teaching. When he replied to Washington
that he wanted Jacky very much, he noted that he might be moving the school
to Maryland where he hoped for a parish. After asking Washington to send
him down "immediately," he concluded:

*Ever since I have heard of Mastr. Custis, I have wish'd to call Him one of my little
Flock; and I am not asham'd to confess to You, that, since the Rect. of yr. Letter, I
have wished it much more. Engag'd as I have now been upwards of seven Years in
the Education of Youth, You will own it must be mortifying to Me to reflect, that I
cannot boast of having the Honr. to bring up one Scholar. I have had, 'tis true,
Youths, whose Fortunes, Inclinations and Capacities all gave Me room for the most
pleasing Hopes: yet I know not how it is, no sooner do They arrive at that Period of
Life when They might be expected more successfully to apply to their Studies than
They either marry, or are remov'd from School, on some, perhaps even still, less
justifiable motive.*

Boucher's letters to Washington tended to be as candid as this expression of
his failures as a teacher. Jacky arrived at the school in early July. Boucher wrote
back that the boy had had stomach trouble, adding "it might be owing to
Worms." Two weeks later he wrote that Jacky had malaria, but, as he later
noted, malaria "easily gives way to Vomits and Bark."

Mrs. Washington was so devoted to her children that she could barely let
them out of her sight. Her ease of mind could hardly have been improved by
this correspondence. Boucher also wrote that while Jacky was of "exceedingly
mild & meek a Temper," he was "far from being a brilliant Genius." Boucher

noted that he had not misunderstood the remark about Jacky's fortune, and he promised to give "more vigilant Attn. to the Propriety and Decorum of his Behvr., & the restraining. Him fr. many Indulgences... allowg. Him more frequently to sit in my Company, & being more careful of the Company of Those, who might probably debase or taint his Morals."

Boucher restored Jacky to his parents about the beginning of September. Washington reported back to him on Sept. 4:

> *Master Custis was so much disordered by an intermitting fever attended with bilious vomitings, that we were obligd... to send for Doctr. Mortimer... He is now better, but not clear of slow fevers, and very weak and low (being much reduced) which induces his Mamma to take him home with us, till he is perfectly restored.*

Boucher wrote that perhaps he should have told Washington more about Jacky's illnesses, which he attributed to eating too many cucumbers.

Jacky stayed under the watchful care of his mother until quite late in the school year. Washington dispatched him back to Boucher on January 26, 1769, with a note: "After so long a vacation, we hope Jacky will apply close to his Studies, and retrieve the hours he has lost from his Books, since your opening School, he promises to do so, and I hope he will." By July, Boucher could write Washington: "I have a Pleasure in informing You that I please Myself with thinking We now do much better than formerly."

On July 25, following his return to Mount Vernon, Washington ordered from London a large library for Jacky's use. It included nearly fifty authors, many in large sets: the works of Cicero (twenty volumes); Livy and Grotius; the Greek New Testament; Greek and Latin grammars; the poetry of Thomson and Milton; histories of Rome, England, and Scotland; and various geographies. Jacky's was a good basic library for the eighteenth century but it was not destined to be extensively used.

THE GOOD LIFE

Between 1762 and 1768, Washington added numerous public duties to his work as Burgess. The first was his election in October 1762 as vestryman of Truro Parish, an office once held by his father. The Anglican church was established by law, and the vestry were responsible not only for church administration but for the care of the parish orphans and the poor. In 1766 he became warden of the parish. As such he was the principal officer to choose a site in 1767 for the new Pohick Church, which he helped to design. Washington,

George Mason, and George Fairfax were on the committee that supervised its building and assigned the family pews.

In 1766, the year he was elected churchwarden, he was also chosen trustee (councilman) for the town of Alexandria. In 1768 he became justice of the Fairfax county court and of the court of oyer and terminer. As Washington added city, church, and court duties to his work at the provincial capital, a note of increasing contentment and happiness appears in his diaries. Paradoxically, for the first time in his life, he began to allow himself more leisure. His daily horseback riding—to check every detail of fencing, seeding, ploughing, reaping, and milling on his farms—was frequently replaced by days devoted entirely to hunting. He went sport fishing and duck hunting. He went to several balls in Alexandria and wrote that he twice stayed up all night to dance. He went to the horse races and took Jacky with him to dine with the governor. Much company came to dinner and cards at Mount Vernon. They included Lord Fairfax as well as his brother Robert and their cousin Bryan, who were later the seventh and eighth lords. The Washingtons also dined out often. By 1770 they were going frequently to plays in Alexandria and Williamsburg. In 1768 Washington ordered a handsome new coach from England for his family. He mentioned, from time to time, staying home all day to write to his London agents or to balance his books. Most of his time, when the weather permitted, was spent out of doors building the strength on which he was to rely during more than eight years of war. He noted only occasional illnesses, usually mild forms of malaria and dysentery.

THE WESTERN LANDS

While king and Parliament in London were busy debating the best means of handling their possessions, Americans went on developing the country in their own way. Washington, who had helped to open the West, took two steps to obtain land beyond the Alleghenies. As he wrote to Colonel John Armstrong of Pennsylvania, who had been with the Forbes army: "I would most willingly possess some of those Lands which we have labord and Toild so hard to conquer." For this work he engaged an old companion of his youthful days in Winchester, Captain William Crawford, who had settled on the Youghiogheny River. He made a proposal to him on September 21, 1767: "I wrote to you a few days ago in a hurry... I then desird the favour of you (as I understood Rights might now be had for the Lands, which have fallen within the Pennsylvania Line) to look me out a Tract of about 1500, 2000 or more Acres somewhere in your Neighbourhood."

Washington wrote also to Armstrong for help in acquiring acreage, saying he had heard Armstrong was to set up a land office in Carlisle. Armstrong said that no such bureau was planned. The Penn Proprietors kept land under such strict control that it was difficult to buy any. Two years later Pennsylvania did start to sell land and Washington got his acreage. Crawford wrote subsequently that he had obtained several choice pieces of land and had them surveyed. Washington did not get out to the wild west of western Virginia until two years later than he had expected.

Washington's views were often well ahead of their time. His opinion that the proclamation line of 1763 was bound to give way was confirmed in 1768 when the British signed treaties with the Iroquois and Cherokees, extending British territory to what is now West Virginia and to the Kanawha and Ohio Rivers. Washington resolved to claim from this territory the 200,000 acres of land promised by Dinwiddie to the three hundred or so volunteer officers and men of 1754. In May 1769, he brought up the subject in conversation with Lord Botetourt who had succeeded Francis Fauquier as governor. On December 8 of that year he formally presented to Botetourt the facts of the soldiers' claims. With the governor's encouragement, he prepared to make his farthest trip west, surveying lands suitable for the bounty.

A NEW BRITISH TAX

Some months after the repeal of the Stamp Act, the king asked Pitt to form a new government. He accepted not only the job but the earldom of Chatham. This lost the Great Commoner much of his popularity. Walpole observed: "That fatal title blasted all the affection which his country had borne to him." Shortly afterwards he fell into a mental disorder, although he did not give up office until 1768.

Pitt's illness left England without a firm guiding hand. His chancellor of the exchequer, Charles Townshend, brilliant and unstable, unguardedly mentioned in Parliament one day that he knew how to tax the Americans without making them angry. Upon a challenge by Grenville, he agreed to make good his words. Many Americans, including Franklin, had argued that Parliament could lay no internal tax in America but that it could levy an external tax. The subsequent Townshend Act, passed in mid-1767, imposed duties on glass, paper, paints, and tea exported from Britain to America. According to the Duke of Grafton, these taxes were presented to Parliament over the objection of every member of the cabinet. They passed without the knowledge of Pitt and with hardly a dissent. After getting the tax through in May, Townshend died in September, leaving a weak government to meet the roar of outrage from America. Lord North was appointed in place of Townshend; in 1770 he succeeded Grafton as the king's first minister.

Massachusetts was the first province to react, since the law established a new customs board at Boston. That colony drew up "a humble, dutiful and loyal petition to the king" and addressed a moderate letter to the legislatures of the other provinces. Lord Hillsborough, the excitable American secretary, ordered Massachusetts to rescind the letter but its legislature refused. Hillsborough then asked the king for troops, which were sent from Halifax. Rioting and general trouble ensued at Boston. In early 1769 Hillsborough proposed to replace the elected Massachusetts council with royal appointees and to threaten the province with revocation of its charter if it questioned an act of Parliament. The king, more moderate and sensible, slapped Hillsborough down:

> *The vesting in the Crown the Appointment of the Council of Massachusetts Bay may from a continuance of their conduct become necessary; but till then ought to be avoided as the altering Charters is at all times an odious measure.*

> *The second Proposition is of so strong a nature that it rather seems calculated to increase the unhappy feudes that subsist than to asswage them.*

The French had followed the growing rift between America and Britain with great interest. In 1767, not long after the Stamp Act's repeal, French diplomats in London got in touch with Benjamin Franklin, praising him as a man of science, and invited him to Paris. There he met Louis XV and many scientists and philosophers.

In 1768 the count du Chatelet reported from London to the French foreign minister: "The ties that bind America to England are three-fourths broken. She must soon throw off the yoke. To make themselves independant, the inhabitants want nothing but arms, courage and a chief... Perhaps this man exists. Perhaps nothing is wanted but happy circumstances to place him upon a great theatre." On April 5, 1769, Washington, who had been studying the economic boycott of Britain adopted in Maryland and Pennsylvania, wrote his neighbor George Mason:

> *At a time when our lordly Masters in Great Britain will be satisfied with nothing less than the deprication of American freedom, it seems highly necessary that some thing should be done to avert the stroke and maintain the liberty we have*

derived from our Ancestors; but the manner of doing it to answer the purpose effectively is the point in question.

That no man should scruple, or hesitate a moment to use arms in defence of so valuable a blessing, on which all the good and evil of life depends; is clearly my opinion; yet Arms I wou'd beg leave to add, should be the last resource... Addresses to the Throne, and remonstrances to Parliament, we have already it is said, proved the inefficacy of; how far then their attention to our rights and privileges is to awakened or alarmed by starving their trade and manufactures, remains to be tryed.

The northern Colonies, it appears, are endeavouring to adopt this scheme. In my opinion, it is a good one, and must be attended with salutory effects, provided it can be carried pretty generally into execution... That there will be difficulties attending the execution of it every where, from clashing interests, and selfish designing men... cannot be denied; but in the Tobacco colonies where the Trade is so diffused, and in a manner wholly conducted by Factors for their principals at home, these difficulties are certainly enhanced.

The more I consider a Scheme of this sort, the more ardently I wish success to it, because I think there are private, as well as public advantages to result from it; the former certain, however precarious the other may prove; for in respect to the latter I have always thought that by virtue of the same power (for here alone the authority derives) which assumes the right of Taxation, they may attempt at least to restrain our manufactories; especially those of a public nature; the same equity and justice prevailing in the one case as the other, it being no greater hardship to forbid my manufacturing, than it is to order me to buy Goods of them, loaded with Duties, for the express purpose of raising a revenue. But as a measure of this sort will be an additional exertion of arbitrary power, we cannot be worsted I think in putting it to the Test.

He concluded by noting that many Virginians were in debt to England and they could only benefit by reducing their expenditures. Washington had already begun to develop political clairvoyance as to the outcome of issues that were still developing. Because of this, his views expressed to Mason were more radical than those of any other leading American. Six years before the outbreak of war, he foresaw that armed hostilities were inevitable if other measures failed. He also stated that Parliament had no more right to interfere with American manufacturing than it had to tax Americans. Probably no American, from Franklin down, would have agreed with him, since they considered the British economic measures to be within their rights. Pitt, the stout defender of America, said that if they overthrew Britain's economic controls, he would be the first to move to crush the Americans.

Mason replied the same day to Washington. He made no mention of Washington's radical ideas, but he did send him a redraft of the Pennsylvania nonimportation agreement that he had adapted to Virginia conditions. Washington had it with him when he arrived in Williamsburg on May 3.

VIRGINIAE DUX

When the Burgesses assembled in 1769, it was the 150th anniversary of this first American parliament, which had met under nine sovereigns and Oliver Cromwell.

Lord Botetourt was an even more popular governor than Francis Fauquier and handled the Burgesses with tact and skill. Nonetheless, he had direct instructions from London to dissolve the Burgesses if they supported the circular letter of Massachusetts. Botetourt's welcoming address was made in a cordial spirit and the Burgesses moved to answer with the same good will. A new delegate, Thomas Jefferson, was assigned to draft a response, but his work was not well-regarded and older members were given the task.

It was Washington who took the lead in persuading his fellow Burgesses to join the nonimportation agreement of the northern colonies and to support the circular letter of Massachusetts. After debate, the House affirmed its exclusive right to tax in Virginia and its resolve to support Massachusetts.

Though the resolutions were worded with care, Botetourt had no choice but to dissolve the House. Washington, who had dined twice with the governor during the legislative meetings, took the Burgesses over to the Raleigh Tavern to discuss the proposed nonimportation agreement. His diary records for May 17, 1769, only this: "Dined at the Treasurer's and was upon a Committee at Hay's [owner of the tavern] till 10 o'clock." There they formed the Virginia Non-Importation Association, which was signed by 94 Burgesses. They then drank loyal toasts to the king and queen, to the governor, and to "the constitutional British liberty in America." On May 19 Washington and his fellow Burgesses attended a ball at the governor's palace, celebrating the queen's birthday.

After this, his first major political move, Washington returned to Mount Vernon on May 22 and noted in his diary that day: "Found my Wheat much better in general than ever it was at this Season before, being Ranker, better spread over the ground, and broader in the Blade than usual."

On July 25, he wrote to Robert Cary, his London agent, ordering various goods, adding that if there were any prohibited goods on the list, "it is my express desire and request that they may not be sent, as I have very heartily entered into an Association... not to Import any Article which now is or hereafter shall be Taxed... until the Acts are repeal'd... I am fully determined to adhere religiously to it."

SIXTEEN

WASHINGTON LOOKS WEST AND EAST

1770–1775

T HE AMERICAN BOYCOTTS broke down when Great Britain again moved to mollify her colonies. On March 5, 1770, Lord North introduced a bill removing all Townshend duties except on tea. An amendment to repeal the tea tax failed adoption by a small parliamentary margin; it was retained as a matter of principle. George III and Lord North wanted peace with America while most Americans viewed the remaining threepence-per-pound tea tax as no great hardship.

On the day that North moved his bill, a large mob of Boston roughnecks, described by John Adams as a "motley rabble of saucy boys, negroes and mulattoes, Irish teagues and outlandish jack tars," attacked a group of British soldiers with oyster shells, icy snowballs, stones, and clubs. The infuriated soldiers eventually fired on them, killing five. Samuel Adams, Paul Revere, and the Boston press attempted to picture the affair as a British massacre but John Adams and Josiah Quincy, Jr., defended the men in court. A jury of honest countrymen acquitted all but two soldiers and effectively acquitted the remaining two, who were branded on the thumb. Thereafter all was calm for more than three years until Lord North, in an offhand way, introduced a measure intended to assist the East India Company to provide cheaper tea for America. To his and the king's surprise, the Boston mobs once again went into action.

With repeal, Americans rushed to buy British goods. Imports which had fallen from £2.2 million in 1768 to £1.4 million in 1769, increased to more than £4 million in 1771. Even taxed tea was imported in increasing volume: 55 tons in 1770 and 370 tons in 1773. The Washingtons again drew up their London shopping lists: fashionable clothing for themselves and Jacky Custis, handkerchiefs, bonnets, many pairs of shoes, hunting caps, brooms, decanters, silver spurs, pencil cases, tea and coffee cups and saucers, hairpins, powder boxes, and food such as walnuts, salad oil, spices, sugar, currants, and figs.

WESTERN LAND

With relations between mother country and colonies once more peaceful, Washington turned again to acquiring western lands. In particular he looked to his share of the 200,000-acre land bonus in the Ohio Valley that Dinwiddie had promised the Virginia Regiment in 1754. He also hoped to make additional land purchases in western Pennsylvania and Virginia. In 1770 Lord Botetourt and the Virginia council gave a favorable report on the soldiers' bonus land claims. In consequence Washington invited his former officers to meet him in Fredericksburg in August to draw up plans. He volunteered to go to the Ohio Valley to look for the best land available and suggested that the officers and men contribute pro rata to the expenses. Court duties and harvesting delayed his trip until autumn. On October 5, 1770, Washington, Dr. Craik, and three servants set out from Mount Vernon for what was to be the farthest inland trip of Washington's life.

After visiting his brother Samuel at Harewood (near the present Charles Town)—a house still owned by a descendent—the party moved toward the northwest. On October 13 they reached Great Meadows, where Washington had capitulated to the French in 1754. It was quite good land, and he bought his old battlefield as a farm in December. They rode across Laurel Hill down "to the Plantation of Mr. Thos Gist [where] the Land appeared charming; that which lay level being as rich & black as any thing could possibly be." Next day, they inspected a mine which produced "Coal of the very best kind, burning freely, & abundance of it." He then recorded their travel to and stay at Pittsburgh:

> *Monday 15th. Went to view some Land which Captn. Crawford had taken up for me near Yaughyaughgane distant about 12 Miles. This Tract which contains about 1600 Acres Includes some as fine Land as ever I saw, a great deal of Rich Meadow... This Tract is well watered, and has a valuable Mill Seat...*

The Lands which I passed over to day were generally Hilly, and the growth chiefly white Oak, but very good notwithstanding; & what is extraordinary, & contrary to the property of all other Lands I ever saw before, the Hills are the richest Land; the soil upon the Sides and Summits of them, being black as Coal, & the Growth, Walnut, Cherry, Spice Bushes, &ca...

Wednesday 17th. Docr. Craik & myself with Captn. Crawford and others arrived at Fort Pitt, distant from the Crossing 43 1/2 Measurd Miles... We passed over a great deal of exceeding fine Land...

We lodgd in what is calld the Town, distant at 300 yards from the Fort at one Mr. Semples who keeps a very good House of Publick Entertainment. These Houses which are built of Logs, & rangd into Streets are on the Monongahela, & I suppose may be abt. 20 in Number, and inhabited by Indian Traders, &ca.

The Fort is built in the point between the Rivers Alligany & Monongahela, but not so near the pitch of it as Fort Duquesne stood. It is 5 sided & regular, two of which (next the Land) are of Brick, the other Stockade. A Mote incompasses it. The Garrison consists of two Companies of Royal Irish Commanded by one Captn. Edmonson.

Thursday 18th. Dind in the Fort with Colo. Croghan & the Officers of the Garrison. Suppd there also, meeting with great civility from the Gentlemen, & engagd to dine with Colo. Croghan the next day at his Seat abt. 4 miles up the Alligany.

Friday 19th. Recd. a Message from Colo. Croghan that the White Mingo & other Chiefs of the 6 Nations had something to say to me... I went up and received a Speech with a String of Wampum from the White Mingo to the following effect:

That as I was a Person who some of them remember to have seen when I was sent on an Embassy to the French, and most of them had heard of; they were to come to bid me welcome to this Country, and to desire that the People of Virginia woud consider them as friends & Brothers...

To this I answered (after thanking them for their friendly welcome)... that I was sure nothing was more wishd and desired by the People of Virginia than to live in the strictest friendship with them...

After dining at Colo. Croghan's we returned to Pittsburgh... Engagd an Indian calld the Pheasant, and one Joseph Nicholson an Interpreter to attend us the whole Voyage. Also a young Indn. Warrior.

Saturday 20th. We Imbarked in a large Canoe with sufficient Stores of Provisions and Necessaries.

CANOEING

The canoe, probably a *Canot du nord*, could hold eight persons, plus supplies. The party drifted rather slowly down the Ohio River, stopping at various points for meals and to inspect properties. Colonel Croghan was offering part of his land for sale. Washington thought it fine and rich, but noted that the country was in too unsettled a state for him to think of buying. The party ran into a snowstorm though it was still only October. When they were seventy-five miles from Pittsburgh, they stopped at an Indian village, Mingo Town (Mingo Junction, Ohio), which had twenty cabins. Washington noted an abundance of ducks, geese, and turkeys, with excellent shooting along the river. They soon passed Wheeling Creek where that city is now located. On the Virginia side, he encountered an old friend who was out hunting:

We found Kiashuta and His Hunting Party incamped. Here we were under a necessity of paying our compliments, as this person was one of the Six Nations Chiefs, & head of them upon this River. In the person of Kiashuta I found an old acquaintance, he being one of the Indians that went with me to the French in 1753. He expressed a satisfaction in seeing me, and treated us with great kindness; giving us a Quarter of very fine Buffalo. He insisted upon our spending that Night with him, and in order to retard us as little as possible movd his Camp down the River... After much Councelling the overnight, they all came to my fire the next Morning, with great formality; when Kiashuta rehearsing what had passed between me & the Sachems at Colo. Croghan's, thanked me for saying that Peace & friendship was the wish of the People of Virginia... and again expressed their desire of having a Trade opend with Virginia... The tedious ceremony which the Indians observe in their Councellings and speeches, detained us till 9 Oclock.

SURVEYING

Washington continued down the river to the big bend of the Ohio and to the junction of the Great Kanawha River, now Point Pleasant, West Virginia. For the first time he saw lands worth patenting for his former soldiers. He also became the first president to go buffalo shooting. He noted:

The young Washington as surveyor. *(The Bettmann Archive)*

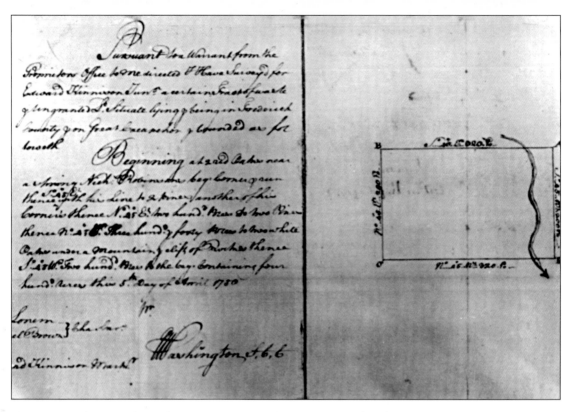

One of Washington's surveying accounts, this one from Frederick County, Va., presumably written in his own hand. It is dated April 5, 1750. *(The Bettmann Archive)*

Washington, delivering an ultimatum to the French for Virginia's Colonial Governor Robert Dinwiddie, being escorted to Fort Le Boeuf in 1753. *(The Bettmann Archive)*

This first portrait of Washington, at age forty wearing his British Colonial uniform, was painted by Charles Wilson Peale (1772). *(The Bettmann Archive)*

Martha Washington by Charles Wilson Peale (1776). *(Courtesy of the Mount Vernon Ladies' Association of the Union)*

Washington, a dedicated planter, directs work on the Mount Vernon plantation (Lithograph, 1853, after a painting by Stearns). *(The Bettmann Archive)*

Carpenters' Hall, Philadelphia, where the first Continental Congress convened in 1775. *(The Bettmann Archive)*

A typical day in the rapidly growing city of Philadelphia in the late 18th century. *(The Bettmann Archive)*

After being named General and Commander-in-Chief by the Continental Congress, Washington took command of the Continental Army in Cambridge, Massachusetts. *(The Bettmann Archive)*

John Adams of Massachusetts. Although lacking a military background, Adams was a critic of Washington's generalship. *(The Bettmann Archive)*

Portrait of General Washington by John Trumball, who served briefly as one of
Washington's aides. *(The Bettmann Archive)*

Wednesday 31st. I sent the Canoe along down to the Junction of the two Rivers abt. 5 Miles, that is the Kanawha with the Ohio, and set out upon a hunting Party to view the Land. We steered nearly East for about 8 or 9 Miles, then bore Southwardly, & Westwardly, till we came to our Camp at the confluence of the Rivers.

November 1st... We set off with our Canoe up the River, to discover what kinds of Lands lay upon the Kanawha. The Land both sides this River just at the Mouth is very fine; but on the East side when you get towards the Hills... it appears to be wet & better adapted for Meadow than tillage...

Novr. 2d. We proceeded up the River with the Canoe about 4 Miles more, & then incampd and went a Hunting; killd 5 Buffaloes & wounded some others... This Country abounds in Buffalo & Wild Game of all kinds as also in all kinds of wild fowl, there being in the Bottoms a great many small grassy Ponds or Lakes which are full of Swans, Geese & Ducks.

Saturday 3rd. We set off down the River on our return homewards, and Incampd at the Mouth; at the Beginning of the Bottom above the Junction of the Rivers, and at the Mouth of a branch on the East side, I mark'd two Maples, an Elm, & Hoopwood Tree as a Cornr. of the Soldiers Ld. (if we can get it) intending to take all the bottom from hence to the Rapids in the Great Bend into one Survey. I also marked at the Mouth of another Gut lower down on the West side... an Ash and hoopwood for the Beginning of another of the Soldiers Survey.

Washington marked off the course of the Ohio and Kanawha Rivers by means of his compass and recorded them in his diary. In company with Captain Crawford, he walked eight miles across the neck of land, which he described as "generally good; and in places very rich. The growth in most places is beach intermixed with walnut... but more especially with poplar... The land towards the upper end is black Oak, & very good; upon the whole a valuable Tract might be had here, & I judge the quantity to be about 4000 acres."

Washington returned slowly to Pittsburgh, spending some two weeks going upriver. He again encountered Kiashuta. Floods and heavy rains delayed him. He used this time to estimate the distances, from point to point, which he had travelled, as 266 miles from Pittsburgh to the mouth of the Great Kanawha.

Washington noted that the Shawnees, Delawares, and Mingos had received little compensation when the English purchased lands from the Six Nations and were, in consequence, quite annoyed at the settlers who were moving in. He wrote that Indian women were as skilled as men in handling canoes. The Indians had camps and cabins all along the river. They hunted during the winter, sometimes moving two hundred or three hundred miles, returning in the spring to their settlements. The women then did all the planting while the men sold furs, gossiped, and led an easy life.

At Mingo Town, Washington obtained horses and crossed the land stretch to Pittsburgh rather than go around by water. On December 1 he was back at Mount Vernon "after an absence of 9 Weeks and one Day."

Upon his return he learned that Lord Botetourt had died while Washington was paddling upriver more than a hundred miles from Pittsburgh. This meant that another governor would come out, and Washington would have to explain anew the situation of the soldiers' land. He also learned of the possibility of trouble from a British group, headed by Thomas Walpole, who were demanding land in the area where Washington had been surveying. Although Washington did not know it at the time, his efforts on behalf of his former officers and men were to involve him in trouble and expense practically the rest of his life. His correspondence in regard to the claims continued for twenty-eight years.

In March 1771, Washington met again with his officers to explain what he had accomplished on his trip and the complications. The governor and council had put an arbitrary limit of 20 tracts to cover the whole 200,000 acres. With Washington's efforts and subsequent surveys by Captain Valentine Crawford, 10 tracts had been found, for a total of 62,000 acres. Over the succeeding two years the remaining acreage was found within the prescribed additional 10 serves. Washington's own share of the land, plus acreage he bought up as a speculation from his former soldiers, increased his holdings in the Ohio Valley to around 24,000 acres. Most of it was far from known civilization and had to be seated, that is, worked as a farm, within a reasonable period. His endeavors to comply with Virginia laws on this cost him more than the land was worth inasmuch as he purchased the claims for around eleven cents an acre.

When the land was being distributed in 1773 in accordance with the patents approved by the governor and council, George Muse, who had been forced to resign from the Virginia Regiment for cowardice at the battle of Fort Necessity, felt that he had been defrauded of a few acres by Washington. Muse sent him an abusive letter. Washington waited only twenty-four hours and then replied on January 29, 1774:

Sir: Your impertinent letter of the 24th ulto. was delivered to me yesterday by Mr. Smith. As I am not accustomed to receive such from any Man, nor would have taken the same language from you personally, without letting you to be cautious in writing me a second of the same tenour; for though I understand you were drunk when you did it, yet give me leave to tell you that drunkeness is no excuse for rudeness; and that but for your stupidity and sottishness you might have known, by attending to the public Gasettes... that you had your full quantity of ten thousand acres of land allowed you... whilst I wanted near 500 acres of my quantity... But suppose you had really fallen short 73 acres of your 10,000, do you think your superlative merit entitles you to greater indulgences than others? or that I was to make it good to you, if it did?... If either of these should happen to be your opinion, I am very well convinced you will stand singular in it; and all my concern is, that I ever engag'd in behalf of so ungrateful and dirty a fellow as you are... I wrote... a few days ago... proposing an easy method of dividing our lands; but since I find in what temper you are, I am sorry I took the trouble of mentioning the Land, or your name in the Letter, as I do not think you merit the least assistance from G. Washington.

In 1775, Lord Dunmore attempted, in one of the last acts of royal authority in the colony, to set aside the land grants on a technicality. The state of Virginia, however, subsequently ratified the transaction and, because of the war, waived the time requirement for seating the lands.

DEVELOPMENT ECONOMIST

a. Canals

Washington, possessing some thirty-seven miles of western land, much of it earned in the service of his country, worked before the revolution to develop it as well as to open up the West to general settlement. Some of his proposals were beyond the existing technical and financial capacity of the country.

As early as 1754 Washington canoed the Potomac from near Cumberland to Great Falls, not far from Georgetown, making extensive notes. By the 1760s, England had begun to build toll canals. After learning of this development, Washington in 1769 drew up a plan for a privately financed system of locks on the Potomac from Georgetown to Cumberland. The old Braddock road thence led to Pittsburgh, from which there was relatively easy water communication with points along the Ohio and on down the Mississippi.

In 1770 Washington sponsored a bill in the Virginia Assembly to promote the navigation of the Potomac; this passed in 1772. It required Maryland to enact similar legislation. He worked actively to promote the company, but political difficulties after 1774 forced the temporary abandonment of the scheme. It was revived after the war, and Washington became president of the company. At the time he made a western trip on which he wrote a brilliant political-economic analysis of the development problems of the new union.

b. Flour Mills

Washington, with a first-class flour mill on his Mount Vernon property, decided to build another on his property on the Youghiogheny River in Pennsylvania. He engaged Gilbert Simpson to settle there and build the mill, thereby acquiring problems that pursued him for many years.

Late in 1772, Washington and Simpson arranged for servants, tools, and necessities for clearing the land, raising grain, and building a mill. By the following April, Simpson was on the land but full of complaints. His cabin, he said, was "leekey Smooke." He told Washington he would stay till fall and then quit. His wife had not wanted to come, and he hated the place. In June he left but assured Washington he had everything in good order and had given directions to his workers. He said he might return in September when there were fewer flies. Washington wrote him a sharp letter, which is now lost, and Simpson replied that he was "Reyley Sorrey," but it was all the fault of his wife, the worthless hands that Washington had sent, the flies, the bad housing, and the colds and boils from which he suffered. Somehow, Washington persuaded him to go back, and Simpson then began asking for money and more helpers, nails, salt, and flour.

The following year war with the Indians broke out. This added to the troubles of Simpson and Washington. More than a thousand fleeing settlers retreated across the Monongahela near Washington's mill property. With wars, interruptions, lack of material, and general inefficiency, Simpson wrote Washington that his mill would probably cost around £700, a figure higher than he had anticipated. He asked for £250 immediately. Simpson acknowledged receipt of the money saying, "I am Sorry you Should Think the Cost of Your Mill So high." Two months later Simpson asked for a further £300. Washington sent this money and Simpson replied: "I am heartyly Sorrey to heare your uneaseyness Concerning Mills Costing so Much... She has alreydy Cost you double the Money I ever Expect She Was to Cost and She Will Cost a Great Deel More yet." Simpson added that it had been so much trouble he would never do it again; but said he agreed with Washington that gold did not grow on trees but he was doing great service in opening the country to poor people.

In February 1775, Simpson asked for more money, and again said he was sorry but hoped that God would bless Washington, who was doing so much for "the good of Amerecay." On August 20 General Washington wrote from Cambridge to Lund Washington at Mount Vernon after Simpson had requested further funds: "Although I never hear of the Mill under the direction of Simpson, without a degree of warmth and vexation at his stupidity, yet if you can spare the money from other Purposes, I could wish to have it sent to him, that it may, if possible, be set agoing before the Works get ruined and spoilt, and my money perhaps totally lost."

Simpson did get the mill in operation and kept it working during the war, but he seems to have kept no accounts, and he offered a settlement in worthless continental currency. Washington figured in 1784 that he had lost some £1,200 on the deal.

c. Land Settlement

Washington was scrupulous in following the Virginia laws relating to settling and clearing land, although the difficulties in attending to this from a great distance were immense.

In March 1774, he got together some twenty slaves and indentured servants and a great quantity of equipment and provisions to send to his lands in the Ohio Valley. The Indian war, known as Lord Dunmore's war, broke out at this time, and the intended settlers fled, abandoning the equipment and leaving Washington considerably out of pocket. On October 10 the battle of Point Pleasant took place near Washington's Kanawha lands.

In 1775 he tried again. The first expedition to settle his lands within the three years required by law cost Washington about three hundred pounds. The second settlement was, temporarily, more successful. On April 2, 1776, his overseers filed at Fincastle a statement of all the improvements made on Washington's lands in the summer of 1775. This showed they had erected four large houses, a barn, and eight smaller cabins. They had also cleared twenty-eight acres and planted corn, potatoes, and turnips as well as two thousand peach stones that Washington had ordered. These improvements were valued at eleven hundred pounds for tax purposes. No record has been found as to the final fate of this enterprise, but it can be assumed that, during the revolution, it was destroyed by Indians.

BOUCHER AND JACKY CUSTIS

While Washington worked on diverse problems, he continued his efforts to provide Jacky Custis with an education. This he did more or less against Jacky's wishes and despite the ineffectual Reverend Jonathan Boucher, who had moved his school to Maryland.

In early 1770, Boucher appears to have been in some financial difficulties. He endeavored to persuade Washington to let him borrow money from Custis' estate. Washington did not like this proposal, and Boucher dropped it. He then took another tack, proposing to take Jacky on a two-year Grand Tour of Europe at Jacky's expense. Boucher's letter of May 9, 1770, assured Washington "it will not be thought that I can possibly have any interested Views in this Matter." The plan was entirely for Jacky's benefit, though Boucher did admit that he wanted to see England again. On May 21 Boucher wrote an exceedingly long amplification of his earlier views, again urging its great advantage to Jacky. He estimated the trip would cost a thousand pounds a year, of which half would be allocated to Mr. Boucher.

Washington replied that he thought travel would be advantageous to Jacky provided that he first had a good classical education. He noted that he was Jacky's trustee and he had to manage Jacky's affairs wisely. Jacky's estate was not too profitable because feeding and clothing the slaves was a very heavy charge, and the lands were of a rather low yield. Having been informed of the possible cost by Boucher, Washington had consulted others who had travelled. Washington wrote that the trip might cost a great deal more than the estimate, and Jacky would have to "break into the capital." To do this, Washington needed court approval.

Boucher persisted with his plan. He asked the governor of Maryland, Robert Eden, for leave to travel and wrote that the governor had granted this in order to oblige Washington and Jacky. He had discussed the value of the estate with the governor, estimating it at a thousand to twelve hundred pounds per annum, which the governor thought would cover their expenses.

On July 9, 1771, Washington sent Boucher a letter to which he had given much thought. He noted that his friends and advisers had conflicting views on the matter. The trip would be expensive, and he had to account to the general court for "every farthing." He then said:

His education, from what I have understood of his improvement... is by no means ripe enough for a travelling tour; not that I think his becoming a mere scholar is a desirable education for a gentleman; but I conceive a knowledge of books is the basis upon which other knowledge is to be built; and that it is men and things more than books he is to be acquainted with by travelling. At present, however well versed he may be in the principles of the Latin language (which is not to be wondered at, as he began the study of it as soon as he could speak), he is unacquainted with several of their classical authors, which might be useful to him to read. He is ignorant of Greek... knows nothing of French... little or nothing acquainted with arithmetic, and totally ignorant of the mathematics; than which, so much of it at least as relates to surveying, nothing can be more essentially necessary to any man possessed of a large landed estate...

I should think myself wanting in candour, if I concealed any circumstances from you... Before I ever thought myself at liberty to encourage this plan, I judged it highly reasonable and necessary, that his mother should be consulted. I laid your first letter and proposals to her, and desired that she would ponder it well, before she resolved, as an unsteady behaviour might be a disadvantage to you. Her determination was, that, if it appeared to be his inclination to undertake this tour, and it should be adjudged for his benefit, she would not oppose it, whatever pangs it might give her to part with him. This declaration she still adheres to, but in so faint a manner, that I think, what with her fears and his indifference, it will soon be declared that he has no inclination to go.

Boucher did not get his trip, nor did he succeed in advancing Jacky's education very much. He was, however, successful in getting him inoculated against smallpox. Washington wanted this done, but the operation had to be concealed from his mother. Washington asked Boucher to write him about it "in a hand not your own... I am sure she cou'd not rest satisfied without knowing the Contents of any Letter to this Family of your writing." Jacky was sent secretly to Baltimore, but he was in such a funk he nearly failed to go through with it. Martha Washington, finally informed of the result by the normally courageous but in this case rather timid Washington, was relieved that her son was now immune.

Washington returned Jacky to school, with a note dated December 16, 1770, which said that his "mind is a good deal released from Study, & more than ever turn'd to Dogs Horses and Guns; indeed upon Dress and equipage, which till of late, he had discovered little Inclination of giving into." He asked Boucher not to let him ramble "about of Nights in Company with those, who do not care how debauched and viceous his Conduct may be." Boucher, though a man of the cloth, was himself rather addicted to drinking, and there is some indication that he had an affair with his housekeeper. For awhile he did watch Jacky, but he then drifted off to more interesting things, including his own courtship and marriage.

In June of 1771 Washington wrote to Boucher to tell him that Jacky had learned very little and that he was giving insufficient attention to his studies. Washington's August letter to his stepson seems to have been lost, but he apparently chided him for inattention and bad spelling. Jacky replied on August 18:

I am exceedingly thankful for your Remarks on my Letters, which I am sorry to say, are but too just. It is however really true, that I was in a hurry, when I wrote; and though undoubtedly I might have found time, I am obliged to own, that I am one of those who put every thing to the last. And how it should or does happen, I know not, but so it is, that tho I can certainly write as good English, & spell, as well as most people yet when hurried I very seldom do either, I might perhaps account for it in a manner less reproachfully to Me, but, as you have attributed it to Carelessness alone, & as Appearances are so much against me, I suppose it is so. All therefore that I can do now is promise to be more attentive & watchful for the future; your gentle yet very striking observations shall have their due weight with me.

By fall Washington was in touch with Dr. John Witherspoon, president of the college at Princeton, who indicated that he thought Jacky Custis was deficient in his education. Washington wrote to his stepson, who showed the letter to Boucher. Witherspoon was a Presbyterian minister and a Whig, while Boucher was an Anglican minister and a Tory. The latter reacted with emotion in his letter to Washington of November 19, 1771:

I have seen your Letter to your Son, &, I will own to You, it has given Me a sensible Concern. That my Attention to Him has not lately been so close nor so rigid, as I wish'd, or, as it ought to have been, is a Truth I will not attempt to deny. The Peculiarities of my Circumstances & Situation, as well as of my Temper & Disposition, are All I have to offer in my Excuse... I know that I might have taught him more than I have... Dr. Witherspoon says I <u>ought</u> to have put Him in Greek. Now, how much Deference soever I owe to his Authority, I will venture to say, that this Declaration, at least, must have been made much at random... I neither have attended, nor dare I promise that I can attend, to Him with the Regularity of a School-Master. But, Sir, tho' the little unessential Minutia of School-Learning may have sometimes been neglected, & thro' my Fault; I think I know You to be too observant & too candid a Man to believe that he has been wholly unattended to... Remiss as I am, or seem to be, I doubt not, in due Time, to deliver Him up to You a <u>good</u> Man, if not a very learned one...

If, after all, You resolve on removing Him, all I have to add is a Request, that it may not be to Princeton.

Washington looked into William and Mary and, not finding it to his satisfaction, decided to send Jacky to King's College (Columbia) in New York. Before he got him placed, there was a new development. George and Martha Washington had visited Annapolis to see Jacky. There they dined with Benedict Calvert and his daughters. Calvert was an illegitimate son of the fifth Lord Baltimore who, in turn, descended from an illegitimate daughter of

Charles II; he had married a distant cousin, Elizabeth Calvert, daughter of a one-time governor of Maryland. In early 1773, when Jacky was eighteen, he abruptly announced that he was engaged to Eleanor (Nelly), their daughter.

The Washingtons were considerably shocked since an engagement was then considered an absolute promise to marry. Boucher heard from the governor of Maryland that the Washingtons blamed him. He protested to Washington that he had not had "the most distant suspicion of any such Thing's being in Agitation." George wrote Benedict Calvert a lengthy letter on the matter, indicating the size of Jacky's estate, saying they would not oppose the marriage but hoped that he would go to college first.

Jacky agreed to enter King's College, then under the direction of the Reverend Myles Cooper, a Tory who, not long afterwards, fled to England. Included on its staff was the Reverend John Vardill, who became a British spy during the revolution. On their way to New York, Washington took Jacky to Annapolis, where they stayed with Eden, whose wife was a sister of the sixth Lord Baltimore. Eden accompanied Washington and Jacky as far as Philadelphia, where they dined with Governor Penn. Washington attended the Philadelphia Assembly ball and met various persons, such as Robert Morris, who would aid him in the revolution.

At New York on May 27, Washington attended a dinner given by the city for General Gage, British commander in chief in North America. Gage had been his old companion-in-arms at Braddock's defeat. A few days later Washington dined privately with him; slightly over two years later they were to face each other as enemies. On Washington's return trip, having deposited Jacky and a hundred pounds in cash at the college, he toured the Pennsylvania Dutch country. After visiting Haverford, Lancaster, and York, he proceeded by way of Baltimore to Mount Vernon.

Washington was always fond of and close to Burwell Bassett, who had married a sister of Martha Washington. To him he wrote letters of cheer and sorrow. On February 15, 1773, he dropped Bassett a note: "Our celebrated fortune, Miss French, whom half the world was in pursuit of, bestowed her hand on Wednesday last, being her birthday (you perceive I think myself under a necessity of accounting for the choice) upon Mr. Ben Dulany, who is to take her to Maryland in a month from this time. Mentioning of one wedding puts me in mind of another, tho' of less dignity. This is the marriage of Mr. Henderson... to a Miss More... remarkable for a very frizzled head, and of good singing, the latter of which I shall presume it was that captivated our merchant."

Not long afterward, tragedy struck the Bassett and Washington households when both families lost daughters. On April 25, Washington wrote to Bassett: "That we sympathize in the misfortune, and lament the decree that has deprived you of so dutiful a child, and the world of so promising a young lady, stands in no need, I hope, of argument to prove; but the ways of Providence being inscrutable, and the justice of it not to be scanned by the shallow eye of humanity, nor to be counteracted by the utmost efforts of human power or wisdom, resignation, and as far as the strength of our reason and religion can carry us, a cheerful acquiescence to the Divine Will, is what we are to aim; and I am persuaded that your own good sense will arm you with fortitude to withstand the stroke, great as it is, and enable you to console Mrs. Bassett, whose loss and feelings are much to be pitied." On June 20, only a few days after his return from New York, Washington again wrote Bassett:

It is an easier matter to conceive, than to describe the distress of this Family; especially that of the unhappy Parent of our Dear Patsy Custis, when I inform you that yesterday... the Sweet Innocent Girl Entered into a more happy and peaceful abode than any she has met with in the afflicted Path she has trod.

She rose from Dinner about four o'clock in better health and spirits than she appeared to have been in for some time; soon after she was seized with one of her usual Fits, and expired in it, in less than two minutes without uttering a word, a groan, or scarce a sigh. This sudden, and unexpected blow, I scarce add had almost reduced my poor Wife to the lowest ebb of misery; which is encreas'd by the absence of her son... and want of the balmy consolation of her Relations; which leads me more than ever to wish she could see them, and that I was Master of Arguments powerful enough to prevail upon Mrs. Dandridge to make this place her entire and absolute home. I should think as she lives a lonesome life (Betsey being married) it might suit her well, and be agreeable, both to herself and my Wife, to me most assuredly it would.

The death of Patsy Custis brought a division of her estate between her brother and Martha Washington, her share going to her husband. Washington received some eight thousand pounds in British bonds, which roughly balanced his British debts. Jacky Custis, on being informed of the death of his sister, wrote moving letters to his mother and stepfather. Almost inevitably, he decided it was time to quit school, and in September he returned to Mount Vernon. He was married the following February to Nelly Calvert.

After Jacky left for college, Boucher wrote Washington to say that he had to forego a planned trip to Mount Vernon, adding that "I have often owned with shame and terror that I did not do so much for him as I could or ought... It is peculiarly vexing to be... disappointed in the pleasure I had promised myself from this visit to a family and some friends, I am proud to rank by far the nearest to me."

In 1775 Boucher took flight for England. He wrote the American commander in chief a farewell note: "You are no longer worthy of my friendship. A man of honour can no longer without dishonour be connected with you." Washington simply noted in his account book a loss of four pounds ten shillings owed him by Mr. Boucher who had "removed" to England.

In his native country Boucher wrote a book about his adventures in Virginia. He said of the man he had troubled so much: "I did know Mr. Washington well... I cannot conceive how he could... have ever been spoken of as a great man. He is shy, silent, stern, slow and cautious, but has no quickness of parts, extraordinary penetration, nor an elevated style of thinking. In his moral character he is regular, temperate, strictly just and honest... excepting... he has lately found out that there is no moral turpitude in not paying what he confesses he owes to a British creditor."

WASHINGTON AND PEALE

Boucher performed one good service in persuading Charles Wilson Peale, who had returned to Maryland after studying in London with Benjamin West, to visit Mount Vernon. Peale arrived at Washington's house with Custis on May 18, 1772. Washington was delighted to have him and to order miniatures of Mrs. Washington, Jacky, and Martha Custis. They promptly got after the colonel to have his portrait made in the uniform of the Virginia Regiment. To his family, to Boucher, and to Peale, therefore, the country is indebted for the first painting of Washington made when he was forty years old. Washington's diary notes on Peale were succinct:

18. In the Evening Mr. Peale and J. P. Custis came to Mount Vernon.
20. I sat to have my Picture drawn.
21. I set again to take the Drapery.
22. Set for Mr. Peale to finish my Face.

Washington described the experience to Boucher on May 21: "Inclination having yielded to Importunity, I am now contrary to all expectations under the hands of Mr. Peale; but in so grave—so sullen a mood—and now and then under the influence of Morpheus, when some critical strokes are making, that I fancy the skill of this gentleman's pencil, will be put to it, in describing to the World what manner of man I am."

For many years thereafter, the reluctant Washington was dragged before the easel by all sorts of painters, good and bad. He sat for Peale at least seven times. In May of 1785, when he was painted by Robert Pine, who had also painted George II, Washington wrote the witty Francis Hopkinson:

> *In for a penny, in for a pound is an old adage. I am so hackneyed to the touches of the Painters pencil, that I am now altogether at their beck, and sit like patience on a Monument whilt they are delineating the lines on my face.*

> *It is a proof among many others of what habit and custom can effect. At first I was as impatient at the request, and as restive under the operation, as a Colt is of the Saddle. The next time, I submitted very reluctantly with less flouncing. Now no dray moves more readily to the Thill than I do to the Painters Chair.*

Washington's diary mentions other houseguests who were at Mount Vernon with Peale. Several of the younger men were out pitching an iron bar when, as Peale related it: "Suddenly the Colonel appeared among us. He requested to be shown the pegs that marked the bounds of our effort; then, smiling, and without putting off his coat, held out his hand for the missile. No sooner did the heavy iron bar feel the grasp of his mighty hand than it lost the power of gravitation, and whizzed through the air, striking the ground far, very far, beyond our utmost limits. We were indeed amazed, as we stood all stripped to the buff, with shirt sleeves rolled up, and having thought ourselves very clever fellows, while the Colonel, on retiring, pleasantly observed, 'When you beat my pitch, young gentlemen, I'll try again.'"

LORD DUNMORE

Virginia had been fortunate in two royal governors, Fauquier and Botetourt, who had been genuinely mourned after their deaths in office. John Murray, earl of Dunmore, was of a different stripe. He was not by nature inclined to be conciliatory like his predecessors; the increasing opposition to British policies served only to raise his natural choler. Although the dispute with Britain began to take a more serious turn after 1773, Washington got along well enough personally with Dunmore, with whom he dined frequently at the palace. Dunmore was interested in acquiring western lands. Washington was about the only Virginian of prominence who had been far west. Dunmore questioned him at length about the area and asked Washington to accompany him on a tour. Washington agreed to this but the death of his stepdaughter forced him to cancel the trip.

In 1774, Dunmore, fearing that the Pennsylvanians would seize Fort Pitt, which Virginia claimed, sent a garrison to that post. There was an Indian uprising shortly afterwards in much of the area over which Washington had travelled in 1770. Dunmore ordered out the militia under Colonel Andrew Lewis. In October 1774, Lewis defeated the Indians at Point Pleasant. By then the colony was in an uproar over British measures in Massachusetts, and Dunmore found Virginians more troublesome than Indians.

THE TEA PARTY

When the East India Company, a pet of the British government, ran into financial trouble, London proposed to allow its surplus of tea to pass through England free of the shilling-a-pound duty. It could then be sold in America with only a threepenny tax and be cheaper than before. Whether Lord North discussed the proposal with the king is not known, but if so it was probably only in passing. There is only a brief reference to it in George III's correspondence in a note by North: "The House went... into the East India Committee, where they came into three resolutions, concerning the Exportation of Tea to America and foreign parts; There was some debate, but the questions passed without a division."

By greatly reducing the price of tea, the act placed the East India Company in the strongest competitive position to the dismay of such a smuggling merchant as John Hancock, who was pro-Tory or pro-Whig, depending on the way the wind blew for John Hancock. Under the leadership of the wooly-minded Samuel Adams, a Boston mob pitched 342 chests of tea into the town harbor on December 16, 1773. Other cities did much the same. These senseless acts, deplored by Franklin and Washington, cast a long shadow on the efforts of Americans to appear responsible and reasonable arguers of constitutional law. They greatly strengthened the hands of English Tories who wanted far stricter control of the colonies. When news of the mob's work reached London, General Gage, the commander in chief in America, called on the king who recorded their conversation in a note to Lord North, dated February 4, 1774:

Since You left me... I have seen Lieutenant General Gage, who came to express his readiness though so lately come from America to return at a day's notice if the conduct of the colonies should induce the directing coercive measures... He says they will be Lyons, whilst we are Lambs but if we take the resolute part they will undoubtedly prove very meek; he thinks the four Regiments intended to Relieve as many Regiments in America if sent to Boston are sufficient to prevent any disturbance; I wish You would see him and hear his ideas as the mode of compelling Boston to submit to whatever may be thought necessary; indeed all men seem now to feel that the fatal compliance in 1766 has encouraged the Americans annually to encrease in their pretensions that thorough independence which one State has of another, but which is quite subversive to the obedience which a Colony owes to its Mother Country.

The king was not a wicked or an ill-intentioned man, but he was wrapped up in cotton wool, away from the world. It is not known that he ever saw or talked with an American other than a royal appointee. Franklin, who was intensely loyal to Britain, was in London for years without ever being questioned about America by George III. The king got his ideas from his royal governors or from army men like Gage, and they were always prejudiced and almost always wrong.

Franklin in London wrote that America never had so few friends in England as after the destruction of the tea. The king, North, and Parliament proceeded to be lions by punishing at once the guiltless majority in Massachusetts as well as the Hancock–Sam Adams mobs. The Boston Port Act, blockading the port and removing the customs house to Salem, passed without a division. This act was to continue in force until the East India Company was reimbursed and the king satisfied that Boston had returned to obedience.

In triumph North then rammed through a series of frontal attacks on all of Massachusetts. The acts bore remarkably innocent titles. A bill for the better regulation of the government of Massachusetts Bay abolished the elected council and established royally appointed councillors, judges, magistrates, and sheriffs. A bill for the impartial administration of justice permitted the governor to send indicted persons outside the province for trial. One of the few voices of protest in Parliament was that of Thomas Pownall, a former royal governor of Massachusetts and a friend of Franklin, who informed North in debate: "I tell you the Americans will oppose the measures, now proposed by you, in a more vigorous way than before. The Committees of Correspondence in the different provinces are in constant communication... As soon as intelligence of these affairs reaches them, they will judge it necessary to communicate with each other. It will be found inconvenient and ineffectual to do so by letters. They must confer. They will hold a Conference; and to what these committees, thus met in congress; will draw up, I will not say. Should recourse be made to arms, you will hear of other officers than those appointed by your governor."

The king closely followed the bills as they moved through first, second, and third readings. At each stage he dropped little notes to Lord North: "Infinitely pleased... Infinite satisfaction... much pleasure." The king informed North that perseverance and firmness were the only sure guides to administering public affairs successfully.

The king had his final pleasure when the Quebec bill became law. From the American point of view this act was ominous because it extended south to the Ohio River the boundaries of Quebec, thus blotting out the ancient charter claims of several American colonies. The act also abolished the Quebec Assembly and established a system of internal and external taxes for that province. The lord chancellor stated that it was the kind of charter the American colonies should have been given originally.

To enforce the new acts the king appointed General Gage, commander in chief of the British army in America, as governor of Massachusetts. On July 1, after talking to Thomas Hutchinson, Gage's predecessor, George III wrote North: "I am now well convinced they will soon submit; he owns the Boston Port Bill was the only wise effectual method... for bringing them to a speedy submission... One of the Regiments arrived the 1st of June the day he sailed, and the People of Boston seem much dispirited." On September 11 he again wrote North: "The dye is now cast, the Colonies must either submit or triumph; I do not wish to come to severer measures but we must not retreat; by coolness and an unremitted pursuit of the measures that have been adopted I trust they will come to submit."

VIRGINIA REACTS

The Boston Port Act, designed to close the harbor on June 1, 1774, and to starve the people into submission, brought a violent wave of reaction throughout the continent. Everywhere, efforts were made to send supplies, food, and money to the city, not only from the other American colonies, but even from Quebec and England itself. Israel Putnam drove 130 sheep from Connecticut to Boston. Washington subscribed fifty pounds to funds for the city.

On May 12, Washington set off for Williamsburg, stopping in Fredericksburg to see his mother. He arrived in the capital on the sixteenth and dined with Governor Dunmore. About the nineteenth, the news of the Boston Port Act reached the Burgesses. On May 24, after they had had a few days to consider it, Robert Carter Nicholas, the colony's treasurer, introduced a resolution:

> *This House, being deeply impressed with Apprehension of the great Dangers to be derived to British America from the hostile Invasion of the city of Boston... whose Commerce and Harbour are, on the 1st Day of June next, to be stopped by an armed Force, deem it highly necessary that the said first Day of June be set apart, by the Members of this House, as a day of Fasting, Humiliation and Prayer, devoutly to implore the divine Interposition, for averting the heavy Calamity which threatens*

Destruction to our civil Rights, and the Evils of civil War; to give us one Heart and one Mind firmly to oppose, by all just and proper Means, every Injury to American Rights; and that the minds of his Majesty and his Parliament, may be inspired from above with Wisdom, Moderation and Justice, to remove… all Cause of Danger from a continued Pursuit of Measures pregnant with their Ruin.

This was a stronger resolve than had ever passed the Burgesses. The British government had assumed that a few regiments would overawe Boston, while other colonies would ignore the measures. Two days after its passage, the governor, saying the resolution reflected highly on the king and Parliament, ordered the House dissolved. Landon Carter noted in his diary that it seemed to be the first time that a prayer asking that king and Parliament might have wisdom, justice, and moderation, a phrase modelled on the Prayer Book, was thought to be derogatory.

The Burgesses moved to the Raleigh Tavern and there passed even stronger resolutions, the most important of which was a call for a congress of all the colonies. They then adjourned to attend a ball for Lady Dunmore at the palace. On May 29 Washington went to Divine Service in the morning and afternoon. On the same or the following day, urgent dispatches reached Williamsburg containing the calls of Massachusetts, Pennsylvania, and Maryland for united action. Virginia, in turn, forwarded them to North Carolina. On June 1, Washington wrote in his diary: "Went to Church and fasted all day." Landon Carter recorded that his rector the same day omitted the usual "God Save the King" and asked God, instead, to preserve the rights and liberties of America.

On August 5 the Burgesses, now calling themselves a convention, voted to send seven men to the general congress of the colonies scheduled to meet at Philadelphia in September. They were Peyton Randolph, speaker of the house, Richard Henry Lee, George Washington, Patrick Henry, Richard Bland, Benjamin Harrison, and Edmund Pendleton. The die was indeed cast; Governor Pownall's prediction of a congress was fulfilled in a matter of months.

From the Virginia convention, a rumor sped through the continent that Washington, in a dramatic speech, had said: "I will raise one thousand men, subsist them at my own expense and march myself at their head for the relief of Boston." There is no evidence that he ever said it, though it may have been a garbled version of something he did say. It was quoted from New England to Charleston and served to recall to many the legendary Colonel Washington of the French and Indian wars.

WASHINGTON'S VIEWS

On June 10, 1774, Washington wrote to George Fairfax who, though resident in England, was strongly pro-American:

> *Our Assembly met at this place the 4th... and was dissolved the 26th for entering into a Resolve... which the Governor thought reflected too much upon his Majesty and the British Parliament... This Dissolution was as sudden as unexpected for there were other resolves of a much more spirited nature ready to be offered to the House wch. would have been unanimously adopted respecting the Boston Port Bill... The day after this Event the Members convend... at the Raleigh Tavern and enterd into the Inclosd Association... the Ministry may rely on it that Americans will never be tax'd without their own consent that the cause of Boston the despotick measures in respect to it I mean now is and ever will be considerd as the cause of America (not that we approve their conduct in destroyg. the Tea) and that we shall not suffer ourselves to be sacrificd by piece meals though god only knows what is to become of us, threatend as we are with so many hoverg. evils as hang over us at present; having a cruel and blood thirsty Enemy upon our Backs, the Indians... with whom a general War is inevitable whilst those from who we have a right to seek protection are endeavouring by every piece of Art and despotism to fix the Shackles of Slavery upon us... Since the first Settlement of this Colony the Minds of people in it never were more disturbed, or our Situation so critical as at present... arising from an Invasion of our rights and Priviledges by the Mother Country; and our lives and properties by the Savages.*

While George Fairfax was supporting the Americans in England, his brother, Bryan, who remained in America, was Loyalist in sympathy. Since he was neither active nor dangerous, Washington saw to it that he was not molested during the war. Early in 1774, he had suggested that Bryan run for the House of Burgesses but the latter declined, feeling, as he explained, that he was almost alone in the county in opposing strong measures. He gave his views to which Washington replied on July 4, 1774:

> *As to your political sentiments, I would heartily join you in them, so far as relates to a humble and dutiful petition to the throne, provided there was the most distant hope of success. But have we not tried this already? Have we not addressed the Lords, and remonstrated to the Commons? And to what end? Did they deign to look at our petitions? Does it not appear, as clear as the sun in its meridian brightness, that there is a regular, systematic plan formed to fix the right and practice of taxation upon us? Does not the uniform conduct of Parliament for some years past confirm this?... Is not*

the attack upon the liberty and property of the people of Boston, before restitution of the loss to the India Company was demanded, a self-evident proof of what they are aiming at? Do not the subsequent bills (now I dare say acts), for depriving the Massachusetts Bay of its charter, and for transporting offenders into other colonies or to Great Britain for trial where it is impossible from the nature of the thing that justice can be obtained, convince us that the administration is determined to stick at nothing to carry its point? Ought we not, then, to put our virtue and fortitude to the severest test?

FAIRFAX RESOLVES

The dissolution of the House required new elections. Washington again stood in Fairfax where he was unopposed. George Mason, in consultation with Washington, drew up a series of resolutions to be discussed and approved by the county voters, subsequent to the election for the House. They were sharp in tone, stating that Americans were subjects and not slaves of the British government. Americans possessed all the rights of Englishmen and of the British constitution and had the sole right to tax themselves through their assemblies. British action to tax them, "if continued," would result in "the most grievous and intolerable species of tyranny and oppression that was ever inflicted on mankind." The resolves then called for nonimportation, a general congress of all the colonies, and a final petition to the king from whom "there can be but one appeal." This last phrase may have been inserted by Washington.

Bryan Fairfax wrote a temperate letter to Washington just before the meeting in which he pointed out that Americans had often been inconsistent. They had said Parliament had no right to tax them, but that in other measures Parliament was supreme. Now they were moving to deny any parliamentary right over America. They should accept the Constitution and petition only. He asked Washington to present his views; Washington handed his letter around, but he informed Fairfax afterwards that no one seeemed to be interested in them. He added:

That I differ very widely from you... I shall not hesitate to acknowledge... I see nothing... to induce a belief that the Parliament would embrace a favourable opportunity of repealing acts, which they go on with great rapidity to pass, and in order to enforce their tyrannical system...

The conduct of the Boston people did not justify the rigour of their measures unless there had been a requisition of payment and refusal of it; nor did that measure require an act to deprive the government of Masachusetts Bay of their charter, or to exempt offenders from trial in the place where offences were committed, as there was not, nor could not be, a single instance produced to manifest the necessity of it. Are not all these things self evident proofs of a fixed and uniform plan to tax us? If we want further proofs, do not all the debates in the House of Commons serve to confirm this? And has not General Gage's conduct since his arrival, (in stopping the address of his Council, and publishing a proclamation more becoming a Turkish bashaw than an English governor, declaring it treason to associate in any manner by which the commerce of Great Britain is to be affected,) exhibit a testimony of the most despotic system of tyranny, that was ever practised in a free government?... What hope then from petitioning... Shall we, after all this, whine and cry for relief, when we have already tried it in vain? Or shall we supinely sit and see one province after another fall a prey to despotism?

As to the resolution for addressing the throne, I own to you, Sir, I think the whole might well have been expunged. I expect nothing from the measure, nor should my voice have accompanied it, if the non-importation scheme was intended to be retarded by it; for I am convinced, as much as I am of my existence, that there is no relief but in their distress; and I think, at least I hope, that there is public virtues enough left among us to deny ourselves every thing but the bare necessities of life... This we have a right to do, and no power upon earth can compel us to do otherwise, till they have first reduced us to the most abject state of slavery that ever was designed for mankind.

Had Washington's letters been published at the time, they would have made a stirring appeal to his countrymen, but his best efforts were reserved for private letters to his friends. On August 5, Washington wrote from Williamsburg to Thomas Johnson in Maryland to inform him that Virginia had agreed to send delegates to Philadelphia on September 5, though they had hoped the meeting would be somewhat later and that it would take place in Lancaster. He noted that they had never had so full an attendance at the legal Assembly as they did at the illegal convention of the same men. On August 7 he wrote to his fellow delegate, Richard Henry Lee, to ask him to obtain from the customs houses figures on commerce with Great Britain. He also mentioned that he would be glad to have Lee's company on the way to Philadelphia. On August 24 he again wrote to Bryan Fairfax to say that he was sure the unanimity of the colonies had been entirely unexpected in Britain, as indeed it was, and that he was also sure that the quiet behavior of the people of Massachusetts Bay was more disconcerting to Gage than anything else could have been. He put in as a lightly needling postscript: "Pray what do you think of the Canada Bill?"

FIRST CONTINENTAL CONGRESS

On August 30, two Virginia delegates, Patrick Henry and Edmund Pendleton, arrived at Mount Vernon. George Mason came over from Gunston Hall to confer with them. The next day Washington recorded in his diary: "With Colo. Pendleton and Mr. Henry, I set out on my journey for Phila. and reached uppr. Marlbro." On September 4 the three men arrived at Philadelphia. Next day the Continental Congress came formally into session under the presidency of Speaker Randolph of Virginia.

Washington's diary records for the Congress are of almost no import. On September 6 he wrote: "Dind at the New Tavern, after being in Congress all day." He noted various people who later served in the revolution, such as Thomas Mifflin and Joseph Reed. He did not mention, though, that he met John Adams, Samuel Adams, Robert Treat Paine, and others from Massachusetts. Adams referred to Washington but once in his diary when he described the speech that he was supposed to have made at the Virginia convention. In his autobiography years later he expanded his notes from memory:

> On the 5th of September Congress assembled in Carpenters Hall. The Day before I dined with Mr. Lynch a Delegate from South Carolina, who, in conversation on the Unhappy State of Boston... after some Observations had been made on the Eloquence of Mr. Patrick Henry and Mr. Richard Henry Lee, which had been very loudly celebrated by the Virginians, said that the most eloquent Speech that had ever been made in Virginia or any where else, upon American Affairs had been made by Colonel Washington. This was the first time I had ever heard the Name of Washington, as a Patriot in our present controversy, I asked who is Colonel Washington and what was his Speech? Colonel Washington he said was the officer who had been famous in the late French war and in the Battle in which Braddock fell. His Speech was that if the Bostonians should be involved in Hostilities with the British Army he would march to their relief at the head of a Thousand Men at his own expence. This Sentence, Mr. Lynch said, had more Oratory in it, in his Judgment, than any that he had ever heard or read. We all agreed that it was both sublime, pathetic and beautiful.

Much of the time was spent by delegates in assessing each other. Tories and Whigs were represented, and those who wanted accommodation with Britain and those who, like Washington, called for radical measures. Washington's common sense and his knowledge of the country gained him wide influence. He had travelled through nine of the thirteen colonies and farther west than any other delegate. Patrick Henry wrote: "Colonel Washington, who has no pretensions to eloquence, is a man of more solid judgment and information than any man on the floor."

One effort was made by the British, perhaps at the instance of General Gage, to woo Washington to their viewpoint. Captain Robert Mackenzie, a former officer of the Virginia Regiment who had purchased a British commission and was then stationed with Gage in Boston, wrote to urge an accommodation with Britain. Mackenzie said Massachusetts was in an unhappy state, its policies aimed at independence, and therefore abler heads and better hearts were needed to draw a line for the guidance of the province. He called the people rebellious and their attacks on authority scandalous while he stressed Gage's efforts to establish full military authority. Washington wrote to Mackenzie (and thus perhaps indirectly to Gage) on October 9, 1774:

> *Permit me with the freedom of a friend (for you know I always esteemed you) to express my sorrow, that fortune should place you in a service, that must fix curses to the latest posterity upon the diabolical contrivers, and, if success (which, by the by, is impossible) accompanies it, execrations upon all those, who have been instrumental in the execution.*

> *...When you condemn the conduct of the Massachusetts people, you reason from effects, not causes; otherwise you would not wonder at a people, who are every day receiving fresh proofs of a systematic assertion of an arbitrary power, deeply planned to overturn the laws and constitution of their country, and to violate the most essential rights of mankind, being irritated, and with difficulty restrained from acts of the greatest violence and intemperance... You are led to believe by venal men, for such I must take the liberty of calling those new-fangled counsellors, which fly to and surround you, and all others, who, for honorary or pecuniary gratifications, will lend their aid to overturn the constitution, and introduce a system of arbitrary government... Give me leave, my good friend, to tell you, that you are abused, grossly abused, and this I advance with a degree of confidence and boldness... having better opportunities of knowing the real sentiments of the people you are among, from the leaders of them... than you have from those whose business it is, not to disclose truths, but to misrepresent facts... It is not the wish of that government, or any other upon this continent... to set up for independencey but this you may at the same time rely on, that none of them will ever submit to the loss of those valuable rights and privileges, which are essential to the happiness of every free state...*

> *Give me leave to add as my opinion, that more blood will be spilt on this occasion, if the ministry are determined to push matters to extremity, than history has ever yet*

*furnished instances of in the annals of North America, and such a vital wound
given to the peace of this great country as time itself cannot cure, or eradicate the
remembrance of.*

This was stronger language than almost any used at the congress but
Washington had long moved to the most radical of positions. Congress,
though having to compromise divergent views, accomplished a great deal.
The members endorsed the resolves of Suffolk County in Massachusetts,
which said the coercive acts were illegal and therefore need not be obeyed.
Congress issued a declaration of American rights, approved an economic boycott of Great Britain, and threatened to cut off American exports in 1775 if
the coercive acts were not repealed.

Washington left Philadelphia on October 27 and reached Mount Vernon on
October 30. On November 17 he wrote to William Milnor in Philadelphia to
order treatises on military discipline and a hundred muskets. He followed with
orders for drums and fifes. By the time he returned to Virginia, numerous county
committees had organized armed companies, and George Washington was
invited by many to be their commander. His own county, Fairfax, adopted the
Whig colors, buff and blue, which General Washington wore through the ensuing war.

BRITAIN REACTS

Massachusetts largely ignored General Gage, the governor and commander in
chief, who remained in Boston. Its legislature moved to Concord, elected
John Hancock its president, and proceeded to take over the government of
the rest of Massachusetts. Independent companies were ordered, trained, and
drilled. A system of espionage was established and relief supplies were
ordered for Bostonians. Boston, with its port shut, saw its merchants in ruins,
unemployment high, and friends of Britain suffering with the rest. Under
their pressure Gage pleaded with London to let him drop the Port and other
acts. The king wrote North on November 18, 1774: "His idea of Suspending
the Acts appears to me the most absurd that can be suggested; the people are
ripe for mischief upon which the Mother Country adopts suspending the measures she has thought necessary this must suggest to the Colonies a fear that
alone prompts them to their present violence; we must either master them or
totally leave them to themselves and treat them as Aliens."

Although the king so wrote, many in England spoke up for the Americans.
The secretary at war, Lord Barrington, wrote to the secretary for the colonies,

Lord Dartmouth, who was Washington's fourth cousin, to say that the contest would bring no gain to Britain. It involved a single point of honor that could not be enforced and was leading to a serious civil war. This could only be won at enormous expense and would thereafter have to be maintained by extensive armies and fleets. In the House of Lords on January 20, 1775, Pitt introduced a resolution to remove all the troops from Boston:

> *I wish, my lords, not to lose a day in this urgent, pressing crisis; an hour lost in allaying ferments in America, may produce years of calamity...*

> *The glorious spirit of Whiggism animates three millions in America; who prefer poverty with liberty, to guilded chains and sordid affluence; and who will die in defense of their rights as men, as freemen...*

> *...I trust it is obvious to your lordships, that all attempts to impose servitude upon such men, to establish despotism over such a mighty continental nation, must be vain, must be fatal. We shall be forced ultimately to retract; let us retract while we can, not when we must. I say we must necessarily undo these violent oppresive acts: they must be repealed—you will repeal them; I pledge myself that you will in the end repeal them.*

Pitt's resolution was voted down 68 to 18. The king was so pleased with his support that he wrote Lord North: "Nothing can be more calculated to bring the Americans to a due submission than the very handsome Majority." Four days later, on January 27, 1775, Lord Dartmouth sent secret orders to General Gage informing him that the king considered the colonies in rebellion, force should be met by force, and reinforcements were on the way for Gage's four thousand or so effectives, including seven hundred Marines, three regiments of infantry, and one of light dragoons from Ireland. Gage, said Dartmouth, had been too long on the defensive; he added:

> *It is hoped however that this large Reinforcement to your Army will enable you to take a more active & determined part...*

> *...It is the Opinion of the King's Servants in which His Majesty concurs, that the first essential step to be taken towards re-establishing Government, would be to arrest and imprison the principal actors & abettors in the Provincial Congress... If the steps taken upon this occasion be accompanied with due precaution, and every means be devised to keep the Measure Secret until the moment of Execution, it can hardly fail of Success, and will perhaps be accomplished without bloodshed; but*

however that may be I must again repeat that any efforts of the People, unprepared to encounter with a regular force, cannot be formidable; and though such a proceeding should be, according to your own idea of it, a Signal for Hostilities yet, for the reasons I have already given, it will surely be better that the Conflict should be brought on, upon such ground, than in a riper state of rebellion.

On February 9, Parliament pledged to the king its support:

We beg leave, in the most solemn manner, to assure Your Majesty, that it is our fixed resolution, at the hazard of our lives and properties, to stand by Your Majesty against all rebellious attempts in the maintainence of the just rights of Your Majesty and the two Houses of Parliament.

PART FOUR

GENERAL AND FARMER
1775–1781

SEVENTEEN

COMMANDER IN CHIEF

1775

L ONDON'S INSTRUCTIONS to General Gage were an order for war. So long as it had to come, the timing for America was, to some extent, lucky. Britain was already advancing into the industrial revolution, which was to make her the world's most formidable power. The growing financial and political troubles of France, under its new weak king, in the course of time might well have made her more cautious about war.

The American War of Independence is often called a civil war, since it split nearly all classes of society in both Great Britain and America. Estimates of those who were Tories in America vary widely. It does appear that, in the initial stages of the war, as high as 40 percent of Americans were opposed to it and to independence. By its end, confirmed Tories may have declined to as low as 10 percent. In England, the opposition at the start was mainly among the better classes. Towards its close, supporters were the king and a few of his friends, with nearly the whole nation in opposition to the war's continuance.

Josiah Quincy, Jr., who was in London as an agent of Massachusetts, talked with so many Englishmen who told him that Americans were fighting their common battle for liberty, that he came to believe that a majority were for the colonies. His diary for January 23, 1775, noted:

Attended a long debate in the House of Commons on American Affairs.

Speakers for the Americans: Burke, Johnston, Charles Fox, T. Townshend, Lord J. Cavendish, Captain Lutterell, Alderman Sawbridge, &c—eighty two. Against the Americans: Sir William Meredith, Lord North, Lord Clare, Sir George Macartney, Sir. G. Eliot, Lord Stanley, &c.—total, one hundred and ninety-seven.

This debate and division show that if King, Lords and Commons can subdue America into bondage against the almost universal sentiment, opinion, wish, and hope of the Englishmen of this island, the deed will be done.

The split affected all of England. Nearly a third of Parliament stood by the Americans. Boswell and Johnson quarreled over the issue, with Tory Boswell for America. The memoirs of the prodigal rake, William Hickey, describe a yachting trip with several Englishmen, including George Dempster, a member of Parliament, Lord George Gordon, and Sir Charles Bingham. Each night on their yacht, renamed *Congress*, they drank treasonable toasts: "Success to the Americans." The generals and admirals divided—Amherst, Cavendish, Pitt, and Keppel, among others, refused to fight them. Other high officers such as Henry Seymour Conway and the duke of Richmond vigorously attacked the war in Parliament. The dukes of Cumberland and Gloucester were against the policy of their brother, the king, the former voting with Pitt on his plan for reconciliation. In the cabinet, too, there was dissension.

THE MINISTRY

The three men principally responsible for the war effort were Lord North, the king's first minister, Lord George Germain, the secretary for American affairs, and Lord Sandwich, first lord of the Admiralty. North, bearing a courtesy title as eldest son of an earl, sat in Commons. He was in power from 1770 to 1782. Short, rotund, and pop-eyed like his king, he was a good-natured man, famous for his wit and debating skill. George III complained that North was lazy and often careless with his accounts. His main drawback for the king, as it turned out, was that he had a conscience in a conscienceless court. He ran a well-oiled machine of corruption, spent the king's money to win elections, and distributed offices, sinecures, titles, and contracts to keep Lords and Commons happy. He himself drew twenty thousand pounds from the treasury, with the king's permission, to pay his personal debts. Yet his scruples were such that, after the battle of Saratoga, he repeatedly told the king the American policies had been wrong and disastrous. He urged the negotiation of peace at almost any price.

Lord George Germain, whose family name was originally Sackville, had served George II as an officer at the battle of Minden, where Lafayette's father was killed. There Germain was accused of cowardice and court-martialed. The probably unjustified verdict was that he was "unfit to serve his Majesty in any military capacity whatever." George III restored him to favor and, at the end of November 1775, following an undignified cabinet dispute over honors, put him in charge of the American colonies. John Montagu, earl of Sandwich, was sufficiently licentious that, even in the freewheeling English eighteenth century, he was regarded as without morals. He was later severely castigated in Parliament, with considerable reason, for corruption and mismanagement in the naval office.

Sandwich was an effective if savage debater. In replying to Pitt's speech on reconciliation with the colonies, he termed Franklin "one of the bitterest and most mischievous enemies this country has ever known," and he said of Americans:

> *The noble Lord [Pitt] mentions the impracticability of conquering America; I cannot think the noble Lord can be serious on this matter. Suppose the Colonies do abound in men, what does that signify? They are raw, undisciplined, cowardly men. Believe me, my Lords, the very sound of a cannon would carry them off... as fast as their feet would carry them.*

Four years later, during the Keppel riots in London, the mob stormed the Admiralty. In Walpole's words, "Lord Sandwich, exceedingly terrified, escaped through the garden *with his mistress*, Miss Ray, to the Horse Guards, and there betrayed a most manifest panic."

On March 2, 1775, just before war began, George Fairfax provided Washington with his appraisal of the situation in England: "What can, or dare I say, about the unhappy difference between this country and America. That you are condemned by the Ministry, and their dependents, and much aplauded by every welwisher to the Antient and Constitutional Rights of Englishmen, whether on this, or the other side of the Atlantic; of which there are a great majority in this County [Yorkshire]. You'll hear probabelly before this reatches you... about the much talked of Motion... I rather think they find they have gone far enough, that the Americans are not so easily duped, and that a War across the Atlantic will be the most expences they have had... It is pretty certain that the Minister has lost ground... A change must soon take place... God grant that it may be for the better, worse I think it cannot be... Yet I fear it never will happen while the Premier has so many lucrative places in his disposal. We can... very justly say that the law is on our side, for all the Law

Lords that do not fill some high office, and many great disinterested Getn. in the Commons, are in support of America."

The king regarded the opposition as personal enemies, if not traitors. He termed them a "motley crew" and "wicked" men. His invective was especially directed at William Pitt, whom he called "a trumpet of sedition."

WASHINGTON IN CONVENTION AND CONGRESS

The Virginia Burgesses met once again in convention on March 20, 1775. Not all the forbidding news from England had reached them, nor could they know of the secret orders to Gage to begin war. It was Patrick Henry who rose to propose measures to put Virginia in a state of defense. He introduced the notion, startling to many but not to Washington, that they might soon have a fight on their hands. Once his resolves carried, Washington was assigned to the military committee for work on recruiting troops in each of the colony's counties. On March 25, he was reelected as delegate to the Second Continental Congress. That same day he wrote his brother John:

> I had like to have forgot to express my entire approbation of the laudable pursuit you are engaged in of Training an Independant Company. I have promised to review the Independant Company of Richmond sometime this Summer, they having made me a tender of the Command of it. At the same time I could review yours and shall very cheerfully accept the honr. of Commanding it, if occasion requires it to be drawn out, as it is my full intention to devote my Life and Fortune in the cause we are engaged in.

Everyone in Virginia with an interest in defense turned automatically to Washington for advice. Two half-pay British officers, Horatio Gates and Charles Lee, who had served with Braddock, came to call at Mount Vernon. The latter, on his second visit, was accompanied by young Harry Lee (not related), who later commanded a troop of light horse.

When, on April 21, a hostile move was made by Governor Dunmore, who removed the powder from the Williamsburg magazine to a British ship, Hugh Mercer, George Weedon, and Alexander Spotswood of the Spotsylvania militia sent an express to Washington to say that "this first Public insult is not to be tamely submitted to," and they proposed to march on Williamsburg. The Prince William and Albemarle companies wrote much the same letters to Washington. The Speaker, Peyton Randolph, however, intervened to stop the use of force while he appealed to the governor. On April 30 Spotswood informed Washington that they had cancelled the proposed march but that he was sure Congress would now want an army. "Their is not the least doubt But youl have the Command of the Whole forces in this Collony." Spotswood assured Washington that he was ready to serve "in the Glorious cause of liberty, at the Risk of my life and fortune Gratis."

LEXINGTON AND CONCORD

Expresses with the news of the battles at Lexington and Concord were ordered to carry the news south while fighting was still in progress. Each town marked its time of arrival. It is possible to trace the news almost hour by hour as the expresses reached Worcester, Norwich, New London, Saybrook, Guilford, New Haven, Fairfield, New York, New Brunswick, Philadelphia, and then south to Annapolis and Alexandria, where the intelligence was forwarded to Williamsburg and the Carolinas. Washington had word of the April 19 battle only a day or two after he heard of Dunmore's actions. This made his trip to Philadelphia the more urgent, as war had begun.

PHILADELPHIA

On May 4, 1775, George Washington left his wife and house for what he hoped would be a rather short absence. He was building a south extension to Mount Vernon, as well as planning to add a front porch, or piazza. He wrote Bryan Fairfax that he always felt the work went a little better when he was around to supervise it. Except for a few days on the way to and from Yorktown in 1781, Washington did not see his house again until Christmas 1783.

Washington was unofficial head of Virginia's troops, through his election as commander of the most important independent county regiments. Automatically he wore his Fairfax County uniform to Philadelphia as a symbol that Virginians would fight alongside their Massachusetts brethren.

At their invitation, Washington reviewed the Baltimore troops on his way north. On May 9 he and his fellow Virginians were escorted into Philadelphia by a band as well as many officers and men of the local volunteer companies. The church bells rang and crowds cheered. The New Englanders, on their arrival, were greeted in the same way. Samuel Curwen, a Loyalist, wrote in his diary that he met Colonel Washington at a dinner. He was "a fine figure and of a most easy and agreeable address." Curwen added that he could find no disposition among the delegates at Philadelphia to make an accommodation with Britain.

Two men were present with firsthand information—Benjamin Franklin, who could give an accurate account of the temper of king and Parliament, and John Adams, who had toured the battlefields of Concord and Lexington and had talked to the American army before Boston. For the first time, Washington, Adams, and Franklin were together, in a war that began near Adams' and Franklin's birthplaces and effectively ended some fifty miles from the farm where Washington was born.

Congress moved swiftly to business. Joseph Warren, physician and soldier, and acting head of the Massachusetts Provincial Congress, rose to say that his colony had voted to raise 13,500 men and that other New England governments were cooperating to establish an American army. The defense of New York came into early focus, and Washington was made chairman of a committee to examine the question.

The delegates were intensely interested in reports on Lexington and Concord and the rapid retreat of the British regulars, who were saved only by the skilled work of the earl of Percy, who was ordered out with relief troops. Lord Percy complained that the Americans fired from behind walls. Washington liked to quote Franklin's subsequent comment that walls had two sides. Franklin wrote Joseph Priestly in England to say the British had had "an *expedition* back again. They retreated twenty miles in six hours." It did not come out at this time what bad shots the embattled farmers were. They scored fewer than three hundred hits out of some ninety thousand rounds expended. Had they been trained marksmen, the effects would have been devastating. Congress examined many affidavits that tended to show that the British fired first but, as Governor Pownall had already observed in Parliament, once blood was shed, it mattered little whose was the first shot. Washington read the affidavits, got as much information as he could, and wrote on May 31 to George Fairfax in England:

> *Before this Letter can reach you, you must, undoubtedly, have received an Account of the engagement in the Massachusetts Bay between the ministerial Troops (for we do not, nor cannot yet prevail upon ourselves to call them the King's Troops) and the Provincials... I inclose you several Affidavits...*

> *General Gage acknowledges, that the detachment under Lieutenant Colonel Smith was sent out to destroy private property; or, in other Words, to destroy a Magazine which self preservation obliged the inhabitants to establish. And he also confesses, in effect at least, that his Men made a very precipitate retreat from Concord,*

notwithstanding the reinforcement under Lord Piercy, the last of which may serve to convince Lord Sandwich (and others of the same sentiment) that the Americans will fight for their Liberties and property, however pusillanimous, in his Lordship's Eye, they may appear in other respects.

From the best Accounts I have been able to collect... if the retreat had not been as precipitate as it was (and God knows it could not well have been more so) the Ministerial Troops must have surrendered, or been totally cut off: for they had not arrived in Charlestown (under cover of their Ships) half an hour before, a powerful body of Men from Marblehead and Salem were at their heels, and must, if they had happened to have been up one hour sooner, inevitably have intercepted their retreat to Charlestown. Unhappy it is thought to reflect, that a Brother's Sword has been sheathed in a Brother's breast, and that, the once happy and peaceful plains of America are either to be drenched with Blood, or Inhabited by Slaves. Sad alternative! But can a virtuous man hesitate in his choice?

When Washington had finished his recommendations for the defense of New York, he was made chairman of a committee composed of Philip Schuyler, Thomas Mifflin, Samuel Adams, Silas Deane, and Lewis Morris, representing colonies from Massachusetts to Virginia, to look into the all-important question of providing ammunition in a country with pitifully little manufacturing. John Adams noted that "Washington... by his great experience and abilities in military matters, is of much service to us."

Congress proceeded slowly but eventually decided to sponsor the New England army serving in Massachusetts, to assist in its financing, to ask for additional recruits from other provinces, and to draft regulations for the new army. Washington moved as chairman from the committee for the defense of New York to ammunitions, then to army finance, and finally to the committee for the regulation of the army. There was only one more step to go.

On May 24 Peyton Randolph was recalled to Virginia to meet with the Assembly called by Lord Dunmore. John Hancock was elected president of Congress in his place. Thomas Jefferson, still on his Charlottesville farm, rode to Williamsburg to join the Burgesses, who, according to Dunmore, displayed such "violence of temper," that he retired to a British warship at sea. Jefferson helped draft resolutions opposing Lord North's conciliatory proposals and then took off, as Randolph's alternate, for Philadelphia. He arrived shortly before Washington left Congress.

On the day after Randolph quit Philadelphia, British reinforcements, including no fewer than three major generals, arrived in Boston on the

Cerberus, a frigate named for the three-headed dog guarding hell. At once a Boston verse was circulated:

Behold the <u>Cerberus</u> the Atlantic plough,
Its precious cargo Burgoyne, Clinton, Howe—
Bow! Wow! Wow!

CONGRESS ADOPTS AN ARMY

The early settlers of America brought with them a strong Anglo-Saxon aversion to a permanent standing army. In part, they disliked the expense, but, more than that, long experience had shown that an army could be instrumental in suppressing liberty. Sending British troops to Boston had done much more to arouse the continent than the imposition of taxes. A citizen militia that could be summoned at need and then disbanded was something else again. The dislike of a permanent army persisted on each side of the Atlantic and hampered the war efforts of both countries. Britain's land and sea forces, which numbered more than 300,000 in the Seven Years' War, had shrunk to 34,000 by the beginning of 1775.

The American army at Boston, consisting of volunteers from four New England provinces, was without a chief. Artemas Ward was general in command of Massachusetts troops only. Other colonies had their own commanders. On June 2 Massachusetts asked Congress to determine how civilian control of the troops could be maintained and to make regulations for the army. When Congress authorized raising troops outside New England, it directed that they be under the commander in chief of the army. Someone therefore had to be selected for this post. John Adams' autobiography suggests that he was the main and almost sole instrument whereby Washington was chosen. His version seems as questionable as his statement that John Hancock was mortified that he was not elected to head the army. About all that seems historically certain is that Washington was chosen by Congress as chairman of all the committees dealing with military affairs. Serving with him were representatives of six provinces outside Virginia. He won the liking and admiration of his committeemen as well as of most of the other delegates. Massachusetts looked to the national congress to assure the fullest help of its sister colonies. Washington had been discussed in Massachusetts as a possible commander in chief and this had won wide approval. Elbridge Gerry wrote on June 4 to the Massachusetts delegation at Philadelphia to say that he was sure that the New England generals would welcome as their generalissimo "the beloved Colonel Washington" from their "sister colony" of Virginia. Gerry added that Dr. Joseph Warren, acting head of the Massachusetts congress, who had been chosen a general of the provincial forces, concurred in his view. It is difficult to believe that so important a letter was not known to Hancock.

There is little doubt that Adams admired Washington and that he, along with his cousin, Samuel Adams, took the lead in presenting his name. John Adams proposed on June 14, in response to the desire of Massachusetts, that Congress adopt the army before Boston. The meeting adjourned, and the talk continued in the lobbies and courtyards, and at dinner tables. On the following day the delegates, probably on the formal nomination by Thomas Johnson of Maryland, unanimously chose George Washington to be general and commander in chief of the armies of the United Provinces. Almost simultaneously Congress authorized the raising of rifle regiments in Pennsylvania, Maryland, and Virginia. By this action Congress intended to show that in choosing a general they were also prepared to give continental military support to New England. What was extraordinary was the ability of a body representing the disparate people and interests of thirteen colonies to choose so unerringly a man who would stay a rugged and foggy course for more than eight-and-a-half years. The hand of Providence clearly worked its wonders in this. Congress did not do so well in selecting his first major generals but the field of choice was narrow.

Washington was so concerned at his lack of qualification for the command that he told Patrick Henry privately that he was not only risking his reputation but that he expected to lose it. Nonetheless, at the official notification of June 16, 1775, he accepted with a modest statement that he read to Congress:

Mr. President: Tho' I am truly sensible of the high Honour done me in this Appointment, yet I feel great distress from a consciousness that my abilities and Military experience may not be equal to the extensive and important Trust: However as the Congress desires I will enter upon this momentous duty, and exert every power I possess in their Service for the Support of the glorious Cause: I beg they will accept my most cordial thanks for this distinguished testimony of their Approbation.

But lest some unlucky event should happen unfavourable to my reputation, I beg it may be remembered by every Gentn. in the room, that I this day declare with the utmost sincerity, I do not think my self equal to the Command I am honoured with.

As to pay, Sir, I beg leave to Assure the Congress that as no pecuniary consideration would have tempted me to accept this Arduous employment at the expence of my domestic ease and happiness I do not wish to make any profit from it: I will keep an exact Account of my expences; those I doubt not they will discharge and that is all I desire.

At dinner that day, the leaders stood and drank a toast "To the Commander-in-Chief of the American Armies." The next day the delegates unanimously pledged their "lives and fortunes" to the support of Washington.

When he heard about the election, Horace Walpole, who had first mentioned Washington as far back as 1754, wrote to a friend on August 3: "The Congress, not asleep, have appointed a Generalissimo, Washington, allowed a very able officer, who distinguished himself in the last war. Well! we had better have gone on robbing the Indies. It was a more lucrative trade." To another friend, after noting that Washington had declined to take any pay, he wrote: "If these folks will imitate both the Romans and the Cromwellians, in self-denial and enthusiasm, we shall be horribly plagued with them."

PAY

Washington kept as exact a record of his expenses as his frequently rapid moves permitted. Since each state had its own currency and the Continental Congress also issued notes, the complications were considerable. Taking the real value of the depreciating paper dollar, together with the expenditures in hard money, the general's headquarters costs, which included those of his staff and the secret service, averaged a little over $6,000 per year. Not only did Washington draw no pay for his services, but his first outlays in the amount of $2,000 were met from his own pocket. He was not reimbursed for eight years. In addition, during the darkest days of the war years, 1778–1780, he lent the government the equivalent of a further $8,000 in hard money, which he did not get back for many years.

During his long absence, Washington's farm and other properties deteriorated through neglect and mismanagement. In addition, many debts due him were paid in depreciating or worthless currency, while he met his own obligations at full value. He emerged from the army a very much poorer man who had the greatest difficulty in meeting his taxes for a long period after the war. By contrast the British commanders in chief were exceedingly well paid. Sir Henry Clinton received more than $57,000 a year in untaxed salary and allowances, and he had, in addition, almost unlimited secret service funds. He was able to save enough, during his years in America, to live comfortably for the rest of his life.

JOHN WRITES ABIGAIL ADAMS

On June 17 John Adams, much pleased, dropped a line to his wife in Braintree: "I can now inform you that the Congress have made choice of the modest and virtuous, the amiable, generous and brave George Washington, Esquire, to be General of the American army, and that he is to repair, as soon as possible, to the camp before Boston. The appointment will have a great effect in cementing and securing the union of these colonies." Abigail met Washington after his arrival in Cambridge, and wrote back to John:

You had prepared me to entertain a favourable opinion of him, but I thought the half was not told me. Dignity with ease & complacency, the Gentleman and the Soldier look agreeably blended in him. Modesty marks every line & fiture of his face. Those lines of Dryden instantly occu'rd to me:

> *"Mark his Majestic fabrick; he's a temple*
> *Sacred by birth, and built by hands divine.*
> *His soul's the Deity that lodges there.*
> *Nor is the pile unworthy of the God."*

John Adams was annoyed by later attempts to deify Washington, whom he had helped to put in office, but his own wife thought the general more than human when she first saw him.

GEORGE WRITES MARTHA WASHINGTON

Washington had a much harder letter to write to his wife for, as he told his brother John, he knew his appointment would "be a cutting stroke upon her." Only two letters from George to Martha Washington appear to survive, both written in Philadelphia in June of 1775. In the first, of the eighteenth, Washington wrote of his concern for the uneasiness his selection would cause his wife. He hoped she would summon her whole fortitude and try to pass her time as agreeably as possible. He mentioned the will he had just drawn up. He was sending her two suits of "the prettiest muslin" he could find.

In the next couple of days he wrote his stepson, Jacky, asking that he and his wife spend as much time as possible at Mount Vernon, as this was "absolutely necessary for the peace and satisfaction of your mother." He also asked Martha's brother-in-law, Burwell Bassett, to go with his wife to see Martha or to ask her to visit them at their house. He also requested John

Washington and his wife to call on Martha, if at all possible. To the captains of the Virginia independent companies, who had elected Washington their commander, he wrote on June 20:

Gentlemen: I am now about to bid adieu to the companies under your respective commands, at least for a while. I have launched into a wide and extensive field, too boundless for my capabilities, and far, very far, beyond my experience. I am called, by the unanimous voice of the Colonies, to the command of the Continental Army; an honour I did not aspire to; an honour I was solicitous to avoid, upon a full conviction of my inadequacy to the importance of the service. The partiality of the Congress, however, assisted by a political motive, rendered my reasons unavailing, and I shall to-morrow set out for the camp near Boston.

I have only to beg of you, therefore before I go, (especially as you did me the honour to put your companies under my direction, and know not how soon you may be called upon in Virginia for an exertion of your military skill,) by no means to relax in the discipline of your respective companies.

To his brother he wrote the same day: "That I may discharge the Trust to the Satisfaction of my Imployers, is my first wish; that I shall aim to do it, there remains as little doubt of, but this I am sure of, that in the worst event I shall have the consolation of knowing (if I act to the best of my judgment) that the blame ought to lodge upon the appointers, not the appointed, as it was by no means a thing of my own seeking, or proceeding from any hint of my friends."

In the same letter he noted that Artemas Ward, head of the Massachusetts troops, was made a major general, along with Charles Lee, Philip Schuyler, and Israel Putnam. Horatio Gates was appointed his adjutant general. Washington and Gates were thus to go to Boston to oppose General Thomas Gage, with whom they had served in the Braddock campaign. On June 23 Washington again wrote his wife:

My dearest,

As I am within a few Minutes of leaving this City, I could not think of departing from it without dropping you a line, especially as I do not know whether it may be within my power to write again till I get to the Camp at Boston. I go fully trusting in that Providence which has been more bountiful to me than I deserve, & in full confidence of a happy meeting with you sometime in the Fall. I have not time to add more, as I am surrounded with Company to take leave of me. I retain an unalterable affection for you, which neither time or distance can change. My best love to Jack and Nelly, & regards for the rest of the Family concludes me with the utmost truth and sincerity

Yr. entire G. Washington

Martha Washington, about whom George worried, turned out to be of stout stuff. When Lord Dunmore raided the coastal towns of Virginia and rumor rose that he would try to capture the general's wife, she remained the most composed person in the colony. And that fall and every autumn for eight years, she climbed into a carriage at Mount Vernon and rode over the rough and icy colonial roads, through rain, snow, and sometimes blizzards, to see the general at his headquarters. Altogether she spent almost two-thirds of the war not only by his side but taking care of the sick and wounded.

Shortly after writing his farewell to Martha, General Washington, accompanied by Generals Lee and Schuyler, and two members of his personal staff, Thomas Mifflin and Joseph Reed, rode off to Boston. John Adams and, probably, Thomas Jefferson saw the departure of the man who would determine whether they would be hanged by a thoroughly offended majesty. Adams wrote, after he watched the glamorous procession: "Such is the Pride and Pomp of War. I poor Creature, worn out with scribbling, for my bread and my Liberty, low in Spirits and weak in Health, must leave others to wear Laurels which I have Sown." Adams soon pulled himself together and not long afterwards proceeded to push America's first authorized naval force through Congress.

EIGHTEEN

CAMBRIDGE

1775

J OHN BURGOYNE, one of the three newly arrived British generals, was a minor playwright. At General Gage's request, he drew up a proclamation designed to subdue the rebellion by dramatic force. As issued by Gage on July 12, it said:

Whereas, the infatuated multitude, who have long suffered themselves to be conducted by certain well known, incendiaries and traitors... have at length proceeded to avowed Rebellion; and the good effects which were expected to arise from the patience and lenity of the King's Government have been often frustrated, and are now rendered hopeless, by the influence of the same evil counsels...

A number of armed persons, to the amount of many thousands, assembled on the 19th of April last, and from behind walls and lurking holes, attacked a detachment of the King's Troops... Since that period, the rebels... have added insult to outrage; have repeatedly fired upon the King's ships and subjects with cannon and small arms... and with a preposterous parade of military arrangements they affected to hold the army besieged...

...I avail myself of the last effort within the bounds of my duty to spare the effusion of blood... I hereby, in his Majesty's name, offer and promise his most gracious

pardon to all persons who shall forthwith lay down their arms… excepting only…
Samuel Adams and John Hancock, whose offenses are of too flagitious a nature to
admit of any other consideration than that of condign punishment.

Many English laughed with the Americans at the document. A London paper commented that the Americans had certainly "effected" a siege, while Walpole asked: "When did you ever read before of a besieged army threatening military execution on the country of the besiegers?"

Gage had taken a very different view in a private dispatch to Lord North, written two days previously. He said that he would need at least thirty-two thousand troops at Boston, New York, and Lake Champlain, and that he saw no possibility of any accommodation. On the same day, a letter, probably written by General William Howe, went to London. It said: "The Situation these wretches have taken in forming the Blockade of this Town is Judicious and Strong, being Well Intrenched… Their Numbers are great… Upon the Alarm being Given, they come from far & near, & the Longer the Action Lasts, The Greater their Numbers Grow… In this State, The General has not Judged it prudent to attack them."

BUNKER HILL

Before Washington left Philadelphia, reports reached the city that there had been another bloody engagement with the British. This was the battle of Bunker Hill, fought at Breed's Hill and Charlestown. Howe mentioned in his letter that he thought Gage should have occupied both Dorchester Neck, south of Boston, and Charlestown, on a peninsula to the north. When the committee of public safety got word that Gage planned to occupy Charlestown, reinforcements were sent to fortify Bunker Hill, near the exit from that town to the mainland.

The five leading American officers who carried the plans through were among the oldest that ever fought a battle. Seth Pomeroy was about 69, Richard Gridley 65, Israel Putnam 57, William Prescott 49, and John Stark 47. All had military experience, some going as far back as the 1745 siege of Louisburg. Joseph Warren, a physician who had been appointed provincial major general and who arrived on the scene as a volunteer, was 34. Putnam commanded the Connecticut troops and Stark those of New Hampshire who joined Prescott's Massachusetts men. Probably owing to the advance of Putnam, the small group, which originally amounted to twelve hundred men and to which were added roughly three hundred later arrivals, decided to fortify Breed's Hill, some six hundred yards farther south than Bunker Hill. Working all night, they had, by morning, constructed a substantial redoubt. According to General Howe's report, the British sentries heard the Americans at work but did not bother to report their activity. The first Gage knew of it was when British ships began firing on the American defense.

With a fort directly threatening Boston, Gage had no choice but to act. At a council of war, General Clinton suggested landings south and north of the redoubt, to encircle it, but his advice was rejected. Gage ordered Howe to make a direct frontal attack under cover of the British fleet in the harbor.

During the course of the battle, the British fleet trained guns on Charlestown and burned it. An American corporal, Amos Farnsworth, wrote afterwards: "The town... supposed to contain about 300 dwelling-houses, a great number of which were large and elegant, besides 150 or 200 other buildings, are almost all laid in ashes by the barbarity and wanton cruelty of that infernal villain Thomas Gage." Abigail Adams and her small son, John Quincy, watched the destruction of Charlestown, the first of a long line of defenseless towns to be burned by the enemy.

Altogether Howe led some 2,400 trained men against the American garrison of 1,500. All afternoon, the British bravely tried to take the American position, which the Americans defended with equal courage and vigor until their water, ammunition, and food ran out. General Warren was killed. The Americans retreated. The British had won but at a terrible price. When the casualties were totaled, the Americans had around 440 killed and wounded, and the enemy 1,054, including 89 officers. It was a staggering loss for the British and, in consequence, General Howe reported to London that he had faced 4,500 to 5,000 Americans and, he said, he had even heard the figure of 6,000 mentioned.

REPERCUSSIONS

The effects of Lexington, Concord, and Bunker Hill were extraordinary. Gage's offensive plan to occupy Dorchester and Charlestown and then to attack the American troops at Cambridge collapsed. There was recrimination and dissension within the British high command; some of the younger officers threatened to resign, having found distasteful the task of killing their fellow subjects.

Shortly after the battles of Lexington and Concord, the Americans dispatched a fast ship to England with the news. It reached there before Gage's dispatches. The king and cabinet simply disbelieved the reports since they were contradictory to the government's statements that Americans would run from a few British regiments. Lord George Germain noted that the opposition was full of smiles. The Whigs attacked the government, both for the disaster and for concealing it, but the government had not yet had confirmation from its own army.

The city of London promptly addressed a petition to the king which, though it was labelled a "humble Address," was perhaps the most insulting one ever handed a reigning British sovereign. The city expressed its "abhorrence of the tyrranical measures pursued against our fellow-subjects in America," referred to "despotism" and "arbitrary power," and declared that American resistance was "their indisputable duty to God." The petition claimed that Gage had begun a civil war, described the king's minister as "notoriously bribed to betray their constituents and Country," and asked the king to dismiss them and dissolve Parliament, for having "by various acts of cruelty and injustice... manifested a spirit of persecution against our brethren in America."

Since the ministers had been wrong in their policy, their orders to Gage, and their assessment of American resistance, they had to find scapegoats. Lord George Germain wrote that the defeat of Gage at Lexington and Concord was similar to that of Braddock and it was obvious he held a command "of too great importance for his talents." The axe was ready for him, even before the news of Bunker Hill reached London. Gage had complained about Admiral Samuel Graves, in sea command at Boston. By fall, both officers were recalled.

The news of Bunker Hill forced the king and cabinet to face a war of a scope beyond anything for which they were prepared. They had believed their own statements; now Britain, with relatively few troops, had to face an enemy willing to fight. To win, desperate measures were required. Thus, in the summer of 1775, Britain undertook policies embracing (a) bribery, treachery, and corruption; (b) burning defenseless towns; (c) hiring foreign troops; and (d) arming Indians and negroes as allies. General Burgoyne, "Gentleman Johnny," was the first to propose such measures to London. As Franklin predicted in 1776, these policies were to make it very difficult for the British to forgive the Americans after the war for having frustrated their knavish tricks.

The news of Lexington, Concord, and Bunker Hill spread through Europe. The reports were cheered at Versailles. The ladies of the court abandoned the English "Whist" to play a new card game, "Boston." The foreign minister, Charles Gravier, comte de Vergennes, followed the reports with satisfaction. In consultation with his king and prime minister, he dispatched two agents, Pierre Caron de Beaumarchais, who continued to write *The Barber of Seville* while going back and forth on secret missions to London, and the aptly named Monsieur Bonvouloir, to Philadelphia. Beaumarchais' dispatches exaggerated the dissension in England, as well as the size of the American armies, but this did the coming United States no harm. After Bonvouloir's arrival in Philadelphia, Congress moved to establish a foreign affairs committee and to dispatch the first American agent to Paris. Another Frenchman, a young king's officer who heard the reports with joy in his heart, was Gilbert Motier de Lafayette, who bore the name of his famous ancestor, a marshal of France who, with Joan of Arc, had driven the English from Orleans.

George III found himself with few friends in Europe. The French and Spanish had long hated England. The king's attempt to rehire Scot troops who had been of the Patriot Party declared that the Americans were "a brave people, defending in a becoming, manly and religious manner those rights which, as men, they derive from God, not from the legislature of Great Britain." Even that towering autocrat, Empress Catherine, rejected British attempts to obtain Russian troops. George III complained to North that she did it in not too "genteel a manner... She... has thrown out some expressions that may be civil to a Russian Ear but certainly not to more civilized ones."

In opening Parliament on October 26, the king declared that a "desperate conspiracy" existed in America, their protestations of loyalty were only meant to "amuse" (trifle) and it was time to increase the army and navy in order to put a quick end to the disorders.

The Whig opposition jeered at the Crown ministers. They threw back at them their speeches saying that Americans were cowards and a few regiments would pacify them. They asked how a physician (Warren) leading a horde of peasants could have done so much damage to the king's troops. If it took a thousand men to capture one hill, they continued, how many hills were there in America? Lord John Cavendish denounced the king's speech as full of falsehoods. Charles James Fox declared that Lord North had lost more territory in one campaign than Caesar, Alexander, and Pitt had ever gained. The heaviest blow came when the duke of Grafton, a member of the cabinet and a former first minister, attacked the government. In Walpole's words, "The Lord Privy Seal deserted and fired on them." Nineteen peers signed a protest that the "ministers have deceived Parliament, disgraced the nation, lost the Colonies... and upon the most unjustifiable grounds, wantonly spilled the blood of thousands of our fellow-subjects."

Nonetheless the king and North proceeded with their policies. Above all, the king wanted a quick war and a cheap war, and these aims were contradictory. In August orders went from London to Gage and, through him, to Sir John Johnson, the British Indian agent, to engage the Indians to attack the colonists. In October, the Royal Navy burned Falmouth (now Portland, Maine). In November, Lord Dunmore issued a decree for the purpose of establishing "peace and good order," calling on all slaves to revolt and be armed as part of His Majesty's troops, thereby gaining their freedom. The decree was perhaps made less effective by being issued on board a ship "off Norfolk."

To get troops as cheaply as possible, a point he emphasized over and over, George III began to recruit and hire Germans. Since he was also king of Hanover, he was quickly able to order 2,355 troops from that country to relieve British garrisons in Gibraltar and elsewhere. By fall intensive negotiations were under way in Hesse-Cassel, Brunswick, Hesse-Hanau, and three smaller states for the purchase of troops, a move that shocked most of Europe. Since close to two-thirds of the nearly 30,000 Germans eventually came from the two Hesses, the term "Hessian," a word ranking with Hun in America, was indiscriminately applied to all of them.

Nevertheless, there was something pathetic about the king's efforts to raise men. Here was a ruler with great power who wrote out in his own handwriting lengthy lists and returns of individual regiments, noting where each was, how many men were sick, or how many men were needed for their full complement. When Lord North asked for two thousand men to begin a campaign in the southern provinces, the king replied on October 15 that it was going to be very hard to find that many but he would try to scrape them together, mainly from Ireland, since "every means distressing America must meet with my concurrence as it tends to bringing them to feel the necessity of returning to their Duty." The difficulties of raising men in Britain and Ireland and the cheapness of the Germans forced this foreign recruiting in order to shorten the time needed to crush America. No policy could have been better calculated to harden resistance.

GENERAL WASHINGTON PROCEEDS TO THE COMMAND

When Washington returned from Boston to Williamsburg in 1756, he was urgently recalled to the frontier to repel French and Indian attacks. In short order, after arriving at Winchester, he absorbed the problems facing his scattered defense command. After reaching Cambridge he wrote reports to Congress and the provincial governors and legislators, reports that showed a similar quick insight into his problems, some quite insoluble under existing conditions.

Washington formulated, almost immediately, the philosophies that carried him through the war years and beyond. The first was that the people were sovereign, they chose their civilian rulers, and military officers were subordinate to them. Within the military, however, discipline and order were necessary. This was a clear distinction but it was difficult to apply in New England, where the men not only voted for their public officials but elected their company and field officers. Washington also set to work to weld the various provincial armies into a single force as a first step towards building a nation. In practice, this proved the most difficult policy of all to execute, but eventually he achieved it to a remarkable degree. Congress had hoped that he might be a resourceful commander. No member could have foreseen the patience, diplomacy, and tact with which he was to handle thirteen sovereign governments, jealous and sometimes treacherous generals, a Congress with few defined powers, and a war effort finally involving armies and navies from the most sophisticated court of Europe.

When Washington arrived in New York on his way to Cambridge, the provincial legislature congratulated him on his appointment, but hastened to add a sentence expressing common Anglo-Saxon concern about an army. They hoped, they said, that as soon as an accommodation with Britain was reached, he would "cheerfully resign" his post. Washington might have been annoyed at such a request, coming only eleven days after his appointment, but he made a graceful reply that quickly circulated through the country: "When we assumed the Soldier, we did not lay aside the Citizen; and we shall most sincerely rejoice with you in that happy hour when the establishment of American Liberty... shall enable us to return to our Private Stations in the bosom of a free, peaceful and happy country."

Washington reached Cambridge on July 2, a quiet Sabbath. The following day he took command without much ceremony. On July 4 he announced to the army that Artemas Ward, Charles Lee, Philip Schuyler, and Israel Putnam had been appointed major generals in "the American Army," the first official use of the term. Thomas Mifflin was made his aide, and Joseph Reed his secretary. He added:

> *The Continental Congress having now taken all the Troops of the several Colonies, which have been raised, or which may be hereafter raised for the support and defense of the Liberties of America; into their Pay and Service. They are now the Troops of the UNITED PROVINCES of North America; and it is hoped that all Distinctions of Colonies will be laid aside; so that one and the same Spirit may animate the whole.*

The general ordered discipline, the observance of the articles of war, "a punctual attendance on divine Service" by all officers and men, and cleanliness of person and camp. To Jonathan Trumbull, the only provincial governor who embraced the American cause and who had been reelected by the Connecticut Assembly, he wrote on July 18: "The uncorrupted Choice of a brave and free people, has raised you to deserved eminence; that the Blessings of Health and the still greater Blessings of long continuing to Govern *such* a People may be yours, is the Sincere Wish of, Sir... G. Washington."

His public letters were tactful and polite and often similar in spirit, but his private communications to friends become ever sharper as he looked at the problems with which he had been so abruptly saddled.

GENERAL PROBLEMS

Washington's first perplexities involved his top officers. He knew that his own appointment had political motivations, although congressional trust in him was perhaps more important. His obvious integrity, military knowledge, friendliness, handsome appearance, and past war record played their part in the delegates' judgment. Congress had to pick other officers by guesswork.

As a matter of politics and courtesy, Artemas Ward of Massachusetts, supplying a majority of the troops, was placed second in command. Ward had been a lieutenant colonel of militia in the French and Indian War and thereafter was often in ill health. He was a colorless leader who failed to appear at Bunker Hill, even though he was head of his colony's forces.

Charles Lee, the third major general, neurotic and unstable, had more extensive military experience than Washington. As a British officer he had been in the battles of Ticonderoga, Niagara, and Montreal. Thereafter he served under Burgoyne in Spain, proceeding finally to Poland where he was an aide to the king and a major general. He subsequently returned to America to settle on his British half-pay. John Adams described him to James Warren: "You observe in your letter the Oddity of a great Man. He is a queer creature. But you must love his Dogs if you love him, and forgive a thousand whims for the Sake of the Soldier and the Scholar." The British captured this letter and made it public. Lee, unoffended, thanked Adams, since everyone now fussed over his dogs, while Abigail Adams wrote that she was made to shake the paw of one of the hounds her husband had made famous.

Philip Schuyler was the only one of the four major generals with a claim to aristocracy. From a patroon family, his was a generous and decent nature but his manners constantly annoyed the New England levellers. He had fought at Oswego, Crown Point, and Frontenac. Washington always trusted him as a man of integrity and judgment. Israel Putnam, last of the four appointed major generals, was by far the oldest. He had been in the French and Indian wars with Roger's Rangers. His bravery at Bunker Hill was not duplicated thereafter. None of the first four major generals served for an extended time. Coming up behind them were unknowns who were to stay with Washington for the entire war: Greene, Knox, Wayne, Morgan, Glover, and many others.

Washington encountered immediate problems with other general officers. Congress had too little knowledge of their ranks in provincial commands. In handing out commissions, men were advanced or demoted without a rational basis. John Thomas of Massachusetts, for example, who outranked two others, found himself below them as a brigadier. Joseph Spencer, who preceded Putnam, was placed under him. The new commander in chief, as he was often to do during the war, had to assuage the hurt feelings of his officers. On July 23 he wrote a long letter to Thomas, pleading with him not to resign:

> *The Retirement of a general Officer possessing the Confidence of his Country and the Army at so critical a Period, appears to me big with fatal Consequences... I think it my Duty to use this last Effort to prevent it... In such a cause as this, where the Object is neither Glory nor extent of territory, but a defense of all that is dear and valuable in Life, surely every post ought to be deemed honourable in which a Man can serve his Country... I admit, Sir, that your claims and services have not had due respect, it is by no means a singular case... For the sake of your bleeding Country, your devoted Province, your charter rights, and by the memory of those brave men who have already fallen in this great cause, I conjure you to banish from your mind every suggestion of anger and disappointment; your country will do ample justice to your merits.*

Thomas accepted his demotion gracefully and soon rose to be major general. Spencer retired, but eventually he, too, returned to the army at his previous rank.

OTHER TROUBLES

As Washington looked around him day after day, the problems seemed to multiply. Field and company grade officers had been selected by the provinces, not by Congress. The size of companies and regiments differed among the colonies, and it was difficult to weld them into a whole. The commander in chief might order everyone to forget provincial distinctions, but practically no one did. Washington became so exasperated that he, too, lapsed briefly into being a provincial Virginian. According to informal reports given him on his arrival, he had 18,000 to 20,000 troops. Almost his first command was to order returns from all headquarters. He later said that he expected them to reach him by nightfall. After a week of repeated orders and complaints, he began to get his reports but many were so faulty they had to be redone. When they were tabulated, he had only 16,000 men, of whom but 14,500 were fit for duty. This was his first shock. His second came when he asked for the supplies of powder on hand and was informed that there were 308 barrels of this most scarce commodity. On checking further, he found only 36 barrels; the returns had included the amounts expended at Breed's Hill and elsewhere. With this powder, and the supplies available in Connecticut and Rhode Island, he had hardly enough for nine rounds per man. According to John Sullivan, Washington sat in stunned silence for a half hour after receiving the corrected report.

Some of Washington's problems were temporary and concerned the long lines established around Boston, but many he mentioned that early July of 1775 continued year after year. They included shortages of engineers, artillery, ammunition, money, and clothing; provincial jealousies; the temporary nature of militia duty; the difficulties of dealing with local officials as well as committees of Congress; and a general air of amateurishness that pervaded the army. Washington did not, at this point, have an intelligence or supply organization, or a paymaster or medical director. As he wrote his brother John on July 20, the troops were fairly numerous but there was "very little command, discipline or order." The British had entire control of the waters and could move their forces to any point on short notice. "Our situation is a little unfavourable, but not so bad but I think we can give them a pretty warm reception if they think proper to make any advances towards us."

Washington slowly began to beat a sense of order into his young army. The camps were cleaned up and the sentries forced to alertness. By July 22 he had formed the forces into three divisions, each consisting of two brigades, under Generals Ward, Lee, and Putnam. His new brigadiers included Nathanael Greene, who was eventually to be commander of the southern army. Washington's order of July 23 revealed one problem: "As the Continental Army have unfortunately no Uniforms, and consequently many inconveniences must arise, from not always being able to distinguish the Commissioned officers, from the non Commissioned, and the non Commissioned from the private; it is desired that some Badges of Distinction may be immediately provided. He ordered field officers to wear red or pink cockades; captains, yellow or buff; and subalterns, green. Sergeants were distinguished by red cloth on their sleeves, and corporals by green. This followed an earlier order by which Washington was to be recognized by a blue ribbon worn across his breast and other general officers by a pink ribbon.

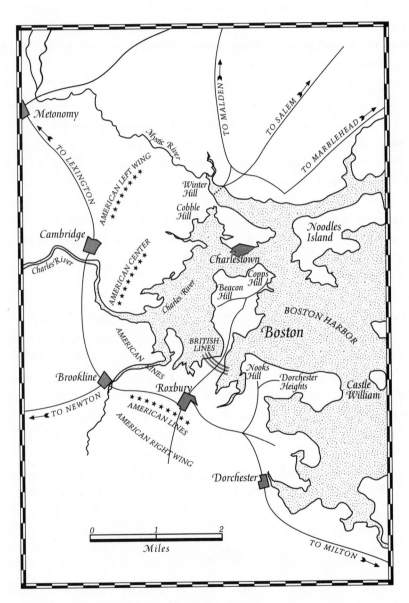

The Siege of Boston, 1775–1776

To introduce discipline and a certain amount of fear into his officers and men, Washington set up a system of courts-martial for offenses, some of which had been committed before he took command. He was particularly angry at any sign of cowardice and dishonor in an officer. The men, rustic and youthful as they often were, were treated with greater leniency. They were fined, whipped, or reprimanded for offenses for which officers were cashiered. He complained to Lund Washington on August 20 of the character of his command:

> *The People of this government have obtained a Character which they by no means deserved; their officers generally speaking are the most indifferent kind of People I ever saw. I have already broke one Colo. and five Captains for Cowardice and for drawing more Pay and Provisions than they had Men in their Companies; there is two more Colos. now under arrest, and to be tried for the same offences; in short they are by no means such Troops, in any respect, as you are led to believe of them from the accts. which are published, but I need not make myself Enemies among them by this declaration, although it is consistent with truth. I dare say the Men would fight very well (if properly Officered) although they are an exceedingly dirty and nasty people.*

When he wrote this, Washington had been in command only seven weeks. The burden of organizing a proper defense, without the backing of an effective government, had fallen on him. He was worried about Mount Vernon and the rumors that Lord Dunmore would try to capture Martha Washington. In addition, sanitary arrangements at the camps were primitive, and this offended his senses of decency and military discipline. In spite of his comments, only one officer in a hundred or so, and one enlisted man in a thousand, were dismissed from the American army during 1775. This was not a bad record for an army of amateurs. Thereafter, except for an occasional outburst, Washington tended more often to praise than to condemn.

CONGRESS

Although it had unanimously voted an army to protect its liberties, Congress was still divided as to procedures. Under the lead of John Dickinson, that body passed another humble petition: "Most Gracious Sovereign: We, your Majesty's faithful subjects..." Even John Adams signed this but most unwillingly.

Adams, in letters, attacked such "Puerilities." He complained to his wife that they should not be wasting their time that way. "We have a Constitution to form... a country to fortify, millions to arm and train, a naval power to begin." On July 24, in a private letter to James Warren, Adams expressed his opinion of Dickinson: "A certain great Fortune and piddling Genius, whose Fame has been trumpeted so loudly, has given a silly Cast to our whole Doings. We are between Hawk and Buzzard. We ought to have had in our Hands a month ago, the whole Legislative, executive and judicial of the whole Continent... to have raised a naval Power; to have arrested every Tory to be found on the continent, and then, perhaps, to have been ready to discuss peace with Britain."

The British captured this letter and published it in order to divide Congress. This worked to some extent, for Dickinson cut Adams dead on the street, and many other members indicated they thought he had been indiscreet. He had pulled the rug out from the humble petition. The reply to it was a thundering London proclamation calling the rebels "wicked and desperate persons," to be brought to "condign punishment."

Congress adjourned on August 1, leaving no central authority with which Washington could deal. Thereafter, for some time, he had to wheedle what he could from the New England provinces. Washington wrote to the president of Congress on August 31 and September 7. Winter was approaching; shelter was required; enlistments were about to expire. He pleaded more urgently but still politely on September 21:

> *It gives me great Pain to be obliged to sollicit the Attention of the Hon. Congress to the State of the Army, in Terms which imply the Slightest Apprehension of being neglected: But my Situation is inexpressibly distressing to see the Winter fast approaching upon a naked Army, The time of their Service within a few Weeks of expiring, and no Provision yet made for such important Events. Added to this the Military Chest is totally exhausted. The Paymaster has not a single Dollar in Hand.*

This letter caused Congress to appoint a committee to attend him at his camp, but it took several weeks until they reached Cambridge. While pleading with Congress, Washington received a rather tart note from Jonathan Trumbull, the able governor of Connecticut, who normally gave him every assistance. On September 2 and 8 Washington ordered the new Connecticut levies, raised for continental duty, to march immediately to Cambridge to replace other troops sent to Canada. The governor protested that the British were raiding Stonington, Connecticut, and asked that the troops remain there, but Washington let his orders stand. Trumbull then wrote him: "I am surprised that mine of the 5th instant was not received, or not judged worthy of Notice, as no mention is made of it... I am, with great Esteem and Regard for your personal character..." Washington replied on September 21 to Trumbull:

> *It gives me real concern... that you should think it Necessary to distinguish between my Personal and Public Character and confine your Esteem to the former.*
>
> *...I have long been sensible that it would be impossible to please, not Individuals merely, but particular Provinces, whose Partial Necessities would occasionally call for assistance; I, therefore, thought myself happy, that the Congress had settled the Point, and apprehended I should stand excused to all, for acting in the Line which not only appeared to me to be that of Policy and Propriety, but of express and positive Duty; If, to the other Fatigues and Cares of my Station, that is to be added that of giving Reasons for all Orders, and explaining the grounds and Principles on which they are formed; my Personal Trouble will perhaps, be of the least Concern, the Public will be most affected.*
>
> *The subject was not so new to me as to require long Consideration; I had occasion fully to deliberate upon it in Consequence of applications for troops from Cape Ann, Machias, New Hampshire, and Long Island... I wish I could extend Protection to all; but the numerous Detachments necessary to remedy the Evil, would amount to a dissolution of the Army, or make the most important Operations of the Campaign depend upon the Piratical Expeditions of 2 or 3 Men of War and Transports.*

Trumbull promptly apologized and thereafter always gave Washington fullest support. In December, Joseph Reed, Washington's military secretary, picked up a report in Philadelphia that the Massachusetts officials were much annoyed because Washington had been insufficiently attentive to them. Washington wrote on December 15 to Reed to say: "I cannot charge myself with incivility... to the gentlemen of this colony; but if such my conduct appears, I will endeavour at a reformation, as I can assure you, my dear Reed, that I wish to walk in such a line as will give most general satisfaction. You know, that it was my wish at first to invite a certain number of gentlemen of this colony every day to dinner, but unintentionally I believe by anybody, we somehow or other missed of it. If this has given rise to the jealousy, I can only say that I am sorry for it; at the same time I add, that it was rather owing to... too much attention to other matters, which caused me to neglect it." While writing this, he was watching much of his army vanish.

WASHINGTON AND GAGE

Though Washington might be far from having all he wanted to make him happy, his opponent, General Gage, was in a worse moral position. The British commander in chief of all America was barely able to hold on to a single port and unable to risk a counterattack for fear of losing the war in one stroke. It was he who had told the king what he wanted to hear, that a few regiments would suppress the rebellion. Now he could only attempt to uphold the Crown's dignity by words. The two former companions-in-arms, Washington and Gage, had an acrimonious correspondence on the treatment of prisoners. The American led off on August 11:

Sir: I understand that the Officers engaged in the Cause of Liberty and their Country, who by the Fortune of War have fallen into your Hands, have been thrown, indiscriminately into a common Gaol appropriated for Felons; That no Consideration has been had for those of the most respectable Rank, when languishing with Wounds, and Sickness; that some have been even amputated, in this unworthy Situation.

Let your Opinion, Sir, of the Principle which Actuates them, be what it may, they suppose they act from the noblest of all Principles, a Love of Freedom, and their Country: But political Opinions I conceive are foreign to this Point; the Obligations arising from the Rights of Humanity, and Claims of Rank are universally binding... These, I should have hoped, Would have dictated a more tender Treatment of those Individuals, whom Chance of War had put in your Power. Nor can I forbear suggesting its fatal tendency, to widen that unhappy Breach, which you, and those Ministers under whom you act, have repeatedly declar'd you wish'd to see forever closed.

If Severity and Hardship mark the Line of your Conduct (painful as it may be to me) your Prisoners will feel its effects.

Gage replied on August 13, in a letter addressed rather contemptuously to "George Washington, Esqr.":

To the Glory of Civilized Nations, humanity and War have been compatible; and Compassion to the subdued is become a general system. Britons, ever preeminent in Mercy, have outdone common examples, and overlooked the Criminal in the Captive. Upon these principles your Prisoners, whose Lives by the Law of the Land are destined to the Cord, have hitherto been treated with care and kindness, and more comfortably lodged than the King's Troops in the Hospitals; indiscriminately it is true, for I acknowledge no Rank, that is not derived from the King. My intelligence from your Army would justify severe recrimination... I would willingly hope, Sir, that the Sentiments of liberality, which I have always believed you to possess, will be exerted to correct these misdoings. Be temperate in political disquisition; give free Operation to truth, and punish those who deceive and misrepresent... Should those, under whose usurped Authority you act, controul such a disposition, and dare to call severity retaliation, to God who knows all hearts, be the appeal for the dreadful consequences. I trust that British Soldiers, Asserting the rights of the State, the Laws of the Land, the being of the Constitution, will meet all events with becoming fortitude... and... will find the patience of Martyrs under misfortune. Till I read your insinuations in regard to Ministers, I conceived that I had acted under the King.

Washington's lengthy riposte of August 30 attempted to outdo Gage in bombast and the result was something of a syntactical mess:

Whether British or American Mercy, Fortitude, and Patience are most preeminent, whether our virtuous Citizens, whom the Hand of Tyrrany has forced into Arms to defend their Wives, their Children, and their Property, or the mercenary Instruments of lawless Domination, avarice and Revenge, best deserve the Appelation of Rebels, and the Punishment of that Cord, which your affected Clemency has forborne to inflict: whether the Authority, under which I act, is usurped, or founded upon the genuine Principles of Liberty, were altogether foreign to the Subject. I purposely avoided all political Disquisition; nor shall I now avail myself of those Advantages, which the sacred Cause of my Country, of Liberty, and human nature, give me over you... I am embarrassed with the Numbers, who crowd to our Camp, animated with the purest Principle of Virtue... You affect, Sir, to despise all Rank, not derived from the same Source with your own. I cannot conceive one more honourable than that which flows from the uncorrupted Choice of a brave and free People.

WASHINGTON'S FLEET

Late in the summer Washington turned from his land operations to organize a small naval force that could tap British supplies. At his urging, the governor of Rhode Island, Nicholas Cooke, sent an armed vessel to Bermuda to seize British powder but this operation failed. In early September, stretching his powers as army commander to the limit, Washington instituted America's first armed naval vessels. On October 16 he issued orders to Captain Nicholas Broughton:

> *You being appointed a Captain in the Army of the United Colonies of North America, are hereby directed to take the Command of a Detachment of said Army and proceed on Board the <u>Schooner Hannah</u>, at Beverly, lately fitted out & equipp'd with Arms, Ammunition and Provisions at the Continental Expence.*
>
> *You are to proceed as Commander of <u>Sd. Schooner</u>, immediately on a Cruize against such Vessels as may be found on the High Seas or elsewhere, bound inward and outward to or from Boston, in the Service of the Ministerial Army, and to take and seize all such Vessels, laden with Soldiers, Arms, Ammunition, Provisions for or from sd. Army.*

Provision was made for prize money for the captain and crew. Broughton was particularly warned not to try to engage British men-of-war. Shortly afterwards the general appointed the enterprising John Manley captain of the *Lee*, and subsequently the fleet's commodore. Manley was to make the first important capture of a British vessel in 1775 and the last seizure of the war in 1783.

In October John Adams led a move in Congress, which encountered bitter opposition, to establish a continental navy. The feeling of many was that any attacks on the British navy or merchant marine would bring retaliation against the coastal towns. Nonetheless Adams won by a small margin and was then put on a committee to draft the fleet's rules and regulations.

Almost at the same time, Congress sent Washington hastily drawn instructions to form a marine corps out of his army. Washington replied on November 10, complaining that he would have to upset his entire existing arrangement "which has cost us so much Time, anxiety and pains to bring into any tolerable form. Notwithstanding any Difficulties which will arise, you may be assured, Sir, that I will use every endeavour to comply with [the] Resolve." Congress then amended the instructions to provide that the corps be enlisted independently of the army.

WASHINGTON IS LIKED

Even working night and day, Washington could scarcely begin to cope with the infinite variety of problems thrust upon him. To trusted friends such as Joseph Reed, Richard Henry Lee, and John and Lund Washington, he poured out his feelings. He wrote to Lee on August 29, less than two months after taking command:

> *There has been so many great, and capital errors, and abuses to rectify—so many examples to make—and so little Inclination in the officers of inferior Rank to contribute their aid to accomplish this work, that my life has been nothing else (since I <u>came here</u>) <u>but</u> one continued round of <u>annoyance</u> and <u>fatigue</u>; in short, no pecuniary <u>recompense</u> could induce me to undergo what I <u>have</u>, <u>especially</u> as I expect, by shewing so little <u>countenance</u> to irregularities and publick <u>abuses to</u> render myself very obnoxious to a <u>greater</u> part of these People.*

This was like old times when young Colonel Washington, out on the cold barren frontier, was the whole force of the British empire. Tired and often discouraged, he wrote to his friends who rallied around him with praise and comfort. Lee, too, replied on September 26: "I assure you, that so far as I can judge from the conversation of Men, instead of there being any who think you have not done enough, the wonder seems to be that you have done so much... Your labours are no doubt great, both of mind and body; but if the praise of the present and future times can be any compensation you will have a plentiful portion of that."

In July, Henry Knox of Massachusetts, soon to be head of Washington's artillery, wrote to his brother: "General Washington fills his place with vast ease and dignity, and dispenses happiness around him." James Warren, president of the Massachusetts legislature, wrote of the "great satisfaction" that Washington gave. A Pennsylvanian, who visited the American camps, wrote a letter on August 9, which appeared in the *Pennsylvania Gazette* of August 23: "We waited on General Washington, who I have the pleasure to inform you is much beloved and admired for his polite condescension and noble deportment. His appointment to the chief command has the general suffrage of all ranks of people here, which I think is no bad omen."

NINETEEN

CAMBRIDGE AND BOSTON

1775–1776

O N SEPTEMBER 26 General Gage received orders to hand his American command to his subordinate, General William Howe, who was an even more determined enemy of the American revolt than his predecessor. On leaving England he stated his belief that most Americans were loyal to the king and only a "frantic" few were prepared to revolt. What was particularly galling to the colonists, including Washington, was that they had greatly admired his elder brother, Lord Howe, who was killed at Ticonderoga. Massachusetts had placed a memorial to him in Westminster Abbey. Shortly after his arrival, Howe led the bloody charge up Breed's Hill. A few days after he assumed command, his forces shelled and burned Falmouth, Maine, destroying 130 houses and the church, library, and town hall. He followed this with an order for the summary execution of any Bostonian caught leaving the city. Later he permitted some of the poorer citizens to depart. Since some had smallpox, Washington believed that he thus attempted to infect the American army. Washington had no illusions about his opposite number but held Howe in personal respect, as he wrote Howe on October 18:

Permit me to add Sir, that we have all here the highest regard and reverence for
your great personal Qualities and Attainments, and that the Americans in general

esteem it not as the least of their Misfortunes, that the name of Howe; a name so dear to them, should appear at the Head of the Catalogue of Instruments, employed by a wicked Ministry for their destruction.

CANADA

On June 25, on his way through New York City, Washington ordered General Schuyler to take command in the province of New York, obeying therein all instructions of the Continental Congress. He asked him to forward regular reports on his activities as well as any important intelligence. He noted that he could not himself command at so great a distance and Schuyler's own "good sense" would have to govern his actions. When Schuyler complained of the numerous difficulties he was encountering, Washington replied sympathetically on July 28: "Mine must be a portrait in full length of what you have had in Miniature... However we mend every Day, and I flatter myself that in a little Time, we shall work up these raw Materials into good stuff. I must recommend to you what I endeavour to practise myself, Patience and Perseverance."

Having raised an army for the support of American liberties that it was unable to equip, feed, clothe, or pay properly, Congress now pushed a campaign for the conquest of Canada. In so doing, that body nearly wrecked America's defenses before the Declaration of Independence was signed. Two men, later to be on George III's payroll, Ethan Allen and Benedict Arnold, appear to have been principally responsible for persuading Congress that capturing Canada would be as easy an operation as Ticonderoga. The argument for invasion was not put forth as a naked aggression. Instead it was argued, with some justification, that the French of Canada were to be freed and British aid to Indian attackers would be stopped. The subsequent operation, nominally under Schuyler's direction but, in fact, under the command of his subordinate, Richard Montgomery, was so bungled that its main objective, an attack on the fortress of Quebec, took place in a Canadian winter.

There is no evidence that the American commander in chief was consulted about the proposed attack to the north. Since he reacted strongly against a similar New England proposal for the conquest of Nova Scotia, it is reasonable to assume Washington would have argued as persuasively against Congress' plans to attack Quebec. He explained to the Massachusetts committee of public safety on August 11: "As to the Expedition proposed against Nova Scotia by the Inhabitants of Machias, I cannot but applaud their Spirit and Zeal; but, after considering the Reasons offered for it, several objections occur, which seem to me unanswerable. I apprehend such an Enterprize inconsistent with the General Principal upon which the Colonies have proceeded. That Province has not acceded, it is true, to the Measures of Congress;... But they have not Commenced Hostilities... To attack *them*, therefore, is a Measure of Conquest, rather than Defence... It might, perhaps, be easy, with the Force proposed, to make an Incursion into the Province... but the same Force must Continue to produce any lasting effects." Washington added that, in any case, he had no powder to spare for such an expedition.

When Arnold appeared in Cambridge, he proposed that an additional force of Americans proceed into Quebec from New England. In outlining this plan to Schuyler, Washington suggested it might be an important "Diversion that would distract Carleton and facilitate your Views." When Schuyler heartily approved, Washington sent Arnold off with a thousand men by way of the Kennebeck River and thence into Quebec province. Washington's instructions were more complete and detailed than those issued by Congress or Schuyler. He stressed the diplomatic difficulties of Arnold's task; Arnold was to turn back immediately if the Canadians resented the invasion. He was to respect absolutely their property and religion. There seems little doubt that the Canadians, under alien rule, felt general sympathy with the Americans. Arnold, in total disregard of orders, was to turn them into enemies. Washington's September 14 instructions stated:

> You are by every Means in your Power, to endeavour to discover the real Sentiments of the Canadians towards our Cause, and particularly as to this Expedition, ever bearing in Mind, that if they are averse to it, and will not co-operate... it must fail of Success... In this Case you are by no Means to prosecute the Attempt...

> ...You will... observe the strictest Discipline and good Order, by no Means suffering any Inhabitant to be abused, or in any Manner injured, either in his Person or Property... You are to endeavour... to Conciliate the affections of those People... convincing them that we come... as the Friends and Supporters of their Liberties, as well as ours...

> ...Crush... every attempt to plunder even those who are known to be Enemies to our Cause...

> Spare neither Pains or Expence to gain all possible Intelligence on your March, to prevent Surprizes...

> In the case of an Union with General Schuyler... you are to put yourself under him and follow his Directions...

If Lord Chatham's son [General Pitt] should be in Canada and in any Way fall in your Power, you are enjoined to treat him with all possible Deference and Respect. You cannot err in paying too much Honour to the Son of so illustrious a Character and so true a Friend to America...

You will be particularly careful, to pay the full Value for all Provisions or other Accommodations which the Canadians may provide for you on your March... Amply compensate those who voluntarily assist you...

As the Season is now far advanced, you are to make all possible Dispatch, but if unforeseen Difficulties should arise or if the Weather shou'd become so severe as to render it hazardous to proceed in your own Judgment and that of your principal Officers, (whom you are to consult)... you are to return...

As the Contempt of the Religion of a Country by ridiculing any of its Ceremonies or affronting its Ministers and Votaries has ever been deeply resented, you are to be particularly careful to restrain every Officer and Soldier from such Imprudence and Folly... You are to protect and support the free Exercise of the Religion of the Country and the undisturbed Enjoyment of the rights of Conscience in religious Matters.

Arnold's expedition pushed forward through such adverse circumstances as to have rendered it prudent, in accordance with his instructions, to have returned. When Washington was facing great difficulties with a vanishing army at the end of the year, he learned that Arnold had joined Montgomery in time to meet disaster at Quebec.

GUNS FOR BOSTON

Although Arnold and many another officer were to give Washington pain, others coming up were prepared to aid him beyond the call of duty. Two were longtime friends: Nathanael Greene, thirty-three, a limping Quaker from Rhode Island, and Henry Knox, twenty-five, a huge Bostonian who had lost two fingers from his left hand. They were both of an agreeable disposition and were alike in their omnivorous reading of military textbooks. Knox had also studied engineering and had seen service with Boston's artillery militia.

When Washington assigned Knox to the artillery, Knox asked him where it was. The commander in chief had to tell him there really wasn't any. Knox said that he would go to Ticonderoga and get some. In doing so, he was to perform one of the great feats of the Revolutionary War. He left Cambridge about November 18. According to his diary of expenses, he had, by late January, delivered to the general fifty-five guns weighing a total of sixty tons, having hauled them for three hundred miles over snow and ice.

DR. CHURCH

One of the many disputes that came to Washington was between Benjamin Church, director general of the hospital, and the regimental surgeons. On September 7, Washington ordered a court of inquiry. Church at once offered his resignation but Washington refused it on the grounds that he could not be spared.

Church was considered a strong patriot. As a member of the Massachusetts legislature, he was sent to Philadelphia to explain the military situation at Boston. He was also chosen to greet Washington on his arrival in the province. Subsequently the general selected Church as his chief medical officer.

Before the court of inquiry could report, a strange tale came to Washington. A woman had attempted, through an acquaintance in Newport, to smuggle a letter to Boston. The person receiving it consulted another patriot and they opened it. The letter, addressed to Major Cane, aide to General Gates, was in code. The woman was brought to headquarters and questioned by Washington. She eventually admitted that it had been written by Church and that she was his mistress. The letter, when decoded, turned out to have somewhat exaggerated information on the American military forces, a note on the planned invasion of Canada, and an appeal to Britain to remove all the oppressive acts.

Church denied any attempt at treason. Washington, uncertain of his authority to try him by court-martial, asked Congress for advice. That body ordered him confined in a Connecticut jail. After two years' imprisonment, Church was permitted to leave for the Caribbean, where he was lost at sea.

Not until many years afterward was it learned from Gage's papers that Church was a paid British spy. He had informed Gage of the cache of American arms at Concord. This brought Gage's hasty action to seize them, thus precipitating war. The British later pensioned Church's widow.

The medical profession, vital to Washington's sick and wounded troops, remained troublesome throughout the war. No sooner had he got rid of Church than he had to cashier a regimental surgeon from Connecticut. His next medical director, John Morgan, quarreled with his fellow physicians and was dismissed from the service by Congress. Morgan's successor, William Shippen, Jr., in turn, was court-martialed. Benjamin Rush, surgeon general of the middle department, having resigned from the army after a dispute, tried to have Washington dismissed from his command.

SECRETARIES AND CORRESPONDENCE

Because of what he said were commitments to his clients, Joseph Reed, a lawyer and Washington's military secretary, returned to Philadelphia in late October. Washington considered Reed's services so important that he intervened with Benjamin Chew, chief justice of Pennsylvania, to see whether Reed's cases could be postponed. The judge replied that the court was not in session and he was sure that Reed could arrange his affairs in order to be able to rejoin his staff. Washington, on hearing this, wrote Reed on November 28: "I could wish, my good friend, that these things may give a spur to your inclination to return; and that I may see you here as soon as convenient; as I feel the want of your ready pen, &c. greatly." This followed a letter he had written on November 20:

> The hint contained in the last of your letters, respecting your continuance in my family, in other words, your wish that I could dispense with it, gives me pain... You cannot but be sensible of your importance to me; at the same time I shall again repeat, what I have observed to you before, that I can never think of promoting my convenience at the expense of your interest and inclination. That I feel the want of you, yourself can judge, when I inform you, that the peculiar situation of Mr. Randolph's affairs obliged him to leave this soon after you did; that Mr. Baylor, contrary to my expectation, is not in the slightest degree a penman, though spirited and willing; and that Mr. Harrison, though sensible, clever, and perfectly confidential, has never yet moved upon so large a scale, as to comprehend at one view the diversity of matter, which comes before me, so as to afford that ready assistance, which every man in my situation must stand more or less in need of. Mr. Moylan, it is true, is very obliging; he gives me what assistance he can; but other business must necessarily deprive me of his aid in a very short time. This is my situation; judge you, therefore, how much I wish for your return, especially as the armed vessels, and the capital change (in the state of this army) about to take place, have added an additional weight to a burthen, before too great for me to stand under with the smallest degree of comfort to my own feelings. My mind is now fully disclosed to you, with this assurance, sincerely and affectionately accompanying it, that whilst you are disposed to continue with me, I shall think myself too fortunate and happy to wish for a change.

There were further pleas to Reed, one on January 23: "Real necessity compels me to ask you, whether I may entertain any hopes of your returning to my family?... At present my time is so much taken up at my desk, that I am obliged to neglect many other essential parts of my duty. It is absolutely necessary, therefore, for me to have persons that can think for me, as well as execute orders." Reed did not return at this time, although he continued in the affection of the commander in chief.

Washington, lacking ammunition, clothing, and, often enough, money to keep his troops contented, had to carry on correspondence with Congress; with the provinces of New Hampshire, Massachusetts, Connecticut, Rhode Island, and New York; and with Arnold in Canada and Schuyler in New York. He prepared addresses to the citizens of Canada and Bermuda; organized and reorganized an army, with all the paperwork involved; and wrote of his personal affairs to his wife, Lund Washington, and others. Though overburdened, the man who had made the phrase "When we assumed the Soldier, we did not lay aside the Citizen" continued his epigrammatic comments. His letters and general orders had crisp, fresh phrases not customary with generals. A few follow:

For God's sake hurry the signers of money, that our wants may be supplied. (to R. H. Lee)

Whilst we have Men therefore who in every respect are superior to mercenary Troops, that are fighting for <u>two pence</u> or <u>three pence</u> a day: Why cannot we in appearance also be superior to them, when we fight for Life, Liberty, Property and our Country? (General Orders)

I am told that Captain Wallace's [Royal Navy] Ships have been Supplied for some time with provisions by the town of New Port... We need not expect to Conquer our Enemies by good Offices. (to the Governor of Rhode Island)

Our Treasury is almost exhausted, and the demands against it, very considerable; a constant supply of money... would much promote the good of the Service; in the common affairs of Life, it is useful: In War, it is absolutely necessary and essential. (to Congress)

I hope it has... enabled the Congress to bestow a little more attention to the affairs of this army, which suffers exceedingly by their overmuch business, or too little attention to it. We are now without any money in our treasury, powder in our magazines, arms in our stores. We are without a brigadier (the want of which has

*been twenty times urged), engineers, expresses (though a committee has been
appointed these two months to establish them), and by and by, when we shall be
called upon to take the field, shall not have a tent to lie in. Apropos, what is doing
with mine?* (to Reed)

*The reflection on my situation, and that of this army, produces many an uneasy
hour when all around me are wrapped in sleep... I have often thought how much
happier I should have been, if, instead of accepting a command under such
circumstances, I had taken my musket on my shoulder and entered the ranks, or, if
I could have justified the measure to posterity and my own conscience, had retired
to the back country, and lived in a wigwam.* (to Reed)

*On reading the Copy of Genl. Wooster's Letter I was much surprised to find, that he
had granted Furloughs to the Connecticut Troops under his Command, in
Preference of Discharges. What Advantage could he imagine they would be to the
Continent, when they were at their own Homes?* (to Schuyler)

*I received your Favour... and am exceedingly sorry to hear, that Congress
countermanded the embarkation of the two Regiments, intended against the Tories
on Long Island... Our Enemies from the other Side of the Atlantic, will be
sufficiently numerous. It highly concerns us to have as few internal ones as
possible.* (to General Lee)

No man upon Earth wishes more ardently to destroy the nest in Boston, than I do.
(to Congress)

*The Clouds gather fast, where they will burst, I know not, but we should be armed
at all points.* (to Congress)

*I observe what you say in respect to my... travelling wagon... I have no doubt but
that the Treasury, by application to Mr. Hancock, will direct payment thereof,
without any difficulty, as Congress must be sensible, that I cannot take the field
without equipage, and after I have once got into a tent I shall not soon quit it.*
(to Reed)

*I have heard of no other valiant son of New England waiting promotion, since the
advancement of Frye... At present he keeps his room, and talks learnedly of emetics,
cathartics, &c. For my own part, I see nothing but a declining life that matters
him.* (to Reed; Frye lived until 1794)

MRS. WASHINGTON AND MOUNT VERNON

Washington found time to write to Williamsburg with regard to the Ohio Valley lands, which he had endeavored to seat in accordance with the law. He asked for help in their registration, noting that he might find them useful as an asylum. He also wrote to Lund Washington in regard to the additions under way at Mount Vernon. Lund's reply stated he did not know how much building he ought to be doing, since the British might come at any time and burn the place down.

Many Virginians were fearful for Martha Washington's safety, though Washington wrote that he did not believe Dunmore would act "so low and unmanly a part" as to seize Mrs. Washington. Lund informed him that Martha was not worried and everyone in Virginia had offered either to take her in for protection or to march to defend Mount Vernon. She eventually went to her old family house at New Kent. While she was there, Washington suggested to her that she join him in Cambridge. He also wrote on October 13 to his brother John:

> *I am obliged to you for your advice to My Wife, and for your Intention of visiting her; seeing no great prospect of returning to my Family and Friends this Winter I have sent an Invitation to Mrs. Washington to come to me, altho I fear the Season is too far advanced (especially if she should, when my Letters get home, be in New Kent, as I believe the case will be) to admit this with any tolerable degree of convenience. I have laid a state of the difficulties, however, which must attend the journey before her, and left it to her own choice.*

According to report, Martha, on receiving George's letter, had to be restrained from setting off without even taking time to pack. The messenger who brought her husband's letter was directed to proceed to Mount Vernon to order a supply of Virginia hams and various delicacies that she could haul to Cambridge to cheer the general's Christmas. Mrs. Washington left the next day, accompanied by her son and daughter-in-law, for a trip that took nearly a month. She was escorted into and out of Philadelphia by troops of light horse and infantry; in Newark the church bells rang on her arrival. As she wrote home later, there was as much pomp for her as if she had been a "some body."

Just before she reached Cambridge, Captain Manley, Washington's naval commodore, captured a ship from London, the *Jenny*, bringing supplies for the king's troops, including limes, lemons, oranges, sweetmeats, and pickles. The general asked Manley politely, through his aide, if he could buy a small portion, so that Mrs. Washington would have them on her arrival.

THE VANISHING ARMY

To get firsthand information on Washington's problems, Congress sent a committee of three to Cambridge in October. Its members were Benjamin Franklin, Thomas Lynch, and Benjamin Harrison, of Pennsylvania, South Carolina, and Virginia, respectively. Its southern composition raised New England eyebrows; General Greene wondered why only "strangers" were sent.

The committee spent many days conferring with Washington, his staff, and representatives of the four New England provinces. Congress had forwarded a number of questions as to the size and pay of his army. Washington, after consulting with his council, had the answers ready when the committee arrived. The army needed a force of 20,372 men; this was a larger number than any Washington had had to date. There were urgent matters of barracks, winter clothing, and firewood to consider. The most troublesome problem was that all enlistments, beginning with the Connecticut troops in early December, were about to expire. Washington had asked how many expected to reenlist; a majority wanted to return home.

Washington took up with the committee the problem of whether, if he attacked Boston, he should destroy the city if necessary. The committee felt that so important a question could be decided only by Congress. As the committee was concluding its work, the news of the destruction of Falmouth reached camp. The committee's report gave support to most of Washington's recommendations, which Congress in turn approved. The resolutions merely gave him authority to try to solve his problems.

The Connecticut troops decided they could not, as they put it, "tarry." Washington and his officers pleaded with them, on every patriotic ground, to stay at least a few extra days until hastily summoned troops from Massachusetts and New Hampshire could take their place. Some went off without leave, others said they might stay a little longer if they got extra money. At this time, Washington was desperately trying to get firewood and blankets, build barracks, and lay in winter supplies, while keeping an eye on the enemy in Boston, who knew from their spies that his army was disintegrating. Washington expressed his feelings in a letter to Reed on November 28:

> *Such a dearth of public spirit, and want of virtue, such stock-jobbing, and fertility in all the low arts to obtain advantages of one kind or another, in this great change of military arrangement, I never saw before, and pray God I may never be witness to again. What will be the ultimate end of these manoeuvres is beyond my scan. I tremble at the prospect. We have been till this time enlisting about three thousand*

five hundred men. To engage these I have been obliged to allow furloughs as far as fifty men a regiment, and the Officers I am persuaded indulge as many more. The Connecticut troops will not be prevailed upon to stay longer than their term (saving those who have enlisted for the next campaign, and mostly on furlough), and such a dirty, mercenary spirit pervades the whole, that I should not be at all surprised at any disaster that may happen.

The first sentence has often been quoted as if it were a denunciation of all New England, but it related to particular circumstances. According to General Lee, the cold and homesick Connecticut farm boys, as they went off, were "so horribly hissed, groaned at and pelted, that I believed they wished their aunts, grandmothers and even sweethearts, to whom the day before they were so much attached, at the Devil's own place." When they got home, they found aunts, sweethearts, and grandmothers so indignant that many were glad to return to Cambridge.

New Englanders understood both themselves and their general. Governor Trumbull wrote that Connecticut had received the reports with "grief, surprise, and indignation." He explained that it was difficult for New Englanders, "high for liberty," to be subordinate to anyone. He had immediately called the Assembly into special session. "You may depend on their zeal and ardor to support the common cause, to furnish our quota, and to exert their utmost strength for the defence of the rights of these colonies. Your candor and goodness will suggest to your consideration, that the conduct of our troops is not a rule whereby to judge of the spirit of the colony." General Greene wrote to Samuel Ward, Rhode Island delegate in Congress, on December 18:

His Excellency is a great and good man. I feel the highest degree of respect for him. I wish him immortal honor. I think myself happy in an opportunity to serve under so good a general... But his Excellency, as you observe, has not had time to make himself acquainted with the genius of this people. They are naturally as brave and spirited as the peasantry of any other country; but you cannot expect veterans, of a raw militia of only a few months's service... The sentiment of honor, the true characteristic of a soldier, has not yet got the better of interest. His Excellency has been taught to believe the people here a superior race of mortals; and finding them of the same temper and dispositions, passions and prejudices, virtues and vices of the common people of other governments, they sink in his esteem. The country round here set no bounds to their demand for hay, wood and teaming. It has given his Excellency a great deal of uneasiness that they... extort... such enormous prices.

Washington's army was pouring out nearly $275,000 a month in unbacked currency for the maintenance of the troops and additional sums for munitions and equipment. Prices were inevitably rising.

The Massachusetts and other enlistments ran out at the end of the year. On Christmas Day, Washington wrote Congress that recruits for the new army were only some 8,500 men—about 40 percent of his authorized strength. This figure was optimistic; a count of January 10 showed that, while his nominal strength was 8,212, only 5,582 men were present and fit for duty. The treasury was almost empty. As Washington wrote Reed on January 4: "It is easier to conceive than to describe the situation of my mind for some time past, and my feelings under our present circumstances. Search the vast volumes of history through, and I much question whether a case similar to ours is to be found; to wit, to maintain a post against the flower of the British troops for six months together, without powder, and at the end of them to have one army disbanded and another to raise within the same distance of a reinforced enemy. It is too much to attempt... For more than two months past, I have scarcely emerged from one difficulty before I have plunged into another."

1776

As America entered upon her most famous year, Montgomery lay dead at Quebec. Arnold was wounded. The Americans had suffered a bloody repulse. On New Year's Day, Lord Dunmore began the shelling and burning of Norfolk, Virginia, nearly obliterating the town. That same day, the commander in chief issued orders to the new army besieging Boston:

> *This day giving commencement to the new Army, which, in every point of View is entirely Continental, The General flatters himself, that a laudable Spirit of emulation will now take place, and pervade the whole of it; without such a Spirit, few Officers have ever arrived to any degree of Reputation, nor did any Army ever become formidable: His Excellency hopes that the Importance of the great Cause we are engaged in, will be deeply impressed upon every Man's mind, and wishes it to be considered, that an Army without Order, Regularity and Discipline, is no better than a Commission'd Mob; Let us therefore, when every thing dear and valuable to Freemen is at stake; when our unnatural Parent is threat'ning us with destruction from every quarter, endeavour by all the Skill and Discipline in our power, to acquire that knowledge, and conduct, which is necessary in War—Our Men are brave and good; Men who, with Pleasure, it is observed, are addicted to fewer Vices than are commonly found in Armies; but it is Subordination and Discipline (the*

*Life and Soul of an Army) which next under Providence, is to make us formidable
to our enemies, honourable in ourselves, and respected in the world.*

THE SIEGE OF BOSTON

Washington's inability to attack the British was most irksome of all. He consulted his council of war on all important questions, usually sending advance written questions to his officers for study. He had often done this in the French and Indian wars, and he continued this policy in obedience to his instructions by Congress. The council's decisions often had to be approved by Congress, which, at times, intervened by sending independent orders. In addition, Washington frequently had to call provincial officials into consultation. This was an inefficient system; some of the indecision attributed to Washington at the time was due to the complex maze erected about him.

Washington held councils in September and October 1775 to decide whether to attack Boston. They voted, each time, that it was too risky. The October meeting, held when the congressional committee was in Cambridge, had raised the question of the destruction of Boston. Not until December 22 did Congress make its determination: "If General Washington and his council of war should be of opinion, that a successful attack may be made on the troops in Boston, he may do it in any manner he may think expedient, notwithstanding the town and property in it be destroyed." John Hancock, one of the richest men of Boston, forwarded the resolve with a note: "May God crown your attempt with success. I most heartily wish it, though individually I may be the greatest sufferer." This resolve did not give the commander in chief, but only his council, the final authority.

Washington was unable to attack, but his fury at the British increased. His letters spoke of the cruelty and barbarity of the enemy. On January 31, referring to the destruction of Norfolk, he told Reed that he hoped this would "unite the whole country in one indissoluble band against a nation which seems to be lost to every sense of virtue, and those feelings which distinguish a civilized people from the most barbarous savages. A few more of such flaming arguments, as were exhibited at Falmouth and Norfolk, added to the sound doctrine and unanswerable reading contained in the pamphlet *Common Sense* will not leave numbers at a loss to decide upon the propriety of a separation." He wrote again on February 10 to Reed:

*With respect to myself I have never entertained an idea of an accommodation, since
I heard of the measures, which were adopted in consequence of the Bunker's Hill*

fight. The king's speech has confirmed the sentiments I entertained upon the news of that affair; and if every man was of my mind, the ministers of Great Britain should know, in a few words, upon what issue the cause should be put. I would not be deceived by artful declarations, nor specious pretenses; nor would I be amused by unmeaning propositions... I would tell them, that we had borne much, that we had long and ardently sought for reconciliation upon honorable terms... that the spirit of freedom beat too high in us to submit to slavery, and that, if nothing else could satisfy a tyrant and his diabolical ministry, we are determined to shake off all connexions with a state so unjust and unnatural. This I would tell them, not under covert, but in words as clear as the sun in its meridian brightness.

Colonel Knox arrived at Framingham on January 25 with his guns. These weapons gave renewed interest to the attack on Boston. With its harbor frozen, Washington presented an urgent plea to his council on February 16 to approve an attack by ice on the city, adding, "a stroke well aimed at this critical juncture might put a final end to the War." His officers voted him down. A disappointed Washington reported two days later to Congress that the vote was "almost unanimous," meaning, probably, that only Washington voted aye. He explained:

The Result... I must suppose to be right although, from a thorough conviction of the necessity of attempting something against the Ministerial Troops, before a Reinforcement should arrive and while we were favour'd with the Ice, I was not only ready, but willing and desirous of making the Assault; under a firm hope, if the Men would have stood by me, of a favourable Issue, notwithstanding the Enemy's advantage of Ground, Artillery, &ca.

Perhaps the Irksomeness of my situation, may have given different Ideas to me, than those which influenced the Gentlemen I consulted, and might have inclin'd me to put more to the hazard than was consistent with prudence. If it had, I am not sensible of it, as I endeavourd to give it all the consideration that a matter of such Importance required.—True it is, and I cannot help acknowledging, that I have many disagreeable Sensations, on Acct. of my Situation; for to have the Eyes of the whole Continent fixed, with anxious expectation of hearing some great event, and to be restrain'd in every Military Operation for want of the necessary means of carrying it on, is not very pleasing, especially, as the means used to conceal my weakness from the Enemy conceals it also from our friends and adds to their Wonder.

As an alternative to a direct attack, the council proposed that Dorchester Heights, commanding Boston and its harbor, be fortified in order to draw the enemy out. Washington wrote Reed that he would follow this plan, though he was still disappointed, "after waiting all the year for this favourable" opportunity, at being told that his plan was "too dangerous!" Now, he said, he would have "to try if the enemy will be so kind to come to us."

In the next few days, Washington formulated a complex plan, involving the placement, as a feint, of guns at points far from Dorchester, planning the kind of fortification that could be erected overnight on the Heights and preparing an amphibious assault on Boston, to be carried out as soon as the British moved to attack Dorchester. This involved an immense secret movement of troops, guns, fortification materials, and boats.

Lieutenant Colonel Rufus Putnam, who was soon thereafter promoted to chief of engineers, devised a prefabricated fort that required little digging into the frozen earth. It consisted of timber frames (gabions) into which were placed tied logs (fascines), hay, and baskets of earth. These could be transported by ox cart from Roxbury and quickly assembled at night. Barrels filled with rocks and earth were added, to be placed in front of the fortification; they could also be an offensive weapon when rolled downhill against attacking troops.

To divert British attention from his plans, Washington ordered the mounting of heavy guns at Lechmere's Point on Philip's farm, opposite Charlestown, and on Cobble Hill to the north. These were on the left of the American lines. Other guns were mounted at Roxbury on the right wing. Four thousand men, under Putnam, were assigned to brigades under Sullivan and Greene, and ordered to prepare an amphibious attack on the British in Boston. All American leaves were cancelled, and militia from nearby areas were summoned. Regimental physicians were ordered to Cambridge to prepare for care of the wounded. Signal flags for a general alarm were established.

On March 2, the Americans began a bombardment of Boston from Lechmere's Point and Cobble Hill. This continued a second night and the British guns replied. On the third night, General John Thomas and a working and armed party of 3,000 men and 360 ox carts, moved onto Dorchester Heights, where they erected the planned fortifications with great gusto. The works were complete on the morning of March 5. General Washington, there with his troops, waited joyfully for action.

GENERAL HOWE FUNKS OUT

As dawn came to Boston, there was tension in the American lines, but little anxiety, since the operation had been carried out exactly as planned. The Americans watched for the British reaction, which was slow in coming.

Admiral Molyneux Shuldham sent at once to General Howe to say he could not keep his ships in the harbor under the guns and that Howe had either to take the fortifications or remove his army to the navy's ships. Howe attempted a bombardment but could not sufficiently elevate his guns. He determined to attack and summoned a force of more than twenty-four hundred men. The Americans heard the general alarm and watched the great movements in the town. The British missed the tide. Late in the afternoon, when rain began, Howe held another council of war, at which most of his officers advised against further action. Howe, who had fought at Breed's Hill and knew, though British honor was at stake, how bloody the assault would be, agreed with his officers. They decided to abandon Boston. That night, around midnight, there arose a storm of near-hurricane proportions that lasted all night. This enabled Howe to announce to his troops that only the intervention of Providence prevented him from dislodging the Americans.

In writing to London on March 21, Howe said that the fortifications erected by the Americans were so strong that they must have required "the employment of at least twelve thousand men." Howe then explained that he had ordered an attack "but the wind unfortunately coming contrary and blowing very hard... the attempt became impracticable." He had therefore decided to leave and thus comply with the king's orders that, when practicable, he sail from Boston.

Howe's reports to London were not precisely truthful, but the British government made them less so by announcing that Howe's troops had embarked for Halifax in good order. The duke of Manchester commented in Parliament that it was a lucky thing that the navy was there to save the British from utter disgrace since it was clear they had been forced out of Boston. Washington had waited in vain for the British to attack. Two days later, on March 7, he expressed his disappointment to Congress:

> It is much to be wished that it had been made. The event I think must have been fortunate, and nothing less than victory and success on our side, as our Officers and men appeared Impatient for the appeal, and to have possessed the most animated Sentiments and determined Spirit... In case the Ministerial Troops had made an Attempt to dislodge our Men from Dorchester Hills, and the number detached upon the occasion, had been so great as to have afforded a probability of a successful attack's being made upon Boston, on a signal given from Roxbury... four thousand men... were to have embarked at the mouth of Cambridge River in two divisions... The first was to land at the Powder House and gain possession of Beacon Hill and Mount Horam. The second at Barton's Point, or a little south of it, and after securing that post, to join the other divisions and force the Enemy's Works and Gates for letting in the Roxbury Troops. Three floating batteries were to have proceeded... and kept up a heavy fire on that part of the

Town where our men were to land... I had reason to hope for a favourable and happy issue.

The evacuation was a difficult task for Howe and Shuldham. There were nearly nine thousand British—including troops, wives, and civilians—to embark, while more than a thousand Tories pleaded to accompany Howe. He permitted them to come, but they took so many possessions that many of the king's stores had to be abandoned. Twelve days were needed to get everyone aboard.

The Boston selectmen appealed to Howe not to destroy the city. He replied that if Washington agreed not to molest the embarkation he would spare the city. The selectmen sent a flag of truce to Washington with this message, but since there was nothing official in it from Howe, he could not reply. Apparently Washington and Howe understood this to be an informal agreement. It was a sad coincidence for the many Irish officers and men among Howe's troops that it was on St. Patrick's Day that the last man embarked and the British set out to sea. On the same day American troops moved into Boston.

March 17 was a Sabbath, and Washington attended church in Cambridge. The Congregational minister took as his text: "The Egyptians said, Let us flee from the face of Israel, for the Lord fighteth for them against the Egyptians."

Washington had last left Boston on March 5, 1756, on the trip occasioned by his annoyance at having to take orders from a former British army captain. Twenty years and thirteen days later he entered the city, according to the posted proclamations, as "His Excellency, George Washington, Captain General and Commander-in-Chief of the Forces of the Thirteen United Colonies," after forcing out an army with five British generals and a Royal Naval force of 150 or more ships. He described the city's condition to John Washington on March 31:

> *The Enemy left all their Works standing in Boston, and on Bunker's Hill, and formidable as they are, the Town has shared a much better Fate than was expected, the damage done to the Houses being nothing equal to report, but the Inhabitants have suffer'd a good deal by being plunder'd by the Soldiery at their departure... King's property [was left] in Boston to the amount... of thirty or £40,000 in Provisions, Stores, &ca. Many Pieces of Cannon, some Mortars, and a number of Shot, Shells... Baggage-Wagons, Artillery Carts... were found destroyed, thrown into the Docks, and drifted upon every shore. In short, Dunbar's destruction of Stores after Genl. Braddock's defeat, which made so much noise, affords but a faint idea of what was to be met with here.*

In the letter, he made one of his rare grumbles about Providence: "That this remarkable Interposition of Providence is for some wise purpose, I have not a doubt: but as the principal design of the Manouvre was to draw the Enemy to an Ingagement under disadvantages... and seemed to be succeeding to my utmost wish... I can scarce forbear lamenting the disappointment."

HONORS

On March 28 Washington was again in the colony's capital to receive the thanks of the province and city. A very Boston account said: "This day, the Thursday lecture, which was established and has been observed from the first settlement of Boston, without interruption until within these few months past, was opened by the Rev. Dr. Eliot."

General Washington attended the lecture and Divine Service and then went to "an elegant dinner... Joy and gratitude sat in every countenance and smiled in every face." The following day, New England reserve further faded when the legislature of Massachusetts expressed its appreciation: "May future peaceful generations, in the enjoyment of that freedom, the exercise of which your sword shall have established, raise the richest and most lasting monuments to the name of Washington." He thanked them for their approval, adding:

> *That the metropolis of your colony is now relieved from the cruel and oppressive invasions of those who were sent to erect the standard of lawless domination, and to trample on the rights of humanity... must give pleasure to every virtuous and sympathetic heart; and its being effected without the blood of our soldiers and fellow-citizens must be ascribed to the interposition of that Providence, which has manifestly appeared in our behalf through the whole of this important struggle...*

> *May that being, who is powerful to save, and in whose hand is the fate of nations, look down with an eye of tender pity and compassion upon the whole of the United Colonies.*

On April 3, Harvard awarded its Doctorate of Laws to "GEORGIUS WASH-INGTON, Armiger, Imperator praeclarus, cujus Scientia et Amor Patriae undique patent; qui propter eximias Virtutes, tam civiles quam militates." However, it reached him too late to find him at Cambridge, for he was off again to the wars.

Byron said that Washington got, from his countrymen, "thanks, and naught else beside," but his warm-hearted nature welcomed them. Washington wrote his brother on March 31 that the Boston addresses showed "a pleasing testimony of their approbation of my conduct, and of their personal regard, which I have found in various other Instances; and which, in retirement, will afford many comfortable reflections." He still hoped that peace and retirement might not be far off.

On March 25 Congress received the news from Boston and, after resolving its thanks to Washington and to the army, ordered a gold medal struck to commemorate the evacuation of the city. Because of war conditions, Washington did not get it until 1786. In forwarding the resolution, John Hancock wrote Washington on April 2: "It gives me the most sensible pleasure to convey to you, by order of Congress, the only tribute which a free people will ever consent to pay, the tribute of thanks and gratitude to our friends and benefactors... As a peculiar greatness of mind induced you to decline any compensation for serving them, except the pleasure of promoting their happiness, they may without your permission bestow upon you the largest share of their affections and esteem."

In a polite reply, Washington expressed his appreciation and, using a phrase of Hancock, said that he had issued the thanks of Congress to his officers and men. "I am happy in having such an opportunity of doing justice to their Merit. They were indeed, at first, 'a band of undisciplined Husbandmen,' but it is (under God) to their bravery and attention to duty, that I am indebted for that success which has procured me the only reward I wish to receive; the affection and esteem of my Countrymen."

TO NEW YORK

Washington concentrated not on honors but on New York, which he assumed would be Britain's next objective. He had ordered General Lee there in January after receiving intelligence of British troop and fleet movements out of Boston. Now that the whole of the enemy forces were out of that city, there were only two ports where they could go—New York or Halifax. For ten days the fleet stayed just outside Boston, in Nantasket Road. Washington had no explanation of this, though his spies reported that repairs were needed on the king's ships before they got under way. His men watched the ships, manned the fortifications, and prepared to repulse any landings. On March 27 the fleet sailed for Halifax. Washington reported its departure to Congress, as well as the fact that he had ordered six regiments, under Sullivan, to march immediately for New York. The rest, except for five regiments left for Boston's defense, would follow shortly. The Massachusetts legislature offered Washington three hundred teams to be added to the British wagons taken at

Boston; these he assigned to Knox to move his artillery and powder. Washington departed Cambridge on April 5. On his way to New York he stopped to call on the governors of Rhode Island and Connecticut and to watch some of his troops leave Connecticut by water. He arrived in New York on April 13; his wife joined him there four days later. On its way to meet him at New York was a British fleet twice the size of the Spanish armada. Admiral Lord Howe commanded this mission with full powers to pardon all offenders and to restore the king's peace.

TWENTY

NEW YORK

1776

ALTHOUGH NEITHER THE king nor his government had expected the rebellion to be so extensive, they moved to mobilize with speed. No expense was spared. British garrisons at home and abroad were stripped. Treaties were negotiated with six German states for nearly thirty thousand troops. The Irish Parliament voted to send four thousand men from that country. Transports were hired and food supplies purchased wherever they could be found. Thousands of men were impressed for the navy from civilian life or the merchant marine. Britain's war expenditures more than doubled from 1775 to 1776. In order to finance the interest on its new debt, the government placed additional taxes on newspapers, deeds, cards, and dice—imposts that Americans had refused to pay in 1765.

In defending the hiring of Germans, Lord North told Parliament this was a quicker and more efficient way of getting troops than any other. Britain, he said, could not stand idly by in the face of an "unprovoked rebellion." He continued: "I believe there is no person in this House who is not firmly persuaded, that the whole united strength of America will not be able to oppose the force which is to be sent out early in the spring. I have the strongest and most confident hopes, that America will submit as soon as she is convinced that Great Britain is determined to act with resolution and vigour."

NEW YORK

London might be aroused but business was going on as usual in New York. The Royal Navy's ships were kept supplied with fresh provisions. British sentries were in cheerful communication with the people and not much was being done about defense. Within six days of his arrival, Washington put a stop to trading with the enemy. On April 17 he wrote to the New York committee on public safety to say that he always wanted to cooperate with civilian bodies but the needs of the country came first. If he took measures that caused pain, he would do so reluctantly, but do it he would. He added:

> That a continuance of the intercourse... between... this Colony and the Enemy, on board the Ships of War, is injurious to the Common Cause, requires no extraordinary abilities to prove... We are to consider ourselves either in a state of peace or War, with Great Britain. If the former, why are our Ports shut up, our Trade destroyed, our property seized, our Towns burnt, and our worthy and valuable Citizens led into captivity and suffering the most cruel hardships? If the latter, my imagination is not fertile enough, to suggest a reason in support of the intercourse.

> ...To tell you, Gentlemen, that the advantages of an intercourse of this kind, are altogether on the side of the Enemy... would be telling what must be obvious to every one... Besides their obtaining supplies of every kind... it also opens a regular Channel of intelligence... It would, Gentlemen, be taking up too much of your time, to use further arguments in proof of the necessity of putting an immediate and Total stop to all future Correspondence with the Enemy. It is my incumbent duty to effect this...

> In effecting the Salutory purposes above mentioned, I could wish for the Concurrence and support of your honorable Body; It will certainly add great weight to the Measures adopted, when the Civil authority Co-operates with the Military.

The committee resolved, two days later, to prohibit sending supplies to the British. Washington added a military proclamation to the same effect. These measures, plus the erection of fortifications, forced the enemy fleet to move thirty miles to Sandy Hook.

DEFENSE

New York's defense problems bore some similarity to those that had faced Howe in Boston. Manhattan was an island connected by a single bridge with the mainland. Boston was a peninsula with a narrow land connection. Brooklyn Heights dominated the city as those of Dorchester did Boston. There the similarity largely ended. New York harbor had many more large and small islands, bays, and sounds. The British could approach from Long Island Sound as well as through the Narrows. Washington had to plan to fight an army and a fleet. The Royal Navy had ships of the line and frigates that were mobile forts. These, with their transports, could move troops rapidly from one point to another under protective firepower. With no naval force of his own, Washington could only divide his small army.

Washington's plan to have General Charles Lee look to the city's defense while he was in Cambridge had been frustrated when Congress ordered Lee to the south. The senior officer at New York, a brigadier, William Alexander, earl of Stirling, took command. He was a collateral descendant of the first earl, a favorite of James I, who, in a fit of generosity, gave him most of eastern Canada and part of Maine. Among his numerous titles was that of Lord Canada. Alexander, with the aid of the duke of Argyll, had successfully established his descent and claim to the earldom by Scottish law. His subsequent efforts to win the approval of the House of Lords, in order to regain his vast ancestral holdings, were blocked in London by powerful interests.

Washington, after taking the command from Stirling, and in the time he could spare from a heavy administrative burden, toured Manhattan, Staten Island, and Brooklyn; the mainland north of the city as far as Tappan Zee on the Hudson; and Long Island Sound up to Mamaroneck. He also looked at Amboy, New Jersey. This was an enormous coastline. Washington ordered street barricades built on lower Manhattan and fortifications at the Battery and in the northwest, at Washington Heights. To prevent the British fleet from sailing up the East River, he added gun emplacements at Governor's Island and at two points in Brooklyn. On the Hudson River, he ordered further fortifications on the Jersey side, at Paulus Hook (now Jersey City) and across from Fort Washington (as it came to be called) at Fort Lee. He also established chevaux-de-frises (wooden barricades with iron points) built on hulks between the two forts on the Hudson and in the channels separating Manhattan from Brooklyn. He ordered further works at King's Bridge leading out of the city to the Bronx, and at points farther north. Every workman who could be hired, as well as most of his troops, were put to building and digging.

A serious problem in regard to defense was the large number of Tories in the city. Some, openly loyal to the king, were known, but others had been secretly recruited as spies or as king's soldiers. In addition, there were many neutrals who were prepared to jump to whichever side proved the stronger. The flame of revolution burned rather low in Manhattan. It was nearly nonexistent on Long Island and Staten Island, or in the Bronx and Westchester.

At Washington's urging, the New York legislature appointed secret committees in May to supervise county subcommittees, empowered to watch or arrest Tories. These committees also channeled intelligence to Washington. Where practicable, Washington preferred to have local governments who knew their people handle the roundup of suspected civilians, leaving the army to deal with military offenders. In emergencies both acted.

One of the first cases involved the mayor of New York and many others, including a member of Washington's bodyguard. The royal governor, William Tryon, after fleeing to the British fleet, sent agents ashore to recruit soldiers for the British army. These were to appear in uniform against the Americans as soon as the British landed. Washington's guard, an Irishman named Thomas Hickey, was convicted by court-martial as a member of the recruiting ring and hanged in view of the American army.

CANADA AND THE SOUTH

Charles Lee, dispatched by Washington to New York to look over its defenses, had arrived there in early February. Congress almost immediately ordered him to the command in Canada. As Adams wrote Lee: "We want you at N. York—We want you at Cambridge—We want you in Virginia—But Canada seems of more importance than any." Rumors then reached Philadelphia that the British would attack in the south. His Canadian orders were countermanded, and he was directed to head a new southern department of the army, stretching from Virginia to Georgia. When Lee went to Virginia, Washington wrote his brother John on March 31, just before leaving Cambridge:

> General Lee, I expect, is with you before this. He is the first Officer in Military knowledge and experience we have in the whole Army. He is zealously attach'd to the Cause, but rather fickle and violent I fear in his temper. However as he possesses an uncommon share of good Sense and Spirit I congratulate my Countrymen on his appointment to that Department.

Lee settled down in the governor's palace in Williamsburg from which Dunmore had been ejected. From this pleasant place, he was ordered south.

The British plan for southern operations had been sent by Lord George Germain to Governor Robert Eden of Maryland. The document, captured by the Americans, revealed that the first landing was to be in North Carolina. The plan went awry when violent storms damaged the vessels bringing troops from Ireland that were to meet additional forces under General Clinton proceeding from Boston. By the time the fleets met, North Carolina had scored a great victory over the Scottish Loyalists at Moore's Creek on February 27. Nearly nine hundred of the enemy were killed, wounded, or captured. This ended any chance for a Loyalist uprising in the province. After hovering awhile off the North Carolina coast, the British decided to attack Charleston.

Lee had gone to Wilmington, North Carolina. Learning that the enemy had departed, he guessed that Charleston would be next and hurried there. South Carolina troops, though not yet continental, were promptly placed under his command by Governor John Rutledge. The British fleet arrived off Charleston about the time Lee got there. Lee's role was largely confined to rather rough treatment of the southern troops and to criticism of their fortifications. He did, however, provide some useful suggestions and encouragement in the fighting. The South Carolinians had constructed their forts well; enemy shells sank softly into the local palmetto wood.

The British forces were routed on June 28. Admiral Sir Peter Parker lost one ship, as well as his breeches when he was wounded in the backside. A number of other ships were badly damaged. There were more than two hundred British casualties as compared with thirty-seven among the Americans. Washington, in his July 21 order to his troops, highly commended Lee and the South Carolinians:

> *The General has great pleasure in communicating to the officers, and soldiers of this Army, the signal success of the American arms under General Lee at South Carolina. The Enemy having attempted to land at the same time that a most furious Cannonade for <u>twelve</u> hours was made upon the Fortifications near Charlestown: both fleet and Army have been repulsed with great loss by a small number of gallant troops just raised. The Enemy have had one hundred and seventy two men killed and wounded... two capital ships much damaged, one Frigate of Twenty-eight Guns entirely lost... The firmness, Courage and bravery of our Troops, has crowned them with immortal Honor. The dying Heroes conjured their Brethren never to abandon the Standard of Liberty, and even those who had lost their Limbs, continued at their posts... This glorious Example... the General hopes will animate every officer, and soldier, to imitate, and even out do them, when the enemy shall make the same attempt upon us.*

When Lee later arrived in Philadelphia, Congress covered him with laurels and also advanced him $30,000 so that he could pay off his debts. From this point on, Lee, raised to an eminence greater than his psychic resources could bear, began the erratic moves that were to destroy his reputation and himself.

The battle of Charleston was the only good news the Americans had after the evacuation of Boston. In Canada, after the death of Montgomery and the failure at Quebec, the situation deteriorated steadily. Canada became a morass into which Congress, alarmed by the reports it received, poured endless troops, supplies, and provisions. In February, Congress resolved to send commissioners there: Benjamin Franklin, Charles Carroll, and Samuel Chase. They were accompanied by John Carroll, a Jesuit priest, who was later to be the first American archbishop. The commissioners did not reach Montreal until the end of April, when they found the situation too desperate to accomplish anything. Franklin, ill from the long journey, had to return before the others.

Washington had issued careful instructions to American troops going to Canada that they were on a mission which was to be as much diplomatic as military. He ordered them to treat the Canadians with the greatest respect and to safeguard absolutely the Canadians' religion and property. His instructions were ignored. The behavior of the twelve hundred or so men who remained in the country after the defeat at Quebec was described by Colonel Moses Hazen, a Massachusetts man living there, in his letter of April 1 to General Schuyler:

> You are not unacquainted with the friendly disposition of the Canadians, when General Montgomery first penetrated into the country; the ready assistance which they gave on all occasions, by men, carriages, or provisions, was most remarkable... His most unfortunate fate, added to other incidents, has caused such a change in their disposition, that we no longer look upon them as friends... The clergy... have been neglected, perhaps in some instances ill-used... The peasantry in general have been ill-used. They have, in some instances, been dragooned with the point of the bayonet to supply wood for the garrison at a lower rate than the current price. For... many articles furnished, certificates have been given, not legible, without signatures... And in a more material point, they have not seen sufficient force in the country to protect them.

Colonel Hazen soon reported to Schuyler that the Canadians were arming against the Americans. He added: "We have brought about by mismanagement, what Governor Charelton himself could never effect." The plan for the conquest of Canada had been Congress' baby. Now that it had failed and the situation was desperate, Congress took further measures without consulting Washington or waiting for the reports of its commissioners. These stripped the commander in chief of a large portion of his best officers and troops, without saving the situation in the north.

In March Congress ordered Brigadier John Thomas, who had brilliantly executed the fortification of Dorchester Heights, to Quebec to command with the rank of major general. This removed one of Washington's best officers. Thomas died of smallpox in June. Subsequently six additional regiments under Brigadier John Sullivan were detached from Washington for Canadian duty. Washington replied no when he was asked if he could spare even more troops.

In June the delegates at Philadelphia ordered Horatio Gates—Washington's adjutant general, on whom he relied for organization and discipline—to proceed to Canada, raising him to major general. When Gates and Schuyler subsequently quarreled over who was in charge, Washington suggested to Congress that he could very well use one of them. He was ignored; by the time Congress got through meddling there were more continental troops engaged on the Quebec expedition than in New York. The commander in chief was left with only the oldest major general in the army and a handful of brigadiers of varying quality.

Early in May General John Burgoyne arrived in Quebec with nearly eight thousand reinforcements. The American army, suffering from smallpox, dysentery, and every kind of shortage, was quickly harried out of the country. According to Gates, American losses there—by death, capture, or desertion—numbered five thousand.

When Arnold's troops left Montreal, they looted the town, thus adding to Canadian enmity. This led to subsequent quarrels between Arnold and Hazen, and between him and Lieutenant Colonel John Brown, who had married Arnold's cousin. In April of the following year Brown published a handbill against Arnold, in which he charged him with many misdeeds. He added: "Money is this man's god, and to get enough of it, he would sacrifice his country."

NERVE CENTER

Although he had been stripped of many of his general officers and troops, Washington resolutely continued to function as the active center of continental military and naval operations. Some indication of their extent is contained in his request of April 23 to Congress for more pay for his aides:

I take the liberty unsolicited by, and unknown to my aid de Camps to inform your Honorable body, that their pay is not, by any means, equal to their trouble and confinement.

*No person wishes to save money to the public more than I do... but there are some
cases where parsimony may be ill placed...*

*I give into no kind of amusements myself, consequently those about me can have
none, but are confined from Morn' 'till Eve hearing, and answering the
applications and Letters of one and another; which will now, I expect, receive a
pretty considerable addition as the business of the Northern and Eastern
departments... must... pass through my hands. If these Gentlemen had the same
relaxation from duty as other Officers have in their common Routine, there would
not be so much in it, but to have the mind always upon the stretch, scarce ever
unbent, and no hours of recreation, makes a material odds; knowing this, and at
the same time, how inadequate the pay is, I can scarce find Inclination to impose
the necessary duties of their Office upon them.*

Congress raised their pay from $33 to $40 per month. By July 25 Washington
was asking for more aides. "The augmentation of my Command, the Increase
of my Correspondence, the Orders to give; the Instructions to draw, cut out
more business than I am able to execute in time, with propriety. The business
of so many different departments centering with me, and by me to be handed
on to Congress for their information, added to the Intercourse I am Obliged
to keep up with the adjacent States and incidental Occurrences, all of which
requiring confidential (and not hack) writers to execute, renders it impossible in the present State of things for my family to discharge the several duties
expected of me with that precision and despatch that I could wish. What will
it be then when we come into a more active Scene, and I am called upon from
twenty different places perhaps at the same Instant?" Congress authorized one
more aide.

Washington's burden can only be understated. He made appeals for militia
to New York, New Jersey, Pennsylvania, and Connecticut, and helped to organize flying camps (mobile forces) in New Jersey. He ordered the Loyalist governor of New Jersey arrested. He was involved in endless problems of discipline
and order among his troops who found New York more exciting than New
England. He saw congressional delegations and asked for more troops and
general officers. The correspondence and instructions to the army in northern
New York and Canada went through his hands. The commander in chief had
to provide boat transportation for the troops ordered north, as well as salt,
powder, tools, and meat for their use. He hired carpenters, boat builders,
painters, and axemen for work on the New York fortifications. Washington was
concerned with shortages of arms, engineers, and working tools such as spades
and shovels. He dispatched whaleboats to patrol New York harbor and to inter-

cept messages and supplies for the Royal Navy. He ordered the building of flat-bottomed boats for troop transport to and from Long Island and New Jersey. He supervised naval operations extending to the Bahamas.

THE BOARD OF WAR AND ORDNANCE

Washington had frequently suggested that Congress appoint a war board with which he could deal directly. The board was established June 12 under the chairmanship of John Adams. His colleagues were Roger Sherman, Benjamin Harrison, James Wilson, and Edward Rutledge. Its membership ranged from New England to South Carolina.

The board having met, its members asked not what they could do for Washington, but how they could impose more paperwork on him. They requested him "as speedily as possible" and "for the more speedy and effectual despatch of military business" to prepare "forthwith" returns of all his troops, being sure that they were fully detailed as to the colonies from which they came, and their time and period of enlistment. Washington was ordered to send these periodically and to conduct "a constant and regular correspondence." This dispatch reached him as the first sails of the British armada came into sight of New York harbor.

The board's next business seems to have been to order three of the five continental regiments stationed at Boston to proceed, not to New York, where they were vitally needed, but northward to Canada. The board gave Washington discretion on ordering the remaining two regiments to New York. On July 6, 1776, the board made a detailed inquiry as to the pay and allowances of drum and fife majors and quartermaster sergeants.

WASHINGTON ASKS FOR CAVALRY

Washington, who had ridden so long as a frontier officer, knew how valuable cavalry could be for reconnaissance and mobile troop support. Though this might seem obvious, a long line of historians has chided him for failing to understand and use cavalry at the August battle of Long Island. The most bitter attack on Washington for negligence was made by Charles Francis Adams, Jr., writing in the twentieth century.

On June 21 Washington requested authority from Charles' great grandfather, John Adams, to enlist a troop of cavalry which, he said, would be "extremely useful... in reconnoitering the Enemy and gaining Intelligence...

and... have it in their power to render many other important benefits." John Adams pigeonholed the request by filing it for later consideration.

On July 22 Washington repeated his request for cavalry authorization, but again he got no answer from Adams. By September, despairing of Congress, he had to turn to temporary Connecticut mounted militia for reconnaissance work. Washington received his authorization to establish a continental cavalry force in December while Adams was on a long holiday.

VIRGINIA VOTES FOR INDEPENDENCE

In the spring of 1776, county meetings were held throughout Virginia for the purpose of advising their delegates at Richmond on whether to vote for a final separation from Great Britain. The results were unanimous. Cumberland County, for example, instructed its representatives "that you solemnly abjure any allegiance for His Britannick majesty and bid him good-night forever." On May 15 the Virginia Convention in turn unanimously asked its congressmen at Philadelphia to vote to forswear all allegiance to the British crown. Washington received this news from his brother John. He replied on May 31:

> *I am very glad to find that the Virginia Convention have passed so noble a vote, and with so much unanimity, things have come to that pass now, as to convince us, that we have nothing more to expect from the justice of G. Britain; also, that she is capable of the most delusive Arts, for I am satisfied that no Commissioners ever were design'd, except Hessians... The Idea was only to deceive... Many Members of Congress... are still feeding themselves on the dainty food of reconciliation...*

> *To form a new Government, requires infinite care, and unbounded attention; for if the foundation is sadly laid the superstructure must be bad, too much time therefore, cannot be bestowed in weighing and digesting matters well... My fear is that you will all get tired and homesick, the consequences of which will be, that you will patch up some sort of Constitution as defective as the present; this should be avoided, every Man should consider, that he is lending his aid to frame a Constitution which is to render Millions happy, or Miserable, and that a matter of such moment cannot be the work of a day.*

Eleven years after he wrote this paragraph, he was elected chairman of the convention called to draft the Constitution of the United States.

CONGRESS VOTES

On June 7, Richard Henry Lee of Virginia—who had entered the House of Burgesses just before Washington and who had, the following year, introduced a bill to end the "iniquitous and disgraceful" slave trade—rose in Congress and offered its most famous resolution:

> *Resolved, That these United Colonies are, and of right ought to be, free and independent States, that they are absolved from all allegiance to the British Crown, and that all political connection between them and the State of Great Britain is, and ought to be totally dissolved.*

When the first vote was taken on July 1, only nine provinces could command a sufficient majority among their delegations in favor of the resolution. South Carolina and Pennsylvania voted no, Delaware was evenly split, and New York lacked authorizing instructions. The next day, with the arrival of a fresh delegate from Delaware, the abstention by two Pennsylvanians, and a reversal by South Carolina, twelve states voted for it. New York subsequently approved. While this was technically unanimous, it was hardly so in spirit. On July 4 Congress approved "A Declaration," as it was called. In it, reliance was firmly placed "on the Protection of Divine Providence." Although the declaration did not so state, Congress had also to rely on George Washington; his one major general, "Old Put" Putnam; and nine thousand troops present and fit for duty in New York. The delegates had reduced Washington's effective force as much as 40 percent for the abortive Canadian expedition, leaving him to face an enemy with six or more times his numerical strength. On July 9 he issued general orders to his troops.

> *The General hopes and trusts, that every officer and man, will endeavour so to live, and act, as becomes a Christian Soldier defending the dearest Rights and Liberties of his country.*

> *The Hon. The Continental Congress, impelled by the dictates of duty, policy and necessity, having been pleased to dissolve the Connection which subsisted between this Country, and Great Britain, and to declare the United Colonies of North America, free and independent STATES: The several brigades are to be drawn up this evening on their respective Parades, at Six OClock, when the declaration of Congress, shewing the grounds and reasons of this measure, is to be read with an audible voice.*

The General hopes this important Event will serve as a fresh incentive to every
officer, and soldier, to act with fidelity and Courage, as knowing that now the peace
and safety of our Country depends (under God) solely on the success of our arms.

That evening a joyful mob, many of them soldiers, clambered over the statue of George III, hitched ropes to it, and pulled away; down it came. George's head was hacked off and rolled along the ground.

The next day, Washington issued a reprimand: "Tho the General doubts not the persons, who pulled down and mutilated the Statue, in the Broadway, last night, were actuated by Zeal in the public cause; yet it has so much the appearance of riot, and want of order, in the Army, that he disapproves the manner, and directs that in future these things shall be avoided by the Soldiery, and left to be executed by proper authority." Revolution or no, its leader wanted law and order.

A SUBSTITUTE

When Rip Van Winkle woke from his twenty-years' sleep through the revolution and beyond and returned to his native village, he found many puzzling changes. On the old tavern sign he recognized "the ruby face of King George, under which he had smoked many a peaceful pipe, but even this was singularly metamorphosed. The red coat was changed for one of blue and buff, a sword was held in the hand instead of a sceptre, the head was decorated with a cocked hat, and underneath was painted in large characters, GENERAL WASHINGTON." Washington Irving thus symbolized the change that was to come to the new nation, though it did not take place immediately. It came the easier because, as Benjamin Rush noted in a letter which was reproduced by a London paper in 1776, every king in Europe, by the side of Washington, would have looked like his valet.

"OUR WORKS ARE MANY, AND THE TROOPS BUT FEW"

In thus appealing to Connecticut for more militia, Washington summed up his situation, but even he had no idea of the size of the opposing force he would face.

On June 25 General Howe arrived in New York from Halifax with three ships. On June 29 Washington reported to Congress that more than 150 ships (though the number was probably somewhat less) had joined Howe. On July

21 Admiral Howe, in his flagship, with another 150 ships, arrived with troops from England. On August 1, Admiral Sir Peter Parker, with 40 ships, and Generals Clinton and Cornwallis hove to off Sandy Hook. On August 8 still another fleet came in. On August 12, 34 more men-of-war and troop transports reported to the Howes. Lord Dunmore, with a small force, also showed up. In September 65 more transports arrived.

Lord Sandwich reported to the king in June that half his naval force of 30,000 had gone to duty in American waters and all but a few small frigates were on the way there. The warships and their transports, many hired in Europe, came from Halifax, Charleston, Glasgow, Emden, Cork, Portsmouth, Spithead, Hamburg, and elsewhere. Altogether around 450 vessels with more than 15,000 sailors and 43,000 troops and marines, all superbly equipped and ready for battle, showed up by September to beat back the rebellion. Included among the officers were no fewer than twenty members of Parliament. On July 7 General Howe described his situation to Lord George Germain in a letter with which Washington would have been in disgusted agreement:

> *I have the satisfaction to inform your Lordship, that there is great reason to expect a numerous body of the inhabitants to join the army from the provinces of New York, the Jerseys, and Connecticut, who in this time of universal apprehension only wait the opportunities to give proofs of their loyalty and zeal for government. This disposition among the people makes me impatient for the arrival of Lord Howe, concluding the powers with which he is furnished will have the best effect at this critical time; but I am still of the opinion, that peace will not be restored in America until the rebel army is defeated.*

Howe quickly disembarked more than nine thousand troops on Staten Island, a Tory stronghold. Tory or not, women were fair game for the British, so long as they were Americans. Francis, Lord Rawdon, a young Irish officer, wrote to his uncle, Lord Huntingdon, on August 5: "The fair nymphs of this isle are in wonderful tribulation, as the fresh meat our men have got here has made them as riotous as satyrs. A girl cannot step into the bushes to pluck a rose without running the most imminent risk of being ravished, and they are so little accustomed to these vigorous methods that they don't bear them with the proper resignation, and of consequence we have the most entertaining courts-martial every day." Lord Howe's secretary, Ambrose Serle, described the fleet's arrival on July 12:

> *We passed Sandy Hook in the afternoon, and about 6 o'clock arrived off the east side of Staten Island. The country on both sides was highly picturesque and*

agreeable. Nothing could exceed the joy that appeared throughout the fleet and army upon our arrival. We were saluted by all the ships of war in the harbour, by the cheers of the sailors all along the ships, and by those of the soldiers on the shore... What added to their pleasure was that this very day about noon the <u>Phoenix</u> of 40 guns and the <u>Rose</u> of 20, with three tenders, forced their passage up the river, in defiance of all their vaunted batteries, and got safe above the town, which will much intercept the provisions of the Rebels.

As soon as we came to anchor, Admiral Shuldham came on board, and soon after Genl Howe... We learnt the deplorable situation of His Majesty's faithful subjects, that they were hunted after and shot at in the woods and swamps, to which they had fled for these four months to avoid the savage fury of the Rebels... and that deserters and others flocked to the King's army continually. We also heard that the Congress have now announced the Colonies to be <u>independent States</u>, with several other articles of intelligence that proclaim the villainy and the madness of these deluded people. Where we anchored was in full view of New York, and of the Rebels' head quarters under Washington, who is now made their generalissimo with full powers.

The forcing of the Hudson was only too true. Washington was furious at his soldiers who gaped at the ships as they passed. His general order the following day said: "The General was sorry to observe yesterday that many of the officers and a number of men instead of attending to their duty at the Beat of the Drum; continued along the banks of the North River, gazing at the ships... A weak curiosity at such a time makes a man look mean and contemptible." Washington dispatched orders to Brigadier James Clinton in the Hudson Highlands to keep a close lookout, since he did not know whether the ships carried troops.

The Howes decided to wait for most of their expected forces to arrive before taking action against the rebels. Many came later than planned. This was of some help to the Americans as the British did not like to fight in the winter. The ship movements up the Hudson were the first and most successful probe of the American defenses. Aside from the alarms they produced in the city and state, their most immediate effect was to force Washington to order the three regiments on their way from Boston to Canada to proceed by land, rather than by water, from Norwich to New York and then to Albany. Washington expressed regret that the men had to march in the summer heat over so long a distance.

The Howes now began their probe of American political defenses. On July 12 a signal came from the British fleet that a messenger would come to the city under a flag of truce. Washington sent Joseph Reed, now back on his staff as adjutant, General Henry Knox, and an aide, Samuel Webb, to meet the officer messenger. The messenger brought with him a letter from Lord Howe addressed to "George Washington, Esq.," which they would not accept because Washington was not addressed officially. Four days later, the British offered another letter for Washington, which added several "et ceteras" after "esquire." This too was refused, and Serle fumed in his diary at the "insolence and vanity" of Washington, "a little paltry Colonel of Militia." On July 17 Lord Howe signalled to ask if Washington would receive his adjutant general. Washington agreed to do so. On July 20 Lieutenant Colonel James Paterson came ashore and called on General Washington. He was excessively polite, addressing Washington as "Your Excellency" with each breath. He assured him that no disrespect had been intended. Colonel Knox described the subsequent talk in a letter of July 22 to his wife:

> He [Paterson] said Lord and General Howe lamented exceedingly that any errors in the transcription should interrupt that frequent intercourse between the two armies which might be necessary in the course of the service. That Lord Howe had come out with great powers. The General said he had heard that Lord Howe had come out with very great powers to pardon, but he had come to the wrong place; the Americans had not offended, therefore they needed no pardon. This confused him.
>
> After a considerable deal of talk about the good disposition of Lord and General Howe, he asked, "Has your Excellency no particular commands with which you would please to honour me to Lord and General Howe?"
>
> "Nothing, sir, but my particular compliments to both." General Washington was very handsomely dressed and made a most elegant appearance. Colonel Paterson appeared awe-struck, as if he was before something supernatural. Indeed I don't wonder at it. He was before a great man indeed.

Colonel Paterson politely refused refreshments, saying that the brothers would be anxious to hear about the interview. Howe had also sent letters to various American officials, including Franklin, whom he called his "worthy friend." Franklin replied on July 20:

> The official despatches to which you refer me, contain nothing more than what we had seen in the act of Parliament, viz., offers of pardon upon submission, which I am sorry to find, as it must give your lordship pain to be sent so far on so hopeless a business. Directing pardons to be offered the colonies, who are the very parties injured, expresses indeed that opinion of our ignorance, baseness, and insensibility,

which your uninformed and proud nation has long been pleased to entertain of us; but it can have no other effect than that of increasing our resentment.

It is impossible that we should think of submission to a government that has with the most wanton barbarity and cruelty burnt our defenceless towns in the midst of winter, excited the savages to massacre our farmers, and our slaves to murder their masters, and is even now bringing foreign mercenaries to deluge our settlements with blood. These atrocious injuries have extinguished every remaining spark of affection for that parent country we once held so dear; but were it possible for us to forget and forgive them, it is not possible for you (I mean the British nation) to forgive the people you have so heavily injured...

I consider this war against us... as both unjust and unwise; and I am persuaded that cool, dispassionate posterity will condemn to infamy those who advised it; and that even success will not save from some degree of dishonor those who voluntarily engaged to conduct it. I know your great motive in coming hither was the hope of being instrumental in a reconciliation; and I believe, when you find that impossible on any terms given you to propose, you will relinquish so odious a command, and return to a more honorable private station.

Franklin's letter was delivered to Lord Howe by Americans who had gone aboard his flagship to discuss the handling of prisoners. Howe commented that he expressed himself very warmly. Franklin's remarks were wasted on the Howes, who were so convinced that the great majority of Americans were loyal to the king that they did not take him too seriously. They were not completely wrong, for less than three weeks before, three states had voted against independence. General Howe's intelligence reports that large groups of citizens in New York and New Jersey were ready to help the British were accurate. Ambrose Serle noted in his August 13 diary entry that many Irish soldiers had already deserted to them from Washington's army.

General Howe had correctly predicted that the British would have to beat the rebel army. However, this attempt could not take place until most of the troops reached New York. When a large fleet arrived on August 12, preparations for attack got under way.

A SKIRMISH ON LONG ISLAND

On August 7, in a further appeal for militia and other help from Governor Trumbull of Connecticut, Washington disclosed that the enemy had 30,000 men ready to attack Long Island and New York. (His intelligence later raised this to 32,000.) He said that much of his army was sick, few levies of new troops had shown up, and he had an enormous extent of ground to defend. He felt that the disgrace to the British arms in the South, plus the fact that the season for fighting was getting short, would force their army and navy to exert every effort against him. He added that he had on hand 10,514 men fit for duty, plus about 3,000 "on command," that is, on detached service. "By this, you will see, we are to oppose an Army of 30,000 experienced Veterans, with about one third the Number of Raw Troops, and these scattered, some 15 miles apart." In his assessment Washington did not mention the enemy's great naval strength. At this point, General Clinton expressed the prevailing British view that the Americans would soon take a drubbing and peace negotiations would quickly follow.

Brigadier John Sullivan returned to New York in early August. He had been dispatched north to take command in Canada and he had then been replaced by General Gates. He left the command in a huff and hurried to Philadelphia to express his resentment and to offer his resignation. Some cooler heads prevailed on him to withdraw it before Congress could act. He was ordered to New York. He had almost no time to assess the situation before going into battle.

On August 12 Washington announced to the army that three of his four brigadiers, Heath, Spencer, and Greene, along with Sullivan, had been made major generals. Shortly thereafter, Greene, who had been in charge of the Brooklyn defense, came down with a serious illness and fever. Washington reported that many of his field officers were also stricken and some regiments had none capable of duty.

Additional reinforcements from Pennsylvania, Massachusetts, and Maryland arrived in New York, as well as some eight thousand Connecticut militia. By the time the British attacked, Washington's paper strength was probably close to nineteen thousand, but many of the additions were farm boys with little or no training.

On August 13 Washington announced to his troops that most of the enemy reinforcements had arrived and they could soon expect battle. He asked them to "be ready for action at a moments call; and when called to it, remember that Liberty, Property, Life and Honor, are all at stake; that upon their Courage and Conduct, rest the hopes of their bleeding and insulted Country... The enemy will endeavour to intimidate by shew and appearance, but remember how they have been repulsed, on various occasions by a few brave Americans; Their Cause is bad; their men are conscious of it, and if opposed with firmness, and coolness, at their first onset, with our advantage of Works, and Knowledge of the Ground, Victory is most assuredly ours."

On August 22 General Howe moved fifteen thousand troops from Staten Island to Gowanus Bay, on Long Island, and landed them without difficulty. On August 25 he sent over five thousand Hessians. On August 27 Lord Howe added two thousand marines. Present on Long Island were Lieutenant Generals Howe, Clinton, Cornwallis, and Percy—four of Britain's top command—plus the experienced German Major General von Heister. In addition, there was Major General James Grant, the officer who had made the foolish attack on Fort Duquesne in 1758 that had cost the lives of many of Washington's Virginians. The four top British officers had suffered humiliation of one sort or another from the Americans. Now they had not only twice the Americans' total strength in Brooklyn alone, but they were a far more effective combat force.

When Howe landed, there were about four thousand Americans in the Brooklyn area. A small Pennsylvania detachment watched the enemy arrive and reported to Washington that there were eight thousand British on the island. This report was so inaccurate that for two or three days Washington groped in the dark, unable to determine whether this was a feint to cover a main landing on Manhattan. He dispatched some eighteen hundred militia to Brooklyn; two-thirds of these were hastily assembled rural volunteers. From time to time, he sent additional troops to Long Island. Their number has been so variously estimated that there seems no possibility of arriving at exactness. The maximum American strength at any point appears to have been more than 10,500, of whom only a third engaged in battle with the 22,000 British troops and marines.

The main American army was stationed on Brooklyn Heights, which commanded, along with guns on Red Hook, Governor's Island, and on lower Manhattan, the entrance to the East River. There was also a series of redoubts and fortifications that extended from Wallabout Bay to a marsh ranging nearly to Gowanus Bay. All the British forces landed south of this area. To reach Brooklyn Heights, they had to pass through, or around, the Heights of Guan, which stretched inland from a point near the bay to central Queens. Along these heights were posted some thirty-five hundred men under Sullivan. They guarded three of the four passes through Guan, but there was only a small mounted patrol at the fourth.

On August 23 Washington went to Long Island to inspect the situation. On August 25 he gave the overall command to his senior general, Israel Putnam, who knew little of military tactics. In his instructions to Putnam, he chided the troops for sporadic and wasteful fire, and asked Putnam to control this. Noting that militia were "most indifferent Troops," he ordered that they be used only in fortified works, leaving the more experienced men for outside

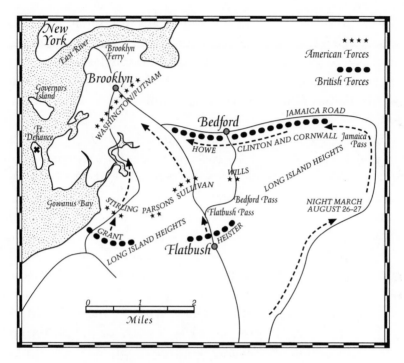

The Battle of Long Island, August 27, 1776

guard and patrol duty. Washington also instructed Putnam to "form a proper line of defence, round your Encampment and Works... The Woods should be secured by Abbatis &c. where Necessary to make the Enemy's approach, as difficult as possible; Traps and ambuscades should be laid for their Parties, if you find they are sent out after Cattle &c." There was little time to do all this.

Guided by Tories, and no doubt by the maps of Captain John Montresor, Howe's aide, who had lived many years in New York, the British under Clinton simply planned to go around Sullivan's forces, through the Jamaica pass.

On August 26 Washington again went to Long Island, where he stayed until the thirtieth. Sullivan remained in command of Guan, with Stirling posted at the Gowanus road along the shore, the only access that did not go through Guan Heights. On the night of the twenty-sixth, Clinton captured a patrol at Jamaica and then, in the early morning of the twenty-seventh, with half the British army, marched through it to outflank the small American detachments under Stirling and Sullivan. Sullivan and his men fought vigorously but were quickly overwhelmed. Some were forced to surrender but many escaped.

On the British left, Stirling with some fifteen hundred men held off seven thousand British troops and marines for an extended period. When Cornwallis came up on his rear with fresh troops, Stirling ordered two-thirds of his men to retreat through the marshes. With the remaining five hundred men, he turned to attack Cornwallis. Five times they fought through until, overwhelmed by a superior force, they surrendered. Many of Stirling's other men got to the American lines, though under the greatest of difficulty.

American battle casualties were about four hundred, mostly killed. The British losses were approximately the same, but perhaps a quarter only were dead. The British took about nine hundred prisoners, including two generals, Sullivan and Stirling.

Ambrose Serle, who was on the flagship, reported that the navy "made a feint of attacking... Many of the principal men of war got under way and sailed backwards and forwards" as a diversion. General Howe received no other naval aid from his brother's ships except for the landing of new supplies of munitions. Washington's planned defense of the East River held throughout the engagement, and his communications with his command post on Manhattan remained secure.

Washington now had nine thousand or more troops—the majority fresh—who held Brooklyn Heights, which could be taken only by direct assault or by siege. Howe and Clinton had had too much experience at Breed's Hill with the cost of an assault, and Howe had refused to attack Washington at Dorchester Heights for the same reason. Had the American defense not kept the British fleet from participating, the Howes might have engaged in a successful combined land and sea operation. Lord Howe could not help, and General Howe therefore moved to his only alternative. To avoid any possible disaster to the British army, he established a siege in the hope of eventual naval support. At some point during this time of decision, Washington received word that a part of the British fleet, unable to get through the East River, had gone around Long Island and was approaching from the north.

The shortage of American supplies, especially tents and food, made their position militarily tenable for only a limited period. The British siege redoubts had moved close to the American lines. On August 29 Washington's council of war approved his move for the return of all troops to Manhattan. That night, John Glover and his regiment of Marblehead fishermen and seamen brought over every available boat from Manhattan. Beginning late in the evening, the entire American army, with practically all its provisions and cannon, was moved quietly across the river. When the British saw the American lines the next morning, they were empty. It was one of the most skillful maneuvers in military history, conducted in the face of an army several times as large and an immense British naval force only a few miles off.

Long Island was a technical defeat for the Americans. Twenty-two thousand troops under famous British generals, including a collateral descendent of Hotspur, had managed to surround thirty-five hundred peasants, two-thirds of whom escaped the trap. Howe reported to London that he had beaten ten thousand Americans and had captured or killed some four thousand of them. The king was so pleased with this amphibious operation that he made Howe a knight of the Bath. It was a victory but not precisely an Agincourt.

Now Washington's army, with its hard core of good troops, was whole again on Manhattan, while the British army was divided. Howe had already been two months in New York harbor but not a single British soldier had set foot on Manhattan.

THE BRITISH WILL NEGOTIATE

When Washington received returns of prisoners from Howe, he was surprised to find more than he had estimated. The discrepancy came in part because additional American militia, operating independently on Long Island under Brigadier Nathaniel Woodhull, were captured after the fight at Brooklyn Heights. According to tradition, when Woodhull surrendered and handed his sword to a Tory officer, he was so badly slashed with it that he died a short time later. Probably because of this, his nephew, Abraham Woodhull, later volunteered to head Washington' s intelligence service during the British occupation of New York.

Stirling and Sullivan, as general officers and in accordance with military custom of the eighteenth century, were entertained by Lord Howe at dinner aboard his flagship. Now that the rebels had apparently been given a crushing blow, Howe returned to his peace mission. Whether Howe misled Sullivan, or Sullivan misunderstood Howe, is not now clear. According to Sullivan, Howe asked him to proceed to Congress to tell them that he could set aside all offensive acts of Parliament and effect a peace settlement. Sullivan agreed to go, and Washington, considering this a political matter, gave him permission to proceed to Philadelphia. John Adams was most annoyed at Sullivan and called him Howe's "decoy duck." He also expressed the opinion that it was too bad that one of the British bullets had not gone through Sullivan's head. After long debate, Congress agreed to send Franklin, Adams, and Rutledge to meet Howe on September 11 at Staten Island.

From his own point of view, Howe was exceedingly tactful in dealing with rebels. He explained that he could talk with them only as individuals, not as congressmen, but this did not matter, since, as soon as peace was declared, Congress would disappear. The irrepressible Adams said Howe could look upon them in any way he wanted but not as British subjects. Howe ruffled a bit at this. The conference got nowhere. At the end Franklin said that Howe seemed still to want unconditional submission and Howe said this was not the case at all. They parted in a polite manner, and the Howes returned to the war. Sullivan did not gain many kudos from this affair but, in the interim, Howe agreed to exchange Stirling and Sullivan. Washington a little later had his two generals back.

GENERAL HOWE ATTACKS NEW YORK

The strain Washington had undergone is noted in his letter to Congress of August 31:

> *Inclination as well as duty, would have induced me to give Congress, the earliest information of my removal of the Troops from Long Island and its dependencies to this City, the night before last; but the extreme fatigue, which myself and family have undergone (as much from the Weather as any thing else) since the incampment of the 27th. rendered me entirely unfit to take a pen in hand. Since Monday, we have scarce any of us been out of the Lines, till our passage across the*

East River was effected yesterday Morning, and for the 48 hours preceeding that; I had hardly been off my horse and I had never closed my Eyes, so that I was quite unfit to write or dictate till this Morning.

Our Retreat was made without any loss of Men or Ammunition and in better order than I expected, for Troops in the Situation ours were, we brought off all our Cannon and Stores, except a few heavy pieces, (which in the condition the Earth was, by a long continued rain) we found upon tryal impracticable... I have inclosed a Copy of the Council of War held previous to the Retreat, to which I beg leave to refer Congress for the reasons...

When Washington was appointed to his command, he received instructions from Congress. His written commission ordered him "punctually to observe and follow such orders and directions... as you shall receive from... Congress... or a Committee of Congress for the purpose appointed." A subsequent directive authorized him "advising with your council of war, to order and dispose of the said army under your command." The first clause, to obey Congress, was clear. The second was less so but Washington understood it to mean that he had to act with the advice and consent of his council. This was not clarified until the spring of 1777, when Congress resolved that Washington was not obliged to follow the recommendation of his general officers. Because he had interpreted the phrase to mean what Congress probably originally intended it to be, he sent them the council's opinion on removing from Long Island. With continued congressional interference in the army and frequent division in his council, he was not fully free in his command until later in the war.

Once both Brooklyn Heights and Governor's Island, from which Washington also withdrew, were in enemy hands, the British fleet was free to operate and New York could be defended for but a short period. The British needed the city for military quarters. Washington posed to Congress the question he had once before asked about Boston: Should the city be destroyed? In the former case, Hancock, a Bostonian, had replied for Congress: Destroy if necessary. This time, Congress, much less brave, hurriedly ordered Washington to leave the city intact.

The remaining question, whether to abandon New York to the enemy, he put to his war council. Washington had informed Congress that he had found the militia so unreliable—they were deserting in such droves—that any hopes he had for the city's defense had almost vanished. The minutes are missing, but the first vote was to defend New York. On September 8 Washington sent Congress the appraisal that he had reached with his council of war. In it, he referred to the "country," meaning the mainland, since American and British forces were still on islands. He wrote:

> *Before the landing of the Enemy on Long Island, the point of attack could not be known… It might be on Long Island, on Bergen or directly on this City, this made it necessary to be prepared for each, and has occasioned an Expence of Labour which now seems useless and is regretted by those who form a Judgement from after Knowledge… By such Works… we have not only delayed… the Campaign, till it is too late to effect any capital Incursion into the Country, but have drawn the Enemy's forces to one point… It is now extremely obvious, from all Intelligence… they mean to enclose us on our Rear, while the Shipping effectually secures the Front, and thus either by cutting off our communication with the Country, oblige us to fight them on their own terms, or surrender at discretion, or by a brilliant Stroke endeavour to cut this Army to pieces…*

> *…On every side there is a Choice of difficulties and every Measure… to be formed with some Apprehension that all our Troops will not do their duty…*

> *History, our own experience, the advice of our ablest friends in Europe… demonstrate, that on our side the War should be defensive. It has even been called a War of costs. That we should on all Occasions avoid a general Action, or put anything to the risque, unless compelled by necessity, into which we ought never to be drawn.*

> *…With these views, and being fully persuaded that it would be presumption to draw out our Young Troops into open ground, against their Superiors both in number and Discipline; I have never spared the Spade and Pick Ax; I confess I have not found that readiness to defend even strong Posts, at all hazards, which is necessary to derive the greatest benefit from them… We are now in a strong Post, but not an impregnable one, nay acknowledged by every man of Judgement to be untenable… To draw the whole Army together in order to arrange the defence proportionate to the extent of Lines and works, would leave the Country open to an Approach and put the fate of this Army and its Stores on the hazard of making a successful defense in the City… On the other hand to abandon a City… on whose Works much Labour has been bestowed, has a tendency to dispirit the Troops and enfeeble our Cause. It has also been considered as the Key to the Northern Country.*

Washington made a point ignored by most subsequent historians that his elaborate defense system for New York, though on a weak troop basis, had thrown away all British plans to take it quickly. Now, he explained, he proposed to move his stores and the large number of sick out of the city, and to concentrate the defense at Fort Washington and King's Bridge to the north and across the river at Fort Lee. His council divided as to holding or abandoning the city. They had worked out a compromise, based on a belief of the majority, that Congress expected them to hold New York at all costs. They therefore planned to leave five thousand men in the city and remove nine thousand. From Washington's letter, it may be guessed that an acrimonious dispute developed among his general officers over leaving any part of the army in the city. Those who were opposed thought the enemy, with naval support, could attack at any point and these five thousand would be lost. Since Congress had resolved the city should not be destroyed and the army could not defend it, the only thing that could be done would be to delay the enemy's taking over. Even this presented problems, since six thousand of the eight thousand Connecticut militia had deserted after the battle on Long Island.

After studying his letter, on September 10 Congress clarified its resolve: Washington was informed that he need hold the city no longer than he thought necessary. However, on October 10, Congress passed a further resolve that Washington, "by every art, and at whatever expense," should prevent the enemy from passing the Hudson River between Fort Washington and Fort Lee on the Jersey side. Washington's war council concluded that Congress had directed that Fort Washington on Manhattan "be retained as long as possible." This congressional backing and filling was to be of serious consequence in a major American disaster.

On September 12 the council resolved that the army should remove from the city to the north, but there were so many supplies and such a shortage of wagons that the task was difficult. The sick alone came to a quarter of the army. They were taken out first. Before the stores could be got out, the enemy struck in force.

KIP'S BAY

On September 15, five British frigates drew up in Kip's Bay, at that time an indentation in Manhattan, running from about the present Thirtieth to Fortieth Streets, and extending in to Second Avenue. The ships began a heavy firing on the rather shallow entrenchments of the militia. In Harlem, Washington, who had expected the enemy to land in the Bronx, heard the sounds. As he wrote Congress the next day:

As soon as I heard the firing, I road with all possible despatch towards the place of landing, when to my great surprize and mortification, I found the Troops that had been posted on the Lines, retreating with the utmost precipitation, and those ordered to support them... flying in every direction... I used every means in my power, to rally and get them into some sort of order, but my attempts were fruitless and ineffectual and on the appearance of a small party of the Enemy... they ran away...

...We are now encamped at... Harlem, where I should hope the Enemy would meet with defeat in case of an Attack, if the generality of our Troops would behave with tolerable resolution, but experience, to my extreme affliction, has convinced me that this is rather to be wished for than expected.

At this point, Washington's factual report merges into legend. The legend is reported by enough persons to bear the mark of fact. Washington rode up, found the troops demoralized, and ordered them behind ditches and walls, and into cornfields. As they continued to flee, he pulled out his riding whip and tried to strike them back into line. No one escaped. Privates, field officers, and even a brigadier got a lashing of whip and tongue. All fled so fast that Washington himself was left, abandoned. His aides forced the stunned general to turn his horse around; he rode back to Harlem to write this comment on his troops.

Putnam was dispatched south to move his troops on the double out of the threatened city. They marched up the West side while the British and the Hessians were pouring in from the East River. The British moved east to Murray Hill to await reinforcements before going north. There Howe called on Mrs. Robert Murray and enjoyed a glass of wine.

HARLEM

Putnam moved rapidly to Harlem, having been forced to abandon many American supplies. Howe also moved north. There was some skirmishing that day but not until next day did the forces meet. The Americans were dug into modest entrenchments on the plateau of Morningside Heights, in the neighborhood of what is now Columbia University. What came close to a major engagement quickly developed.

Washington sent out a small patrol under Colonel Thomas Knowlton to scout the British defenses. They were soon discovered by a body of enemy infantry, who pursued them, blowing an insulting fox-hunting call. Washington added a newly arrived unit of Virginia troops under Major

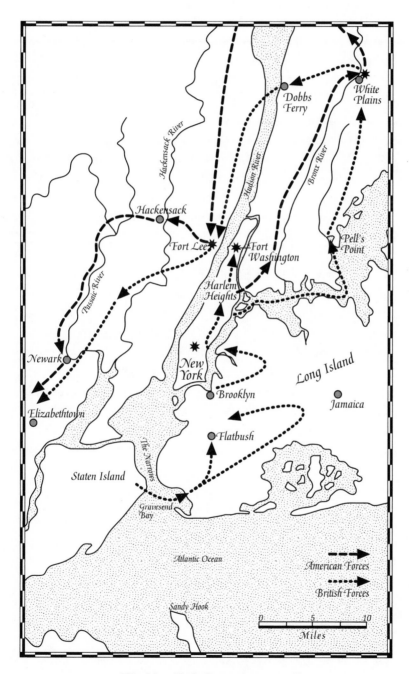

The New York Campaign, 1776

Andrew Leitch to encircle the British, while sending further detachments, as a feint, to hit them in the center as they advanced. Though there were blunders, and the Americans attacked on the flanks instead of the rear, the British were driven back for more than a mile. It was cheering for Americans to see the backs of redcoats and the Black Watch regiment as well as the Hessians. Washington added more troops, singling out particularly the New Englanders who ran at Kip's Bay. They moved forward and when the enemy finally stopped, they fought as vigorously as the rest. For the first time in the war, Americans from New England to Virginia were on the firing line together and successfully. Howe finally had to send in five thousand troops, and Washington, not wanting a general engagement, ordered his men back to the lines. Americans had around sixty casualties, including Knowlton, who was killed, and Leitch, who later died of his wounds. The British lost nearly three hundred men. Howe reported to London that he had engaged three thousand Americans, though the number who drove back his troops was only a few hundred. It disturbed Howe to be beaten in the open for the first time, and he began to be more cautious.

This affair greatly cheered Washington after the disaster at Kip's Bay. His general order of September 17 said: "The Behaviour of Yesterday was such a Contrast to that of some Troops the day before, as must shew what can be done, where Officers and Soldiers will exert themselves.—Once more therefore, the General calls upon officers, and men, to act up to the noble cause in which they are engaged." Washington also referred to "the gallant and brave Colonel Knowlton, who would have been an Honour to any Country."

Many army tents had been lost in New York because Washington had given priority to moving out several thousand sick troops. Many of his men were now without shelter. He directed his colonels "to store their men thicker in their tents, and lend all they can spare, to their suffering fellow-soldiers."

FIRE AT NEW YORK

About midnight on the night of September 20, 1776, a great fire broke out at several places in New York. It seems to have been set by Americans, probably New Englanders, but whether this was done from patriotic motives, or to cover looting, or both, cannot be determined. Washington watched the city burn. He wrote about this on October 6 to Lund Washington:

> *Had I been left to the dictates of my own judgment, New York should have been laid in Ashes before I quitted it; to this end I applied to Congress, but was*

absolutely forbid; that they will have cause to repent the Order, I have not a moments doubt... It will be next to impossible for us to dispossess them of it again as all their Supplies come by Water, whilst ours were derived by Land... By leaving it standing, the Enemy are furnished with warm and comfortable Barracks, in which their whole Force may be concentrated, the place secured by a small garrison (if they chuse it) having their ships round it, and only a narrow Neck of Land to defend, and their principal force left at large to act against us, or to remove to any other place for the purpose of harrassing us. This in my judgment may be set down amg. one of the capitol errors of Congress.

In speaking of New York, I had forgot to mention that Providence, or some good honest Fellow, has done more for us than we were disposed to do for ourselves, as near One fourth of the City is supposed to be consumed. However enough of it remains to answer their purpose.

General Howe had to call in many of his troops, as well as sailors from the ships, to put the fires out. When it was over, more than a quarter of the town had gone up in flames. This was a great disadvantage to the British, who had to house not only thousands of Tories, but the British armed forces, many naval officers, and the British civil authority.

NATHAN HALE

On September 22, Howe's aide, Captain John Montresor, came to Washington's camp under a flag of truce to arrange for the exchanges of Generals Stirling and Sullivan. In passing, he mentioned that they had captured and that day hanged a spy, Captain Nathan Hale of Knowlton's regiment. Hale had volunteered to go to Long Island and get information. Though the documentation is not too clear, he may have been captured while nearing the American lines. Hale was hanged without trial directly after the fire at New York. The British may have thought he was involved in it. Montresor reported, at a later date, that Hale had murmured as he was going to the gallows, "What a pity it is that we can die but once to serve our country," a line from Joseph Addison's *Cato*.

Washington made no written comment on Hale's death, which indicates that he probably had no knowledge of his selection, although he may have encouraged Knowlton to find someone to go to the enemy lines.

WASHINGTON AND THE BOARD OF WAR

Washington again had to face his old problems: shortages of tents and winter clothing in an army of soldiers many of whose enlistments were shortly to expire. His strength of men fit for duty had dwindled to fourteen thousand or fewer. Many of these were short-term militia, ungovernable and without discipline. The board of war continued to function. As the army was going into battle in October, the board requested from Washington a detailed list of all his ordnance. A polite reply was returned to the effect that the guns were being used on the enemy and they were a little difficult to count. Washington went on to suggest that the board might bestir itself to provide more ordnance.

When John Adams rode to Staten Island to see Howe, he noticed on the way many soldiers loitering and hanging around taverns. This offended him. He induced Congress to pass a resolution that "the commander in chief... be directed... that the troops may, every day, be called together, and trained in arms... and inured to the most exemplary discipline." On its receipt, Washington, on September 24, sat up late in order to write a letter to Congress, giving them the facts:

From the hours allotted to Sleep, I will borrow a few Moments to convey my thoughts on sundry matters to Congress...

It is in vain to expect, that any... part of this Army will again engage in the Service on the encouragement offered by Congress... As the War must be carried on systematically, and to do it, you must have good Officers, there are, in my Judgment, no other possible means to obtain them but by establishing your Army upon a permanent footing; and giving your Officers good pay... They ought to have such allowances as will enable them to live like, and support the Characters of Gentlemen; and not be driven by a scanty pittance to the low, and dirty arts which many of them practice, to filch the Public of more than the difference of pay would amount to... Besides, something is due to the Man who puts his life in his hands...

With respect to the Men, nothing but a good bounty can obtain them upon a permanent establishment; and for no shorter time than the continuance of the War, ought they to be engaged... If this encouragement is given to the Men, and such Pay allowed the Officers as will induce Gentlemen of Character... to engage... We should in a little time have an Army able to cope with any that can be opposed to it...

To place any dependence upon Militia, is, assuredly, resting upon a broken staff. Men just dragged from the tender Scenes of domestick life; unaccustomed to the din of Arms; totally unacquainted with every kind of Military skill... when opposed to

Troops regularly train'd, disciplined and appointed... makes them timid and ready to fly from their own shadows... To bring Men to a proper degree of Subordination is not the work of a day, a Month or even a year...

The Jealousies of a Standing Army, and the evils to be apprehended from one, are remote... but the consequence of wanting one... is certain and inevitable Ruin.

John Adams did, at times, appear rather foolish. Aside from asking Washington to discipline troops in daily battle, he suggested the officers take time to study military history and science. They ought to be able, like Sallust, to write great reports where "You see the combatants, You feel the ardor of battle. You see the blood of the slain, and you hear the wounded sigh and moan."

Washington's long letter aroused Congress, which began to face the issues for the first time. Adams said it was a lot easier to get action after a couple of defeats than it had been before. Congress authorized a permanent army of eighty-eight regiments, raised the pay of officers, gave bonuses and clothing to enlisted men, and otherwise attempted to introduce major reforms. Unfortunately this was paper legislation for a paper army, backed by paper money, and it did not materially help Washington for some time to come. Having got these measures through, Adams then took a long vacation from his labors and left Congress on October 13. Jefferson had already resigned, leaving the implementation of the Declaration of Independence to others.

Washington did not complain of one aspect of his command, that he had to be chief of staff of the American army, as well as a field commander, without ever having a day of rest. The generals with the best reputations, though they were not necessarily the best officers—Gates, Schuyler, and Lee—were elsewhere, while Sullivan and Stirling were not released from captivity until October. Washington's devoted associates recognized this problem. Colonel John Haslet of Delaware wrote on September 4: "The General I revere, his Character... Patience and Fortitude will be had in Everlasting Remembrance, but the Vast Burthen appears to be too much his own... w'd to Heaven Genl Lee were here is the Language of officers and men." General Knox wrote his brother on September 23: "The general is as worthy a man as breathes, but he cannot do everything nor be everywhere. He wants good assistants. There is a radical evil in our army—the lack of officers."

Another appraisal of Washington's command was made on September 25 by General Howe in a report to Lord George Germain: "The enemy is too strongly posted to be attacked in front, and innumerable difficulties are in our way of turning him on either side... [I have] not the smallest prospect of finishing the combat this campaign." Howe requested further recruits from

Europe, more seamen to manage his boats, and an additional ten ships of the line. Since king and cabinet had scraped the bottom of the military, naval, and money chests in order to provide a knockout blow to the rebellion, this was rather poor thanks from Howe. Although the British commander had received two setbacks, he could still count on further reinforcements, which were already on their way. On October 12 more British and Hessian troops arrived, bringing the grand total of all ranks of enemy soldiers, sailors, and marines who crowded New York and its harbor to nearly seventy thousand. This contrasts with the approximately thirty thousand men in Philip II's Armada. George III wrote to Lord North on November 4: "Nothing can have been better planned nor with more alacrity executed than the taking of the city of New York and I trust the Rebel army will soon be dispersed." The rebel army was, in fact, soon dispersed, but not for long.

TWENTY-ONE

HARLEM TO MORRISTOWN

1776–1777

T HE DAY AFTER Howe reported to Germain that the American defenses were too strong to attack, Washington wrote to Brigadier Hugh Mercer, head of the flying camps in New Jersey: "If the Troops at this Post, can be prevailed upon to defend it, as they should do, it must cost General Howe a great many Men to carry it, if he succeeds at all. If this should happen to be *his* Opinion there is scarce a doubt but that he will turn his thoughts another way, as inactivity is not to be expected from him."

Washington indicated that Howe might move to New Jersey and Philadelphia or even attack farther south. He asked Mercer to get all the intelligence he could and to keep a close watch from the coast on all ship and troop movements. He added: "In doing this Money may be required, and do not spare it." While waiting to see what Howe would do, Washington began to plan a counterattack on Long Island, where the enemy was getting food supplies and many recruits for its army. When Howe landed in the Bronx, Washington abandoned this scheme.

Washington urged Congress to give greater attention to his need for troops. He said that the enemy now offered a bounty of ten pounds to each American recruit and he was afraid that Howe might be more successful in getting enlistments than he was. On October 4, he pointed out to its president that, while Congress had authorized a larger army, there was a difference between voting men and raising them. "Give me leave to say, Sir, I say it with due deference and respect... that your Affairs are in a more unpromising way than you seem to apprehend." He pointed out that he was likely to lose his most valuable officers for lack of pay and that letting states appoint officers, subject to ratification by Congress, brought him men who, too often, owed their appointment to politics, or to their ability to recruit, rather than merit. In congratulating Patrick Henry on October 5 for his election to the governorship of Virginia, Washington gave him lengthy advice on choosing Virginia officers for continental regiments. He said that officers needed character, honor, and martial spirit, and should have a good reputation that they would not want to lose. In his letter, Washington referred to Virginia as "your Colony," an indication of his newly national sentiment. Independence was so recent that he forgot to call it a state.

Jonathan Trumbull, governor of Connecticut, approached the question with his usual good sense. He asked if Washington could get his generals to supply a merit rating of Connecticut officers, which would then be used in determining promotions. In forwarding these to Trumbull, Washington expressed his gratitude for so novel a scheme, which put merit ahead of politics. He added that he was pleased that the governor's son, Joseph Trumbull, had been given particular praise. The general subsequently suggested to Massachusetts and Rhode Island that they adopt a similar plan.

On October 5 Washington wrote to his brother Samuel, who said that he had read in the gazettes of all the militia coming to his camp: "The pompous Acct. of the Marches, and Counter Marches of the Militia, tho' true so far as relates to the Expence, is false with respect to the Service, for you could neither get them to stay in Camp or fight when they were there, in short, it may truely be said they were eternally coming and going without rendering the least Earthly Service, altho' the expence of them surpasses all description." He added that he had heard from others that Howe's troops "were scarce a mouthful for us," which was hardly true.

By the early part of October, the first of a long line of French volunteers—some men of character, others soldiers of fortune—had begun to arrive in camp. Washington wrote Congress that he did not know what to do with them. Officer appointments were made by the states and not by him. He asked advice on a problem that later became most serious.

FROG'S NECK TO WHITE PLAINS

On October 12, Howe finally attempted the mainland, landing at Frog's Neck (now Throggs Neck). Washington reported to Congress that this was effected

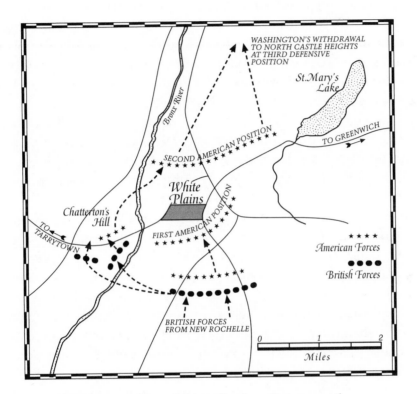

Battle of White Plains, October 28–29, 1776

in order to cut off American communications at King's Bridge. He added that the area, with many stone walls, was strongly defensible, so that Howe's army and artillery could advance only on the main road. He assured Congress his men posted there were in good spirits.

Howe, with 10,000 men, had not, as he expected, landed on the mainland itself. In effect, Frog's Neck was an island, isolated by a brook and marshes. The Americans, under Colonel Edward Hand, had removed the planking from its only bridge connection and proceeded, with 225 men, to hold off the whole British army. Additional American reinforcements came up and Howe and Cornwallis were held for six days in this ridiculous position.

At this point, General Lee was on his way back from Philadelphia. On October 12 he wrote from Amboy to Congress to warn them that the British would not attack Washington's army; instead they would probably move into New Jersey to take Philadelphia. He told Congress to start raising men immediately for defense of the city. On October 12 Lee reached New York. He was assigned to command north of King's Bridge, which Washington expected to be a focal point for the British attack.

On October 9 two enemy ships of the line and a frigate sailed up the Hudson, past Forts Washington and Lee, going easily through the secret channel within the chevaux-de-frises. Tory spies may have given the British sufficient information to make a move that greatly annoyed Washington. Two days later Washington received the directive of Congress that ordered him "by every art, and whatever expense, to obstruct effectually the navigation of the river, at the two forts on the Hudson." His war council of October 16 voted that, in view of this directive, Fort Washington should be retained as long as possible. At the same time, the council voted against holding Harlem because the troops might be cut off by the British. The army, leaving a garrison of about twelve hundred men at Fort Washington, moved north. A further garrison of three thousand men was ordered across the river to New Jersey. Forts Lee and Washington were placed under the command of General Greene, who had a further source of reserves in New Jersey's flying camps.

On October 18 the British moved from Frog's Neck to Pell's Point, south of New Rochelle. They were held there temporarily by 750 Americans under the command of Colonel John Glover, who subsequently received high praise from Washington. By October 21 the American commander in chief was in Westchester and on October 23 the main American army was heading towards White Plains in a move to outflank Howe. Four days later, the enemy was on the way there.

By then the Americans were placed along a line of low hills, south of the village, with their right on Chatterton's Hill. As the British moved towards that point, Washington increased the force to 1,500 men. Howe advanced 4,000 British and Hessians who easily stormed the hill. Though called the battle of White Plains, it was no more than a skirmish, in which each side suffered about 250 casualties.

After this, Washington pulled the Americans back to a stronger and higher position on Northcastle Heights. Howe's troops, now numbering some twenty thousand men, waited for several days, probing the American defenses. On November 2 William Demont, a lieutenant and adjutant of a Pennsylvania regiment, escaped from Fort Washington, carrying with him to the enemy a plan of the fort, an estimate of the strength of the garrison, and, presumably, a list of the valuable stores located there. On November 4, Howe's army began to withdraw from White Plains towards Dobbs Ferry and Manhattan. Howe made preparations for an assault on Fort Washington and then for a crossing to New Jersey, while Washington waited in Westchester.

FORT WASHINGTON FALLS

Washington had left Greene in charge of the key points on the Hudson when he moved north on October 16. He now had to make a number of decisions in the light of Howe's unexpected retreat. Washington was certain that Howe would move on Fort Washington, but he had to guess whether Howe would also move north on the Hudson or cut into New Jersey. He decided to leave General Lee with half the army at White Plains and to move General Heath with four thousand men farther north to Peekskill. On November 7 Washington sent an urgent warning to Greene to watch for an attack on Fort Washington and for a possible move into Jersey. On November 8 he followed with a further letter:

> *The late passage of the 3 Vessels up the North River... is so plain a Proof of the Inefficacy of the Obstructions we have thrown into it, that I cannot but think, it will fully Justify a Change in the disposition which has been made. If we cannot prevent Vessels passing up, and the Enemy are possessed of the surrounding Country, what valuable purpose can it answer to attempt to hold a Post from which the expected Benefit cannot be had; I am therefore inclined to think it will not be prudent to hazard the men and Stores at Mount Washington, but as you are on the Spot, leave it to you to give such Orders as to evacuating Mount Washington as you Judge best... The best Accounts obtained from the Enemy, assure a considerable Movement among their Boats last Evening... From various sources of Intelligence, they must design a Penetration into Jersey and fall down upon your Post. You will*

therefore immediately have all the Stores &c removed, which you do not deem necessary for your defence.

Greene replied the next day from Fort Lee:

The passing of the ships up the river is, to be sure, a full proof of the insufficiency of the obstructions to stop the ships from going up; but that garrison employs a double the number of men to invest it, than we have to occupy it. They must keep troops at Kingsbridge to prevent a communication with the country, and they dare not leave a very small number for fear our people should attack them. Upon the whole, I cannot help thinking that the garrison is of advantage; and I cannot conceive it to be in any great danger. The men can be brought off at any time, but the stores may not so easily be removed. Yet I think they can be got off in spite of them, if matters grow desperate. This post is of no importance, except in conjunction with Mount Washington. I was over there last evening. The enemy seems to be disposing matters to besiege the place; but Colonel Magaw thinks it will take them till December expires before they can carry it. If the enemy do not find it an object of importance, they will not trouble themselves about it; if they do, it is a full proof that they feel an injury from our possessing it. Our giving it up will open a free communication with the country by way of Kingsbridge.

On November 10 Washington wrote Lee that, in view of the enemy's probable move to New Jersey, he would go there with a small body of troops. The command of the army near White Plains devolved upon Lee, who was warned to be on guard, since any British moves across the Hudson might be a feint. If they crossed in force, Lee was to join him "with all possible despatch." The next day Washington and Heath examined the passes and terrain of the Hudson Highlands. He was instructed to remain there with his troops, to guard the area and its three forts, but to be ready to aid Lee, should he be attacked.

Late in the evening of November 13, Washington reached Hackensack near Fort Lee. There he consulted with Greene who, repeating his firm conviction that Fort Washington could be held, indicated that he had not removed the supplies but had strengthened the garrison. He referred to the order of Congress to hold these guardians of the Hudson, Forts Lee and Washington, at almost any cost. Putnam, in charge of the Manhattan fort's engineering, supported Greene. Colonel Magaw, in command at Fort Washington, had already indicated his certainty that the fort could hold until December. To order it abandoned at the last minute, Washington would have had to overrule the senior officers who had been on the spot, as well as disobey Congress' directives. Even so he hesitated but it was soon too late for decision.

On November 15, the day Howe demanded that the garrison surrender, Washington set out across the Hudson. On the way he met Generals Putnam and Greene, who informed him that the troops were "in high Spirits and would make a good Defence." The next day Washington, Greene, Mercer, and Putnam crossed the river but battle had begun and they returned to the Jersey shore. Howe sent 8,000 troops smashing in, with a full knowledge of the defense system. While the fort was under attack, Washington sent a messenger to tell the defenders that if they could hold till dark, he would try to bring them all out. By this time the outer works had fallen and the messenger was nearly captured. Shortly afterwards the fort surrendered. The troops on the outside had fought bravely, but inside many of the militia panicked in the crowded edifice. Magaw had to surrender in order to avoid their complete slaughter by British artillery. The British lost 450 men, killed and wounded, and the Americans around 150. The British captured 2,800 rebels, one of the most serious losses of the war. These, with the prisoners taken on Long Island, added up to more than 4,000 in enemy hands. They were confined in close ship's quarters or crowded prisons and brutally mistreated; many died. Washington protested vigorously to Howe on his lack of humanity. Three years later Washington wrote that his anguish at the loss of the fort was made far more "poignant" by the sufferings of the prisoners.

In addition the Americans lost much of their ordnance and munitions and such scarce supplies as tents and flour. Demont, English born, received sixty pounds for his treason but it took him seventeen years to collect from the British government. Greene, the day after the loss of the fort, expressed his feeling to Knox: "I was afraid of the fort. The redoubt that you and I advised was not done... This is a most terrible event; its consequences are justly to be dreaded." On November 19 Washington finished a letter to his brother John, which he had begun thirteen days previously at White Plains: "This is a most unfortunate affair, and has given me great Mortification... I had given it... as my opinion to Genl Greene, under whose care it was, that it would be best to evacuate the place; but as the order was discretionary, and his opinion differed from mine, it unhappily was delayed too long, to my great grief, as I think Genl Howe, considering his army and ours, would have had but a poor tale to have told without it and would have found it difficult... to have reconciled the People of England to the Conquest of a few pitiful Islands, none of which were defensible, considering the great number of their Ships."

There was little time to mourn. On the night of November 19, Lord Cornwallis and a British force of four thousand crossed the Hudson and raced to Fort Lee to capture Washington and Greene. An American warned Greene just in time and he informed Washington. Before departing in great haste,

Washington wrote to Congress asking them to get clothing and blankets to the prisoners at New York.

TREASON ON THE STAFF

Although Washington, Greene, and Putnam were chagrined at the quick fall of the fort, they had no hesitation about going on fighting. The new adjutant general, Colonel Joseph Reed, however, was totally shaken by the event; even a month later he was writing to Washington of the desperate plight of the army, and his worry about his wife and children and the poverty and ruin that he faced. Reed proceeded, almost immediately after the fort fell, to acts of treason. Treason is defined in the Oxford dictionary as "betrayal of... trust; breach of faith; treachery." Had he succeeded, the war might have quickly ended with the capture of Washington.

Some parts of the action and correspondence are missing, but enough is available to reconstruct events. On November 16 Washington sent to Lee a factual account of the surrender of Fort Washington. At the same time, Reed wrote to Lee complaining about Greene's influence on Washington, which had led to the loss of the fort. Lee, after hearing from Reed, wrote to Washington on the nineteenth: "Oh, General, why would you be over-persuaded by men of inferior judgement to your own? It was a cursed affair." This phrase about men of inferior judgement very probably came from Reed, who, in a later letter of December 22 to Washington, used an almost identical sentiment urging him not to be subject "to the Influence of Opinions of Men in every Respect your Inferiors."

When the British landed in New Jersey, Washington asked his aide, William Grayson, to send Lee a quick order. Grayson much too politely informed Lee that Washington now thought it "advisable" for Lee to cross the Hudson.

On November 21 Washington asked Reed to draft further orders to Lee. Reed sent them to Lee that day. The first two paragraphs, with the probable exceptions of the first sentence and the last two sentences, are in Washington's unmistakable style. The two paragraphs, with the orders to Lee, were entirely rewritten by Reed. In the file copy at the Library of Congress, they are on the inside of a four-page folded sheet:

> *With respect to your Situation, I am very much at a Loss what now to determine, there is such a Change of Circumstances since the date of your Letter, as seems to call for a Change of Measures. Your Post undoubtedly will answer some important Purposes; but whether so many or so great as your Removal... is well worthy of*

*Consideration... Upon the whole therefore, I am of Opinion and the Gentlemen about
me concur in it, that the publick Interest requires your coming over to this side...*

*My reasons for this measure and which I think must have weight with you, are,
that the Enemy are evidently changing the Seat of War to this side of the North
River... It is therefore of the utmost Importance, that at least an Appearance of
Force should be made, to keep this Province in the Connection with the others, if
that should not continue, it is much to be feared, that its Influence on
Pennsylvania would be very considerable... Unless therefore some new event should
occur... I would have you move over by the easiest and best Passage... Perhaps it
may not be agreeable to the troops [but it] will at least have an effect to discourage
the desponding here.*

With this letter, Reed enclosed another of his own to Lee. The first sentence
indicated that the "order" had been written by Reed rather than Washington,
but this may easily have been overlooked by Lee, in reading what his military
secretary had to say: "The letter you will receive with this contains my
sentiments with respect to your military situation. But besides this I have some
additional reasons for most earnestly wishing to have you where the principal
scene of action is laid. I do not mean to flatter, nor praise you at the expense
of any other, but I confess I do think it is entirely owing to you that this army
and the liberties of America, so far as they are dependent on it, are not totally
cut off. You have decision, a quality often wanting in minds otherwise
valuable, and I ascribe to this an escape from York island—from Kingsbridge
and the Plains—and I have no doubt had you been here the garrison at
Mount Washington would now have composed a part of this army... I ardently
wish to see you removed from a place where there will be little call for your
judgement and experience to the place where they are likely to be so necessary... Every gentleman of the family [Washington's staff]... have a confidence
in you."

Reed continued: "Col. Cadwalader... has been liberated from New York
without any parole. He informs us that the enemy... hold us very cheap in consequence of the late affair at Mount Washington where both the plan of
defense and execution were contemptible... General Washington's own judgment, seconded by representations from us, would I believe have saved the
men and their arms, but unluckily General Greene's judgment was contrary;
this kept the general's mind in a state of suspense until the stroke was struck.
Oh! General—an indecisive mind is one of the greatest misfortunes that can
befall an army—how often have I lamented it this campaign. All circumstances considered we are in a very awful and alarming state... As soon as the

season will admit I think yourself and some others should go to Congress and form the plan of the new army."

As the army left Hackensack, Reed scribbled a hasty note to Lee: "We are flying before the British." By his actions, Reed warned Lee, who had already formed such an idea in his mind, that Washington was weak, timid, and indecisive. When Lee first saw Grayson's note, he told Heath that it almost seemed an order to move. He demanded that Heath, as the officer nearest the ferrying point, send two thousand of his men to Washington. Heath properly refused; he informed Lee that Washington had ordered him to keep his men there. Furious, Lee asked Heath if he thought he held an independent command. Washington, he said, was far away, and Greene was the officer to be obeyed. "By your mode of reasoning, the General's injunctions are so binding that not a tittle must be broke though for the salvation of the General and his army."

The harassed Heath did his duty. He replied with the sharp implication that Lee himself was disobeying orders: "Be my mode of reasoning as it may, I conceive it my duty to obey instructions... The least recommendation from him, to march my division or any part of them, over the river, should have been instantly obeyed, without waiting for a positive order."

On November 23 Lee wrote to James Bowdoin, president of the Massachusetts council, to say that he had always assumed, even before the fall of Fort Washington, that there should be separate American armies, each "on its own bottom," on the west and east sides of the Hudson River. Now, he said, it was "absolute insanity" for him to move across the river. The next day, having received the Washington order drafted by Reed, he sent extracts of it to Bowdoin, saying he could make his own comment on it. Lee added that "the resolves of the Congress must no longer too nicely weigh with us... There are times when we must commit treason against the State, for the salvation of the State." He asked for reinforcements for "his" army.

While all this was going on, Reed had become so concerned for the safety of his wife and children that Washington sent him to Burlington on November 23 to look after them, and also to appeal to the governor of New Jersey for assistance. Totally unaware of Reed's treachery, Washington opened a letter from Lee to Reed, dated November 21, which said that Washington had recommended his moving across the river but that his troops would be too late "to answer any purpose... I have therefore ordered General Heath who is close to the only ferry which can be passed to detach two thousand men, to apprize His Excellency, and wait his further orders, which I flatter myself will answer better what I conceive to be the spirit of the orders... Withdrawing our troops from hence would be attended with some very serious consequences which at present would be too tedious to mention."

Washington at once wrote sharply to Lee: "From your letter to Colo. Reed, you seem to have mistaken my views entirely, in ordering Troops from Genl Heath... Colo. Reed's second Letter, will have sufficiently explained my intention... that it was your division I want to have over." In response to a further equivocal letter from Lee, Washington wrote him on the twenty-seventh: "My former Letters were so full and explicit, as to the Necessity of your Marching, as early as possible, that it is unnecessary to add more on that Head. I confess I expected you would have been sooner in motion." Washington also commended Heath for obeying the instructions of the commander in chief.

Lee at last reluctantly crossed the Hudson on December 2, after engaging in a quarrel with Heath. He slowly ambled into New Jersey while Washington and Congress sent him impatient letters. About November 27, Washington, who had retreated to Brunswick, opened a letter to Reed from Lee, which said: "I received your most obliging, flattering letter–lament with you that fatal indecision of mind which in war is a much greater disqualification than a stupidity or even want of personal courage–accident may put a decisive blunderer in the right–but eternal defeat and miscarriage must attend the man of the best parts if curs'd with indecision." On November 30 Washington forwarded the letter to Reed, who by then had resigned as adjutant general, with an accompanying note:

> *The enclosed was put into my hands by an Express from the White Plains. Having no Idea of its being a Private Letter, much less suspecting. This, as it is the truth, must be my excuse for seeing the contents of a Letter, which neither inclination or intention would have prompted me to.*
>
> *I thank you for the trouble and fatigue you have undergone in your Journey to Burlington... My best to Mrs. Reed.*

It is well that the governor of New Jersey, William Livingston, wrote Washington a letter on November 27, which arrived shortly after the letter from Lee to Reed: "I can easily form some Idea of the Difficulties under which you labour and particularly of one for which the public can make no allowances because your Prudence and fidelity to the Cause will not suffer you to reveal it to the public, an instance of Magnanimity superior perhaps to any that can be Shewn in Battle. But depend upon it, my dear Sir, the impartial world will do you ample Justice before Long. May God support you under the Fatigue both of Body and Mind to which you must be constantly exposed."

ACTION ELSEWHERE

While Washington was fighting in the New York area, there were important developments elsewhere. In March Congress sent Silas Deane to Paris as the first American agent. With the help of the French government, Beaumarchais and Deane quickly set up a secret dummy trading corporation to supply arms and ammunition to Washington's troops. In October 1776, Franklin left America for France. In early 1777 the American army began to receive some foreign supplies as well as a number of adventurers, to whom Deane promised commissions as general and field officers in the American army. Washington needed officers but not the type who, too often, came.

Meanwhile Britain had built up its forces in Canada to thirteen thousand troops under the command of General Guy Carleton, aided by John Burgoyne. In September British troops moved southward into the United States. This action indicated the strategy being developed at Whitehall to cut the United States in half in 1777 through joint operations with Howe in New York. The British movements were delayed by the need to build vessels to bring troops and guns southward on Lake Champlain. Benedict Arnold, who had some merchant marine experience, moved urgently to build a small defensive fleet. In October he met the British in battle and was quickly swept from the lake. He and his men escaped to Fort Ticonderoga. However, Arnold had delayed the British sufficiently for Carleton to feel it was too late in the season to attack the fort. The British retired to winter quarters in Canada. An encouraged Congress permitted Washington to order Gates, with six regiments, to march to the defense of Philadelphia.

Washington's rapid retreat across New Jersey convinced Howe that he could now release troops for an additional offensive. At the end of November he ordered General Clinton and Admiral Peter Parker, the mismated pair who blamed each other for the failure at Charleston, to take Newport. This was easily done in December. Newport provided an additional base for Lord Howe's fleet and a possible staging area for operations against New England when the British again moved south from Canada in their next offensive.

HACKENSACK TO MORRISVILLE

Washington had somewhat more than four thousand men under his command when he left Hackensack on November 21, but the number dwindled rapidly during his retreat across New Jersey. Lord Rawdon, who saw the mess left by the retreating Americans at Fort Lee, commented that "their army is all broken to pieces." By November 29, Washington was at Brunswick. Many enlistments were to expire at the end of the month; other enlistees had deserted before their time was up. Washington, in writing to Congress, now referred to his forces as a "handful." On December 1 he again appealed to Lee to hurry, or he might be too late. On the same day he appended a post-mark to his letter to Congress: "½ after 1 o'clock P.M. The Enemy are fast advancing, some of 'em are now in sight. All the Men of the Jersey flying Camp under Gen Herd being applied to, have refused to continue longer in service."

He immediately appealed to Governor Livingston for whatever men he could send and asked him to secure every boat on the Delaware for his troops. The news that Cornwallis was moving fast threw Philadelphia into a panic; all roads west were crowded with people and wagons. That evening Washington informed Congress that he could not hold New Jersey and would cross the Delaware. On December 2 he was at Princeton, the next day at Trenton. He reported to Congress that he had not had a word from Lee for a week and had dispatched an officer to find him.

On December 3 Washington sent his sick into Philadelphia. He took time to repeat his complaints to Congress about militia and short-term enlistments. If, he said, any troops had rallied around him while crossing New Jersey, he was sure he could have made a stand there. He urged a larger standing army that, when trained, would no longer be "a disorderly Mob." He reported that General Howe and Lord Howe had issued a joint proclamation, offering pardons to everyone in New Jersey who would submit to the king within sixty days.

The British now moved so fast that Washington ordered all troops to Pennsylvania. The tiny American army crossed the Delaware on December 7 and 8 to what is now Morrisville. Every boat was secured on the west side to prevent the enemy from following. On December 9 Washington finally heard from Lee, who was at Morristown but doubtful that he could join Washington. He thought, however, that he might be able to make some diversion on Howe's flanks and would let Washington know. By this time, Washington's troops were down to three thousand, but Pennsylvania militia came in to add a little strength.

Washington advised Congress to fortify Philadelphia immediately, adding that he was sending Generals Mifflin and Putnam to the city to assist in the work. Cornwallis, having reached the Delaware and finding no transportation, established his headquarters at Pennington. Howe, who had posted British and Hessian troops at all important towns from Amboy to Trenton and Burlington, now ordered his army into winter quarters. He was induced to do this by the increasingly severe weather, the weak and broken state of

Washington's army, and because thousands of Jerseyans were flocking to take the oath of allegiance to the king in response to his amnesty proclamation. Howe reported to London: "I conclude the troops will be in perfect security."

A fast ship carried to London the news of Cornwallis' movements across New Jersey. On January 1 George III dropped one of his usual little notes to Lord North. He said he was sorry that General Howe had received such bad bread and flour from the European contractors who supplied the army. "I trust Sir William Howe is now in possession of so extensive a Country that he will not require to be entirely provided from Europe; I have seen a private letter from the General that his posts will extend from the River Delaware to Rhode Island consequently my opinion seems well grounded."

On December 10 Washington again asked Lee to move because he had only "weak and feeble forces... Do come on, your arrival may be happy, and if it can be effected without delay, may be the means of preserving a City, whose loss must prove of the most fatal consequences to America." He wrote to Lund Washington on the same date: "I tremble for Philadelphia. Nothing... but Gen. Lee's speedy arrival... can save it... It is next to impossible to guard a shore for sixty miles." On December 11 he asked Lee to "push on with every possible succour you can bring."

That day he sent Major Elisha Sheldon of the Connecticut volunteer cavalry to Congress to plead once again for an authorization for continental cavalry regiments. In his letter he said: "I can only say the Service of himself and his Troop, has been such as merits of the public, and deserves a handsome Compensation for their Trouble... From the Experience I have had this Campaign, of the Utility of Horse [cavalry], I am convinced there is no carrying on the war without them." Congress, now thoroughly scared, at once granted a request that had been lingering in Adams' committee for six months. Immediately thereafter Congress fled to Baltimore.

On December 16 Washington gave Sheldon his commission as "Lieut. Colo. Commandant of a Regiment of Horse." That dark December day, the United States cavalry service was born on the banks of the Delaware.

On December 14 the exasperated Washington wrote again to Lee: "I am much surprized that you should be in any doubt respecting the Route you should take, after the information you have had upon that Head... Let me once more request and entreat you to march immediately for Pitts Town." The letter did not reach Lee, who the day before had finished a letter to General Gates:

> *The ingenious maneuver of Fort Washington has unhinged the goodly fabrick we had been building. There never was so damned a stroke. Entre nous, a certain*

great man is most damnably deficient. He has thrown me into a situation where I
have my choice of difficulties. If I stay in the Province I risk myself and army, and
if I do not stay the Province is lost for ever...

In short unless something which I do not expect turns up we are lost. Our counsels
have been weak to the last degree... If you think you would be in time to aid the
General I would have you by all means go.

Lee had just enough time to get the letter out to Gates before he was
captured. He had gone three miles away from his army to an inn, for reasons
that have never been satisfactorily determined. Colonel William Harcourt,
leading a body of British cavalry, captured American soldiers who told him,
under threats of death, where Lee could be found. Harcourt was instantly on
the trail to get him. To the British, it was a great triumph to capture the man
who had become second in command of the American army after the resignation of Ward; to the Americans it seemed the severest of a long series of misfortunes. The capture, however, turned out to be a blessing for Washington.
Once rid of Lee, Sullivan, next in command, marched his troops straightway
to Washington.

In his letters, Washington occasionally hinted at a "stroke" he had in mind.
With almost no army, no equipment, no supplies—and while waiting for Lee
and Gates—Washington had been constantly turning in his mind an attack on
the enemy. Before he heard of Lee's capture, he told Gates to hurry to
Pittstown. "I expect Genl. Lee will be there this Evening, or tomorrow, who
will be followed by Genl. Heath and his Division. If we can draw our forces
together, I trust, under the smiles of providence, we may yet effect an important stroke." To Heath, who had been ordered from Peekskill, he wrote on
December 14: "If we can collect our forces speedily, I should hope we may
effect somthing of importance."

Enlistments for nearly the whole Continental Army were to expire on
December 31. George wrote Lund Washington that he was less afraid of
Howe's army than of total disaffection to the cause in New Jersey and
Pennsylvania. Unless he could get a new army and support from these states,
the game was pretty well up. Already two former Pennsylvania members of
Congress had taken the oath to George III. He asked Lund to send all his per-
sonal papers from Mount Vernon to Berkeley County, in what is now West
Virginia. He told Reed in November that, if necessary, he would go into the
Shenandoah Valley to continue fighting, and beyond that he was prepared to
retreat over the Alleghenies. The flame of revolution, so long as he was alive,
was never to be allowed to flicker out. He wrote his brothers on December 18

and 19 that, knowing the cause was just, "I cannot entertain an Idea that it will finally sink tho' it may remain for some time under a cloud."

On December 19, Thomas Paine, who had followed the retreating army across New Jersey, published a famous pamphlet with the now-familiar opening words:

These are the times that try men's souls...

...No great deal is lost yet. All that Howe has been doing for this month past is rather a ravage than a conquest, which the spirit of the Jerseys, a year ago, would have quickly repulsed, and which time and a little resolution will soon recover.

...In the fourteenth century the whole English army, after ravaging... France, was driven back like men petrified with fear; and this brave exploit was performed... by a woman, Joan of Arc. Would that heaven might inspire some Jersey maid to spirit up her countrymen.

I shall not now attempt to give all the particulars of our retreat to the Delaware... Both officers and men, though greatly harassed and fatigued... bore it with a manly and martial spirit. All their wishes centred in one, which was that the country would turn out and help them drive the enemy back.

Voltaire has remarked that King William never appeared to full advantage but in difficulties and in action; the same remark may be made of General Washington... God has given him a mind that can even flourish upon care.

The pamphlet circulated from hand to hand in the army and throughout the new nation in its darkest hours.

On December 20 Washington wrote a lengthy letter to Congress, asking what had happened to his October requests for corps of engineers and artillery. He had not been able to wait any longer and he had ordered the enlistment of three artillery regiments. Congress, on leaving Philadelphia, had given him emergency powers; with these he had ordered Knox to raise his artillerymen. He urgently asked Congress to authorize additional infantry regiments and a corps of engineers, authority to pay a bonus to keep his men past the end of the month, and better pay, a clothing department, a commissary of prisoners, magazines, tents, small arms, and officers on the national establishment. General Greene wrote to Congress on December 21: "Greater powers must be lodged in the hands of the General... Time will not permit nor circumstances allow of a reference to Congress... There never was a man that might be more safely trusted, nor a time when there was a louder call."

On December 30 Congress, in "perfect reliance on the wisdom, vigor and uprightness of General Washington," gave him everything he asked, including full powers to raise additional regiments of infantry and to appoint the officers, and to enlist three thousand cavalry, three regiments of artillery, and a corps of engineers. Before he received his directives, Washington stretched his powers to offer a ten dollar bonus to men who would stay six weeks beyond their enlistment period.

Sullivan brought about two thousand men to camp, while Gates arrived with another six hundred, bringing Washington's total forces to six thousand. Gates, who had been warned by Lee that Washington was "damnably deficient," refused to accept a command at Bristol. Pleading illness, he went to Baltimore to try to persuade Congress to move the army to the south. As it turned out, his timing was most inept. Washington's "stroke" was already set in his mind.

TRENTON

On the night of December 24, the American commander in chief held a conference with his general officers in a house not far from what is now Washington's Crossing. Those present included Greene, Stirling, Sullivan, Knox, Mercer, and St. Clair. He outlined plans that called for crossing the river with twenty-four hundred troops, then moving south to Trenton. Brigadier James Ewing, with a thousand militia, would go over at a point below Trenton and move north. Colonel John Cadwalader, with a few hundred men, would cross still further down in a diversionary attack on the Hessians at Mount Holly and Burlington.

Washington's troops assembled after dark on Christmas night. His tiny army was remarkably national, with ten out of thirteen states represented. It included future presidents Washington and Monroe, cabinet members Hamilton and Knox, and Chief Justice Marshall. Colonel John Glover and his Marblehead fishermen, who had ferried Washington's troops across the East River on a hot August night, were there with Durham boats used for river freight. These were forty to sixty feet long, of very shallow draft, and capable of holding up to fifteen tons. They easily carried the horses and Knox's seventeen guns. It was bitterly cold, snow alternating with sleet, and ice cakes forming in the river.

Washington was giving orders, which Knox relayed in his bullhorn voice. Wind, river ice, and sleet delayed the crossing some three hours longer than planned. Although Washington did not know of it until later, Ewing was unable to get over to New Jersey, while Cadwalader moved some troops but not his guns. Washington therefore had to improvise new plans.

The troops had a nine-mile march to Trenton. The command was split, going on two roads of an approximately equal distance, with Greene on the left, Sullivan on the right. The severity of the weather had called off the Hessians' usual morning patrol. Washington's restrained report of the action was sent to Congress the next day:

> *The quantity of Ice, made that Night, impeded the passage of the Boats so much, that it was three O'Clock before the Artillery could all get over, and near four, before the Troops took up their line of march.*
>
> *This made me despair of surprizing the Town, as I well knew we could not reach it before the day fairly broke, but... I determined to push on... The upper Division arrived at the Enemys advance Post, exactly at Eight O'Clock, and in three Minutes after, I found, from the fire on the lower Road, that that Division had also got up. The out Guards made but small Opposition, tho' for their Number, they behaved very well, keeping up a constant retreating fire from behind Houses. We presently saw their main Body formed, but from their Motions, they seemed undetermined how to act Being hard pressed by our Troops, who had already got possession of their Artillery, they attempted to file off by a road on their right leading to Princetown, but perceiving their Intention, I threw a Body of Troops in their Way which immediately checked them. Finding from our disposition that they were surrounded, they agreed to lay down their arms.*

This modest summary failed to convey that it had been a brilliant encircling movement, devised after he found that Ewing's force had not arrived. Washington sent his troops to choke off the only escape route, while others surrounded two Hessian regiments. These regiments surrendered after their commander, Colonel Johann Roll, was mortally wounded. The third regiment, driven to a creek, held out only a short time thereafter.

More than a thousand Hessians were killed, wounded, or captured. Included was a brass band that was to play for the Americans the following July 4 in Philadelphia. American casualties numbered perhaps four wounded. On January 1, Washington, replying to congratulations from Robert Morris, said: "The Accounts you give me... of the good effects that are likely to flow from our Success at Trenton, add not a little to the Satisfaction I have felt on that occasion. You are pleased to pay me many personal Compliments as if the Merit... was solely due to me; but I assure you, the other General Officers, who assisted me in the plan and Execution, have full as good a right to your

Encomiums as myself." He wrote Congress that everyone had behaved with "the highest honour."

Washington was especially pleased with Knox and his artillerists, singling them out for praise. Before the news of Trenton could reach Congress, that body had ratified Knox's promotion to brigadier. In sending Colonel George Baylor, his aide, to Congress with his victory dispatch, Washington added a particular commendation of the bearer. Congress voted Baylor a fully equipped horse and a cavalry command. Washington thus lost a badly needed aide but told Baylor that he "cheerfully" acquiesced.

PRINCETON

On December 27 the general wrote to Cadwalader that they should follow up the success at Trenton as soon as possible by beating up all the enemy's posts on the Delaware. He suggested an early conference, but Cadwalader, heading militia, had shown unexpected enterprise by saying he had already planned a crossing and suggested that Washington join him there. Cadwalader had done this in spite of the equivocal role played by Joseph Reed. The latter had been assigned to Cadwalader's forces because of his special knowledge of the Burlington area. Reed had forwarded a pessimistic report from Philadelphia to Washington on Christmas Day, but the general wrote Cadwalader that this would not influence his plans. The next day, while Washington was counting his Trenton prisoners, Reed appeared in Bristol. According to Cadwalader's later account, Reed stated how discouraged he was. There were only "the remains of a broken army," he had a family to take care of, and General Howe's amnesty would soon expire. He said that he had advised his brother in New Jersey to seek British protection if necessary. Inasmuch as a letter had already arrived at camp from the Hessian commander who agreed to see Reed, Cadwalader's suspicions were aroused. He said that he thought Reed ought to have been placed under arrest, but he was afraid of the discouragement this would give to his troops. He took Reed with him to New Jersey but kept an eye on him.

On the other side Cadwalader found that the Hessians in posts below Trenton had panicked and fled. He wrote Washington that if they could all be driven "from west Jersey, the success will raise an army by next spring." The general's troops were exhausted from the two river crossings and the battle at Trenton, but this possibility of regaining much of New Jersey made him spring to action. He wrote to Heath, on his way south from Peekskill, to hurry as fast as possible to Hackensack. He asked McDougall at Morristown to order out all the Jersey militia. With help, he could drive "the Enemy from the whole province of Jersey."

Washington, desperately short of food and money, appealed to Robert Morris, who had been left by Congress in Philadelphia as caretaker of its business. In this period Morris was the commander's stoutest supporter, saying he would assume powers rather than let the cause suffer. He got him the food needed and on December 31 forwarded £124 7s. 6d. to Washington, in gold and silver coins, which he had borrowed, so that Washington could pay his New Jersey spies. With it was a note saying, "The year 1776 is over. I am heartily glad of it, and hope you, nor America will never be plagued with such another." Washington's further request for $50,000 in paper money, to pay his promised bonus to his troops, reached Morris late that night. The next day Morris forwarded the money, saying he had gotten up early the next morning and awakened everyone in town to get it. When Washington made out his accounts at the end of the war, he remembered the £124 7s. 6d. exactly, "the time and circumstances of it being too remarkable ever to be forgotten by me."

On December 30 Washington again crossed the Delaware with even worse weather and ice conditions than those of Christmas night. From Trenton he issued a proclamation announcing that the American army was back in the province and calling on the whole population and the militia to rise against the enemy. On January 1 when Mifflin joined him with sixteen hundred men, Washington had a total force of around thirty-four hundred men.

Trenton had shocked the British into counteraction. Cornwallis cancelled his planned leave to England and raced across Jersey with seven thousand men. Although harassed and delayed by American troops along the way, he reached Trenton late on January 2, with darkness setting in. That night, using intelligence gathered by his and Cadwalader's spies, including a map of Princeton, Washington determined to counterattack the forces left by Howe and Cornwallis at Princeton. After he ordered the army's baggage moved to Burlington and leaving all the campfires brightly lit at Assunpink Creek, the army quietly decamped on the Sandtown road. Circling around Cornwallis, they advanced against Howe's regiments at Princeton, quickly defeating them. On January 5 Washington reported to Congress:

> We found Princeton about Sunrise with only three Regiments of Infantry and three Troops of Light Horse in it, two of which were upon their March for Trenton; these three Regiments (especially the two first) made a gallant resistance and in Killed, wounded and Prisoners must have lost near 500 Men...

> The rear of the Enemy's army Laying at Maidenhead (not more than five or Six

Miles from Princeton) were up with us before our pursuit was over, but as I had the precaution to destroy the Bridge over Stony Brook (about half a Mile from the field of Action) they were so long retarded there, as to give us time to move off in good order for this place. We took two Brass field pieces from them, but for want of Horses could not bring them off. We also took some Blankets, Shoes, and a few other trifling Articles...

My original plan when I set out from Trenton was to have pushed to Brunswick, but the harassed State of our own Troops (many of them having had no rest for two Nights and a day) and the danger of losing the advantage we had gained by aiming at too much, Induced me, by the advice of my Officers, to relinquish the attempt, but in my judgement Six or Eight hundred fresh Troops upon a forced March would have destroyed all their Stores, and Magazines; taken (as we have since learnt) their Military Chest containing £70,000 and put an end to the War...

...The Militia are taking Spirit, and, I am told, are coming fast from this State; but I fear those from Philadelphia will scarce Submit to the hardships of a Winter Campaign much longer, especially as they very unluckily sent their Blankets with their Baggage to Burlington; I must do them the justice however to add, that they have undergone more fatigue and hardship than I expected Militia (especially Citizens) would have done at this Inclement Season. I am just moving to Morristown where I shall endeavour to put them under the best cover I can, hitherto we have lain without any, many of our poor Soldiers quite barefoot and ill clad in other respects.

As usual, others present had to report on Washington's personal bravery, which encouraged his troops but made them concerned for his safety. At Princeton were three enemy troops of light horse and three regiments, the first two of which were already on the march to aid Cornwallis. Having heard firing the preceding night from Trenton, their initial surprise was complete.

Brigadier Hugh Mercer was sent to the left, with orders to destroy Stony Brook Bridge and then to join Washington and the remainder of the troops who were proceeding by the back road to Princeton. They soon encountered a British regiment which, not expecting Americans there, was driven back. They rallied and Mercer received a wound that was to be fatal. Washington forwarded additional militia under Cadwalader, but both forces were driven back rapidly. Washington himself came up with the greater part of his men. Charging ahead on his horse he rallied the Americans, telling them to hold their fire. The enemy shot first and there was a great cloud of smoke around the general. One aide put his hands over his eyes, afraid to see the commander in chief fall. Then

Washington called the order to charge and fire and the British lines broke. Washington and his cavalry pursued them, while others chased the enemy as far as four miles on foot.

A part of a second British regiment nearby retreated to Princeton, where the other enemy forces had taken a position in Nassau Hall. After the artillery was turned on them, the majority surrendered. The remainder escaped to the north. Cornwallis, having pursued the enemy up from Trenton, reached the Princeton area as the tired Americans were on their way north to Morristown. Afraid for his supply depot and his seventy-thousand-pound treasure at Brunswick, the British commander moved eastward. British casualties at Princeton amounted to about four hundred, while the Americans lost forty, including Mercer and Colonel John Haslet, who had been commended by Washington for his bravery at Harlem.

Within a few days the British abandoned every post in New Jersey except Brunswick, Amboy, and Paulus Hook. On January 6 the Americans captured Hackensack, the point from which Washington had fled across the state not quite seven weeks before. It had taken the general and his ragged, often shoe-less, army from Christmas to Twelfth Night to beat an enemy with forces numbering, in their entirety, nearly twelve times his combat forces, and to drive them back to what he had once described as their "pitiful islands." The British suffered fourteen hundred casualties in the period, the Americans around forty-five.

Not quite four years later the chevalier de Chastellux, a French general who tried to visit all of Washington's battlefields, went to Princeton with Colonel Stephen Moylan, Washington's aide. He was immediately seized by President Witherspoon, who engaged him in conversation in bookish French about his college. Chastellux wrote: "I confess... that I was rather impatient to seek out the traces of General Washington, in a country where every object recalled his successes, I passed rapidly therefore from Parnassus to the field of Mars, and from the hands of President Witherspoon into those of colonel Moylan. They were both upon their own ground; so that while one was pulling me by the right arm, telling me 'Here is the philosophy classroom' the other was pluck-ing me by the left, telling me 'This is where one hundred and eighty English laid down their arms.'"

MORRISTOWN

By the time he reached his new headquarters in Morristown on January 6, Washington was already thinking of attacking New York. He wrote to General Heath the next day, ordering him and General Lincoln to move towards the city to blockade it and, if possible, to prepare for an assault upon it. His hopes, however, were dashed when Heath marched against Fort Independence in the Bronx on January 18. Heath demanded that the fort surrender within twenty minutes or take the consequences. The British ignored this and fired at him. Heath attempted a siege but the British sortied ten days later and drove him off. Heath got a lot of ridicule and Washington sharply reproved him.

Washington took some pleasure in writing to Lord Cornwallis on January 8 to say that his army would not molest convoys of money and stores intended for the German and British prisoners at Trenton and Princeton. But, he added, he could not answer for the militia of the state, who were "exceedingly exasperated at the treatment they have met with, from both Hessian and British troops." He therefore would send one of his officers to escort the convoy across New Jersey, indicating thus that Cornwallis' men would not otherwise be safe.

In moving across New Jersey, the British, but far more the Hessian troops, had ravaged, plundered, and raped on such a scale as to turn the state from Tory or neutral to Whig. The Hessians took no account of the difference between loyal and rebel inhabitants. The fact that the king could not give protection to those who had sworn allegiance to him made a great difference in the attitude of the population. The militia swarmed into Washington's camp, a change from the days when Washington could raise no more than one hundred men when he was retreating across New Jersey. British foraging and raiding parties were regularly attacked by continentals and militia. On January 7, a German foraging party was set upon and around fifty killed, wounded, or captured. Throughout the spring, guerrilla operations of this kind continued against the enemy. Washington used the original French term, *la petite guerre*, for these actions. George III's hope that Howe could now draw on the country for provisions was not fulfilled.

Washington had hardly arrived in Morristown before he wrote to Robert Morris and his friends to get the gun foundry at Philadelphia going again. He would need "a large number of field pieces" for the spring campaign.

REED

On January 13 Washington announced that Colonel George Weedon, once a captain in his Virginia Regiment, had been made adjutant general, *pro tempore*, in the place of the resigned Joseph Reed. The commander in chief soon offered the post to General Gates, who declined on the ground that this would be a comedown after having a northern command. He did not disclose his real reason that, following the work of Reed and Lee, he had developed a deep mistrust of Washington. Gates subsequently persuaded Congress to send him to the north, far from the commander in chief.

That spring Washington offered the command of the cavalry service to Joseph Reed, who declined to serve. In June he wrote Washington, apologizing for his letter to Lee, assuring him there was nothing in it that was "inconsistent with that respect and affection" he had always borne to the general. The statement was false, but Washington, not knowing it to be so, answered by thanking Reed for his "friendly and affectionate sentiments." He added that he had always unreservedly welcomed Reed's "advice on any point in which I appeared to be wanting. To meet with any thing, then, that carried with it a complexion of witholding that advice from, and censuring my conduct to another, was such an argument of disingenuity, that I was not a little mortified at it. However, I am perfectly satisfied that matters were not as they appeared from the letter alluded to."

PRISONERS

The reports that Washington received of the Howes' mistreatment of prisoners brought him almost to tears. An American officer described them as "miserable starved objects... mere skeletons, unable to creep or speak in many instances."

Washington wrote separate letters to the Howe brothers on January 13. To General Howe, he said: "I am sorry that I am again under the necessity of remonstrating to you upon the Treatment which our prisoners continue to receive in New York. Those, who have lately been sent out, give the most shocking Accounts of their barbarous usage, which their Miserable, emaciated Countenances confirm. How very different was their Appearance from that of your Soldiers, who have lately been returned to you, after a Captivity of twelve months; And, whether this... was owing to a difference of treatment, I leave it to you... to determine... If you are determined to make Captivity as distressing as possible, to those whose Lot it is to fall into it, let me know it, that we may be upon equal terms, for your Conduct must and shall mark mine." To Lord Howe, he wrote: "I hope that, upon making the proper Inquiry, you will have the matter so regulated, that the unhappy Creatures, whose Lot is Captivity, may not in future have the Miseries of Cold, disease and Famine, added to their other Misfortunes." An acrimonious correspondence continued between Washington and the British for an extended period. On June 10 he wrote General Howe:

To prove that the Prisoners did not suffer from any ill treatment...

you say "they were confined in the most airy Buildings and on Board the largest Transports in the fleet"...

That airy Buildings were chosen to confine our Men in, is a fact I shall not dispute. But whether this was an Advantage or not in the Winter Season, I leave you to decide. I am inclined to think it was not; especially as there was a general Complaint, that they were destitute of fire...

...I wish their sufferings may not have been increased in the Article of clothing, by their being deprived of what they had thro' the rapacity of too many of their Captors...

...You ask "How is the Cause of debility in Prisoners to be ascertained?" This seems to be considered as a perplexing Question. For my part, I cannot view it as involving any great difficulty. There is no more familiar mode of reasoning than from Effects to causes... In the Subject before us, the appearance of the Prisoners and what eventually happened, proved that they had been hardly dealt with.

In this last sentence, Washington referred to the fact that many prisoners had been so weakened that they died shortly after reaching the American lines. By October of 1777, there were far more British in American hands than the other way around, and Washington had greater leverage in his negotiations.

In April, Benjamin Franklin appealed, in turn, to Lord Stormont, British ambassador at Paris, to obtain better treatment for American prisoners in England. Stormont returned the letter with a note saying that he would receive no letters from rebels unless they came to implore "his Majesty's mercy." Franklin returned it to Lord Stormont, with a note saying that it was a matter of common humanity "between two nations, Great Britain and the United States of America," and Stormont's reply was "*indecent.*" Franklin complained again by a message that reached Lord North and was forwarded by him to George III. The king, with his usual astuteness, replied that Franklin's letter was an obvious trick to gain recognition and perhaps to have some propaganda value, since no British officer would ever act with cruelty, even to rebels. He added: "If they have erred I should rather think it has been in too much civility towards them."

LEE

Lee was the top prisoner of the British and a favorite of Congress, which took great interest in his welfare and the possibility of his being exchanged. Howe at first tried to consider Lee a deserter from the British army and wrote home for instructions. London suggested that he be sent to Britain for trial, but Congress' threat to retaliate caused a change in directives. Lee's reported bad treatment complicated Washington's negotiations, since Congress ordered a British officer, Colonel Archibald Campbell, and several Hessian officers kept to close confinement. Washington protested and eventually got this changed. He maintained a policy of treating British and Hessian prisoners well, not only for humanitarian reasons but on the simple ground that this was a much easier way to obtain enemy deserters.

Contrary to reports to Congress, Lee was handled more as a prisoner of state than of war. Some of the British officers were old friends and he had them to dine. The Howes again tried to get Congress, through their captive, to send negotiating commissions but, though Lee begged them to do so, Congress refused. Lee, feeling the American cause was all but hopeless and that—as he later explained to Elias Boudinot, Washington's agent to the prisoners—American troops could not stand up to British forces, wrote out and gave to Henry Strachey, General Howe's secretary, a long plan whereby the Howes could obtain the submission of the United States. Howe paid it little heed. Congress continued to apply pressure for Lee's exchange and unfortunately succeeded the following year.

FORGED LETTERS

Sometime late in 1776 a series of letters—purportedly written by Washington to his wife, stepson, and Mount Vernon manager—were printed in London and subsequently republished in New York. Washington guessed they were composed by John Randolph, once attorney general of Virginia, who had gone to England. Possibly a more likely candidate was Randolph's brother, Beverley, since they show considerable knowledge of activities at Washington's headquarters and his problems. Beverley Randolph was on active duty with the British forces in New York and knew something of Virginia politics and Washington's family affairs. The letters are not especially vicious, but they have a despondent Washington protesting both his loyalty to the king and worry about his wife's suspicions. The London press expressed doubt that they were genuine. They were republished by the Jeffersonian press in 1796. Other forgeries appearing in New York thereafter described lewd behavior on the part of Washington. Since his conduct was open to all, they made no impression.

SICKNESS AND SPRING

A new aide, the twenty-two-year-old Alexander Hamilton, was appointed on March 1 and, like all who held that post, bore the rank of lieutenant colonel. He had gone from New York to White Plains and on to Trenton and Princeton with the army. He entered the general's family just before Washington's first illness of the war.

Washington, who had been nearly two years without a day's rest, came down with a severe peritonsillar abscess. Hamilton and the other aides had to keep visitors and business from him, and to act as nursemaids to a general who was highly aggrieved at being in bed. Washington became very sick; the household and staff passed through agony, hearing the general's difficult breathing. Before he fully recovered, Martha Washington arrived in camp from Mount Vernon and helped to put him on his feet again.

For the first time in the war, with Mrs. Washington around to see to it, Washington began to take better care of himself and to get the exercise and sport he had too long denied himself. With the British beaten back to New York, he became—for a little while—the old cheerful, smiling Washington, taking long horseback rides and playing ball with his officers. This was a form of the "base-ball" enjoyed as a boy by George III, an early patron of the game. Colonel Theodorick Bland of Virginia came with his wife, Martha, to join Washington. She wrote a fine, gossipy letter to her sister, Frances Randolph:

> *Now let me speak of our noble and agreeable commander (for he commands both sexes) one by his excellent skill in military matters, the other by his ability, politeness and attention. He is generally busy in the forenoon—but from dinner till night he is free for all company. His worthy lady seems to be in perfect felicity while she is by the side of her Old Man, as she calls him. We often make parties on horseback—the General, his lady, Miss Livingston, and his aides-de-camp... at which times, General Washington throws off the hero, and takes on the chatty, agreeable companion. He can be downright impudent sometimes.*

As for Martha Washington, one of the matrons of Morristown told of visiting her with several ladies. They had heard that she was a very grand person. "So we dressed ourselves in our most elegant ruffles and silks... And don't you think we found her knitting and with a (checked) apron on... There we were, without a stitch of work, and sitting in state, but General Washington's lady with her own hands was knitting stockings for herself and husband. She seems very wise in experience, kind-hearted and winning in all her ways. She talked much of the poor soldiers, especially the sick ones." Washington was to have only a brief taste of domestic bliss before the spring campaign.

MARCH 17, 1777

It had been a year since Washington had driven Howe out of Boston and, in the interim, New Jersey. Howe held two seaports and a bit of the mainland, and that was all. In New York, Lord Rawdon and his Irish troops made a brave showing as they marched up Broadway in a Saint Patrick's Day parade. On the same day Colonel William Harcourt, who had captured Lee and who was later to be a field marshal, wrote to his father, Lord Harcourt, lieutenant of Ireland: "Though it was once the fashion of this army to treat them in the most contemptible light, they are now become a formidable enemy. Formidable, however, as they may be, I flatter myself as we are a good deal more so, and I have therefore little doubt that, provided affairs continue quiet in Europe, and the expected reinforcements arrive in good time, we shall soon bring this business to a happy conclusion."

Lord Howe's secretary, Ambrose Serle, who had been calling Americans "poor mad Quixotes," wrote in his March 28 diary that he expected "a speedy termination of the war." He added that he and Joseph Galloway, a Pennsylvania Tory, agreed that in the future Americans should have little to say about their government, since they could not be trusted with power.

By March the news of Washington's victories at Trenton and Princeton had spread through Europe. Every foreign and war office began to scramble for maps and to ask, who is General Washington? Frederick the Great, regarded with awe as the greatest soldier of his time, told his ambassador in London that, in his view, Americans could be expected to gain their independence. Howe had informed his government that there was no possibility of ending the war with the 1777 campaign. Everyone in Europe watched, with no little malice, to see what George III and Lord North would do now.

TWENTY-TWO

MORRISTOWN TO VALLEY FORGE

1777

DUPLICITY WAS A common practice in European diplomacy, but those who used it were often duped by others. In 1775 the comte de Vergennes, French foreign minister, told the British ambassador to Versailles that his government regarded the American rebellion as deplorable and France would do nothing to help an insurrection against a lawful sovereign. Although the British cabinet had reason to doubt such assurances, North repeatedly declared to Parliament that there was no possibility of war with France. By 1776, trusting both Vergennes and their own ability to crush the rebellion quickly, the British had the bulk of their armed forces in America. In the same year, France and Spain began sending secret arms and supplies to America. These arrived in some quantity in 1777.

Silas Deane, the first American representative in Paris, worked closely with Beaumarchais in setting up the trading company that purchased arms, ammunition, and clothing for the rebels. He was rather too sharp a trading Yankee and some government purchases managed to end up as his own. In addition he may have tried to charge Congress for goods given free by the French. Using his private knowledge of French plans, he also speculated on the London stock exchange, through Edward Bancroft and Mrs. Jacobus van Zandt, American spies on George III's payroll. By 1781, or perhaps earlier, Deane was also a paid agent of the British king.

Benjamin Franklin in Paris was surrounded by intrigue. The French police and court agents kept their eyes on his doings. The British also spied on him through their secret service in Europe, headed by William Eden, brother of the last royal governor of Maryland. Eden's French agent was Paul Wentworth, a New Hampshire Tory who enlisted the services of Bancroft, secretary to the American legation, and a Major Thornton, secretary to Arthur Lee of the mission. Wentworth later brought Deane into the network. For his money the king got some remarkably bad intelligence, such as the information that Congress had been advised by Franklin not to ratify the treaty with France. Where the information was accurate it was often too painful for the king to believe. He also mistrusted his spies who, he correctly thought, were too often "stockjobbers" (speculators).

Arthur Lee, after joining Franklin as the third United States commissioner in Paris, quickly suspected Deane and Bancroft. In this he was remarkably astute; his suspicions were confirmed but not until many years had gone by and archives were opened. Franklin, much more interested in high level international politics than in business details, paid insufficient attention to Lee's complaints. Lee finally suspected that Franklin, too, was involved, and he may well have been justified. Lee complained to Congress about Deane, who was recalled from France. John Adams took his place.

The news of Trenton and Princeton had been well received by the French, who quickly gave Franklin further secret funds in the amount of $400,000. In England, the situation became acute for the king because he and his government were in financial difficulties with victory nowhere in sight. Lord North had some very unhappy times with his Parliament that spring.

In April of 1777 North announced that the king was more than £600,000 short in his accounts, and Parliament would have to vote the sums necessary. It was a sad picture, for the palace servants and fuel bills were unpaid. Most— and probably all—of the money had been spent for such purposes as the bribery of press and Parliament. The immensity of his debts is shown by the fact that before the war, the British budget, other than the king's civil list, had been less than £5 million a year. Parliament not only had to vote him £600,000 but also an extra £100,000 a year for purposes that were not disclosed but that were well known to Parliament.

The House of Commons passed the requisite acts only after lengthy debates and a call by the Whigs for a full statement of the facts. The king, pleased at the passage, told North the money had been voted because he had placed the management of Commons in "the most able and honest hands." When the king went to Parliament to assent to the bills, the speaker rose, addressed his majesty, and said:

*At a time of public distress, full of difficulty and danger, their constituents
labouring under burdens almost too heavy to be borne, your faithful Commons...
have not only granted to your Majesty a large present supply, but also a great
additional revenue; great, beyond example, great beyond your Majesty's highest
expense. All this, Sir, they have done in a well-grounded confidence that you will
apply wisely what they have granted liberally.*

This was a first sign of parliamentary revolt. The House of Commons not only
subsequently unanimously approved the statement but then congratulated
the speaker on having said it. The king complained to North that this tended
to spoil everything, "for the manner may enhance or diminish any gift."

Not long afterwards North had to turn to Parliament for £5 million more
in supplementary war expenditures, which meant new taxes and loans. All this
became a part of Britain's system of corruption. To the bribes and pensions
from the king's purse, and the titles and ribbons he could give, were added
lucrative war contracts that often went to George III's friends in Parliament.
In addition, loans at exorbitant rates were placed through the same channels.
Yet, at the same time, there were increasing signs of a popular desire to return
to the old British standards of decency and honor that had been brought to
America by the early settlers.

DEANE AND THE FRENCH OFFICERS

Silas Deane was plagued after his arrival in Paris by visitors who wanted something from Americans: intelligence, supply contracts, or jobs. Many who came
to his office were adventurers or retired officers who saw a chance to advance
in the only war going on at the time. They often exaggerated their military
rank, added nonexistent hereditary titles to their names, and pretended to
more knowledge than they had. Without much discrimination, Deane hired
many and promised them they would be generals or colonels as soon as they
got to America. This became a source of great embarrassment to Congress,
and to Washington, when that body unloaded them onto him.

Deane selected some good officers, including Johann Kalb, who, calling himself a baron, came as an ostensible volunteer, but he was engaged in a plan to
make the comte de Broglie commander in chief of the American army. Another
man he chose was Gilbert Motier, marquis de Lafayette, connected by marriage,
as Deane knew, to the great house of Noailles, which had enough field marshals,
governors, and ambassadors in the family to be itself a small empire.

Lafayette's father was killed at Minden, the battle that resulted in the cashiering of Lord George Germain. His son had already had a precocious career; he was a military cadet at age twelve, married and a captain in the French army at sixteen, and a father at eighteen. He too was promised a major general's commission in America. The romantic stories about him are well known: his visit to the English court where the marquis de Noailles was ambassador; his introduction to George III and Germain; his return to France and the purchase of his own ship; and his escape from his king's police after being ostensibly forbidden to go to America. Congress, having had their fill of adventurers, treated him rudely when he arrived at Philadelphia in July, but his dignified plea that he had the right to volunteer, without pay, won him his commission as major general just before his twentieth birthday. Shortly after receiving his July 31 commission, he met Washington in Philadelphia. Lafayette found him impressively tall and majestic and his welcome most friendly. Nonetheless he embarrassed Washington, the more so because he said he only came to learn and, of course, to fight. Washington asked Congress on more than one occasion what they intended for Lafayette. He considered Lafayette's appointment as a general officer honorary, while Lafayette did not think it such at all. "The Marquis," as he was soon called by everyone, earned his field command by sheer persistence and personal bravery. He turned out to be a good soldier who improved as the years passed. Six months after his arrival he was writing to his wife, Adrienne: "My presence... is more necessary to the American cause than you can think... In the place that he occupies one may be surrounded by flatterers or secret enemies; he finds in me a sure friend to whom he can open his heart, and who will always tell him the truth."

CONGRESS

The great Congress, which had assembled in Philadelphia, soon deteriorated. Washington had left even before independence and Franklin and Jefferson not long after, the former to assume his important duties in Paris. By May of 1777, Adams was complaining to Jefferson that Congress consisted of only "twenty hands," all that were still on deck to do the work. He added: "Your country is not yet quite secure enough to excuse your retreat to the delights of domestic life." Jefferson did not return until the war was securely won. Adams himself departed for Paris before the year was out.

The weakness of Congress became a recurring complaint of the army. By 1778 Hamilton was asking the governor of New York why his state was not represented by men of the stature of Livingston and Jay. That same year

Washington asked Benjamin Harrison about Virginia's representation: "Where is Mason, Wythe, Jefferson, Nicholas, Pendleton, Nelson and another I could name?" meaning the letter's recipient.

The small representation, in a Congress divided into numerous committees, had one advantage for the commander in chief. In 1775 and 1776, its members had interfered at numerous points, directed an invasion of Canada, and stripped him of officers, troops, and supplies. By 1777 Congress was too weak to try to control overall strategy and left its management very largely where it belonged. As a result, American military planning was much more efficient in the third year of the war than it had been at first. Congress meddled in more minor matters and often struck at the morale of the officers' corps.

STRATEGY

On February 25 Congress suggested to Washington that he should keep the enemy confined, stop further supplies from reaching them, and beat Howe before additional reinforcements arrived from Europe. He replied on March 14 that he would be happy to do just this but, at the moment, he had exactly 981 continentals with him, plus militia who were engaged only till the end of the month.

Two days earlier Washington had informed General Schuyler, who held the northern command, that American operations would have to continue on the defensive. He planned to station his forces in post "so central to the theatre of War, that they may be sent to the support of any part of the country. It is a military observation, strongly supported by experience, 'that a superior Army may fall sacrifice to an inferior, by an injudicious division.'" Americans ought therefore to avoid "being beaten in detachments."

Washington went on to say that there should be a garrison at Ticonderoga to prevent a penetration from Canada. The principal defensive point, however, was to be the Hudson Highlands. The force there would act to prevent the enemy from moving up the Hudson. It could promptly march north if an incursion came from Quebec province or south to New Jersey, if the British moved across the state, to attack Philadelphia. Troops could easily reach Peekskill from New England, and then shift north or south as required. This, with variations taking place that year, remained the core of his strategy. It involved keeping the various parts of the American army in full communication. The British were to be attacked "if they formed an injudicious division."

The original British plan for the conquest of America projected an invasion from Canada to join with the forces taking New York. These would then cut off New England. Washington had upset them by grimly holding onto Manhattan until the fall of 1776 and then by stopping Howe at White Plains. The Canadian portion of the British plan had also stalled in the north. The original plans were changed in 1777 when Howe decided to take Philadelphia, leaving New York with only a defensive garrison. Washington quickly learned from his agents in Philadelphia that Howe was trying to recruit pilots with a knowledge of the Delaware. At least a part of Howe's army would be coming by sea, if this plan were to be executed.

Washington did not know that Howe had requested heavy reinforcements—fifteen thousand troops—from England so that he could make a combined attack across New Jersey and up the Delaware. His failure to receive the needed men and ships, along with Washington's New Jersey defenses, made him eventually decide to take his troops on the sea route.

That winter General John Burgoyne had sold the king and Germain on a plan for a new enterprise from Canada that would involve fifteen thousand men of all ranks. Leaving behind a garrison in Quebec, Burgoyne himself would descend into the United States by Lake Champlain. An additional force would sail up the Saint Lawrence and then move across New York's Mohawk Valley from Lake Ontario. No one in authority bothered particularly about the long supply lines involved. Burgoyne's operations seem to have been planned and approved independently of General Howe's schemes to go south. As it was to turn out, there were six separate British armies operating in 1777: three maintaining stations in Quebec, Newport, and New York; a fourth moved eastward across New York state; a fifth marched south from Montreal; and a sixth wallowed for weeks at sea before landing at the head of the Chesapeake. Throughout, Washington's strategic plans held until they were, in part, wrecked by the vainglory of General Gates. Nonetheless, by the end of the year, at least twelve enemy general officers had been killed, captured, or driven from the country. In addition, the British commander in chief offered his resignation to London.

By early May Washington had reports of the invasion projected from Canada. He automatically assumed that Howe would cooperate with it and that an attack on Philadelphia seemed less probable. He ordered General McDougall to survey all sources of food on both sides of the Hudson, in case he brought his troops north. He urged each of the northern states to raise more men, particularly to reinforce Ticonderoga. He detached six of his brigadiers for northern service and ordered eight Massachusetts regiments, recently recruited, to Peekskill. He also asked Greene, Knox, and Wayne to examine and strengthen the fortifications of the Hudson Highlands.

In mid-May Sullivan was assigned to Princeton, with instructions to keep a close watch for any movements by Howe. If Howe headed for the Delaware, he was to harass and impede Howe's movements but to be ready at all times to retreat to hilly country. If the enemy moved to Morristown or the Hudson, they were to be annoyed night and day by small parties. Sullivan was ordered always to have his troops ready to march at a moment's notice and never to risk a general engagement.

General Howe had spent the winter comfortably in New York with his mistress, Mrs. Elizabeth Loring, wife of Howe's Loyalist commissary of prisoners. Her fame became lasting because of various verses that circulated, including one from Francis Hopkinson's "Ballad of the Kegs," which is, perhaps, the most widely quoted of revolutionary rhymes:

> *Sir William, he, snug as a flea,*
> *Lay all this time a-snoring*
> *Nor dreamed of harm, as he lay warm*
> *In Bed with Mrs. Loring.*

Another poem commented: "Awake, Sir Billy... leave your little filly, and open the Campaign." As spring began, Sir Billy did, in fact, make numerous moves to open it, but it was not till July that his campaign to take Philadelphia was under way. In March, British troops attacked Peekskill and did substantial damage before being driven off. In April an expeditionary force burned many houses and barns in Danbury, Connecticut. Brigadier Benedict Arnold, who helped to repel the enemy, was promoted by Congress.

GENERAL PROBLEMS

The commander in chief worked hard attempting to keep his top officers happy. On February 24 he wrote Sullivan: "Do not, my dear General Sullivan, torment yourself any longer with imaginary slights... No other officer of rank, in the whole army, has so often conceived himself neglected, slighted and ill treated, as you have done, and none I am sure has had less cause." Lord Stirling and his sister-in-law got into a squabble over a house she rented from him, and she complained to Washington, who asked him to treat her with all the respect due her sex. Stirling replied, in a rather persuasive letter, that she had caused all the trouble. Washington had assuaged Arnold's feeling of annoyance at not being made a major general prior to Danbury. Others of his command threatened to resign over their treatment by Congress, and

Washington was kept busy with their grievances. In turn John Adams complained they were scrambling for promotion, like apes after nuts.

Meanwhile Gates had gone to Ticonderoga, believing he was to take command in the north. Subsequently Congress reaffirmed that Schuyler was in command, to the annoyance of Gates, who was told he could report either to Schuyler or to Washington. Prior to that time, Gates had sent his reports of enemy movements to Congress only, from which source they belatedly reached the commander in chief. Washington complained to Gates, saying Howe would concert his actions with those of Burgoyne, and it was vital that he have the earliest intelligence of all British activities. Subsequently Gates told Washington he was depriving the northern army of tents and should not keep everything for himself. He added that he would appeal to Congress, "the common parent body of all the American armies," thus attempting to establish that he was independent of the commander in chief, who was holding back his needed supplies.

Washington was further plagued by the French, who demanded high rank and command. As early as February, Washington asked Gates, then still in Philadelphia, "to stop the shoals of French Men that are coming on to this Camp... For these ten days past, it has taken up half my time to hear their pretensions." Later, exasperated, he told Richard Henry Lee that many were adventurers whose effrontery was far greater than their merit. They often impressed Congress, however, and John Adams was particularly taken in by them. On June 19 Washington wrote to James Warren: "We have three capital characters here, Monsr. de Coudray, General Conway and Monsr. de la Balme. These are great and learned men. Coudray is the most promising officer in France." As it turned out, all were intriguers who made trouble for the American commander in chief.

Phillippe Tronson du Coudray had helped Beaumarchais to select artillery for America. He then arranged with Deane to proceed to the United States as a major general and inspector general of engineers and artillery, with a commission dated to make him senior to every officer in the army except Washington. Hearing of this, Washington wrote to John Hancock, protesting that this might cost him the valuable services of Henry Knox, who had labored so long with the American artillery service. When rumor reached camp that Congress had confirmed the appointment, Knox, Greene, and others threatened to resign. Congress was furious, and John Adams wrote angrily to Greene, saying that many members wanted the generals arrested or dismissed from the service. This storm blew over but resentment continued in Congress; this eventually spewed over onto Washington. Congress made du Coudray a major general but subsequently appointed him inspector general of ordnance, which was intended as a staff rather than a line appointment. When Washington informed du Coudray that some of the artillery sent from France was too cumbersome to move and he was having it recast, du Coudray wrote tartly, implying that Washington was ignorant of the subject and had been too easily influenced by another French officer, the chevalier du Plessis. Washington sent a long, polite reply to du Coudray outlining in detail the reasons the guns could not be easily transported "through the Mountainous and Woody country in which our operations most commonly are." He added: "I am at a loss to conceive how you could imagine that I had been governed in my determination in this matter by the advice of Monsieur Du Plessis... It can hardly be supposed that either Genl. Knox or myself would repose so implicit a confidence in his representations and counsels, as to regulate our measures entirely by them, in an affair of so much consequence." Du Coudray was drowned in September while crossing the Schuylkill River, to the ill-concealed relief of many in the American army. Even the kindly Lafayette called it "a happy accident."

Augustin de la Balme got Congress to appoint him inspector general of cavalry. After creating difficulties and doing nothing, he resigned in October. Conway, an Irishman in the service of France, was made a brigadier and then a major general, following which he attempted to oust Washington from the army in order to get the command for Gates.

BOUND BROOK

From January to May Washington continued his partisan attacks on British foraging parties. Hamilton estimated that as many as five hundred British were killed or wounded that spring, with relatively light American losses. In addition the enemy suffered greatly from sickness and desertion. Howe's army was less formidable than it had been the preceding year and few reinforcements came from England.

By the middle of May Washington had built his strength in New Jersey to about nine thousand men, in addition to the regiments that he had stationed from Peekskill to Ticonderoga. On May 28 he marched them to Middle Brook, in order to give them exercise and training after the long winter at Morristown. The army soon saw some action when Howe and Cornwallis endeavored to bring them to a general engagement. As Hamilton, reflecting Washington's views, wrote at the time, this was the only way the British could win the war, but it was the one thing the Americans had to avoid. Their army was increasing while time was diminishing the enemy forces, but Washington was still too weak for a major battle. As long as the American army existed, the British could hold only one or two posts; if they held more, they had to divide and the Americans could then attack.

Howe sent eighteen thousand men to New Jersey on June 12 to try to draw Washington's army, half its size, into battle. Howe and Cornwallis did all they could for nearly three weeks to draw Washington into a trap, but he eluded their maneuvers. At the end of June, Howe gave up and withdrew all British troops from New Jersey to Staten Island. On July 24 Lord North sent the king a report "by which his Majesty will see that Sir Wm. Howe has found Mr. Washington's camp too strong to venture to attack it, & has embarked his troops as Lord North supposes for Chesapeake Bay in order to attack Philadelphia." Howe's embarkation was so slow that he did not set sail until the day before the king received this letter.

TICONDEROGA

In the meantime, Gentleman Johnny Burgoyne had set out from Canada with high hopes and many Indian braves to restore the king's peace to the United States. Burgoyne had drafted the proclamation issued by General Gage from besieged Boston. Now, on his own, he produced another, which resulted in even more laughter in America and England and a parody by Francis Hopkinson. On June 23, 1777, he announced to Americans: "By John Burgoyne, Esq., etc., etc., Lieut. General of his Majesty's Forces in America, Colonel of the Queen's Regiment of Light Dragoons, Governor of Fort-William in North-Britain, one of the Representatives of the Commons of Great-Britain in Parliament, and commanding an Army and fleet in an Expedition from Canada etc. etc. etc... At the Head of Troops in the full Powers of Health, Discipline, and Valour, determined to strike where necessary, and anxious to save where possible, I, by these Presents, invite and exhort all Persons, in Places where the Progress of this Army may point, and by the Blessing of God I will extend it FAR, to maintain such a Conduct as may justify me in protecting their Lands, Habitations, and Families... If notwithstanding these Endeavors and sincere Inclination to assist them, the Phrenzy of Hostility should remain, I trust I shall stand acquitted in the Eyes of God and Men in denouncing and executing the Vengeance of the State against the wilful Outcast. The Messengers of Justice and of Wrath await them in the field, and Devastation, famine and every concomitant Horror." Hopkinson's parody said, in part:

I Issue This My Manifesto
By John Burgoyne and Burgoyne, John, Esq.
And Graced with titles still more higher,
For I'm Lieutenant-general too,
Of George's troops both red and blue...
And furthermore, when I am there,
In House of Commons I appear
(Hoping ere long to be a Peer),
Being a member of that virtuous band
Who always vote at North's command...
And all my titles to display,
I'll end with thrice et cetera...
I will let loose the dogs of Hell,
Ten thousand Indians, who shall yell
And foam and tear, and grin and roar,
And drench their moccasins in gore...
They'll scalp your heads, and kick your shins,
And rip your —, and flay your skins...
If after all these loving warnings...
You shall remain as deaf as adder...
I swear by George and by St. Paul
I will exterminate you all.

John Burgoyne commanded king's troops, who wore red coats; Hessians, who wore blue; and Indians, who largely wore skin—altogether some nine thousand officers and men. With them were an enormous baggage train and many women, ranging from officers' wives to prostitutes. Baroness von Riedesel, wife of the general in command of the Germans, wrinkled up her nose at Burgoyne, who, she wrote, spent his nights in his tent drinking champagne with his mistress.

At Ticonderoga, the American defenders had thirty-four hundred troops under General St. Clair, many inexperienced militia. When General Gates inspected Ticonderoga, a proposal was made to him to fortify Sugar Loaf Mountain, a mile from the fortress, but he ruled out this scheme as impracticable. The British, more skilled in military matters, quickly seized Sugar Loaf when they got to Ticonderoga and mounted guns on it. By this maneuver, they drove out St. Clair and the Americans on July 6 for an easy victory. This was a heavy blow to morale in the north.

Germain received the dispatch announcing the fall of Ticonderoga on August 23 and sent it with a note to the king: "Lord George Germain has the honour of Congratulating your Majesty upon the great and Glorious success of Lt. General Burgoyne in taking Ticonderoga, in destroying vessels Boats, Stores, Artillery &c &c &c."

WASHINGTON MOVES NORTH

On July 1 Washington reported to Congress that the British had evacuated New Jersey. Throughout July Washington continued to assume that Howe, in all probability, would go up the Hudson to make a juncture with Burgoyne. During this period General Henry Clinton was, in fact, trying to argue Howe into this plan. Washington's counter-strategy continued the policy of maintaining the Hudson Highlands as the key to an American defense system that would be flexible enough to meet any British moves.

After Howe abandoned Amboy, Washington urgently warned the American General George Clinton in the Highlands to be on a sharp lookout for an attack. He asked that militia be ordered out immediately: "the least delay may be productive of the most fatal consequences." He also ordered two regiments to proceed at once to Peekskill. He asked General John Nixon and four regiments to proceed north, to reinforce Schuyler as soon as the two new brigades got to Peekskill. Washington continued to think there was a preconcerted plan between Burgoyne and Howe, though none existed in reality. On the other hand, he could never be certain that Burgoyne's moves might not be a feint to enable Howe to attack Philadelphia. By July 4, Washington had moved his army to Morristown in order to be ready to march north if Howe attacked there. He put troops on the alert and ordered his officers to strip themselves of heavy baggage. "If after this second notice, they continue to fill and encumber wagons with old tables, chests, chairs, &c., they are not to be surprised if they are left in the field."

Shortly afterward, Washington dispatched Sullivan to the Highlands to get intelligence of possible enemy movements. By July 7, on the basis of his information from Staten Island and Manhattan, he began to question whether Howe really planned to go north. At this time Henry Clinton was still trying to argue Howe into so doing but his commander was unshakable. When Howe heard that Washington had sent more troops into upper New York, he was determined to take an additional brigade with him to Philadelphia.

Washington learned from Schuyler on July 12 that Ticonderoga had fallen to Burgoyne. At Schuyler's request he immediately sent cannon, entrenching tools, kettles, and gunpowder, and regretted that he had no tents or further regiments to spare. However, he added, he had some reserve troops who could go north in an emergency. Soon thereafter, Washington moved his army to Smith's Clove, near Haverstraw, in order to head off any move by Howe. From there he wrote to Schuyler not to despair over Ticonderoga. He added: "I hope a Spirited Opposition will check the progress of General Burgoyne's Arms and that the confidence derived from his success, will hurry him into measures, that will in their consequence be favourable to us." He requested Schuyler to send down every boat from Albany so that he could move troops north by water if necessary.

The next day he informed Schuyler he had decided to order Benedict Arnold, an aggressive officer, to help him. Arnold, he said, knew the country; he was a New Englander, and he would give spirit to New England troops. A few days later he wrote to Schuyler to suggest that Arnold might be especially useful in western New York, if the enemy attacked Fort Schuyler. This turned out to be an accurate forecast.

Washington made other efforts to help the northern army. He wrote to Schuyler on July 22 that he had found some tents and was sending them on; he had also decided to send General Glover and his Marblehead regiment north. He ordered General Lincoln, who was popular with the Massachusetts militia, to take charge of similar forces in Vermont. He advised Schuyler that it was particularly important to attack Burgoyne's left flanks from that area. By August Burgoyne was complaining to London that the militia on his left were like "a gathering storm." In sending three New England officers, Washington recognized that New England disliked Schuyler. He gave both political and military support, in the expectation that New York and New England would then work together to destroy Burgoyne. He appealed to Massachusetts and New Hampshire to add all the militia they could. Washington wrote further to Schuyler on July 22:

I yet look forward to a fortunate and happy change. I Trust General Burgoyne's Army will meet, sooner or later an effectual check, and I suggested before, that the success, he has had, will precipitate his ruin. From your accounts, he appears to be pursuing that line of conduct, which of all others, is most favourable to us; I mean acting in Detachment... Could we be so happy, as to cut one of them off, supposing it should not exceed four, five or six hundred Men. It would inspirit the people and do away with much of their present anxiety... They would fly to Arms and afford every aid in their power.

On July 24 Washington received confirmed intelligence that Howe had sailed with an armada of 260 warships and transports. The fleet was observed off Sandy Hook; this meant that it was heading south. Washington wrote that he found it "unaccountable" that Howe had abandoned Burgoyne, but he moved immediately to defend Philadelphia. He and his army raced south and, by July 31, they were again crossing the Delaware.

This was one of the more peculiar periods of the war and totally nerve-wracking for Washington and his army. From July 23 until August 25, the greater part of the British army rolled around the Atlantic Ocean and Chesapeake Bay. Washington could never be sure of what would happen, whether Howe would turn north again or go farther south. Howe was sighted off Delaware on July 30 and then his fleet disappeared. Washington was uncertain whether Howe would head back to the Hudson. On August 10, the fleet appeared off Maryland and then for a long period again disappeared. Washington was now in Pennsylvania but nearly two weeks went by with no news. Howe was again sighted, this time coming up the Chesapeake. On August 25 he anchored at Head of Elk (Elkton) in Maryland and began to dis-embark his troops. Howe was now farther from Philadelphia than he had been in Amboy two months before, but the terrain was much easier for him than it was in New Jersey. Washington would have found it militarily prefer-able to have attacked New York, held by Clinton with only seven thousand troops, but to do so meant abandoning the capital and Congress to the enemy. Politically this was impossible, and Washington was forced to fight the main British army with inferior forces.

The campaigns from August to November 1777 were one of the two most extensive campaigns the British undertook in America. Fighting ranged from Maryland and Delaware in the south to the New York Highlands, the Mohawk Valley, Ticonderoga, and into Vermont in the north. In the end, American strategy, employing forces inferior to those of the enemy, bent but never broke. Britain gained a single limited objective, Philadelphia, but her strategy lay in the dust.

BATTLES IN NEW YORK AND VERMONT

Schuyler made every effort to obstruct Burgoyne's march southward by destroying all bridges and felling trees along the roads. He also pulled out all cattle, food, and forage along the way, leaving the country bare. Burgoyne himself decided to cut a road from Skenesborough to Fort Edward rather than go by water. This delayed him more than three weeks.

In the meantime the second invading army of some eighteen hundred men under Brigadier Barry St. Leger moved eastward from Fort Oswego, on Lake Ontario, through the Mohawk Valley to Fort Stanwix, near the present Rome.

There two American forces, one in the fort under Colonel Peter Gansevoort, and the other militia under Brigadier Nicholas Herkimer, held St. Leger until Schuyler could send Benedict Arnold with relief. Arnold's timely approach forced St. Leger to raise the siege on August 22. He retreated to Lake Ontario and Canada. One of the six British armies of 1777 was knocked out of the war. Burgoyne could no longer count on a junction with St. Leger.

Burgoyne, desperate for food, forage, and transport, largely because of Schuyler's actions, dispatched into the New Hampshire grants (now Vermont) a force of Hessians and Indians to get horses, meat, and grain. A party of militia under Colonel John Stark (who had been refused a promotion by Congress) killed or captured almost all of the enemy at the battle of Bennington on August 16. A relief party sent to their aid by Burgoyne was also badly mauled. Altogether Burgoyne lost more than nine hundred men. Congress quickly promoted Stark to his brigadiership.

The Indian allies of Burgoyne were considered a particular threat both to the army and to the inhabitants of upper New York. To counteract them, on August 22 Washington ordered his best partisan regiment, Colonel Daniel Morgan's corps of riflemen, north to fight them on their own terms. He also added additional regiments from New York to the northern forces.

Schuyler did not reap the benefits of Washington's efforts on his behalf. New Englanders in Congress savagely attacked him for the loss of Ticonderoga, which was more properly attributable to Gates. In an atmosphere that Washington on August 4 called "Suspicion and Fear," John Adams led a successful move to dismiss Schuyler from his command. In a gesture, Congress asked Washington to nominate a successor but he sidestepped this as a political trap. Congress then chose the man New England wanted, Horatio Gates. He was an enemy of Washington and the choice was to have unfortunate consequences. Schuyler bore the outrage with dignity and continued his efforts to help the American forces. Gates took over the command on August 19, after the victory of Bennington and just before St. Leger was beaten. Schuyler's successes brought such an accretion of militia to Gates' camp that he soon had twelve thousand men, while Burgoyne's army had fallen to fewer than five thousand effectives.

For the first time Washington asked Congress to define his authority if he moved north to join Gates. His August 4 letter noted that the northern department had always been considered by Congress as "under their direction." On August 21 he repeated his request to define his powers. On August 23 Congress resolved that they had never intended, by setting up a departmental command, "to Supercede the power of General Washington as the Commander-in-Chief of all the Continental Land Forces within the United

States." This did not mean quite what it said. Congress, at Gates' request, did subsequently and unfortunately circumscribe the powers of Washington with relation to Gates.

THE BATTLE OF BRANDYWINE

Washington was now back in Pennsylvania, the state with the largest percentage of Tories. Philadelphia was the capital of the confederacy. These were two factors that led Howe to choose it for attack. Washington decided, in consequence, to march his army in strength through Philadelphia in order to give pause, if not to the Tories, at least to those who wanted to save their skins by being on the winning side.

The ten thousand men made as brave a show as they could on August 24 as they marched through the capital. Their uniforms, ragged and worn, had been washed or brushed. Every man wore a sprig of green in his hat. Washington, impeccably uniformed, rode with Lafayette by his side, and the young marquis got his first cheers and taste of glory. The parade took two hours to pass the watching Congress and only John Adams complained, undoubtedly correctly, that they didn't quite look like soldiers or quite march in step.

Howe took a long time to unload his troops, baggage, and horses. Many of his men were sick, while the draft and cavalry horses that had survived the trip were weak from lack of fodder. Howe took his time getting fresh meat, provisions, and forage, a task quite easy in the cooperating Quaker country of southern Maryland. Washington, along with Greene and Lafayette, reconnoitered Head of Elk on the next two days. Thereafter he ordered out Delaware and Maryland militia to harass Howe's flanks as his army marched and to remove all cattle and forage from the enemy's paths. He reported to Congress that Captain Henry Lee and his cavalry had captured twenty-four British prisoners.

On September 5 Washington issued general orders to the army. In these he indicated that this was the enemy's "last attempt" to take Philadelphia. They had tried to capture it the preceding year and failed. They had begun another campaign to cross New Jersey that summer and that, too, failed. Howe's attempt to come up the Delaware had been frustrated by American fortifications on the river, and he had been forced to use the longer Chesapeake route. Howe would now gamble on taking Philadelphia. If he were beaten "the war is at an end... One bold stroke will free the land from rapine, devastations and burnings, and female innocence from brutal lust and violence... If we behave like men, this third Campaign will be the last... The eyes of all America, and of Europe are turned upon us, as on those by whom the event of the war is to be determined."

By September 6 the British army was on the move, its baggage left behind. Washington too ordered his army to travel light to meet an expected "speedy and rapid movement" of the enemy. Lord Howe's fleet put down the bay in order to return up the Delaware and meet the army at Philadelphia. On September 9 the two armies were two miles apart. Washington reported to Congress that Howe had started to move, his obvious plan was to flank his right, to cross the Brandywine, and to make straight for Philadelphia. To off-set this, he proposed to cross the river, and take post on the high ground at Chadd's Ford.

Washington took a few minutes out, while waiting for battle, to direct Putnam, commanding at Peekskill, to move part of his forces down to New Jersey to prevent an expected attack by Clinton on that state. He added that the enemy was advancing but he trusted "under the smiles of Providence... that we shall give them a repulse or at most... a painful and dear bought victory."

The best description of the battle was written three years later by the French general, the chevalier de Chastellux. He spent many hours at the Brandywine battlefield with French and American officers who had fought there. The ter-rain had not changed in any essential detail; Chastellux noted that many trees still bore the marks of bullets and cannon shot. Prior to his visit he discussed the battle in detail with Generals Washington, Wayne, Sullivan, and Lafayette. In tracing the movements of the armies, he used a copy of Howe's map of the battle. Chastellux commented, after his inspection of December 7, 1780:

> *The English, having finished their debarkation, were ready to advance into the country; [Washington's] right flank was exposed, and he was leaving both Philadelphia and the whole of Lancaster County uncovered. It was determined therefore that the army should cross back over Brandywine Creek and encamp on the left [eastern] bank of this river. The position chosen was certainly the best that could be taken to dispute the passage. The left of the position was very good and was supported by thick woods extending as far as the junction of the creek with the Delaware... A battery of cannon with a good parapet was pointed towards Chadd's Ford, and everything appeared secure on that side; but to the right the ground was so covered that it was impossible to judge of the movements of the enemy... The only precaution that could be taken was therefore to place five or six brigades in echelon, to watch that sector. General Sullivan had the command of these brigades; he received orders to keep abreast of the enemy, should they march by their left; and on the supposition that they would unite their forces near Chadd's Ford, he was himself to cross the river and make a powerful diversion of their flank.*

When a general has foreseen everything, when he has made the best possible dispositions, and when his activity, judgment, and courage in the action are equal to the wisdom of his measures, has he not already triumphed in the eyes of every impartial judge? And if by some unforeseen misfortunes, the laurels he has merited drop from his hands, is it not for History to gather them up carefully and replace them on his brow?... Let us now observe how such wise dispositions were upset by the mistakes of a few officers and by the inexperience of the troops.

On the 11th of September, General Howe occupied the heights on the right [west] of the creek; he there formed part of his troops in line of battle and had batteries placed opposite Chadd's Ford, while his light troops were attacking and driving before them a corps of riflemen, who had crossed over the right bank to observe his motions more closely. General Washington seeing that the cannonade was continuing without any disposition on the part of the enemy to cross the river, concluded that they had another object. He was informed that a great part of their army had marched up the creek and was threatening his right; he realized how important it was to keep an attentive eye on all movements of this corps; but the country was so covered with thickets, that the patrols could discover nothing; It must be observed that General Washington had only a very small number of horsemen, and that he sent these to the right towards Dilworth to scout that sector. He ordered an officer, whom he judged an intelligent one, to cross the river and inform himself accurately of the route Lord Cornwallis was taking, for it was Cornwallis who commanded this separate corps. The officer returned and assured him that Cornwallis was marching by his right to join Knyphausen, in the direction of Chadd's Ford... Another officer was then sent, who reported that Cornwallis had changed his direction, and that he was rapidly advancing by the road to Jefferies's Ford, two miles above Birmingham Church. General Sullivan was immediately ordered to march thither with all the troops of the right. Unfortunately the roads were badly reconnoitred, and not all open: with great difficulty General Sullivan got through the woods, and when he came out of them to gain a small eminence near Birmingham Church, he found the English columns were coming up the same height on the opposite side. It was no easy matter to range into order of battle such troops as his; he had neither the time to choose his position nor to form his line. The English reached the eminence, drove the Americans back on the woods, and pursued them to the edge of these woods, where they finally dispersed them.

During the short time that this rout lasted, Lord Stirling and General Conway had time to form their brigade on rather advantageous ground: this was a sort of hillock, partly covered by the woods which backed it up. Their left was protected by these same woods, and on the right of this hillock, but a little in the rear, was the Virginia line, which had been ranged in battle formation, on slightly rising ground and on the edge of a sort of grove. The left column of the enemy, which had not been engaged with Sullivan, deployed rapidly and marched against these troops with as much order as vivacity and courage. The Americans made a very smart fire, which did not check the English, and it was not till the latter were within twenty yards of them, that they gave way and plunged into the woods. Lord Stirling, M. de La Fayette, and General Sullivan himself, after the defeat of his division, fought with this body of troops, whose post was the most important, and who resisted the longest. It was here that M. de La Fayette was wounded in his left leg, while rallying the troops who were beginning to waver. On the right, the Virginia line made some resistance; but the English had gained a height, from which their artillery took them obliquely.

General Knyphausen heard the firing... He descended from the heights in two columns, one at Jones's Ford, which turned the battery of the Americans, and the other lower down at Chadd's Ford. The latter marched straight to the battery of General Wayne, whose brigade was in line of battle, the left on a height and the right inclined towards the battery, withdrew his right and strengthened the heights, thus operating a sort of change of front. In a country where there are neither open columns, nor successive positions to take in case of misfortune, it is difficult to make any provision for retreat. The different corps which had been beaten all rushed headlong into the Chester Road... At nightfall, General Wayne also took the road, but in better order.

Chastellux's description makes clear a point that subsequent historians have overlooked, that the country was so thickly wooded that reconnaissance was extremely difficult. Chastellux could not know that the flanking turn over the ford to the north of Washington's army was led by Pennsylvania Tories, headed by Joseph Galloway. In effect, Washington was in enemy territory, and he found intelligence hard to get from local farmers. By midnight most of the American army was at Chester. Though overcome with fatigue, Washington reorganized his troops, and he found the strength to report to Congress:

I am sorry to inform you, that in this day's engagement, we have been obliged to leave the field. Unfortunately the intelligence received of the enemy's advancing up the Brandywine, and crossing at a ford about six miles above us, was uncertain and contradictory, notwithstanding all my pains to get the best. This prevented my making a disposition, adequate to the force with which the Enemy attacked us on the right; in consequence of which the troops first engaged, were obliged to retire before they could be reinforced. In the midst of the attack on the right, that body of the Enemy which remained on the other side of Chad's Ford, crossed it, and attacked the division there under General Maxwell who, after a severe conflict, also retired... Though we fought under many disadvantages, and were from the causes, above mentioned, obliged to retire, yet our loss of men is not, I am persuaded, very considerable, I believe much less than the enemy's. We have also lost about seven or eight pieces of cannon.

Notwithstanding the misfortunes of the day, I am happy to find the troops in good spirits; and I hope another time we shall compensate for the losses now sustained. The Marquis La Fayette was wounded in the leg, and Genl. Woodford in the hand.

History has rightly given the victory to Howe but has failed to second Chastellux's award of laurels to Washington for his placement of troops. The American army that fought at Brandywine had not read the future verdicts and many thought they had won against a much larger British army. Their morale was high. This was unlike the battle of Long Island where the army thought it was worse beaten than it was and despair caused nearly a third of the troops to desert. Casualties for the British were under six hundred, and for the Americans around one thousand. The wounded Lafayette, who had just passed his twentieth birthday, emerged as a hero to the Americans.

On September 13 Washington issued a general order from Germantown: "The Honble. Congress, in consideration of the gallant behaviour of the troops on Thursday last, their fatigue since and from a full conviction they will manifest a bravery worthy of the cause they have undertaken to defend, having been pleased to order thirty hogshead of rum to be distributed among them... the Commander in Chief... orders the Commissary... to deliver to each officer and soldier, one gill [4 oz.] per day, while it lasts."

Congress and Washington had given much thought to the defenses of the Delaware River and here French engineers were most helpful. Washington had no more continentals to spare for the river's defense and informed Congress that militia would have to be used. While watching Philadelphia, he also kept an eye on the Hudson. As soon as Sir Henry Clinton made a sortie into New Jersey, he asked Putnam to dispatch reinforcements to the state. At the same time he warned him they might also move up the Hudson and Putnam could not be "too vigilant."

Washington reported to Congress on September 15 that Howe and the main body of the British were at Dilworth, "not far from the field of Action where they have been busily employed in burying their Dead." He added that he was moving northwest and would recross the Schuylkill to prevent the enemy "from turning our right flank, which they seem to have a violent inclination to effect, by all their Movements."

This letter referred also to the case of General Sullivan, who had conducted an earlier and abortive raid on Staten Island. At that time Congress had suggested a court-martial for him. Now, much annoyed at his failure to spot Cornwallis' flanking move at Brandywine, Congress ordered Washington to hold the court. The commander had been adopting an increasingly tough approach to Congress; he firmly said this was impossible. "We are now most probably on the point of another Action, and to derange the Army by withdrawing so many General Officers from it, may and must be attended with many disagreeable, if not ruinous, Consequences... How can the Army be possibly conducted with a prospect of Success, if the General Officers are taken off, in the moment of Battle?... I am obliged to observe... that I cannot be answerable for the consequences."

A near-battle with the British the next day failed to materialize when heavy rains poured down on both armies. Much of Washington's ammunition was made useless, and he marched his men to the powder magazine at Warwick Furnace. From there the army moved towards Valley Forge. An American detachment stationed at Paoli under General Wayne was routed when British troops caught them in ambush. By this time Howe had moved to White House Tavern, west of Philadelphia.

On September 18 Alexander Hamilton urgently warned Congress that Howe was able to send troops into Philadelphia in greater force than any militia stationed there and its members should leave the capital. Aroused between midnight and three in the morning, they fled the city angry and dispirited. Their chagrin they later took out on Washington. John Adams let out a bellow in his diary of September 21. This has often been quoted for its blast at Washington, usually omitting his even more bitter comment on Gates in the north. Adams criticized Washington for his false alarm (the British did not occupy Philadelphia until September 26) and for maneuvering his army very injudiciously. He remarked that a brigade from him, along with the town's militia, could have cut Howe's army to bits. Adams added that he thought Gates was acting "the same timorous, defensive Part, which has involved us in so many disasters.—Oh Heaven! grant Us one great Soul!" Congress, after its dispersion, settled first at Lancaster and then York, where Adams complained that their quarters were too crowded. Not long afterward, he requested and was given leave by Congress. He went home intending to resign.

Before leaving, Adams informed everyone that the eighteen thousand troops that Howe had brought with him were, in reality, only half that number. On his part, Washington had been putting out greatly exaggerated figures of his strength in order to fool Howe. It is doubtful that Washington succeeded with the British but he seems to have persuaded many Americans. In consequence of Adams' and Washington's statements, members of Congress and others thought Washington far stronger than Howe, and they bitterly resented his defensive tactics and the fact that he had been beaten.

To augment his army, Washington ordered reinforcements from New Jersey that had gone to the state to meet an expected attack by Sir Henry Clinton. These arrived in time to induce Washington to attack the British at Germantown. On September 19 Washington recrossed the Schuylkill. Two days later Howe moved to Valley Forge and then north along the river. Washington followed in a parallel column on the other side. Washington had two fears: that Howe would try either to turn his right flank or try to capture Reading, where the major American army stores were located. Howe's march had been a feint. He suddenly backtracked and crossed the river on September 22 to Germantown. This placed him between Washington's army and the capital. A few days later he sent Cornwallis into the city with advance troops who received many welcoming cheers from the Tories.

FREEMAN'S FARM

On the day that Congress left Philadelphia a major battle took place in the north. A few days before, Burgoyne had crossed the Hudson and moved south with his dwindling forces and supplies. He met Gates' army at Freeman's Farm, where Gates had entrenched on Bemis Heights, north of Stillwater. Gates intended to hold this position and wait for the enemy to attack, but Arnold and Morgan persuaded him to send them and their men forward on the left flank. Morgan and his crack riflemen broke up an advancing group of Indians and provincials, but they were temporarily pushed back by British regulars. Arnold came up with his troops to help and then asked for more men from Gates. These were refused and angry words were exchanged between them. German reinforcements came in and drove Arnold back. By night the indecisive battle was over, but Burgoyne received a message from Sir Henry Clinton saying he could make an attack on the Hudson Highlands to provide a diversion if Burgoyne so desired. Burgoyne asked him to do so with all urgency.

WASHINGTON MOVES

While Burgoyne waited for Clinton, and Gates for Burgoyne, Washington began a march towards Philadelphia. On September 26 he advanced from what is now Pottstown to the present town of Schwenksville. He also moved to reinforce, as fast as he could, the forts on the Delaware in order to prevent Lord Howe from coming up the river to join his brother. He informed Congress that he was having difficulty in marching his army because 10 percent of his men were barefoot. On September 28 he issued orders to the army:

> *The Commander in Chief has the happiness again to congratulate the army on the success of the American Arms, at the northward. On the 19th. instant an engagement took place between Gen. Burgoyne's army and the left wing of ours under Gen. Gates... our troops fighting with the greatest bravery and not giving an inch of ground... A detachment from the northern army under Col. Browne... have got possession of the old French lines at Ticonderoga.*

The same day he called a council of war and informed it that he would soon have about eight thousand continentals and three thousand militia. According to his best estimate, Howe had only eight thousand men at Germantown, the remainder being in Philadelphia with Cornwallis. He asked if they should now attack the enemy. The council voted ten to five against but suggested that the army move closer to them. He so informed Congress, adding his opinion that "we may count upon the total ruin of Burgoyne." He wrote to Putnam on October 1 to say that he did not think Clinton planned an attack in the Highlands because of Burgoyne's perilous situation. This was written while Clinton was preparing such an action. Washington soon learned, however, that Clinton had received reinforcements from Europe and this changed his opinion. He urgently requested the governor of Connecticut to send militia reinforcements to Putnam, from whom he had drawn a substantial force. On October 2 he issued a further order to his army: "The whole army are to strike their tents tomorrow morning at 8 O'clock, and get ready to march. At *nine* the march is to begin."

The four days from October 4 to 7 were among the most critical of the war for the American and British armies. Around fifty thousand troops of both sides engaged in battle from Pennsylvania to northern New York. The enemy, led by six British and German lieutenant generals, won two Pyrrhic field victories and lost one army. Within a few weeks the British were shut up in Philadelphia and in the area around New York City. Except for Newport with its small garrison, the rest of the country was liberated and Versailles was free to take advantage of Britain's difficulties.

GERMANTOWN—OCTOBER 4

On October 3 Washington's orders to his troops further praised Gates' successes in the north. He also mentioned a victory by the American frigate *Randolph*, which had taken four out of the five enemy ships it had met. He went on:

> *This army, the main American army, will certainly not suffer itself to be outdone by their northern Brethren; they will never endure such disgrace... Covet! my Countrymen, and fellow soldiers! Covet! a share of the glory due to heroic deeds!... Let the enemy no longer triumph. They brand you with ignominious epithets. Will you suffer the wound given to your Country to go unrevenged... The term of <u>Mercy</u> is expired, General Howe has, within a few days proclaimed all who had not then submitted, to be beyond the reach of it, and has left us no choice but <u>Conquest</u> <u>or</u> <u>Death</u>... My fellow soldiers!... Be firm, be brave; shew yourselves men, and victory is yours!*

Washington's war council now unanimously approved an immediate attack on the British forces at Germantown, which were somewhat greater than Washington's intelligence had estimated. Though his plans came fairly close to succeeding in the subsequent battle, they were nonetheless very complex for inexperienced troops and officers. Chastellux was much more critical of them than of his plan at Chadd's Ford. Accidents, ineptness, and fog threw them awry. Some idea of what they involved is shown by his orders the day before the battle:

> *The divisions of Sullivan and Wayne to form the right wing and attack the enemy's left; they are to march down the Monatany road. The divisions of Green and Steven to form the left wing and attack the enemy's right; they are to march down the Skippack Road, General Conway to march in front of the troops that compose the right wing, and file to attack the enemy's left flank. General McDougall to march in front of the troops that comprise the left wing, and file off to attack the enemy's left flank. General Nash and General Maxwell's brigade to form the corps de reserve and to be commanded by Major General Lord Stirling. The Corps de reserve to pass down the Skippack Road. General Armstrong to pass down the ridge road, pass by Leverings Tavern and take guides to cross the Wissahikon creek up*

the head of John Vandeering's mill-dam so as to fall above Joseph Warner's new house. Smallwood and Forman to pass down the road by a mill formerly Danl. Morris and Jacob Edges mill into the White marsh road at the Sandy run: thence to Whitemarsh Church, where take the left hand road, which leads to Jenkin's tavern, on the old York road, below Armitages, beyond the seven mile stone, half a mile from which turns off short to the right hand, fenced on both sides, which leads through the enemys incampment to German town market house. General McDougall to attack the right of the enemy in flank. General Smallwood and Forman to attack the right wing in flank and rear.

General Conway to attack the enemy's left flank and General Armstrong to attack their left wing in flank and rear.

Washington further wrote that each column should be within two miles of the enemy by 2 A.M. All were to attack simultaneously at five in the morning. The plan, more simply put, called for the army to march sixteen miles in the dark, two columns on main roads, and two partly across country, using rather vague landmarks. All were supposed to arrive at the same time, but one never got to Germantown, and a second reached there as the Americans began their retreat. Washington accompanied Sullivan and the left wing, perhaps because of congressional criticisms of that general's moves at Brandywine. The main army, moving along what is now Germantown Avenue, saw the sun rise as Chestnut Hill was crossed.

At Mount Airy, near Germantown, there was a first encounter with the enemy, which quickly developed into full-scale battle as British reinforcements moved up. The Americans determinedly used the bayonet, forcing a British retreat. Howe himself came up but was forced by the Americans back to Germantown. A morning mist soon turned to fog, making operations thereafter difficult for both sides. At this point of their retreat, the British, under Colonel Thomas Musgrave, got into the Benjamin Chew house on the Germantown road, quickly turning it into a small fortification.

The Americans had now to decide whether to go around or attack the house; the latter decision was made, primarily at Knox's urging. His artillery was unable to demolish a house built in the solid stone of Pennsylvania. From this point on, trouble developed for the Americans. Howe sent in further reinforcements and ordered Cornwallis to come from Philadelphia. In the meantime, Adam Stephen, Washington's mistrusted companion from the French and Indian War days, turned off from Greene's approaching column and headed for the firing. He had taken on too much rum against the morning chill and, seeing men in the fog, he ordered his command to fire on them.

They were Wayne's troops, from Sullivan's division, and they returned the fire. Each side retreated from the supposed enemy.

While this was occurring, Sullivan's men, who had carried out a major part of the attack, were running out of ammunition. They were forced to retire. Greene's fresher men took on the enemy, now reinforced by Cornwallis and his cavalry. Greene fought as long as he could, but he too had to retreat. Washington had taken personal command, exposing himself to every kind of danger, as he had often done before, but he could not rally his men. The tired army, which had marched all night and fought all morning, began its weary retreat. By noon they were at Chestnut Hill, from which they moved on twenty miles to Schwenksville.

Green forces had done well in attacking, without hesitation, well-led professionals and they had scented at times the near-proximity of victory. Americans killed, wounded, or missing totalled around one thousand, although the losses included a fair number of deserters. Each side had a general officer killed. Four days later, Howe expressed his opinion of the battle by writing urgently to Sir Henry Clinton in New York to send down four thousand reinforcements. Two weeks after that he pulled his army back from Germantown to Philadelphia and began to erect fortifications.

Washington's report to Congress on the following day is nearly as complicated as his line of march. His summary conclusion seems justified, for the Americans thought they had done well. Washington went out of his way to praise Sullivan, who was on Congress' black list. He wrote:

> *Upon the whole it may be said that the day was rather unfortunate than injurious. We sustained no material loss of Men and brought off all our Artillery, except one piece which was dismounted. The Enemy are nothing the better by the event; and our Troops, who are not in the least dispirited by it, have gained what all young troops gain by being in Action...*

> *In justice to Genl Sullivan and the whole right wing of the Army, whose conduct I had an opportunity of observing... I have the pleasure to inform you, that both Officers and Men behaved with a degree of Gallantry, that did them the highest honor.*

On October 6 the American commander sent a note to his British counterpart: "General Washington's compliments to General Howe. He has the pleasure to return him a dog, which accidentally fell into his hands, and by the inscription on the Collar, appears to belong to General Howe."

The news of Germantown reached Versailles before that of Saratoga. Vergennes, the foreign minister, remarked to the American commissioners, perhaps with diplomatic tact, that he was much impressed that Washington could build up a brand-new army that year and then go out and attack the British. That, he said, promised everything. Congress, too, congratulated Washington for attacking the enemy.

FORTS MONTGOMERY AND CLINTON
OCTOBER 5 AND 6

The day after Germantown, a battle took place in which the British general Henry Clinton faced the American generals, George and James Clinton, for possession of Fort Clinton, which was named for George Clinton. It was the only one of the three battles of the four days in which British naval forces participated.

When Sir Henry Clinton received reinforcements from England and an appeal from Burgoyne to do something, he moved with considerable speed to establish his diversion on Gates' rear. Forts Montgomery and Clinton were located on the west bank of the Hudson near Bear Mountain, across from Fort Independence and Peekskill. Putnam was stationed near Peekskill with some fifteen hundred troops, a garrison much reduced by Washington's urgent call for men. About six hundred men were on the west bank.

Sir Henry Clinton left New York with four thousand men in troopships guarded by three frigates and moved up the Hudson. On October 5, in the same kind of fog that had belabored Howe and Washington, he landed troops on the east bank as a feint to Putnam and his main force, who retired into prepared positions. The next day, the main British force of about twenty-one hundred men landed across the river and, without too much difficulty, took the two forts. The British destroyed these and then Fort Independence across the Hudson. Clinton sent his naval forces further up the river to burn Esopus (Kingston), the temporary state capital. They retired after receiving news of Burgoyne's surrender. Soon Clinton received Howe's urgent request for four thousand troops. He abandoned the Hudson Highlands and retired to New York.

BEMIS HEIGHTS — OCTOBER 7

The battle of Bemis Heights, more widely known as that of Saratoga, took place between an American army, commanded by an Englishman of the servant class, and an English army containing six officer members of the Houses of Lords and Commons.

Gates, with all his faults, had some of the patience of Washington and a willingness to let the enemy make mistakes. He told Governor Clinton of New York that Burgoyne, whom he had known in London, was a gambler. He would wait for him to stake his all. Arnold and others violently opposed this policy, which caused further dissension between Gates and Arnold. While he waited, additional strength poured into his camps. General Lincoln's militia were north of Burgoyne, busily cutting his supply lines and setting siege to Fort Ticonderoga. Other militia forces were operating to the east and west of Burgoyne's lines in a slowly strangling network.

Burgoyne's only hope was that Sir Henry Clinton's forces, moving north to attack Gates' rear, would force him to detach troops to the south, but the Highlands were far away and Gates did not swallow the bait. Clinton's messages of encouragement to Burgoyne were captured by the Americans. Forage for his horses and food for his troops became ever scarcer. There was no longer a possibility of retreat. Burgoyne had to fight or surrender.

On October 7 the British general determined on the gambling attack that Gates had awaited for more than two weeks. He ordered out a reconnaissance force of sixteen hundred, a mixed bag of Germans and British. Gates sent in only a portion of his forces, mainly Morgan's riflemen, keeping most of his troops in reserve. Burgoyne's right was rolled back, leaving the center open. At this point, Arnold, grumbling in his tent, dashed out, got on his horse, and took command in the center and helped to drive the enemy back. British General Simon Fraser was killed by Morgan's riflemen and Gates sent more men into the attack. Gates himself stayed in his quarters, a move that gained him no honor among his fighting men. Arnold and Morgan swept into the redoubt on the British right, killing its commander. Burgoyne's casualties were 600, the Americans' 150, including Generals Arnold and Lincoln, who were wounded. Burgoyne ordered a retreat towards Saratoga.

On October 13 Burgoyne opened a parley with Gates, who was now worried about Sir Henry Clinton's moves up the river. Gates somewhat weakly accepted a convention rather than a full surrender. This allowed Burgoyne's army to return to Great Britain after agreeing not to serve again in America. On October 17 the British army surrendered fifty-seven hundred prisoners, seven general officers, and a large quantity of guns and small arms. The tonic effect on the morale of the new United States was extraordinary and Gates became a great hero.

The convention caused endless complications, with both sides claiming breaches of faith. The captured forces were expected to sail from Boston, but Howe endeavored to change this to New York. There he hoped to exchange them for American prisoners, thus saving endless time and expense to the

British in sending replacements. Although Congress could not know this, they suspected some trick and asked that the British government and king ratify the terms. With one delay and another the captured army was not returned to Europe till after the war.

Gates' deplorable actions subsequent to the battle have tended to obscure a superb aspect of his achievement. By building his strength and patiently waiting, in spite of the outrage of some of his subordinates, for Burgoyne to take rash and impetuous action, he secured the surrender of an army at a cost, in final battle, of only one hundred fifty American casualties. This feat was not duplicated by any other commander, British or American, in the war.

The enemy garrisons at Ticonderoga and elsewhere in northern New York soon retired to Canada. Clinton had brought his men back from the Highlands, leaving all of the Hudson-Champlain area from the Canadian border to Westchester County clear of the British. Howe, with the major part of his forces, including the Royal Navy, was still struggling to clear the Delaware. Washington now saw that he could get back from the north a large portion of the regiments he had dispatched to Schuyler, in order to make the northern victory possible.

THE HESSIANS AND THE AMERICANS

The Continental Army has been so often pictured as ragged and shoeless that it is sometimes forgotten that it contained a remarkably large and tough breed of men in comparison to Europeans. The Germans who served with Burgoyne were much impressed. One officer wrote: "The colonists are... big, handsome, sinewy, strong, healthy men." Another commented on the Americans at Saratoga: "Nature had formed all the fellows who stood in rank and file so slender, so handsome, so sinewy, that it was a pleasure to look at them, and we were all surprised at the sight of such a finely built people. And their size!... Quite seriously, English America excels most of Europe in respect to the stature and beauty of its men."

The Hessians who went with Howe to Pennsylvania, Maryland, and New Jersey were even more impressed with the well-stocked and fertile farms, particularly those of the Pennsylvania Germans. They also picked up some new notions of equality and freedom. While Howe was showing the old flag there, the state was displaying itself to the Germans. Desertions by Hessians and Brunswickers became increasingly common thereafter. By the end of the war, nearly 17 percent of the German army (which had cost Great Britain almost £5 million) had deserted.

COLONEL HAMILTON ON MISSION

There was no flicker of jealousy in Washington's remarks on Gates' victory, of which he and Schuyler had been the principal architects, but he was thoroughly displeased that Gates reported it to Congress and not to him. This intelligence was crucial to the operations of the army from Peekskill to Philadelphia. Gates was dilatory in sending the information, even to Congress; this upset the exiled legislators. In the excitement, they tended to overlook his casualness.

On October 18 Washington received indirect news of the victory from Generals Putnam and Clinton, and he notified Congress. He also announced it to the army, ordering small arms fired in celebration. Six days later he wrote anxiously to Congress that he had received no confirmation or communication from Gates. When that body had the northern commander's letter on October 30, Washington was informed. He immediately wrote Gates:

> *By this Opportunity, I do myself the pleasure to congratulate you on the signal success of the Army under your command, in compelling Genl. Burgoyne and his whole force to surrender themselves prisoners of War. An event that does the highest honor to the American Arms, and which, I hope, will be attended with the most extensive and happy consequences. At the same time, I cannot but regret that a matter of such magnitude and so interesting to our General Operations, should have reached me by report only.*

The letter further advised Gates that Washington was sending Alexander Hamilton north to explain the needs of his army and the enemy dispositions. If he sent them by post, the facts might reach the British. What Washington did not know was that, a few days before, Gates had received a letter from Brigadier Thomas Conway, the Irish officer admired by John Adams. This letter followed the old Reed–Lee argument that Washington was weak and incompetent, and served further to minimize Gates' already feeble desire to cooperate with his commander in chief.

Hamilton, only twenty-two, had the disagreeable task of negotiating with the fifty-year-old Gates, now exalted into eminence. In doing so, he displayed some of the same toughness and resourcefulness that Washington had once displayed as a twenty-one-year-old emissary to the French. While Hamilton was en route north, Congress voted Gates a gold medal and limited the number of troops Washington was permitted to draw from him.

On arriving at Peekskill, Hamilton ordered continental troops under Putnam's command to march south immediately. He reported to Washington that Morgan's riflemen were already on their way. The more delicate task began at Albany. From there, about November 6, he wrote that Gates was very uncooperative. He had told Hamilton that the intelligence that additional troops were being sent from New York to Philadelphia was unconfirmed; Sir Henry Clinton might again come up the Hudson, and he had to defend New York and New England. Hamilton added that he had done all he could, without avail, to persuade Gates: "I felt the importance of strengthening you as much as possible, (but) on the other hand I found insuperable inconveniences in acting diametrically opposite to the opinion of a gentleman whose successes have raised him to the highest importance. General Gates has won the intire confidence of the Eastern States; if disposed to do it, by addressing himself to the prejudices of the people he would find no difficulty to render a measure odious... General Gates has influence and interest elsewhere."

Gates finally agreed to send a brigade. Hamilton wrote him on November 5: "By inquiry, I have learned that General Patterson's brigade, which is the one you proposed to send is by far the weakest of the three now here." After further discussion, Hamilton got Gates to add Glover's brigade to those ordered south. When Hamilton got to the Highlands, he wrote Washington that he found that Putnam had been negligent in sending on continental troops, since he had in mind an attack on New York. At the advice of Governor Clinton, Hamilton ordered Putnam "in the most emphatic terms" to send the troops. He added that he had written Gates again, giving him a full account of the situation in New York and the departure on November 5 of troops from the city to aid Howe against Washington. By this, he said, he hoped to "extort from him a further reinforcement... I doubt whether you would have had a man from the Northern Army, if the whole could have been kept at Albany, with any decency."

While Hamilton had got brigades from Gates and hurried on the men from Putnam's command, the bulk of them did not arrive in time to keep Howe from smashing the Delaware fortifications. On the trip Hamilton learned of the existence of a Gates faction that was opposed to Washington. This he duly reported to his commander. Washington always remembered that Hamilton had done his duty very well on this occasion.

HOWE OPENS THE DELAWARE

Though he had occupied the American capital and received his additional troops from Clinton, Howe was still in a dangerous position. His brother's ships were cut off from Philadelphia by American forts on the Delaware while the city was besieged by the rebel army. Washington thought that if northern reinforcements arrived in time, he could force Howe out of Philadelphia by holding the river forts, but his troops present were too few to do this for more than a brief period.

In early October Lord Howe's fleet moved up the Delaware to cooperate with Sir William. On October 21, Count Carl von Donop led some two thousand Hessians against Fort Mercer on the Jersey side. Its commander was Colonel Christopher Greene, the general's cousin, who had only four hundred men. Before the attack was over, Americans had killed or wounded an equal number of Hessians including von Donop, their commander, who later died of his injuries. Two British warships went aground and were blown up the next day by the Americans. The strong defense delayed the British advance. Not for a month could the enemy bring up enough naval and armed forces to destroy Fort Mifflin on Mud Island and to clear the river for the Royal Navy. On November 22 the Americans evacuated Forts Mifflin and Mercer; the Howes had control of the access by sea.

Just as the forts fell, the most important of the northern regiments reached the Philadelphia area. On November 26 Washington wrote his brother John "Had the reinforcement from the Northward arrived but ten days sooner it would I think have put it in my power to have saved Fort Mifflin which defended the Cheveaux de Frieze, and consequently have rendered Philadelphia a very ineligible situation for them this winter."

On November 25, with added forces, Washington proposed an attack on Philadelphia but the great majority of his general officers strongly opposed such a risk. General Knox was among those who voted against it. Knowing that Washington was being severely criticized for waiting tactics, he wrote to him on November 26 that he was certain his reputation would not suffer if he avoided rash action. He added: "I know to the contrary, the people of America look up to you as their Father, and into your hands they entrust their all, fully confident of every exertion on your part for their security and happiness and I do not believe there is any man on earth for whose welfare there are more solicitations at the Court of Heaven, than for yours."

On December 4 Howe moved with most of his army from Philadelphia to Germantown, to tempt Washington into battle. Although his forces were far larger, he did not himself try to attack the rebel positions, which, he concluded, were too strongly entrenched. Howe's ploy failed, and he returned to spend the winter in Philadelphia. The Americans then had to decide where to station their men.

On the day that Howe suffered his disaster at Fort Mercer, he forwarded to London his resignation as commander in chief of the British forces in

America. He did not say that he had been continuously outmaneuvered by Washington for more than two years, but he complained that he had never had sufficient forces and support from Britain. This was a tacit admission that he could not beat him. The battle of Brandywine was the last time in the war that a British army attempted to attack Washington and his army.

LAFAYETTE GETS A COMMAND

Lafayette, after being wounded in the leg at Brandywine, was taken to Bethlehem where he was cared for by Moravian sisters. On October 16 he wrote his wife: "Let us talk then of the wound... The surgeons are astonished by the promptness with which it healed. They go into ecstacies every time they dress it, and pretend that it is the most beautiful thing in the world. That depends on taste." Lafayette added that he was getting the best of care thanks to the orders of General Washington, "that inestimable man, whose talents and virtues I admire." He told his wife to explain to everyone in Paris that Washington's army had been much smaller than Howe's but that he would soon retake Philadelphia.

While Lafayette was recuperating, Conway came to see him and told him how marvelous Gates was as a soldier. Lafayette sent Gates a letter of congratulation, noting that he was anxious to meet him. This was Conway's opening move to maneuver Lafayette into an anti-Washington position, but the young Frenchman was too clever to be trapped.

Lafayette, not fully recovered, returned to Washington's army and begged to join General Greene, who was protecting southern New Jersey from Cornwallis. There he asked Greene to let him go on a reconnaissance mission to Gloucester. As Washington reported to Congress on November 26, Lafayette was "not inactive" there. He quoted a letter from Greene to himself of the same date:

> *The Marquis with about 400 Militia and the Rifle Corps, attacked the Enemie's Picket last Evening, killed about 20, wounded many more and took about 20 prisoners. The Marquis is charmed with the spirited behaviour of the Militia and Rifle Corps. They drove the Enemy above half a Mile and kept the ground till dark. The Enemeys Picket consisted of about 300 and were reinforced during the skirmish. The Marquis is determined to be in the way of danger.*

Lafayette's action had, in fact, brought out Cornwallis and much of the British army to save the fleeing Hessians. Darkness made both sides withdraw.

Lafayette added to his éclat by sending a modest little note to the new president of Congress, Henry Laurens: "I was there almost nothing but a witness, but I was a very pleased one in seeing the behavior of our men."

Washington had issued general orders on November 20 appointing Lieutenant John Marshall to be deputy judge advocate and James Monroe to be aide to General Stirling. The orders also approved the court-martial verdict cashiering Adam Stephen for misbehavior at Germantown.

Lafayette had strongly urged Washington to give him a line command and threatened to return to France unless he got it. His social and political connections there were such that this would have been unfortunate. Now that he had proved his devotion at Brandywine and in New Jersey, Washington recommended to Congress that Lafayette be given his command. Congress responded enthusiastically and on December 4 Washington issued orders: "Major General, the Marquis La Fayette is to take the command of the division lately commanded by General Stephen." It was fitting that Lafayette, who tried to emulate Washington, should command Virginia troops.

DUCHÉ AND HOPKINSON

On October 15, two days before Burgoyne's surrender, Washington received a letter from Jacob Duché, an Anglican clergyman of Philadelphia, who had been chaplain to Congress. He wrote: "Your harbours are blocked up, your cities fall one after another; fortress after fortress, battle after battle is lost. A British army, after having passed almost unmolested through a vast extent of country, have possessed themselves with ease of the capital of America. How unequal the contest now! How fruitless the expense of blood!" Duché attacked Congress, referring to its members as "dregs," adding that America had no navy, while the army had let Washington down. With Great Britain united, there was no further hope for the cause. He asked Washington to negotiate an accommodation "at the head of your army... 'Tis to you, and you alone, your bleeding country looks... May Heaven inspire you." Washington, calling it a "ridiculous, illiberal performance," sent the letter to Congress. Duché's brother-in-law, Francis Hopkinson, a Signer, was shaken by the plea. On November 14 he forwarded an open letter to Washington, which he asked to be forwarded to Duché:

Words cannot express the grief and consternation that wounded my soul at the sight of this performance. You have by a vain and weak effort attempted the integrity of one whose virtue is impregnable to the assaults of fear or flattery; whose judgment needed not your information and who, I am sure, would have resigned his charge the moment he found it likely to lead him out of the paths of virtue and honour.

Although Duché had gone over to the Tories and Hopkinson remained a patriot, both looked to Washington as the one man to save the country. This was increasingly the national opinion, but there were those ready to increase their denunciations of Washington for timidity, indecision, and incompetence. Their deadliest attacks were to be made while he kept together his half-starved army at Valley Forge.

TWENTY-THREE

BITTER WINTER

1777–1778

W HILE WASHINGTON AND his staff were settling into a crowded
Valley Forge farmhouse, the palaces at London, Versailles, and
Madrid churned with the news from the wilderness. Philadelphia's
fall was depressing to Franklin, whose town it was, but he put on a good front
for the French as he received Vergennes' congratulations for Germantown. The
news of Burgoyne's capture reached Paris on December 4, a day or two after
London had the news. The French, who had been waiting for just such an event,
moved quickly. Two days later Conrad Alexandre Gérard, an official of the foreign ministry who was to be the first diplomatic representative to the United
States, called on Franklin. He asked the Americans to resubmit their earlier proposal for a treaty of alliance. On December 17 Vergennes informed Franklin
that the French government would accept the treaty but would not formally ratify it until Spain had expressed its opinion. From December to March Franklin
received an extraordinary number of callers from London offering whatever he
wanted if America would choose anything but independence.

On February 6, 1778, France and the tiny new nation, its Congress in exile,
signed the treaty. On March 20 Franklin, cheered by all Paris, formally called
on Louis XVI, a scene too well known to need another telling.

For George III this was a trying winter but he bore it with a fortitude worthy of a better cause. Parliament had been in an uproar even before Saratoga.

Governor Pownall, who had accurately forecast events, told Parliament: "I tell this House and this Government that the Americans never will return to their subjection to this country." Pitt was in a fury in the Lords over the use of Hessians and Indians as allies:

> As to conquest, my Lords, it is impossible! You may swell every expense and every effort, still more extravagantly; pile and accumulate every assistance you can buy or borrow; traffic and barter with every little prince that sells his subjects to the shambles of a foreign Prince; but your efforts are for ever vain and impotent... If I were an American, as I am an Englishman, while a foreign troop was landed in my country, I never would lay down my arms—never—never—never!

> But, my Lords, who is the man that—in addition to these disgraces and mischiefs of our army—has dared to authorize and associate to our arms the tomahawk and scalping-knife of the savage?... My Lords, these enormities call aloud for redress and punishment... [They are] a violation of the Constitution... They shock every sentiment of honour.

On December 1 Lord George Germain reported to the king that Washington's army was "still in force" and that Sir William Howe, claiming he had had insufficient support from home, wanted to resign. The next day Lord Sandwich forwarded the "unpleasant accounts" of Saratoga. When the news was reluctantly announced in Parliament, the Whigs turned on the ministers with such scorn that Lord North was moved to tears. Two days after receiving the news, the king, who had a sense of military strategy, told North that henceforth British military activity in America would have to be defensive. George III dismissed the capture of Philadelphia as of little significance. The king gave more tribute to Washington than he intended, for it had been only fifteen months since the latter had said that the Americans would have to fight a defensive war. That same day Lord North gave his first hint to the king that it would be better if he resigned. On December 18 the king received news of the success at Mud Island. This offered him a brief ray of hope that Howe would be able to defeat Washington in a general engagement.

When Parliament met on January 20, the government lost a vote on a motion to call for papers relating to the failure of Burgoyne's expedition. The opposition split on the question of American independence, Pitt being against and Lord Rockingham for it. British recognition of independence was the only way in which a long and expensive war with France could have been averted. North was in a dilemma. The king had recognized that America could not be conquered unless Great Britain redoubled its efforts, and this could not be done with France ready to go to war. The strain on North was such that he wrote the king that "the anxiety of his mind for the last two months [has] deprived Lord North of his memory and understanding... The whole of this matter had been an additional proof to Lord North of his incapacity for the high and important office in which he has been placed. A pacifick proposition appears to him necessary both for this country and America." He again strongly suggested that he retire.

Although Lord North had been wholly on the king's side in willingness to crush America, by January 1778 he realized that the policy had been fruitless. There began a long struggle between North and the king over his retirement that did not end until 1782. The king cajoled, threatened, praised, and bribed Lord North to keep him. He appealed to his "honour," a word that did not have quite the same connotation to the king as it did to Washington. North, often weary and embittered, continued in office at the command of a king who had the hand but not the heart of his prime minister. George III was just clever enough a politician to realize that war with France would be much more popular than war with America. He was correct since many of the Whigs and others who opposed the American policy heartily joined him in fighting the trans-channel enemy. The king reluctantly agreed that North should introduce measures in Parliament to pacify America so that Britain could concentrate its forces against France. If that country were beaten, any concessions to America could be quickly scrapped.

On February 17 Lord North rose in Commons to say: "The forces of Washington are not sufficient to make him quit his defensive plan. Our army is great, our navy is great, our men in health, in spirits, and well supplied; but the resistance of America is greater, and the war has lasted longer, than was at first apprehended." He added that the government was prepared to grant everything that America had asked for—in 1775. The tea and other taxes were to be repealed, many concessions were to be made, and commissioners were to go to America with the usual power to grant pardons. (The offer of pardons always irked Americans. Governor Trumbull of Connecticut said they needed to ask God for pardon every day but they needed none from the English king.) After North introduced these proposals, Charles James Fox rose to ask if Lord North knew that the Americans had signed a treaty with France. Fox suggested that Versailles had beaten North by ten days and the house was in an uproar. Walpole made his usual tart comment: "Such... criminality, ignorance and incapacity in the Ministers has never been equalled." Even the bills introduced by North stated that nothing signed by the peace commissioners would be binding unless ratified by Parliament. This maintained the principle over which America had revolted.

The bills passed handily but everyone knew their chance of succeeding was slim. With the prospect of war with France, the British nation almost to a man called for Pitt, who had once before led Britain to victory. When North suggested him to the king, George III answered: "No advantage to this country nor personal danger can ever make me address myself for assistance either to Lord Chatham or any other branch of the Opposition honestly I would rather lose the Crown." To the king's great relief Pitt died soon afterwards.

The treaty with France made Britain hurry the peace commissioners to America. They were instructed to head off the French envoy and prevent ratification of the pact. A remarkably ill-assorted mission was chosen. Lord Carlisle, its chairman, was a macaroni, gambler, and poetaster. William Eden had been head of the secret service, while George Johnstone was a naval officer who had been governor of West Florida. Secretaries, servants, wine, and mountains of baggage accompanied them. The expedition brought John Wilkes' comment: "To captivate the rude members of Congress, and civilize the wild inhabitants of an unpolished country, a noble peer was very properly appointed chief of the honourable embassy. His lordship, to the surprise and admiration of that part of the new world, carried with him a green ribbon, the gentle manners, winning behaviour, and soft insinuating address of a modern man of quality and a professed courtier. The muses and graces with a group of little laughing loves were in his train, and for the first time crossed the Atlantic."

As the peace commissioners sailed up the Delaware they were fired at from every point. They did not know that orders to abandon Philadelphia had already gone out from London. By the time they arrived, the British forces were packing and Congress had ratified the French treaty.

On March 17, Madame de Lafayette's uncle, the French ambassador in London, handed a note to the foreign secretary. It was couched in the bantering Shakespearean humor of the dauphin's gift of tennis balls to Henry V. The note declared that, in view of the good relations between the two countries, France was pleased to forward information that Great Britain would find "interesting." Since the United States of America were "in full possession of their independence," France had concluded a treaty of friendship and commerce with them. Inasmuch as the United States had reserved the right to negotiate such treaties with other countries, the note suggested Great Britain might approach the Americans, requesting a similar pact.

PENNSYLVANIA AND THE ARMY

Pennsylvania, the most Tory or neutral state, gave Washington the least help of any. In writing to his brother John on October 17, he said: "This State acts most infamously, the People of it I mean as we derive little or no assistance from them." On the same day he complained bitterly to the president of the Pennsylvania council, Thomas Wharton, Jr., that, although the main British army was in Pennsylvania and had occupied the capital, the state's continental regiments were less than half full. Only twelve hundred of the local militia had come to his aid. He pointed out that Pennsylvania was the richest and most populous of the northern states but was doing far less for him than New England had done for Gates. While he did not mention that most of the continental troops on the river defenses were from Rhode Island, he wrote his brother that Virginia had as many troops in the state as Pennsylvania.

Nothing pained the Quaker general, Nathanael Greene of Rhode Island, more than the attitude of the Pennsylvania Quakers. He was exasperated by their eagerness to provide food and provisions to Howe for gold and silver, their refusal of continental currency, and their lending money to Howe. Washington complained that, in some areas of the state, he could get no help or information from the inhabitants, while some of them went out of their way to give information to the enemy. Howe's victory at Brandywine was in part owing to the intelligence he was able to obtain from local citizens.

Pennsylvania might have been last in war but it was first in criticism. When the decision was taken to send the army to Valley Forge, the state's legislature complained angrily that the army was retiring to winter quarters, away from battle, leaving the state to be ravaged. In fact, Washington had reluctantly chosen this site as the nearest defensive post to Philadelphia, even though it was in an area short of supplies. Three days after he received the letter from Congress, December 20, he wrote a reply from Valley Forge designed to take the skin off the senders.

We have, by a field return this day made, no less than 2898 Men now in Camp unfit for duty because they are bare foot and otherwise naked... Our whole strength amounts to no more than 8200 In Camp fit for duty. Notwithstanding which, and that, since the 4th Instt., our Numbers fit for duty from the hardships and exposures they have undergone, particularly on Acct. of Blankets (numbers being obliged and do set up all Night by fires, instead of taking comfortable rest in a natural way) have decreased near 2000 Men. We find Gentlemen without knowing whether the Army was really going into Winter Quarters or not (for I am sure no resolution of mine would warrant the remonstrance) reprobating the measure as if they thought Men were made of Sticks or Stones and equally insensible of frost and Snow and moreover, as if they conceived it practicable for an inferior Army, under the disadvantages I have described ours to be, which is by no means exaggerated, to confine a superior one (in all respects appointed and provided for a Winter's Campaign) within the city of Phila., and cover from depredation and waste the States of Pensa., Jersey, &ca., but what makes the matter still more extraordinary in my eye is, that these very Gentn., who were well apprized of the nakedness of the Troops from ocular demonstration... advised me near a Month ago to postpone the execution of a Plan I was about to adopt for seizing Cloathes under strong assurance that an ample supply would be collected in ten days, agreably to a decree of the State, not one article of which by the bye is yet come to hand, should think a Winters Campaign, and the covering these States from an invasion of an Enemy so easy a business. I can assure these Gentlemen it is a much easier and less distressing thing to draw remonstrances in a comfortable room by a good fireside than to occupy a cold bleak hill and sleep under frost and Snow without Coats or blankets; however, although they seem to have little feeling for the naked and distressed Soldier, I feel superabundantly for them, and from my Soul pity those miseries.

THE WINTER ENCAMPMENT

When Washington decided to move his troops to a point twenty miles from Philadelphia, he explained it to the army in general orders of December 17:

The Commander in Chief, with the highest satisfaction, expresses his thanks to the officers and soldiers for the fortitude and patience with which they have sustained the fatigues of the Campaign. Altho' in some instances we unfortunately failed, yet upon the whole Heaven hath smiled on our Arms and crowned them with signal success; and we may upon the best grounds conclude that, by a spirited continuance of the measures necessary for our defence we shall finally obtain the end of our Warfare, Independence, Liberty and Peace... Every motive therefore irresistably urges us, nay commands us, to a firm and manly perseverance in our opposition to our cruel oppressors... The General ardently wishes it were now in our power, to conduct the troops into the best winter quarters. But where are these to be found? Should we retire to interior parts of the State, we should find them crowded with virtuous citizens, who, sacrificing their all, have left Philadelphia... To their distresses, humanity forbids us to add. This is not all, we should leave a vast extent of fertile country to be despoiled and ravaged by the enemy... Many of our firm friends would be exposed to all the miseries of the most insulting and wanton depredation… These conditions make it indispensably necessary for the army to take such a position, as will enable it most effectually to prevent distress and to give the most extensive security… With activity and diligence Huts may be erected that will be warm and dry… [The General] will share in the hardships, and partake of every inconvenience.

Washington thus warned they were going to a hardship post. On December 19 the troops marched to Valley Forge and began to erect log cabins. Designed by the commander in chief, they were fourteen by sixteen feet. The supply services were disorganized; shortages of food, clothing, and fodder grew increasingly acute. On Christmas Day four inches of snow fell. That same day Washington worked on a plan for a surprise attack on Philadelphia. This was where his heart lay but the task was not possible. The capital was too well fortified and his men were as worn out as their uniforms and shoes. The general's energy had to be diverted to keeping his army alive; in this he only partly succeeded.

The winter at Valley Forge is so great a part of American life that it is worth telling again because it was worse than the legend. Typhus was common, and the scant supplies of drinking water were often polluted. From January on, heavy snows blocked delivery of supplies. The hospital and medical services were primitive and inefficient. Provisions were so scarce that, for days on end, the only food was firecake, a mixture of flour and water baked on stones. Twenty-five hundred or more soldiers died that winter. Fodder was so scarce that some five hundred horses died and could not be buried in the frozen ground. Some two thousand men decamped to the British and took the king's oath. Most were foreign born, the majority Irish. The remaining soldiers who lived stayed on in camp, to the amazement of the French officers, including Lafayette.

Joseph Galloway, Tory superintendent of police in Philadelphia, prepared a memorandum for George III in January 1779 during the British occupation. In it he took pride in the degree to which Pennsylvania had cooperated with the British. He estimated that Philadelphia had nearly 26,000 inhabitants who had not fled the city prior to Howe's arrival. "The above number of 25,767 People with the British Army and Navy supposed in the whole to amount to near 55,000 persons were fed and supplied with all manner of fresh provisions and every other necessary that the Country usually produced in great plenty by the well affected Inhabitants from without Sir William Howe's Lines; though Washington's Patroles and Picquets continually cirrounded these Lines… At the same Washington's Army both Foot and Horse were starving."

On the last day of 1777 Washington wrote to the governor of New Jersey: "Our difficulties and distresses are certainly great and such as wound the feelings of Humanity. Our sick naked, our well naked, our unfortunate men in captivity naked!" Five days later one of his officers, John Brooks, wrote to a friend in Massachusetts:

> You make me smile when you observe that you are not so sanguine about matters in this quarter at present as you were. My dear friend, whatever made you sanguine?... Could a large superiority of numbers on the side of Mr. How through the whole campaign have made you sanguine?

> ...For a week past we have had snow, and as cold weather as I almost ever knew at home. To see our poor brave fellows living in tents, bare-footed, bare-legged, bare-breeched, etc., etc., in snow, in rain, on marches, in camp... is really distressing... Another thing which has been the occasion of much complaint is the unequal distribution and scanty allowance of provisions... The cursed Quakers and other inhabitants are the cause of the latter... Our regiment has never received but two months pay for twelve months past... In my opinion nothing but virtue has kept our army together...

> The States of Pennsylvania and Maryland do not seem to have any more idea of liberty than a savage has of civilization... They have ever supposed (till wofull experience taught them otherwise) that the King's troops were as kind, mercifull and just as they represented themselves to be. But now the tone is altering fast. Even some of the Thees and Thous, who have had their wives ravished, houses plundered and burned, are now ready... to take their arms and oppose them.

THE CONWAY CABAL

The ill-bred Thomas Conway comes down in history with his name attached to a plot against Washington. The paradox arises because Conway was to complain of the cabal that, in the end, formed against him. This included nearly the whole of Congress and the army.

Two strands of thought, the first developed by John Adams and the second by Joseph Reed, met and fused in the cabal. Conway, described by Washington as an "incendiary," tossed a match into highly flammable material.

Although no trace of complaint of John Adams by name can be found in Washington's reports and papers, it is clear that, as head of the board of war, he was a considerable cross. When Adams issued his directive of September 1776 to Washington to "Call his troops in every day and discipline them," he was much hurt by Washington's tart reply. He sent a lengthy complaint to Colonel William Tudor that there were imperfections in the American generals and any indiscipline or cowardice among the men was the fault of the officers. He mentioned to Tudor the need for a great mind in the army. On October 1, 1776, he wrote to Colonel Hitchcock that the army was mismanaged. By February 1777, Adams was complaining to Congress of the "superstitious veneration that is sometimes paid to General Washington." In the summer he praised Conway and other troublesome foreign officers. In October Adams spread the word that Howe had only half the number of troops that he had, in reality, brought to Pennsylvania and that Washington was acting in a timorous and defensive way. On October 26 he wrote his wife that he was pleased that Gates' victory at Saratoga had not been "immediately due to the commander in chief. If it had been, idolatry and adulation would have been unbounded; so excessive as to endanger our liberties."

Just before the battle of Trenton, Joseph Reed informed Dr. Benjamin Rush that all the troubles of the army were the fault of Washington, who was not fit to command a regiment. He had written to Washington, as he had to Lee, that he was too much influenced by men of inferior judgement. Reed, in turn, knew Conway, and it is of some significance that Conway also wrote to Washington to complain that he had a "confidence in men who are much inferior to you in judgement."

Charles Lee had blasted Washington to Gates, declaring America's counsels "weak to the last degree." Gates refused thereafter to serve directly under Washington, and he told Benjamin Rush that Patrick Henry had declared him to be unfit for his job. Thomas Mifflin, the army's quartermaster, had, in turn, been miffed with him for neglecting Philadelphia's defense, when he was uncertain where Howe would land, and for criticizing the management of his department. Mifflin spent little time with the army, and the supply services broke down.

In the middle of this backbiting, the battles of Brandywine, Germantown, and Saratoga took place; Congress fled to York; and Philadelphia fell to the enemy. General Conway thereupon tossed his match. In a letter to Gates praising his leadership, Conway wrote a strong critique of Washington's generalship. Gates cordially responded that his views seemed to confirm reports he had from others. Gates was not very discreet in showing Conway's letter around camp, and word of it soon reached Pennsylvania. Gates mentioned to General Morgan at Saratoga that there was great dissatisfaction with Washington, and many officers had threatened to resign unless he were replaced. Morgan, however, told Gates never again to bring up such a subject, for he would serve under no other commander in chief.

While this was going on, Dr. Benjamin Rush was active in Pennsylvania. Having heard of the Conway correspondence, he added his own criticisms in an October 13 letter to John Adams: "We lost a city, a victory, a campaign... General Conway wept for joy when he saw the arder with which our troops pushed the enemy from hill to hill... But when he saw an officer low in command give counterorders to the Commander in Chief... his distress and resentment exceeded all bounds. For God's sake do not suffer him to resign... He is moreover the idol of the army... Some people blame him for calling some of *our generals* fools, cowards, and drunkards... But these things are proofs of his integrity... Be not deceived, my dear friend. Our army is not better than it was two years ago." Eight days later Rush followed with another letter to Adams:

> *General Gates' unparalleled success gave me great pleasure, but it has not obliterated the remembrance of the disorders I have seen in the army in this department... I have heard several officers who have served under General Gates compare his army to a well-regulated family. The same gentlemen have compared General Washington's imitation of an army to an unformed mob. Look at the characters of both! The one on the pinnacle of military glory... the other outgeneraled and twice beated, obliged to witness the march of a body of men only half their number through 140 miles of a thick-settled country, forced to give up a city the capital of a state, and after all outwitted by the same army in a retreat...*

> *"A great and good God," says General Conway in a letter to a friend, "has decreed that America shall be free, or [Washington] and weak counselors would have ruined her long ago."*

> *General Mifflin must not be suffered to resign... If he is you will soon receive a hundred others.*

Before Washington learned of Conway's critiques, he heard that Congress was considering making Conway a major general. He wrote to Richard Henry Lee on October 17: "If there is any truth in a report which has been handed to me, Vizt., that Congress hath appointed, or, as others say, are about to appoint, Brigadier Conway a Major General in this Army, it will be as unfortunate a measure as ever was adopted... I must speak plain... General Conway's merit, then, as an Officer, and his importance in this Army, exists more in his own imagination than in reality... For it is a maxim with him, to leave no service of his untold, nor to want any thing which is to be obtained by importunity... Allowing him every thing his warmest Friends will contend for, I would ask why the Youngest Brigadier (for I believe he is so) should be put over the heads of all the Eldest... This truth I am very well assured of... that they will not serve under him... These Gentlemen have feelings as Officers... All our Officers are tired out: Do not, therefore, afford them good pretexts for retiring... I have been a slave to the service: I have undergone more than most Men are aware of, to harmonize so many discordant parts, but it will be impossible for me to be of any further service, if such insuperable difficulties are put in my way."

Lee informed Washington, mistakenly, as it turned out, that he was sure Conway would not be promoted over the army's objections. On October 27, James Wilkinson, Gates' aide, passed through Reading with the victory dispatch. In what seems to have been a drinking bout, Wilkinson mentioned the Conway letter to the aide of Lord Stirling. The latter, calling it "wicked duplicity of conduct," forwarded the information to Washington. Wilkinson then went on to Congress which, upon Gates' recommendation, promoted him to brigadier. On November 9 Washington dropped a note to Conway:

Sir: A Letter which I received last Night, contained the following paragraph.

In a Letter from Genl. Conway to Genl. Gates he says: "Heaven has been determined to save your Country; or a weak General and bad Councellors would have ruind it."

I am Sir Yr, Hble Servt. G. Washington.

The effects of the note were to be out of all proportion to its length. There were quarrels, recriminations, duels, and the tarnishing of reputations. When it was all over, Washington was undisputed commander in chief of all the American armies. On November 13 he wrote to Patrick Henry: "I was left to fight two Battles, in Order, if possible, to save Philadelphia, with less numbers than composed the Army of my Antagonist, whilst the world had given us at least double. This, though mortifying in some points of view, I have been obliged to encourage; because, next to being strong, it is best to be thought so by the enemy... My own difficulties, in the course of this Campaign, have been not a little encreased, by the extra aid of Continental Troops which the gloomy prospect of our affairs in the North... induced me to spare... If the cause is advanced, indifferent it is to me, where, or in what quarters it happens."

After receiving Washington's November 9 note, Conway wrote him, repeating twice that he was governed by men of inferior judgement. At the same time he offered his resignation to Congress, which postponed action on it. He also consulted Mifflin, who sent Gates a warning that, although Conway had expressed "just sentiments," the northern commander should have been more discreet. When Wilkinson returned to his headquarters, he found Gates in an ugly temper, claiming that Alexander Hamilton had stolen letters from his files. He added that he intended to disgrace both the stealer and the receiver, Washington. Wilkinson, who had tossed out Conway's incriminating remarks over a bottle, always claimed he had no recollection of having done so. He gave Gates no information on his own actions but suggested that Robert Troup, a staff member who had been a college roommate of Hamilton, might have passed along the information. Gates wrote to Conway for help in finding out who stole the letters, and he asked which one had been copied. He also wrote to Washington on December 8: "I conjure your Excellency to give me all the assistance you can in tracing out the author of the infidelity which put extracts from General Conway's letters to me into your hands. Those letters have been *stealingly copied*... I shall have the honour of transmitting a copy of this to the President of Congress." Gates added that he did not know whether an officer or a member of Congress had given him the information.

After his victory Gates received numerous letters of congratulation, some noting the contrast, expressed by Rush, between his victories and Washington's defeats. Joseph Reed wrote that Saratoga would "enroll him with the happy few who shine in history... I have for some time volunteered with this army, which, notwithstanding the labors and efforts of its amiable chief, has yet gathered no laurels." James Lovell, head of Congress' foreign affairs committee, said: "You have saved our northern hemisphere... We have had a noble army melted down by ill judged marches... How much are you to be envied, my dear general! How different your conduct and fortune... Conway [and] Mifflin [have] resigned... This army will be totally lost, unless you come down... We want you most near Germantown... Come to the Board of War if only for a short season." Among Conway's words to him were: "What a pity there is but one Gates! But the more I see of this army, the less I think it fit for general action under its actual chiefs and actual discipline... I wish I could serve under you."

Some who wrote to Gates complained that Washington was too much idolized. Not all the criticism was of the commander in chief. Those who complained of his "council" referred mainly to his principal advisor, Nathanael Greene, whose responsibility for the loss of Fort Washington had not been forgotten. Conway, as Rush pointed out, had been publicly denouncing Washington's officers as drunks, fools, and cowards.

For some time Congress had been considering the appointment of a board of war not composed of members of Congress. This was a first step towards the organization of an executive body. Because of congressional backing and filling, the old and new boards overlapped. Gates was elected president, although he did not appear at congressional headquarters until January 1778. Mifflin was placed on it; thus, Washington had a board with two men who mistrusted him. Also on the board were Joseph Trumbull; Richard Peters, who had been secretary of the old board; and Timothy Pickering.

On December 13 Congress raised Thomas Conway to the rank of major general and appointed him inspector general. Congress soon received the protests of brigadiers from seven states who said they represented all the brigadiers in the army. Their dissent was approved and forwarded by Major General Greene. At almost the same time forty-seven colonels of the line denounced the promotion of Colonel Wilkinson.

When Washington received Gates' letter, he gave him a candid version of events, quoting exactly the correspondence he had obtained from Stirling and the information the latter had received through Wilkinson. He included a copy of his letter to Conway. He assured Gates that no one except Lafayette, outside his personal staff, had seen the correspondence, since it was his duty to conceal from the enemy all signs of internal dissensions. He expressed surprise that Gates had sent Congress a copy of his letter. He would therefore have to do the same. He continued:

> *Thus, Sir, with an openess and candour which I hope will ever characterize and mark my conduct have I complied with your request; the only concern I feel upon the occasion… is that… I have necessarily been obliged to name a Gentn. whom I am persuaded (although I never exchanged a word with him upon the Subject) thought he was rather doing an act of Justice, than committing an act of infidelity; and sure I am that till Lord Stirlings Letter came to my hands, I never knew that General Conway (who I viewed in the light of a stranger to you) was a corrispondant of yours, much less did I suspect that I was the subject of your confidential Letters; pardon me then for adding that… I considered the information as coming from yourself; and given with a friendly view to forewarn, and consequently forarm me, against a secret enemy; in which character, sooner or later, this Country will know General Conway.*

As the controversy developed, the army rallied around Washington. They showed their feelings in vigorous protests to Congress against the promotions of Conway and of Gates' favorite, Wilkinson, and in extensive correspondence. General Knox gave his opinion to Elbridge Gerry, a member of Congress from his own state: "Every military character on this continent, taken collectively, vanishes before him." General Greene wrote to his brother, Jacob: "A horrid faction has been forming to ruin his Excellency… Mifflin has quarelled with the General because he would not draw off the force to the southward last summer... before the enemy's object was ascertained... Mifflin thought Philadelphia was exposed by it, and went there and raised a prodigious clamour against the measure, and against me for advising it. But the General, like the common father of all, steadily pursued the great Continental interest without regard... to the discontents of individuals... General Conway is a man of much intrigue and little judgment." Colonel Hamilton summarized the situation to New York governor George Clinton, who had informed him in November that a plot was brewing against Washington: "All the true and sensible friends to their country, and of course to a certain great man, ought to be on the watch to counter the secret machinations of his enemies. Have you heard anything of Conway's history?... There does not exist a more villainous calumniator and incendiary." Dr. Craik, assistant director of the medical services, wrote to Washington: "Notwithstanding your unwearied diligence and the unparalleled sacrifice of domestic happiness and ease of mind which you have made for the good of the country, yet you are not wanting in secret enemies who would rob you of the great and truly deserved esteem your country has for you... The method they are taking is by holding General Gates up to the people, and making them believe that you have had a number three or four times greater than the enemy; that Philadelphia was given up by your management, and that you have had many opportunities of defeating the enemy. It is said they dare not appear openly as your enemies; but that the new Board of War is composed of such leading men, as will throw such obstacles and difficulties in your way as to force you to resign." Colonel Morgan had already declared to Gates his absolute loyalty to Washington and Stirling had shown it by his actions. General Varnum wrote to Greene: "Next to God Almighty and my country, I revere General Washington and nothing fills me with so much indignation as the villainy of some who dare speak disrespectfully of him." Mercy Warren summed it all up in telling her husband that the soldiers' toast was "Washington or no army."

Conway had been arrogant with Congress. In putting forth his claims to promotion he listed all his merits and demanded an immediate reply. Now he proceeded to handle the commander in chief in similar fashion. He informed Washington that his new rank was absolutely essential for his inspector generalship. Washington replied on December 30:

> *Your appointment of Inspector General... I believe has not given the least uneasiness to any Officer... By consulting your own feelings upon the appointment of the Baron de Kalb you may judge what must be the Sensations of those Brigadiers, who by your Promotion are Superceded... For my own part I have nothing to do in the appointment of Genl. Officers... nor have I any other wish on*

that Head, but that good attentive officers may be chosen, and no Extraordinary promotion take place, but where the Merit of the Officer is so generally acknowledged as to Obviate every reasonable cause of Dissatisfaction thereat.

To this Conway answered the following day: "What you are pleased to call an extraordinary promotion is a very plain one. There is nothing extraordinary in it, only that such was not thought of sooner. The general and universal merit, which you wish every promoted officer might be endowed with, is a rare gift. We see but few men of merit so generally acknowledged. We know but the great Frederick in Europe and the great Washington on this continent. I certainly was never so rash as to pretend to such a prodigious height... I do not mean to give you or any officer in the army the least uneasiness therefore I am ready to return to France."

Washington forwarded the correspondence to Congress, but Conway was not through putting the commander in chief in his place. He wrote him on January 10: "I remain in a state of inaction until such time as your Excellency will think fit to employ me... I cannot believe, Sir, neither does any other officer in your army believe, that the objection to my appointment originates from any body living but from you." Washington never again wrote to Conway, who had thus implied he was a liar. His aides, however, were livid with rage.

LAFAYETTE'S SUPPORT OF WASHINGTON

The twenty-year-old marquis moved through these troubled scenes with a sure touch and understanding. There was nothing he was not prepared to do to help America and Washington. From his cold hut at Valley Forge, he forwarded plans to the French prime minister on ways to hurt Great Britain. He also sent his father-in-law, lieutenant general the duc d'Ayen, a message that he knew would circulate at the highest court levels:

Our General is a man truly made for this revolution, which could not be successfully accomplished without him. I see him more closely than any man in the world and I see that he is worthy of the adoration of the country. His tender friendship and his entire confidence in me in regard to all military and political subjects, great and small which occupy him, place me in a situation to judge of all that he has to do, all that he has to conciliate and overcome. I admire him more each day—the beauty of his character and of his soul. Certain foreigners, offended at not having been placed, although that in no wise depended on him, and some whose ambitious plans he was not willing to serve, certain jealous caballers, have tried to tarnish his reputation; but his name will be revered in all ages by all lovers of liberty and humanity.

Friend and father confessor to the commander in chief, Lafayette was equally the friend of his soldiers and dug into his own pockets to try to get them food and clothing. He was often miserable and homesick, missed his family, and wrote to Paris that Valley Forge was about as gay as a dungeon. He told his wife he wanted to go home but honor required him to stay by Washington's side. "So many foreigners... have made powerful cabals. They have tried by all sorts of traps to disgust me with this revolution and with him who is its chief. They have spread about, as much as they could, that I was going to leave the continent... The English have announced it openly. I cannot, in all conscience, make it appear that they are right. If I leave... many Frenchmen, useful here, will follow my example. General Washington would be truly grieved... His confidence in me is greater than I dare to avow, because of my age... Adieu, adieu; love me always, and do not forget for an instant the unhappy exile who thinks always of you with a new tenderness." Lafayette found the intrigues in Congress distressing and the work of Conway even more so. He poured out his feelings in a letter of December 30, 1777, to Washington:

When I was in Europe, I thought that here almost every man was a lover of liberty, and would rather die free than live a slave. You can conceive my astonishment when I saw that Toryism was as apparently professed as Whigism itself... There are open dissensions in Congress; parties who hate one another as much as the common enemy; stupid men who, without knowing any thing about war, undertake to judge you, to make ridiculous comparisons. They are infatuated with Gates, without thinking of the different circumstances, and believe that attacking is the only thing necessary to conquer. These ideas are entertained by some jealous men, and perhaps secret friends to the British government, who want to push you, in a moment of ill humour, to some rash enterprise upon the lines, or against a much stronger army.

[Conway] calls himself my soldier, and the reason such behaviour for me is that he wishes to be well spoken of at the French court, and his protector, the Marquis de Castries, is an intimate acquaintance of mine; but since the letter of Lord Stirling I inquired in his character. I found that he was an ambitious and dangerous man. He has done all in his power, by cunning maneuvers, to take off my confidence and affection for you. His desire was to engage me to leave this country... I have the warmest love for my country and for every good frenchman; their success fills my heart with joy; but, sir, besides Conway is an irishman I want countrymen who

deserve, in every point, to do honour to their country... I am now fixed to your fate, and I shall follow it and sustain it as well by my sword as by all means in my power.

Washington responded the next day:

Your favour of Yesterday conveyed to me fresh proof of the friendship and attachment which I have happily experienced since the first of our acquaintance... It will ever constitute part of my happiness to know that I stand well in your opinion... Happy, thrice happy, would it have been for this Army and the cause we embarked in, if the same generous spirit had pervaded all the Actors in it. But one Gentleman, whose Name you have mentioned, had, I am confident, far different views... How far he may have accomplished his ends, I know not, and but for considerations of a public Nature, I care not. For it is well known that neither ambitious, nor lucrative motives led me to accept my present Appointments; in the discharge of which I have endeavored to observe one steady and uniform conduct, which I shall invariably pursue, while I have the honour to command, regardless of the Tongue of slander or the powers of detraction. The fatal tendency of disunion is so obvious that I have, in earnest terms, exhorted such officers as have expressed their dissatisfaction at General Conway's promotion, to be cool and dispassionate... We must not, in so great a contest, expect to meet with nothing but Sun shine. I have no doubt but that everything happens for the best; that we shall triumph over all our misfortunes, and shall, in the end, be ultimately happy; when, My Dear Marquis, if you will give me your company in Virginia, we will laugh at our past difficulties and the folly of others.

When Gates took over as head of the war board, he and Congress went back to the old chimerical vision of the capture of Canada. Ignoring Washington, they developed another scheme for a midwinter invasion without advance planning or supplies. This expedition may have originally been intended to provide a command for Conway, but his increasing unpopularity and the marquis' renown gave Gates a chance to detach Lafayette from Washington. He was offered the command directly by Gates, with Conway to be his second. Washington refused to give Lafayette advice on what to do. The young officer leaped at this chance to revenge the British capture of French Canada. Though dazzled, he kept his head. He informed Congress that he would accept only on condition that he serve under Washington. He went to York and explained further, by a superficially naive but very clever letter to Henry Laurens, that he had Washington's permission to go to Canada, but he was surprised that he had not had the orders from the general himself. No doubt, he went on, it was ridiculous the way he sometimes misinterpreted things, for he knew Congress meant him to be directly under Washington, and in any case he would find it a much higher honor than having an independent command. Furthermore, said Lafayette, *all Frenchmen* felt exactly the same way. He also indicated he wanted Johann Kalb as his second in command, and if Congress would kindly approve all this, he would then return to camp to take leave and "the last orders of my general."

Congress might push Washington around, but Lafayette could put that body in its place. On the eve of the expected French alliance the representatives surrendered completely. That day Gates gave a dinner for the marquis followed by the usual toasts. Lafayette rose and said that they seemed to have forgotten one which he would give: "To the Commander-in-Chief of the American Armies!" Lafayette later wrote of the look of pain on some faces as the men got to their feet.

Conway was sent on ahead of the main group. Lafayette, Kalb, and several other French officers departed in the middle of the winter, with Gates' promises of all the soldiers, supplies, and money that would be waiting for them in the northern country. For fourteen days they travelled across frozen rivers and landscapes to Albany where Schuyler and Arnold told Lafayette that it was a mad scheme, for there were few soldiers and no money or supplies. Lafayette wrote to Washington: "Why am I so far from you, and what business had the board of war to hurry me through the ice and snow without knowing what I should do, neither what they were doing themselves... Your excellency may judge that I am very distressed by this disappointment... It will soon be known in Europe... I am afraid it will reflect on my reputation and I shall be laughed at." Washington replied on March 10:

> I... hasten to dispel those fears respecting your reputation, which are excited only by an uncommon degree of Sensibility... It will be no disadvantage to you to have it known in Europe, that you had received so manifest a proof of the good Opinion and confidence of Congress... and I am persuaded that every one will applaud your prudence in renouncing a Project... in which you would have attempted Physical Impossibilities. Indeed, unless you can be chargeable with the invariable effects of natural causes, and be arraigned for not suspending the course of the Seasons... the most prone to slander can have nothing to found blame upon... Your Character stands as fair as ever it did.

Three days later Congress authorized Washington to recall Lafayette and Kalb to commands in his army. Henry Laurens, president of Congress, wrote John Rutledge on March 11 that he remembered only three votes, in addition to his own, in opposition to "that indigested romantic scheme" but now everyone was remarking: "I never liked that Canada expedition." Its failure did not enhance Gates' reputation.

THE COLLAPSE OF THE CABAL

While this was going on, the Pennsylvania council, which had given the minimum cooperation to Washington's campaigns and the maximum criticism of his going to Valley Forge, decided that action should be taken against Howe. The state determined to organize its militia and drive Howe out of Philadelphia. Benjamin Rush busied himself with trying to persuade Gates to place his friend Mifflin at the head of the enterprise, but nothing came of this. Rush was also engaged in a quarrel with his superior medical officer and had taken his case to Congress.

While operating in this manner, Rush sent two letters to Washington, one on December 25, which he signed "With the most perfect esteem," the other February 25, which he concluded "with the warmest sentiments of regard and attachment." In between he wrote an anonymous letter on January 12 to Patrick Henry. What induced him to try to bring Henry into the coalition seems to have been Gates' remark that Henry considered Washington unfit for his command. It is certain that he never made such comment. Rush said to Henry:

> *America can only be undone by herself. She looks up to her councils and arms for protection, but alas! where are they?... But is our case desperate? By no means... The northern army has shown us what Americans are capable of doing with a GENERAL at their head. The spirit of the southern army is in no ways inferior to the spirit of the northern. A Gates, a Lee, or a Conway would in a few weeks render them an irresistible body of men. The last of the above officers has accepted of the new post of inspector general of the army in order to reform abuses. But the remedy is only a palliative one.*

In another letter to a friend Rush wrote, "A great and good God hath decreed America to be free, or the [commander in chief] and weak counselors would have ruined her long ago."

Three days later Rush wrote his wife: "As there is a rupture between General Gates and General Washington, it is feared no great things will be accomplished by this proposed army reform. Conway has banished himself from Headquarters by speaking disrespectfully of the Commander in Chief. These things occasion great uneasiness to all the true whigs, who foresee from General Washington's coolness to the two first officers in his army a continuation of all the calamities under which we have groaned... The Congress act a prudent part. They consult General Washington in every-thing, but they are determined to support the authority and influence of Gates and Conway."

Not long afterwards an anonymous document was found in the halls of Congress demanding a change in generals and detailing many reasons for it. When this was placed in the hands of Henry Laurens, president of Congress, he forwarded it to Washington with a note of apology. He was an exceedingly strong partisan of Washington but at the same time anxious to heal any split in the army. Two weeks or so after Gates arrived in York on January 19, Laurens informed him of some of Conway's actions, including his sarcastic comparison of the great Washington and Frederick the Great. Gates began to view Conway with distaste and made efforts to conciliate his commander. Washington replied to Laurens on January 31:

> *I cannot sufficiently express the obligation I feel to you for your friendship and politeness upon an occasion in which I am so deeply interested. I was not unapprized that a malignant faction had been for some time forming to my prejudice; which, conscious as I am of having ever done all in my power to answer the important purpose of the trust reposed in me, could not but give me some pain on a personal account; but my chief concern arises from an apprehension of the dangerous consequences, which internal dissentions may produce to the common cause.*

> *As I have no other view than to promote the public good, and am unambitious of honours not founded in the approbation of my Country, I would not desire in the least degree to suppress a free spirit of enquiry into any part of my conduct that even faction itself may deem reprehensible.*

> *The anonymous paper handed you exhibits many serious charges, and it is my wish that it should be submitted to Congress; this I am the more inclined to, as the suppression, or concealment, may possibly involve you in embarrassments hereafter; since it is uncertain how many, or who may be privy to the contents.*

> *My Enemies take an ungenerous advantage of me; they know the delicacy of my situation, and that motives of policy deprive me of the defence I might otherwise make against their insidious attacks. They know I cannot combat their insinuations, however injurious, without disclosing secrets, it is of the utmost moment to conceal. But why should I expect to be exempt from censure; the unfailing lot of an elevated station: Merits and talents, with which I can have no pretensions of rivalship have ever been subject to it.*

Patrick Henry, after receiving Rush's anonymous letter, wrote on February 20 to Washington: "You will, no doubt, be surprised at seeing the enclosed letter... I am sorry there should be one man who counts himself my friend, who is not yours. Perhaps I give you needless trouble in handing you this paper. The writer of it may be too insignificant to deserve any notice... But there may possibly be some scheme or party forwarding to your prejudice... Believe me, Sir, I have too high a sense of the obligations America has to you, to countenance so unworthy a proceeding. The most exalted merit has ever been found to attract envy. But I please myself with the hope, that the same fortitude and greatness of mind, which have hitherto braved all the difficulties and dangers inseparable from your station, will rise superior to every attempt of the envious partisan. I really cannot tell who is the writer of this letter... The handwriting is altogether strange to me."

When Gates arrived in Pennsylvania, he found Washington's January 4 letter awaiting him. On January 23 he replied in the devious manner he often employed with the army's head. "[Your] letter... has relieved me from unspeakable uneasiness... The paragraph which your Excellency has condescended to transcribe, is spurious. It was certainly fabricated to answer the most selfish and wicked purposes. Conway's letter was perfectly harmless." Gates went on to say that it ought not be shown "to those who stand most high in the public esteem... Honour forbids it." He added a tortuous explanation as to why he had sent a copy of his own letter to Congress. He called Wilkinson treacherous, in having first made an unscrupulous forgery and then accusing Troup of having tipped off Hamilton. Washington delayed a reply until February 9, informing Gates that he had been engaged in more urgent business. He then demolished the victor of Saratoga:

> *It is my wish to give implicit credit to the assurances of every Gentleman but... I am sorry to confess, there happen to be some unlucky circumstances, which involuntarily compel me to consider the discovery you mention, not so satisfactory and conclusive as you seem to think it.*

> *I am so unhappy as to find no small difficulty in reconciling the spirit and import of your different Letters, and sometimes of the different parts of the same Letter. It must appear somewhat strange that the forgery remained so long undetected; and that your first Letter to me from Albany of the 8th. of Decemr. should tacitly recognize the genuineness of the paragraph in question; while your only concern at that time seemed to be "the tracing out the author of the infidelity..."*

> *Throughout the whole of that Letter, the reality of the extracts is by the fairest*

implication allowed... Your Letter of the 23d. Ulto. to my great surprize, proclaims it "in words as well as in substance a wicked forgery."

It is not my intention to contradict this assertion, but only to intimate some considerations, which tend to induce a supposition, that though none of Genl. Conways Letters to you contained the offensive passage mentioned, there might have been something in them too nearly related to it, that could give such an extraordinary alarm... If this were not the case, how easy in the first instance, to have declared there was nothing exceptionable in them, and to have produced the Letters... Concealment in an affair, which had made so much noise, tho' not by my means, will naturally lead men to conjecture the worst... The anxiety and jealousy you apprehended from revealing the letter, will be very apt to be increased by suppressing it.

You are pleased to consider General Conway's Letters as of a confidential nature... Permit me to enquire, whether, when there is an impropriety in communicating, it is only applicable with respect to the parties, who are the subject of them... Your not knowing whether the Letter... "came to me from a Member of Congress, or from an Officer," plainly indicates that you originally communicated it to at least one of that honorable body; and I learn from General Conway... it had been communicated to the perusal of several of its members, and was afterwards shewn by himself to three more. It is somewhat difficult to conceive a reason, founded in generosity, for imparting the free and confidential strictures of that ingenious Censor, on the operations of the Army under my command to a Member of Congress.

Washington clearly indicated that many members of Congress had seen Conway's correspondence, and it is reasonable to suppose, Congress not being very adept at keeping secrets, that Washington knew precisely what Conway had been writing and saying. Wilkinson himself later wrote to Washington that his quotation had been nearly exact. At this point, Henry Laurens, much distressed by the dispute, intervened and implored Gates to end it. Gates washed his hands of Conway in a letter to Washington:

I earnestly hope not more of that time, so precious to the public, may be lost upon the subject of General Conway's letter... I have no personal connection with him, nor have I any correspondence, previous to his writing the letter... He therefore must be responsible; as I heartily dislike controversy, even upon my own account, and much more in a matter in which I was only accidentally concerned... I solemnly declare that I am of no faction... After this, I cannot believe your

Excellency will either suffer your suspicions or the prejudices of others to induce you to spend another moment upon this subject.

Washington immediately replied: "I am as averse to controversy as any Man and had I not been forced into it, you would never have had occasion to impute to me, even the shadow of a disposition towards it... Your Solemnly disclaiming any offensive views... makes me willing to close with the desire, you express, of burying them in silence... My temper leads me to peace and harmony with all Men; and it is particularly my wish, to avoid any personal feuds or dissensions with those who are embarked in the same great National interest with myself."

Patrick Henry followed his first letter with another. Jacky Custis had called on him and told him that General Mifflin had been working against Washington. Henry said: "It is very hard to trace the schemes and windings of the enemies to America. I really thought that man its friend; however, I am too far from him to judge of his present temper. While you are facing the armed enemies of our liberty in the field, and by the favor of God have been kept unhurt, I trust your country will never harbor in her bosom the miscreant who would ruin her best supporter. I wish not to flatter; but when arts, unworthy of honest men, are used to defame and traduce you, I think it not amiss, but a duty, to assure you of that estimation in which the public hold you... I cannot help assuring you... of the high sense of gratitude which all ranks of men in this our native country bear to you... I do not like to make a parade of these things, and I know you are not fond of it; however, I hope the occasion will plead my excuse... your ever affectionate friend." Washington's responses to Henry's first and second letters were dispatched in the same outgoing mail of March 28:

Your Friendship, Sir, in transmitting me the Anonymous Letter you had received, lays me under the most grateful obligations...

I have ever been happy in supposing that I had a place in your Esteem, and the proof you have afforded on this occasion, makes me peculiarly so. The favourable light in which you hold me, is truly flattering, but I should feel much regret, if I thought the happiness of America so intimately connected with my personal welfare as you so obligingly seem to consider it. All I can say is, that she has ever had, and I trust she ever will have, my honest exertions to promote her Interest. I cannot hope that my services have been the best. But my heart tells me, they have been the best I could render...

The Anonymous Letter... Was written by Doctor Rush so far as I can judge from a similitude of hands. This Man has been elaborate, and studied in his professions of regard for me; and long since the letter to you.

My caution to avoid any thing, that could injure the service, prevented me from communicating, but to a very few of my friends, the intrigues of a faction, which I know was formed against me, since it might serve to publish our internal dissensions; but their own restless Zeal to advance their views has too clearly betrayed them, and made concealment, on my part fruitless… It appeared in general, that General Gates was to be exalted, on the ruin of my reputation and influence. This I am authorised to say, from undeniable facts in my possession… General Mifflin, it is commonly supposed, bore the second part in the Cabal; and General Conway, I know was a very Active and malignant Partisan; but I have good reasons to believe that their machinations have recoiled most sensibly upon themselves.

Washington thus accurately appraised the cabal. Its subsequent collapse can be summarized as follows.

WILKINSON

When this officer learned that Gates had attempted to make him the scapegoat of the affair, he demanded an apology for a slur on his honor. Gates replied with a tart note, enclosing a copy of Washington's letter. Wilkinson challenged Gates to a duel. According to the latter's unconfirmable version they met; Gates assured him that he had not meant it, and the affair ended with Gates in tears. Later, while Wilkinson was secretary of the war board, he asked to see Washington's correspondence with Gates on Conway. After reading it, he immediately resigned his post with the board, in a letter to the president of Congress: "After the acts of treachery and falsehood in which I have detected Major General Gates, the president of that board, it is impossible for me to reconcile it to my honor to serve with him."

RUSH

This physician carried his bitter dispute with Dr. William Shippen, Jr., to Congress but got nowhere with his complaints. He resigned in disgust at the end of January. He assured Shippen: "You have supposed that I am busy in traducing you. Far from it. I declare solemnly I feel no personal resentment against you." Before and after this note Rush wrote severe castigations of

Shippen to Washington, John Adams, Nathanael Greene, and others. He continued to make bitter comments on Washington in some of his letters but had no further role in the war. Washington was so anxious to keep dissensions quiet that, though he saw Rush on many occasions over the years, he never mentioned his letter. In 1804 Rush learned with horror that John Marshall had received it from Bushrod Washington and planned to publish it in his life of Washington. Rush protested; Marshall published it without his name, thus preserving the anonymity.

GATES

The general's behavior in the Conway affair did not increase his esteem in Congress. After the collapse of the Canadian campaign he was invited by that body to leave the board of war and place himself under the command of General Washington.

MIFFLIN

Mifflin, as quartermaster of the army, had not exercised his functions and the army suffered greatly. He resigned his commission but was persuaded to retract and go on the board of war. He was one of the principal movers of Gates' election as the board's president. After the army's roar of support for Washington, Mifflin quickly retreated and denied that he had any role in wanting to displace him. He too was taken off the board of war and put under Washington's orders. Washington was not cheered by this addition to his army. He wrote Gouverneur Morris on May 18:

> *I was not a little surprized to find that a certain Gentleman who some time ago (when a cloud of darkness hung heavy over us and our affairs looked gloomy) was desirous of resigning, now stepping forward in the line of the Army. But if he can reconcile such conduct to his own feelings as an <u>Officer</u> and Man of Honour and Congress hath no objection to his leaving his Seat in another department, I have nothing <u>personally</u> to oppose it, yet I must think, that Gentleman's stepping in, and out, as the Sun Happens to beam forth or obscure is not <u>quite</u> the thing, nor <u>quite</u> just with respect to those Officers who take the bitter with the sweet.*

Congress not long afterwards ordered an inquiry into Mifflin's management of the quartermaster's department, and he resigned his commission.

CONWAY

This Irishman soon had Congress and practically all the army, including Gates and the French officers, against him. The only position the inspector general could obtain was third in command of the small Canadian expeditionary force under Lafayette. When this failed, Congress ordered the two top officers to return, leaving Conway wandering around upstate New York. Conway wrote protesting letters to Congress and to Washington. The latter informed Gouverneur Morris on May 18: "I am told that Conway (from whom I have receiv'd another impertinent letter... *demanding* the comd. of a division of the Continental Army) is, through the medium of his friends, solliciting his commission again. Can this Be?" In writing Congress, Conway offered to resign if his complaints were not remedied. Morris replied to Washington: "[I] took the earliest opportunity to express [in Congress] in the very strongest terms my satisfaction my joy at the receipt of the letter from him and of consequence to assign the reasons why this event gave me so much pleasure... No opposition was made... [to] accepting his resignation."

Conway, protesting that he had not meant to resign, hurried down to York. From there he wrote to Gates, who had left the war board: "I never had a sufficient idea of Cabals until I reached this place my reception, you may imagine was not a warm one... Mr. Carroll from Maryland upon whose friendship I depended is one of the hottest of the Cabal. He told me a few days ago almost literally, that any body that displeas'd or did not admire the commander in chief ought not to be kept in the army. Mr. Carroll might be a good papist, but I am sure the sentiments he expresses are neither roman nor catholick."

Conway continued to give out sentiments hostile to Washington. In return General John Cadwalader expressed his opinion that Conway had been a coward at Germantown. Conway challenged Cadwalader to a duel and the latter shot him in the mouth. Conway recovered and hung around the United States till the end of the year. He then disappeared from American history until he turned up in Lafayette's house in Paris to claim the Order of the Cincinnati along with Rochambeau and the French officers who had won at Yorktown. Lafayette wrote Washington that he had given it to him; otherwise Conway would have claimed that there was a plot by Washington and Lafayette against him.

TWENTY-FOUR

HOPEFUL SPRING

1778

ASIDE FROM HAVING to bear the attacks of treacherous American generals and congressmen, Washington had also to manage an army and conduct a war from Valley Forge. He maintained his sense of humor although on one occasion he found it unappreciated. General William Smallwood had captured two British vessels near Wilmington, with arms, ammunition, food supplies, and a number of British officers' wives. The news of the captives made an impression in camp. Lafayette wrote his father-in-law that the wives were dreadfully afraid they were to be put to servicing the American army. Washington congratulated Smallwood and said if there were any supplies of liquor aboard, not to forget "the poor fellows" in his camp.

When the wives were released, Smallwood asked how he should account for their food rations. Washington replied on February 23: "With respect to the board of the Officers' Wives, it is a matter you must determine yourself. I imagined they had been sent to Philadelphia, soon after the prize was taken. I do not suppose that the public will suppose themselves liable for it... and it might be deemed ungenerous to make the Ladies pay it themselves... As you and your Officers only have had the pleasure of their company and conversation, I believe you must adjust the matter among you."

Smallwood replied with heavy earnestness: "Even had I have enjoyed the pleasure of their company and conversation I should not have thought myself liable... Upon reflection you must be conscious I have been fully employed in a less agreeable way [with] little relaxation and leisure to enjoy the ladies' company if I discharge my duty which I have endeavored to do."

Washington replied on March 6: "I... am sorry to find that what I meant merely as a joke, has been taken by you in a serous light. I can assure you I never had the least suspicion that any part of your time was sacrificed or your duty neglected, on account of the Ladies who fell into your hands... The Board... in my opinion properly becomes an incidental charge, to be deducted from the gross amount of the prize."

Congress and its board of war were supposed to negotiate for troops and clothing with the individual states but, as a practical matter, Washington was forced to send pleading letters to individual governors. He wrote politely on January 18 to the president of Pennsylvania, the state that had toyed with the idea of raising its own militia to capture Howe and thus show up Washington. He noted again that the state's regiments were very depleted in numbers and had little clothing. Previously he had told their officers to go out in the state to buy clothing. A committee of the state legislature asked him to desist for they had sent out commissioners for this purpose. Washington added: "What these Commissioners have done I do not know, but no clothing has come to the army thro' their hands." He suggested that, since so many of the inhabitants were staying home because of their principles, they might be able to do weaving and spinning. He also sent appeals for clothing to North Carolina, Virginia, Delaware, Connecticut, and New Jersey.

On New Year's Day 1778, Washington complained to Congress that he had long been without a quartermaster general. His first draft noted that General Mifflin had quit the post in July. He had pleaded indisposition but recovered on being offered a post on the board of war.

When a congressional committee was appointed to look into the army's problems, Washington prepared a thirty-eight-page document for them. He particularly asked for a pension plan, explaining that the men had made great financial sacrifices and that there was no provision for their families in case of disability or death. He discussed the need for more cavalry, which had proven invaluable for intelligence purposes. He proposed eighty regiments for the army with a total of forty thousand rank and file. He asked for a provost marshal, with mounted troops, for the maintenance of order and discipline, camp security, and counterintelligence. He requested an assistant inspector general for each regiment, in order to institute a uniform system of training. He complained that the congressional methods of promotion had brought so much bickering and so many resignations that he had to spend too much time on officers' grievances. The commissary department needed reorganization. The army, he said, lived "from hand to mouth if I may be allowed the phrase." The hospital department was in a deplorable condition, partly because of the lack of supplies but also because of the constant quarreling among the physicians in charge. He asked for extra pay for his engineers, who were often in great danger, building or blowing up fortifications in the face of the enemy. He wanted more riflemen for guerrilla purposes.

Many of the requests and plans Washington made were far in advance of army practices of the time, while others such as pensions were copied from the British army. In his organizational thought, he was always ahead of the country and he was now thoroughly professional. The amateur critics in Congress continued to maintain that he needed only a few thousand temporary extra militia from the farms to beat a trained and formidable enemy. His proposed pension plan aroused almost implacable opposition on the ground that it would establish a favored class in society.

By the middle of February, the army was so close to starvation that Washington was begging, in the word's most literal sense, the governors of Maryland, Virginia, Connecticut, New Jersey, and New York for food, informing them the army was naked and starving. He appealed to the loyal citizens of Pennsylvania and the neighboring states to provide what food they could to keep the army together. He sent out such fighting officers as Greene, Wayne, and Henry Lee to forage. Washington expected the army to revolt or leave him but there were only plaintive murmurings. One French officer heard a man say: "No bread, no soldier."

On March 1 Washington expressed his gratitude to those who stuck by him through the hardships: "The Commander-in-chief again takes occasions to return his warmest thanks to the virtuous officers and soldiery of the Army for that persevering fidelity and Zeal which they have uniformly manifested in all their conduct... The recent Instance of uncomplaining Patience during the scarcity of provisions in Camp is a fresh proof that they possess in an eminent degree the spirit of Soldiers and the magnanimity of patriots... Defects in the Commissaries department, Contingencies of weather and other temporary impediments have subjected and may again subject us to a deficiency for a few days, but soldiers! American soldiers! will despise the meanness of repining at such trifling strokes of adversity, trifling indeed when compared to the transcendent Prize... Glory and Peace."

On March 24 Washington announced that Major General Greene was appointed his quartermaster general. This unexpected assignment of one of his ablest general officers had taken all of the commander in chief's very persuasive powers to accomplish. Greene had remarked: "No one ever heard of a quartermaster general in history." This turned out not to be true. He handed in a brilliant performance before returning to a field command. He later wrote Washington that he had taken the job "out of compassion" for the commander in chief, who was acting as quartermaster general as well.

Washington's next problem was the army's urgent need for training and discipline. Had Conway not made so many enemies, Washington would have welcomed him for this task. In January, while he was wrestling with the Conway intrigues, he had a note from Baron Frederick von Steuben, who had arrived at Portsmouth, New Hampshire, with an introductory letter from Franklin. This described him as a lieutenant general and former aide to Frederick the Great. Steuben wrote Washington:

> The object of my greatest ambition, is to render your country all the services in my power and to deserve the title of a citizen of America by fighting for the cause of your liberty...

> If the distinguished ranks in which I have served in Europe should be an obstacle, I had rather serve under your Excellency as a volunteer, than to be an object of discontent to such deserving officers as have already distinguished themselves amongst you...

> ...I could say moreover (were it not for the fear of offending your modesty) that your Excellency is the only person under whom (after having served under the King of Prussia) I could wish to pursue an art to which I have wholly given up myself.

Much has been made of the fact that Steuben seems to have had no higher rank than major in the Prussian army. However, the rank of lieutenant general, which corresponded with that of the English brigadier, may have been conferred on him—as his barony was—by one of the minor German courts. It is of little importance since Steuben was immediately liked by Congress and, after arriving at Valley Forge, made himself indispensable.

On February 27 Washington wrote to Henry Laurens, president of Congress: "Baron Steuben... appears to be much of a Gentlemen, and as far as I have had an opportunity of judging, a man of Military knowledge and acquainted with the World." A few days later, John Laurens informed his father that he thought Steuben would make an ideal inspector general. Training and discipline were so badly needed that, however "obnoxious" Conway had been to the whole army, it would have been better to have had him than no one. The baron was liked by everyone and it might be just the job for him. Washington's letters and orders thereafter were full of praise for Steuben's ability, zeal, cheerfulness, and intelligence. By March 8 John Laurens was writing his father: "The Baron Steuben has had the fortune to please uncommonly, for a stranger, at first sight. All the general officers who have seen him, are prepossessed in his favour, and conceive highly of his abilities."

Though Steuben was horrified at conditions in camp, he plunged into his duties with tact and understanding. As he wrote to a friend in Europe, he quickly found that American soldiers could not be ordered around as soldiers were at home. Once the need for doing things was explained to them, however, they responded with alacrity.

On March 17 Washington chose one hundred men for drilling. Steuben found an assistant, Captain Benjamin Walker, who translated for him. Soon he acquired the ability to swear a little in English, mixed with French and German, and this put the army in good humor. He had the ability to make drilling, marching, and musket drill seem like games, and those who passed through his command emerged proud of their new abilities. The army clamored to take part. Soon Washington was appointing inspectors in each brigade and ordering everyone to take the drills. Steuben himself sat up late at night composing manuals of training and discipline. Washington quickly extended the system to troops in New Jersey and Delaware. On April 30 Washington warmly praised Steuben to Congress and asked that he be appointed inspector general. On May 8 after the army had paraded in celebration of the French alliance, Washington announced in general orders:

> *The Commander in Chief takes particular pleasure in acquainting the Army that their Conduct yesterday afforded him the highest Satisfaction; The Exactness and order with which their movements were performed is a pleasing Evidence of the Progress they are making in military Improvement... The General at the same time presents his thanks to Baron Steuben and the Gentlemen under him for the indefatigable Exertions in the duties of their Office, the good effects of which are already so apparent.*

On May 9 Washington informed the army that Congress had made Steuben major general and inspector general.

An exasperated Washington had written to Congress on April 10 in reply to a resolve authorizing him to call in five thousand militia from Pennsylvania, Maryland, and New Jersey. He pointed out that he needed an army, not militia. That winter he had been able to raise fewer than one thousand militia in Pennsylvania to help him against the enemy and usually there were no more than one hundred. A congressional committee had visited him and extensively gone over his problems. They had reached agreement as to his needs but nothing happened. The committee had led him to expect that Congress would support him with forty thousand troops, but he had heard nothing further of these. His requests for pensions for officers had been ignored; many officers were so dissatisfied they had resigned. His urgent needs for "the horse establishment, Companies of Sappers, Provost Marshalseys &ca., &ca., &ca. as agreed to by the Committee, and recommended for Congress's consideration, are entirely at a stand."

Shortly afterwards he received a letter from John Banister, a new Virginia member of Congress and an old acquaintance. Banister was optimistic that Congress would establish a pension scheme for officers. Washington replied on April 21 that he was pleased but that he regretted the long delay. He added: "I find it a very arduous task to keep the officers in tolerable humour." Washington then analyzed congressional attitudes towards the army:

> The other point is, the _jealousy_ which Congress unhappily entertains of the Army, and which, if reports are right, some Members labour to establish. You may be assured, there is nothing more injurious, or more unjustly founded. This jealousy stands upon the common, received Opinion, which under proper limitations is certainly true, that standing Armies are dangerous to a State... The prejudices in other Countries has only gone to them in time of _Peace_... It is our policy to be prejudiced against them in time of _War_; though they are Citizens having all the Ties, and interests of Citizens, and in most cases property totally unconnected with the Military Line. If we would pursue a right System of Policy... there should be none of these distinctions. We should all be considered, Congress, Army, &c. as one people, embarked in one Cause, in one interest; acting on the same principle and to the same End. The distinction, the Jealousies set up, or perhaps only incautiously let out, can answer not a single good purpose. They are impolitic in the extreme... The very jealousy, which the narrow politics of some may affect to entertain of the Army, in order to assure a due subordination to the supreme Civil Authority, is a likely mean to produce a contrary effect... It is unjust, because no Order of Men in the thirteen States have paid a more sanctimonious regard to their proceedings than the Army; and, indeed, it may be questioned whether there has been that scrupulous adherence had to them by any other... [At this point in the draft letter, Washington's feelings in regard to the army got the upper hand. In redrafting it he inserted the following addition.] ...for without arrogance, or the smallest deviation from truth it may be said, that no history, now extant, can furnish an instance of an Army's suffering such uncommon hardships as ours have done, and bearing them with the same patience and Fortitude. To see Men without Cloathes to cover their nakedness, without Blankets to lay on, without

Shoes, by which their Marches might be traced by the Blood from their feet, and almost as often without Provisions as with; Marching through Frost and Snow, and at Christmas taking up their Winters Quarters within a day's March of the enemy, without a House or Hutt to cover them till they could be built and submitting to it without a murmur, is a mark of patience and obedience which in my opinion can scarce be parallel'd.

Washington went on to say that from time to time the army had remonstrated against certain measures taken by Congress. Only slaves would be denied the right to petition and Congress should not consider this as an infringement of civil authority.

Washington's remark that the legislature seemed to dislike having a standing army, when the country was at war for its liberties, was a severe condemnation of a body that was fearful of a starving army whose bare feet had bloodied the snows of Valley Forge. Washington did not need to add to Banister that he bore the brunt of the attacks, though he had gone far out of his way to support civil authorities, maintained in office only by the existence of the army itself.

It is worth noting that whereas Congress remained throughout the war as the supreme authority, the British allowed only military control in occupied areas. The single exception was thinly populated Georgia, where a royal governor was reinstalled. The American Tories frequently protested that the British did not trust them or permit them to reestablish civil government, but their complaints were ignored.

On April 22 Washington received copies of Lord North's reconciliation bills from William Tryon, last royal governor of New York, who had become a major general of Tory troops. He sent them to Congress with a letter saying that Tryon had made the "extraordinary and impertinent request" that he communicate them to his army. Congress then passed a resolution requesting the states offer pardons to all Tories who should surrender prior to June 10. Washington replied on April 26 to Tryon:

I had had the pleasure of seeing the Draughts of the two Bills... I can assure you they were suffered to have a free currency among the officers and men under my command, in whose fidelity to the United States, I have the most perfect confidence...

I take the liberty to transmit you a few printed copies of the resolution of Congress of the 23d. instant, and to request, you will be instrumental, in communicating its contents... to the persons who are the objects of its operation. The benevolent purpose, it is intended to answer, will, I persuade myself, sufficiently recommend it to your candour.

On the day he had the note from Tryon, he received a resolve of Congress that he call a general council of his officers to devise plans for the ensuing campaign. Washington had already, through memoranda circulated to his senior officers, asked their opinions whether to attack Philadelphia or New York, or to adopt a waiting policy. Very roughly (though some voted for more than one policy), a third of his generals wanted him to attack New York, a third Philadelphia, and a third asked him to wait till the army was better trained.

The resolution authorized Generals Gates and Mifflin to attend the council. Gates was ordered to the command in New York State but placed under Washington's orders. He and Mifflin were to appear at camp when directed by the commander in chief. In forwarding the resolves, Gouverneur Morris strongly suggested that his council's decisions not be sent to Congress, which could never keep a secret. This was a clear hint not to let the members interfere with military strategy. Washington was now, in fact as well as by commission, commander in chief of all the armies and his authority was never again in serious question.

JOLLITY

While the cabal was collapsing, Mrs. Washington arrived at headquarters after a long, rough trip in a blizzard. She wrote Mercy Warren on March 7: "The General's apartment is very small; he has had a log cabben built to dine in which has made our quarters much more tolerable than they were at first." A miniature of her husband made by Major Nicholas Rogers was presented to Martha that month. John Laurens wrote his father, probably reflecting her views, that he had made the general too aged. His associates thought, in fact, that he had begun to look a great deal older, but Mrs. Washington did not care to notice this.

An effort was made to keep up a little social life in the waste of Valley Forge. The army band played for the commander in chief on February 22. He gave them some of his small personal stock of hard money. There was singing in the evening over cups of tea or coffee, and this was almost the only entertainment. General Greene's wife, Kitty, could speak French and found herself a center of attraction for the French officers. She was more active in promoting the French alliance than some thought proper. Baron Steuben allowed his aides to have a dinner in his quarter, to which all American officers were invited who had not a whole pair of breeches. His aide, Pierre Duponceau, described it as a meal of tough beefsteak and potatoes, the drink "salamanders," liquor set on fire then drunk "flame and all. Such a set of ragged and at the same time merry fellows were never brought together. The Baron loved to speak of that dinner, and his sans-culottes." Mrs. Washington herself had to patch the breeches of John Laurens, the general's aide, so he could be fit for duty.

SPRING

Washington tried several times to attack British ships frozen in the Delaware. By the end of February he wrote that the thaw in the river had made this impossible. There was more snow in March, but on the twenty-third the weather began to turn warm. By the middle of April spring was in full bloom. Schools of patriotic shad raced past the British fortifications and up the Schuylkill to feed the army. The camp was thoroughly cleaned. Washington ordered his men to wash their clothes even though they were but "rags." The lean, tough, and disciplined army, which had survived the winter, had a vital élan that promised well.

On May 1 maypoles were erected throughout the camp and the day was given up to celebrating King Tammany, the old Delaware chieftain who was a symbol of resistance to oppression. The procession was led by a sergeant dressed as an Indian chief. The soldiers who wore blossoms in their hats paraded and cheered. The enlisted men were all given a drink of whiskey. In the evening the officers held a dance in honor of their own chief.

That day Washington received the news of the French alliance and immediately sent word to Congress, adding: "I believe no event was ever received with a more heartfelt joy." Although he did not announce it officially to the army until Congress had acted, his delight and gratitude clearly appeared in his general orders of Saturday, May 2:

The Commander in Chief directs that divine Service be performed every Sunday at 11 oClock in those Brigades to which there are Chaplains; those which have none, to attend the places of worship nearest them. It is expected that Officers of all Ranks will by their attendance set an Example to their men.

While we are zealously performing the duties of good Citizens and soldiers we certainly ought not to be inattentive to the high duties of Religion. To the distinguished Character of Patriot, it should be our highest Glory to add the more distinguished Character of Christian. The signal Instances of providential Goodness which we have experienced and which have now almost crowned our labours with complete Success, demand from us in a peculiar manner the warmest returns of Gratitude and Piety to the Supreme Author of all Good.

Congress received the news too late for action on Saturday, and on the Sabbath it did not meet. The treaty was read on Monday, May 4, and ratified that afternoon. The following day Washington announced it to the army:

It having pleased the Almighty Ruler of the Universe propitiously to defend the Cause of the United American States and finally by raising us up a powerful Friend among the Princes of the Earth to establish our liberty and independence upon lasting foundations, it becomes us to set apart a day for gratefully acknowledging the divine Goodness and celebrating the important Event which we owe to his benign Interposition.

The French officers were smothered with congratulations and joy. The following day the whole army paraded in celebration after prayers. Two French officers, Kalb and Lafayette, were given preferred positions. The men marched with unusual precision. Thirteen cannon were discharged. The infantry then fired in a running line from right to left on the front line and from left to right on the second line. There were cheers by the whole army: "Long live the king of France" and "God save the American states." A discharge of thirteen cannon finished the ceremony. The enlisted men were given a gill of rum. All military prisoners were released and two soldiers under sentence of death were pardoned by Washington.

After the ceremony Washington gave a dinner for all his officers and such of their wives as were in camp. The army band played. According to John Laurens, Washington was given "such proofs of the love and attachments of his officers as must have given him the most exquisite feelings." The general, in fact, suddenly looked years younger. One officer noted that his face had a look of "uncommon delight." When he left the table the whole assembly rose and cheered, and as he rode off the shouts continued and hundreds of hats were flung into the air. The general returned the greetings with great waves of his hat and "huzzaed" back several times.

Throughout the country a new anthem was being sung to an old tune: "God Save Great Washington," ending with a rousing "God Damn the King."

PHILADELPHIA

The well-fed British army stayed comfortably in the nation's capital all winter. Balls, plays, dinners, and cards kept the officers contented, but some of their doings had not been previously known in quiet Philadelphia. The British and their mistresses were much frowned upon by the Quakers in whose houses they were billeted.

The previous December George III had taken no joy in the capture of Philadelphia. On March 23 he wrote North that, with a French war certain, "it is a joke to think of keeping Pennsylvania for we must form from the Army now in America a corps sufficient to attack the French Islands." It had not been an easy winter for the king. A few days before, he had written North: "I am fairly woren down."

North continued to offer his resignation so that "*new* and *able* men" could take over the government, but the king replied that North's "Honour and Integrity" were at stake. The king added that North was too diffident of himself. At this point, on March 25, Lord North, the only man in the kingdom who dared to do so, bluntly gave George III the facts:

> *From the situation of public and private credit, Lord North doubts very much whether this country can borrow for two years more... The power of borrowing has been hitherto the principal source of the greatness and weight of Great Britain.*
>
> *...The condition of the country as to its facilities is deplorable. It is totally unequal to a war with Spain, France, and America, and will, Lord North fears, be over match'd if the contention is only with the House of Bourbon, and, therefore, although the offence received from France is great He owns that he should be glad if an accommodation with America would prevent for the present moment, a war with France, as he thinks that Great Britain will suffer more in the war, than her enemies, He does not mean, by defeats, but by an enormous expense, which will ruin her, and will not in any degree be repaid by the most brilliant victories. Great Britain will undo herself while she thinks of punishing France.*
>
> *Lord North begs leave to trouble his Majesty for a moment on a disagreeable subject, but in which he is bound to speak the truth, the bad situation of affairs will with great appearance of reason be attributed to the obstinate perseverance in the American War... Ld. North's diffidence of himself is grounded upon seven years' experience, and will for ever render it fatal to his Majesty to continue him at the head of affairs. His Majesty's own sentiments will make him prefer the salvation of this country to every personal consideration, impress'd as he is, with that*

affectionate regard to his people which becomes a good Prince. Lord North having said this much, is silent, but this much he could not, with peace of mind, refrain from saying.

Lord North has received the obloquy of history but it has not been a just appraisal. At this critical stage of world affairs North appealed for reason and sanity. Had the king listened, five more years of bloodshed in America, a war with France, and the French revolution might have been averted. The king's only reply to North was that it was necessary to end the war with America "to be enabled with redoubled ardour to avenge the faithless and insolent conduct of France." To do so, he was prepared even to open "the channel of intercourse with that insidious man," Benjamin Franklin. North continued to plead to be allowed to quit, saying his abilities and memory were greatly impaired, and he could no longer continue. In the modern world North would have resigned, but in the eighteenth century the king had the means to force him to stay as he dragged his kingdom and North down to destruction. So long as the war had to continue, it was at least good for America that a halfhearted man conducted it. The king shortly thereafter made him warden of the Cinque Ports, a sinecure that added £ four thousand a year to his income.

The news that France had dispatched to America a fleet under the comte d'Estaing caused great commotion in the cabinet and in Parliament. The Royal Navy was totally unprepared for this sudden move, and the king himself went to Portsmouth to try to expedite a relief fleet. Its commander was Admiral Byron, uncle of Lord Carlisle, peace commissioner. They were the grandfather and cousin of the poet, who described Carlisle's rhyming as "paralytic puling," but wrote of Washington:

> *...The first—the last—the best—*
> *The Cincinnatus of the West,...*
> *To make man blush there was but one!*

On May 8 the king received correct but belated reports that there had been many desertions in Washington's army and that "they are sickly and in want of cloathing, and not above six thousand in camp." Two days earlier the wholly cheerful American army had paraded in celebration of the French alliance.

On May 13 General Burgoyne arrived in England on parole. Washington had been particularly desirous that he be allowed to return since his only defense for his defeat would be to describe the overwhelming strength of the Americans. Burgoyne was not allowed a court of inquiry, for Lord George

Germain was not anxious that Parliament look into the war office. He was coldly received and stripped of the offices in which he had taken so much pride in his American proclamation: colonel of the Queen's light dragoons and governor of Fort William. He was forced to turn to producing dramas and illegitimate children. In this latter enterprise he fathered a son who became a field marshal 146 years after his father's birth.

On April 9 Sir William Howe was recalled to England. He was the second of the three unlucky generals who had arrived in Boston in May 1775 to join the unfortunate Gage. Now he and Burgoyne were on their way home to be scapegoats, leaving Sir Henry Clinton, the last of the trio, to be the final sacrificial goat offered up for London's sins. As the new commander in chief, he reached Philadelphia from New York on May 8. The following day he received the king's instructions to abandon the city and retire to New York and permitting him a further retreat to Halifax. He was informed that peace commissioners were on the way, but Clinton clearly saw that America was not likely to accept terms when the British were giving up a major post.

On the eve of General Howe's departure, the British gave him a regatta and a great ball called the "Meschianza." Letters went to London praising the glory of it. Ladies in Turkish costume were attended by knights of the blended rose and of the burning mountain who jousted in tournaments. Magnificent arches led into a ballroom decorated with 85 mirrors and 34 sconces covered with flowers and ribbons. The 430 guests dined in a brilliant supper room adorned with 56 more mirrors and more than 700 candles. Toasts were given to the king, queen, army, and navy, and to the knights and their ladies. Dancing continued till four in the morning.

In his life of Washington, Washington Irving could not restrain his contempt for "this tawdry and somewhat effeminate pageant... this silken and mock heroic display [when] the number of British chivalry in Philadelphia was nineteen thousand five hundred and thirty, cooped up in a manner by an American force at Valley Forge, amounting according to official returns, to eleven thousand eight hundred men. Could any triumphal pageant be more ill-placed and ill-timed." It was especially so for the American Tories who had been risking their property, liberty, and even lives, in order to maintain the king's cause in America. The ball, held just before the British abandoned the capital, greatly shocked them, the more so as General Howe rather casually suggested they ought to make their peace with the rebels. Joseph Galloway, according to Lord Howe's secretary, Ambrose Serle, was filled with "horror and melancholy." Serle tried to console him but noted in his diary: "Nothing remains for him but to attempt reconciliation with (what I may now venture to call) the United States of America." Less than two years before Serle had described the "villainy and madness" of the Americans for rebelling. Now he thought, as did Howe, that they had won de facto independence. Clinton, however, was now in command, and he feared that the provincial Tory troops in New York might give up unless the Philadelphia Loyalists were protected. He offered to take them to New York by ship. Since there were so many, he was forced to march the main part of his army across New Jersey and this gave Washington an opportunity for action.

When Sir William Howe saw the king on July 3 he pledged his support. George III drafted for Lord North a little memorandum of this talk: "I had a very long conversation with him... the Substance of which was his very strongly declaring nothing shall make either His Brother or Him join Opposition, but that Lord G. Germaine and His Secretaries Nox and Cumberland have everywhere loaded him with obloquy that he must therefore be allowed some means of justifying himself."

General Howe was not allowed what he thought a proper defense and he and his brother finally swung over to the opposition. Nonetheless, he lost his seat in the house at the next election, his constituents showing their disapproval of the American war and his part in it.

CHARLES LEE

The Americans had more good news on top of the French alliance. After long negotiations, they succeeded in swapping General Richard Prescott, another unlucky British general who had been captured twice, and once before exchanged, for General Charles Lee, the ranking major general of the American army.

Lee had been taken in the darkest days of the war and since then had been under strong British influence. He had a low opinion of Washington at the time of his capture, and he had not been with the army since it had acquired a wholly different spirit from that following the fall of Fort Washington.

General Lee was received in May with great ceremony by Washington, who rode out four miles from camp with his principal officers and an army band to meet him. He was given all military honors and escorted to camp, where the general and his wife gave him a splendid dinner with music. Lee soon told Elias Boudinot, Washington's commissary of prisoners, who had arranged his transfer, that he thought the army was in deplorable condition and that Washington was unfit to be a sergeant. He later told others that the army could never stand up to British professionals.

When Lee was asked to sign the oath to the United States, including a renunciation of his allegiance to George III and his successors, he put his hand on the Bible and then took it away. When asked why, he said he was glad to abjure his allegiance to George III but he had some scruples about the Prince of Wales. This was taken as a joke by the army, which knew nothing of Freudian interpretations of wit. Lee had told Sir Henry Clinton in March that he thought the war would end by negotiation and if he and Clinton were at the heads of the armies there would soon be an accommodation.

On May 3 Lee wrote to British General Robertson that America should forget about independence. After Sir Henry took command, Lee dropped him a note from Valley Forge on June 4: "General Lee presents his most sincere and humble respects to Sir Henry Clinton. He wishes him all possible happiness and health and begs, whatever may be the event of the present unfortunate contest, that he will believe General Lee to be his most respectful and obliged humble servant."

On the following day, Lord Howe's confidant, Ambrose Serle, recorded in his diary that Lee had told a member of a British flag party that "he was very unhappy in and very averse to the present course of affairs, and that he might assure Lord Howe that he had acted entirely as he had promised him and wished for nothing so much as to promote every idea of peace."

Serle, who undoubtedly reflected the views of the British high command, loathed Lee. His diary refers to him as "a damned scoundrel" and "as ill-looking a rebel in appearance as he really is." While Lee was committing treason to be on the winning side, Serle had come to a different conclusion as to their position. After learning that the British army was to abandon Philadelphia, he wrote on May 21: "I now look upon the contest as at an end."

LAFAYETTE AND BARREN HILL

Washington's spies were so active that, days before the Philadelphia Tories learned the bad news, he heard that the enemy appeared ready to abandon the city. He assigned Lafayette the command of an advanced unit of twenty-two hundred troops to proceed to Barren Hill, about half way between Valley Forge and Philadelphia. His orders of May 18 to his young commander were:

> *... To be a security to this camp and a cover to the country between the Delaware and the Schuylkill, to interrupt the communication with Philadelphia, obstruct the incursions of the enemy's parties, and obtain intelligence of their motives and designs... You will endeavour to procure trusty and intelligent spies, who will advise you faithfully of whatever may be passing in the city.*

A variety of concurring accounts make it probable the enemy are preparing to evacuate Philadelphia. This is a point, which it is of the utmost importance to ascertain; and if possible the place of their future destination...

You will remember that your detachment is a very valuable one, and that any accident happening to it would be a severe blow to this Army. You will therefore use every possible precaution for its security, and to guard against a surprise. No attempt should be made nor anything risked without the greatest prospect of success and with every reasonable advantage on your side.

Lafayette's troops included infantry, militia for patrol duty, detachments of cavalry, and fifty Indians he had persuaded to come with him from his expedition to Canada. The enemy got word of his movements as he approached Barren Hill. As a last gesture before quitting America, Howe decided to lead out nearly half the British army under Clinton, Grey, and Grant to capture him. They were so confident that they invited their officers to dinner that night "to meet General Lafayette." They set out on what was to be a brilliant encircling movement, surrounding Barren Hill on three sides, with Lafayette trapped at the river. On the nineteenth, General Grant marched a roundabout way through Whitemarsh to arrive to the north. Grey was assigned to go through Germantown to hit the center, while Clinton was to take a road along the river. Lafayette had posted militia along the Whitemarsh Road to watch for the British but they simply disappeared. Grey reached his position. Clinton and Howe were spotted and Lafayette was warned. British cavalry came unexpectedly on the Indians. They let out such loud whoops of fear that the dragoons beat a hasty retreat, while the Indians moved off rapidly in the opposite direction.

Below Barren Hill was a road unknown to the British that was concealed by thick woods. Lafayette, after sending out a few guards to divert the enemy, got all his men safely down this road, across the Schuylkill, and back to Washington and Valley Forge. British columns under Clinton and Grant raced from opposite sides to the top of the hill and encountered each other. They glared, cursed, and returned to Philadelphia. Lafayette, who hardly needed it, had more acclaim then ever.

THE PEACE COMMISSION ARRIVES

The three commissioners—Carlisle, Eden, and Johnstone—sailed up the Delaware, astonished at the American siege, and landed at Philadelphia on June 6. They found four hundred or so British transports being loaded with baggage and Tories, and all preparations under way for flight. They considered their government had made fools of them. Their instructions for public behavior were such that they could only continue to look foolish, but privately Lord Carlisle and William Eden viewed the situation objectively. Carlisle wrote his wife: "We all look grave, and perhaps we think we look wise... I don't see what we have to do here." To George Selwyn in London he noted: "I have this morning at five o'clock been taking a ride into the country, about ten miles; grieved I am to say, eight miles beyond our possessions." William Eden wrote a friend: "It is impossible to see even what I have seen of this country and not to go nearly mad at the long train of misconducts and mischances by which we have lost it."

Though the commissioners were pessimistic they pleaded with Clinton not to leave Philadelphia until they had approached Congress. His orders from London were so positive that he could not delay. The commissioners complained of the "perfidy" of the ministers, yet it is possible that the cabinet had deluded itself into thinking that the Americans would accept their offers. Lord George Germain had indicated to Clinton that "the generous terms now held out... will be gladly embraced, and... a negociation will immediately take place upon the arrival of the New Commission, and be so far advanced before the season will admit of military operations as to supersede the necessity of another campaign. So speedy and happy a termination of the war could not fail to give the greatest pleasure to the King."

The commissioners asked Washington for permission for their secretary, Dr. Adam Ferguson, professor of natural philosophy at Edinburgh, to proceed to York. Washington sent the request to Congress, which refused to receive him. This forced the commission on June 13 to write to His Excellency, the President of Congress, thereby formally recognizing Congress as an official body. They expressed the desire to avoid further bloodshed and to re-establish "the tranquillity of this once happy empire." The letter offered everything that was in the limit of their instructions, including American seats in Parliament and internal freedom of legislation and government in America. There was more than a hint that Britain recognized the military importance of America, which, after reconciliation, would act "in peace and war, under our common sovereign." The commissioners attacked "the insidious interposition of France," an enemy to both Britain and America. They concluded by threatening calamities, horrors, and devastations if America did not submit.

Before Congress could reply, the commissioners had to scurry to join the British fleet retreating to New York. President Laurens sent them an answer on June 17, which did not reach them for nearly three weeks:

Nothing but an earnest desire to spare the further effusion of blood could have induced [Congress] to read a paper containing expressions so disrespectful to his most Christian majesty, the good and great ally of these states, or consider propositions so derogatory to the honour of an independent nation.

The acts of the British parliament, the commission from your sovereign, and your letter suppose the people of these states to be subjects of the crown of Great Britain, and are founded on the idea of dependence, which is utterly inadmissible.

I am further directed to inform your excellencies that Congress are inclined to peace, notwithstanding the unjust claims from which this war originated and the savage manner in which it hath been conducted. They will, therefore, be ready to enter upon the consideration of a treaty of peace and commerce not inconsistent with treaties already subsisting, when the king of Great Britain shall demonstrate a sincere disposition for that purpose. The only solid proof of this disposition will be an explicit acknowledgement of the independence of those states, or the withdrawing of his fleet and armies.

The commissioners on July 11 asked Congress by what authority it dared to sign a treaty with France. They threatened to appeal over their heads to the American people. Congress ignored the letter, which reached them after the arrival in Philadelphia of Conrad Gérard, his most Christian majesty's minister to the United States.

On June 8 Martha Washington left for Mount Vernon, having received what her husband liked to call her "marching orders." Washington had picked Benedict Arnold late in May to be the American commander in Philadelphia. When the British evacuated the city, Arnold moved into General Howe's house and proceeded to use his new authority to try to make a fortune.

TWENTY-FIVE

MONMOUTH TO MIDDLEBROOK

1778–1779

WHILE ESPIONAGE IS an ancient practice, Washington was the first military commander to have an extensive intelligence organization in his operational command. His apparatus embraced security, counterintelligence and positive intelligence, penetration of the enemy's operations, and placement of false information with enemy agents. Most of the system operated from Washington's own cocked hat. This prevented trouble when counterintelligence agents picked up his spies going into the enemy lines. After they were brought to his office for severe "questioning," Washington arranged for their escape to the enemy, carrying bitter tales of their mistreatment.

As the war progressed, Washington's network included an array of bright young college graduates, respectable businessmen, state governors, tavernkeepers, semiliterate farmers, barmaids, dear old ladies in Quaker bonnets who carried vegetables to the enemy, young boys who could wriggle past the enemy lines, the American lady who owned the waxworks museum in London, several of Sir Henry Clinton's trusted agents, Lord Cornwallis' valet, and one of Lord North's diplomatic emissaries. Washington's operations were kept secret even after the war. The identities of several agents were not discovered until the twentieth century. Many are still known only by initials or numbers.

In the campaigns around New York every move of the British fleet and army was watched. Washington had spies at Trenton, before he attacked, and his agents gave him information on all the roads in the area. After the second battle of Trenton, their intelligence enabled him to elude Lord Cornwallis with ease. Long before the British occupied Philadelphia, Washington had his agents planted there. They reported to Major John Clark, Jr., and to Captain Allan McLane. They tipped off Washington that the British would try to draw him into a general engagement at Whitemarsh. They also warned Lafayette just in time that the British would try to capture him.

Washington particularly liked having his fearless young cavalrymen as intelligence officers. These included Captain McLane, Benjamin Tallmadge, and Henry Lee. His aides, Robert Hanson Harrison, John Laurens, and Alexander Hamilton, also became adept in the work. By the summer of 1778 Washington had designated Tallmadge to head his network; he occupied this post for five years. In his deliberately restrained memoirs Tallmadge referred only to the "private correspondence" he had undertaken for the general. Congress scraped together five hundred guineas in gold for this service and subsequently added another two thousand guineas.

It is remarkable that a Virginia farmer was able to outwit the more sophisticated British in this deadly game. They had experience and unlimited secret service funds in solid specie, but their operations, though aided by many Tories, were far more clumsy. From the time Washington left Manhattan in October 1776 until his return there at the end of 1783, it appears that only one American agent was caught and sent to the gallows, while Washington hanged at least ten enemy spies, including the head of British intelligence.

PLANS

Washington cried out frequently in his letters to spare no expense in getting information. Indian raids on the frontier, stimulated by British agents, caused him much concern. He reluctantly dispatched two Pennsylvania and Virginia regiments to Fort Pitt in May for frontier protection. In the same month he informed his war council that approximately three thousand of his men were ill, some from disease, many from inoculation for smallpox. In weighing reports of the projected British evacuation of Philadelphia, he had to take into account his own natural inclination to attack and the need to protect his sick and his military supplies. His councils were divided and the advice he received from his senior generals was too often deficient.

On June 8 Gates, stationed in Peekskill, wrote Washington that he was sure the British would attack up the Hudson and then move into New England.

Washington replied in an appraisal, which turned out to be correct, that he thought they would try only coastal raids in the area. On June 12 Charles Lee informed Washington, whose intelligence had made it almost certain that Clinton would cross New Jersey, that the British would not go to New York. Instead they would either move westward in Pennsylvania in order to connect with the Indians or try to get hold of a large tract of land somewhere else. He added: "I have particular reasons to think that they have cast their eyes on the lower counties of the Delaware, and some of the Maryland counties on the eastern shore." Lee had sent them a plan, while a prisoner, for ending the war by taking possession of that area.

Washington made early preparations to counter British moves across New Jersey. He ordered Brigadier William Maxwell into the state with 1,200 continentals and asked Major General Philemon Dickinson to alert the state's militia. His general officers in the state were requested to get intelligence, to destroy all bridges the enemy might use, and to block the roads with felled trees. Washington's great worry was that the British, moving directly across the Delaware while he was proceeding from Valley Forge to that river, would gain a day's march on him. As nearly as he could calculate in June, he had about 12,000 troops fit for duty in Pennsylvania and somewhat under 1,000 militia. According to the reliable figures of Joseph Galloway, the British had around 29,000 men of all ranks in the military and naval forces in Philadelphia. Although Washington could not know this accurately, Clinton planned to march around 16,500 of these to New York, the remainder going by sea.[*]

---

[*] In general, histories of the revolution give wildly varying numbers of troops present at battles. The discrepancies appear to have risen from the differing forms of returns: (a) total effectives of all ranks; (b) effectives, excluding officers; (c) rank and file, omitting sergeants, drummers, and fifers, and those "on command," that is, on detached duty; and (d) rank and file present and fit for duty. This last figure leaves out those who were sick, wounded, or on furlough.

Washington's troop returns for August 1776 ranged from 17,200 under (a) down to 10,500 under (d). Total British forces in the United States, just before Monmouth, vary in the same categories from 42,000 to 27,000.

Clinton always preferred to underrepresent his troop strength while exaggerating Washington's. Lord George Germain, who could also count, protested, with much asperity, against Clinton's practice of minimizing the strength of the troops sent at such expense from Great Britain. Clinton's memoirs state that there were 18,000 continentals facing him in New Jersey and these had increased to 20,000 by the time he got to New York.

Using Clinton's numbering, Washington had around 9,800 rank and file present and fit for duty at Monmouth to oppose Clinton's 14,700. Even if the militia are added to Washington's total, the British outnumbered the Americans by a third. The difference remains approximately the same if category (b) is used to describe the opposing forces.

Washington estimated to his war council that Clinton had 10,000 rank and file present and fit for duty. There is reason to suppose, in view of the timidity of his general officers, that he understated the enemy in order to give them more courage in their decisions.

Washington's May war council had concluded that he should remain on the defensive. A further meeting was held on June 17 to consider alternative plans if the British moved, including attacking their flanks or bringing them to a general engagement. Only two of the fifteen general officers present voted for the latter policy.

At 11:30 the next morning Washington received word that Clinton had abandoned Philadelphia and was on his way across New Jersey. Within three hours, twelve of his regiments were marching to the Delaware. The rest of the army was on its way early the following morning. From then on, each Washington letter cried out for every scrap of information from his generals in New Jersey as well as from the state's governor.

On June 21, at what is now New Hope, Washington again crossed the Delaware, this time in suffocating heat. Heavy and repeated thunderstorms added to the humidity and discomfort and made the primitive roads a morass. They delayed his march but equally hindered the enemy, who were burdened by a baggage train of fifteen hundred wagons, guarded by five or six thousand rank and file. They also had to move trees and other obstacles and repair the bridges that the Americans had destroyed. In a week they had covered only 40 miles. This gave Washington his much-desired chance to march directly east across New Jersey and intercept Clinton, moving northeast from Mount Holly to Allentown, New Jersey.

VICTORY AT MONMOUTH

From this point on Washington put the exact time of writing on requests for intelligence and asked his reporting officers to do the same, stressing that even a half hour would make a difference in his operations.

On June 24 he called a council of his general officers. Present were Lee, Greene, Stirling, Lafayette, Steuben, Knox, Poor, Wayne, Woodford, Paterson, Scott, and Du Portail. Alexander Hamilton was secretary.

The psychologically acute Lafayette, like nearly everyone, had taken his measure of Lee after his arrival from the British lines: "His visage was ugly, his spirit sarcastic, his heart ambitious and mean, his character inconsistent; on the whole a queer fellow." Lee spoke, almost too symbolically, during a full eclipse of the sun. He argued against an attack. The Americans, if necessary, he said, should build a bridge of gold to help the British to cross New Jersey, for they could never beat the better-trained British army. Lee was persuasive and a number of generals supported his view. The meeting finally advised Washington only to go so far as to detach fifteen hundred men to harass the British flanks.

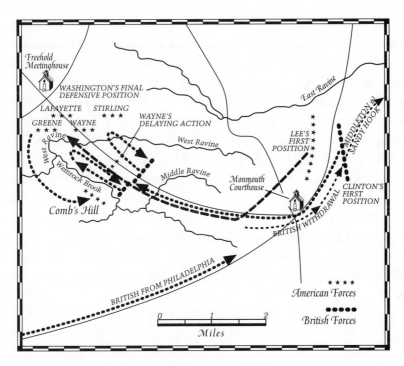

Battle of Monmouth, June 28, 1778

Hamilton subsequently described the meeting in a letter to Elias Boudinot: "The General unluckily called a council of war, the result of which would have done honour to the most honourable society of midwives, and to them only. The purport was, that we should keep at a comfortable distance from the enemy, and keep up a vain parade of annoying them in detachment... General Lee was the *primum mobile* of this sage plan. The General, on mature reconsideration of what had been resolved on, determined to pursue a different line of conduct at all hazards." In this he was joined by Greene, Lafayette, and Wayne, who pleaded with him to do more. Greene wrote Washington: "I am not for hazarding a general action unnecessarily, but I am clearly of opinion for making a serious impression with the light troops and for having the army in supporting distance... If we suffer the enemy to pass through the Jerseys without attacking, I think we shall ever regret it... People expect something from us and our strength demands it. I am by no means for rash measures but we must preserve our reputations and I think we can make a very serious impression without any great risk and if it should amount to a general action I think the chance is greatly in our favour."

After the meeting Washington dispatched Morgan to the enemy's right flank, Maxwell to the left, and Scott to the left and rear. Washington wrote Scott:

> *You are immediately to march with the detachment, under your command, towards Allen Town, in order to fall in with the enemy's left flank and rear, and give them all the annoyance in your power. You will carefully collect intelligence as you advance and govern your motions accordingly; and you will take every precaution for the security of your detachment consistent with the objects it is intended to promote. You will co-operate, as far as may be proper, with the other troops in the neighbourhood of the enemy. You will keep me continually and punctually advised of every occurrence that happens, either with respect to the Enemy or yourself. Lt. Colo. White is ordered to join you with the detachment of Cavalry under his command.*

Washington next day selected a delighted Lafayette to march with approximately fifteen hundred troops to join Scott, to take over the command and, in Washington's words, "if a proper opening shd. be given, by operating against them with the whole force of your command." Washington added that if Lafayette attacked in force he would be "supported or covered, as circumstances should require, by the whole army." Washington consulted Lee about his command because of the latter's seniority. He initially agreed but then, hearing that Lafayette would have an additional body of troops, numbering five thousand or more, and that other generals thought his absence would

One of at least seven portraits of Washington painted by Charles Wilson Peale. *(The Bettmann Archive)*

Alexander Hamilton, a valued
and trusted aide of Washington's during the Revolution.
(The Bettmann Archive)

LAFAYETTE.

The Marquis de
Lafayette, who
sailed to America
at his own expense
to assist Americans
in the war for
independence.
He was wounded
at the Battle of
Brandywine and
stood by
Washington at
Valley Forge
during the terrible
winter of 1777-
1778. *(The
Bettmann Archive)*

Benedict Arnold, the most infamous man in American history. Arnold helped the Americans win important victories at Ft. Ticonderoga and at the Battle of Saratoga before committing treason. *(The Bettmann Archive)*

General "Mad" Anthony Wayne also endured the harsh conditions at Valley Forge. Later he fought in the great victory at Monmouth, led an audacious attack on Stony Point, N.Y., and participated in the siege of Cornwallis at Yorktown, Va. *(The Bettmann Archive)*

GENERAL WAYNE.

Daniel Morgan, one of Washington's fiercest officers. Morgan crushed the British at the Battle of the Cowpens on Jan. 17, 1781. *(The Bettmann Archive)*

"Light Horse Harry" Lee, one of Washington's finest cavalry leaders. In July, 1779, he accomplished one of the most daring raids of the war, surprising the British post at Paulus Hook, New Jersey, and capturing 160 prisoners. *(The Bettmann Archive)*

The Compte de Rochambeau, selected by King Louis XVI because of his *savoir-faire* to command the French troops assisting Washington. In mid-August, 1781, he and Washington began marching their troops from New York towards Virginia's peninsula, where they trapped the British under Lord Cornwallis (portrait by Raynaud). *(The Bettmann Archive)*

Admiral Lord Charles Cornwallis became Washington's central military foe. On Oct. 19, 1781 he surrendered his forces at Yorktown, thus effectively ending the American Revolutionary War. *(The Bettmann Archive)*

To the Right Hon.ble Lady Louisa Brome?

This Portrait of **MARQUIS CORNWALLIS** is by Permission

Dedicated by her obedient humble Serv.t J.W. Dewis?

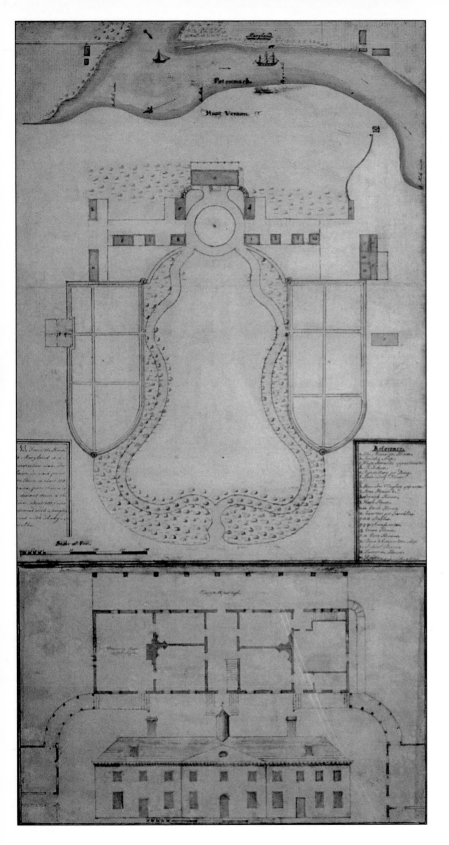

Map of the Mount Vernon mansion and its grounds (by Samuel Vaughan, 1787). *(The Mount Vernon Ladies' Association of the Union)*

Martha Washington by Archibald
Robertson (1782). *(The Bettmann Archive)*

Bust of George
Washington by Houdon.
(The Bettmann Archive)

Another Houdon bust of Washington (1785). *(The Mount Vernon Ladies' Association of the Union)*

look peculiar, he protested that he should have it after all. Hamilton afterwards commented that Lee's conduct "was very childish." He told Lafayette that his "fortune and honor" were at stake. The French general said that, if it were a matter of his honor, he would cheerfully acquiesce in any decision by Washington. This put the commander in chief in a dilemma. Lee had told him that he would be "disgraced" while Washington did not want to offend Lafayette. He reached an unfortunate compromise decision, which he relayed to Lee on June 26:

> *Your uneasiness, on account of the command of yesterday's detachment, fills me with concern, as it is not in my power fully to remove it, without wounding the feelings of the Marquis de la Fayette. I have thought of an expedient which though not quite equal to either of your views, may in some measure answer both; and that is to make another detachment for this Army for the purpose of aiding and supporting the several detachments now under the command of the Marquis and giving you the command of the whole, under certain restrictions; which, circumstances arising from your own conduct yesterday, render almost unavoidable. The expedient which I would propose is for you to march towards the Marquis with Scott's and Varnum's brigades. Give him notice that you are advancing to support him, that you are to have command of the whole advanced body; but as he may have formed some enterprise... which will not admit of delay or alteration, you will desire him to proceed as if no change had happened, and you will give him every assistance and countenance in you power.*

He wrote Lafayette the same day, ending on a much more affectionate note: "General Lee's uneasiness on account of Yesterday's transaction rather increasing than abating, and your politeness in wishing to ease him of it, has induced me to detach him from this Army, with a part of it, to reinforce, or at least cover, the several detachments under your command, at present. At the same time I felt for General Lee's distress of mind, I have had an eye to your wishes, and the delicacy of your situation; and have, therefore, obtained a promise from him, that when he gives you notice of his approach and command, he will request you to prosecute any plan you have already concerted for the purpose of attacking or otherwise annoying the Enemy. This is the only expedient I could think of to answer both your views... I wish it may prove agreeable to you, as I am with the warmest wishes for your honour and glory, and with the sincerest esteem and affection."

On June 25 Lee was dispatched to Englishtown with two additional regiments, making the American vanguard more than five thousand men stationed five miles from the enemy. He ordered Lafayette not to move too fast and exhaust his men in the excessive heat. That night a heavy rainstorm added to the discomfort. Ferocious New Jersey mosquitoes indiscriminately attacked British and American troops.

From the twenty-fifth to the twenty-eighth Hamilton was everywhere, acting as the eyes and ears of Lafayette and Washington. His written intelligence reports were models, giving necessary information without an unnecessary word. Late on the night of the twenty-sixth, the prescient Lafayette wrote Washington: "I do not believe General Lee intends to make any attack tomorrow, for then I would have been directed to fall immediately upon them without making eleven miles entirely out of the way. I am here as near as I will be at Englishtown."

On the twenty-seventh Lee took command of the advance forces. That day he was called to Washington's headquarters and given orders to attack the enemy. Washington promised to bring up the main body of troops to his support. He was told to post a patrol to give instant warning if Sir Henry Clinton decided to move during the night. General Dickinson and his militia were assigned this duty. At a conference with the officers under his immediate command Lee gave no indication as to his plans for the morning.

On June 27 the British were encamped around the Monmouth County Courthouse at Freehold. Lee and Lafayette were just beyond Englishtown, while the main army under Washington was about five miles to the rear. Late that night Lee informed Washington he thought the British would attack him, though there is no evidence that they had anything in mind but heading away to the heights at Middletown. At four in the morning the van of the British army began to move off towards the coast. Washington had this information from Dickinson by 5 A.M. He sent a hurried order to Lee to attack, adding that he was bringing forward the rest of the army. Washington had around sixty-seven hundred men, with Stirling in command on the left and Greene on the right. Morgan and his riflemen were far off on the enemy's left flank, too far as it turned out, to do any good that day. That Sunday, June 28, soon became unbearably hot with the temperature going to ninety-six degrees. The British nonetheless moved off rapidly.

Lee reacted very slowly to Washington's orders and to information of the British movement. Not until seven did he march with the main part of his troops. From this point on Lee had no plans and no control. He hesitated, waiting at one point a half hour, during which he told Dickinson he had provided false intelligence. The various bodies of troops moved without command; where Lee did give orders, they were confused and contradictory. Wayne, Lafayette, and Scott endeavored to come up with the enemy but other troops remained behind. When British cavalry and infantry appeared, Lee began to move back with some of his troops, leaving the forward parties to fend for themselves. They were forced to rejoin him though without orders to do so; suddenly the whole advance force was retreating, after having fired almost no shots.

This was an unexpected bonus for Sir Henry Clinton, whose only objective to that point had been to leave Monmouth as rapidly as possible. Clinton had his best troops nearby including such famous regiments as the Black Watch, Guards, and Grenadiers. He ordered Lord Cornwallis to attack and sent word to General Grant, with Knyphausen's advance troops, to join with his forces. Clinton complained many years later that Grant refused to obey "under most frivolous pretenses."

Washington's aides whom he had sent forward found disorder, Lee twice telling Richard Meade, "They are all in confusion." Another aide, Harrison, asked Lee's aide the reason for the confusion. He was told that British foot and horse were coming along. Harrison replied that the American army was there to meet them. Washington in the rear was puzzled by the absence of battle sounds. He spurred forward and, on encountering Lee, demanded an explanation for the disorder and his failure to obey. Lee missed the question and Washington repeated it. Lee said that there had been confusing intelligence and contradictory orders, people had interfered, and he could not fight the British under such conditions. He added that in any case he had consistently opposed an attack. Washington told him that he was expected to obey orders and that he should not have undertaken the advance unless he intended to go through with it. It is unclear whether Lee went to the rear or stayed at the scene, but thereafter he played no important role in the battle. Washington himself took over the command.

By this time the American van had retreated more than two miles with the British in hot pursuit. Wayne had fought a delaying action and Washington ordered two additional regiments to stand with Wayne. He then hurried back to get his remaining troops, throwing Greene's division to the right, Stirling's to the left, and Lafayette to the rear of center. Knox and Du Portail directed the highly effective artillery. Officers and men responded with a disciplined enthusiasm previously unknown in the American army. Washington's report to Congress of July 1 gave the essentials of the subsequent battle:

> *After marching about five miles, to my great surprise and mortification, I met the whole advanced Corps retreating, and, as I was told, by General Lee's orders, without having made any opposition, except one fire given by a party under the command of Colo. Butler, on their being charged by the Enemy's Cavalry, who were repulsed. I proceeded immediately to the Rear of the corps, which I found closely*

pressed by the Enemy, and gave directions for forming part of the retreating troops, who, by the brave and spirited conduct of the Officers, and aided by some pieces of well served Artillery, checked the Enemy's Advance, and gave time to make a disposition of the left wing and second line of the Army upon an eminence, and in a wood a little in the Rear covered by a morass in front. On this were placed some Batteries of Cannon by Lord Stirling who commanded the left Wing, which played upon the Enemy with great effect, and seconded by parties of Infantry detached to oppose them, effectually put a stop to their advance.

…The command of the Right Wing… was given to General Greene. For the expedition of the march, and to counteract any attempt to turn our Right, I had ordered him to file off by the new church, two miles from English Town, and fall into the Monmouth Road, a small distance in the Rear of the Court House, while the rest of the Column moved directly on towards the Court House. On intelligence of the Retreat, he marched up and took a very advantageous position on the Right.

The enemy by this time, finding themselves very warmly opposed in front made an attempt to turn our left flank; but they were bravely repulsed and driven back by detached parties of Infantry. They also made a movement to our Right, with as little success, General Greene having advanced a Body of Troops with Artillery to a commanding piece of Ground, which not only disappointed their design of turning our Right, but severely infiladed those in front of the Left Wing. In addition to this, General Wayne advanced with a Body of Troops and kept up so severe and well directed a fire that the Enemy were soon compelled to retire behind the defile where the first stand in the beginning of the Action had been made.

In this situation, the Enemy had both their flanks secured by thick Woods and Morasses, while their front could only be approached thro' a narrow pass. I resolved nevertheless to attack them, and for that purpose ordered General Poor with his own and the Carolina Brigade, to move round upon their Right, and General Woodford upon their left, and the Artillery to gall them in front, but the impediments in their way prevented their getting within reach before it was dark. They remained upon the Ground they had been directed to occupy, during the Night, with intention to begin the attack early the next morning, and the Army continued lying upon their Arms in the field of Action, to be in readiness to support them… About 12 OClock the Enemy marched away…

Were I to conclude my account of this day's transactions without expressing my obligations to the Officers of the Army in general, I should do injustice to their merit, and violence to my own feelings. They seemed to vie with each other in manifesting their Zeal and Bravery. The Catalogue of those who distinguished themselves is too long to admit of particularising individuals; I cannot however forbear mentioning Brigadier General Wayne whose good conduct and bravery thro' the whole action deserves particular commendation.

The Behaviour of the troops in general, after they recovered from the first surprise occasioned by the Retreat of the advanced Corps, was such as could not be surpassed.

In general orders after the battle Washington expressed his particular thanks to Dickinson and the Jersey militia, and to Knox, who invariably at every battle received special encomia from the commander in chief. Wayne, who was honored by a mention in the dispatch to Congress, expressed his opinion of the battle in more earthy prose than Washington's: "Tell the Phil'a ladies, that the heavenly, sweet, pretty red coats—the accomplished gentlemen of the Guards and Grenadiers have humbled themselves on the plains of Monmouth."

London had repeatedly urged its commanders in America to bring Washington to a general engagement and to defeat him. The king and cabinet correctly believed that this was the only way to suppress the rebellion and to reestablish British rule. The opportunity was at hand. The British army, though badly mauled, was larger than Washington's and included many of the crack regiments of Great Britain. Washington was there and prepared to fight a general action the next day. Sir Henry Clinton declined. Shortly after midnight the British picked up and ran. They had been moving across New Jersey at six miles a day. By midmorning they were thirteen miles away, after one of the most rapid retreats in history. Thereafter, in the north, the British army largely confined its operations to war on civilians.

Washington did not learn for several days the extent of his victory. During the following week his army and the local inhabitants buried around 300 enemy dead. The number of wounded generally ran in a ratio of three or four to one killed. Prisoners taken on the battlefield and by desertion numbered about 800. Washington's estimate that the enemy suffered 2,000 casualties is probably accurate and may even have been conservative. American losses were around 350, some being from heatstroke rather than enemy action.

Washington praised everyone except Lee and himself for the day's action against superior forces and the largest British army Washington was ever to fight. Those who were closest to him that day gave their opinion. Hamilton wrote to Elias Boudinot: "I never saw the General to so much advantage. His coolness and firmness were admirable. He instantly took measures for checking the enemy's advance, and giving time to the army, which was very near, to form and make a proper disposition... on a very advantageous piece of ground... America owes a great deal to General Washington for this day's work. A general rout, dismay, and disgrace would have attended the whole army in any other hands than his. By his own good sense and fortitude, he turned the fate of the day. Other officers have great merit in performing their parts well, but he directed the whole with the skill of a master workman... Our troops, after the first impulse from mismanagement, behaved with more spirit and moved with greater order than the British troops." John Laurens wrote his father: "The merits of restoring the day, is due to the general; and his conduct was such throughout the affair as has greatly increased my love and esteem for him." James McHenry noted that Washington had "unfolded surprising abilities which produced uncommon effects." Lafayette wrote at a much later date: "Never was General Washington greater in war than in this action. His presence stopped the retreat. His dispositions fixed the victory. His fine appearance on horseback, his calm courage roused by the animation produced by the vexation of the morning, gave him the air best calculated to arouse enthusiasm."

Elias Boudinot replied to Hamilton: "The general I always revered and loved ever since I know him, but in this instance he rose superior to himself. Every lip dwells on his praise, for even his pretended friends (for none dare to acknowledge themselves his enemies) are obliged to croak it forth."

The cruel winter at Valley Forge and the Conway cabal made Washington commander in fact of the armies. The great victory at Monmouth made him, by acclamation, father of the nation.

TWO LETTERS

On July 10 Washington received the unanimous thanks of Congress for his "distinguished exertions in forming the line of battle; and for his great good conduct in leading on the attack and gaining the important victory at Monmouth over the British grand army." Henry Laurens, president of Congress, wrote: "Love and respect for your excellency are impressed on the heart of every grateful American, and your name will be revered by posterity." There were further thanks by Congress to the "gallant officers and men under this command." This latter resolution Washington published. Four days later Washington received a letter from Admiral the comte d'Estaing, who had arrived off the American coast with twelve ships of the line and six frigates:

I have the honor to inform your Excellency of the arrival of the King's fleet, charged by his Majesty with the glorious task of giving his allies, the United States of America, the most striking proofs of his affection... The talents and great actions of

*General Georges Washington have secured to him, in the eyes of all Europe, the
truly sublime title of Liberator of America. Accept, Sir, the homage that every man,
that every military man, owes you; and be pleased that I solicit with military and
naval frankness from the first moment so flattering a friendship as yours; I will try
to render myself worthy of it by my respectful devotion to your country; It is
prescribed by my orders and inspires my heart.*

For Washington and Lafayette this direct military assistance by France and the
first effort to implement the alliance were cheering, but they introduced new
problems that were to test Washington's developing diplomatic skills to the
utmost. After handling the turbulent congressmen and sensitive generals who
were his countrymen, Washington often found it easier to deal with the
courtly and usually more tactful French.

IDYLLIC DAYS

The American army rested for two days not far from the battlefield and then
made a long, hot, and nearly waterless march of twenty miles to Brunswick,
where Washington kept headquarters for nearly a week. On July 4 the army
paraded to celebrate the second anniversary of American independence.
Thirteen cannon were discharged and three cheers were given for the United
States. Washington again invited his principal officers to dine with him and
that night they held a ball. From Brunswick they moved on through the then-
beautiful New Jersey countryside to Paramus. James McHenry, a physician
who had recently been appointed aide to the commander in chief, left a
record of their stop at Passaic Falls and of their subsequent movements:

*After viewing these falls we seated ourselves round the General under a large
spreading oak within view of the spray and in hearing of the noise. A fine cool spring
bubbled out most charmingly from the bottom of the tree. The travelling canteens were
immediately emptied and a modest repast spread before us, of cold ham, tongue, and
some biscuit. With the assistance of a little spirit we composed some excellent grog.
Then we chatted away a very cheerful half hour and then took our leave of the
friendly oak—its refreshing spring—and the meek falls of Passaic—less boisterous
than those of Niagara, or the more gentle Cohoes or the waters of the Mohawk.*

*From hence we passed thro' a fertile country to a place called Paramus. We stopped
at a Mrs. Watkins whose house was marked for headquarters. But the General
receiving a note of invitation from a Mrs. Provost [later Mrs. Aaron Burr] to make*

*her Hermitage, as it was called, the seat of his stay while at Paramus, we only
dined with Mrs. Watkins and her two charming daughters, who sang us several
pretty songs in a very agreeable manner.*

*At Mrs. Provost we found some fair refugees from New York who were on a visit to
the lady of the Hermitage; with them we talked—and walked—and laughed—and
danced and gallanted away the leisure hours of four days and four nights and
would have gallanted—and danced and laughed and talked and walked with
them till now had not the General given orders for our departure. We left them...
without much sighing.*

McHenry and Alexander Hamilton, who were later in Washington's cabinet,
were highly competitive in pursuit of women, on the rare occasions the
general let them have free time. At Doylestown McHenry found a pretty
Quaker girl and wrote: "Hamilton thou shalt not tread on this ground." Three
days later he described with pleasure the "charming girls" on the Jersey side,
adding that one of the general's guards was more favored than Hamilton.

THE FRENCH FLEET

Bad luck and quite a lot of bad manners on the part of some Americans and
French soured the first months of the alliance between the ancient French
kingdom and the two-year-old United States.

The French dispatched their fleet to America with great promptness before
Britain could organize for a French war. They had chosen a soldier, General
d'Estaing, for the command and commissioned him vice admiral. This paper
act did not make him a skilled sea lord and it annoyed other admirals. The fleet
encountered bad weather on its way to America and the trip took nearly three
months. The French had no idea that the British had abandoned Philadelphia,
and they went first to the Delaware and then north to Sandy Hook, which they
reached on July 11. Had they arrived eleven days earlier they might have cut off
Clinton at the Hook, isolating most of the British army on a land spit.

Washington had heard of the fleet's arrival before he received d'Estaing's
letter and wrote him a warm letter of welcome. D'Estaing, in saluting
Washington, also sent a note introducing the marquis de Chouin, a relative of
the French naval minister, who would concert French plans with him.
Washington responded to d'Estaing on July 17:

The arrival of a fleet, belonging to his most Christian majesty, on our coast, is an event that makes me truly happy and permit me to observe that the pleasure I feel on the occasion is greatly increased by the command being placed in a Gentleman of such distinguished talents, experience and reputation as the Count d'Estaing. I am fully persuaded that every possible exertion will be made by you to accomplish the important purposes of your destination...

I esteem myself highly honored by the desire you express, with a frankness which must always be pleasing, of possessing a place in my friendship; at the same time allow me to assure you that I shall consider myself peculiarly happy if I can but improve the prepossessions you are pleased to entertain in my favour, into a cordial and lasting amity.

Major de Chouin, who arrived this day at my Quarters, has given me a very full and satisfactory explanation of your situation and views and in return I have freely communicated to him my ideas of every matter interesting to our mutual operations.

Washington had already sent his French-speaking aide, John Laurens, of Huguenot descent, to see d'Estaing. He now added Hamilton and the marquis de fleury. Washington found two experienced pilots and four merchant marine captains to aid d'Estaing in the coastal waters. He appealed to the state governors to order their privateers and frigates to cooperate with the French. As a hospitable Virginian, he also dispatched two hundred sheep, fifty head of cattle, and a quantity of poultry for the French navy. He sent his commissary to help procure further supplies. He asked Sullivan, who commanded in Rhode Island, to call up five thousand New England militia, in case d'Estaing decided to attack the British in Newport rather than New York.

By July 21 Washington had his main army at White Plains, about fifteen miles from Manhattan. There he reported to his war council that the Continental Army numbered 16,700 rank and file, the highest figure of the war. However, around 4,700 were on duty in New England, western New York, and the Hudson Highlands. His immediate command had slightly under 12,000 rank and file. His council advised against attacking New York, where at this time Clinton, in addition to his 3,600 troops in Rhode Island, had over 28,000 rank and file who were under siege by an enemy of less than half its numbers. On August 20 Washington wrote to Thomas Nelson of Virginia:

It is not a little pleasing, nor less wonderful to contemplate, that after two years' Maneuvering and undergoing the strangest vicissitudes that perhaps ever attended any one contest since the creation, both Armies are brought back to the very point

they set out from, and that that which was the offending party in the beginning, is
now reduced to the use of the spade and pick axe for defence. The hand of
Providence has been so conspicuous in all this that he must be worse than an
infidel that lacks faith, and more than wicked that has not gratitude to
acknowledge his obligations, but it will be time enough for me to turn preacher
when my present appointment ceases.

For a brief period the French operated outside Sandy Hook, with Washington
on tenterhooks hoping the French fleet could attack Lord Howe's ships. The
British peace commission felt humiliated. They had arrived in Philadelphia
without knowledge that the British army would retreat. That army had suffered a severe defeat. Their overtures to Congress had been rejected with contempt. As a last straw, a French fleet, which they had not even been warned
about, was off the coast of New York and obviously eager for battle. By July 22
Carlisle was writing George Selwyn: "We are blocked up by a French fleet. We
are kept in prison, as we dare not ride beyond our posts towards the country ...
If certain events, which are not improbable, should take place, we shall be
inevitably starved."

The French-American land and naval siege was brief. French warships drew
around five feet more water than their British counterparts. Though several
French sailors lost their lives, and d'Estaing and Laurens were nearly drowned
in looking for channels, the admiral had to conclude that his ships could not
pass the bar at New York harbor. With American encouragement d'Estaing
turned to Newport, the only other point in the United States that the British
occupied.

The tempestuous Sullivan, who, Washington had once written, complained
more than any other general officer, was in command in Rhode Island.
Washington dispatched two brigades to him under Lafayette, who was more
than anxious to fight alongside French forces. Washington subsequently sent
General Greene, a native Rhode Islander, to the state. Lafayette had to divide
his expected command with Greene. Washington tactfully appealed to him to
consent. Lafayette replied in his usual graceful way: "I willingly part with the
half my detachment... Any thing, my dear General, which you will order or
even wish, shall always be infinitely agreeable to me."

Greene had considered himself hurt when Washington mildly rebuked him
for not coming to headquarters when ordered to do so. He wrote Washington
on July 21: "Your Excellency has made me very unhappy. I can submit very
patiently to deserved censure; but it wounds my feelings exceedingly to meet
with a rebuke, for doing what I conceived to be a proper part of my duty." He
offered his resignation. The commander in chief replied to him the same day:

"I cannot at this time (having many People round me, and Letters by the Southern Post to read) go fully into the contents of your letter of this date, but with the same truth I have ever done, I still assure you, that you retain the same hold of my affections... With equal truth I can, and do assure you, that I have ever been happy in your friendship, and have no scruples in declaring, that I think myself indebted to your Abilities, honour and candour, to your attachment to me, and your faithful Services to the Public, in every capacity you have served it since we have been together in the Army. But my dear Sir, these must not debar me the privileges of a friend (for it was the voice of friendship that spoke to you) when I complained of Neglect; I was four or five days without seeing a single person in your department, and at a time when I wished for you in two capacities, having business of the utmost importance to settle with the Count de Estaing... But let me beseech you my dear Sir not to harbor any distrusts of my friendship, or conceive that I mean to wound the feelings of a Person whom I greatly esteem and regard." Greene, fully mollified, went off to his command.

In informing Sullivan of his orders on July 27, Washington told him that he assumed d'Estaing would send some of his troops ashore to join the attack on the British. D'Estaing's wishes as to who should command should govern Sullivan completely. He added: "Harmony and the best understanding between us should be a Capital and first object. The Count himself is a Land Officer and of the high rank of Lt. General in the French Army."

D'Estaing wrote Washington of his many problems and difficulties, his shortages of supplies and water, and his ignorance of the American coast. On August 8 Washington took time to express his appreciation to the admiral: "I most sincerely sympathize with you in the regret you feel at the obstacles and difficulties you have heretofore encountered. Your case has certainly been a case of peculiar hardship, but you justly have the consolation which arises from a reflection that no exertions possible have been wanting in you to insure success... The disappointments you have experienced proceed from circumstances which no human foresight or activity can control." He added that he had written to the governor of Connecticut to send water as soon as possible "to relieve the sufferings of the brave officers and men under your command."

Washington exerted every effort to get intelligence of British fleet movements that might endanger d'Estaing. On August 8 he sent information that Lord Howe was on the way to Rhode Island with part of his naval force. To his agent, Caleb Brewster, who operated a whaleboat between Connecticut and enemy-held Long Island, he wrote: "Let me entreat that you will continue to use every possible means to obtain intelligence of the Enemys motions, not only those which are Marching Eastward, upon Long Island, but others...

Have a strict watch kept upon the Enemy's Ships of War, and give me the earliest notice of their sailing from the hook... Let an eye also be had on the Transports, whether they are preparing for the reception of Troops... Know what number of Men are upon Long Island; whether they are moving or stationary; what is become of their draft Horses; whether they appear to be collecting of them for a move. How they are supplied with Provisions; what arrivals; whether with Men, or Provisions. And whether any troops have Imbarked for Rhode Island or Elsewhere."

Sullivan sent back highly optimistic reports that he would take the British garrison at Newport. When d'Estaing arrived off Narragansett Bay, the British burned several of their own frigates. Sullivan was so wound up with excitement that he ordered d'Estaing, a more experienced officer, to do things with his fleet and troops that were not practical. There was early friction between the allies. The Americans were slow in their preparations and the French tended to look down on them. De Chouin reported to d'Estaing that the American militia looked like "Tartar hordes," while John Hancock, who had shown up as a militia general, was "old, gouty and infirm." Hancock's gout was famous, but he was eight years younger than d'Estaing.

After many discussions the French and Americans agreed on a combined land and sea assault for August 9 but Sullivan, to d'Estaing's annoyance, moved a day in advance. Just as the French got under way, Lord Howe and his fleet showed up. The French abandoned their plans in order to chase the British. Sullivan's chance for glory was gone and he was furious, particularly as most of his militia then went home.

At this point, after the French fleet had outmaneuvered the British, the famous gales of Narragansett Bay, usually coming later, rose and badly damaged both fleets. D'Estaing lost the masts and rudder of his flagship. Howe took his damaged fleet to New York, while d'Estaing briefly put into Narragansett Bay to inform Sullivan that he would go to Boston for repairs. This was in accordance with orders from the French naval minister, but Sullivan and his officers reacted vehemently against the proposal.

Sullivan induced all of his generals except Lafayette to protest to d'Estaing that his actions were derogatory to French honor and injurious to the alliance. Lafayette was furious and threatened to draw his sword on Sullivan but the other officers apologized to him. Nonetheless Lafayette wrote Washington that he felt himself more an enemy in the American camp than he might have in the British, and he wrote in anguish to d'Estaing. Sullivan did not stop there but informed his troops in general orders that their allies had refused to help. At this point Greene intervened and Sullivan issued a halfhearted apology the next day.

In the meantime Sullivan fought a pitched battle with the British on Rhode Island. The Americans somewhat bested the enemy, and Sullivan then brought his troops to the mainland. He got off just in time to avoid Sir Henry Clinton, who arrived in the bay with four thousand troops. When d'Estaing reached Boston, the city blamed him for the failure of the Newport expedition. American sailors fought the French. A French officer was killed in the riot. The first fruits of the alliance were bitter for each side. The whole affair was immediately dumped onto Washington as everyone, including Congress, turned to him. With infinite tact he saw to it that the enemy gained no advantage from the disputes. To General William Heath, in command at Boston, he wrote on August 28:

The unfortunate circumstance of the French fleet having left Rhode Island at so critical a moment, I am apprehensive, if not prudently managed, will have many injurious consequences, besides merely the loss of the advantages we should have reaped from succeeding in the Expedition. It will not only tend to discourage the people, and weaken their confidence in the new alliance, but may possibly produce prejudices and resentments, which may operate against giving the fleet such effectual assistance in its present distress, as the exigence of our affairs and our true interests demand. It will certainly be sound policy to combat these effects, and whatever private opinion may be entertained, to give the most favorable construction of what has happened to the public, and at the same time to put the French fleet, as soon as possible, in condition to defend itself and be useful to us. The departure of the fleet from Rhode Island is not yet publicly announced here, but when it is, I intend to ascribe it to necessity, from the damage suffered in the late storm. This, it appears to me, is the Idea which ought to be generally propagated. As I doubt not the force of these Reasons will strike you equally with myself, I would recommend to you to use your utmost influence to palliate and soften matters, and induce those, whose business it is to provide succours of every kind for the fleet, to employ the utmost zeal and activity in doing it. It is our duty to make the best of our misfortunes, and not to suffer passions to interfere with our interest and the public good.

To Sullivan he wrote two letters. The first, on August 28, said: "Should the expedition fail, thro' the abandonment of the French fleet, the Officers concerned will be apt to complain loudly. But prudence dictates that we should put the best face upon the matter... The Reasons are too obvious... that our British and internal enemies would be glad to improve the least matter of complaint and disgust against and between us and our new allies into a serious rupture." He followed this with another letter on September 1: "The disagreement between the army under your command and the fleet has given me very singular uneasiness... first impressions, you know, are generally longest remembered, and will serve to fix in a great degree our national character among the French. In our conduct towards them we should remember that they are a people old in war, very strict in military etiquette and apt to take fire where others scarcely seem warmed. Permit me to recommend in the most particular manner, the cultivation of harmony and good agreement, and your endeavors to destroy that ill humour which may have got into the officers. It is of the greatest importance, also, that the... soldiers and the people should know nothing of the misunderstanding... I have one thing more... to say. I make no doubt but you will do all in your power to forward the repairs of the French fleet."

To Greene he wrote: "I depend much upon your temper and influence to conciliate that animosity which I plainly perceive by a letter from the Marquis, subsists between the American officers and the French in our service. This you may depend will extend itself to the Count and the officers and men to his whole fleet, should they return to Rhode Island, except upon their arrival, they find a reconciliation has taken place. The Marquis speaks kindly of a letter from you to him upon this subject. He will therefore take any advice coming from you in a friendly light, and if he can be pacified, the other French Gentlemen will of course be satisfied as they look up to him as their Head... I beg you will take every measure to keep the protest... from being made public... I fully depend upon your exerting yourself to heal all private animosities."

To Lafayette, who told Washington that his heart had been wounded "by that very people I came from so far to love and support," he wrote on September 1: "I feel every thing that hurts the Sensibility of a Gentleman; and consequently, upon the present occasion, feel for you and for our good and great Allys the French. I feel myself hurt also at every illiberal and unthinking reflection which may have been cast upon Count D'Estaing or the conduct of the fleet under his command; and lastly I feel for my Country. Let me entreat you my dear Marquis to take no exception at unmeaning expressions, uttered perhaps without Consideration, and in the first transport of disappointed hope. Everybody, Sir, who reasons, will acknowledge the advantages which we have derived from the French fleet, and the Zeal of the Commander of it, but in a free and republican Government, you cannot restrain the voice of the multitude; every man will speak as he thinks, or more properly without thinking, consequently will adjudge of Effects without attending to the Causes. The censures which have been levelled at the French fleet would more than probably have fallen in a much higher degree on our own (if we had one) in the same situation... Let me beseech you therefore my good Sir to afford a healing hand to the wound… I, your friend, have no doubt but that you will use your utmost endeavors to restore harmony, that the honour, glory and mutual Interest of the two Nations may be promoted and cemented in the firmest manner." Finally, Washington sat down and wrote a lengthy letter to d'Estaing:

If the deepest regret that the best concerted enterprise and bravest exertions should have been rendered fruitless by a disaster which human prudence is incapable of foreseeing or preventing can alleviate disappointment, you may be assured that the whole Continent sympathizes with you; it will be a consolation to you to reflect that the thinking part of Mankind do not form their judgement from events; and that their equity will ever attach equal glory to those actions which deserve success, as to those which have been crowned with it. It is in the trying circumstances to which your Excellency has been exposed that the virtues of a great Mind are displayed in their brightest lustre; and that the General's Character is better known than in the moment of Victory; it was yours, by every title which can give it…

I exceedingly lament that in addition to our misfortunes, there has been the least suspension of harmony and good understanding between the Generals of allied Nations, whose views, like their interests must be the same. On the first intimation of it I employed my influence in restoring what I regarded as essential to the permanence of a Union founded on mutual inclination and the strongest ties of reciprocal advantage.

Thanks to Washington everything quieted down. General Heath, in command at Boston, gave the fullest assistance in repairing the French fleet and in suppressing anti-French talk and action. The Massachusetts council called on d'Estaing to offer all the help the state could provide. Congress sent a resolution to d'Estaing praising him "as a brave and wise officer" who had rendered every benefit to the United States that circumstances permitted. Sullivan informed Washington that, having subdued his "passion," he had sent an apology to d'Estaing and dispatched Lafayette to Boston to help get the French fleet repaired. John Hancock and General Greene also went to Boston to aid d'Estaing. Bostonians gave it out that it was British prisoners who had attacked the French.

By September 16 Greene was writing Washington: "All the French officers are extravagantly fond of your Excellency but the Admiral more so than the rest." D'Estaing, fully appeased, sent Washington a message that might serve more than two hundred years later, when French-American friendship runs into storms:

If during the coming centuries, we of America and France are to live in amity and confidence, we must banish recriminations and prevent complaints. I trust the two nations will not be forced to depart from moderation in their conduct but that they will reflect in all their public affairs that firmness and consideration for public interests necessary to unity between the two great nations.

John Hancock presented a copy of a Peale portrait of Washington to Admiral d'Estaing. Lafayette wrote enthusiastically to Washington that Hancock had also promised him one. He mentioned that he had never seen a man so glad to have a picture "as the Admiral was to receive yours." Those who dined aboard the *Languedoc*, the flagship commanded by naval Captain and army General Louis de Bougainville (after whom the plant was named), noticed it hung in a conspicuous place, its frame decorated with laurels. In early November, d'Estaing sailed with all his ships and troops, and Washington's picture, for the West Indies, leaving the British in control of the seas off North America.

On September 23 Washington expressed his disappointment to his brother John: "Had the British garrison at Newport been captured," he said, it would "have hastened the departure of the Troops in New York as fast as their Canvas wings could convey them."

LAFAYETTE CHALLENGES CARLISLE

With the alliance repaired, Lafayette turned back to fighting the British. The commissioners of Albion called France a land of "perfidy." Lafayette immediately wrote to d'Estaing to tell him he would send Lord Carlisle a billet-doux challenging him to a duel. "I have nothing to do here that is very interesting and, while killing Lord Carlisle, I can at the same time transact more interesting business at White Plains." Washington was immediately dragged into this affair. Lafayette had requested Washington's "advice," by which he meant approval, but the latter replied on October 4:

The generous Spirit of Chivalry, exploded by the rest of the World, finds a refuge, My dear friend, in the sensibility of your Nation only. *But it is in vain to cherish it, unless you can find Antagonists to support it... In our days it is to be feared that your opponent, sheltering himself behind Modern opinion, and under this present public Character of Commissioner, would turn a virtue of such ancient date, into ridicule... Besides, experience has proved, that chance is as often as much concerned in deciding these matters as bravery... I would not therefore have your life, by the remotest possibility, exposed, when it may be reserved for so many greater occasions. His excellency the Admiral, I flatter myself, will be in Sentiment with me.*

D'Estaing and Carlisle reacted precisely as Washington predicted. The fatherly admiral was horrified and asked Washington to intervene to stop the duel. This he had already done and he replied to d'Estaing on October 24:

The coincidence between Your Excellency's sentiments… and those which I expressed to him on the same subject, are peculiarly flattering to me. I am happy to find that my disapprobation of the measure was founded on the same arguments…

I omitted neither serious reasoning nor pleasantry to divert him from a Scheme in which he could be so easily foiled… He intimated that Your Excellency did not discountenance it, and that he had pledged himself to the principal Officers of the French squadron… The charms of vindicating the honor of his country were irresistible… Though his ardour was an overmatch for my advice and influence, I console myself with the reflexion that his lordship will not accept the challenge… [He] has probably answered it in a strain of pleasantry.

Lord Carlisle, after considerable discussion at British headquarters, decided that he need not accept. He wrote rather ironically to Lafayette that he could not take the proposed duel very seriously, for he had spoken only as the king's commissioner, and Admirals Byron and d'Estaing were better fitted to decide national disputes. Lafayette had, however, made his point about French honor. The younger French and American officers thought highly of his action.

BRITISH TROUBLES

When Lord Cornwallis returned to America with the British commissioners and looked at the situation and the orders to retreat, he offered his resignation to London. This was refused on the ground that he was next in line to succeed Sir Henry Clinton.

There was not much for the commissioners to do in New York, especially as Congress ignored their communications. They occasionally lectured Americans, pointing out that America belonged not to them but to the British empire. A member of the commission, George Johnstone, probably acting on his own, wrote letters to Robert Morris and Joseph Reed, implying that they were men of great integrity but if they restored America to Great Britain, suitable rewards would be forthcoming for them, as well as for Washington and

Henry Laurens if they also helped. Washington correctly described these approaches as of a pulse-feeling cast but Congress decided to make the most of them. They published Johnstone's letters with a stern warning that they would have nothing further to do with a man who had made such "Daring and atrocious attempts to corrupt [our] integrity."

Johnstone in a great huff denied the allegations. Washington commented in a letter of September 12 to Henry Laurens: "He tries to convince you that he is not at all hurt by, or offended at, the interdiction of Congress. That he is not in a passion, while he exhibits a striking proof of his being cut to the quick, and actually biting his fingers in an agony of passion."

Carlisle was not at all pleased with this development, nor was William Eden who noted that Americans lacked "those principles of implied honour and confidence under which it is usual to transact business in Europe," that is, they complained out loud when offered bribes. Johnstone resigned from the commission and sailed back to England to tell the king that Congress should be destroyed.

On July 27 Sir Henry Clinton wrote to London to say that Washington's armies now numbered nearly 28,000 troops, and further additions to his forces could be expected after the harvests. (Washington, in fact, had the previously mentioned 16,700 men stretching from Boston and Rhode Island to New Jersey.) Clinton complained that he himself had only 26,000 rank and file who were fit for duty. He therefore did not know what his future plans might be. According to orders he had received from London, he was to dispatch 8,000 to the West Indies and Florida, plus troops to Canada which, he said, would make his command very small. Lord George Germain replied that, according to his own calculations, even after sending them, Clinton would still have more than 22,000 rank and file.

Sir Henry's projected attack on Newport, which was intended to capture the American forces there, totally failed when Sullivan evacuated Rhode Island. In frustration, Sir Henry sent General Charles Grey, later Earl Grey, to burn the towns of New Bedford and Fairhaven and to steal sheep from the farmers of Martha's Vineyard. Grey's activities were slightly repaid that spring when John Paul Jones raided Whitehaven, England, and also seized HMS *Drake* and several other prizes in English waters. On August 9 Lord Sandwich reported to the king that a French fleet under d'Orvilliers had fought a British fleet under Keppel and "the damage sustained [by the English] is very great indeed."

Lord Howe, after an abortive attempt to blockade d'Estaing at Boston, returned to New York and turned his command over to Admiral Byron. Howe sailed for England, having earlier asked for his recall.

The two remaining peace commissioners, Carlisle and Eden, decided that they too had had enough and they resigned. Carlisle had been pessimistic almost from the day he landed. On July 21 he informed his wife that "the common people hate us in their hearts, notwithstanding all that is said of their secret attachment to the mother country." By October he was writing his friend, George Selwyn: "Everything is upon a great scale on this continent. The rivers are immense; the climate violent in heat and cold; the prospects magnificent; the thunder and lightening tremendous.... We have nothing on so great a scale with us but our blunders, our misconduct, our ruin, our losses, our disgraces and misfortunes."

Though he wrote such private letters, Carlisle knew on which side his bread was sugared and he took care not to tell the same story to the king and ministers. He informed Germain in October: "The spirit of revolt is much abated... The French connection is generally disliked." On returning home the commissioners reported that there was a great upsurge in American loyalty to the king, which would further increase as soon as British strength was shown. Sir Henry Clinton commented in his memoirs that they painted a false picture of sentiment in America.

Before they left the United States, the peace commissioners issued a manifesto to the "British colonies," ordering them to break their alliance with the wicked French; otherwise Great Britain would be forced to lay the country waste to make it useless to France. By this time Americans were benumbed by threats and reacted only mildly. The severest castigations came from Englishmen of the character of Lord Rockingham who called it an "accursed proclamation." Washington commented to d'Estaing on October 27: "The British Commissioners, I believe, will not trouble us with any more of their harangues. They authorize us to consider the last as a farewell speech, preparatory to their final exit. They will not need our aid to accelerate their political death." On October 4 he had written to Gouverneur Morris: "God grant [the enemy] may embrace the opportunity of bidding an eternal adieu to our, once quit of them, happy land."

Lord Cornwallis took advantage of the serious illness of his wife to sail home with the commissioners. He did not expect to return to America. Generals Grey and Pigot and a General Jones also asked London for permission to return to England. On October 8 Sir Henry Clinton sent in his resignation to Lord George Germain, the second British commander in chief to do so within a year. Clinton said that, in accordance with his instructions, he had despatched troops to Bermuda, Halifax, Georgia, and the West Indies, and the forces remaining to him were too few to mount an offensive.

This scurrying to quit was a shock to the British cabinet. A long red and blue line of heroes had come up against the modest and humorous George Washington: Gage, the two Howes, Burgoyne, von Heister, Pigot, Cornwallis, St. Leger, Percy, Riedesel, Phillips, Fraser, Grey, Grant, Clinton, and Jones. By the end of 1778 only Clinton and Pigot were left in America, along with Phillips and Riedesel, who were prisoners. Pigot departed in 1779. George III was running out of generals. He and Germain placated Clinton with long flattering letters and sinecure appointments. Like Lord North, he was doomed to stay to the end. In November Lord North again beseeched the king to let his servant depart. The king replied on November 14 with more firmness than syntax:

> *If Lord North can see with the same degree of enthusiasm I do, the beauty, excellence, and perfection of the British Constitution as by Law Established, and consider that if any one branch of the Empire is allowed to cast off its dependency, that the others will infallibly follow the Example, that consequently though an arduous struggle that is worth going through any difficulty to preserve to the latest Posterity what the Wisdom of our Ancestors have carefully transmitted to us; he will not allow despondency to fill a place in his breast, but resolve not merely out of Duty to fill his post, but will resolve with Vigour to meet every obstacle that may arise he shall meet with most cordial Support from me; but the times require Vigour or the State will be ruined.*

Lord North answered that he would serve his master with all the firmness and resolution he could muster but that "his spirits, strength, memory, judgement and abilities [are] sensibly and considerably impaired."

THE FRONTIERS AND CANADA

The king's troops, aided by Tories and Indians, were also active on the frontiers of Pennsylvania and New York. In July they raided Wyoming Valley near the present Wilkes-Barre, destroying a thousand houses, scalping 227 Americans, and torturing many to death. The town of German flats in the Mohawk Valley was levelled to the ground and all the cattle and provisions of the inhabitants were taken. In November the houses in Cherry Valley went to the flames and more than thirty women and children, as well as many soldiers, were massacred.

This needless brutality put Washington in the difficult position intended. He had far fewer troops than the British, and these were stretched over a wide area. In July he detached a Pennsylvania and a New York regiment and part of

Morgan's corps to meet the attacks. By September he was writing the governor of New York that he was willing to send another regiment though he could ill spare it. In October he assigned General Hand to command all troops engaged in protecting the frontiers. The Indian and British ravages persuaded him that in the next campaign he should send troops against the Indians in order to break their power as an ally of Great Britain.

Congress gave him another problem when that body decided that the troops who had surrendered at Saratoga should be moved from Massachusetts to Charlottesville, Virginia. He had to arrange this difficult task primarily with the help of state militia. Sir Henry Clinton, knowing Washington had dispatched forces against the Indians, attempted to move up the Hudson to rescue the convention troops, but he arrived well after they had crossed the river. On December 12 Washington wrote Joseph Reed:

> *Sir Harry's late extra Maneuvre up the North River kept me upon the March and countermarch from the 5th until yesterday... What did, or could prompt the Knight to this expedition I am at a loss to discover... [I cannot conceive] that he could be so much out in point of intelligence to mistime matters so egregiously... I could not help being uneasy lest disaster might happen and posted back from Elizabeth Town at 4 O'clock on the Morning of the 5th and got within 12 or 15 Miles of King's Ferry, when I was met by an Express informing me that the Enemy had landed at that place, burn'd two or three small logged cabins with 9 Barrels of spoilt Herrings, and had reimbarked... for New York... Thus ended this notable expedition which was conducted... with so much secrecy that all the flag boats to and from the City were stopped and not a mouse permitted to move within their lines.*

Congress now returned to its old dream of taking Canada. This time Washington decided that Congress should make no more disastrous moves in that direction without carefully weighing every factor involved. Busy as he was, he worked much of the summer in appraising the situation, since Canada was the principal supply point for the Six Nations, who were attacking on the frontiers. In September he asked General Jacob Bayley, stationed in northern New York, to make an intelligence assessment of the Canadian garrison and defense system, the attitude of the people and clergy, the disposition of the Indians, the system of government, the size of the crops, and whether Canadians would welcome Americans as liberators. He also asked Generals Gates and Bayley to formulate a plan for a military invasion. In sending this first appraisal to Congress he suggested that, so long as the British were in the United States, "we shall find employment enough in defending ourselves, without meditating conquests."

On November 4 Washington received a resolution and plan from Congress for a full-scale invasion of Canada to be undertaken in cooperation with the French. This plan provided for attacks on Quebec and Montreal and invasions from Detroit and Niagara. During the following week Washington wrote a critique that was one of his most admirable state pieces. With political clairvoyance he wrote that someday France might no longer be an ally and could be a greater threat to American independence than Great Britain. Washington outlined his letter, then drafted and redrafted it before forwarding it on November 11. Congress had requested that he send a copy of his reply to Lafayette as a means of getting French help for the invasion. Washington suggested that this was unwise because he had to discuss the many weaknesses and wants in the army and these should be known only to Americans. He then indicated he thought the Canadian plan was unsound:

> *I consider it as my duty and what Congress expects from me, to give my reasons for this opinion, with that frankness and candour which the importance of the subject demands...*

> *It seems to me impolitic to enter into engagements with the Court of France for carrying on a combined operation of any kind, without a moral certainty of being able to fulfill our part...*

> *So far from being a moral certainty of our complying with our engagements, it may, in my opinion, be very safely pronounced that if the enemy keep possession of their present posts at New York and Rhode Island, it will be impracticable either to furnish the men or the necessary supplies...*

> *If I rightly understand the plan in consideration, it requires for its execution 12,600 Men, rank and file. Besides these, to open a passage through a Wilderness for the march of the several bodies of Troops, to provide the means of... transportation by land and Water, to establish posts... to build and man Vessels... these and many other purposes... will demand a much larger proportion of Artificers and persons to be employed in manual and laborous Offices, than are usual in the Ordinary course of military operations. When we add the whole together, the aggregate number of men requisite... will be little less than double the number heretofore in the field...*

> *The State of our Supplies for transporting and subsisting the troops will stand upon a footing equally bad... We have encountered extreme difficulties in these respects... in the Heart of the country... In Canada we should be carrying on the*

War at an immense distance, in a country… incapable of affording any aid, and the great part of it hostile…

…All the reasons which induce France and the United States to wish to wrest Canada and Halifax from the dominion of England, operate with her, perhaps more forcibly to use every possible effort for their defence. To hope to find them in a defenceless state, must be founded in a supposition of the total incapacity of Britain… We may run into a dangerous error by estimating her power so low…

A strong garrison has been lately sent to Halifax… The English are not greatly superior to the French by Sea in America…

…If the French troops should arrive before Quebec, I think their success against that strong place, fortified by every advantage of nature and of art would be extremely doubtful… [an attack] on Detroit… if well conducted, should [succeed] without very great difficulty. The case is very different with respect to Niagara. This I am informed is one of the strongest fortresses in America; and can only be reduced by regular approaches or by famine. (In accomplishing this last war and a conquest as far as Montreal… General Amherst exhausted two campaigns, with all the advantages he derived from the United Efforts of Britain and America… with plenty of Seamen… and money…)

The body of Troops to penetrate by way of the River St. Francis must meet with great obstacles… We may find ourselves in the bosom of an enemy's Country, obliged to combat their whole force with one inferior and reduced by a tedious and wasting march…

The plan proposed appears to me not only too extensive… but too complex. To succeed, it requires such a fortunate coincidence of circumstances as could hardly be hoped and cannot be relied on.

One draft of this letter contains typical Washington phraseology: "Your Number of Eaters will be little, if any, under 20,000… This Provision… is to be transported in wagons or by Pack horses some hundreds of miles the great part of which thro' an uninhabited Country." But he gave it a more dignified turn in the final polish. Washington added a political critique of the plan in a private letter to Henry Laurens, president of Congress:

I have one objection, untouched in my public letter, which is in my estimation, insurmountable, and alarms all my feelings for the true and permanent interests of my country. This is the introduction of a large body of French troops into Canada, and putting them in possession of the capital of that Province, attached to them by all the ties of blood, habits, manners, religion and former connexions of government... Let us realize for a moment the striking advantages France would derive from the possession of Canada; the acquisition of an extensive territory... the opening of a vast... commerce with the Indian nations... the having ports of her own on this continent... the facility of awing and controuling these states, the natural and most formidable rival of every maritime power in Europe.

France acknowledged for some time past the most powerful monarchy in Europe, able now to dispute the empire of the sea with Great Britain... possessed of New Orleans on our right, Canada on our left and seconded by the numerous tribes of Indians on our Rear... a people... whom she knows so well how to conciliate; would, it is much to be apprehended have it in her power to give law to these states... I am heartily disposed to entertain the most favourable sentiments of our new ally... but it is a maxim founded on the universal experience of mankind, that no nation is to be trusted farther than it is bound by interest; and no prudent statesman or politician will venture to depart from it.

Laurens replied that his military arguments against the attack on Canada were sufficiently persuasive that there was no need to bring up political objections in Congress. Thereafter Canada was left alone.

THE FALL OF CHARLES LEE

On December 22, 1778, Washington announced the results of the courts-martial of Generals Arthur St. Clair, Philip Schuyler, and Charles Lee. In a fit of vindictiveness over the loss of Ticonderoga in the summer of 1777, Congress had ordered St. Clair tried for treachery and cowardice and Schuyler for negligence. The fort had fallen to overwhelming British forces and the only negligence had been that of General Gates. St. Clair and Schuyler were acquitted unanimously and "with the highest honor." The trial of Lee was held at his request. Following the battle of Monmouth he wrote to Washington on June 30:

From the knowledge I have of your Excellency's character, I must conclude that nothing but the misinformation of some very stupid, or misrepresentation of some very wicked person, could have occasioned your making use of such very singular expressions as you did on my coming up to the ground where you had taken post. They implied that I was guilty either of disobedience of orders, or want of conduct, or want of courage. Your Excellency will therefore infinitely oblige me by letting me

know on which of these three articles you ground your charge, that I may prepare
for my justification which I have the happiness to be confident that I can do to the
army, to the Congress, to America, and to the world in general... I ever had, and
I hope I ever shall have the greatest respect and veneration for General
Washington; I think him endowed with many great and good qualities, but in this
instance, I must pronounce that he has been guilty of an act of cruel injustice... I
have a right to demand some reparation for the injury committed and unless I can
obtain it I must... retire from the service... In justice to you, I must repeat that I
from my soul believe, that it was not a motion of your own breast, but instigated
by some of those dirty earwigs who will for ever insinuate themselves near persons
in high office.

Washington issued orders that day for the arrest and court-martial of Lee. He
wrote him: "I received your Letter (dated thro' mistake the 1st. of July)
expressed as I conceive, in terms highly improper. I am not conscious of having made use of any very singular expression at the time of my meeting you,
as you intimate. What I recollect to have said was dictated by duty and war-
ranted by the occasion. As soon as circumstances will permit, you shall have
an opportunity, either of justifying yourself to the army, to Congress, to
America, and to the world in General; or of convincing them that you were
guilty of a breach of orders and of misbehaviour before the enemy of the
28th. Inst. in not attacking them as you had been directed and in making an
unnecessary, disorderly, and shameful retreat."

Lee's court-martial was held under considerable difficulties since the army
was in movement from New Jersey to White Plains. The court reached its verdict about August 12. It found Lee guilty of disobedience of orders, misbehaviour, and disrespect to the commander in chief. He was sentenced to
suspension from the army for a year.

St. Clair was tried subsequently to Lee, and Schuyler after St. Clair.
Congress did not act on the results until December when all three verdicts
were confirmed. Before his year of suspension was up, Lee wrote a sarcastic
letter to Congress, and that body dismissed him from the army.

Lee had very little to do until his death in 1782, and he spent much of the
time denouncing Washington. He suggested on one occasion, in a letter published July 6, 1779, in the *Maryland Journal* that Joseph Reed certainly knew
the truth about the commander in chief. Reed, however, had become very
nimble in shifting with the prevailing winds. He informed Washington that all
he had ever said to Lee was: "With a thousand good and great qualities, there
is a want of decision to complete the perfect military character." Reed
denounced Lee's "malevolence" and his attempts to make Reed a "false wit-

ness." He congratulated Washington on the "public affection" enjoyed by him. John Laurens, Washington's aide, challenged Lee to a duel and shot him in the side. Lee's mind deteriorated; late in 1779 he described Washington to Gates as "dark, designing sordid ambitious vain proud arrogant and vindictive," adding that he was planning Lee's assassination.

After Lee's death, Washington wrote his sister in England on April 30, 1783, expressing "condolence of the loss of so near a relation; who was possessed of many great qualities." For his epitaph Washington, consciously or not, selected a phrase from Lee's letter to him of June 30, 1778.

PHILADELPHIA

Washington established his headquarters at Middlebrook, New Jersey, on December 11 and put his army in winter quarters there. This village was in a much more fertile area than Valley Forge. The army was better housed and fed than in the preceding winter and, thanks to French supplies, more warmly clothed. The winter was a remarkably mild one with relatively little frost or snow after the middle of January. To Joseph Reed, who had been elected head of the executive council of Pennsylvania, Washington wrote on December 12:

> *Were I to give into private conveniency and amusement, I should not be able to resist the invitation of my friends to make Phila. (instead of a squeezed up room or two) my quarters for the Winter; but the affairs of the army require my constant attention and presence, and circumstanced as matters are at this time, calls for some degree of care and address to keep it from crumbling. As Peace and retirement are my ultimate aim, and the most pleasing and flattering hope of my Soul, every thing advancive of this end, contributes to my satisfaction... and will reconcile any place and all circumstances to my feelings whilst I continue in Service.*

Congress, however, summoned Washington to Philadelphia for consultation on the 1779 campaign. He slipped quietly into the city on December 22. His wife was already there from Mount Vernon. The couple stayed with Henry Laurens who, having resigned his post as president of Congress, was replaced by John Jay, also of Huguenot descent. To assist in discussions with Congress, Washington had with him General Greene as well as his aides Laurens, Tilghman, and Hamilton. All five army men were shocked by Philadelphia. Under the influence of war, the British occupation and the greatly depreciated currency, the once-sober Quaker capital had become dissipated, with gambling, theatres, and all night balls and routs interfering with the work of

Congress. Joseph Reed's party to celebrate his election cost two thousand pounds; nearly a hundred glasses were broken. General Benedict Arnold, the city's military commander, was living in high style and courting the Tory Elizabeth Shippen. Washington was revolted. He wrote his stepson, Jack Custis, on January 2: "You say I shall be surprised at the slow progress made by [the Virginia] assembly in the passage of the bills through both houses. I really am not, nor shall I, I believe, be surprised at anything; for it appears to me that idleness and dissipation seem to have taken such fast hold of every body, that I shall not be at all surprised if there should be a general wreck of everything." To Benjamin Harrison in Virginia he wrote eight days after his arrival:

Our Affairs are in a more distressed, ruinous, and deplorable condition than they have been in Since the commencement of the War. By a faithful labourer then in the cause. By a Man who is daily injuring his private Estate without even the smallest earthly advantage not common to all in case of a favourable Issue to the dispute. By one who wishes the prosperity of America most devoutly and sees or thinks he sees it, on the brink of ruin, you are beseeched most earnestly, my dear Colo. Harrison, to exert yourself in endeavouring to rescue your Country, by... sending your best Men to Congress; these characters must not slumber, nor sleep at home, in such times of pressing danger... While the common interests of America are mouldering and sinking into irretrievable (if a remedy is not soon applied) ruin... If I was called upon to draw a picture of the times, and of Men; from what I have seen, heard, and in part know, I should in one word say that idleness, dissipation and extravagance seem to have laid fast hold of most of them... An insatiable thirst for riches seems to have got the better of every other consideration... That party disputes and personal quarrels are the great business of the day whilst the momentous concerns of an empire, a great and accumulated debt; ruined finances, depreciated money, and want of credit (which in their consequences is the want of every thing) are but secondary considerations and postponed from day to day, from week to week as if our affairs wore the most promising aspect; after drawing this picture, which from my Soul I believe to be a true one I need to repeat to you that I am alarmed and wish to see my Country men aroused. I have no resentments, nor do I mean to point out any particular character; this I can declare upon my honour for I have every attention paid me by Congress that I can reasonably expect and have reason to think that I stand well in their estimation... Your Money is now sinking 5 pr. Ct. a Day in this city... And yet an assembly, a concert, a Dinner, or Supper (that will cost three or four hundred pounds) will not only take Men off from acting but even from thinking of this business while a great part of the Officers of your Army from absolute necessity are quitting the Service and the more virtuous few rather than do this are sinking by sure degrees into beggary and want.

On December 28 Washington attended a Masonic festival in honor of St. John the Evangelist as well as services at Christ Church. There Dr. William Smith, later rector of the college at Chestertown, Maryland, renamed for Washington, referred to him as the "American Cincinnatus." He had also been called, most inappropriately, the "American Fabius Maximus," in praise and in sarcasm, but the "masterly inactivity" of Fabius, "the delayer," was totally foreign to his nature and desire. Nonetheless he had to conclude that with a weak Congress, inadequate public backing for the army's needs, and no credit, he could only continue a defensive war. He made clear that under these circumstances the Canada conquest was a mirage and Congress acquiesced. He proposed instead an expedition to end the Indian attacks on the frontier, and Congress approved this plan. For the rest the army could act only to contain Clinton in his two northern ports. Congress at this time gave Washington full authority to direct all military operations in all parts of the country, the most comprehensive power he had received.

Before he left Philadelphia, Washington learned that some of the British troops sent south from New York had taken Savannah in December and had moved on to Augusta. Much of Georgia came under their control. This was of no great military significance, but it added a new dimension to Washington's problems. He did not yet know that the king and Germain had decided that the war could be won more easily in the south than in the north.

On January 6 the Washingtons attended a dance at the house of Mrs. Samuel Powel, whose husband had been mayor of Philadelphia. Benjamin Franklin's daughter, Sarah Bache, was there and she wrote her father in Paris a few days later: "I have lately been several times invited abroad with the General and Mrs. Washington. He always inquires after you in the most affectionate manner, and speaks of you highly. We danced at Mrs. Powel's your birthday [old style] or night I should say, in company together, and he told me it was the anniversary of his marriage; it was just twenty years that night."

Washington's officers bore the gaiety of Philadelphia with disapproval. Tench Tilghman wrote to his fellow aide, James McHenry, at Middlebrook: "I suppose you think we must be by this time so wedded to sweet Philadelphia that it will break our hearts to leave it. Far from it... we anxiously await the moment that gives us liberty to return to humble Middlebrook. Philadelphia may answer very well for a man with his pockets well lined, whose pursuit is idleness and dissipation. But to us, it is intolerable... By the body of my father, as honest Sancho used to swear, we have advanced as far in luxury in the 3d year of our independency as... Greece and Rome did in twice as many hundred." General Greene summed it up to General McDougall in February: "I spent a month in the most agreeable and disagreeable manner I ever did a month in my life. We had the most splendid entertainment imaginable; large assemblies, evening balls, etc. It was hard service to go through the duties of the day. I was obliged to rise early and go to bed late... Our great Fabius Maximus was the glory and admiration of the city. Every exertion was made to show him respect and make his time agreeable; but the exhibition was such a scene of luxury and profusion they gave him more pain than pleasure."

On January 29, after posing for a portrait by Charles Peale at the request of Pennsylvania, Washington urgently asked Congress to let him return to the army. He and Martha went off a few days later, arriving at Middlebrook on February 5.

About the end of the year a Pennsylvania German almanac was published for 1779. On its cover was a laureled head labelled "Waschington." Above it was an angel trumpeting the words "Des Landes Vater," the first known use of this term.

MIDDLEBROOK

Washington, no *cunctator*, at once set to work to organize all possible intelligence for the frontier campaign. His knowledge of the Indian tribes and of much of the territory involved was clearly revealed in his letters. He sent out a heavy correspondence, with detailed questions to his officers and agents, westward to Detroit and north to New Hampshire. He also appealed to Pennsylvania to collect all state maps and surveys of the areas around the Allegheny and Susquehanna Rivers.

To General McIntosh at Pittsburgh he had addressed lengthy instructions before leaving Philadelphia: "I would wish you to have the Country well explored between Pittsburgh and Detroit... also the water conveyances to that post (Detroit) by the Scioto and other waters, leading out of the Ohio towards Lake Erie, and the distance of portage between the heads of those Rivers and the Waters of the lake... I would also have you make yourself perfectly informed of the water and land communications between Pittsburgh and Presquile; what kind of Craft can pass up French Creek (or River la Beuf) and whether such Craft can be transported across from French Creek to the Lake... When the Northern Indians go to War with the Southern, they fall into the Allegheny River and come down from thence to Fort Pitt... whether they make use of any water Carriage is a matter worth enquiring into... Let it also be inquired how far this route is wide of the falls of Niagara and Lake Erie."

Other letters went to his officers: "Let me know... how far Rochester is from Mahcomac? and how far is it from Middle Brook to Mahcomac, what kind of road, and which is the best Route? I wish to be informed of the distances from Chemung and Ononaquaga to Niagara? Which is the easiest and best route to the principal settlements of the Six Nations... How far it is from Cannedessago to Chessie a capital Seneca Village?"

By March he sent more standardized questionnaires to all general and field officers having knowledge of the Indian country. They were sweeping in detail and covered road and water routes, distances, limits of navigation, when grass would grow for forage, the best types of batteaux and canoes to use, and the strength and fortifications of all Indian villages.

To his quartermaster General Greene he sent orders to provide 150 batteaux, 1,500 axes, 1,000 spades and shovels, 2,000 knapsacks, 3,000 canteens, 6,000 horse shoes, 1,000 horse bells and a great miscellany of saws, files, quill pens, orderly books, ink stands, paper, and candlesticks.

With some reluctance Washington chose Gates to head the army going west but Gates refused, in a letter the commander in chief thought rather brusque. He therefore selected Sullivan, whose tactlessness would matter little in the West. By early summer he and his army were ready to move.

CAMP LIFE

Though Washington's officers had complained of the constant gaiety at Philadelphia, life at camp was not entirely ascetic. On the first anniversary of the French alliance Washington gave a dinner followed by fireworks and a ball. According to General Knox, the dance was attended by seventy or more ladies and four to five times as many officers. Washington opened the dance with Mrs. Knox, perhaps the fattest woman there. A few days later General Greene and his wife gave a ball at which Washington and Mrs. Greene danced for three hours without sitting down.

On February 25 Dr. James Thacher, a surgeon attached to the army, attended a headquarters dinner where George and Martha Washington presided. He wrote in his journal the next day: "It is natural to view with keen attention the countenance of an illustrious man, with a secret hope of discovering in his features some peculiar trace of excellence, which distinguishes him from and elevates him above his fellow mortals. These expectations are realized in a peculiar manner, in viewing the person of George Washington.

His tall and noble stature and just proportions, his fine, cheerful open countenance, simple and modest deportment, are all calculated to interest every beholder in his favour, and to command veneration and respect... In conversation his Excellency's expressive countenance is peculiarly pleasing and interesting; a placid smile is frequently observed on his lips... He is polite and attentive to each individual... Mrs. Washington combines in an uncommon degree, great dignity of manner with the most pleasing affability, but possesses no striking marks of beauty."

On May 2 the United States army paraded for the first time for distinguished foreign visitors, Conrad Gérard, the French minister, and Don Juan de Miralles of Spain. Spain was displaying little enthusiasm for revolution in the western hemisphere. Miralles had been sent as an unaccredited agent to Philadelphia. Dr. Thacher recorded the event:

> *The whole of our army in this quarter was paraded... in a spacious field... At the signal of thirteen cannon, the great and splendid cavalcade approached... A very beautiful troop of light horse, commanded by major Lee, a Virginian, marched in front, then followed His Excellency the Commander in Chief and his aids... next the foreign ministers... and the general officers... [They] passed in front of the line of the army, from right to left in review, and received the military honours due their rank; after which the gentlemen dismounted and retired to the stage, and took seats with Mrs. Washington, Mrs. Greene, Mrs. Knox and a number of other ladies... The army then performed the field maneuvers and evolutions, with firing of cannon and musketry.*

Thacher noted that Washington looked "incomparably more majestic" than the foreigners. Gérard and Miralles politely praised everything. Later Miralles sent the Washingtons some Cuban products, chocolate, sugar, guava jelly, and crystal flasks.

The main purpose of the meeting was to enable Gérard and Washington to discuss overall strategy in the event d'Estaing could return with his fleet from the West Indies. Washington was cautious, in view of what had happened at Newport, his limited supplies and troops, and his planned expedition to the West. Gérard talked of attacks on Nova Scotia and Newfoundland, but these points were too far removed. Washington wanted a second joint operation against Newport, provided that this time the French had superiority of sea power, but Gérard could not assure this. The conversations ended with an agreement that a Franco-American attack on Savannah, now held by the British, offered the most feasible immediate operation. If this were successful, further joint operations in the North could be reviewed. Gérard clearly found

Washington a relief after dealing with Congress, about which he often complained to Versailles. He wrote from Middlebrook to the French foreign minister: "I have had many conversations with General Washington, some of which have continued for three hours... I will now say only that I have formed as high an opinion of the powers of his mind, his moderation, his patriotism, and his virtues, as I had before from common report conceived of his military talents and of the incalculable services he has rendered to his country." Washington quickly turned from the French to another group of allies, the Delaware Indian chiefs. He made them a simple and humorous speech on May 12:

Brothers: I am happy to see you here... I am glad also you have left all our friends of the Delaware Nation well.

Brothers: I have read your paper. The things you have said are weighty things, and I have considered them well... I rejoice in the new assurances you give of your friendship...

Brothers: I am a Warrior. My words are few and plain; but I will make good what I say. 'Tis my business to destroy the enemies of these states and to protect their friends. You have seen how we have withstood the English for four years; and how their great Armies have dwindled away and come to very little; and how what remains of them... are glad to stay upon Two or three little Islands... The English, Brothers, are a boasting people. They talk of doing a great deal; but they do very little. They fly away on their Ships from one part of our Country to another; but as soon as our Warriors get together they leave it and go to some other part. They took Boston and Philadelphia... but when they saw our Warriors... they were forced to leave them.

Brothers: We have till lately fought the English all alone. Now the Great King of France... has taken up the Hatchet with us, and we have sworn never to bury it, till we have punished the English and made them sorry for All the wicked things they had in their Hearts to do against these States...

Brothers: I am glad you have brought three of the children of your principal Chiefs to be educated with us. I am sure Congress will open the Arms of love to them... This is a great mark of your confidence... You do well to wish to learn our arts and ways of life, and above all, the religion of Jesus Christ. This will make you a greater and happier people...

Brothers: When you have seen all you wish to see, I will then wish you a good journey to Philadelphia. I hope you may find there every thing your hearts can wish, that when you return home you may be able to tell your Nation good things of us.

Two days later Washington held another army parade for the Indian chiefs. Dr. Thacher commented: "His Excellency, with his usual dignity, followed by his mulatto servant, riding a beautiful grey steed, passed in front of the line and received the salute. He was accompanied by a singular group of savages, whose appearance was beyond description ludicrous, their personal decorations equally farcical having their faces painted of various colors, jewels suspended from their ears and nose... tufts of hair on the crown... and dirty blankets." Martha Washington nearly collapsed with laughter. She described the sight of her husband surrounded by Indians as "funny" and "ridiculous." She mentioned that some of them "were fairly fine-looking but most of them appeared worse than Falstaff's gang... The General says it was done to keep the Indians friendly towards us." The general also extracted every ounce of intelligence he could from them.

Martha Washington was bundled off in a hurry to Mount Vernon at the beginning of June with a lot of good stories to tell. Sir Henry Clinton, prodded urgently by London to beat Washington, had moved up the Hudson to Stony Point.

TWENTY-SIX

MIDDLEBROOK
TO WEST POINT

1779–1780

WHEN THE CAMPAIGN of 1778 closed, Lafayette asked permission to return to France to offer his services to Louis XVI. On October 6 Washington endorsed his request to Congress for a furlough, adding that he was reluctant to part with an officer "who unites to all the military fire of youth, an uncommon maturity of judgment." In praising his "bravery and conduct," he suggested that Congress give Lafayette a suitable testimonial.

Congress voted him leave and their hearty thanks for his "services... courage and abilities on many signal occasions." They ordered Benjamin Franklin to procure an "elegant sword... to be presented in the name of the United States" to the young general. In addition the president wrote "To our Great, Faithful, and Beloved Friend and Ally, Louis the Sixteenth," praising Lafayette for his wisdom, gallantry, and patience under the hardships of war.

Washington also sent a note to Franklin describing Lafayette's many brave exploits and his own "particular friendship for him." He forwarded it to Lafayette on December 29 with a letter:

I am persuaded, My dear Marquis, there is no need of fresh proofs to convince you either of my affection for you personally or of the high opinion I entertain of your military talents and merit. Yet as you are on the point of returning to your country, I cannot forbear indulging my friendship by adding to the many honourable testimonies you have received from Congress, the inclosed letter [to Franklin.] I have there endeavoured to give him an idea of the value this country sets upon you; and the interest I take in your happiness cannot but make me desire you may be equally dear to your own.

Adieu, my Dear Marquis. My best wishes will ever attend you.

From Boston Lafayette wrote a farewell note: "To hear from you, my most respected friend, will be the greatest happiness I can feel... I hope you will quietly enjoy the pleasure of being with Mrs. Washington, without any disturbance from the enemy, till I join you again... Farewell, my most beloved general... The sails are just going to be hoisted... I hope your french friend will ever be dear to you... With what emotion I now leave the coast you inhabit, and with what affection and respect I'll for ever be, my dear General, your respectful and sincere friend."

Lafayette had violated the king's orders when he went to the United States. Louis XVI had to place him under technical arrest on his arrival in Paris. In a graceful gesture he was confined for one week in the great Hotel de Noailles. He was then released to call on the king and to receive wild popular acclaim. Louis XVI promoted him from captain to colonel of the king's dragoons and assigned him to the army that was assembling to invade England. The failure of the Spanish and French fleets to cooperate led to the abandonment of the plan. Lafayette looked around for other ways to help Americans.

Lafayette asked Franklin whether the French cabinet was doing all it could for him and whether America needed anything more. Franklin replied that the ministers were splendid, that America did need more money and supplies, but he knew that France had heavy war expenditures and he did not want to ask. Lafayette did the asking; as he later told Franklin, he could be much more demanding than the American minister. He requested ships, troops, supplies of every sort, and money loans and grants. The cabinet, particularly Vergennes, had not planned to send an army to America or to bankrupt France but Lafayette eventually won many points. He was so importunate that the prime minister, the comte de Maurepas, grumbled that he wanted everything but the furniture at Versailles for "his dear Americans. The king can deny him nothing."

Washington had noted Lafayette's maturity of judgement. With all his romantic nature and desire to place the French flag on the soil of "insolent" England, he was down to earth in detailing the kind of officers needed for

America. He said the French would find the Americans rather difficult people; tough officers should be selected who could live on little, be tactful to the natives, endure boredom, and get on without any of the pleasures of France. His romanticism came out when he asked to head the troops but the king could not nominate a captain, just raised to colonel, over all his generals.

Washington's letters to Lafayette did not reach him before he left Boston. They did not hear from each other for months, although each bombarded the other with letters. Lafayette wrote in June that he was afflicted at being so far from his dearest friend, particularly with the campaign opening. He added, "I have a wife, my dear General, who is in love with you... She begs you will receive her compliments and make them acceptable to Mrs. Washington." He also asked Washington to tell Congress not to go on "loudly disputing together," for it was making a poor impression in Europe. Soon he was hinting to Washington that troops might be on their way and that Madame de Lafayette was expecting a child.

He expressed to Congress the "unbounded affection and admiration which I shall ever feel for them... To the letter congress was pleased to write on my account, I owe the many favours the king has conferred upon me; there was no time lost in appointing me to the command of his own regiment of dragoons, and everything he could have done, everything I could have wished, I have received on account of your recommendation."

Washington did not get Lafayette's July letter until the end of September, but he expressed his pleasure at receiving it, in two inordinately long letters, one of which, he said, reached nearly from West Point to Paris. He was delighted by the reception Lafayette had received and said how pleased he would be to have him return, either as "head of a corps of gallant French or as a Major Genl. commanding a division of the American Army." He hoped he would bring his wife. "I love every body that is dear to you." He congratulated Lafayette and his wife on their expected child, "this fresh pledge she is about to give you of her love." He made a complete summary of all the operations to October 1779, concluding his letter of the twentieth: "It only remains for me now to beg the favour of you to present my respectful compliments to *your* (but have I not a right, as you say she had made a tender of her love to *me*, to call her *my*) amiable and lovely Marchioness." On December 24 a son was born to the marquise and christened George Washington de Lafayette, names that were to be regarded with horror by the reactionary regimes of Napoleon and the Bourbons.

Partly because of a delay in receiving it, and perhaps from some modesty on his part, Lafayette did not show his letter from Washington to Franklin until he was in France nearly a year. On March 5, 1780, Franklin wrote

Washington that he had only lately received it but he had formed the same regard and esteem for Lafayette that Washington held for him. He continued:

> *Should peace arrive after another campaign or two, and afford us a little leisure, I should be happy to see your Excellency in Europe and to accompany you, if my age and strength would permit, in visiting some of its ancient and most famous kingdoms. You would, on this side of the sea, enjoy the great reputation you have acquired, pure and free from those little shades that the jealousy and envy of a man's countrymen... are ever endeavouring to cast over living merit. Here you would know, and enjoy, what posterity will say of Washington. For a thousand leagues have nearly the same effect with a thousand years... At present I enjoy that pleasure for you; as I frequently hear the old generals of this martial country, who study the maps of America, speak with sincere approbation and great applause of your conduct; and join in giving you the character of one of the greatest captains of the age.*

Washington's generalship—even more than Franklin's diplomatic skills, which could not operate in a vacuum—produced the final financial, naval, and military support of the court of France. Another factor favored the Americans. France was largely fighting a naval war and the army had found little chance for glory. The younger officers in particular were more than anxious to do as Lafayette in America and their attitude influenced the court.

Franklin forwarded to Lafayette the congressional sword inscribed with an account of his battles together with a letter: "By the help of the exquisite artists France affords, I find it easy to express everything but the sense we have of your worth and our obligations to you." Lafayette replied that the "goodness of the United States... far surpasses any idea I could have conceived... In some of the devices I cannot help finding too honourable a reward for those slight services, which, in concert with my fellow soldiers, and under the god-like American Hero's orders, I had the good luck to render. The sight of these actions, where I was a witness of American bravery and patriotic spirit, I shall ever enjoy with that pleasure, which becomes a heart, glowing with love for the nation and the most ardent zeal for their glory and happiness."

Franklin had complained to Congress that they were wasting some of the money lent by France, for he found orders from Philadelphia for tea, gewgaws, and frivolities. (His own daughter did not escape censure when she asked him for feathers from France and he answered: "*Feathers...* feathers, my dear girl, may be had in America from every cock's tail.") When France made a grant of six million livres early in 1780, Franklin was told it was to be spent only by Washington since it might be wasted by the various committees of

Congress. Franklin protested, but very mildly, and forwarded the information to Congress with a note that the giver had the right to make the terms. Congress was outraged at this rather justifiable slap, but, at Washington's insistence, the French minister found a qualifying clause that enabled the legislature to regain control.

In the autumn of 1779 the king tapped Lieutenant General the Comte de Rochambeau to head the French army in America. He had been a soldier since he entered military academy when Washington was eight. Like Washington, he was a colonel at twenty-two. He had served under Saxe, once a famous French marshal; fought at Klostercamp; and became inspector general of the French infantry. He was short and stocky, solid and cool, and a disciplinarian intensely knowledgeable in his profession. He was carefully selected as a man who would be tactful with Americans while maintaining an army of high discipline in a foreign country.

ENGLAND'S TROUBLES

A well-known characteristic of George III and his war ministers was their quite human preference for hearing what they wanted to hear and believing what they wanted to believe. They expected flattery, servility, and reports that cheered. The American Tories, British officers, and courtiers were more than willing to supply these. They contributed to the king's determination to proceed with the war at all costs. His papers are full of reports that the great majority of Americans were loyal to him, the Congress and the French alliance were hated, and the American army was small and starving. All that had to be done was to beat Washington, to destroy the coastal towns, and to get the Indians to provide "a diminution of the number of Americans." Some of the reports were quite accurate—that Washington had been reduced to 3,300 men at the end of 1776, to 6,000 at Morristown, and to 4,000 at Valley Forge. George III may have wondered what the more than 75,000 soldiers, sailors, and marines he had sent to America had been doing and why there were contradictory reports from Sir Henry Clinton claiming that Washington had moved from Valley Forge to Monmouth with an army of 18,000, which grew to 20,000 a month later.

The court might be euphoric and the king in constant expectation that Americans were about to "sue for pardon," but many of his subjects were far more realistic. The growth of royal power and corruption, the prolonged war with its constant increase in loans and taxes, the casualty lists with nothing to show for them, and the sympathy of the best English for the Americans resulted in a continuous growth of opposition that came close to revolution in England.

The defeat in July 1778 of Keppel's fleet by the French, in which, as Sandwich reported to the king, their fleet was badly damaged, shocked British naval pride. A Tory vice admiral, Hugh Palliser, brought charges against Keppel, a Whig, and the affair became a heated political dispute. Keppel had the ardent support of the great Whig lords, two of the king's brothers, and Burke and Fox. When he was acquitted on February 11, 1779, there was a great outburst of popular enthusiasm for the Whigs and a harrying of the Tories. Mobs broke loose and burned Palliser's house to the ground. An attack was made on the houses of North and Germain. The mob then surged over to the admiralty and, as Walpole reported, forced the very frightened Lord Sandwich to flee with his mistress, Martha Ray. A few weeks later, Miss Ray was murdered by a disappointed lover, and the kindly king sent his condolences to the first lord of the admiralty.

From London William Eden wrote Sir Henry Clinton that he had better take every action possible, including the bribing of American leaders, before the mischief makers succeeded in stopping the war. Germain also suggested to Clinton the extensive use of bribes, adding that he would "cheerfully" approve such expenditures.

Resolutions in Parliament denouncing Sandwich for sending Keppel out against a larger French fleet were beaten, but other attacks were made on the Germain ministry. General Grey, who had served with Howe and Clinton, said that the idea of conquering America was impractical, and Lord North told the king that his statement had caused a great stir. Further resolutions petitioning the king to stop the "unnatural war" with America and to withdraw all his forces in order to fight France failed. The king told North on June 11 that there was "but one Sensible, one great line to follow, the being ever ready to make Peace when to be obtained without submitting to terms that in their consequence must annihilate this Empire."

On June 15 North wrote the king that his "faculties of mind & body are daily diminishing, & he is sorry to say, that the difficulties of this country are increasing," and he ought to resign. The king answered that "the times are certainly hazardous, but that ought to rouze the Spirit of Every Englishman to support me." Two days later he received the Spanish declaration of war on England.

In the autumn two cabinet members quit in protest. North continued to be depressed about the war, the dissensions in the cabinet, and the fact that others were permitted to resign. On November 3 he wrote the king that he could not come around to the palace that day "having been detained... by a most material and perplexing public distress arising from the great quantity of bills drawn at New York and Quebec... the greater part of which will become due before Christmas... and there has not yet occurd any method of paying them." The following day Charles Jenkinson reported to the king that the attorney general, after threatening to resign, had decided not to, but he would have nothing to do with Lord North thereafter.

The king told North that he had not treated his fellow cabinet members well and that was why they were quitting. North replied that he had been unhappy in his post for ten years, he had been "criminal" in keeping it, and now he felt miserable and guilty when no one, including the king, approved of his conduct.

A fresh wind in British politics appeared in Yorkshire, where voters overwhelmingly passed a petition to Parliament stating that the great sums voted in the budgets had been squandered and used too often for corrupt purposes. The increase in the power of the Crown was endangering the liberties of the country and it should be curtailed. The Yorkshire Resolves inflamed England. Soon twenty-six English counties endorsed them. Committees of association and correspondence were established in counties, towns, and cities, which voted to send delegates to a general convention. So great was the voice of the country that Parliament could not brush aside the petitions as it had those from Philadelphia.

After a bitter struggle, Parliament, by a majority of eighteen votes, passed the famous resolve of John Dunning: "It is necessary to declare that the influence of the Crown has increased, is increasing, and ought to be diminished." North, in reporting this to the king, said he ought now to quit and that he had been warning him for four years this would occur. The king assured North the resolutions "can by no means be looked on as personal to him; I wish I did not feel at whom they are *personally levelled*." Four days later the king felt more assured and told North: "It is attachment to my Country that alone actuates my purposes and Lord North shall see that at least there is one person willing to preserve unspoiled the most beautiful Combination that was ever formed." The king soon regained control and the Dunning resolution for the moment was the high point of opposition to the Crown.

THE HUDSON

Lord George Germain had informed Sir Henry Clinton in January that the members of the Carlisle commission had given the cabinet "a perfect knowledge of the real state of affairs in America." In consequence Clinton should bring Washington to "a general and decisive action" but in any case drive him back to the Highlands of New York or to New Jersey, whereupon, as the commissioners had reported, the inhabitants would freely return to allegiance to their king. In addition Clinton should continue burning the coastal towns of New England and Virginia and bring renewed Indian raids on the frontier farms. He promised Clinton nearly seven thousand reinforcements in 1779.

On May 5 Clinton sent an expedition to Virginia to ravage the tidewater region. When this force returned, Sir Henry moved up the Hudson on May 30 with six thousand troops and easily took the poorly defended American works at Verplanck's and Stony Points. The British set to work to improve the fortifications. This greatly inconvenienced the American army, whose connection with New England now had to be maintained by a route farther up the Hudson. The move also threatened West Point, which Washington considered the key defense post in America. Washington moved his army to Smith's Clove in Orange County, some fourteen miles west of the West Point area, to meet any attempt Clinton might make on the fort. Not long afterwards he changed his headquarters to New Windsor, near Newburgh, and then to the Moore house, a mile north of West Point.

Clinton left around eleven hundred men at the two forts with orders to make Stony Point a strong fortress. He then moved back to New York and sent a pillaging expedition into Connecticut. Its commanders were William Tryon, former royal governor of New York, and Sir George Collier, a naval commodore who had taken part in the raids on Virginia. They landed near New Haven where, after doing much damage, they were driven off by the militia. They then proceeded to burn down the towns of Fairfield, Norwalk, and Horse Neck (now more elegantly called Greenwich). As a result of their activities, the New England societies for preserving antiquities have had less work to do.

At Washington's request General Parsons made a survey of the damage. He reported that the British at Fairfield had burned 97 houses, 67 barns, 3 churches, 2 schoolhouses, and numerous shops. At Norwalk they destroyed 130 houses, 87 barns, and 2 churches, as well as numerous other buildings. On September 12 Washington wrote Lafayette of the destruction by "the intrepid and magnanimous Tryon who, in defiance of all the opposition... by the Women and Children... of these towns, performed this notable exploit with 2000 brave and generous Britons, adding thereby fresh lustre to their Arms and dignity to their King."

Washington, with no naval force of consequence, could not prevent such raids but the burning of the towns made him anxious to retaliate. He had picked General Wayne to command at Fort Montgomery, five miles north of Stony Point, and urged him to get every intelligence on the work being done there, adding that he had an attack on the fort "much at heart." Wayne selected Captain Allan McLane to go into the fort, under a flag of truce, where he made a rapid assessment of the situation. Wayne, McLane, and Light Horse Harry Lee subsequently held the fort under continual observation. On July 6 Washington himself came over to look at the works. He and Wayne went over all possible means of attack, Washington writing these out in detail. After receiving reports of the destruction in Connecticut, he told Wayne it was "infinitely desirable" that the attack be made in the near future.

Captain McLane's diary report of the July 15 engagement was brief: "At ten o'clock rode with Majors Posey and Lee to reconnoitre the enemy's lines. Genl. Waine moved down from the forest... At 8 o'clock at night moved my company close to the enemy's sentrys... At 30 minutes past 12 o'clock the light infantry began the attack on the lines, Genl. Waine at their head. They rushed on with fixed bayonets and carried the lines in 25 minutes—killed one capt., 21 privates, wounded 4 subalterns, 66 privates, took one colonel, 4 captains, 15 subalterns, 468 men."

At 2 A.M. Wayne sent a dispatch to Washington: "Dear Genl. This fort & Garrison with Coln. Johnson are our's. Our Officers & Men behaved like men who are determined to be free." American casualties were about ninety.

Sir Henry Clinton, greatly shocked, recalled his troops who were planning further raids on Connecticut. The American Tories in New York and London bitterly attacked Clinton for the defeat, while the English Whigs raised horrified hands at his destruction of defenseless towns.

On July 21 Washington sent Wayne's report to Congress with a lengthy letter. He said: "to the encomiums he has deservedly bestowed on the officers and men under his command, it gives me pleasure to add that his own conduct throughout the whole of this arduous enterprise, merits the warmest approbation of Congress. He improved upon the plan recommended by me and executed it in a manner that does signal honour to his judgment and to his bravery. In a critical moment of the assault he received a flesh wound in the head with a musket-ball; but continued leading on his men with unshaken firmness." Washington explained to Congress that he and his engineers had gone over the fortifications after the battle and had decided that Stony Point would need far more troops and materials than he could spare. It would have to be fortified against both land and river and this was too expensive. He had therefore ordered the British guns and supplies removed and the fortifications destroyed.

Washington followed with another blow at the British that was less complete. Light Horse Harry Lee itched to emulate Mad Anthony Wayne. Washington and Lee together planned the attack on Paulus (or Powle's) Hook on the point near the present Jersey City. Several plans that Lee proposed were rejected by Washington as risking too many troops, but they finally agreed on an expedition of four hundred men. It was an impudent plan, to be carried out under the nose of the British garrison at New York and the Royal Navy in the Hudson. The attack was set for shortly after midnight on August 18. A part of the attacking force got lost on the way and the remainder arrived much later than the plan anticipated. Lee pushed through nevertheless, carried the fort by surprise, largely because of British negligence, and took off 158 officers and men.

Congress passed resolutions of high praise for Washington, Wayne, and Lee, awarding the latter two gold medals. According to his usual habit, Washington published to his troops everything but congressional praise of the commander in chief.

CLINTON AND WASHINGTON

The blow at Paulus Hook, only a short distance by water from the great British fortifications on Manhattan, quite unnerved Clinton. Both the army and the Tories blamed him for two humiliating episodes. From Clinton's headquarters Colonel Charles Stuart reported to his father, Lord Bute, that Clinton was "tremendously depressed... His temper from these two unlucky blows... became much soured."

Two days after Lee's raid, Sir Henry Clinton again offered his resignation to Lord George Germain, suggesting that Lord Cornwallis was much more suitable for the command. Cornwallis had departed with the peace commissioners to see his ill wife and had not intended to return. When she died, he found England gloomy and he again offered his services to the king. He returned to America in July and this gave Clinton his chance. Again London refused, saying how badly he was needed in America. With the political troubles at home and the wide criticism of the American war, the government could not afford further resignations by its commanders. Washington was in a much more cheerful mood than Clinton. On August 16 he wrote from West Point to John Cochran, one of his army physicians:

I have asked Mrs. Cockran and Mrs. Livingston to dine with me to morrow; but ought I not to apprize them of their fare?...

It is needless to premise that my table is large enough to hold the ladies... To say how it is usually covered is rather more essential... Since our arrival at this happy spot, we have had a Ham (sometimes a shoulder) of Bacon, to grace the head of the table; a piece of roast Beef adorns the foot; and a small dish of Greens or Beans (almost imperceptible) decorates the center.

When the Cook has a mind to cut a figure (and this I presume he will attempt to do to morrow) we have two Beefsteak Pyes, or dishes of Crabs, in addition one on each side the center dish, dividing the distance between dish and dish to about Six feet, which without them, would be near twelve a part. Of late, he has had the surprizing luck to discover that apples make pyes; and it's a question if amidst the violence of his efforts, we do not get one of apples instead of having both of Beef.

If the ladies can put up with such entertainment and will submit to partake of it on plates, once tin but now Iron; (not become so by the labour of scowering) I shall be happy to see them.

INTELLIGENCE

Washington, aided by his small special congressional fund, continued to develop his intelligence apparatus. He informed Congress that he often had to use "ambiguous characters," and to let them carry goods in to the enemy, as "cover to their mission." However some of them had been picked up for violating state laws against trading with the enemy; he had then to intervene to save them from prosecution but he thereby lost their services. He developed an unexpected talent in writing crude dialogue to be used by his double agents:

Where is Mr. Washington and what number of men has he with him?

Cant tell the number exactly. Some says eight thousand and very knowing has ten thousand. I dont think he has 8000 with himself, besides the Jersey Brigade, another brigade at which I hear is at Paramus…

Whether there is any discontent among the soldiers.

I cant say theres much discontent among the sodgers, tho' their Money is so bad. They get plenty of provisions and have got better cloes now than ever they had. They are very well off only for hatts. They give them a good deal of rum and whiskey, and this I suppose helps with the lies their officers are always telling them…

PS dont send your next letter by the same hand, for I have reason to be suspitious. I would not send this by him. When he left me he went strait to Washingtons head quarters.

He instructed "Samuel Culper, Sr." (Abraham Woodhull), through Benjamin Tallmadge, to try to get his messages out through New Jersey instead of the slower Long Island-Connecticut route, to note the numbers of each British regiment moving, whether they were being recruited, and what they were doing with their wagons and horses. He had observers on the Jersey coast to watch all enemy ship movements. He heard that Lord Cornwallis was back in New York within two days of his arrival.

To one of his double agents, operating within Clinton's command, Washington wrote on August 12 requesting that he report to Clinton that Washington had about 18,000 men present and fit for duty, plus another 2,000 levies on the way. He had arranged for more who could be assembled at any time. He had sufficient boats on hand to transport 5,000 of these troops. Washington had, in reality, about 9,500 rank and file on hand, fit for duty. It is not clear whether Sir Henry Clinton's greatly exaggerated reports to London of Washington's strength were in consequence of these false reports, or whether Clinton enlarged them in order to draw reinforcements from England.

"Samuel Culper, Jr." (Robert Townsend) was particularly asked not to change his employment but to be "under cover of his usual business." This was the merchant firm of Oakman and Townsend, which supplied British ships. Both "Culpers" were provided with a secret ink developed by Sir James Jay that could be brought to light only by use of another chemical. They were instructed by Washington to use good paper and to write ordinary business and family letters "in the Tory stile," and to use almanacs and ledger books with blank space for the secret ink. Washington referred to Culper, Jr., whom he did not know, as "the old gentleman," though Townsend was only twenty-five. Washington frequently praised the reports of these two most trusted agents who reported for years from enemy-held territory.

Philadelphia was the one place from which Washington could get little information. On August 1, 1779, he wrote to Edmund Randolph, a member of Congress from Virginia, to say: "I shall be happy in such communications as your leizure... will permit you to transmit me, for I am as totally unacquainted with the political state of things, and what is going forward in the great National Council, as if I was an alien; when a competent knowledge of the temper and designs of our Allies... and the complexion of Affairs in Europe might, as they ought to do, have a considerable influence on the operations of our Army, and would, in many cases, determine the propriety of measures which, under a cloud of darkness, can only be groped at."

GENERAL ARNOLD

Benedict Arnold had been in trouble with his accounts and handling of government property almost since he had entered the service. As soon as he became military commander of Philadelphia, he made an agreement with the army's clothier general, James Mease, about whose incompetence Washington had long complained. This agreement provided that a portion of the goods bought with public funds for the army's account would be sold in what was essentially a grey market. The public would be reimbursed the original purchase price and Arnold and his confrere would pocket the difference. There were also opportunities for trading with the British, who paid for supplies in good money at New York. It is probable that Arnold also used wagons, requisitioned from the state by his authority, for transporting his goods. He gave a pass to a Miss Hannah Levy, who was trading with the enemy, to proceed to New York; she had been associated with David Franks, who had been arrested for passing intelligence to the British.

Arnold was considered by many in Philadelphia to be too close to the Tories there. He married Elizabeth Shippen, a friend of Captain John André, aide to Sir Henry Clinton. Amidst all this smoke, the Pennsylvania council, headed by Joseph Reed, brought charges in Congress against Arnold for giving Miss Levy a pass, using requisitioned wagons for his purposes, and other misdemeanors. As usual any problem was dumped onto Washington and he, at the insistence of Congress, had to order Arnold court-martialed. This he did a few days after Arnold's marriage. Because of rapid army movements the court could not sit until the end of the year.

Exactly when Arnold decided that the British paid better is not known. Carl Van Doren, in his classic *Secret History of the American Revolution*, believes it may have been late in 1778 but that his first overtures to the British took place not long after Washington issued his court-martial order. Sir Henry Clinton handed the assignment of dealing with Arnold to Captain André, who headed British intelligence. André had done the millinery and costumes for the Meschianza ball in Philadelphia and while there got to know Peggy Arnold quite well. Working with André was another intelligence officer, Captain George Beckwith, aide to the German General Knyphausen in New York. In corresponding with André and Beckwith, Arnold first called himself "Monk," after the general who turned from the Puritans to the Cavaliers and thereby earned a dukedom. He later used "Gustavus" after the Swedish king who freed his country from the Danes.

Arnold offered to supply André with intelligence but information meant fighting Washington and this was not what the British craved. André made this clear very early in the correspondence. He wanted Arnold to surrender an army with an important post, offering to pay two guineas per American head. This was a very cheap method of winning. To this point, each American killed, wounded, or captured had cost the British treasury over three thousand guineas. From the beginning, Arnold insisted on a proper reward if he succeeded and on ten thousand pounds if he failed. There was much haggling over this latter point for more than a year. In the meantime Arnold continued to transmit valuable information as an evidence of good faith.

When Sir Henry Clinton went with André to South Carolina in December 1778, the negotiations temporarily broke off but resumed the following year. That same month Arnold had his court-martial. One of the charges preferred by Pennsylvania was that he had been too friendly to Tories. Since Reed was the prime mover, Arnold replied in court: "I can with boldness say to my persecutors... and to the chief of them... that in the hour of danger, when the affairs of America wore a gloomy aspect, when our illustrious General was retreating through New Jersey with a handful of men, I did not propose to my associates basely to quit the General, and sacrifice the cause of my country, by going over to the enemy... I can say I never basked in the sunshine of my General's favour, and courted him to his face, when I was at the same time treating him with the greatest disrespect and villifying his character when absent."

Though he put in an energetic defense, Arnold was convicted on two charges and ordered reprimanded by the commander in chief. Not until April 1780 did all the papers go through the court to Washington, then to Congress, and back to Washington. In public orders Washington noted that he would have preferred to commend Arnold, but he now had to declare that his conduct had been imprudent and improper. With this light sentence, Arnold was free to take a command, but he did not request one until summer.

SULLIVAN AND THE INDIANS

Sullivan had been a rather tempestuous and none too lucky general, and there were protests when he was selected to head the campaign against the Indians. Washington answered that he had to work with the material available and with due respect to seniority. He would have preferred Schuyler but neither he nor Gates wanted the job.

Sullivan, after taking command on March 6, complained of everything, including his lack of intelligence, troops, supplies, boats, roads, maps, boots, uniforms, and money. He was, in fact, handed a difficult assignment: to march from eastern Pennsylvania through the wilderness to the Finger Lakes of New York, and to coordinate with New York forces moving west and troops marching from Fort Pitt northward. He complained so much that Congress, the Pennsylvania council, and, finally, Washington, found him exasperating. Some of Sullivan's complaints to Congress were forwarded to Washington, who had worked with great energy on plans, intelligence, and supplies for the expedition. On August 15 and 21 Washington sent long replies to Congress, with copies of much of his extensive correspondence preparing for the expedition. He said: "I am sorry to find... Genl. Sullivan... has mistaded several particulars of importance, and that in providing for his own justification in case of misfortune, he had left the matter upon such a footing as to place me in a delicate situation." He quoted Sullivan as saying: "The plan for carrying on the expedition was not agreeable to his mind, nor were the number of men for it sufficient." Washington noted that he wanted "to have two bodies, each superior to the whole force of the enemy" and this was not practical. Sullivan said he had finally gotten supplies for General James Clinton's army in the north, but in fact Washington had ordered these months before. He also complained that his men were bare; Washington quoted his orders or authorizations for 10,000 pairs of shoes, 3,500 shirts, and large supplies of overalls. Though a complainer, Sullivan drove through the final expedition with dispatch. On October 17 Washington issued general orders to his troops:

> *The Commander in Chief has now the pleasure to congratulate the Army on the complete and full success of General Sullivan... against the Senecas and other tribes of the six Nations... Their whole country has been overrun and laid waste and they themselves compelled to place their own security in a precipitate flight to the British fortress at Niagara... The whole of this has been done with a loss of less than 40 men on our part, including the killed, wounded and captured and those that died natural deaths.*

CABAL

Sullivan resigned from the army in December, for reasons of health and because his criticisms of Congress and the board of war had made him many enemies. In his farewell letter to Washington, he referred to a speech made by Colonel William Tudor in Boston in March 1779. Tudor had been John Adams' law clerk. Presumably owing to Adams' influence he was made judge advocate of the army in 1775, wherein he acted as Adams' eyes and ears. The pair thereafter exchanged gossipy letters on the faults of the army and its generals.

Tudor's speech raised the danger signal that a popular general, at the head of a victorious army, might be even more threatening to America than the British tyrant. Others had already cried that Washington was not only too popular but also too virtuous and good, which made him even more danger-ous. Sullivan wrote to Washington on December 1: "Permit me to inform your Excellency, that the faction raised against you in 1777, into which General Conway was unfortunately and imprudently drawn, is not yet destroyed. The members are waiting to collect strength and seize some favorable moment to appear in force. I speak not from conjecture but from certain knowledge. Their plan is to take every method of proving the danger arising from a com-mander who enjoys the full and intimate confidence of his army... They will endeavor to convert your virtue into arrows with which they will seek to wound you... If you will take the trouble to read Mr. Tudors oration... you will find every line calculated to answer this purpose: The words are Tudor's but the thoughts are borrowed... The next step is to persuade congress that the military power of America should be placed in three or four different hands, each having a separate quarter of the continent assigned him, each comman-der to answer to congress only for his conduct. This, they say, will prevent one aspiring commander from enslaving his country and put it in the power of congress, with the assistance of the commanders, to punish the attempt... The present time is unfavorable to their designs, they well know that the voice of citizens and soldiers would be almost unanimously against them... I am well convinced that they cannot succeed, yet I thought it my duty, in the moment of my departure, to give your Excellency this notice... Could you have believed four years since that those adulators, those persons so tenderly and so friendly used as were General Gates, Mifflin, Reed, and Tudor, would become your secret and bitter, though unprovoked enemies." Washington replied to Sullivan on December 1:

I assure you, my Dear Sir, I am sensibly touched by so striking an instance of your friendship...

I am particularly indebted to you for the interesting information you give me of the views of a certain party. Against intrigues of this kind, incident to every man in a public station, his best support will be a faithful discharge of his duty, and he must rely on the justice of his country for the event.

I flatter myself it is unnecessary for me to repeat to you how high a place you hold in my esteem. The confidence you have experienced, and the manner in which you have been employed on several important occasions, testify the value I set upon your military qualifications and the regret I must feel that circumstances have deprived the army of your services.

The French also picked up stories similar to Sullivan's. The marquis de Fleury, who had been commended by Washington and Wayne and given a medal by Congress for bravery at Stony Point, reported to France that New England and Pennsylvania were again pushing Gates as a rival to Washington. He added that Congress was "eternally barking" that Washington had too godlike a virtue.

On April 16, 1780, the new French minister, the chevalier de La Luzerne, informed his foreign minister that members of Congress, in expressing fear of Washington's influence, spoke of "his virtues as an additional reason for taking alarm." By June the opposition in Congress was strong enough to place Gates in command in the South, without consulting the commander in chief.

WASHINGTON ON THE 1779 CAMPAIGN

Washington continued to send long, chatty letters to his friends about the campaign and future prospects. On October 25 he wrote from West Point to Benjamin Harrison in Virginia:

The Pennsylvania Gazettes… will have conveyed official accts. to the public of all occurrances of any importance… It may not be amiss to observe that, except the plundering expedition to Virginia and the burning one in Connecticut, the enemy have wasted another campaign… in their ship-bound Islands and strong-holds, without doing a single thing advancive of the end in view, unless by delays and placing their whole dependance in the depreciation of our money, and the wretched management of our finances, they expect to accomplish it.

In the meanwhile they have suffered, I do not know what other term to give it, a third part of the Continental Troops which altogether were inferior to theirs, to be employed in the total destruction of all the Country inhabited by the hostile tribes of the Six Nations, their good and faithful Allies! While the other two thirds… confined them within very circumscribed bounds, at the same time bestowing an immensity of labour on this Post, more important to us, considered in all its consequences, than any other in America.

There is something so truly unaccountable in all this that I do not know how to reconcile it with their own views, or to any principle of common sense… The latter end of May… Genl. Clinton moved up to Kings-ferry in force, and possessed himself of Stony and Verplanks Points... since which these Posts have changed Masters frequently, and after employing the enemy a whole campaign, costing them near a thousand men... and infinite labour, is at length in Status-quo...

It is now 30 days since Congress gave me official notice of Count D'Estaing's intended co-operation, and no authentic acct. of him is since come to hand. The probability therefore is that we shall have hot work in a cold season.

D'ESTAING AWAITED

When Washington heard that a French fleet was on its way north from the West Indies, he redoubled his efforts to get information from New York and Clinton's headquarters. He also had observers on the coastal points looking hopefully for the fleet. He drew up intelligence and operating plans and had French officers and Alexander Hamilton ready to dash to sea with them. D'Estaing, however, got no farther north than Georgia.

In the meantime, the governor of Jamaica, expecting d'Estaing to attack him, had sent an urgent appeal to Clinton to send relief troops. Clinton dispatched Lord Cornwallis south with four thousand men but they got very quick word that d'Estaing was heading for the American coast. The British fleet returned to New York. Clinton decided to gather all his forces into New York for a stout defense. He abandoned his outposts on the Hudson. He also pulled his ships and nearly four thousand men from Newport to New York, a move that opened the harbor to its later use by the French fleet.

Gates was in command at Rhode Island and was, as usual, slow in transmitting this major development to Washington. In his restrained way Washington sent Gates a note, with very veiled sarcasm, that he had word of the British evacuation but "not hearing from you I have concluded that your express had met with some accident." Later he received a report from Gates, but the officer messenger had not come by his headquarters, explaining that he had to take this important intelligence to Congress. In acknowledging Gates' letter, Washington said he regretted not having been able to ask the officer for details. He added another quiet prod: "Altho' your letter is silent upon the subject, I cannot doubt that you are on the march before this for Hartford... Indeed I hoped the instant the Enemy had embarked that you would have pushed the Troops on." On November 1 Washington wrote to Edmund Pendleton, another Virginia friend:

I will, while my eyes are turning Southwardly (impatiently looking for or expecting to hear something decisively of Count d'Estaing) make my acknowledgements for [your letter]...

Stony Point which has been a bone of contention the whole campaign... is totally evacuated. Rhode Island is also abandoned and the enemys whole force is drawn to a point at New York...

...Another Campaign having been wasted; having had their Arms disgraced, and all their projects blasted, it may be conceiv'd that the enemy, like an enraged Monster summoning his whole strength, will make some violent effort, if they should be relieved from their present apprehension of the French fleet. If they do not detach for the West Indies (and I do not see how this is practical while they remain inferior at Sea) they must from the disagreeableness of their situation, feel themselves under a kind of necessity of attempting some bold, enterprizing stroke, to give, in some degree, eclat to their Arms, spirits to the Tories, and hope to the Ministry.

Washington's prediction turned out to be accurate. The wounded British lion from this point on showed unexpected ferocity. The next eighteen months were the most bitter of all the war years for America. The British came close to cutting off the South and New England both by sea and by the Hudson. Had these operations succeeded, a new British invasion was scheduled from Canada into western New York and Pennsylvania. Further attacks were planned on Baltimore and Philadelphia.

D'ESTAING IS BEATEN

The French regarded the West Indies as more important than the United States and this was a major defect in the alliance. Whenever the French could spare ships for American waters, they did so for very brief periods only, as when d'Estaing first appeared off New England and then sailed for the Indies. It happened again at Savannah. It was also to happen at Yorktown when the French fleet just barely gave Washington time to effect a successful siege.

Congress had dispatched General Benjamin Lincoln to Charleston to command its defense. He arrived there with reserve troops in time to break a British attack on the city in May 1779. Savannah, however, and much of Georgia, remained in British hands. The South Carolinians appealed to d'Estaing in the West Indies to aid a combined land and sea assault on the port. D'Estaing agreed, provided that he had American supporting troops. He arrived off Savannah on September 8 with 22 ships of the line, 11 frigates, and 100 transports with some 5,000 troops. Lincoln marched from Charleston with around 1,600 continentals, to which were added Casimir Pulaski's cavalry of 500. Other American militia came in during the attack. Defending the city were 2,500 of the enemy, to which were added about 800 rushed from nearby Beaufort.

D'Estaing began the regulation eighteenth-century siege, which could be calculated with precision but which also gave time to the Savannah garrison to strengthen its defenses. Although it got under way a little more than two weeks after d'Estaing's arrival, it was not fully ready to operate until October 3. D'Estaing, with an anxious eye on possible storms or hurricanes and on British activity in the Caribbean, decided on October 9 to abandon the siege and make a direct assault on the town. The attackers were beaten back with a loss of more than eight hundred in killed and wounded. On October 20 the French departed for the West Indies. Washington termed it a "disaster."

General Lincoln sent John Laurens north with a full account and pleas for help. Laurens, Washington's former aide, had volunteered for duty in South Carolina when his own state was threatened. Washington ordered his Virginia and North Carolina troops to march the long distance from West Point to Charleston. He told Lincoln they could be "ill spared" but he would do what he could. At the same time he ordered the New England and New York militia, whom he had summoned in hope that D'Estaing would proceed north, to return home.

Sir Henry Clinton called the British victory "the greatest event that has happened the whole war." He began preparations for what was most unusual for the British, a large-scale winter campaign in the South.

WINTER AT MORRISTOWN

Washington established his quarters in the Jacob Ford house in Morristown on December 1. Those weather experts, the oldest inhabitants, had complained that the summer of 1778 was the hottest on record. Now they were to have new tales, for the winter of 1779–1780 was the severest of the eighteenth century and perhaps in the history of the United States. Valley Forge is the most famous of the war winters but Morristown was even crueler.

The winter began early. In January it was sixteen below zero in New York. The New Jersey rivers were ice three feet thick. The Hudson River and New York Bay were so solidly frozen that cavalry and cannon crossed from Manhattan to New Jersey and Staten Island. Undrifted snow was four feet deep in New Jersey. Dr. Thacher's January journal noted: "The weather for several days has been remarkably cold and stormy. On the 3d... we experienced one of the most tremendous snow-storms ever remembered; no man could endure its violence many minutes without danger of his life. Several marquees were torn asunder and blown down over the officers' heads in the night, and some of the soldiers were actually covered in their tents and buried like sheep under the snow."

To add to the misery of weather, which prevented supplies from reaching the troops, there had been a severe drought that summer. The water mills for grinding flour had dried up and there were few reserves. Washington reported to Congress on January 5 that "the late violent storm has so blocked up the Roads that it will be some days before the scanty supplies in this quarter can be brought to camp. The Troops, both Officers and Men have borne their distress with a patience scarcely to be conceived. Many of the latter have been without meat entirely and short of bread and none but on very scanty supplies." Washington had to order the horses' corn fodder served to his troops, preferring to let the animals starve.

In desperation, Washington appealed to the civil authorities in every county of New Jersey to ask the inhabitants to help feed his starving men. He told his officers that he would, if necessary, requisition the food, but he would avoid this until the last possible minutes. The inhabitants, many of them poor and with very little themselves, gave everything asked. Washington wrote General Schuyler on January 30:

> We have had the virtue and patience of the army put to the severest trial... I hardly thought it possible that we should be able to keep it together, nor could it have been done but for the exertions of the Magistrates in the several counties of this state, on whom I was obliged to call, [and] expose our situation... I allotted to each county a certain proportion of flour or grain and a certain number of cattle... and for the honour of the Magistrates and good disposition of the people I must add that my requisitions were punctually complied with and in many Counties exceeded... At one time the Soldiers ate every kind of horse food but Hay.

Washington was so distressed that he became waspish, and Greene, his quartermaster general, suffered. Martha Washington reached Morristown just after Christmas, in time for the great blizzards. A few days later Mrs. Greene, pregnant, came to camp with her small son, George Washington. Greene constructed a kitchen for his wife but had not, after repeated requests, built one for Washington's wife and staff. Washington fired a note to Greene on January 22:

> I have been at my prest. Quarters since the 1st. Of Decr. and have not a Kitchen to

Cook a Dinner in, altho' the Logs have been put together some considerable time by my own Guard... Eighteen belonging to my family and all Mrs. Fords are crowded together in her Kitchen and scarce one of them able to speak for the colds they have caught.

I have repeatedly taken notice of this inconveniency... and have been told that boards were not to be had. I acquiesced... To share a common lot and participate [in] the inconveniencies which the Army... are obliged to undergo has, with me, been a fundamental principle; and while I conceived this to be the case universally, I was perfectly content; that it is not so, I [appeal] to your own observation...

Equally opposed is it to my wishes that you should be troubled in matters respecting my accomodations, further than to give the necessary orders and furnish materials, without which orders are nugatory; from what you said I am fully satisfied that the persons to whom you entrusted the business are alone to blame; for certain I am they might, by attention, have obtained (equally with others) as many boards as would have answered my purposes long 'ere this.

Greene in February, having asked Washington for money for supplies, was told there was not a dollar in the military chest. At this time Greene wrote to Joseph Reed, head of the Pennsylvania council, to say that "a southern gentleman" was severely criticizing his state for not supplying food to save the army. He asked Reed not to mention the source from which he had this information. "I have difficulties enough without adding to them."

The weather was still bitter in March. On the eighteenth Washington wrote Lafayette that he had sent North Carolina and Virginia troops to Charleston, "but the extreme cold, the deep Snows and other impediments have retarded the progress of the march. The oldest people now living in this country do no remember so hard a Winter... The severity of the frost exceeded anything of the kind that had ever been experienced in this climate before."

That winter Congress practically ceased to function as a legislature. Its currency and credit were nearly worthless. Thereafter, Congress merely issued requests, which Washington described as timid, to the various states for troops and supplies. On March 26 he bluntly told Congress that the supplies requested were far below the minimum needs of the army and that there was no power to enforce the requisitions. On the following day Washington estimated his total northern army strength at 10,400 rank and file but the terms of service of around 2,500 were about to expire. In spite of this, he decided on April 4 to send his Maryland and Delaware lines south to aid in the defense of Charleston.

The French minister reported to Versailles that, in his judgement, not only were American finances disordered, but the supply services were so swollen that they employed "nine thousand men... receiving enormous salaries who devour the army's substance while it is suffering from famine."

FALL OF CHARLESTON

On Boxing Day 1779, just before the harbor froze, Sir Henry Clinton and Lord Cornwallis left New York with more than a hundred ships and transports, five thousand seamen, and eight thousand rank and file. The ill winds that were blowing so bitterly at Morristown also blew at sea. Many of the ships and transports foundered, including one carrying Clinton's artillery. Clinton also lost most of his cavalry and transport horses on the way. Not until February 11 did the first of the ships put into the Savannah River. Clinton stripped the navy of many of its guns and ordered replacements of supplies, horses, and powder from the Bahamas, Saint Augustine, and Jamaica.

After learning that Lincoln intended a serious defense of Charleston, Clinton called for Lord Rawdon to bring more troops from New York. After providing a jolly St. Patrick's Day dinner—where the volunteers of Ireland sang that, like the good saint, they would drive the rebellious vermin from the land—Rawdon sailed for Charleston with three thousand reinforcements. By the time Clinton was ready to move, he had an army of more than ten thousand rank and file, in addition to the navy.

Lincoln, in command at Charleston, was moderately experienced but not very able. After learning on January 23, from a captured British transport, that Clinton was coming south with ninety sail, he wrote Washington: "It is, my dear Sir, among my first misfortunes that I am not near enough to your Excellency to have the advantage of your advice and direction. I feel my own insufficiency and want of experience. I can promise you nothing but a disposition to serve my country."

Lincoln had only a small naval force. His continentals were few, at first no more than twelve hundred but reinforcements, slowly drifting in from the north brought them to more than two thousand. South and North Carolina provided militia but when their enlistment period ended, they went home. Lincoln had trouble getting powder and arms from the state government, which insisted on orders from Congress.

By March 15 John Laurens was writing Washington a lengthy and accurate appraisal of the situation, referring in his letter to a map of Charleston that he knew the general had. He pointed out that it was going to be nearly impossible to stop the enemy navy from passing the bar at the harbor and that the fortifications to the north at Charleston Neck were incomplete. He appealed to Washington to come in person to save the situation. On April 26 Washington replied: "The impracticability of defending the bar, I fear amounts to the loss of the town and garrison... The propriety of defending the town depended on the probability of defending the bar, and when this ceased, the attempt ought to have been relinquished."

After explaining that the disorders in the northern army were such that he could not leave nor could he propose such a move to Congress, he added: "Be assured my dear Laurens that I am extremely sensible to the expressions of your attachment and that I feel all for you in your present situation which the warmest friendship can dictate. I am confident you will do your duty and in doing it you must run great hazards. May success attend you, and restore you with fresh laurels to your friends, to your Country, and to me. With every sentiment of regard and Affection."

By March 29 Clinton was a mile from the forts on the neck. On April 8 Admiral Arbuthnot's fleet moved across the bar into the harbor. A strangling network was drawn around the city, cutting its food supplies. On April 14 American cavalry guarding an escape route in the north were beaten by Colonel Banastre Tarleton's dragoons. On May 12, after long negotiations, Lincoln and his army surrendered. Clinton counted as prisoners some 5,500 men, but he did this by including all males of military age in the town. The Continental Army prisoners, including the sick, were somewhat over 2,000, with perhaps another 2,000 militia. Each side lost under 300 in killed and wounded. It was the most classic and best conducted British victory and the worst American defeat of the war.

The British military forces, on taking the city, engaged in wholesale official and private looting. The division of spoils between the Royal Army and Navy was still being disputed in London while Washington was serving his second term as president.

With most of the southern American army captured, Clinton easily established posts across the interior of South Carolina, to add to those in Georgia. A detachment of the Virginia line under Colonel Abraham Buford, which had made the weary march from West Point through the bitter winter and snows encountered Tarleton's cavalry at Waxhaws near the South Carolina border. They were quickly beaten and surrendered. More than half the men were killed immediately or so badly wounded they died within a few days. Thereafter Tarleton was known as the Butcher. South Carolina was now under the king's peace.

LONDON

No news could have been more timely for London or well received than the fall of Charleston. Lord George Germain wrote Clinton on the fourth anniversary of American independence that the victory was "glorious" and had given "his Majesty the highest satisfaction."

The king needed cheering. The British lower classes, not represented at all in Parliament, had parodied the polite petitioning rebellion of the upper classes by erupting in mob action in June. Technically the cause was a protest against parliamentary bills to relieve the disabilities of Roman Catholics. As Trevelyan noted, the gathering mobs had fewer and fewer good Protestants and more and more bad citizens. The lower classes had long been harassed by harsh penal laws, press gangs, rising prices, and higher taxes. Many of the imposts added by North each year fell on such necessities of the poor as candles, salt, sugar, and beer.

The London mobs, stimulated by Lord George Gordon, grew in size and then in venom. They surged to Whitehall and attacked the House of Lords. Many lords, including two members of the king's cabinet and the archbishop of York, were roughed up and two peers nearly killed. Lord Mansfield's house and those of three London judges were burned to the ground. The prime minister's house and the Bank of England were attacked. Huge fires burned for several nights. Nearly three hundred persons were killed and many more wounded. The riot was finally suppressed by the king and army. Twenty-three of those involved were hanged. Gordon was clapped in the tower, where he was joined in October by Henry Laurens, who had been captured by the British. Charleston and the Gordon riots combined temporarily to strengthen the king's hands in domestic and foreign policy. He now could persuade many that the war was proceeding with success in America and that domestic opposition was a form of revolution. In addition, following the fall of Charleston, he received a peace feeler from the French prime minister.

On August 3 Germain wrote Clinton: "The reduction of the whole Province [of South Carolina] and the concurrence of all our accounts from the provinces in rebellion of the distress of the inhabitants and their anxious desire to return to the King's obedience, together with the reduced state of Mr. Washington's force, the decay of the power of Congress, and the total failure of their paper money, open a flattering prospect of a speedy and happy termination of the American war. Your able and vigorous conduct in your respective commands [warring general and peace commissioner] leaves no room to apprehend anything will be wanting to accelerate this happy event."

WASHINGTON, I AM HERE

Here I am, my dear general, and, in the midst of the joy I feel in finding myself again one of your loving soldiers, I take but the time of telling you that I came from France on board a fregatt which the king gave me for my passage. I have affairs of the utmost importance I should at first comunicate to you alone... Tomorrow we go up to the town, and the day after I'll set off in my usual way to join my beloved and respected friend and General... Adieu...

Lafayette.

Writing this in Boston Harbor on April 27, he thus informed the surprised Washington of his return. Boston, too, had not known he was coming but the word passed fast. When Lafayette got off the ship, nearly the whole town was out cheering. The church bells rang, the cannon boomed, and he was hauled in a coach through immense crowds to John Hancock's house on Boston Common. By May 10 he was at Morristown with a full report of the French military and naval reinforcements on their way. After their conference Washington sent Lafayette directly to Congress to arrange American cooperation with the French forces.

The army's distresses increased the nearer Rochambeau approached the coast. On May 26 Washington wrote that the army was meatless and for the first time troops had mutinied. The Connecticut line decided to go home to eat. He informed Governor Trumbull that his state's troops were finally persuaded to stay but he did not know how long he could keep starving men in camp. He wrote Congress that in addition to having no food, they had not been paid for five months and could not even attempt to buy rations.

To Joseph Jones, a member of Congress, Washington wrote on May 31: "I see one head gradually changing into thirteen; I see one Army branching into thirteen; and instead of looking up to Congress as the supreme controuling power of the United States are considering themselves as dependent on their respective States... I see the powers of Congress declining too fast for the consequence and respect which is due them as the grand representative body of America, and I am fearful of the consequences of it."

By June 20 Washington was writing anguished but polite letters to Congress saying the French would expect plans for cooperation and attack, but he had heard nothing of the supplies and troops he could expect from the states. He could make no plans, therefore, though American "honor and reputation" were at stake as well as "the justice and gratitude due our allies." He added an especially distressed note that his men were without shirts or overalls. He found "mortifying" and "distressing" the prospect of marching an American army as naked as savages before the elegant French. On June 30 he pleaded with the governors of all states north of Maryland to forward their recruits since he had only a handful of men in his army. On July 4 Washington wrote to the head of New Hampshire that, six weeks after the states had been called upon for recruits, only thirty had shown up.

THE SUMMER

If anything, Lord George Germain had underestimated the troubles facing Washington in 1780. Although Clinton reported to London in July that Washington had an army of twelve thousand, the American commander had only thirty-two hundred men fit for duty.

Sir Henry Clinton returned to New York on June 18, covered with laurels. There he was informed that General von Knyphausen, upon hearing of Washington's general plight and of the mutiny, had sent five thousand men to Springfield, New Jersey, eight miles from the main American base at Morristown. The militia were able to drive them back to Connecticut Farms (now Union, New Jersey), where the British and German forces burned a church, a parsonage, and a number of houses. Knyphausen was then forced back to the coast.

Clinton, while in Charleston, had been planning just such an attack, to be undertaken on his return, but the British high command in America had now begun to disintegrate. The frigate, bringing Clinton's plans, was mistaken for an enemy ship and driven from New York by the Royal Navy. Many transports carrying troops ran aground in a fog near New York. Clinton, on his arrival, found that, instead of his planned all-out war against Washington, he had to rescue Knyphausen. In this situation he received a message from Benedict Arnold that French troops and naval forces were on their way to America. Clinton, perturbed by this news, felt no part of New Jersey could be held. He ordered a diversionary move up the Hudson to Verplanck's Point, but finding that Admiral Arbuthnot had given his fleet entirely different sailing orders, he abandoned the plan.

In the meantime Washington, alarmed for the safety of West Point and Morristown, moved with part of his troops to Pompton, which would bring him within fairly quick marching distance to the Hudson. Knyphausen made one last effort at attack, again reaching Springfield, where he was routed by Greene and his continentals, together with the local militia. He retreated to Staten Island. Sir Henry was furious when he found that the whole futile business had cost the British more losses than they had suffered in taking Charleston.

On July 10, Rochambeau, his fifty-one hundred troops, and eight ships of the line under Admiral the Chevalier de Ternay, arrived off Newport and began their disembarkation. They were rather coldly received by the town, which had been occupied by Americans and then British and again by Americans, but General Heath in command at Boston soon appeared to see that they were warmly welcomed. He wrote Washington that he was "charmed" by the French officers.

Before they landed, Washington had one more diplomatic problem. On May 24 he had ordered Dr. James Craik, his personal physician and head of the army's hospital services, to set up a medical service for the French in Providence. He asked the governor of Rhode Island to help, assuring him that the French would reimburse the state in hard money for any expenses. The French commissary, Louis Ethis De Corny, went with Craik to help organize the hospital. The state government, because of Washington's interest, assigned the French the Rhode Island College building, now Brown's University Hall. This caused a great uproar and no end of trouble for De Corny. The college president, the Reverend James Manning, excitedly warned that Providence would soon be infected with French diseases. Two members of the Brown family, Nicholas and Joseph, declared that the citizens of the town ought to blow up the hospital. They threatened the carpenters who were at work with loss of employment and suits for damages. De Corny had to pacify the workers with bonds of indemnification. He complained to Washington, who apologized for the "reprehensible" conduct of the persons connected with the college.

Washington's foresight had been fortunate, since more than twenty-three hundred French soldiers and sailors, most of whom had been on board ship for ninety days, were hospitalized with scurvy. Till they could recover the French forces were much weakened.

On July 13 Rear Admiral Thomas Graves, who had been dispatched in a hurry by Lord Sandwich to intercept the French fleet, arrived off New York with six ships of the line, having crossed much more quickly than the French. Vice Admiral Marriot Arbuthnot thus acquired heavy naval superiority over de Ternay's fleet.

By this time Washington's intelligence service had become more effective than Sir Henry Clinton's. The British service under Captains André and Beckwith was, at this point, more interested in playing Benedict Arnold on its line than in arranging to fight. Washington learned on July 15 of the arrival of Graves' ships, but Clinton did not hear until July 18 that the French had landed eight days earlier in Newport. This gave the allies much needed time to begin their fortifications before Clinton could start to make plans. Fortunate for them also was the bad blood existing between Clinton and Arbuthnot, which made their cooperation minimal at a critical period. With their superior fleet the British by July 21 had established an effective blockade of Newport, but they had not coordinated their plans with Clinton.

Washington had expected large French supplies of arms and powder but he heard on July 22 that these had not arrived with the fleet. That day he begged the state of Connecticut to lend him arms. He also wrote Lafayette: "Another thing that gives me concern is the non-arrival of our arms and powder... With every effort we can make we shall fall short by at least four or five thousand arms, and two hundred tons of powder. We must, of necessity, my Dear Marquis, however painful it is to abuse the generosity of our friends, know of the French, whether they can assist us with a loan of that quantity." On July 24 Washington learned that Clinton had embarked on an expedition against Rochambeau. By July 27 he was marching his troops from New Jersey to the east bank of the Hudson. Washington planned to move south as rapidly as possible to King's Bridge in order to strike at New York if Clinton moved a major portion of his forces to Newport. When Clinton got into a dispute with Admiral Arbuthnot and returned to New York, Washington recrossed the Hudson.

GREENE RESIGNS

General Greene, who had been an effective quartermaster general, but now was without money or credit, had complained to Congress. After the representatives recommended changes in his organization, he resigned. His letter was abrupt enough for Congress to be incensed, and many members wanted to throw him out of the army. Washington's trusted friend in Congress, Joseph Jones, so informed Washington, who answered on August 13:

In your letter... an idea is held up as if the acceptance of General Greene's resignation of the Qr. Mrs. department was not all that Congress meant to do with him. If by this is in contemplation to suspend him from command in the line (of which he made an express reservation at the time of entering on the other duty) and it is not already enacted, let me beseech you to consider <u>well</u> *what you are about before your resolve.*

I shall neither condemn, or acquit Genl. Greenes conduct for the act of resignation, because all the antecedents are necessary to form a right judgment of the matter, and possibly, if the affair is ever brought before the public, you may find him treading on better ground than you seem to imagine; but this is by the by. My sole aim at present is to advise you of what I think would be the consequences of suspending him from his command in the line... without a proper trial. A procedure of this kind must touch the feelings of every Officer; it will shew in a conspicuous point of view the uncertain tenure by which they hold their commissions. In a word it will exhibit such a specimen of power that I question much if there is an Officer in the whole line that will hold a Commission beyond the end of the Campaign if they do till then. Such an act in the most Despotic Government would be attended at least with loud complaints.

...The suspension of Genls. Schuyler and St. Clair, tho it was preceded by the loss of Ticonderoga... was by no means viewed with a satisfactory eye by many discerning Men... Suffer not my Friend, if it is within the compass of your abilities to prevent it, so disagreeable an event to take place... I _fear_... I _feel_ it must lead to very disagreeable and injurious consequences. Genl. Greene has his numerous Friends out of the Army as well as in it, and from his Character and consideration in the world, he might not, when he felt himself wounded in so summary a way, withhold from a discussion that could not at best promote the public cause. As a Military Officer he stands very fair and deservedly so, in the opinion of all his acquaintances.

These sentiments are the result of my own reflections on the matter... I do not know that Genl. Greene has ever heard of the matter and I hope he never may.

Greene presumably never knew of Washington's impassioned plea on his behalf. By the time Washington's letter got to Jones, Congress had cooled down. Arrangements were made with Greene that he temporarily continue as quartermaster general, on his own terms, until a new appointee, Colonel Timothy Pickering, could take over.

BATTLE OF CAMDEN

On August 16 General Gates suffered a disastrous defeat at Camden, South Carolina. Washington had pleaded with him on July 18 to keep him fully informed of his operations in the South. On August 12 he repeated his request, assuring Gates that he would send him all intelligence of value. Gates did not write, and, as he had done before, informed Congress of the battle on August 20 but did not report it to Washington for another ten days.

Much has been written about the battle, but the facts, particularly in relation to American losses, are obscure. Lord Cornwallis with 2,200 troops, most of them regulars, unexpectedly encountered Gates with approximately 3,000 troops, two-thirds untrained militia. With Cornwallis were Lord Rawdon and his tough Irish volunteers and Tarleton and his even rougher legion. When battle began, the Virginia militia on the American left broke and ran and the North Carolina militia quickly followed. Only the 1,100 continentals under General Kalb stood up and in fact drove back the British until they were overwhelmed by numbers. Kalb was killed after fighting bravely. The American army was pursued from the field and scattered in every direction. Gates himself that night reached Charlotte sixty miles away. Three days later he was at Hillsborough, 180 miles from Camden. The British suffered around 325 casualties, while the Americans lost about 1,000 killed, wounded, and captured. One hundred and fifty of these were later retaken by Colonel Francis Marion. More than two-thirds of the continentals who had done most of the fighting showed up later to fight again. When Gates did not write Washington two weeks after the battle, he sent a straightforward manly letter:

My public letter to Congress has been surely submitted to your Excellency... The militia broke so early in the day... that very few have fallen into the hands of the enemy.

By the firmness and bravery of the Continental troops the victory is far from bloodless on the part of the foe, they having upwards of 500 men, with officers in proportion, killed and wounded. I do not think Lord Cornwallis will be able to reap any advantages of consequence from his victory as this State seems animated to reinstate and support the army. Virginia, I am confident, will not be less patriotic. By the joint exertions of these two states, there is good reason to hope that, should the events of the campaign be prosperous to your Excellency, South Carolina might be again recovered. Lord Cornwallis remained with his army at Camden... I am cantoning ours at Salisbury, Guilford, Hillsborough and Cross Creek. This is absolutely necessary as we have no magazine of provisions and are only supplied from hand to mouth. Four days after the action of the 16th, fortune seemed determined to distress us; for Colonel Sumter... halted with the wagons and prisoners he had taken on the 15th; by some indiscretion the men were surprised, cut off from their arms, the whole routed and prisoners retaken.

What encouragement the numerous disaffected in this State may give Lord Cornwallis to advance further into the country I cannot yet say. Colonel Sumter... has reinstated and increased his corps to upwards of 1,000 men. I have directed him to continue to harass the enemy on that side. Lord Cornwallis will therefore be cautious how he makes any considerable movement to the eastward... The main body is cantoned in his front. Anxious for the public good I shall continue my unwearied endeavours to stop the progress of the enemy, to reinstate our affairs, to recommence an offensive war and recover all our losses in the southern States. But if being unfortunate is the sole reason for removing me from command, I shall most cheerfully submit to the orders of Congress and resign an office few generals would be anxious to possess, and where the utmost skill and fortitude are subject to be baffled by the difficulties which must for a time surround the chief in command here.

Five days later Gates followed with another letter to Washington: "If I can yet render good service to the United States, it will be necessary it should be seen that I have the support of Congress and your Excellency; otherwise some men may think they please my superiors by blaming me, and thus recommend themselves to favour. But you, sir, will be too generous to lend an ear to such men, if such there be, and will show your greatness of soul rather by protecting than slighting an unfortunate. If, on the contrary, I am not supported and countenance is given to everyone who will speak disrespectfully of me it will be better for Congress to remove me at once... This, sir, I submit to your candour and honour, and shall cheerfully await the decisions of my superiors."

Washington had too much experience with militia, and with the conditions under which Gates had fought, to criticize. On the contrary, as soon as he had studied Gates' reports, he wrote Congress at length, strongly attacking the militia system of the South, noting that they would always break in battle as they had done at Camden. He recommended a permanent southern Continental Army of at least six thousand men, plus cavalry and artillery, together with sufficient supplies of food and forage. To Gates, Washington wrote on October 8, apologizing for the delay occasioned by his conference with the French:

The behaviour of the Continental Troops does them infinite honour. The accounts, which the Enemy give of the action, shew that their Victory was dearly bought. Under present circumstances, the system which you are pursuing seems infinitely proper. It would answer no good purpose to take a position near the enemy, while you are so far inferior in force. If they can be kept in check, by the irregular troops under Colo. Sumter and other active Officers, they will gain nothing by the time which must be necessarily spent by you, in collecting the new Army, forming Magazines and replacing the Stores which were lost in the Action...

It was owing to the fatal policy of temporary enlistments, that the enemy were enabled to gain the footing which they hold in the southern States, and it is much to be feared that the same Cause will be attended with an increase of disagreeable effects...

Preparations have been sometime making for an embarkation from New York. The destination is publickly said to be to the southward, and I think probability is in favour of that report. Should a further extension of their conquests in that quarter be their object, I am in hopes that the force collecting by the exertions of North Carolina, Virginia and Maryland, will keep them confined to the limits of South Carolina at least.

Gates and his reorganized, if small, force were sufficient to prevent Cornwallis (who was burdened by his sick and wounded and a shortage of supplies) from moving into North Carolina for three weeks after his victory. One of the enemy armies was soon knocked out completely while Gates was still in command. Cornwallis was forced to retreat to South Carolina, precisely as Washington hoped.

Congress was neither as understanding nor as generous as Washington was to Gates. On the day the successful battle of King's Mountain took place, the delegates instructed the commander in chief to recall Gates, to hold a court of inquiry on his conduct, and to nominate another general to head the southern department. Other people were even harsher. On September 11, Benedict Arnold took time off from his correspondence with British intelligence to tell General Greene: "It is an unfortunate piece of business to that hero and may possibly blot his escutcheon with indelible infamy." Alexander Hamilton, without Washington's knowledge, wrote on September 6 to James Duane, a New York congressman: "What think you of the conduct of this great man? I am his enemy personally for unjust and unprovoked attacks on my character... Did ever any one hear of such a flight? His best troops placed on the side strongest by nature, his worst, on the weakest... 'Tis impossible to give a more complete picture of military absurdity... Was there ever an instance of a General running away, as Gates has done, from his whole army? And was there ever so precipitous a flight? One hundred and eighty miles in three days and a half. It does admirable credit to the activity of a man at his time of life. But it disgraces the General and the Soldier... Will he be changed or not. If he is changed, for God's sake overcome prejudice, and send Greene."

This was total insubordination on Hamilton's part. His letters tended to be considered by their recipients as conveying the views of the commander in chief. The attempt to get Congress to dismiss Gates was an infringement of the legislative prerogative, which Washington himself never attempted.

THE ARMY TAKES A FEW COWS

By the middle of August the troops again faced starvation, since the states had been backward in sending supplies. To his agonized distress, Washington had to send out forage parties to take, by requisition, the little the inhabitants of Bergen County had. In his urgent appeal to the governors of New England and the middle states, he explained his actions and needs:

> *I am under the disagreeable necessity of informing you that the Army is again reduced to an extremity of distress... The greater part [was] without Meat from the 21st to the 26th. To endeavour to obtain some relief, I moved down to this place [Englewood], with a view to stripping the lower parts of the County of the remainder of its Cattle, which after a most rigorous exaction was found to afford two and three days supply only, and those, consisting of Milch Cows and Calves of one or two years old. When this scanty pittance is consumed, I know not what will be our next resource... Military coercion is no longer of any avail, as nothing further can possibly be collected from the Country in which we are obliged to take a position, without depriving the inhabitants of the last morsel...*

> *It has been no inconsiderable support of our cause to have had it in our power to contrast the conduct of our Army with that of the enemy, and to convince the inhabitants that while their rights were wantonly violated by the British Troops, by ours they were respected. This distinction must now unhappily cease, and we must assume the odious character of the plunderer instead of the protectors of the people... We have not yet been absolutely without flour, but we have <u>this</u> day but <u>one</u> days supply...*

> *...Altho' the troops have upon every occasion hitherto borne their wants with unparalleled patience, it will be dangerous to trust too often to a repetition of the causes of discontent.*

On August 30 he wrote his brother Samuel: "The flattering prospect which seemed to be opening to our view in the Month of May is vanishing like the Morning Dew. The States, instead of sending the full number of men required of them by the first of July [and] the consequent supplies, have not furnished one half of them yet... At best, the Troops we have, are only fed from hand to Mouth and for the last four or five days have been without Meat. In short, the limits of a letter would convey very inadequate ideas of our disagreeable situation; and the wretched manner in which our business is conducted. I shall not attempt it, therefore, but leave it to some future Pen, and a more favourable period for truths to shine."

CONFERENCE WITH ROCHAMBEAU

Lafayette had been acting as American liaison with Lieutenant General Rochambeau. While he might be major general in the American army, to the French commander he was a twenty-two-year-old French captain who had recently received the rather honorary rank of colonel. Washington wanted to plan a joint French-American attack on New York but this was difficult with the French blockaded. In addition, Rochambeau expected a second French division, with additional naval forces, and he did not intend to move until they arrived.

Washington's instructions to Lafayette of August 3 were clear: "I would not wish to press the French General and Admiral to any thing to which they show a disinclination... Only inform them what we can do, what we are willing to undertake, and let them intirely consult their own inclination for the rest. Our prospects are not so flattering as to justify our being very pressing to engage them in our views. I shall however go on with all our preparations and hope circumstances will ultimately favour us."

Nonetheless, Lafayette pushed Rochambeau hard to do something, telling him that the French could always beat the British. Rochambeau chided him firmly but with great politeness. He said that he had had forty years' experience, French troops could be beaten even by the British, he had seen too many Savannahs, and he did not intend to take chances with the lives of his men. He made it clear that he would make all arrangements directly with Washington and wanted to confer with him. This was a difficult meeting to plan since Washington had to be on the alert against any move by Clinton into the Highlands or New Jersey, and Rochambeau equally so for attacks on Newport.

On August 25, while his army was rounding up cattle, Washington received dispatches from Rochambeau, saying that the long-awaited second division of French troops and its supporting fleet had been blocked up in Brest and no one knew when they might get out. Thus both sections of the French forces were paralyzed and with them any offensive plans Washington might want to undertake.

On September 14 Admiral Sir George Rodney, with ten ships of the line, arrived in New York from the West Indies, an unexpected bonus for Sir Henry Clinton. This gave him overwhelming naval as well as military superiority. Rodney was an unscrupulous fellow and so greedy that Lord Sandwich had to assure the king that the admiralty commissioners in the West Indies had enough control of supplies there to prevent Rodney from taking too much for his own pocket. Nonetheless he was a fighting admiral and more than welcome to Clinton, who was fed to the teeth with Arbuthnot. Clinton took him immediately into his confidence on his plan to purchase West Point from Benedict Arnold. Rodney agreed to make his naval forces available for any "attack."

On September 20 Washington held his meeting with Comte de Rochambeau in Hartford. Since each was prepared to like the other, the conference was successful so far as human relations went, but in planning nothing was accomplished. The French could only say that they had been in touch with Count de Guichen, in command of the French fleet in the West Indies, but they did not know whether he would come to their aid. Claude Blanchard, the French commissary, recorded in his diary that the French officers had "returned enchanted" by Washington.

On October 4 Washington summarized the meeting to James Duane: "The interview at Hartford produced nothing conclusive, because neither side knew with certainty what was to be expected. We would only combine possible plans on the supposition of the possible events; and engage mutually to do every thing in our powers against the next campaign."

On September 23 Washington left Hartford for West Point, where he intended to go over the defense system with Benedict Arnold. Not long after he set out, three American militiamen captured a prisoner near Tarrytown who identified himself as a British officer but who was carrying extensive documentation of West Point's fortifications.

TWENTY-SEVEN

WEST POINT

1780

WHEN EVERYTHING LOOKED bleakest for Washington, the British made two capital blunders. In the North, their intelligence handled a major operation so ineptly that its chief was hanged on October 2. Three days later a new breed of southern mountaineers destroyed a British army at King's Mountain. As enemy power disintegrated with increasing momentum, Washington made ready to strike and kill.

CAPTAIN ANDRÉ

John André, aide to Major General Charles Grey, had been the chief designer of the 1778 ball at Philadelphia to honor Sir William Howe. André was enraptured by his own costume. He wore, he said, a "hat of white satin... enlivened by red, white and black plumes." His "hair tied with contrasted colors of the dress, hung in flowing curls." He had a coat "of white satin... the sleeves made very full, but of pink, confined with a row of straps of white satin laced with silver upon a black edging." He also wore "a large pink scarf... with a white bow... and a pink and white sword belt and pink bows... Fastened to the knees."

André had been quartered with General Grey in Franklin's house in Philadelphia. Had Franklin ever learned of the costume André designed there, he could have written one of his merriest pieces. When the British army retreated, André took many books and pieces of china belonging to Franklin. He also removed, presumably on General Grey's orders, a portrait by Benjamin Wilson. This was presented to the White House many years afterwards by one of Grey's descendants.

André was thirty in 1780. He was an excellent linguist, a fair artist, and a mediocre poet. Above all he had a gift of the tongue and high ambition. In three years he moved from subaltern to Clinton's intelligence and administrative chief. Before Grey left America, he recommended André to Clinton, who made him his aide and gave him the intelligence assignment. In 1779 when Clinton's adjutant general and deputy adjutant both resigned, André was made deputy adjutant. Clinton asked London to give him a majority, but Lord Amherst ruled that he was too far down the captain's list to be promoted. André continued to call himself a major, presumably as an acting or local rank. André's intelligence assignment was of utmost importance to the British, but William Smith, Tory chief justice of New York, observed in his diary that André spent more time performing on the stage than getting information about Washington's army.

André's 1779 negotiations with Arnold, in which he urged him to take an important command that he could surrender, were broken off when Clinton and André went to Charleston. During their absence, Captain George Beckwith took over British intelligence in New York. He formulated a plan to kidnap Washington but nothing came of it. He sent urgent inquiries to one of his spies for information on Washington's forces, supplies, recruiting, militia, and cavalry. The agent, who was in the American service, forwarded them to Washington. On March 7 Washington himself carefully wrote out misleading answers to "Beekwith's letter." When Beckwith received reports of the May 30 mutiny of the Connecticut line, he sent three spies to the American lines. They were caught and later hanged on Washington's orders the following month.

Benedict Arnold resumed negotiations with British intelligence in May 1780. In correspondence with Arnold, Beckwith used the names of "G. B. Ring" and "M. De l'Anneau," symbolic of an identical pair of rings, one of which he sent to Arnold for identification. On June 4 Washington asked Arnold to undertake, very secretly, the printing in Philadelphia of a proclamation in French to the inhabitants of Canada declaring that the French were coming to rescue them. Washington and Lafayette had devised this as a ruse to fool the British. Arnold immediately forwarded a copy to British intelligence, which perhaps took it more seriously than if it had come from a less reliable channel.

When Arnold resumed his correspondence, he moved to meet André's demand that he take command of a major post. He asked General Schuyler to intercede with Washington to get him West Point. As he was frequently to do, he pleaded that his war wounds prevented him from taking a field command. On June 12 he was at Morristown on his way to Connecticut. He hinted his desire for West Point to Washington. The commander in chief seems to have told Arnold that he would think it over. Arnold informed Beckwith, nevertheless, that he was certain to have it. The day after his interview with Washington, Arnold inspected the West Point fortifications and sent a full report on them to British intelligence. At the same time Arnold let them know that six French ships of the line and six thousand troops would soon arrive in America. To make sure of his West Point appointment, he subsequently asked Robert Livingston, New York's chancellor, to put in a good word for him with Washington. This Livingston did at the end of June.

When Arnold returned from his Connecticut trip, he again talked with Washington and thought he was assured of the command. On July 7 he so informed André, who had resumed his post as head of British intelligence. Sir Henry Clinton was so elated that he told William Smith that he thought the rebellion would soon end in a crash. André had offered Arnold two guineas per American head in 1779. The blood bargaining resumed in earnest in early July of 1780. Arnold again insisted that he get ten thousand pounds whether he succeeded or failed, but André balked at this. He proposed they meet under a flag of truce to discuss it. Arnold said he wanted £20,000 for West Point. André, in turn, suggested he could give £20,000 provided the British captured at least three thousand troops. Thus the price per man was upped from about two guineas to a little more than six guineas, but this was still a bargain. At the same time André informed Arnold he would have to break off the negotiations temporarily, since Sir Henry Clinton was going to make some attempt against the French at Newport.

During the summer the agents of General Robert Howe, who had the West Point command, picked up a New York rumor that an American general was about to sell out. Howe informed both Washington and Greene but nothing further seems to have been done about it. At about the same period, Arnold told André that some of his trusted agents were, in fact, working for Howe.

Around July 21 Arnold left for Washington's camp; his wife, Peggy, remained in Philadelphia as an intermediary, forwarding letters between her husband and British intelligence. On July 31 the commander in chief told Arnold he was being given command of the army's left wing. Washington later recalled that Arnold remained completely silent when told this. Peggy Arnold, informed of it a few days later at Robert Morris' house, fell into a state of hysterics. Those present interpreted this as concern for her husband, which in fact it was. Subsequently Arnold told Washington's aides that his wound still prevented him from the hard riding of a campaign. Because of this the commander in chief announced on August 3 that Arnold would command the Hudson River area, including West Point.

Earlier, on July 15, Washington had written to the board of war, approving the promotion of Major John Jameson, following the resignation of a lieutenant colonel in Sheldon's dragoons who formed an important part of his intelligence operations. On August 4 he further announced that he had appointed Lieutenant Colonel James Livingston to command the forts at Stony and Verplanck's Points.

Arnold continued to send messages to the British through Philadelphia but this was a slow process, sometimes taking as much as three-and-a-half weeks to reach them. In turn, Arnold did not receive André's offer of £20,000 for West Point and three thousand troops until August 24. On August 30, however, Arnold contrived to send a note to New York by an Irish-born member of the Connecticut legislature, William Heron, who had offered, through William Smith in New York, to spy for the British. Heron appears to have opened Arnold's letter and to have noted that it was written in commercial form, disguising his acceptance as a business deal. It was signed "Gustavus," Arnold's code name, and addressed to "John Anderson," André's feigned name. Heron decided that Arnold was conducting a speculation in New York. To ingratiate himself with the American army, he handed the letter to General Samuel Parsons, who filed it.

On September 3 Arnold found means to transmit another letter to André by a flag boat bringing a woman from Quebec into New York. He suggested a meeting between them, with André posing as an American secret agent, at the headquarters of Colonel Elisha Sheldon of the second dragoons. That same day Major Jean-Louis Villefranche, the West Point engineer, sent Arnold plans of three of the redoubts and promised to forward the remaining drawings as soon as possible. Arnold in turn wrote to Colonel Livingston to say that he was sending him sixty flatboats. If the enemy attacked the fort, Livingston was to embark all his troops and cannon from the east bank of the Hudson and "come with them to West Point." The next day, in response to his earlier order, Arnold received from Major Sebastian Bauman, head of artillery, lists of ordnance and the alarm guns and signals to be used in case of an enemy assault.

In a clumsy move on September 7, the British intelligence chief sent a letter to Sheldon, suggesting that he see Mr. G. at Dobbs Ferry on September 11. This was signed "John Anderson." Sheldon, puzzled by it and odd references to Anderson entering the lines by stealth, forwarded the letter to Arnold the next day asking its meaning. He added that he had never heard of Mr. G. or of Anderson. In any case he was not in good health and he could not ride to Dobbs Ferry.

Arnold had apparently forgotten to inform Sheldon of the name of his supposed agent and of the proposal for a meeting. On September 10 Arnold wrote to André not to trust Sheldon with any further communication. It is hardly possible that the next move, the sudden arrest of Colonel Sheldon, could have been coincidental. Somewhere between September 10 and 12, a Dr. Darius Stoddard preferred charges that led to Sheldon's being relieved of his command and ordered court-martialed. John Jameson, just promoted to lieutenant colonel, became acting commander of the second dragoons at this critical point. Sheldon was subsequently acquitted with honor and Stoddard was severely reprimanded by the court for bringing false and malicious accusations.

Washington had reports from New York, as early as September 2, that the enemy might be preparing to move up the Hudson. He informed Arnold that he was ordering two Connecticut regiments to join Sheldon's dragoons at North Castle. On September 10, Washington had further reports that the British were drawing in troops from Long Island.

On September 6 Peggy Arnold left Philadelphia to join her husband at West Point. André soon became more and more open in his actions and desires to talk to Arnold. On September 11 he and Colonel Beverley Robinson, the New York Tory who owned the house that Arnold used for headquarters, went to Dobbs Ferry. Arnold came down by barge late in the evening, but André had made no arrangements for his reception and a British gunboat fired on him. He was forced away and André returned to New York.

On September 13, Colonel Livingston, in command on the Hudson's east bank, wrote to Arnold that Robinson had been seen around Tarrytown in a boat, pretending to establish a flag contact but Livingston was sure he had espionage in mind. He asked Arnold if he should not try to give him "a check." Arnold cautioned him against this. The same day Arnold wrote to Benjamin Tallmadge that if "Anderson" reached his lines, he was to send him to Arnold with a cavalry escort.

By September 14 Rodney and his ten ships were in New York. This addition to the British forces made André even more eager and impetuous to establish early contact with Arnold. That same day Washington informed Arnold that he would be at Peekskill on September 18, on his way to see Rochambeau, and to keep his trip very secret. Arnold encoded the message and sent it to André. On the eighteenth, Washington wrote General Greene, who was to take command in his absence, that he was much worried about Rodney's arrival, particularly as Colonel Jameson had told him that Clinton had seventy troop transports ready to move "at a moment's warning." There might be an early attack on West Point and Greene should move his troops towards Tappan.

On September 16, time being of the essence for the British and Arnold having proposed a meeting on the twentieth, André sent Colonel Robinson up the Hudson on a British war sloop, appropriately named *Vulture*. The ship anchored off Tellers Point, only five miles below Verplanck's Point, which was under the command of the suspicious Colonel Livingston. That same day Clinton and Rodney met to discuss plans for taking either West Point or Newport. The following day Clinton wrote Rodney he hoped that they would agree on the former post. At the same time Robinson sent a letter to Arnold, under a flag of truce, enclosing another letter ostensibly addressed to General Putnam. Robinson hinted that he wanted to discuss his private affairs, including the house used by Arnold, which had been taken by the New York state government. These arrived so openly at his quarters that he spoke of them to his aides, as well as to Colonel Lamb, who commanded at West Point. They all heartily damned Robinson and suggested that Arnold show the letters to General Washington. Arnold escorted Washington across on the ferry, from which all could see the spy ship anchored below. Arnold showed Robinson's letters to Washington, who said that letters on civilian affairs should go to the governor of New York.

On the following day Arnold sent Robinson a "public" reply, indicating that he could not discuss any civil business of this kind, but he enclosed private letters saying that he would meet the British emissaries on the twentieth. He enclosed a copy of an earlier letter to André, pointing out that he had twenty-five hundred troops towards the needed three thousand and he would be able to get more. The original had already gotten to Beckwith in New York, who had forwarded it to André. On its receipt André started for Dobbs Ferry. He arrived there on the twentieth and proceeded by sloop to the *Vulture* to be in time for the meeting.

In the meantime Arnold had engaged the services of a Joshua Smith, who lived in a farmhouse down the river from West Point. He was the brother of William Smith, Clinton's chief justice. Because of this he seems to have leaned over backward to show his loyalty to the patriots by an extra willingness to help Arnold. When the latter requested his assistance in getting an intelligence agent from New York, he agreed. Smith was also to recruit two brothers, tenant farmers, who lived on his property on the Hudson's west bank. They were to be engaged to row to and from the *Vulture* as needed. On the night André waited on his ship, one of the brothers decided he was just too tired to row out and pick him up. Having waited all night in vain, André wrote worriedly to Clinton that this was the second meeting that had failed, Robinson had been seen with him before, and people might begin to ask questions. He said that he would wait another day, pretending to be too sick to return to New York. Arnold, too, was much annoyed at this miscarriage.

On September 21 there was a skirmish between the *Vulture's* gunboat and Livingston's troops. The British were driven off. American and enemy versions differ as to the cause. The British claimed the shore battery had waved a flag of truce. Livingston insisted the British had attempted to come ashore "to steal sheep." Using this as an excuse for correspondence, the captain of the *Vulture* sent a protest to Arnold at a violation of flags. It was in André's handwriting and signed for the *Vulture's* captain by John Anderson, secretary. Enclosed was a letter from Robinson saying that they would expect Mr. Smith that evening.

That night, September 21, Arnold again had to deal with Smith's very independent tenant farmers, Joseph and Samuel Cahoon. Samuel allowed to Arnold as how it was risky to row about at night with American patrols on the river. He asked Arnold why he didn't do it in the daytime like everyone else, and, in any case, his wife did not want him to go. Joseph later testified in New England tones: "I... told him I did not choose to go. He then said there was no hurt in going, at all; and if anything should come against me, he would defend me... I told him he could not clear me if there was any bad in it." Finally both brothers told Arnold they "had no mind to go."

The fate of the British empire was at stake. Fortune and titles were waiting for Arnold. The whole British high command and Admiral Rodney were "a tiptoe" but everything had to wait while he argued with two pigheaded American farmers. Arnold, in desperation, said they were unpatriotic, the country needed their services, and if they refused to go he would arrest them immediately. They consented with bad grace but they were even more intractable in the morning.

About midnight the Cahoons rowed Smith to the *Vulture* to pick up "John Anderson," who wore a cloak over his red coat. Arnold took two horses and rode downriver from Smith's house to meet them at a point below Haverstraw. For four days thereafter, no one on the *Vulture* had any word of André.

Arnold and André conferred all night while Smith and the boatmen waited. Near dawn Smith mentioned to Arnold that it would soon be light. He asked the Cahoons to take André back to his ship but they said they were too tired. Smith and the Cahoons rowed back to the Smith farm, while André and Arnold proceeded there by horseback.

On the opposite side of the Hudson Colonel Livingston had also been busy. Late the preceding afternoon Arnold had complained to him about the firing on the *Vulture's* boat. Livingston expressed his annoyance at having the ship there, with Robinson aboard, and he asked Arnold for heavy guns to drive the *Vulture* away. Arnold brushed him aside. Livingston hauled a light four pounder that night from Verplanck's Point to Tellers Point. At daybreak, just as Arnold and André turned into Smith's house, they saw firing from the opposite side. Livingston kept up his attack on the *Vulture* for two hours, accurately hitting the rigging, hull, sails, and boats. He stopped only when his magazine exploded. André saw the *Vulture* pull off down the Hudson.

In the morning, after delivering all the West Point documents to André, Arnold returned to Robinson's house across the Hudson, while Robinson himself floated downstream. Smith was nearly as thick about everything as his tenants. He knew that André wore a British officer's uniform, but Arnold had assured him that he was only a merchant and wore it for vanity. That night Smith told him to take it off and gave him civilian clothes. André was informed he was to be delivered across the Hudson and go back by land. He did not care much for this change and protested but Smith seems to have told him he would have no trouble. André slipped Arnold's documents into his boots.

Smith and André proceeded to King's Ferry and crossed to Verplanck's Point. Smith had a jolly conversation with Colonel Livingston, who invited him in for a drink, but Smith said he had a friend with him and they had to go on.

On September 19, the day that André received Arnold's note inviting him to a meeting the following day, an American militiaman, John Paulding, escaped from a British prison in New York and made for Westchester. This was the second time he had been captured and had suffered brutal treatment. His good coat had been taken by the British, who gave him a ragged one of a kind worn by Tories and called a "refugee coat." He rejoined his militia unit in Westchester.

Not long after leaving Livingston, Smith and André were stopped and questioned by an American patrol. Their pass from Arnold was sufficient but they were warned not to proceed because of the large number of Tory partisans on the road. They spent the night in a small farmhouse. The next morning they were up early. At Pine's Bridge, Smith said goodbye to André and returned to Peekskill, feeling he had done good service for General Arnold.

André rode on with the West Point papers in his boots, his plans completed, and glory near. Just north of Tarrytown, John Paulding in his refugee coat stepped out of the bushes and levelled his gun. With him were two other young militiamen, Isaac Van Wart and David Williams. André noticed Paulding's coat and asked him if he were of the "lower Party." Paulding said yes and André said good, for he was a British officer on urgent business. When they announced they were Americans, he produced Arnold's pass but they would have none of it. The three men took him into the woods, searched him, and found the hidden documents. André offered every kind of bribe in golden guineas but the three "simple peasants," as Alexander Hamilton was to term them, hauled him off to Colonel Jameson at North Castle.

Much of what happened thereafter, in the period from September 23 to 25, during which Arnold was permitted to escape, is a still an unresolved riddle. It is known that Jameson took actions that were subsequently described by Washington as "the egregious folly, or the bewildered conception of Lieut. Colo. Jameson who seemed lost in astonishment and not to have known what he was doing."

As nearly as can be determined, André, an accomplished actor, attempted, with some success, to bluff. He claimed to be acting on urgent business for Jameson's commanding officer, General Arnold, and demanded to be taken to him at once, so the matter could be cleared up. It is nearly certain that Jameson knew that Arnold was, in fact, expecting such a man. It was apparent at the same time that there were flaws in the story. André was going in the wrong direction, and he did have highly secret papers on American defenses. Jameson devised a compromise to protect himself against any possible charges by Arnold. He decided to send André to Arnold, while forwarding the papers to General Washington. In so doing Jameson informed Arnold that he had caught "a certain John Anderson going into New York. He had a pass signed with your name. He had a parcel of papers... which I think of a very dangerous tendency." At the same time he wrote Washington:

> *Inclos'd you'll receive a parcel of Papers taken from a certain John Anderson who has a pass signed by General Arnold as may be seen. The Papers were found under the feet of his Stockings he offer'd the Men that took him one hundred Guineas and as many goods as they wou'd please to ask. I have sent the Prisoner to General Arnold he is very desirous of the Papers and every thing being sent with him. But as I think they are of a very dangerous tendency I thought it more proper your Excellency should see them.*

Washington was en route back from his Hartford conference. The messenger, thinking he was returning by the more southern route, headed for Danbury. It is unclear at this point why Jameson, after thinking it over, decided it might be wrong to dispatch André to Arnold. He sent a further rider out to ask the escorting party to deliver the prisoner to lower Salem, to be held in tight security. Nonetheless the messenger was to proceed to Arnold with the Jameson note.

Sometime during the afternoon of September 24, the day after he was caught, André confessed to the chief of his guard. He also wrote a letter to General Washington, identifying himself as Major André, adjutant general of the British army, who was involuntarily out of uniform. There was still a chance to catch Arnold and, as it turned out, more than ample time. The Robinson house was little over three hours' ride from lower Salem but the messenger, with the note from Jameson to Arnold, took eighteen or more hours to cover the distance. Jameson's subsequent excuse to Washington was that he had expected Arnold to come to his camp where he would have been seized. It never occurred to him, he said, that a British warship, the *Vulture*, was in the Hudson.

Sometime that day, after André's confession, the messenger with the papers for Washington reappeared, saying he had not been able to find him. Jameson added André's confession to the documents and directed the messenger to try to find him on the northern route from Hartford. Meanwhile, Washington, on his way to Fishkill, had planned to spend that night at the Robinson house with Arnold. On his way south from Fishkill, he met the French minister, the chevalier de Luzerne, who was overjoyed and begged General Washington to have the goodness to dine with him and spend the night, so he could hear all about the conference with Rochambeau. Washington politely agreed to his request. On the night of September 24, Washington, Lafayette, and Luzerne dined and slept in Fishkill. Mr. and Mrs. Arnold were in the Robinson house seven miles to the south. André was a prisoner sixteen miles to the southeast of Arnold. Robinson was on the *Vulture*, near Ossining, writing a worried letter to Sir Henry Clinton.

ARNOLD FLEES

Washington got up early in the morning of September 25 and rode for Arnold's headquarters. He sent two of his aides ahead to say he was on his way. Near the house, about half past nine, he and Lafayette turned off to examine two redoubts. While they were doing so, a messenger rode to the house and delivered the note from Colonel Jameson. With Washington expected at any moment, Arnold dashed upstairs to tell his wife that the conspiracy was broken and he was leaving immediately. He came down and informed his aides that he had an urgent summons to West Point and he would return within the hour. As he was mounting his horse, he met four of Washington's dragoons, who told him that his excellency was nearby. Arnold asked them to stable their horses and then rode rapidly down the hill to his waiting barge. He ordered the men to pull off, saying he had a matter of great importance and they were to row him to the *Vulture*. When he got aboard, he gave Beverley Robinson the first news of André for which they had been waiting since Thursday evening.

Robinson at once adopted what was to be the official British line. He wrote Washington that André had come ashore under Arnold's flag and pass and under his direction. "Under these circumstances Major André cannot be detained by you... I must desire you will order him to be set at liberty." Arnold also wrote Washington a letter in which the handwriting shook and the ink blotted noticeably at two points: first, when he proclaimed that his wife was "innocent," and again when he expressed a hope that Washington would protect her against American "fury." He concluded "With great regard and esteem." The *Vulture* then pushed off for New York.

When Washington got to Arnold's quarters, he was informed that Arnold was at West Point. He crossed the river to meet him there. Colonel Lamb, the puzzled commandant, apologized profusely for not knowing that Washington was coming and said that he had not seen Arnold for two days. On looking over the fortifications Washington found signs of neglect and disrepair everywhere. He recrossed the river about two hours later. At around four in the afternoon, Jameson's long-delayed letter reached him.

Washington sent Hamilton racing down the river to see if he could find any way of stopping Arnold but it was too late. At Verplanck's Point he was handed the letters that had been sent ashore from the *Vulture* by Arnold and Robinson. Hamilton immediately sent an urgent note to Greene outlining what had happened and asking him to send additional troops to West Point.

When he returned with the news, Washington talked to Arnold's two aides, Major David S. Franks and Lieutenant Colonel Richard Varick, telling them he was sure they were not involved but for their protection he would have to place them under temporary arrest and examine their and Arnold's papers. They informed him of the frequent exchanges of visits between Arnold and Joshua Smith. Upstairs Mrs. Arnold was having hysterics, and Varick said she had had them earlier in the day when Washington was across the river. When the commander in chief went to see her to help calm her, she said he was going to kill her baby. She went on this way for some time, her acting aided by a natural tendency to emotion.

Washington ordered Jameson to send André to headquarters "under the care of such a party and so many officers as to preclude him from escaping... General Arnold... went off to day to the enemy. André must not escape." Washington turned at once to organizing the defenses on both banks of the Hudson against a British attack which, he wrote, might even come that night. He called in everyone, including Colonels Lamb and Livingston, who were in command at the nearby forts. He sent urgent messages putting the whole army on the alert.

Washington ordered Wayne's division to come at top speed from Haverstraw to West Point. They set off at two in the morning, scrambled through sixteen miles of dark and rutted roads in four hours, showing up just as dawn broke. Wayne wrote six days later to H. A. Sheel: "When our approach was announced to the General he thought it fabulous, but when convinced of the reality he received us like a god, and retiring to take a short repose exclaimed, 'All is safe. I again am happy.' May he long, very long continue so!"

Not long after the arrival of Wayne, Tallmadge and a hundred dragoons arrived with André in tow. At about the same time Joshua Smith was brought as a captive to headquarters.

PAULDING, VAN WART, AND WILLIAMS

John Paulding was sent by Colonel Jameson to Washington, shortly after André was brought to camp, to explain the circumstances of the capture and to enable Washington to express his gratitude. On October 7 he wrote Congress: "I have now the pleasure to communicate the names of the Three persons who captured Major André, and who refused to release him notwithstanding the most earnest importunities and assurances of a liberal reward on his part. Their conduct merits our warmest esteem and, I beg leave to add, that I think the public will do well to make them a handsome gratuity. They have prevented in all probability our suffering one of the severest strokes of the war that could have been meditated against us. Their names are John Paulding, David Williams and Isaac Van Wart." On November 3 Congress awarded each of them silver medals and lifetime annual pensions of two hundred dollars.

SIR HENRY CLINTON

Arnold's arrival in New York on September 26 was a severe shock to Clinton, whose great dream of bringing the rebellion to an abrupt end lay crushed. He reacted with increasing hysteria over the next two weeks.

William Smith, his chief justice, noted in his diary: "The *Vulture* has been ten days up the river with Major André and Colonel Robinson... The Secret is now out, for... General Arnold came... this day to town. The people exult much, but it is not known yet that André was catched with his papers... Some great error has been committed by André or Sir H. Clinton... I fancy that Sir H. Clinton has intrigued with Arnold for some time, and that his reliance upon its success is the cause of his neglecting Rhode Island." Two days later Clinton told Smith that the war would have been over, and Washington and Rochambeau his prisoners, had all gone well. Now, as Smith correctly surmised, he had wasted a whole summer depending on Arnold, and he was nowhere.

Not until the following day was Clinton certain that André was to be treated as a common spy. On September 26 he had written Washington: "The King's Adjutant General in America has been stopt under Major General Arnold's Passports, and is detained a Prisoner... A flag of Truce was sent to receive Major André." He therefore expected him to be released. On September 30 Washington forwarded to Clinton the court-martial verdict, adding that André had come ashore to execute measures "very foreign to a flag to truce" and André himself had said it was impossible to suppose he had come ashore under such protection.

Clinton was utterly shaken. Not only had the plot failed but a British officer and gentleman who was his most trusted adviser was to be hanged. He hastily called a council of his generals and legal officers to draw up a memorandum proving André was not a spy. The conference was not entirely happy. Two lawyers, William Franklin, former governor of New Jersey, and John Kempe, attorney general of New York, raised questions that indicated they thought André had been properly convicted. Clinton, however, was so distressed about this discussion that they all finally voted that André was not guilty. Clinton ordered his New York governor, General James Robertson, his lieutenant governor, Andrew Elliot, and his chief justice to call on Washington and explain why André was not a spy. At Dobbs Ferry only Robertson, as a military officer, was allowed ashore. He held an extended conversation with General Greene that got nowhere. Robertson proposed that Washington check with Rochambeau and Knyphausen on the European laws concerning spies but this suggestion did not go over well. Greene may have hinted that André would be released in exchange for Arnold. After the conference adjourned, Robertson informed Clinton that he was sure "André will not be hurt." Clinton was writing to Washington and the British ship was still anchored at Dobbs Ferry, awaiting favorable news, when André's effects were delivered to the British.

Both Clinton and Washington thought that André had not been very clever when he met John Paulding. Clinton said: "I wish our poor friend André had not been a little too much off his guard when the militia questioned him." Washington wrote: "An unaccountable deprivation of presence of Mind in a man of the first abilities and the virtuous conduct of three Militia men, threw the Adjutant General of the British forces in America... into our hands." Unlike some on Washington's staff, General Greene had instantly perceived the truth about André. In announcing to the army the defection of Arnold and the capture of the adjutant general, he wrote: "Our Enemies despairing of carrying their point by force are practicing every base art to effect by bribery and Corruption what they cannot accomplish in a manly way."

ANDRÉ HANGED

A board of fourteen general officers, headed by Greene, tried André for espionage and on September 29 sentenced him to death. The head of British intelligence was hanged at noon on October 2. The purchase price he had offered per American head worked out at a little under thirty silver dollars.

No more unlikely candidate for canonization could have been chosen than André, who had masterminded the West Point plot and bumbled it into ruin. During his captivity he displayed vanity, great gifts of speech and charm, and an absence of all guilt feelings. Throughout André maintained that he was there because of bad luck only. He said nothing of his offers to Arnold to come into the American lines by stealth, to meet him under a false flag, nor did he ever admit to a lengthy correspondence with Arnold, nor to urging him to seek a post for betrayal that he would buy. He maintained to the last that he was a gentleman of honor. With charm and good manners, he persuaded many Americans to believe this, including Hamilton and Major Tallmadge, America's own intelligence chief, whose memoir of the events following the capture of his opposite number is highly suspect. Washington, who never saw André, seems to have been persuaded by them that he was "more unfortunable then criminal." André was helped in his pose because the whole army exploded in fury at Arnold, and the pleasant actor seemed to be a victim rather than the author of the plot.

When Tallmadge took André down the Hudson to his trial at Tappan, the prisoner pointed to the plateau where he was to land with British troops and gallantly attack the fort that he had arranged with Arnold to surrender. For this act, he told Tallmadge, he expected to be made a brigadier. He boasted a great deal about his importance to Sir Henry Clinton. He so impressed Tallmadge that the latter wrote on September 30 to Colonel Samuel Webb: "He is a young fellow of the greatest accomplishment, and was the prime minister of Sir Harry on all occasions... Unfortunate Man! He will undoubtedly suffer death tomorrow and tho' he knows his fate, seems to be as cheerful as if he was going to an Assembly... Had he been tried by a Court of Ladies, he is so *genteel, handsome, polite* a young Gentleman, that I am confident they would have acquitted him."

THE ROLE OF HAMILTON

Alexander Hamilton was more moved by Peggy Arnold and John André than anyone else. His biographer and editor, Henry Cabot Lodge, ascribed this to "the tenderness of his nature." His feeling for Mrs. Arnold is the more understandable since female conspirators were hardly thought possible in America. Hamilton wrote to his fiancée, Elizabeth Schuyler, daughter of the general, on September 25:

> *Arnold, hearing of it being detected, immediately fled to the enemy. I went in pursuit... On my return, I saw an amiable woman frantic with distress for the loss of a husband she tenderly loved... It was the most affecting scene I ever was witness to. She for a considerable time intirely lost her senses. The General went up to see her, and she upbraided him being in a plot to murder her child: One moment she raved; another she melted into tears... All the sweetness of beauty, all the loveliness of innocence, all the tenderness of a wife and all the fondness of a mother showed in her appearance and conduct...*
>
> *This morning she is more composed... She received us in bed, with every circumstance that could interest our sympathy. Her sufferings were so eloquent that I wished myself her brother, to have a right to become her defender. As it is, I have entreated her to enable me to give her proofs of my friendship.*

Hamilton frequently visited André and was completely charmed by him. André did not want to be hanged but to die in front of a firing squad as became a soldier. They talked it over and Hamilton agreed to take a letter from André to Washington:

> *Buoyed above the terror of death by the consciousness of a life devoted to honourable pursuits, and stained with no action that can give me remorse, I trust that the request I make to your Excellency... will not be rejected. Sympathy towards a soldier will surely induce your Excellency and a military tribunal to adopt the mode of my death to the feelings of a man of honour. Let me hope, Sir, that... if aught in my misfortunes marks me as the victim of policy and not of resentment, I shall experience the operations of these feelings in your breast, by being informed I am not to die on a gibbet.*

Washington ignored the letter. Hamilton was bitter about this intransigence. On October 2 he wrote his fiancée: "I must inform you that I urged a compliance with André's request to be shot and I do not think it would have had an ill effect; but some people are only sensible to motives of policy, and sometimes from a narrow disposition mistake it. When André's tale comes to be told, and present resentment is over, the refusing him the privilege of choosing the manner of death will be branded with too much obduracy."

After the execution Hamilton praised André in an October 11 letter to John Laurens: "There was something singularly interesting in... André. To an excellent understanding well improved by education and travel, he united a peculiar elegance of mind and manners, and the advantage of a pleasing person. 'Tis said he possessed a pretty taste for the fine arts... His sentiments were elevated, and inspired esteem; they had a softness that conciliated affection. His elocution was handsome; his address easy, polite and insinuating."

THE COW CHASE

That summer André, whose father was in trade, had begun a lengthy satirical poem in the style of the ballad of Chevy Chase, mocking a raid by Anthony Wayne on a British outpost at Bull's Ferry on July 21. The raid was not successful though Wayne succeeded in driving off some cattle. The poem expressed André's contempt for Americans as a lesser breed. He called Wayne a tanner by trade and rhymed that "steers shall know / And tauntingly deride / And call to mind in ev'ry low / The tanning of his hide." He mocked at Hamilton who "Rode like a soldier big," at Henry Lee, a "drover," adding an unkind comment about Parson Caldwell, whose wife had been killed, and two of whose churches had been burned by the British. André included schoolboy references to emetics and nature's needs. He spoke of Irvine's troops joining Wayne like two sewers flowing into a drain: "So meet these dung-born tribes in one." The last canto was published on the day that André was caught. It concluded:

> And now I've closed my epic strain,
> I tremble as I show it
> Lest this same warrior-drover, Wayne
> Should ever catch the poet.

Wayne's troops were guards at André's execution. After it was over, an anonymous American added a verse:

When the epic strain was sung
The Poet by the neck was hung
And to this cost he finds too late
The <u>dung born tribe</u> decides his fate.

EFFECT ON GENERAL CLINTON

Sir Henry Clinton reacted to André's execution with fury at Washington, the intended victim. He wrote his family in England a letter, amounting to four printed pages, that is often quite incoherent. In its self-pity, guilt, hatred, and fear, it contrasts sharply with Washington's letters of the period:

> *[October 4]...The Circumstances of poor André's capture throws a damp upon all, upon me greater than I can describe. Should he suffer you will easily believe it will be impossible for me to continue to serve... Respecting the coup manquee I do not feel it... Washington seems a moderate man all my friends say... he will not dare execute the sentence... I wish I may obtain leave to resign this command... Good God what a coup manquee... I am of course in very bad spirits... If I can return to my country without any more shocks I may live to enjoy a good old age...*

> *[October 9] The horrid deed is done. Washington has committed premeditated murder... I feel beyond words to describe... He is become a murderer and a Jesuit.*

Clinton's next problem was to inform the British government of the fiasco for which he was responsible as commander in chief. His government had encouraged him to use bribery, treachery, and corruption as the means to victory, but did not care for failure. Sir Henry therefore had to lie. He sent back only such documents, dating from the last days of the negotiation, as might support his case that André had been invited by Arnold to accept the surrender of West Point. He summarized the earlier negotiations in a mass of disingenuous phrases and falsehoods.

The British government reacted angrily against what appeared to be an unjust murder of a gallant soldier. The case presented to the British public caused a great outcry against Washington. A friend of André, Ann Seward, "the Swan of Lichfield," produced a rather dreadful "monody," indicting Washington, whose "Nero-thirst of guiltless blood" had made him "a cool, determined murderer of the brave." She hoped he would be hanged and have "eternal mildew on the ruthless head." From all this André received an unjustified immortal glory. The king gave him a posthumous baronetcy. Many years later he was reburied in Westminster Abbey. Altogether he got more recognition than Sir Henry ever did.

The ignominious end of the André-Arnold plot paralyzed Clinton's will to fight. Years later he wrote in his memoirs: "The unfortunate discovery of my design put an end, of course, to the proposed move up the Hudson River." There was no military reason to add "of course." The British military and naval forces in New York were far superior to anything Washington could mobilize for West Point's defense. Rodney wrote privately to Lord George Germain on December 22: "The Highlands up Hudson's River... cut off all communication between the northern and southern provinces... This is the post Arnold was to have betrayed, and which he assured me, as he did [Clinton] he would answer with his head should be taken in ten days. But, to my infinite surprize, cold water was immediately thrown upon it, notwithstanding it had but a few days before the arrival of Arnold been told me that it was of infinite consequence, and if taken would ruin the rebels."

The following summer Arnold again proposed an attack on West Point, to which Clinton replied that he was willing to consider it, "provided Washington was at a safe distance." Nothing developed even after the American commander headed for Virginia.

From the time of André's capture, Clinton made no important move against Washington until his abortive sortie from New York on the day that Cornwallis surrendered. His memoirs after October 1780 are concerned almost exclusively with Cornwallis' southern operations, which he heartily criticized. However wrong Cornwallis might have been in strategy and tactics, he fought in this period, and the British forgave him but not Clinton.

THE BATTLE OF KING'S MOUNTAIN

Clinton's later memoirs described the effects of King's Mountain, the battle fought three days after André was hanged, as "an event which was immediately productive of the worst consequences to the King's affairs in South Carolina, and unhappily proved the first link in a chain of evils that followed each other in regular succession until they at last ended in the total loss of America."

Cornwallis in moving north had split his forces in three. Far to the left was Major Patrick Ferguson with twelve hundred men who moved towards King's Mountain just inside the South Carolina line. Lord Rawdon later reported that "a numerous army now appeared on the frontiers, drawn from Nolachucky and other settlements beyond the mountains whose very names had been unknown to us." These attacked from Augusta north. Some who went after Ferguson came from what is now Tennessee, though most were North Carolinians. Ferguson retreated onto King's Mountain. Nine lines of Americans surrounded the hill and moved up, inexorably, shooting from behind the trees. Ferguson was killed, and every member of the enemy force of one thousand (two hundred being absent foraging) were killed, wounded, or captured. Fourteen thousand small arms were taken. American casualties were under one hundred.

Lord Cornwallis rapidly retreated into South Carolina from Charlotte. According to Clinton, this American victory "overset in a moment all the happy effects of Charleston... and... Camden and so encouraged that spirit of rebellion in both Carolinas that it could never be afterwards humbled. For no sooner had the news of it spread than multitudes of disaffected flew to arms from all parts, and menaced every British post on both frontiers, 'carrying terror even to the gates of Charleston'... Lord Cornwallis must have experienced extreme mortification from... the return of an army which he had, three months before, as he thought, so completely annihilated that not even a guard of six men could be collected to cover its General's flight to Hillsboro."

MR. AND MRS. ARNOLD

Two days after her husband's defection, Washington sent Peggy Arnold to Philadelphia with an escort and a pass. The latter expressed Washington's faith in her innocence and requested his countrymen to treat her with "delicacy and tenderness." She was not unaware, as she travelled, and while she stayed in Philadelphia, of a universal outburst of gratitude to God, which culminated in Congress setting aside a day of thanksgiving for preserving "the person of our commander in chief."

Peggy Arnold knew, too, that effigies of her husband were being burned throughout the nation. What was harder to take when she got to the house of her father, Edward Shippen, was her family's detestation of her husband. They denounced him as base and treacherous, while warmly sympathizing with her misfortune. This was rather hard on a participant in the plot.

The Pennsylvania council had searched Arnold's house and found evidence of his peculations and a letter from André to Peggy. While it referred to millinery and feminine things, it was in fact a greeting to a fellow conspirator. The Pennsylvania press suggested she might have had other correspondence. The council, in spite of her family's protests, exiled her. Her father took her to the British lines at New York.

Sir Henry Clinton gave the king's commission as colonel to the "trusty and well beloved Benedict Arnold," with temporary rank of brigadier in America. He also gave him an immediate cash settlement of £6,315 as an addition to a small earlier payment made by André. It was not long before the Americans intercepted a London banker's letter that said that he had bought for Arnold £7,000 worth of British 4 percent consols at a discount of 30 percent. This was a last service to Arnold by Washington, whose resistance had sent British bonds to new lows.

Carl van Doren listed all of Arnold's rewards. In addition to cash, he had half-pay for life, while his wife and children received pensions or king's commissions. The Arnolds and their children drew nearly £50,000 from the British government over the next sixty-seven years. This was a high return for Arnold's fifteen months of active service subsequent to his treason.

Arnold was faithful neither to Clinton nor to his wife. It was not long before Clinton discovered that Arnold was intriguing with Germain against him. Eventually he tried to get Clinton's high post. Five years later he took a mistress by whom he had an illegitimate child.

Four months after he received his British commission, Arnold, on an independent command in Virginia, got into an unseemly quarrel with the Royal Navy over a division of loot. He wrote to Commodore Thomas Symonds on February 5, 1781, objecting to a letter by him which failed, so Arnold complained, to live up to a verbal agreement on the spoils: "How far these sentiments can be reconciled with the strict honour which ought to govern among gentlemen, the world will judge... I shall bring the matter to the attention of the Commander in Chief."

TWENTY-EIGHT

WEST POINT TO WESTCHESTER

1780

WASHINGTON HAD FOUGHT a holding operation for five-and-a-half years against forces superior by sea and by land. Large doses of French sea power had been vitally needed from the first days of the alliance but except for d'Estaing's disappointing appearances, they had never come. Rochambeau and his French troops were tied to Newport; they had been of little help to Washington and drained America's limited food supplies. On September 12, 1780, Washington appealed to Admiral the Comte de Guichen for naval support from the West Indies. He pointed out the great efforts that America had made in hope of French sea support:

> *The Chevalier de Ternay has informed you of his being blocked in the port of Rhode Island, by a superior British fleet; and the French troops are of course under a necessity of remaining there for the security of the fleet... Nor indeed could they be more useful to us in any other position, a naval superiority being essential to every enterprise in these States.*
>
> *In consequence of the expected [naval] aid, great exertions have been made on our part for offensive operations; an additional expense (immense to this country in its present exhausted state) has been incurred; great expectations have been excited among the people...*

The situation of America at this time is critical; the Government without finances; its paper credit sunk... the resources of the country much diminished by a five Years war, in which it has made efforts beyond its ability. Clinton... In possession of one of our capital towns, and a large part of the State to which it belongs; the savages desolating the other frontier; [with] a fleet superior to that of our allies, not only to protect him against any attempts of ours, but to facilitate those he may project against us. Lord Cornwallis... in complete possession of two States, Georgia and South Carolina; a third, North Carolina, at his mercy...

...General Gates... [has] met with a total defeat near Camden, in which many of his troops have been cut off, and the remainder dispersed...

The enemy are said to be now making a detachment from New York for a southern destination; if they push their successes in that quarter, there is no saying where their career may end. The opposition will be feeble, unless we can give succour from hence, which, from a variety of causes, must depend on a naval superiority.

...Any succour you could send in consequence of this letter, must arrive too late for an enterprise against New York; but an unequivocal naval superiority would I hope enable us to act decisively in the Southern extremity.

Convinced as I am that the independence of America is the primary object of war, with your Court, it is unnecessary to offer any other motives to engage your exertions in our favor. I might otherwise remark that the destruction of the enemy here would greatly facilitate the reduction of their [the British West Indian] Islands...

I am happy in this opportunity of congratulating you on the advantages you have reaped in your different combats... My happiness would be complete if the coasts of this Continent should add to your laurels.

Guichen returned to France, and this request never reached him. Instead, Washington had to face the arrival of Admiral Rodney and new British reinforcements. Soon thereafter the British moved southward, in a climax of violence, for a final attempt to break America's will to resist. At the same time, the comte de Vergennes was negotiating with other European powers to get France out of an expensive war, even at the price of leaving the United States dismembered. Repeated American appeals for naval assistance were ignored until the summer of 1781. Then, in an overwhelming gesture, the French threw their entire West Indian naval garrison to Washington's support, leaving their Caribbean posts nearly defenseless.

A DIFFERENCE OF OPINION

When he returned to the West Indies, Rodney wrote Lord George Germain on December 22, 1780:

> *Believe me, my dear Lord, you must not expect an end of the American war till you can find a general of active spirit, and who hates the Americans from principle. Such a man with the sword of war and justice on his side will do wonders, for in this war I am convinced the sword should cut deep. Nothing but making the Americans feel every calamity their perfidy deserves can bring them to their senses.*

Rodney noted that Arnold was "greatly beloved" by American troops and that Washington's soldiers would desert if they were promised land and their pay arrears. Washington, he added, could be "bought" with a peerage. Rodney thought the sword of justice had not cut deeply enough but Americans differed. John Rutledge, governor of South Carolina, had written two weeks before to his state's delegates in Congress:

> *It is really melancholy to see the desolate condition of Mr. Hill's plantation... all his fine iron-works, mills, dwelling houses... reduced to ashes... I was shocked to see the ragged, shabby condition of our brave and virtuous men, who would not remain in the power of the enemy but have taken to arms.*
>
> *This, however, is but a faint description of the sufferings of our country, for it is beyond a doubt the enemy have hanged many of our people... Tarleton has... hung one Johnson, a magistrate of respectable character. They have also burnt a prodigious number of houses, and turned a vast many women... with their children, almost naked into the woods.*
>
> *In short, the enemy seem determined, if they can, to break every man's spirit, if they cannot ruin him. Engagements of capitulations and proclamations are no security against their oppressions and cruelties.*

GREENE TO THE SOUTH

Having previously selected three generals—Robert Howe, Lincoln, and Gates, who had been defeated—Congress now directed Washington to choose the new southern commander. He had no hesitation; on October 14, the day after receiving the order, Washington informed Greene:

As Congress have been pleased to leave the Officer to command on this occasion to my choice, it is my wish to appoint You; and from the pressing situation of affairs in that quarter, of which You are not unapprised, that You should arrive there, as soon as circumstances will possibly admit. Besides my own inclination to this choice I have the satisfaction to inform You, that from a Letter I have received, it concurs with the wishes of the Delegates of the three Southern States most immediately interested in the present operations of the Enemy; and I have no doubt it will be perfectly agreeable to the sentiments of the Whole.

To John Matthews, who had written Washington on behalf of Georgia and North and South Carolina, he replied on October 23: "You have your wish in the officer appointed to the Southern command; I think I am giving you a General; but what can a General do, without men, without arms, without clothing, without stores, without provisions?" He added that he was also sending south a partisan corps under Henry Lee, an officer, he said, who had "great resources of genius." Shortly afterward Washington informed Congress that he had also decided to send General von Steuben there, since the new army had to be organized and trained. Steuben was competent not only to do this but was well-suited for a field command. These moves were typical of Washington, who sent officers he could ill spare.

Washington wrote many letters of introduction for Greene to his southern friends. Greene noted that the commander in chief's name was far more potent in opening all doors than his own reputation. He took command of an infinitesimal army on December 3, with fewer than 1,500 men fit for duty and only half of these regulars. The enemy under Lord Cornwallis had altogether about 13,300 effectives in the southern states, though many were on garrison duty.

Gates, whose only son had just died, retired from the war to await the holding of a court-martial that never assembled. Greene, with some of his commander's magnanimity, wrote Washington that many officers thought well of Gates and that he would be able to acquit himself honorably. The Virginia Assembly passed a resolution expressing their "high regard and esteem" for Gates, which made his retirement in that state easier. On January 9, 1781, a little more than a month after taking over, Greene wrote Joseph Reed, describing the usual difficulties the American army had faced for so many years:

Measures are taking in Virginia which promise us some aid though very trifling... I overtook the army at Charlotte... The appearance of the troops was wretched beyond description... The wants of this army are so numerous and various that the shortest way of telling you is to inform you that we have nothing... We are living upon charity... An army naked and subsisted in this manner, and not more than one-third equal to the enemy will make but a poor fight, especially as one has been accustomed to victory and the other to flight... General Morgan is upon Broad River with a little flying army, and Colonel Washington since his arrival there has defeated a party of Tories.

BATTLE OF COWPENS

Eight days later, General Daniel Morgan won the most brilliant single victory of the Revolutionary War. Military historians have gone back to Hannibal's victory over the Romans at Cannae in 216 B.C. to find its counterpart. The Dupuys' *Compact History of the Revolutionary War* considers it "probably the closest approach to tactical perfection ever seen on the American continent—a complete double envelopment, the dream of every professional soldier." Morgan's force, according to his own account, consisted of 800 men, of whom 300 or so were continentals. Others credit him with as many as 1,040 but Sir Henry Clinton wrote that Morgan's "number and species of troops were greatly inferior to Tarleton, who had 1,100 men, including 300 cavalry."

The American militia had been accustomed to breaking and running at the first sign of battle. The British came to depend on this, expecting then to move on to victory. This time Morgan devised a planned militia retreat, which would bring Tarleton's forces forward to meet experienced continentals. Placing expert southern riflemen on his front, he stationed the militia under Colonel Andrew Pickens directly behind them. The riflemen were instructed to hold their fire, then to pick off British officers and sergeants, and to retreat in orderly fashion, continuing to shoot. As Tarleton's troops moved forward, riflemen and militia fired, bringing down more than one hundred British. The militia then moved rapidly to the rear. Sir Henry Clinton, in describing the battle's next stage, failed to guess what happened. He wrote that American "militia were driven back and everything seemed to promise victory... It was suddenly wrested from [Tarleton] by an unexpected fire from the Continental troops while the King's troops were... charging in loose, flimsy order." Colonel William Washington, a cavalryman, had yelled to Morgan: "They are coming on like a mob. Give them one fire and I'll charge them."

Although there was the usual confusion of battle among the Americans, the ensuing moves were perfect. The withdrawing militia, led by Pickens, went around the American rear to come in the left, while Colonel Washington's cavalry moved in to the British right. The whole enemy force was encircled.

Tarleton, with a few dragoons, escaped and was pursued for nearly twenty-five miles by Washington's horsemen.

It was an astonishing victory. More than 900 of Tarleton's 1,140 men were killed, wounded, or captured. American casualties were 73. Morgan took an immense baggage train, more than 100 horses and 800 muskets. In sending his much-admired guerrilla general to the South, Washington had calculated well. As a result, Cowpens was the second notable victory, after King's Mountain, on the road to Yorktown.

THE GENERAL AND THE CHEVALIER

One of the most attractive of the Frenchmen who came to America was Major General the Chevalier (and later Marquis) de Chastellux. While he was chief of staff to Rochambeau and an experienced soldier, he was also a man of letters, interested in poetry, music, philosophy, and even economics; a member of the French Academy; and a friend of Voltaire and Franklin. Of all the French who came, he left the most extensive and interesting diary account: *Travels in North America.* He was not always quite tactful, for he described Mrs. Washington as "fat," and looking "like a German princess" and Mrs. Schuyler as a "big Dutchwoman."

George Washington took to him at once. Chastellux in turn greatly admired the general and has given posterity admirable accounts of his battles. His description of his visit to Washington's camp in 1780 has often been mined by biographers:

November 23... After riding two miles beyond the right flank of the army, and after passing through thick woods on the right, I found myself in a little plain, where I saw a rather handsome farm: a small camp which seemed to cover it, a large tent pitched in the yard, and several wagons round it convinced me that this was the headquarters of "his Excellency"... M. De La Fayette was conversing in the yard with a tall man, six feet two inches high, of a noble and mild appearance. It was the general himself. I soon dismounted and approached him. The greetings were brief; the feelings which animated me and his kindly disposition towards me were not feigned. He conducted me into his house, where I found the company still at table, although the dinner had long been over. He presented me to Generals Knox, Wayne, Howe, etc., and his "family," then composed of Colonels Hamilton and Tilghman... A fresh dinner was prepared for me... A few glasses of claret and Madeira accelerated the acquaintances I had to make, and I soon felt myself at ease near the greatest and best of men. The goodness and benevolence which characterize him are evident in all that surrounds him; but the confidence he calls forth is never familiar, for the sentiment he inspires has the same origin in every individual, a profound esteem for his virtues and a high opinion of his talents...

November 24... We availed ourselves of the opportunity of following [Washington] to [Lafayette's] camp. We found all his troops in order of battle... himself at their head, expressing by his bearing and countenance that he was happier in receiving me here than at his estate in Auvergne. The confidence and attachment of the troops are to him invaluable possessions, well-acquired riches, which nobody can take from him; but what, in my opinion, is still more flattering for a young man of his age, is the influence, the consideration he has acquired in the political, as well as in the military order. I do not fear contradiction when I say that private letters from him have frequently produced more effect on some states than the strongest exhortations from congress...

November 26... I got on horseback, after breakfasting with the General. He thoughtfully gave me the horse he had been riding two days earlier and which I had greatly commended. I found the horse as good as he was handsome, but above all, perfectly well broken and well trained, having a good mouth, easy in hand, and stopping short in gallop without bearing the bit. I mention these minute particulars, because it is the general himself who breaks in all his own horses, and because he is a very excellent and bold horseman, leaping the highest fences and going extremely quick, without standing upon his stirrups, bearing on the bridle, or letting his horse run wild...

...General Knox... took us back to headquarters... He is a man of thirty-five, very fat, but very active and of a gay and amiable character... On our return to headquarters... I had an opportunity of conversing more particularly with General Wayne... He is sensible and his conversation is agreeable and animated...

Here would be the proper place to give the portrait of General Washington, but what can my testimony add to the idea already formed of him? The continent of North America, from Boston to Charleston, is a great book, every page of which presents his praise... The strongest characteristic of this respectable man is the perfect harmony which reigns between the physical and moral qualities which compose his personality. One trait alone enables you to judge of all the rest. If you are shown medals of Caesar, or Trajan or Alexander, you will still, upon examining their faces, ask what was their stature and the form of their bodies; but if you discover, in a heap of ruins, the head or the limb of an antique Apollo, be not curious about the other parts, but rest assured that all belong to a god... It is not my intention to exaggerate. I wish only to express the impression General Washington has left on my mind, the idea of a perfect whole... This is the seventh year that he has commanded the army, and that he has obeyed Congress; more need not be said, especially in America, where they know how to appreciate all the merits contained in this simple fact... If anything can be more marvelous than such a character, it is the unanimity of the public suffrage in his favor. Soldier, Magistrate, People, all love and admire him; all speak of him only in terms of affection and admiration...

In speaking of this perfect whole... I have not excluded exterior form. His stature is noble and lofty, he is well built, and exactly proportioned; his physiognomy mild and agreeable, but such as to render it impossible to speak particularly of any one of his features, so that on leaving him, you have only the recollection of a fine face... His smile is always the smile of benevolence.

But it is interesting, above all, to see him in the midst of the general officers of his army. General in a republic, he has not the imposing pomp of a <u>Marechal de France</u> who gives <u>the</u> order; a hero in a republic, he excites another sort of respect, which seems to spring from the sole idea that the safety of each individual is attached to his person... When one sees the battalion of the General's guards encamped within the precincts of the house; nine wagons, destined to carry his baggage, ranged in his yard; a great number of grooms holding very fine horses belonging to the general officers and their aids-de-camp; when one observes the perfect order that reigns... one is tempted to apply to the Americans what Pyrrhus said of the Romans: "Truly these people have nothing barbarous in their discipline!"*

DISTRESSES

Washington, with his customary courtesy, effectively concealed from Chastellux the worries that gnawed at him.

On November 12, 1780, Sullivan had written to suggest that he urge the French to move to the Hudson. Such a move would introduce a new threat to Sir Henry Clinton, and thus keep the British from sending further reinforcements southward. On November 28 Gouverneur Morris proposed that the General attack New York for the same reason. Washington replied to Sullivan,

---

* Washington did not see this comment on him by Chastellux until the summer of 1786. With his usual humor he wrote him on August 18: "Colonel Humphreys has put into my hands the translation of that part in which you say such, and so many handsome things of me; that (altho' no sceptic on ordinary occasions) I may perhaps be allowed to doubt whether your friendship and partiality have not, In this one instance, acquired an ascendancy over your cooler judgment."

who understood his problems, and to Morris, who did not. He informed Sullivan that he had strongly urged Rochambeau to move to the New York area but Rochambeau declared that he was tied completely to the blockaded French fleet. Washington further noted that, as usual, the army lacked clothing. "We are *feelingly* reminded of it... Congress will deceive themselves if they imagine that the Army... can rub through a second campaign as the last. It would be as unreasonable as to suppose that because a man had rolled a Snowball 'till it had acquired the size of a horse that he might do so till it was as large as a House." He detailed to Morris his deficiencies and inferiorities and noted that it "was with difficulty I could remove the army to its places of Cantonment where it would be well for the Troops, if like Chameleons, they could live upon Air, or like the Bear, suck their paws for sustenance during the rigor of the approaching season."

On January 1 General Stark wrote Washington pleading for money since he had not received a penny of pay for two years. Washington replied two days later that the army did not have a farthing in the military chest and it had been three months since he himself had been able to draw even for his own food. Chastellux had no hint of any of these problems.

Martha Washington made her usual long winter trip from Mount Vernon to the Hudson. She arrived at Washington's winter headquarters at New Windsor in time for Christmas and for the first major mutiny in the American army.

THE MUTINIES

Washington had frequently predicted that American troops could not be pushed around much more or he would have no army. On December 16 General Wayne described to President Reed of Pennsylvania the miserable conditions of his state's troops—their dry bread and beef; their worn coats and tattered linen; their threadbare blankets, each of which had to be shared among three soldiers; their lack of pay for a year; and "their more than Roman virtue."

On January 1, 1781, the Pennsylvania line mutinied. In the calmer atmosphere of April 18, Washington could write to Greene that it had arisen "more from the effect of an over charge of spirits on the first of January than of premeditated design." Before he reached the stage where he could appraise it with some humor, he had to live with it, as it spread to the troops of other states.

Late on the night of January 1, rockets and guns went off in the Pennsylvania camp at Mount Kemble. When the officers found it was a mutiny, they tried to quell it, and two of them were shot. General Wayne appeared, but the mutineers said their quarrel was not with him but with Congress and Pennsylvania. After great disorder half the camp set out for Philadelphia, "being much agitated with liquor when they went off." The amount of alcohol each man had that day was only half a pint but it had been downed on almost empty stomachs.

Word quickly reached the British. Sir Henry Clinton rushed troops across Staten Island to a point near Amboy. He also sent out proclamations offering the Pennsylvanians pardons and all their back pay, but this was a patriotic revolt, and the men repeatedly said that if the enemy appeared they would turn around and fight. The Pennsylvanians halted at Princeton, where two British spies caught up with them. They were held by the revolters and later turned over to the army, which hanged them.

President Reed of Pennsylvania, acting under the authority of his state and of Congress, moved to address the grievances of the men. As he put it so handsomely, he had only one life and his country deserved it. In anxiety to please, he agreed to meet all their complaints, real or imaginary. They were to be given their back pay and some clothing, which were reasonable adjustments, but then Reed listened to the plea that some men were being held beyond their enlistment dates. He agreed that if they signed a paper stating when they had enlisted and under what terms, and this showed that they had finished their service, they would be released. This was too easy a way out, and more than thirteen hundred men claimed their discharges. The remainder, about eleven hundred men, were given a two-month furlough. With one swoop, Reed knocked out about 20 percent of Washington's army.

Washington made various comments. His January 22 letter to New York and the New England states said that "an accommodation took place, which will not only subvert the Pennsylvania Line, but have a pernicious influence on the whole army." On January 27 he wrote the New Jersey commissioners: "In transacting terms of enlistments with the Pennsylvanians, for want of proper care, the greatest part of the line has been dismissed, though only a small proportion was intitled to a dismissal. Authentic and unequivocal proofs have been since found that a majority of the discharged men were fairly and explicitly enlisted for the war. The evil arose from admitting the oaths of individuals before the vouchers could be assembled." On February 3 he wrote to General St. Clair to say that perjury did not relieve the soldiers from their engagement to serve and they should be rounded up. St. Clair replied there were so many this would be difficult. In any case it might be considered a governmental "breach of faith."

After the Pennsylvanians revolted, Washington appealed to the states to produce more clothing and pay. His letter to New Jersey succeeded in part, for their troops received extra cash, which they promptly spent on liquor. With a whoop and a holler, on the evening of January 20, the New Jersey troops at Pompton set off for Trenton to seek redress of their grievances. This time Washington took the strongest possible steps to keep civilians out and to suppress the mutiny himself. He sent an urgent message to the congressional committee at Trenton not to talk to them. He asked the governor of New Jersey for militia help and requested that he make no "compromise with the mutineers." He selected General Howe to march with a large detachment for Ringwood with orders of January 22, "to compel the mutineers to unconditional submission... I am to desire you will grant no terms while they are with arms in their hands or in a state of resistance... If you succeed in compelling the revolted troops to a surrender you will instantly execute a few of the most active and most incendiary leaders."

Heavy snows blocked the roads but Washington got through to Ringwood by sleigh. One problem he had was outlined in his January 25 letter to his quartermaster general, Timothy Pickering: "My horses, I am told, have not had a mouthful of long or short forage for three days. They have eaten up their mangers and are now (though wanted for immediate use) scarcely able to stand. I should be glad to know if there is any prospect of relief for them."

Howe's troops, as Washington wrote in their praise on January 30, marched from West Point to Ringwood "through rough and mountainous roads rendered almost impassable by snow." As it turned out, the New Jersey mutiny was small scale, with only two hundred or so men involved. When Washington got to Ringwood on January 27, Howe marched to the scene and surrounded the huts of the mutineers with heavy guns. There were no negotiations. They were ordered out in five minutes. They came out without arms. Fifteen ringleaders were selected, tried by court-martial, and sentenced to death. Twelve of the fifteen were then chosen to shoot the other three. After the first two were shot, the third was pardoned. The revolt was over. Washington then wrote to the New Jersey commission that "having punished guilt and supported authority, it now becomes proper to do justice." He urged the commissioners to give the fullest hearing to all complaints.

VIEWS ON NATIONAL UNITY

Washington had earlier received a letter of January 8 from Robert R. Livingston, chancellor of New York and a member of Congress. He hoped Washington would not mind his saying that the economic distresses of the state were great. The inhabitants, poor as they were, were so heavily taxed that they were sending many complaints and petitions to the state Assembly. Since New York's government was weak and subject to popular pressure, it would be impossible to raise any more money, at least until they could see that other states bore an equal burden.

Washington during the war often expressed the country's need for union and a strong central government, the more so as the authority of Congress grew weaker and weaker. The previous October 22 he had told William Fitzhugh that "instead of one head and director, we have, or soon shall have, thirteen, which is as much a monster in politicks as it would be in the human form." After apologizing to Livingston on January 31 for a delay in answering, because of the mutinies of troops without pay, clothing, and provisions, Washington continued:

> To learn from so good authority as your information that the distresses of the Citizens of this State are maturing into complaints which are likely to produce serious consequences, is a circumstance as necessary to be known, as it is unpleasing to hear...

> To trace these evils to their sources is by no means difficult; and errors once discovered are more than half corrected. This, I hope, is our case at present; but there can be no radical cure till Congress is vested by the several States with full and ample Powers to enact Laws for general purposes, and till the executive business is placed in the hands of able Men and responsible characters. Requisitions, then, will be supported by Law. Jealousies, and this ill timed compliances arising from distrust, and the fear of doing more than a Sister State, will cease. Business will be properly arranged; System and order will take place, and economy must follow; but not till we have corrected the fundamental errors enumerated above.

> It would be no difficult matter to prove that less than half the present expenditures... is more than sufficient if we had money, and these alterations in our political movements were adopted, to answer all our purposes. Taxes of course would be lessened, the burthen would be equal and light, and men sharing a common lot would neither murmur nor despond.

COLONEL HAMILTON MUTINIES

Amidst Washington's unceasing major troubles, Alexander Hamilton, his aide, engaged in a unilateral quarrel with the commander in chief.

Hamilton's longtime feeling that he was doing mere clerical work and finding no chance for glory boiled over when Washington failed to heed his pleas for Captain André. Not long after André met his death, Hamilton began to pull wires to obtain a staff assignment or field command. He asked Greene and Lafayette to recommend that he be made adjutant general. Washington politely pointed out to both generals that he could not appoint a lieutenant colonel to the post. The adjutant was second in command to the inspector general. His staff colonels would find it "disagreeable" to report to him. Lafayette informed Hamilton that the general's "friendship and gratitude" to him were extensive. "When he thinks he can do it," he would give him a suitable post. In December, Hamilton married Betsy Schuyler, the well-connected daughter of General Schuyler.

Hamilton did not lack for friends. When Congress asked John Laurens if he would accept appointment as special minister to France, to request further aid, he suggested Hamilton as more suitable. The members said they did not know him very well; they preferred Laurens. On January 29, General John Sullivan, now sitting in Congress for New Hampshire, wrote Washington that Congress had decided to have ministers of war, foreign affairs, marine, and finance. He wondered what Washington would think of "Colo. Hamilton as a Financier." The general replied that he had never discussed this field with him but he thought "that there are few men to be found, of his age, who has a more general knowledge than he possesses... or who exceeds him in probity and Sterling virtue."

On February 16, the twenty-six-year-old Hamilton contrived a dispute with Washington. He subsequently wrote a version that tells only part of the story and this not necessarily accurately. The missing portion, which involved a letter misplaced by Hamilton, can be deduced from Washington's correspondence. On January 25 Washington sent to the British fleet commander in New York a formal complaint that American prisoners were "suffering all the extremities of distress from a too crowded and in all respects disagreeable and unwholesome situation on board the prison-ships, and from the want of food and other necessities." A Captain George Dawson of the Royal Navy, replying on February 2, rejected the charges. He listed the Americans' rations, thereby unwittingly disclosing that they had a diet below that of British prisoners in American hands. Washington sent the correspondence to Congress on February 13 indicating that he was studying what action to take.

On February 16 Washington and Hamilton worked out a lengthy letter to Abraham Skinner, American commissary of prisoners, on proposals for an exchange of General Burgoyne and other British prisoners. When Washington asked Hamilton to get Dawson's letter, he could not find it. The exact circumstances are unimportant but Washington was annoyed, and Hamilton, according to camp reports, said he would not be talked to like a menial. On February 18 Hamilton wrote to General Schuyler: "Two days ago, The General and I passed each other on the stairs. He told me he wanted to speak to me. I answered that I would wait upon him immediately. I went below, and delivered Mr. Tilghman a letter to be sent to The Commissary, containing an order of a pressing and interesting nature. Returning to The General I was stopped in the way by the Marquis De La Fayette, and we conversed together about a minute on a matter of business. He can testify how impatient I was to get back, and that I left him in a manner which, but for our intimacy, would have been more than abrupt. Instead of finding the General as usual in his room, I met him at the head of the stairs, where, accosting me in a very angry tone, 'Colonel Hamilton' (said he,) 'you have kept me waiting at the head of the stairs these ten minutes. I must tell you Sir you treat me with disrespect.' I replied without petulancy, but with decision: 'I am not conscious of it Sir, but since you have thought it necessary to tell me so we part.'"

Hamilton then said that, within the hour, Tench Tilghman came with a verbal message from Washington expressing praise of Hamilton's abilities and integrity and a hope that he would come around and talk to him so that the breach could be healed. Hamilton reported to Schuyler that he had rejected the proposal but agreed to stay on Washington's staff until two absent aides returned to camp. He continued:

> *I always disliked the office of an Aide de camp as having in it a kind of personal dependence... Infected however with the enthusiasm of the times, an idea of the General's character, which experience taught me to be unfounded, overcame my scruples, and induced me to <u>accept his invitation</u> to enter into his family. I believe you know the place I held in The General's confidence and councils which will make it the more extraordinary to you to learn that for three years past I have felt no friendship for him and have professed none. The truth is our own dispositions are the opposites of each other & the pride of my temper would not suffer me to profess what I did not feel. Indeed when advances of this kind have been made to me on his part, they were received in a manner that showed at least I had no inclination to court them... You are too good a judge of human nature not to be sensible how this conduct in me must have operated on a man to whom all the world is offering incense. With this key you will easily unlock the present mystery.*

> *...The General is a very honest man. His competitors have slender abilities, and less integrity. His popularity has often been essential to the safety of America, and is still of great importance to it...*

I wish what I have said to make no other impression than to satisfy you I have not been in the wrong.

It is probable that Hamilton preferred that only his own version circulate. Two days later, the missing letter from Dawson was found. Washington then dictated a letter to Hamilton ordering Abraham Skinner to give British prisoners the same diet as American prisoners in New York. Hamilton, as the only French-speaking aide, stayed through the subsequent conferences with Rochambeau. Thereafter he found other work and no little glory at Yorktown.

LAURENS TO PARIS

John Laurens had studied in Geneva and spoke French well enough for his mission as a special American minister to Versailles. He had been wounded three times and exchanged as a prisoner of war. For these reasons, and because his father had been its president, he was better known to Congress than Hamilton. Henry Laurens had been appointed minister to Holland, but the British picked him up at sea. The first American president to visit England, he was clapped in the Tower of London and rigorously treated. In sending John Laurens to France, Congress gave him a chance to institute negotiations for his father's release by offering Burgoyne in exchange.

Rochambeau had sent his own son from Newport to the French court to plead for more money for his troops, for the additional division of five thousand men that had been promised America, and for naval support. Rochambeau, though writing of American needs, concentrated on his own irksome position. Laurens was sent to explain that the American army had nearly reached the end of its rope. Before he left, he held lengthy conversations with Washington on the presentation to be made at Versailles. Lafayette, still only twenty-three, sent Vergennes a sharp and brilliant summary of the American position on January 20:

With a naval inferiority, it is impossible to make war in America. It is that which prevents us from attacking any point that might be carried with two or three thousand men. It is that which reduces us to defensive operations, as dangerous as they are humiliating. The English are conscious of this truth, and all their movements prove how much they desire to retain the empire of the sea. The harbours, the country, and all the resources it offers appear to invite us to send thither a naval force. If we had possessed but a maritime superiority this spring, much might have been achieved with the army that M. De Rochambeau brought with him, and it would not have been necessary to have awaited the division he announced to us. If M. De Guichen had stopped at Rhode Island on his way to France, Arbuthnot would have been ruined, and not all Rodney's efforts could have prevented our gaining victories.

Since the hour of the arrival of the French, their inferiority has never for one moment ceased, and the English and the Tories have dared to say that France wished to kindle, without extinguishing, the flame. This calumny becomes more dangerous at a period when English detachments are wasting the South; when under the protection of some frigates, corps of fifteen hundred men are repairing to Virginia without our being able to get to them...

The result, sir, of all this is that... it becomes, from a political and military point of view, necessary to give us... a decided naval superiority for the next campaign; and also, sir, to give us money enough to place the regular army and ten thousand... militia in this part of the country; a Southern army... formed by the five southern states... Immense sums of money could not transport resources of equal value from Europe to America, but these, without a succour of money, although established on the very theatre of war, will become useless... All that credit, persuasion and force could achieve has been done—but that can hold out no longer.

...The Continental troops have as much courage and real discipline as those that are opposed to them. They are more inured to privation, more patient than Europeans... The recruits whom we are expecting... have seen more gunshots than three-fourths of the European soldiers... The militia... are not deficient in ardour and in discipline but would be most useful in the labours of a siege.

It had not occurred to Lafayette, the soul of honor, that French policy towards the United States was deliberately machiavellian. France's aim was to separate the country from Great Britain, while keeping America sufficiently weak to make it a French satellite. There is a long-standing myth that the American war was responsible for France's subsequent bankruptcy and revolution. France's financial aid to the United States was small and grudging. From 1775 to 1780 grants totalled only $600,000, of which a portion disappeared in internal French bribes. France advanced a further $1.6 million in loans at ungenerous terms.

Before Laurens' departure, Congress forwarded to Franklin a copy of his instructions to ask for a loan of $5 million. Franklin discussed the request with Vergennes who dismissed it but agreed to a grant of $1.1 million, equivalent to twenty months' pocket money for Marie Antoinette. Vergennes' subsidy was carefully calculated to barely keep the American army in being. Laurens reached Paris with a shopping list far in excess of the grant. He asked the ministers to reconsider and advance the larger sum in repayable loans. Franklin complained that he was too brusque with the government but this made no difference in French policy. Vergennes did say he would guarantee a loan in the Netherlands to the amount of $2 million. Since he knew the money could not then be raised, the offer was entirely *pro forma*.

The French court decided to send a fleet under the comte de Grasse to the West Indies, to cooperate with the Spanish against the British in the Caribbean. De Grasse was given an option to go to American waters, if circumstances permitted. Laurens returned to America just in time to join Washington and Rochambeau on their way to Virginia.

UTI POSSIDETIS

The European powers played war as a form of musical chairs. When they tired of fighting, the belligerents kept whatever real estate they occupied at the time the music stopped, though they might thereafter swap countries and islands.

While John Laurens was in France begging for help, Vergennes was engaged in arranging for other courts to "mediate" the war. Maurepas, the prime minister, had sent peace feelers to England as early as 1780. Necker, the finance minister, had also proposed peace with Great Britain, suggesting that partial independence be allowed a few American states. George III concluded that France was in financial difficulties and he should therefore hold out for complete American submission.

At this point the British held most of Georgia and South Carolina, a large part of North Carolina, much of Virginia and New York, and a naval base in Maine. In addition they controlled substantial areas of the Northwest Territory. Under Vergennes' mediation, America would have been left with the ports of Boston and Philadelphia and not much else on the sea, with the British and Spanish across the mountains. Washington was aware of the danger. He wrote Thomas Jefferson on June 8: "The progress which the enemy are making in Virginia is very alarming not only to the State immediately invaded but to all the rest, as I strongly suspect from the most recent European intelligences, that they are endeavouring to make as large seeming conquests as possible, that they may urge the plea of uti possidetis in the proposed mediation."

JOHN ADAMS

Fortunately John Adams, who had been a headache for Washington and Franklin, was in Europe, fully ready to take on the French foreign ministry.

Franklin had won all hearts in Paris but this had not deflected, to the slightest degree, French government policy based on its own self-interest. What the United States needed was a man to stick up for his country, and this Adams did to a degree that alarmed Franklin and Vergennes. Adams' touch of paranoia was often misdirected but in this case it gave him dazzling insight.

Adams' vanity was attractive because he could be humorous about it. He had no humor about his country. Arriving in France as minister, with full powers to make a treaty of peace and commerce with Great Britain, he aroused Vergennes' suspicions, while Adams was won over, at first, by Vergennes' charming insincerity. With time on his hands, he busied himself addressing the comte de Vergennes as a representative of a fully equal power: "The state of things in America has really become alarming, and this merely for want of a few French men-of-war on the coast... The flourishing state of France's maritime and commerce, and the decisive influence of her councils... all the world will allow to be owing in great measure... to her new connections with the United States... The United States of America are a great and powerful people, whatever European statesmen may think of them."

By the following year, while Vergennes was busy with his scheme to dismember the United States, Adams was writing him: "The dignity of North America does not consist in diplomatic ceremonials or any of the subtleties of etiquette; it consists solely in reason, justice, truth, the rights of mankind and the interests of the nations of Europe... The United States have assumed their equal station among the nations. They have assumed a sovereignty which they acknowledge to hold only from God and their own swords."

Vergennes' reactions were direct and simple. He ordered Luzerne, his minister at Philadelphia, to instruct Congress, which eagerly desired their crumbs of gold from France, to clip the wings of John Adams. In June 1781 Congress directed Adams to place himself under the authority of Vergennes and to do nothing without his knowledge and concurrence. In addition Congress appointed three other ministers coequal with him in peace negotiations. Adams received these revised instructions as he was on his way to the Netherlands. He conveyed his suspicions to his diary: "Keep us poor. Depress us. Keep us weak. Make us feel our obligations. Impress our minds with a sense of gratitude. Let Europe see our dependence. Make Europe believe we are in great distress and danger... Propagate bad news, to discourage the merchants and bankers from lending us money. Is there anything in these jealousies and insinuations?"

LONDON

On December 17, 1780, Lord North complained to the king that Britain's declaration of war on Holland would cause him great trouble in raising more loans. He again said his mind and body were going and he ought to resign. On January 14, North wrote the king that Britain would have to raise an extra £3 million for the army in America, which he had not anticipated. The expenses, he said, "are increased to an amazing degree." Lord Stormont, a few days later, suggested to the king he might try to bribe Russia to enter the war by offering her Minorca.

In the newly elected Parliament, a young man named William Pitt was returned from Appleby, Westmorland, where Washington's father, uncle, and two half brothers had gone to school. By June Horace Walpole was writing that Pitt, with all his father's oratory, had "answered Lord North and tore him limb from limb." As Greene and Cornwallis fought throughout the South, Pitt described Cornwallis' efforts as "a series of ineffective victories or severe defeats—victories only celebrated with temporary triumph over our brethren whom we would trample down, or defeats which fill the land with mourning for the loss of dear and valuable relations, slain in the impious cause of enforcing unconditional submission." Lord North continued to command heavy majorities for continuing the war but he was hammered at from all sides, and his heart had long gone out of the business.

WAR IN VIRGINIA

In December Sir Henry Clinton sent Benedict Arnold to Virginia with orders to take a post at Portsmouth, to move up the James River destroying supplies, and, if possible, to block any attempt by Washington, Congress, or Governor Jefferson to relieve Greene's army in the Carolinas. Clinton was not entirely sure of Arnold's trustworthiness or judgement. He assigned to his staff Lieutenant Colonels Thomas Dundas and John Simcoe; Arnold was ordered to consult with them on all operations.

Arnold arrived in Virginia on December 30 and proceeded rapidly up the James to Westover and Richmond. Jefferson heard by December 31 that a British fleet had arrived but he took little action and, when he did act, it was too late. By January 3, Arnold had driven Jefferson out of the capital at Richmond. He destroyed arms, ammunition, government records, and the state's most important foundry. Arnold then returned to Portsmouth, where he remained until spring. Steuben, in command of the handful of Continental troops in the state, wrote of his disgust, for the northern governors had done far better when invasion came than the southern governors had.

Washington advised Jefferson in early February that, despite sporadic raids of this kind, he should not neglect to send all possible aid and reinforcements to Greene, who was fighting the main British army in the South; the longer it was kept out of Virginia the better. At almost the same time Washington wrote Jefferson that a chance had come to send aid south since a severe storm had damaged the British fleet blockading Rhode Island. For a glorious moment it looked as though relief could go by sea and Arnold could be captured and hanged.

THE FRENCH ENVOY INTERFERES

The chevalier de La Luzerne had, once before, accidentally prevented Washington from capturing Arnold when, on his way to Rhode Island, he persuaded Washington to spend a night at Fishkill rather than West Point. The next morning Arnold went off to the enemy. Luzerne again managed to foul up a daring plan to close in on Arnold. The French minister at Philadelphia was engaged in diplomatic pool, which looked to Spanish and French interests rather than American. He had two objectives: to prevent the Northwest Territory, the future middle west of the United States, from becoming American at the peace, and to keep the navigation of the Mississippi in Spanish hands.

In his operations, conflicting private and public interests were at work. The private Illinois-Wabash Company owned or claimed large parts of the Northwest Territory that Virginia considered hers by original charter. The company's stockholders included a number of prominent Marylanders, as well as the former French minister, Conrad Gérard, brother of Joseph Gérard de Rayneval, French undersecretary of foreign affairs; and the French consul at Philadelphia, John Holker.

The Articles of Confederation, supposed to form a more perfect union of the states, had never been ratified. Maryland refused to sign unless Virginia and other states surrendered their claims to western lands. Luzerne was anxious to accomplish this in order to facilitate France's operations at the peace table. In addition, he wanted the Articles approved, since under the new constitution four states, rather than the previous six, could block foreign treaties.

This would make it easier for pro-French factions to control American foreign policy. While the minister was pushing the states to ratify, he proposed to Vergennes that future French financial aid be directed to individual states rather than to Congress. Thus he hoped further to divide and conquer the new weak nation.

It was not difficult to get Jefferson's Virginia to surrender the western lands. This left Maryland as a holdout. With the British raiding the Chesapeake, Luzerne had only to hint that future French aid was contingent on the Articles being passed. Ratification came quickly in February 1781. Without consulting Washington, Luzerne then requested Rochambeau and Destouches to send a small naval force to the Chesapeake.

Washington received word on February 7 of the storm that had broken the British blockade of Newport on January 29. He immediately forwarded to Rochambeau his latest information of Arnold's movements, suggesting that Destouches and his fleet ought to proceed to the Chesapeake. By February 15, having had further Virginia intelligence, Washington sent a rather hurried letter, clumsily drafted by Hamilton, proposing to Rochambeau an immediate plan to capture Arnold. Washington would detach Lafayette and twelve hundred continentals to move as rapidly as possible by land to Virginia. He hoped, in turn, that Rochambeau would cooperate by sending the whole of the French fleet southward, together with a thousand troops and as much siege artillery as he could spare. He noted that "the capture of Arnold and his detachment will be an event particularly agreeable to the Country; a great relief to the Southern states and of important utility in our future operations." On February 20, Lafayette, with his continental detachment, headed rapidly south, the young general marching his troops thirty or more miles a day.

On February 20 Rochambeau replied that Luzerne had only asked for some frigates and one ship of the line and had not mentioned any troops. He had sent these to Virginia under Captain Armand de Tilly. Arnold, who had been a merchant mariner and had fought naval battles on Lake Champlain, was too clever to be caught by de Tilly, who had no ground forces. He moved his small boats up the Elizabeth River. The French expedition was not totally unsuccessful, for the fleet caught a British warship and several merchantmen. The French returned to Newport fifteen days after leaving port.

On February 27 Washington received word from Rochambeau and Destouches that, following their initial failure, they had decided to proceed with his plan. He wrote immediately to Lafayette to wait at Head of Elk for word of French naval movements. He informed Destouches that he had received the news "with peculiar pleasure" and he would proceed, as soon as possible, to Newport, to discuss the plans. By March 5 Lafayette was at Head of Elk.

THE NEWPORT MEETING

Washington left New Windsor on March 2, riding at his best speed to Newport. He was met at Jamestown, Rhode Island, on March 6 by the French admiral's barge, which carried him to the flagship, the *Duc de Bourgogne*. His one anxiety was to see everything start. He was informed the next day that the French fleet, loaded with troops and provisions, was ready to sail. Several days elapsed before they were under way.

Rochambeau had often expressed the wish of the French army to see "their general." This was Washington's first chance to review allied troops. The French formed an honor guard stretching from the wharf to Rochambeau's house, where Washington stayed. The next night Newport was illuminated, the town council having voted funds so that every house could have candles. The French held a ball in his honor, which he opened by dancing with Margaret Champlin; French officers took the instruments for the appropriate opening tune: "A Successful Campaign."

Washington greatly impressed the French. Claude Blanchard, their commissary, noted that he was "handsome, noble and gracious... I mark, as a fortunate day, that in which I have been able to behold a man so truly great." Another officer wrote to an American about "the arrival of the celebrated Washington, the Atlas of your country... We had not eyes enough to see him with. Man is born with a tendency to pride and the further he progresses in his career in an elevated rank the more his self love nourishes this vice in him but, so far from this, Washington, although born with every superior quality, adds to them an imposing modesty, which will always cause him to be admired by those who have the good fortune to see him; as for esteem he has already drawn to himself that of all Europe."

Washington stayed a week with the French then headed back to his camp. At Bristol, the principal people of the town rode out on horseback to greet him. The entire population was out to cheer and to drop flowers and evergreens in his way through the town. At Providence everyone again turned out. Count Dumas noted in his memoirs that the children, carrying torches, crowded so thickly around "their father," that no one could move. Washington pointed to them and told Dumas: "We may be beaten by the English but there is an army they can never beat." By March 17 he was back at New Windsor, anxious for every letter from the south.

WASHINGTON APOLOGIZES

The second French naval expedition returned to Newport in nearly as fast time as the first eighteen days. The British fleet had been allowed six weeks for repairs after the storm. A superior British force chased the French to the Chesapeake. An indecisive battle was fought in which two French and three British ships were damaged. Destouches quickly retired to Newport, leaving Arbuthnot in command of the Chesapeake. Sir Henry Clinton at once dispatched Major General William Phillips and twenty-five hundred troops to Virginia, where they arrived on March 26. Clinton mentioned in his memoirs that the French expedition could not have failed had it got under way earlier, but a seven weeks' delay can be long in war.

Washington heard on March 30 that the whole enterprise had fallen through, making it the fourth time the French navy had failed to cooperate effectively with American plans. Nonetheless he wrote the French minister on March 31 that he was sure there would be "universal admiration of the good conduct and bravery of the French forces." He sent similar letters to Rochambeau and Destouches.

Two days before writing the French, Washington had sent a note to Lund Washington, his Mount Vernon manager, mainly about his farm and personal affairs but he added: "It was unfortunate, but this I mention in confidence, that the French fleet and detachment did not undertake the enterprize they are now upon, when I first proposed it to them; the destruction of Arnolds Corps would then have been inevitable before the British fleet could have been in a condition to put to Sea... The small squadron... could not, as I foretold, do anything without a land force." The letter was a highly restrained comment on a disaster that put the southern states in an even more critical situation. The British captured the letter and printed it in *Rivington's Gazette*.

It is difficult to see why American historians have chided Washington for the remarks. Douglas Southall Freeman was perhaps the most critical, for he has a whole chapter called "Washington's Pen Runs Away with Him," and he terms the letter "imprudent," "unrestrained," and "offensive," adding that it was humiliating for Washington and insulting to the allies.

Rochambeau wrote Washington a dignified complaint, saying that the proposal had not reached him until ten days after the first French squadron sailed. He said nothing about the failure of the French to consult the commander in chief about their operations. On April 30 Washington offered Rochambeau a straightforward regret that he had unintentionally given pain to the French, but he deftly placed a thorn amidst the roses: "I have lately learnt (though not officially) that the cause of the delay I have alluded to was a want of Supplies for the fleet. Impressed with a real esteem for, and confidence in the Chevalier Des Touches, I heard this circumstance with satisfaction."

With spring, Washington could not help thinking that he had not seen Mount Vernon for nearly six years. He wrote General John Armstrong on March 25:

Our affairs are brought to an awful crisis, that the hand of Providence, I trust, may be more conspicuous in our deliverance.

The many remarkable interpositions of the divine government in the hours of our deepest distress and darkness, have been too luminous to suffer me to doubt the happy issue of the present conflict; but the period for its accomplishment may be too far distant for a person of my years, whose Morning and Evening hours, and every moment (unoccupied by business), pants for retirement; and for those domestic and rural enjoyments which in my estimation far surpasses the highest pagentry of the world.

In his letter to Lund Washington criticizing the slow tactics of the French, he had asked: "How many Lambs have you had this Spring? How many Colts are you like to have? Is your covered way done? What are you going about next? Have you any prospects of getting paint and Oyl?... Have you made good the decayed trees... Have you made any attempts to reclaim more Land for Meadow?... An acct. Of these things would be satisfactory to me, and infinitely amusing... as I have these kind of improvements very much at heart."

On April 18 Lund Washington wrote him that a British vessel had anchored off Mount Vernon, stolen some slaves, and destroyed a boat. Lund said he had taken refreshments on board the ship in an endeavor to regain the negroes. On April 30 Washington sent a sharp reply: "I am very sorry to hear of your loss. I am a little sorry to hear of my own; but that which gives me most concern is that you should go on board the enemy's vessels, and furnish them with refreshments. It would have been a less painful circumstance for me to have heard that, in consequence of your non-compliance with their request, they had burnt my House and laid the Plantation in ruins. You ought to have considered yourself as my representative, and should have reflected on the bad example of communication with the enemy." Washington added that he knew Lund was trying to protect his property but the whole thing was "ill-Judged." He added that so long as the British controlled the seas, there was no way to stop the raids, and he expected his house to be burned. He suggested that Lund move out the most valuable and least bulky objects.

WAR IN THE SOUTH

According to his published notes on the state, Thomas Jefferson, as governor of Virginia, was commander in chief of its fifty thousand militia. When Steuben asked for two thousand men to march south to reinforce Greene against the main enemy, Cornwallis, Jefferson rejected the request, although this strategy had been strongly urged on him by Washington. Steuben then asked him to move against the British at Portsmouth but the governor again disapproved.

Lafayette reconnoitered the Chesapeake after learning that a fleet had been sighted to the south. To his distress he found the ships to be British. Moving to Annapolis, he was temporarily blockaded there. On his own credit, he provided his men with $9,000 worth of clothing. When the joint forces of Phillips and Arnold moved to Petersburg, he marched rapidly south to save Richmond at the end of April, even though his forces were only a quarter of the enemy's. On May 10 the Virginia Assembly resolved to meet thereafter in Charlottesville. Shortly afterwards, on May 24, Lafayette wrote to Washington from Richmond, describing his situation:

I ardently wish my conduct may meet with your approbation. Had I followed the first impulsion of my temper, I would have risked some things more. But I have been guarding against my own warmth, and this consideration that a general defeat… would involve this State and our affairs in ruin, had rendered me extremely cautious in my movements. Indeed, I am… more crippled in my projects than we have been in the Northern States.

…Public stores and private property being removed from Richmond, this place is a less important object. I don't believe it would be prudent to expose the troops for the sake of a few houses… Was I to fight a battle, I'll be cut to pieces, the militia dispersed, and the arms lost. Was I to decline fighting, the country would think herself given up. I am therefore determined to skirmish, but not to engage too far…

Was I any ways equal to the enemy, I would be extremely happy in my present command. But I am not strong enough even to get beaten. Government in this state has no energy.

On June 5, Tarleton and 250 dragoons rode swiftly to Charlottesville to capture the governor and legislature. Virginia's commander in chief, warned just in time, fled to the West. Tarleton seized one congressman and eight members of the Virginia Assembly. Thus Thomas Jefferson, who had pledged his fellow Signers' lives, fortunes, and sacred honor, ignominiously ended his governorship. He was replaced by a militia general, Thomas Nelson, Jr.

From this point on, thanks in large part to Washington's foresight, Lafayette's position began to improve. Steuben had spent the winter drilling a continental battalion, intended to aid Greene in North and South Carolina. When Jefferson, to Greene's anger, intervened to forbid this part of the Virginia line from leaving the state, they were added to Lafayette's forces in June. Wayne had also spent much time that winter and spring in rebuilding the Pennsylvania line, which had been decimated by Reed. He marched south with his new troops that same month, bringing Lafayette's total to twenty-five hundred regulars. To these were soon added nearly eight hundred North Carolina riflemen. The new governor of Virginia restored energy to the state government, especially its defenses. Before long Lafayette had an additional twenty-two hundred militia, making his force opposed to Cornwallis much more formidable than it had been. While he was not strong enough for a general engagement, he was sufficiently so to stop further raids and to harry the enemy onto the peninsula between the James and the York Rivers. That summer of 1781 the entire success of the allied operations and the future of the United States of America was to depend on Lafayette's skill in keeping Cornwallis bottled up.

On May 2, 1781, Lord George Germain sent peremptory orders to Sir Henry Clinton: "I am commanded by His Majesty to acquaint you that the recovery of the southern provinces and the prosecution of our conquests from south to north is to be considered as the chief and principal employment of all the forces which can be spared... until it is accomplished." It was the American army, however, that was to carry out Germain's plan almost to the letter.

Presumably Germain viewed the three southernmost states as safely under British control. With their rear secure, the British could then move on to Virginia and then up into Maryland. Whatever Germain may have believed, the southern states were in fact anything but secure.

Lord Cornwallis had received Clinton's instructions that Charleston was to be kept at all costs, and South Carolina be made perfectly secure, before he moved north for further operations. In the March 15 battle of Guilford Court House, North Carolina, Cornwallis had beaten Greene, but he thereby lost a quarter of his forces. He thereupon retreated to Wilmington, the state's principal seaport, from which he moved north to Virginia. Greene almost immediately determined to push straight into South Carolina. There he was defeated by Lord Rawdon at Hobkirk's Hill on April 25, but, as he put it in words that became famous, "We fight, get beat, rise and fight again."

This battle's effect was outweighed by a general uprising in South Carolina and Georgia, encouraged by the presence of an American army. Partisans under Henry Lee, Andrew Pickens, Thomas Sumter, and Francis Marion attacked throughout the area. Within six weeks almost every interior post in the two states had fallen to the Americans. By July Lee was almost at the gates of Charleston. Before Washington set foot in Virginia, the British were effectively confined to three ports in the three southernmost states.

WETHERSFIELD CONFERENCE

When Rochambeau's son returned from France discouraged because few of his father's requests had been granted, the French general asked for a further conference with Washington to plan the 1781 campaign.

As Washington was getting ready, he received news of a signal honor. In early 1776, before independence was declared, Harvard had given him its honorary degree. Less-giddy Yale waited five years. In May 1781, he was awarded the college's doctorate, with a letter from President Ezra Stiles: "We cannot add to the accumulation of glory which shines around the name of Washington, and which none but himself thinks unmerited." Stiles also had the grace to recognize and compliment Washington's "literary merits."

On May 1 Washington resumed the diary he had broken off in June 1775. It contains interesting points that are not always covered in letters, such as verbal instructions to intelligence agents and where he stayed while travelling. Washington reached Wethersfield, Connecticut, in time for extensive conversations with the state's governor, before Rochambeau and Chastellux arrived on May 21. He attended church with Connecticut's chief executive. The minister's text: "Blessed are the poor in spirit, for theirs is the kingdom of heaven," was painfully apt in view of the deficiencies of supplies, men, and money that Washington listed in his diary.

Admiral the Comte de Barras, who had arrived from France to take command from the Chevalier Destouches, intended to attend the conference but the British admiral, Arbuthnot, showed up off Newport and de Barras stayed put.

The French found Wethersfield as picturesque as it is, in large degree, today. Baron Cromot du Bourg thought the town charming. "It would be impossible to find prettier houses and a more beautiful view." From the steeple of the church where Washington, in Congregational fashion, had worshipped all day, du Bourg noted the rich country he could see for fifty miles around.

Washington informed Rochambeau at their conferences of May 22 and 23 that he had brought along intercepted dispatches from Germain to Clinton, in which Lord George said that he expected the southern states to be conquered and thereafter every effort should be made to bring Maryland and Pennsylvania back to "obedience." Neither Washington nor Rochambeau knew at this time that Cornwallis had reached Virginia. Rochambeau told Washington, in turn, that none of the additional troops he had asked for from France would be forthcoming. Indeed his government had even cancelled the second division, which they had promised the Americans in the spring of 1780.

Washington and Rochambeau agreed that, in spite of the distances and difficulties, the main objective in a combined operation would probably be the southern states. It was necessary to make every effort to deceive the enemy. A plan for this purpose was devised, which was described by Washington in a letter of July 31, 1788, to Noah Webster. The American general, by letter and otherwise, was to make it clear that New York was to be the sole objective. The plan was the easier to carry out because de Barras did not have sufficient transports to move Rochambeau's army from Newport to Virginia, and therefore the French would march by land, joining the American army on the Hudson. The deception was so skillfully carried out that it not only fooled Sir Henry Clinton but also a remarkable number of later biographers and historians, who believed that Rochambeau forced the march to Yorktown on a reluctant Washington.

LETTERS TO JOHN HANCOCK

Washington had promised Rochambeau that he would make every effort to fill his continental battalions, to raise supplies and ammunition from the states, and to provide militia from Massachusetts and Rhode Island to guard the French guns at Providence.

Washington began at Wethersfield, and continued in the spring and summer from other points, an extensive unilateral correspondence with John Hancock, governor of Massachusetts. By July 8 he was writing Hancock: "I have not been honored with an answer to my several letters of the 24th and 25th of May, of the 2nd, 4th, 15th, and 25th of last Month, and am of course unable to form any estimate of what may be expected in consequence of my requisitions. This puts me in rather an awkward situation, as I cannot give His Excellency Count Rochambeau, who has formed a junction with me, that official assurance of support which I had promised upon the faith of the States." Washington wrote further letters on July 14, July 30, and August 4. On August 24 Washington apologized to the governor of Rhode Island for "the neglect or Inattention of your Sister State, who have been repeatedly requested to send on their Quota."

Washington had also asked Hancock to send Massachusetts militia into the Albany region in order to release continental troops for his army. When he ordered his Albany continentals to join the main forces, the inhabitants there protested that there were no militia and they would be without protection. Washington ordered one New York regiment to remain there temporarily, which delayed their march for Yorktown.

In a confused reply of August 15 Hancock acknowledged receipt of "several" letters. He seemed surprised about everything: the militia requests for Newport and Albany, and Washington's requisitions of powder. Some of these he said he had forgotten about or he thought maybe he had taken care of them. By the time Washington received this letter he was on his way to Virginia.

As soon he returned to New Windsor, Washington learned that Thomas Jefferson's government in Virginia had collapsed. His diary for June 7 noted that he had received a letter from Pennsylvania's Joseph Reed which "afforded little hope of provision or other things from that State and was more productive of what they had done than what they meant to do." Slightly offsetting his lack of aid from the states were letters from Greene, who reported that Lord Rawdon had abandoned Camden; Orangeburg, Fort Motte, and Granby were recaptured; and the American army was investing Ninety Six and Augusta.

BRITISH INTELLIGENCE AND THE PILOTS

On June 10 Rochambeau informed Washington that de Grasse would definitely appear in American waters that summer. Washington replied on June 13 that, while they had decided New York was the only possible point of attack under existing circumstances, if de Grasse brought naval superiority or, even better, his whole fleet, other areas of operation might be "more practicable." Both officers knew this meant Virginia.

The British intercepted messengers carrying Rochambeau's accounts of Wethersfield to Luzerne and Washington's to Lafayette. These outlined the plans for attacking New York, but Sir Henry failed to detect that they were to be flexible and contingent upon circumstances. Clinton quite correctly noted in his memoirs that Washington had been much alarmed by the British invasion in the South, but Washington's supposed plans to attack him equally alarmed Clinton. He wrote Cornwallis that, in view of Lafayette's feeble forces of continentals in Virginia and Washington's proposal to besiege New York with as many as twenty thousand men, he was to return a part of his forces as soon as possible.

On June 23 Clinton received intelligence from Newport that the French frigate *Concorde* was taking ten American pilots to the West Indies. He did not know that Rochambeau's letters were also aboard; these pleaded with de

Grasse to bring with him all the ships, troops, and money that he could scrape together. On June 28 Clinton forwarded the intelligence about the pilots to Rodney in the West Indies, not then realizing that de Barras had, in fact, sent thirty pilots, allowing one for each ship that de Grasse might be in a position to bring.

About July 12 Captain George Beckwith received corrective and more accurate information from Newport, which noted that, in addition to the ten pilots from Rhode Island, the *Concorde* had previously taken on fourteen at Boston. "Their destination is for the West Indies, to pilot the Count de Grasse's squadron upon the Coast, who certainly comes with a powerful body of troops and ships. I conceive their design is to give Mr. Rodney the slip, and their object at present is certainly New York; if that is thought impracticable, Virginia." This was perhaps the most important single report received by British intelligence during the war, but there is no indication that it made the slightest difference to Sir Henry Clinton's planning.

This was the year when the British military and naval high commands were seized with idiocy. In the spring Germain informed Clinton's aide in London that he considered the war as practically finished, with Washington's small army reduced to starvation, the French cooped up in Newport, and the South nearly reconquered. He wrote Clinton that he was sending him four thousand additional troops and, with these, he should surely have enough men to end the rebellion. He assured him that, while de Grasse had gone to the Indies, Rodney would be watching him so carefully that Clinton had nothing to worry about from that source.

Clinton did not fret about de Grasse until it was too late. He spent his time writing Germain that he did not have enough troops to end the war. He said that Washington and the French together had thirty thousand men, in the North and South, plus many thousand militia and what could he do? (In fact, Clinton with his reinforcements had nearly thirty-seven thousand effectives, whereas the continentals and the French numbered around sixteen thousand.) Cornwallis marched back and forth in Virginia with no warning whatsoever of what was impending, before settling down on a peninsula, where the Royal Navy would assure his security.

Rodney in the West Indies, although he heard of the arrival of thirty American pilots before he returned to England, took no hint from this. He had already ordered fourteen British ships of the line to go north under Sir Samuel Hood and saw no reason to change his plans. He informed the British admiral at New York, eight days after de Grasse had sailed for the Chesapeake with twenty-eight ships, that he thought de Grasse would take "at least 12" ships north. Sir Samuel Hood, as he proceeded with a fleet half the size of de

Grasse's, informed Sir Henry Clinton, on August 25, that he was bringing enough force "fully to defeat any designs of the enemy, let de Grasse bring or send what ships he may in aid of those under de Barras."

THE FRENCH AND AMERICANS JOIN

The French were more than glad to get away from the small island and town they had occupied since the preceding summer. But they did not leave with undue haste. Washington at one point asked Rochambeau if he could hurry a bit in order to put pressure on Clinton to remove troops from the South.

The French marching routes were planned and drawn by Alexandre Berthier, later chief of staff to Napoleon. Rochambeau left Wethersfield on May 23, but his army did not quit Newport until June 10. By June 17 the French were no farther than Providence. Thereafter they moved at about half the speed of Lafayette on his way to Virginia. The troops were well disciplined and behaved, and this made a lasting and pleasant impression on the Americans. The officers were delighted with the acacia trees in bloom and found the Connecticut town of Windham and its girls charming. They did not reach Westchester and their Phillipsburg encampment until July 6. On July 15 Washington noted that the British sloop of war, the *Savage*, which had been the American *General Washington*, and several other vessels went easily up the Hudson past his defenses.

While waiting for the French, Washington had moved his headquarters to Dobbs Ferry, to be nearer Manhattan. On July 9 he noted in his diary: "Received a Letter from the Marqs. De la Fayette [dated June 28] informing me of Cornwallis' retreat to Williamsburg—that he had pushed his Rear and had obtained advantages—having killed 60 and wounded an hundred with small loss. Southern accts. Though not official speak of the reduction of Augusta and Ninety Six by the Arms of Major Genl. Greene."

Cornwallis' move towards Yorktown had been, in part, occasioned by Clinton's capture of the Wethersfield documents and his immediate call on Cornwallis for more troops. There began a series of misunderstandings between Cornwallis and Clinton, resulting in squabbles that lasted for years and that Clinton rehashed till his death. Clinton suggested that Cornwallis move against Philadelphia and Baltimore, that he return troops to protect New York, and that he establish bases in Virginia, which would have access to Britain's sea power. For his part, Cornwallis established only one base, which proved inadequate for its purpose. Furthermore, not only did he refuse to return troops to New York, he suggested instead that Clinton move all his troops to Virginia. Amidst this squabbling, Clinton neglected to warn Cornwallis that a heavy French sea and land force might be going to Virginia.

On July 20 Washington wrote in his diary: "Count de Rochambeau having called upon me... for a definitive plan of campaign [for de Grasse]... I could not but acknowledge that the uncertainties under which we labour—the few Men who have joined [as continentals or militia] and the ignorance in which I am kept by some of the States on whom I mostly depended—especially Massachusetts from whose Governor I have not received a line... rendered it impracticable for me to do more than prepare, first, for the enterprise against New York, and secondly for the relief of the Southern States, if after all my efforts and earnest applications to these States, it should be found at the arrival of Count de Grasse, that I had neither Men nor means adequate to the first object." Washington noted the same day that he had ordered General Knox to "suspend the Transport of the heavy Cannon and Stores from Philadelphia lest we should have to carry them back."

Though Washington thus gave a clear indication that everything pointed to the South, sound tactics indicated that he continue all preparations for a siege of New York. If more continentals were sent by the states and de Grasse arrived with sufficient troops and naval support, the operation might still be carried out. If not, the preparations would worry and harass Sir Henry Clinton and put pressure on him to recall troops from Virginia. In addition, some portion of the efforts would be useful either way. Washington, for example, ordered the building of a hundred new boats and the repair of all existing vessels on the Hudson. These could be used for ferrying southbound troops across the river or for waterborne attacks on Staten or Manhattan Island.

On July 20 Lafayette had written Washington that he wanted to rejoin the main army for its operations. On July 30, using indirection for fear the enemy would capture the letter, Washington told Lafayette to stay in Virginia "until matters are reduced to a greater degree of certainty than they are at present, especially when I tell you that, from the change of circumstances with which a removal of part of the Enemy's force from Virginia to New York will be attended, it is more than probable that we shall also entirely change our plan of operations." He noted that the proposed change would be difficult, not because they lacked sufficient force to move south but because of transport problems by land. "I should not however hesitate in encountering these difficulties great as they are, had we prospects of transporting ourselves in a manner, safe easy and expeditious. Your penetration will point out my meaning"; that is the march south would be foreshortened by 175 miles if de Grasse could move the troops by sea from the head of the Chesapeake. He noted that he had asked de Barras to proceed to Virginia to aid Lafayette, but he preferred to sit in Newport to await "greater plans."

On August 1 Washington asked Knox to estimate all the ordnance and stores that would be available south of the Hudson. He also requested Robert Morris, who had been made superintendent of finance in the government, to look into the amount of shipping that could be made ready quickly at Philadelphia and in the Chesapeake Bay, in order "to carry a Body of Men suddenly round by Water."

The time around New York was not wasted, for the Americans and French got to know each other during numerous reconnaissance and skirmishing parties. On July 3 a first attempt by Washington at a landing from the Jersey shore, above Spuyten Duyvel, failed when the duke de Lauzun's cavalry, who had a long ride through excessive heat, did not arrive in time to support General Lincoln. On July 18 Washington, with Rochambeau and Duportail, crossed the Hudson to reconnoiter the enemy's Manhattan defenses. Although he had left the island more than five years previously, Washington remembered and noted in his diary many details of the fortifications and the ensuing changes. In particular he remarked that the island's trees had all been cut down (for firewood) and a new growth of waist-high bushes had taken their place. On July 21 the French and American commanders, with a large part of both armies to screen them, reconnoitered the Bronx from King's Bridge, Clinton's only connection with the mainland, to Frog's Neck. Washington noted that the British defenses at Forts Knyphausen (once Washington), Tryon, and Laurel Hill were "formidable." By the end of July he had about abandoned all hope of an attack on New York as too strong for his few troops. During the operations, the French were assessing their American commander. They also studied his campaigns, leaving around maps of Princeton and Trenton in compliment to him. The French at their first meeting with Washington in 1780 had been, as Blanchard reported, "enchanted." They were now all curious to see him in action. Luckily many were diarists and letter writers. Baron Cromot du Bourg wrote: "Washington is a very fine looking man, but this did not surprise me as much as I expected from the descriptions I had heard of him. His physiognomy is noble in the highest degree, and his manners are those of one perfectly accustomed to society, quite a rare thing certainly in America." After their reconnaissance at Morrisania, du Bourg added: "I need not mention the sang froid of General Washington, it is well-known; but this great man is a thousand times more noble and splendid at the head of his army than at any other time."

Comte Louis-Philippe de Ségur, son of the French war minister, wrote: "When I looked at Washington I found a perfect accord between the impression made by his appearance and the idea I had formed of him... His figure was noble and tall; the expression in his face was pleasant and kind; his smile was gentle, his manners simple without being familiar. He did not flaunt the magnificence displayed by generals under our monarchies; he was the embodiment of the republican hero. He inspired rather than commanded respect and, in the eyes of all the men around him, one could read their real affection and whole-hearted confidence in a chief, upon whom they seemed to rely entirely for their security."

Ségur had heard of the hordes of ill-dressed peasants who had swarmed around Gage at Boston, and he noted that he expected the American troops to be a rabble in unkempt camps. "One may imagine how surprised I was when I saw a well-disciplined army, presenting in every detail, the very image of order, reason, training and experience." Other officers noted their relief at finding that the American troops, though they had inadequate clothing and few resources, were disciplined and well-trained.

The French were particularly pleased to observe Washington at close quarters at the dinner table where, after the meal, he relaxed in long conversations over glasses of wine. Claude Blanchard, the French quartermaster general, noted that he had a "most gracious and amiable smile. He is affable and converses with his officers familiarly and gaily." The comte de Dumas commented that he enlivened all the after-dinner conversations with his "unaffected cheerfulness."

The doughty little padre of the Soissonais regiment, Abbé Claude Robin, went with the French army on horseback from Providence to Yorktown. He wrote that he found the trip very hard, with the marches beginning at two in the morning, and the long, hot days going by without food or drink. He commented that he felt embarrassed because the young nobles of the army, who had every luxury in France, bore it all so cheerfully. On August 4 he achieved his desire to see the commander in chief: "I saw Washington... I gazed at him eagerly to find... the marks of genius... He has a tall, noble, and well-proportioned figure, and an open, kind and calm expression... Throughout all [this country] he appears like a benevolent God; old men, women, children all flock eagerly to catch a glimpse of him; people follow him through the towns with torches, his arrival is marked by public illuminations... The Americans, a cold people... are inflamed by the very mention of his name."

TWENTY-NINE

WESTCHESTER TO YORKTOWN

1781

ALTHOUGH IN RETROSPECT the Yorktown operations appear remarkably smooth and speedy, the odds against their success were great. De Grasse had promised the fullest aid but Washington's past experience of French assurances had not been good. Hurricanes or the Royal Navy might have delayed or stopped de Grasse. The strength of the British fleet in American and Caribbean waters, with expected reinforcements under Admiral Digby, was near that of the French. The British were the more experienced seamen, and their copper-bottomed ships were faster. Had they used any skill de Grasse might never have been master of the Chesapeake. Even so the French fleet, when it achieved clear superiority, came close to ruining the operation.

In his first proposal de Grasse gave Washington no more than sixty-two days to achieve his objective. Possibly the time was even less, for de Grasse said he had to be back in the Caribbean by October 15. The French army had taken six weeks to march from Newport to Westchester. Washington now had to move far larger forces three times this distance, in the heat of the summer, with immense ferrying problems over seven major intervening rivers. Upon reaching Virginia he had to conduct a siege. Sir Henry Clinton had required sixty-six days to effect the conquest of Charleston, with British forces welded together in years of warfare. The French and American armies had been together for the first time and for only a few weeks. The French officers were knowledgeable in engineering and siege warfare, but only the oldest had ever been in battle, and that was twenty years before. Rochambeau's last previous siege had been in 1756; his troops were green and untested. Nevertheless Washington took all the risks on his shoulders. Four days after hearing that de Grasse was on his way, the combined armies with their artillery and stores were crossing the Hudson.[*]

AUGUST 14–16

Washington had received the dispatch from de Barras on August 14, informing him that de Grasse would leave Cap François on August 3 with twenty-five to twenty-nine ships of the line and thirty-two hundred troops. De Grasse hoped that everything would be in perfect readiness to begin operations at once, since he could spare only a few weeks. At the same time de Barras informed Washington that he himself had decided to go off on an expedition to Newfoundland. As he explained to Rochambeau, de Grasse had once served under him as a cadet but was now his superior in rank. Rochambeau wrote to de Barras to protest, with Washington adding a footnote that he had heard a reinforcement was coming under Admiral Digby. This might endanger de Grasse's fleet if de Barras did not stay. De Barras then agreed to abandon his northern expedition, but he did not get under way from Newport until two weeks after his receipt of the message announcing de Grasse's departure from Cap François.

On August 15 Washington wrote to Lafayette, ordering his express horsemen to "ride Night and Day" with the letter. He informed Lafayette that de Grasse would soon be off the Virginia coast, and he was to take every possible step to prevent Cornwallis from escaping to North Carolina. At this point Washington did not know of Cornwallis' plans, but the next day he recorded heartening intelligence.

Letters from the Marqs. de la Fayette and others inform that Lord Cornwallis with the Troops from Hampton Road, had proceeded up York River and landed at York and Gloucester Towns where they were throwing up Works on the 6th. Inst.

---

[*] The distance from Dobbs Ferry to York varied from about 440 miles by land and to 550 miles by sea. The latter was longer because ships had to round the lower peninsula to reach the York river.

On August 15 Cornwallis reported to Clinton that he had seventy-five hundred army rank and file, plus around fifteen hundred Tories, marines, and sailors for his defenses. The following day he wrote that he was working on the Gloucester fort but that he had not yet removed all of his forces from Portsmouth.

In the meantime, the twenty-eight French ships of the line under de Grasse were moving north between the Bahamas and the Florida coast, a channel not usually used and therefore away from prying British eyes. De Barras, with his eight ships, was moving reluctantly and slowly to join but taking care to bring with him the heavy French siege guns from Rhode Island.

The Royal Navy, for its part, was everywhere. Admiral Graves, who had been on sea patrol, returned to New York on August 16 with his seven ships of the line. Clinton thought he and Graves should prepare an attack on de Barras at Newport, but Graves said two of his vessels had to be repaired. Hood was approaching the American coast with fourteen ships. Somewhere in the North Atlantic were Admiral Digby and three ships that Lord Sandwich had persuaded the cabinet to send to America as reinforcements. Rodney, claiming illness, though probably his main objective was to take home loot from his capture of St. Eustatius, sailed for England on August 1 on his flagship. He also detached two other ships for eastward convoy duty home, thus neatly neutralizing the westward-moving Digby. Rodney left six other ships under the charge of Admiral Sir Peter Parker in the Caribbean. Parker kept one; three he sent to England on convoy. He dispatched two more to America, but too late to be of help. Thus, while two French admirals were moving to join thirty-six French ships, five British admirals were scattering thirty-three of theirs over the wide Atlantic.

On August 17 Clinton received intelligence that de Grasse was on his way north with twenty-eight ships and seven thousand troops. Clinton informed Graves that he did not credit the report. Graves replied that it seemed to be someone's "heated imagination."

AUGUST 18–31

As Washington put it in his diary, the Jersey troops and the Canadian regiment were quickly "thrown over at Dobbs Ferry." They were marched down to Chatham and Springfield, opposite Staten Island, as if they were the vanguard of an attacking force. The French proceeded to build a bakery there, indicating it was to be a permanent encampment. For security reasons the remainder of the troops were sent north to cross at Kings Ferry. By August 21 all American troops were west of the Hudson. The French were slow in getting under way. Washington commented in his diary that their horses were in bad condition and they needed "better management" of them.

The French, in moving north, crossed Pine's Bridge, near which Joshua Smith had left André almost eleven months before. Claude Blanchard, sent on with a message from Rochambeau apologizing for the slowness of his troops, found Washington quietly taking tea in the Smith house, where André had spent the day after meeting Arnold. The French, more encumbered with baggage and stores than the Americans and having the larger number of troops, took five days to cross the river. While waiting for them, Washington took Rochambeau on a tour of West Point. He also, according to his diary, mounted "30 flat Boats (able to carry about 40 Men each) upon carriages, as well with a design to deceive the enemy as to our real movement, as to be useful to me in Virginia when I get there." Clinton quickly received intelligence warnings that they might be used for an attack on Staten Island.

The American army was full of rumors on their destination, but Washington kept his confidence from all but a trusted few. He had long given up calling formal councils of war; instead, where necessary, he asked his officers for written opinions. That way, he said, he could make the decision and keep it secret instead of sharing it with a dozen others. His new military secretary, Jonathan Trumbull, Jr., who had taken the place of Robert Hanson Harrison, noted on August 21 that the many "conjectures" were "curious [and] indeed laughable." Dr. James Thacher also recorded his impressions that day and the next:

> Our destination has been for some time a matter of perplexing doubt and uncertainty; bets have run high on one side that we were to occupy the ground marked out on the Jersey shore... and on the other, that we... are actually destined to Virginia...

> We crossed at King's Ferry, 21st instant, and encamped at Haverstraw. A number of batteaux, mounted on carriages, have followed in our train, supposed for the purpose of conveying troops over to Staten Island.

> Resumed our line of march, passing rapidly through Paramus, Acquackanack, Springfield and Princeton. We have now passed all the enemy's posts and are pursuing our route with increasing rapidity towards Philadelphia; wagons have been prepared to carry the soldiers' packs, that they may press forward with greater facility. Our destination can no longer be a secret. The British army under Lord Cornwallis is unquestionably the object.

Washington's burdens became greater when his quartermaster general,

Timothy Pickering, went off for a holiday visit to his family. The commander in chief had to assume that job as well as his own. Washington's letters flowed out in streams from Dobbs Ferry, Kings Ferry, Chatham, New Brunswick, and Trenton. He asked his intelligence officers to get every scrap of information from New York on Sir Henry Clinton's movements and reactions to his march. He sent his geographer, Simeon De Witt, to make surveys and sketches of the roads from New Brunswick to Elkton (to use their modern names). He asked the governors of Connecticut and Rhode Island to rush provisions to de Barras at Newport, which he could carry to Virginia. He wrote Lafayette requesting information on horses and wagons that would be available for use in Virginia. He also requested him to send as many boats as possible to Head of Elk, adding that he depended on Lafayette's "Military Genius and Judgment" to keep Cornwallis from escaping. He gave Rochambeau detailed marching instructions for his troops and where boats might be available for speedier transport than by land. He dispatched expresses to Trenton to assemble all vessels to ferry the armies across the Delaware. He wrote Robert Morris, superintendent of finance, that there was great discontent in the American forces at not having been paid for so long. He asked him to scrape some specie together. "I make no doubt that a little douceur of hard money would put them in proper temper."

Washington ordered Brigadier Louis Du Portail, his able French chief of engineers, to proceed at full speed south with letters to Lafayette and de Grasse. Du Portail was later to be Louis XVI's war minister, while General Knox held a similar position in Washington's cabinet. While the armies were crossing New Jersey in good fashion, Washington went on to Philadelphia with Rochambeau and Chastellux. He noted in his diary for August 30:

> *I set out myself for Philadelphia to arrange matters there, provide Vessels and hasten the transportation of the Ordnance, Stores, &ca., directing, before I set out, the second York regiment [which had been delayed because of John Hancock's negligence] to follow with the Boats, Intrenching Tools &ca. the French Rear to Trenton.*

About one in the afternoon Washington and his French colleagues were escorted into the city by the Philadelphia Light Horse Troop amid, as Robert Morris noted in his diary, the "universal acclamations of the citizens." That afternoon the president of Congress gave a dinner where toasts were drunk to the United States, France, Spain, and the Netherlands. The local press next day reported: "In the evening the city was illuminated, and his Excellency walked through some of the principal streets, attended by a numerous concourse of people, eagerly pressing to see their beloved General."

Washington found too few ships at Philadelphia to move both stores and troops south, and he and Rochambeau agreed to march the armies to Head of Elk. As Washington was entering Philadelphia, Admiral de Grasse was moving into Chesapeake Bay with his twenty-eight warships and accompanying frigates and transports. Intelligence reports had been reaching Sir Henry Clinton which indicated that Washington's army appeared to be moving towards Baltimore and that de Grasse was coming with a large fleet. Clinton wrote to Cornwallis on August 27:

> *I cannot well ascertain Mr. Washington's real intentions by this move of the army. But it is possible he means for the present to suspend his offensive operations against this post and to take a defensive stand at the old post of Morristown, from whence he may detach to the southward... This move of the enemy may be only a feint and they may return to their former position, which they certainly will do if de Grasse arrives.*

Clinton, in conjunction with Admiral Graves, had been making preparations for an attack on de Barras at Newport and was paying relatively little attention to Washington. The French admiral, who had been so slow the preceding winter, was now equally dilatory in getting under way from Newport but not as slow as the British. He sailed south on August 25. Fortunately for de Barras, the two British ships were slow in being repaired. By the time Graves was ready to move, de Barras had gone. On August 25 Hood reached New York with fourteen ships; the two admirals decided to drop the Newport plan and go south.

On September 2 Clinton reported to Cornwallis that the newly arrived HMS *Pegasus* had sighted forty French sail. "However," Clinton continued, "as Rear Admiral Graves (after being joined by Sir Samuel Hood) sailed from hence on the 31st. *ultimo* with a fleet of nineteen sail besides some fifty-gun ships, I flatter myself Your Lordship will have little to apprehend from that of the French."

SEPTEMBER 1–15

On the day that Clinton wrote this letter, de Grasse began landing the Marquis Claude-Anne de Saint-Simon's army division. Lafayette did his best to tidy up the ragged continentals but he did not have much to work with. When they met, although Saint-Simon was a major general in the French army and Lafayette only a colonel, the former graciously agreed to go under his command. On the same day, Du Portail reached de Grasse's flagship, the *Ville de*

Paris, of 110 guns, the largest warship then afloat. He gave him Washington's letters and an account of the march that was being made to Yorktown. Immediately thereafter de Grasse dispatched a letter by a fast cutter to Baltimore to let Washington know of his arrival.

De Grasse was almost as tall as Washington though much fatter. He was notable for his short temper, a quality possessed by most admirals, and for his nervousness, a quality not always associated with the sea. In his conferences with Lafayette and Du Portail, de Grasse seemed chagrined that Washington and his armies were not already at Yorktown and ready to start. He mentioned the approaching hurricane season and his need to leave in six weeks. He suggested that Lafayette and Saint-Simon, together with some marines that de Grasse offered to send ashore, proceed to demolish Cornwallis. This was a remarkable request since de Grasse had been present with d'Estaing at Savannah where, in his great hurry, d'Estaing changed a siege into an assault and was badly beaten. Lafayette and Du Portail advised against this. At the same time they assured him that Washington would shortly be at Head of Elk, ready to move troops down the Chesapeake Bay by water. He would need the help of de Grasse's frigates and transports.

On September 5 Graves and Hood, with their nineteen ships of the line and a few frigates, appeared off Chesapeake Bay looking for de Barras' fleet which, they expected, might be reinforced by de Grasse. The British scouting ship reported fourteen French ships of the line present in the bay. A curious feature of the ensuing battle is that the British admirals never guessed that de Barras was not part of the large fleet they fought.

De Grasse had been rather negligent in his watches. When Graves moved in, two thousand of his men were ashore and four of his ships were too far away to do any good. De Grasse signalled his fleet to move without the missing men; they hoisted sail in disorderly fashion. The British were amazed to count twenty-four ships of the line straggling out of the bay.

Not much can be said for the seamanship of either European power in the ensuing battle, which has many names, including the battle of the Chesapeake. De Grasse had the advantage of about three hundred more guns, but he failed to used them decisively. De Barras showed up while both fleets were off the coast but, claiming that he could not distinguish French ships from English, he did not join the battle. In the early stages, five ships of the French van separated from their main body. They should have been tempting targets for the British, but Graves was more concerned with maneuvering his fleet on a parallel with the French. This gave the French time to improve their formation. In moving towards the French, Graves deployed his ships in such fashion that Hood, who had led the British van, was left straggling in the rear.

In turn, the rear of the French fleet failed to hold their line and drifted south. The British admiral gave confused and conflicting signals. In the end, only fifteen of the French ships engaged twelve of the British. Seven British and three French ships were severely damaged and three others of Graves' fleet suffered minor damage. Later, four French ships became detached and were very ineffectively attacked by the enemy van. The engagement ended at dusk. British casualties were 336 and French 220. One English ship, later found to be leaking, was blown up on Graves' order.

Although de Grasse was the technical victor, he did not care to re-engage; indeed, he avoided it and eventually moved to join de Barras. The two French fleets were united by September 13; there were now thirty-six warships forming the sea defenses of Yorktown. The British admirals decided "to proceed with all despatch for New York," where their ships were put in repair.

During his five Philadelphia days, Washington was busier than ever giving orders, holding conferences, and sending out letters. He directed General Lincoln to send all heavy ordnance and baggage by water and lighter pieces by land. He added: "You will please to use every Exertion for dispatch in your Movement, as not a Moments Time is to be lost." He directed part of his troops to move by water from Jersey to Delaware. He forwarded to Lafayette intelligence of the movement of the British fleet to the Chesapeake. He dispatched an officer to Christiana, Delaware, to direct the unloading of ordnance and troops at the head of the creek there, and to repair the road to Elkton. He sent an engineering officer to Williamsburg by way of Baltimore, Georgetown, and Fredericksburg to survey the roads and to request all government officials and militia to get them into quick repair. He wrote the governors of Maryland, Delaware, and New Jersey to beg for supplies and clothing. He provided Rochambeau with routes and distances for the French wagons that were going overland. He wrote General Greene a lengthy letter giving intelligence of all his moves. He noted that he had no word of de Grasse and that a British fleet had apparently gone to the Chesapeake. "You will readily conceive that the present Time is as interesting and anxious a Moment as I have ever experienced." He sent General Heath, in command on the Hudson, an urgent request to send down one hundred head of cattle each week for his army.

On September 2 he wrote to Lafayette who, although four days short of his twenty-fourth birthday, was the kingpin of the whole operation, to say that he calculated that the troops to be assembled at Yorktown would be sufficient for a siege. What chiefly worried him was being able to move enough heavy cannon, stores, and ammunition to prosecute "a Siege with rapidity, energy and success." He reported that Knox was making every exertion possible. He also

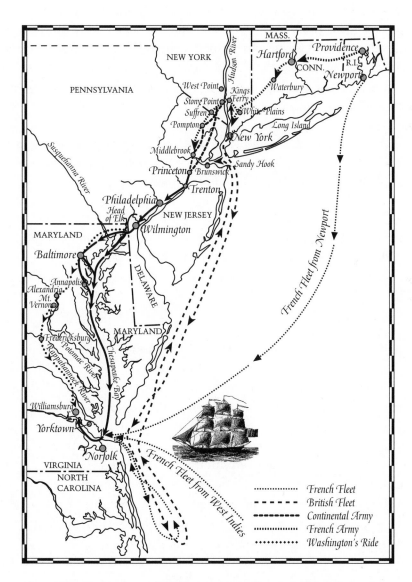

The Approach to Yorktown and the Battle of Chesapeake,
August–September, 1781

noted the problem of feeding, clothing, and getting medicines for the troops. He concluded:

> *But my dear Marquis, I am distressed beyond expression, to know what is become of the Count de Grasse, and for fear that the English fleet, by occupying the Chesapeake (towards which my last accounts said they were steering) should frustrate all our flattering prospects in that quarter. I am also not a little solicitous for the Count de Barras, who was to have sailed from Rhode Island on the 23d Ulto. and from whom I have heard nothing since that time. Of many contingencies we will hope for the most propitious events.*

> *Should the retreat of Lord Cornwallis by water, be cut off by the arrival of either of the French fleets, I am persuaded you will do all in your power to prevent his escape by land. May that great felicity be reserved for you!*

> *You See how critically important the present Moment is: for my own part I am determined still to persist with unremitting ardour in my present Plan, unless some inevitable and insuperable obstacles are thrown in our way.*

> *Adieu my dear Marquis! If you get any thing New from any quarter, send it, I pray you, on the Spur of Speed, for I am almost all impatience and anxiety.*

On September 5 all the American troops being south of Philadelphia and the French rearguard having reached it, Washington left at high speed for Head of Elk, the principal point for shipments by water or land to Williamsburg. Rochambeau decided to go by riverboat from Philadelphia to Chester in order to examine the fortifications along the Delaware. When Washington was a few miles south of Chester, an express from Baltimore met him with de Grasse's letter, announcing that he had arrived safely and that he had debarked troops to join Lafayette. The French officers said that they had never seen a man so moved with joy. On the instant, he whirled around to gallop back to Chester to await Rochambeau. As his boat moved in, the rather serious Rochambeau was astonished to see Washington jumping up and down, waving his hat and handkerchief in sheer exuberance, as he shouted the news. According to Cromot du Bourg, Washington gave Rochambeau the Gallic embrace when he landed.

Washington moved on to Christiana to inspect the landing places there and to give instructions for unloading supplies sent by ship. He then rode across the Delaware peninsula to Head of Elk. There he found far less shipping available than he had hoped but enough to transport two thousand Americans and French to Williamsburg. He sent expresses to Baltimore to find out how much additional shipping could be provided at that port. He added urgent letters to everyone he knew on Maryland's eastern shore, asking them to send to Baltimore all available "craft and vessels." He wrote Comte de Grasse to congratulate him on his arrival and to let him know that the van of the French and American armies was now going aboard transports and would shortly be on their way. He told Lafayette how prudently he had acted and that they would meet in a few days. He sent detailed instructions to General Lincoln on the embarkation of troops and supplies, even covering such points as baking bread and providing salt provisions. He acknowledged Du Portail's letter, telling him that de Grasse would stay only a few weeks. Washington added: "Our measures must be forced, and every intermediate moment employed to the greatest advantage." It was a great misfortune, he added, that they did not have enough sea transport and that he would have to march a large part of the army to Baltimore. He wrote to the governors of Maryland and Virginia to raise all the forage they could for the teams that were on their way. He directed the payment to the army of a month's salary, which Robert Morris had forwarded from Philadelphia. He asked his quartermaster general, Timothy Pickering, to report for duty from his vacation.

Now more anxious than ever to get to Williamsburg and Yorktown, Washington started out with Rochambeau and Chastellux for Mount Vernon. With tact (and possibly also because Washington was riding too fast for them), the French officers persuaded him to go on ahead so that he would have a day at Mount Vernon with his wife before they appeared. As he rode through Baltimore, the city was illuminated in his honor. The citizens, as usual, fired salutes and gave him a speech. Early on September 9, 1781, Washington and three aides set out to ride the sixty miles from Baltimore to Mount Vernon. That evening he was home for the first time since May 4, 1775.

The moment Washington arrived he wrote to the Fairfax County Lieutenant, Peter Waggoner, to hold all the country militia that had been assembled to go to Yorktown. Instead, Waggoner was ordered, "with out a moment's loss of time," to repair the roads from the Georgetown ferry landing to the Occoquan ford. He added to Waggoner that French and American army wagons and their cavalry and cattle would be travelling the roads in a very few days. He also instructed General Weedon to repair all the roads further down, from the Rappahannock to Caroline Court House, and to provide carriages and fresh horses for Rochambeau and Chastellux.

The following day Washington wrote to his deputy quartermaster at Alexandria to inform him that he had heard the landings at Georgetown were in disrepair. He was ordered to look to them at once and also to make ready proper ferry service from Georgetown to Virginia. General Weedon was further directed, if he did not have enough shipping at Baltimore for all his troops, to start them marching south. "The time is fast slipping away; the most expeditious Mode should be taken to collect our whole Force at the Point of Operation." That same day he wrote Lafayette:

We are thus far, My Dear Marquis, on our way to you. The Count de Rochambeau has just arrived, General Chastellux will [soon] be here, and we propose (after resting tomorrow) to be at Fredericksburg on the night of the 12th; the 13th we shall reach the New Castle and the next day we expect the pleasure of seeing you at your Encampment.

Should there be any danger as we approach you, I shall be obliged if you will send a party of Horse towards New Kent Court House to meet us…

P.S. I hope you will keep Lord Cornwallis safe, without Provisions or Forage until we arrive.

On September 14 an anxious Washington reached Williamsburg. Colonel St. George Tucker described the scene in a letter to his wife next day:

I wrote you yesterday that General Washington had not yet arrived. About four o'clock in the afternoon his approach was announced. He had passed our camp… before we had time to parade the militia. The French line had just time to form. The Continentals had more leisure. He approached without any pomp or parade, attended only by a few horsemen and his own servants. The Count de Rochambeau and Gen. Hand, with one or two more officers, were with him. I met him as I was endeavoring to get to camp from town in order to parade the brigade; but he had already passed it. To my great surprise he recognized my features and spoke to me immediately by name. Gen. Nelson, the Marquis, etc., rode up immediately after. Never was more joy painted in any countenances than theirs. The Marquis rode up with precipitation, clasped the General in his arms and embraced him with an arder not easily described.

The whole army and all the town were presently in motion. The General—at the request of the Marquis de St. Simon—rode through the French lines. The troops were paraded for the purpose and cut a most splendid figure. He then visited the Continental line. As he entered the camp the cannon from the park of artillery and from every brigade announced the happy event. His train by this time was much increased; and men, women and children seemed to vie with each other in demonstrations of joy and eagerness to see their beloved countryman.

Within hours Washington received word from de Grasse that he was back in

Chesapeake Bay, with de Barras, and that he had captured two British frigates on the way in. Washington immediately gave orders to start all troops moving down the Chesapeake. He sent a letter of congratulation to de Grasse for driving off the British fleet. This, he said, will "give us happiest Presages of the most complete Success in our combined Operations on this Bay." He asked de Grasse to send a cutter to pick up Rochambeau and him for an early conference with the admiral. He expressed his thanks that French transports were moving his troops to the Yorktown peninsula.

General Thomas Nelson, Jr., Virginia's governor, was of double assistance to Washington. As commander of the state militia, he had seen to it that almost 30 percent of Washington's American forces present were state troops. As chief executive of the commonwealth, he stretched his powers to the fullest to requisition food, fodder, teams, and entrenching tools. Maryland's governor, Thomas Sim Lee, also worked industriously to forward provisions and tools for the troops.

In New York, Sir Henry Clinton continued in a state of euphoria and inaction, while American and French troops moved across Pennsylvania and Maryland. Benedict Arnold, who had been recalled from Virginia, pleaded with him to be allowed to attack West Point, Philadelphia, or elsewhere. Clinton finally allowed him an expedition to New London, a few miles from his birthplace at Norwich. Arnold burned the town, destroying some 65 houses and numerous other buildings. He took two small forts, bayoneting more than 75 men after they surrendered. This was the last effective action Clinton was able to take against the Americans.

Two days later the last major battle of the revolution, south of Virginia, was fought at Eutaw Springs. There Greene, Marion, Henry Lee, Otho Williams, Andrew Pickens, and William Washington fought so savagely that the British forces suffered a loss of 40 percent. The survivors retreated hurriedly to Charleston, their only remaining post in South Carolina. The British now held only five fortified points in America, but these were on the sea, and the French commanded the sea.

SEPTEMBER 16–30

Once word came from Washington, the immense machinery was again in motion. French and American transports moved south from Annapolis, Baltimore, and Head of Elk. The duc de Lauzun and his cavalry galloped across the Virginia countryside. Wagons, with flour, guns, and ammunition, moved creakily down bad roads and across ferries over the Potomac,

Pamunkey, Rappahannock, and York Rivers. De Barras unloaded the French siege guns. American vessels, which had accompanied him from Newport, sent ashore the supplies Washington had ordered from Connecticut and Rhode Island. Horses and teams were impressed everywhere to move the guns and food. Bakeries were set up and roads repaired.

The great nagging question for Washington was whether all forces and supplies could be assembled and the siege effected before de Grasse had to take off for the West Indies. On September 17 Washington, Rochambeau, Chastellux, Knox, and Du Portail boarded the captured *Queen Charlotte*, which had been His Majesty's ship, named for His Majesty's wife. They arrived next day at the *Ville de Paris*, where they were given full military honors. Washington opened the conference with praise of France and de Grasse:

> *The noble and generous Support which is given to this Country by His Most Christian Majesty does, as it ought, fill the breast of every American with gratitude and Love: The zeal and alacrity with which His Officers strive to carry his Royal intentions into execution, merit our highest admiration and applause.*

Washington then came to his main point. The operation he was engaged in was difficult because he had to bring troops from such a distance. Peace for Europe and independence for the United States hung on success at Yorktown. It was impossible to determine how long the siege would take. It could be done slowly but surely. The alternative, if French fleet support were to be withdrawn, would have to be an assault without "regard to the lives of men." This would be "bloody and precarious." He begged de Grasse to let him know how long he would stay. De Grasse answered that he had planned to leave by October 15, but he could now assure Washington that he would stay till the end of the month, and he would not take Saint-Simon's troops before then. De Grasse was less satisfactory in his reply to other questions. He said he was prepared to lend marines only for an assault (a coup de main) and he would have to think over Washington's request for ships to be stationed above the British fortifications on the York River.

Violent storms faced the American and French officers when they attempted to go ashore. They did not reach Williamsburg for four days while Washington fumed with impatience. He found that everything had been going smoothly in his absence and almost all the troops from Head of Elk had landed. Three days later most of the remaining troops from Annapolis and Baltimore were debarking.

In New York Clinton had received firsthand accounts from Graves that he had fought twenty-four French ships of the line and that he was sure de Barras' ships had been part of the squadron. Two British ships in New York, which had not sailed with Graves, had completed their repairs, bringing total British naval forces to a possible twenty-one. With the expected arrival of Digby's three ships and two from Jamaica, Clinton figured the British and French fleet would be about equal. Not until September 23, while Washington was rolling on the seas, did Clinton hear from Cornwallis that de Barras' squadron had indeed joined with de Grasse's. There was still hope, though, and Clinton prepared to move with five thousand troops to the relief of Cornwallis. He informed him that he expected to be ready by October 5.

On September 11 Digby reached New York; aboard his flagship was the sixteen-year-old Prince (later King) William. He wrote his father that he had been greeted by "an immense concourse of people who appeared very loyal, continually crying out, 'God bless King George!'... They appear in general very well affected to our Government, but particularly the Dissenters and Quakers... [one of whom said] 'God bless thy father. It is not for want of respect I do not take my hat off, but because my religion requires it.'" William Smith, the Tory chief justice, who had long held a dim view of Clinton and of the British war efforts, noted that the population, after learning of the Chesapeake defeat, had raved at the navy. He wrote with irony that the prince's presence "may supply our deficiency."

Washington received quick word that Digby had reached New York with reinforcements but the number of his ships was variously reported as three to ten. He did not take the news too seriously since the French still had a wide margin of superiority. He wrote to General David Forman, who was watching enemy movements at New York, that Digby's arrival "cannot... have any influence on our projects, or in the least retard our operations, while there are 36 French ships of the line in the bay. Every thing has hitherto succeeded to our wishes... In a very few days, I hope the Enemy at York will be completely invested. And although Lord Cornwallis has endeavored to strengthen himself as much as possible, and has a considerable Army with him, yet the prospects of his reduction, from the superiority of the Naval and land force, are as favorable as possibly could have been expected."

The following day, Rochambeau's aide, Baron von Closen, handed Washington an unpleasant shock in the form of a letter written by de Grasse only five days after their conference. Washington had sent the intelligence of Digby to de Grasse by the baron, who reported that "the news of Digby's arrival and of the approaching departure of Hood's fleet from New York alarmed and disquieted these excitable gentlemen of the navy." De Grasse informed Washington he was leaving as soon as he could hoist sail. He did not dare risk having his fleet trapped in the bay. He might go outside the capes, or to New

York, or perhaps be forced to return to Martinique. Rochambeau and Washington, greatly alarmed, sent urgent pleas to de Grasse to stay. Washington said, "I cannot conceal... the painful anxiety under which I have laboured since the receipt of your letter." He emphasized that the reduction of Cornwallis was certain and would go a long way towards terminating the war. He noted the "uncommon exertions and fatigues" undergone by both armies and the disgrace that would ensue. He flattered and praised the admiral, saying he was sure he could stop any British attempt to force the bay. His ships were vitally needed to transport food and artillery for the army. He added that de Grasse was superior to any force the British could bring. Fortunately the Admiral received word from the French naval minister that only three ships had been sent out with Digby, and he replied to Washington that he would stay.

As the army got ready to move, Washington took care of one minor item. He wrote to Robert Morris in Philadelphia: "It is of such essential consequence, in my opinion, that the Army should be regularly supplied with rum during the present operation, that I cannot forbear interesting myself on the subject. When we take into consideration how precious the lives of our men are, how much their Health depends upon a liberal use of spirits, in the judgment of the most Skillful Physicians, who are best acquainted with the climate; how meritorious their Services have been, and what severe and incessant duties are expected from them, we cannot hesitate to determine that the Public ought to incur a small expense, to answer the most valuable purposes." He asked him to ship fifty hogsheads as soon as possible. He also marked "warmly endorsed" a request to the board of war for blankets for the "poor fellows" in the hospitals. On September 27 the commander in chief issued general orders at Williamsburg: "The whole Army will March by the right in one Column at 5 o'clock tomorrow Morning precisely."

By nightfall the French and Americans had reached the outskirts of York. The following day Cornwallis, to save his men and ammunition, and in expectation of relief from Clinton, abandoned his outer works and holed in for the siege. Washington noted in his diary: "Immediately upon which we possessed them, and made those on our left (with a little alteration) very serviceable to us."

OCTOBER 1–17

The total land forces under Lord Cornwallis' command numbered approximately eighty-five hundred British, Hessian, and Anspach infantry, artillery, and cavalry. There were also around fifteen hundred naval rank and file on about twenty-six transports and frigates and many small vessels.

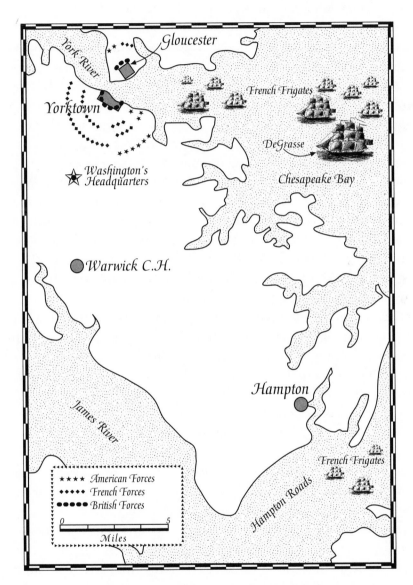

The Siege of Yorktown, September–October, 1781

Americans and French continued to straggle into the peninsula by foot, ship, boat, wagon, and horse until the day of Cornwallis' surrender. At their peak the combined armies under Washington numbered close to twenty thousand, the largest force he had ever commanded.

On the extreme left (all figures being rank and file rather than totals) were the Marquis de Saint-Simon's West Indian regiments—Gatinois, Touraine, and Agenois—numbering 3,000. Next were Rochambeau's regiments—Saintonge, Soissonois, Royal Deux-Ponts, and Bourbonnois—3,600 men under Baron Antoine de Viomenil. The American continental line—around 5,700—was in three divisions under Steuben, Lincoln, and Lafayette. In addition there were 3,200 Virginia militia and state troops. Half of these were placed under the governor of Virginia on the extreme right, behind a rather large creek, where they would be secure but also act as a reserve.

Across the York River, facing Dundas' infantry and Tarleton's cavalry, were the duc de Lauzun's 600 cavalry, half the Virginia militia, and a battalion of 800 French marines, added by the comte de Grasse, and placed under the command of the marquis de Choisy. From Washington's point of view, his most important officers were Du Portail, head of the engineers, who was to erect the parallels; and Knox, chief of artillery, who had to smash the British fortifications before an infantry attack could take place.

From October 1 to 6, as Washington wrote in his diary, "nothing occurred of Importance. Much diligence was used in debarking and transporting the Stores, Cannon, &ca. from Trebells Landing (distant 6 miles) on James River to Camp; which for want of Teams went on heavily, and in preparing Fascines, Gabions, &ca. for the Siege, as also in reconnoitering the Enemies defenses, and their situation as perfectly as possible, to form our parallels and mode of attack. The Teams which were sent around [by land] from the head of Elk, having arrived by this time, we were enabled to bring forward our heavy artillery and Stores with more convenience and dispatch and everything being prepared for opening Trenches, 1500 Fatigue men [working parties] and 2800 to cover them, were ordered for service."

The one weakness, in Washington's view, was that the whole of the York River above Gloucester and York remained unguarded. At his conference with de Grasse, he asked that ships be stationed there, though they would have to pass the English batteries. On October 1 he repeated to de Grasse his fear that Cornwallis, with most of his force, might escape up the river and head for New York. With a touch of humor he reported that his own experience with shore batteries had been that they were not very effective against ships. In again asking for naval support, he added reassuring intelligence from New York as to the number of British vessels laid up for repairs. De Grasse continued to raise objections, saying that he would have to send naval observers ashore and that he did not have proper pilots or protection against fireships. De Grasse and Washington were still discussing this when Cornwallis made a final attempt to escape by that route sixteen days later.

The trenches were dug by the working parties operating under fifty-five detailed instructions prepared by Washington and completed by the morning of October 6. Washington commented that the work had been done with such "secrecy and dispatch" that the enemy was unaware it was going on. "The next two days were employed in completing our parallel, finishing the redoubts in them and establishing Batteries." By this time the allied forces were 600–800 yards from Cornwallis. The French under Saint-Simon opened fire on October 9; later Washington himself fired the first American shot. He recorded in his diary:

About 3 o'clock P.M. the French opened a battery on our extreme left of 4 Sixteen pounders, and Six Morters and Howitzers and at 5 o'clock an American battery of Six 18s and 24s; four Morters and 2 Howitzers began to play from the extremity of our right. Both with good effect as they compelled the Enemy to withdraw from their ambrazures the Pieces which had previously kept up a constant firing.

In the next two days the French and Americans opened up with thirty more guns. On the tenth the French destroyed a British frigate and three smaller craft. On the same day Cornwallis sent a desperate message to Clinton at New York: "Nothing but a direct move to York River—which includes a successful naval action—can save me... On the evening of the 9th the enemy's batteries opened and have since continued firing without intermission... We have lost about seventy men, and many of our works are considerably damaged. With such works on disadvantageous ground, against so powerful an attack we cannot hope to make a long resistance." By October 12, Washington was running his parallels within three hundred yards of the enemy's lines. On October 14 the batteries were moved up to the second parallel.

At Clinton's headquarters in New York there was a panic atmosphere as the Royal Navy and Army screamed at each other to do something quickly. Graves worked day and night to get his fleet ready to move Clinton's relief troops. Press gangs were at work to obtain sailors. The richer Tories aided in any way they could. Admiral Hood wrote to London on October 14 that the repairs on the ships "have gone on unaccountably tedious, which has filled me with apprehension that we shall be too late to give relief to Lord Cornwallis... I think very meanly of the ability of the present commanding officer [Graves.]"

Two strong British redoubts on the right still kept the allied armies from extending their full parallel. These had to be taken by assault, but they were first subjected to heavy bombardment. Redoubt nine was given to the French and ten to the Americans. Count William Deux-Ponts (also known as Zweibrucken) led the French attack. Alexander Hamilton, who had finally won the field command about which he had raised so much fuss, successfully appealed to lead the assault on the other redoubt. Accompanying him was John Laurens, back from France, and once more Washington's aide. Hamilton, with 400 men, stormed the redoubt, which had 45 men, and captured it quickly. The other was occupied by 120 British. The French had much more trouble but it too was carried. The second parallel was complete and new batteries were hauled up.

On October 16 the enemy made a sortie but this accomplished little except to knock out a few guns temporarily. That night Cornwallis made a last attempt to move his men across to Gloucester, hoping that he could break through de Choisy and move north. He got some troops across but a rain, referred to by Tarleton as a "squall" and by Cornwallis as "a most violent storm," made him abandon his plan.

October 17 was the anniversary of Burgoyne's surrender, and the American officers who had been at Saratoga were planning a celebration dinner. Soon after the allied batteries opened fire, a drummer beat a "parley" and a British officer waved a white flag. All firing ceased. The officer was led into the American lines where he handed over a letter for delivery to Washington:

Sir

I propose a cessation of hostilities for twenty four hours, and that two officers may be appointed by each side, to meet at Mr. Moore's house, to settle terms for the surrender of the posts of York and Gloucester. I have the honour to be

> *Sir*
> *Your most obedient &most humble servant*
> *Cornwallis*
> *His Excellency*
> *General Washington*

It had taken but sixty-four days from the receipt of de Barras' letter at Dobbs Ferry for Washington to have in his hand this offer to surrender the posts at Gloucester and York (later Yorktown). The rest of the story is well-known. Washington gave him two hours to forward his proposals in writing. Cornwallis attempted to get the terms that had been given Burgoyne.

Washington rejected these and outlined what he was prepared to grant. The following day the British commissioners, Lieutenant Colonel Thomas Dundas and Major Alexander Ross, Cornwallis' aide, met with Vicomte Louis-Marie de Noailles, representing the French, and Colonel John Laurens, Washington's aide, of Huguenot descent, for the Americans. For Laurens this was a particularly noteworthy day, inasmuch as Lord Cornwallis was titular governor of the Tower of London, where his father was imprisoned.

The British haggled and procrastinated all day, possibly in a forlorn hope that Clinton might arrive. A main problem was the treatment of American Tories who were serving with Cornwallis. Washington considered them governed by the civil laws of their states rather than military law. A tacit agreement seems to have been made that a number were allowed to go to New York as paroled prisoners, and thus be saved from possible death, but the principle was maintained. The draft treaty was ready late that night between "His Excellency General Washington Commander in Chief of the combined Armies of America & France... His Excellency the Count de Rochambeau Lieutenant General of the Armies of the King of France... His Excellency the Count de Grasse Lieutenant General of the Naval Armies of His Most Christian Majesty... And the Right Honourable Earl Cornwallis Lieut. General of his Majesty's Forces... and... Thomas Symonds Esq. Commanding His Britannick Majesty's Naval Forces."

On October 19 Washington wrote in his diary: "In the Morning early I had them copied and sent word to Lord Cornwallis that I expected to have them signed at 11 o'clock and that the Garrison would March out at two o'clock, both of which were accordingly done." Dr. James Thacher left a more extensive portrait of the surrender:

> *This is to us a most glorious day... Preparations are now making to receive as captives that vindictive, haughty commander and that victorious army, who by their robberies and murders, have so long been a scourge...*

> *At about twelve o'clock, the combined army was arranged and drawn up in two lines extending more than a mile in length. The Americans were drawn up... on the right, and the French occupied the left. At the head of the former, the great American commander... took his station, attended by his aides. At the head of the latter was posted the excellent Count Rochambeau and his suite. The French troops, in complete uniform, displayed a martial and noble appearance, their band of music... is a delightful novelty and produced while marching to the grounds, a most enchanting effect... Every countenance beamed with satisfaction and joy. The Concourse of spectators from the country was prodigious...*

It was about two o'clock when the captive army advanced... Every eye was prepared to gaze on Lord Cornwallis... but he disappointed our anxious expectations; pretending indisposition, he made General O'Hara his substitute as the leader of his army... Having arrived at the head of the Line, General O'Hara, elegantly mounted, advanced to his excellency the commander-in-chief... With his usual dignity and politeness, his excellency pointed to Major General Lincoln for directions, by whom the British army was conducted into a spacious field, where it was intended they should ground their arms.

The tradition is that the British band played "The World Turned Upside Down," with its appropriate lines "Goody Bull and her daughter together fell out. Both squabbled, and wrangled, and made a damned rout." However, this is unsupported by tangible evidence.

Aside from having conducted one of the great concentrations of military history and its speediest large-scale siege, Washington had achieved victory with remarkably little loss of life. He had written to Robert Morris "how precious the lives of our men are," and all his movements at the siege were destined to preserve rather than squander lives. Winston Churchill has said: "Battles are won by slaughter and maneuver. The greater the general, the more he contributes in maneuver, the less he demands in slaughter." The battle of Blenheim, where the great grandfather of Martha Washington's first husband was Marlborough's aide, cost the duke 12,000 men in killed and wounded. The battle of Yorktown, of far greater significance than Blenheim, resulted in around 350 casualties among the French and Americans.

The British lost a force close to 10,000 and numerous ships and small vessels which had been sunk. Twenty-four transports were captured, along with more than 200 cannon and 7,300 small arms. Numerous horses and wagons were also taken, many of which had been seized from Virginians. A great grandnephew of Marlborough, Lord Chewton, was among the prisoners.

On the day of the surrender, Graves and Clinton sailed from Sandy Hook to rescue Cornwallis.

THE VICTORY DISPATCHES

Unofficial news went north in one of de Grasse's ships sailing to Annapolis. When Governor Lee of Maryland got the word on October 20, he ordered an express to "ride night and day" for Philadelphia. Lee's messenger roused the president of Congress at two in the morning of October 22.

The carrying of a victory dispatch was considered the highest honor a general could bestow on a member of his staff. Washington chose Lieutenant Colonel Tench Tilghman, his aide of longest service, about whom he had written on May 11 to Congress:

This Gentn. came out a Captn. of one the light Infy. Companies of Philadelphia, served in the flying Camp in 1776. In August of the same Year he joined my family and has been in every action where the Main Army was concerned. He has been a zealous Servant and slave to the Public, and a faithful assistant to me for near five years, a great part of which time he refused to receive pay. Honor and gratitude interests me in his favour, and makes me solicitous to obtain his commission.

While Congress and the capital anxiously waited for official word, Tilghman ran into bad luck on his way north. He wrote Washington that the stupidity of his boatman had cost him a night's run, while, because of a calm, he had taken a day to cross the bay from Annapolis. He did not reach Philadelphia till early in the morning of October 24.

Jacky Custis had been present at the siege. He was taken ill and it is not certain whether he witnessed the surrender. When his great great grandfather handed Marlborough's dispatch to Queen Anne, she rewarded him with a thousand guineas, a diamond-studded miniature of herself and, later, a governorship. On Tilghman's arrival, the members of Congress each contributed one dollar to cover his expenses. They later voted him a horse and sword. Philadelphia was ordered illuminated from six to nine that night. All citizens were warned to behave and give "a general discountenance to the least appearance of riot," which did not prevent the breaking of windows in Quaker houses.

On October 29 Congress ordered "that two stands of colours taken from the British army under the capitulation of York, be presented to His Excellency General Washington in the name of the United States." The duke of Marlborough was awarded Blenheim palace.

The news of Yorktown spread rapidly. On October 23 Tories in New York heard cannon fire from New Jersey and rightly guessed that Americans were celebrating a dreaded event. The next day Sir Henry Clinton picked up refugees at sea who informed him that Cornwallis had offered to capitulate on the seventeenth and no firing had been heard thereafter. That same day an American schooner reached Newport with the news. Riders carried it into Massachusetts and Connecticut. General Greene and his army in South Carolina celebrated it when they had the news a few days later. De Grasse dispatched two of his fastest frigates across the Atlantic, one carrying the comte des Deux-Ponts, the other the duc de Lauzun, with duplicate reports, as well as letters from Washington to Franklin and Adams. They were so fast that Paris newspapers with the account of Yorktown reached London the day Germain received Clinton's melancholy report. Maurepas, the French prime minister, heard of the victory from Lauzun before his death on November 21.

THE SNATCHES

During the move to Virginia and the subsequent siege, Washington's intelligence network worked at top form. Its members operating from Philadelphia, New York, and elsewhere accomplished two of the great feats of intelligence history.

Richard Peters, secretary to the board of war, had opened communication with a member of the staff of James Rivington, publisher of the violently Tory *New York Gazette*. Rivington was also the king's printer, entrusted with confidential official documents. When Admiral Graves gave him his secret naval signals to print, Peters' spy smuggled a copy to Philadelphia by another trusted agent. Peters took the signals to the French minister for immediate transmission to de Grasse. When additional signals were developed for Graves and Clinton to use on their expedition to the Chesapeake, these were forwarded to Peters. In sending them to Washington, Peters asked him what other intelligence he might like from Rivington's shop.

De Grasse, after copying the second set, returned them to Washington who, in turn, on October 29 transmitted them to the French minister for the use of the whole French fleet, adding: "I... hope they may be of signal Advantage to the Commanders of his Most Christian Majesty's Naval Armies."

Another success was recorded at Philadelphia when congressional operators discovered that Cornwallis was getting some of his letters out from Yorktown to New York by way of Tangier Island. Among the letters seized was one written in Clinton's secret code. James Lovell, a member of Congress, cracked the code and forwarded the cipher, as well as vital intelligence on Cornwallis' troops and supplies, to Washington. He replied to Lovell on October 6:

I am much obliged by the Communication you have been pleased to make me in your Favr. of 21st ulto.

My Secretary has taken a Copy of the Cyphers, and by help of one of the Alphabets has been able to decypher one paragraph of a Letter lately intercepted going from Ld Cornwallis to Sir Hy Clinton.

THE WAR CONTINUES

Generals Clinton and Washington reached identical conclusions as to what would happen if de Grasse remained in American waters. On October 20 Washington wrote de Grasse:

> *Charles Town, the principal Maritime port of the British in the southern parts of the Continent, the Grand Deposit and point of Support for the present Theatre of the War, is open to a combined attack, and might be carried with as much certainty, as the place which has just surrendered.*

> *The capture would destroy the last hope which induces the Enemy to continue the war.*

> *It will depend upon Yr. Excellcy. therefore to terminate the War, and enable the allies to dictate the Law in a Treaty. A Campaign so glorious and so fertile in consequences could be reserved only for the Count de Grasse.*

> *It rarely happens, that such a combination of means as are in our hands at present, can be seasonably obtained by the most strenuous of human exertions.*

> *A decisively superior fleet, the Fortune and talent of whose Commander overawe all the naval force that the most incredible efforts of the enemy have been able to collect. An army flushed with success and demanding only to be conducted to new attacks, and the very session which is proper for operating against the points in question.*

Washington further appraised the situation to Lafayette, indicating that if de Grasse agreed to stay an additional sixty days, the three remaining British armies at Wilmington, Charleston, and Savannah would be captured. While still at sea, Sir Henry Clinton wrote to Germain on October 29 in much the same terms: "I beg leave to prophesy... that every station we hold in America is in peril, if the enemy can retain a naval superiority in these seas only for a few weeks."

Throughout the siege of Yorktown, Washington thought constantly about the valiant Greene who had driven the enemy to Charleston and who needed only the help of de Grasse, and part of the northern army, to win final glory. Washington kept him fully apprised of the situation at York but told him he was pessimistic about de Grasse. He praised highly the action at Eutaw Springs: "How happy am I, my dear Sir, in at length having it in my power to congratulate you upon a victory as splendid as I hope it will prove important. Fortune must have been coy indeed had she not yielded at last to so persevering a pursuer as you have been; I hope now she is yours, she will change her appelation of fickle to constant." He sent Colonel Robert Morris to Greene with instructions to tell him that Washington wished "from principles of generosity and justice to see him crowned with those Laurels which from his unparalleled exertions, he so richly deserves." Morris was told to emphasize that, if Washington went south, it was not to take glory from Greene, but because only he could command French troops.

Although Washington went aboard de Grasse's flagship to ask for further aid, the admiral rejected his request. Washington then asked him if he could at least land troops near Wilmington, North Carolina. De Grasse at first agreed, and Washington made arrangements; he then refused to do even this. By October 28 Washington was reduced to begging the admiral to remain a few more days in order to protect his movements of troops, stores, and sick and wounded in the Chesapeake area. De Grasse agreed after Graves' fleet, with Clinton aboard, returned to New York.

A commander who stretches his instructions is praised rather than condemned if he wins. De Grasse, in the face of an opportunity for certain victories that would have been of inestimable value to France as well as America, sailed away in early November. In February he captured the flyspeck island of Saint Kitts. In April he was disastrously defeated by Rodney and carried prisoner to England.

DEATH OF JACKY CUSTIS

In the days before de Grasse left, Washington's time was spent in getting his troops ready to return to the Hudson and in preparing Wayne's and Gist's brigades for their march south. Washington's diary of November 5 noted that they "began their March and were to be joined by all the Cavalry that could be equipped of the first, third and fourth Regimts. at"—the diary thus abruptly broke off, apparently when Washington heard that Jacky Custis was dying at nearby Eltham of typhus, which he had contracted at Yorktown. Washington arrived at the house a few hours before Custis died in the presence of his stepfather, mother, wife, and daughter. It was a crushing blow for Martha Washington, who had borne so much for more than six years, to lose her last living child. Washington's aides had ridden with him and waited at a nearby tavern. The kindly Washington, with all his troubles, thought of them and sent a note over to Jonathan Trumbull, Jr.:

> My dear Sir: I came here in time to see Mr. Custis breathe his last. About Eight
> o'clock yesterday Evening he expired. The deep and solemn distress of the Mother,

and affliction of the Wife of this amiable young Man, requires every comfort in my power to afford them; the last rites of the deceased I must also see performed; these will take me three or four days; when I shall proceed with Mrs. Washington and Mrs. Custis to Mount Vernon.

As the dirty tavern you are now at cannot be very comfortable; and in spite of Mr. Sterne's observation, the House of Mourning is not very agreeable.* It is my wish, that all of the Gentn. of my family, except yourself, who I beg may come here and remain with me, may proceed on at their leizure to Mount Vernon and wait there for me. Colo. Cobb will join you on the road at the Tavern we breakfasted at (this side Ruffens.) My best wishes attend the Gentn. and with much sincerity and affection.

On November 13 Washington reached Mount Vernon with the grieving ladies.

VERGENNES AND THE AMERICANS

Horace Walpole recorded a rumor, circulating in London, that the dying French prime minister, having been told of the British defeat at Yorktown, quoted from Racine: "Mes derniers regards ont vu fuir les Romains."

On November 26 Franklin in Passy, and Adams in Amsterdam, sent each other similar letters. Franklin said: "Most heartily do I congratulate you on the glorious news!" Adams wrote: "With unfeigned joy I congratulate your Excellency on the glorious news."

The United States had been instrumental in giving France what turned out to be her only decisive victory of the war. Her reward was a sneer from Vergennes to the French minister at Philadelphia that perhaps now the Americans would snap out of their lethargy. He instructed his minister to inform Congress that the United States would receive no further monetary help from France. Congress had already written Franklin to ask for more aid. On December 31 Vergennes returned a brusque reply to Franklin, referring to the "successive variations and augmentations of your demands on me for funds." After going into the status of the current loan, he continued: "There will be nothing more supplied than the million [$185,000] above mentioned; and, if the drafts which you have already accepted, exceed that sum, it must be for you to contrive the means of meeting them." Having thus refused

---

* It is difficult to choose precisely the quotation Washington had in mind in his reference to *Tristram Shandy.* Possibly it was Laurence Sterne's observation: "Labour, sorrow, grief, sickness, want, and woe, are the sauces of life."

further help to a country, an ally, which had borne nearly seven years of war, Vergennes concluded that he could now control the coming peace. John Adams, at Vergennes' request, had been ordered by Congress to subordinate his activities to the wishes of the French foreign—and now prime—minister. With Yorktown in his pocket, John Adams proceeded to push for the total independence of the United States. Against the disapproval of Vergennes and the undercover intrigues of the French ambassador at The Hague, Adams determined to win the Netherlands' recognition of the United States. He worked on the old Dutch spirit of republicanism and liberty as well as that country's mistrust of France and Britain. At the end of February, the province of Friesland instructed its delegates to vote for recognition. Other provinces and cities fell into line. On April 19, 1782, the seventh anniversary of Lexington, the States General formally recognized the United States of America. By August subscriptions were pouring into the Dutch bankers for the first private American foreign loan raised abroad. Adams was able to raise nearly $700,000 on the same terms as Dutch loans to France. In October he set out for the peace table.

APPENDIX A

BIBLIOGRAPHICAL NOTE

EDITING

This biography was developed as a primary work on George Washington. Its objective was to make his story as autobiographical as possible, with added comments by Washington's contemporaries in their own words.

Editing of quoted manuscripts has been confined to changes that clarify the texts. Punctuation has been added or deleted; obscure abbreviations have been spelled out; slips of the pen and other errors have been corrected; and a few modern terms have been substituted for obsolete words. Material inserted within a quote is bracketed.

In numerous cases several copies exist of original documents, while various recipients got much the same letter. There are progressive drafts, a copy for the Washington files, later transcripts, and the final document. In some cases only a file copy is available. In a few others, all originals have disappeared and only a printed version exists. In all quoted manuscripts, the closest available approach to the final paper has been chosen.

The Fitzpatrick transcripts of the diaries and writings were extensively used, and corrections were made when needed according to the new Virginia edition. The original manuscripts were employed (a) for the presidency and (b) where there was doubt as to the transcription.

Although the existing manuscripts are extensive, a considerable part is missing. Tampering with and careless handling of the papers began almost at the moment of Washington's death. Martha Washington is presumed to have burned all but two letters from her husband. Martha and Bushrod Washington and Nelly Lewis gave away letters as souvenirs. Other papers, stored by John Marshall, were subject to the indignity of being eaten by rats. Various papers were simply stolen. Surviving correspondence of Washington's parents, brothers, and sisters is scarce. In some periods, such as the campaign of 1758, various letters have disappeared, making reconstruction of some events difficult.

MANUSCRIPTS AND OTHER PRIMARY SOURCES

George Washington

The principal collection of Washington's writings is the 64,786 documents in *The Papers of President Washington* at the Library of Congress. There is a 295 page index to the original documents that are in its collection. The Manuscript Division has numerous copies of papers in other libraries, thanks to the indefatigable work of John C. Fitzpatrick.

In 1788 David Humphreys, who had been a wartime aide to General Washington, came to stay at Mount Vernon. He started a draft biography of the man, and Washington himself made some interesting comments and additions, which showed his vivid memory of events. In 1991 the University of Georgia Press published an edited version of Humphreys' work, which was put together from three archival sources. Unfortunately the result is disappointing because Humphreys seems to have lacked the curiosity to ask about aspects of Washington's life that modern biographers would love to know.

The biography by John Marshall, the first writer to have unlimited access to Washington's papers, is of special interest. He lived through and participated in many events of the period, and some of his writings have a ring of authenticity which no later biographer can hope to capture. The judicious manner in which he treated Washington's presidency and final years maddened his distant cousin, Thomas Jefferson. The value of Mason Weem's biography is noted in the text and in Appendix C.

The main published source of pre-1775 letters to Washington has been the five-volume work of Stanislaus Murray Hamilton, which appeared in 1901. It is also valuable for transcripts of various Washington family wills. Jared Spark's

1853 edition of letters to Washington and his 1834–1837 *Writings* are less trustworthy for, being a Harvard man, he thought he could improve Washington's prose.

Washington's Contemporaries

In using the writings of those around Washington, efforts were made to secure the most authentic texts available. In numerous cases, these were at the Library of Congress. For the years 1789–1797, in particular, letters and memoranda to Washington, in the presidential papers, were employed. The major printed sources of original documents that supplemented these are well known.

Collected Writings

The Adams Papers, ed. L. H. Butterfield (Harvard, 1961).

The Papers of Alexander Hamilton, ed. Harold C. Syrett (Columbia, 1961–1976).

The Works of Alexander Hamilton, ed. Henry C. Lodge (Putnam's, 1904).

The Papers of Thomas Jefferson, ed. Julian P. Boyd (Putnam's, 1950).

The Works of Thomas Jefferson, ed. Paul L. Ford (Princeton, 1904).

The Correspondence of King George III, ed. Sir John Fortescue (Macmillan, 1927–1928).

The American Rebellion: Sir Henry Clinton's Story, ed. William B. Willcox (Yale, 1954).

Anthony Wayne: Correspondence 1792–6, ed. Richard C. Knopf (Pittsburgh, 1960).

The Correspondence of John Jay, ed. Henry P. Johnson (Putnam's, 1891).

Letters of Benjamin Rush, ed. L. H. Butterfield (Princeton, 1951).

The Correspondence of William Shirley, ed. Charles R. King (Putnam's, 1894).

The Life and Correspondence of Rufus King, ed. Charles R. King (Putnam's, 1894).

The Life and Correspondence of James McHenry, ed. Bernard C. Steiner (Burrows, 1907).

The Papers of George Washington, (University Press of Virginia, 1976–).

Benjamin Franklin: Writings, ed. J. A. Leo Lemay (Library of America, 1987).

George Washington: A Collection, ed. W. B. Allen (Liberty Classics, 1988).

Diaries, Journals, and Memoirs

Christopher Gist (Kennikat reprint, 1964).

Claude Blanchard (Albany, 1876).

Ambrose Serle (Huntington Library, 1940).

James Thacher (Cottons and Barnard, 1823).

Benjamin Tallmadge (Giliss, 1904).

Jacob Hiltzheimer (Philadelphia, 1893).

Albigence Waldo (*Pennsylvania Magazine*, 1897).

François-Jean de Chastellux, ed. Howard C. Rice, Jr. (North Carolina, 1963).

Josiah Quincy, Jr. (Wilson, 1874).

Claude Robin (Paris, 1782).

Cromot du Bourg (*Magazine of American History*, 1880–1881).

William Byrd, Vol. II (Dietz, 1942); Vol. III (Oxford, 1958).

Ludwig von Closen (North Carolina, 1958).

Ewald, Johann. *Diary of the American War: A Hessian Journal*, (Yale, 1979).

Philadelphia Merchant: The Diary of Thomas P. Cope, ed. Eliza Cope Harrison (Gateway, 1978).

Others

The U. S. Geological Survey Maps, Fredericksburg and Wakefield Quadrangels, and the U. S. Coast and Geodetic Survey Chart of the Rappahannock were of particular value in attempting to locate early Washington farms.

Statutes at Large (Richmond, Virginia [Henning], 1810–1823).

Hoppin, Charles A., "The House in Which George Washington Was Born," Tyler's Quarterly (Vol. VIII, October, 1925: The Washington Ancestry, 1931).

Private Affairs of George Washington, Stephen Decatur, Jr. (using Tobias Lear's presidential account for his first term, Houghton Mifflin, 1933).

Commager, H. S. and R. B. Morris, *The Spirit of Seventy-Six* (Bobb-Merrill, 1958).

Songs and Ballads of the American Revolution (Kennikat reprint, 1964).

Letters from America, by German officers, ed. Ray W. Pettengill (Kennikat reprint, 1964).

Baker, W. S., *Itinerary of George Washington*, 1775–1783 (Lippincott, 1892).

D. A. R., *Patriot Index*, (1966) has dates of birth and death, and names of wives, not always available elsewhere.

Hinchcliffe, E., "The Washingtons at Whitehaven and Appleby," *Transactions of the Cumberland and Westmorland Antiquarian Society* (vol. LXXI, 1971).

Campaigns of the American Revolution: An Atlas of Manuscript Maps, eds. Douglas W. Marshall and Howard H. Peckham (Michigan, 1976).

The American Campaigns of Rochambeau's Army, 1780, 1781, 1782, 1783, eds. Howard C. Rice, Jr. and Anne S. K. Brown (Princeton, Brown 1972).

Notes on Debates in the Federal Convention of 1787, reported by James Madison, introduction by Adrienne Koch (Ohio, 1966).

Leonard Baker, John Marshall: A Life in Law (Macmillan, 1974).

George Washington Atlas (George Washington Bicentennial Commission, 1932).

Peter Oliver's Origin and Progress of the American Rebellion: A Tory View, eds. Douglass Adair and John A. Schutz (Stanford, 1961).

Thomas, Peter G. D. *Lord North* (St. Martin's Press, 1976). No mention is made of General Washington.

Currey, Cecil B. *Code Number 72 Ben Franklin: Patriot or Spy* (Prentice Hall, 1972).

The West Point Atlas of American Wars, Brigadier General Vincent J. Esposito (USA edit., Praeger, 1959).

The Statistical History of the United States: Colonial Times to the Present, prepared by the Census Bureau (Basic Books, 1976).

Pellew, George, *John Jay* (Chelsea House Reprint, 1980).

Brighton, Ray. *The Checkered Career of Tobias Lear* (Portsmouth (PH) Marien Society, 1985).

Randall, Willard Sterne. *Benedict Arnold Patriot and Traitor* (Morrow, 1990).

Leckie, Robert. *George Washington's War* (Harper Perennial, 1992).

Higginbotham, Dan. *War and Society in Revolutionary America* (South Carolina, 1988).

George Washington's Beautiful Nelly, ed. Particia Brady (South Carolina, 1991).

Minutes of the Vestry, Truio Parish, Virginia 1932–1785 (Gateway Reprint, 1995).

THE CHIEF JUSTICE
AND THE ANGLICAN PRIEST

I N 1800, AS the eighteenth century was ending, two Virginians worked on biographies of George Washington. The first was John Marshall, Chief Justice of the United States, who had access to all Washington's papers through Associate Justice Bushrod Washington, who had inherited them. Marshall began describing Washington's life with the "Birth of Mr. Washington," unintentionally suggesting that Washington, like Athena, had arrived fully grown and armed. He summed up Washington's ancestry, birth, and upbringing in four paragraphs, mentioning however that Washington's mother had instilled in him "principles of religion and virtue."

The Reverend Mason Locke Weems, who had been ordained in England, wanted to emphasize Washington's virtues in private life as a model for young Americans. Possibly he was influenced by Light Horse Lee's funeral oration, from which, when quoted, an important part is omitted: "First in war, first in peace, first in the hearts of his countrymen, he was second to none in the humble and endearing scenes of private life."

Weems wrote: "Of those private deeds of Washington very little has been said. In most of the elegant orations pronounced to his praise, you see nothing of Washington beneath *the clouds*—nothing of Washington the *dutiful son*—the affectionate brother—the cheerful schoolboy—the diligent surveyor—the neat draftsman—the laborious farmer—the widow's husband—

the orphan's father—the poor man's friend. No! This is not the Washington you see; 'tis only Washington the HERO, and the Demigod...."

Weems had the advantage of being able to interview many relatives and friends of Washington who had known him from early childhood and who remembered his father. Weems' wife was a niece by marriage of Dr. James Craik, Washington's intimate friend for almost half a century. It was James Craik, Jr., who introduced Weems to Washington at Mount Vernon. Later he occasionally preached in Washington's Phick Episcopal Church.

Without Weems far less would be known about Washington's earliest years. It was a kinswoman of Washington who recalled that, at his Potomac farm, Washington's father, a giant of a man, worked to instill the proper virtues in George, particularly to be truthful at all times. So the story of the hatchet and the cherry tree, related by this lady to Weems, has its own ring of truth. The recollection of Washington's cousin, Lewis Willis, that he was the only boy strong enough to throw a stone across the Rappahannock River is perhaps more endearing. Weems wrote with verve, rollicking humor, and rolling and occasionally Homeric prose, all intermingled with bad dialogue. He made a lasting impression on one reader.

On his way to Washington in 1861, Abraham Lincoln, the fifteenth successor to the first president, addressed the New Jersey State Senate: "I cannot but remember the part that New Jersey holds in our early history.... May I be pardoned if upon this occasion, I mention that away back in my childhood... I got hold of a small book, such as one as few of the younger members have ever seen, 'Weems' Life of Washington'.... I recollect thinking then, boy even though I was, that there must have been something more than common that these men struggled for.... something that held out great promise to all the people of the world to all time to come."

GEORGE WASHINGTON: SPURIOUS AND DUBIOUS DOCUMENTATION

"I would have the National character of America be pure and immaculate."
— Washington to George William Fairfax, July 10, 1783.

The well-known myths and legends surrounding Washington were not troublesome in writing his biography. What was disconcerting was to find that numerous documents, many prepared by his own countrymen, were questionable or false. This addendum to the biography reviews a fair sampling of them, including many that were uncritically used by various Washington biographers.

The first fabrication appeared in 1754 when the August issue of *The London Magazine* was published, along with a June 4th letter from Williamsburg purportedly written by "Major General" Washington on May 31 to an unidentified brother. The report was based primarily on Washington's May 29 dispatches to Lieutenant Governor Dinwiddie. His brothers lived on the Northern Neck, quite far from Williamsburg. The distances involved would have made it virtually impossible for a genuine letter to have reached London, by this indirect route, in time for an August publication. The letter is also suspect because of its uncharacteristic phraseology, which subjected Washington to some ridicule in England. He was made to say that expected reinforcements "will enable us to exert our noble courage with spirit. P. S. I fortunately escaped without any wound... I heard the bullets whistle, and, believe me, there is something charming in the sound." Washington was a soldier and an experienced shot; the last sentence was a silly attribution. George II put it very well when he was quoted as saying: "He would not say so, if he had heard many."[1] In 1756 the French government published *Mémoire*, which included a partial distortion, for propaganda purposes, of the Washington journal notes which they had captured shortly after the battle.[2] Thomas Paine drew on this for a portion of his 1796 attack on the president.[3] In 1777 the London government produced a series of forged letters from General Washington to his wife, stepson, and Mount Vernon manager, which even the English press viewed with skepticism.[4] They were republished in 1796 by Benjamin Bache, in an attempt to discredit Washington. During the revolution, the British produced other crude fabrications, such as additions to genuine captured letters and an "account" of the trial of Thomas Hickey at New York in 1776. Many were intended to portray the dissolute behavior of the American commander-in-chief.[5]

After Washington's death, not much attention was paid to the minutiae of his early life. John Marshall's five volumes devoted less than two pages to his ancestry, birth, education, and growth to manhood. Mason Locke Weems, however, who had interviewed old friends and relatives, referred to his birth at Pope's Creek, his subsequent removal, as a small boy, to a house across from

---

[1] John C. Fitzpatrick, ed., *The Writings of George Washington*, Washington, D.C., 1931-1944, Vol. 1, pp. 63-66 and 70-71, and *The London Magazine*, August, 1754, pp. 370-371. In quoting George II, Horace Walpole referred to Washington's "rodomontade."

[2] Fitzpatrick, *Writings*, Vol. 1, pp. 84-89 and Douglas Southall Freeman, *George Washington*, New York, 1948-1957, Vol. 1, pp. 540-545.

[3] Freeman, Vol. 7, Prepared by J. A. Carroll and M. W. Ashworth, p, 428.

[4] Worthington C. Ford, ed., *The Writings of George Washington*, New York, 1889, Vol. IV, pp. 132 et seq. has the text of the letters. On March 3, 1797, the President, in an official letter to the Secretary of State, dismissed them as forgeries. Fitzpatrick, Writings, Vol. 35, pp. 414-416.

[5] This anti-American propaganda, circulated by the British in 1775-1778, would be too trivial to mention but for the fact that some of the tales were revived in 1970 by a New York scribbler for the same purpose.

Rupert Hughes, *George Washington*, Vol. 2, pp. 290-291 and 402-405, included them as forgeries. According to Hughes, the *Gentleman's Magazine* also published a doctored version of a genuine Washington letter.

Fredericksburg, and his return to Pope's Creek to attend school, at age 11, while living with his half brother, Augustine Washington, Jr.[6]

In 1815, George Washington Parke Custis placed a monument at a spot near Pope's Creek, as the supposed birthplace of Washington. Eighty-one years later the United States government erected a more permanent shaft near the place chosen by Custis. With the approach of the 1932 bicentennial, the federal government, in cooperation with private groups, made efforts to locate the places where Washington had lived until he settled permanently at Mount Vernon in 1754. While the available documentation turned out to be scanty, this did not prevent the government from making categorical declarations about his youthful years; many of these appear to be wrong or unproven.

When Augustine Washington, George's father, came of age he inherited 1,100 acres of land in Westmoreland County. Some of the land was on Mattox Creek and, presumably, the rest was mostly in Washington's parish, which included Bridge's Creek and may have been bordered to the east by Pope's Creek. After 1717 Augustine extended his holdings on the peninsula. By the time he died in 1743, he was able to leave seven hundred acres west of

---

[6] Mason Locke Weems, *The Life of Washington*, Harvard, 1962, pp. 7, 8 and 19-20. In a remarkable piece of research, Edgar Hinchcliffe, Librarian of Appleby School, Cumbria, England, in "The Washingtons at Whitehaven and Appleby," *Transactions of the Cumberland & Westmoreland Antiquarian & Archaeological Society*, Vol. LWWI, 1971, pp. 151-198, indicated that Lawrence and Augustine Washington, Jr., had been ushers (assistant masters) on the teaching staff of the Appleby Grammar School, a notable public school. They were well qualified therefore to be George's tutors.

Weems did introduce into his "Life" several tales which some thought dubious but a couple of these, including the cherry tree, came from an elderly kinswoman of the general. A great deal of what Weems reported has been verified in other sources, much as the research of Mr. Hinchcliffe has confirmed the statement that George went to live with Augustine, Jr., after their father's death. One of Weems's principal informants was Dr. James Craik, whose wife was aunt to Mrs. Weems, and whose son, Dr. James Craik, Jr., introduced the clergyman to Washington at Mount Vernon. Craik was an intimate friend of Washington from the French and Indian War days until the general's death. As a result, Weems has some remarkable details not available elsewhere. He noted, for example, that while the young Washington was in Frederick County, "he boarded in the house of the widow Stevenson, generally pronounced *Stinson*. This lady had seven sons—William and Valentine Crawford, by her first husband; and John, Hugh, Dick, Jim and Mark Stinson, by her last husband. These seven young men, in Herculean size and strength, were equal, perhaps, to any seven sons of any one mother in Christendom." The widowed Mrs. Honora Stephenson and all seven of her sons are mentioned, some of them frequently, in Washington's diaries and correspondence. His letter to Tobias Lear, November 30, 1786, confirms the pronunciation, by noting that Col. John Stephenson, whom Lear was to see, was "commonly called Stinson." Weems also reported that Hugh Stevenson would say that, in their younger days, when wrestling, "He and his brother John had often laid the conqueror of England on his back."

It is curious that Weems is endlessly attacked by those who have never read him. Essentially his life of Washington is one written for Americans. He is recommended reading.

Bridge's Creek to his son, John, and much, perhaps most of the area from Bridge's Creek to Pope's Creek, to another son, Augustine, Jr.[7]

Around 1723–1724 Augustine engaged a carpenter to build what he called "my house."[8] While the phrase has been interpreted to mean what it would currently imply, his residence, this is by no means a certain rendering. The various Washington deeds and wills of the period contain such phrases as "all houses, edifices, buildings, tobacco houses, etc.," indicating there were numerous structures through the wide area inherited or acquired by Augustine Washington. A trust deed of February 23, 1726–7 indicates that he was then living on the Abingdon tract, between Pope's and Bridge's Creeks.[9] This statement can be taken to refer only to the day on which it was written. It is possible to infer that, four years later, he brought his second wife to live in the same house, but there is no supporting evidence for or against it. Furthermore, no description of the 1724 house exists other than an implication it was frame and of modest size. The current elegant "Birthplace," erected for the Washington bicentennial, probably bears little relation to the early house, while the term "Wakefield" was applied to the farm well after George Washington's departure.

Augustine Washington was elected in 1735 to the vestry of Truro Parish, where the future Mount Vernon farm was located. The vestry met rarely, twice in 1735, once in 1736, and three times in 1737. Augustine Washington missed one meeting in 1736 and in 1737. To some this seemed to indicate that young George at three, and for two years afterwards, was roaming his future estate. Too much was read into this. The area around Little Hunting Creek was still largely unsettled wilderness. Mrs. Augustine Washington was pregnant in 1735 and 1736, the year her husband departed for England. It is highly unlikely that he moved his family from their many relatives and accustomed life in Westmoreland to a pioneer venture while he was absent from Virginia.[10]

The Bicentennial Commission also appears to have been responsible for the misnomer "Epsewasson" being applied to the farm that was to be Mount Vernon. In 1674 Nicholas Spencer and John Washington received a patent

---

7 Wills of Lawrence and Augustine Washington, Stanislaus Murray Hamilton, ed., *Letters to Washington*, New York, 1901, Vol. III, pp. 392–402. See also Westmoreland Co. Deeds, No. 9, Agreement between Augustine and John Washington, Deed of Exchange, March 29, 1743, with a plat of Augustine Washington's holdings. Copy supplied by Virginia Historical Society. For consistency, Pope's and Bridge's Creeks have been spelled in current fashion but, historically, the apostrophe was often dropped and sometimes the possessive as well.

8 Freeman, Vol. 1, pp. 536–536.

9 Westmoreland Co. Vol. 8-1, p. 226. Copy supplied by George Washington Birthplace.

10 Truro Parish records, photostat, Library of Congress. Family members told Weems that Augustine Washington and children moved directly from Pope's Creek to the Rappahannock.

from Lord Culpepper for an estimated 5,000 acres located between Little Hunting and Epsewasson Creeks, the latter apparently an early name for Dogue Run. In 1690 the tract was divided between the Spencer and Washington heirs. If Epsewasson was ever used descriptively, it applied only to the Spencer half. The Washington wills call their land Little Hunting or Hunting Creek.[11]

In 1932 the United States government introduced what was to be a troublesome document for future biographers. This was a map purporting to be of a farm on the Rappahannock River, where the Washingtons supposedly moved when George was six or seven. The drawing made by Lawrence Martin, chief of the map division of the Library of Congress, employed Washington's own handwriting along the plat prepared for the government. This was taken from the hasty survey notes Washington made on September 13, 1771 "of the Fields where my Mother lives."[12] The absurdity of the Martin claim was that he placed it on a U.S. topographic map at a place where neither his mother nor George had ever lived. Indeed the farm where she was living in 1771 was considerably up the river and west of the Rappahannock Falls and Falmouth. She had moved there about 1747 when her brother, Joseph Ball, wrote her a letter marked "nigh the falls." George Washington's notes indicate that her farm was north of the Fitzhugh lands and bordered on the property of James Hunter, Jr., who ran the ferry next to Mrs. Washington's property.

It is clear that the farm where Washington's mother lived was west of Falmouth because the road to Stafford Court House (now Stafford) running more or less northeast would have gone there directly. The 1932 map, placing the farm well below Falmouth, so located the Stafford Road that it would lead down to King George County. Where the Washingtons lived on the Rappahannock until Augustine Washington's death has never been accurately determined. It is not of much importance. From the evidence suggested by Weems it may have been located in parkland about Catham.

There is a tendency for centennial observances to bring out bad history. In July, 1876, an American novelist, Constance Cary Harrison, announced to the world in *Scribner's* magazine that Sarah Cary Fairfax, her great great grandaunt, had been the "object of George Washington's early and passionate love." On March 30 of the following year, *The New York Herald* published a purported letter by Washington to Mrs. Fairfax, dated Fort Cumberland,

---

[11] The patent by Lord Culpepper is quoted in the 1972 *Annual Report*, Mount Vernon Ladies Association of the Union, p. 38. Mr. Morse's research indicated that Epsewasson may have been first applied as a name to a 19th century farm on Dogue Run.

[12] *George Washington Atlas*, Washington, 1932, Plate 9, and Washington's Survey notes, September 13, 1771.

September 12, 1758.[13] This letter then subsurfaced for many years; it was given to Harvard's Houghton Library in 1958. A second letter in a similar vein, dated September 20, 1758, was sold at auction in New York in 1969. The author, convinced that most of the text of the letters did not sound like anything Washington ever wrote, undertook an investigation into their authenticity. In this he had the aid of Mount Vernon and the Manuscript Division of the Library of Congress. He alone is responsible for the conclusions.[14] The historical discrepancies are too great for them to have been written by George Washington. They have, nonetheless, fooled many biographers, the media, such great corporations as GM and NBC, and the *Smithsonian* magazine at least twice. The letters sound as if they were written by a Victorian lady novelist; it seems hardly a coincidence that the letters were discovered by such a novelist. It is hard to believe that anyone could suppose their purple prose emanated from the crisp, direct pen of Colonel Washington. Nor is it possible that the colonel, in writing to George Fairfax about the reconstruction of Mount Vernon in preparation for his new bride, would enclose a love letter to his friend's wife.

A comparison was made between the September 12 letter and two notes sent by Washington to Mrs. Fairfax in February of the same year.[15] The formal and restrained terminology of the latter is quite different but very typical of his prose. The elongated G. and W. of his signature, in contrast with the later letter, correspond to his handwriting of the period. There are other discrepancies. Washington was made to refer to "the unseasonable haste" of

---

[13] Fitzpatrick, *Writings*, Vol. 2, pp. 287–289.

[14] The *Smithsonian*, November, 1973, reproduced the Sally letters as if genuine and also an extract of the "letter" from Lord Fairfax to Mrs. Mary Washington, which was composed about 1903 by S. Weir Mitchell for *The Young George Washington*, New York, 1904, p. 76. The noted Washington scholar, John C. Fitzpatrick, rightly pronounced it spurious, though it was "naively printed in various places," in *George Washington Himself*, Indianapolis, 1933, p. 518.

When Henry Cabot Lodge and Woodrow Wilson undertook their lives of Washington in the 1890s, they were well aware of the Sally letters. Wilson ignored them, while Lodge made only an oblique reference to them. Rupert Hughes, writing for the sesquicentennial year, 1926, devoted page after page to Mrs. Fairfax. When Washington was supposed to have written: "'Tis true, I profess myself a votary of love,'" Hughes added: "this is George Washington writing! And he professes himself a votary of love!" The repellence of the phrase ought to have served as a warning.

[15] The Historical Society of Pennsylvania and the Boston Public Library supplied copies of George Washington's letters to Mrs. Fairfax, the first written about February 11 and the second dated February 13, 1758. The former was incorrectly listed in Fitzpatrick, *Writings*, Vol. 1, pp. 476–477, as written in 1756. Internal evidence in the first letter (its reference to "the President" who was John Blair, acting governor) together with Blair's letter of February 5 to GW (Hamilton, *Letters to GW*, Vol. II, pp./ 262–264) make it reasonably probable that the "Saturday morning" of the letter was February 11.

his express rider who left the Fairfax house September 1, not reaching Fort Cumberland until September 11. By contrast the extant historical letter from George Fairfax to Washington, at the Library of Congress, indicates that the return rider left the fort on September 12, arriving at Belvoir two days later.[16] Washington was made to write that Mrs. Spotswood had "already become a reigning Toast in this Camp."[17] Wilson Miles Cary subsequently identified her as Mrs. John Spotswood, widowed in 1757. However, there is an existing letter at the Library of Congress, from Captain Charles Smith to Washington, September 7, 1758, referring to Col. John Spotswood's death "about seven days ago."[18] In any case this was a frontier post in a savage war, and Washington was a disciplinarian who did not tolerate highjinks in his camp. Finally Washington was supposed to have written that his hours were "melancholy dull." In fact, this able and energetic commander had received orders, a few days previously, to be prepared to move all his effective troops to Ray's Town (Bedford, Pennsylvania) en route to Fort Duquesne, the moment he received the orders of his commanding general, John Forbes. He was instructed to bring all his ammunition, many tons of food supplies, 50 head of cattle, and 200 horses.[19]

The second Sally letter also contains discrepancies in relation to historical fact. A copy in the Hamilton auction catalogue is dated September 19th at Ray's Town. However, General Forbes wrote that Washington left there for Fort Cumberland on September 18, probably reaching there on the 19th. He was there on September 20th, not at Ray's Town, and thus he was nearly two days' march from General Forbes' headquarters. Late in the evening of the 20th Forbes received a preliminary report of a military disaster. Yet, in his letter, Washington provided Mrs. Fairfax with details of the battle, which he could not have had for another three days. He also acknowledged receipt of a letter from her that day, although the mail from Belvoir did not reach him until the 21st. On the 25th Washington prepared an urgent summary of the battle for Virginia's governor.[20]

---

[16] George William Fairfax to GW, September 15, 1758, Hamilton, Vol. III, p. 100.

[17] W. M. Cary, *Saily Cary: A Long Hidden Romance of Washington's Life*, New York, 1916.

[18] A. Hamilton, *Letters to GW*, Vol. III, p. 87.

[19] Henry Bouquet to GW, September 4, 1758, *ibid*, pp. 82–85.

[20] Fitzpatrick, *Writings*, Vol. 37, pp. 482–3. Copy of original supplied by Mount Vernon. The addressee was George William Fairfax, not John Augustine Washington as stated by Fitzpatrick.

INDEX